THE STATUTORY REGULATION OF BUSINESS TENANCIES

THE STATUTORY REGULATION OF BUSINESS TENANCIES

by

MICHAEL HALEY

OXFORD

UNIVERSITY PRESS

This book has been printed digitally and produced in a standard specification
in order to ensure its continuing availability

OXFORD
UNIVERSITY PRESS

Great Clarendon Street, Oxford OX2 6DP

Oxford University Press is a department of the University of Oxford.
It furthers the University's objective of excellence in research, scholarship,
and education by publishing world-wide in

Oxford New York

Auckland Bangkok Buenos Aires Cape Town Chennai
Dar es Salaam Delhi Hong Kong Istanbul Karachi Kolkata
Kuala Lumpur Madrid Melbourne Mexico City Mumbai Nairobi
São Paulo Shanghai Taipei Tokyo Toronto

Oxford is a registered trade mark of Oxford University Press
in the UK and in certain other countries

Published in the United States
by Oxford University Press Inc., New York

ISBN 0-19-826898-X

Antony Rowe Ltd., Eastbourne

This book is dedicated with all my love to Lara

PREFACE

During the last century the law of landlord and tenant has developed, often haphazardly, by virtue of fragmentary statutory intervention and a vast array of judicial decisions. It is not surprising that lawyers (whether practitioners, academics or students) can feel overwhelmed by the extent and ever increasing complexity of the subject area.

This book is concerned only with the law as it affects business tenancies. Part II of the Landlord and Tenant Act 1954 is pivotal to this analysis. This Act gives business tenants security of tenure by offering the general right to remain in occupation, following on from the contractual term, and to obtain a new lease. By way of a counterweight, the landlord is entitled to a market rental income and, in delimited circumstances, can defeat the tenant's claim for renewal. The tenant who fails to obtain a new tenancy might be entitled to claim compensation for loss of renewal rights. The ability to carry out improvements and to obtain compensation for them is available under Part I of the Landlord and Tenant Act 1927.

Albeit of a highly technical nature, the 1954 Act attempts to strike a balance between the interests of both parties and to offer some equality of bargaining strength. Apart from a number of amendments made by the Law of Property Act 1969, the statute remains largely unchanged. Unlike other areas of landlord and tenant law, it remains largely untouched by shifts in policy and political viewpoint. Although the 1954 Act is widely regarded as a success, in 1992 the Law Commission put forward an extensive catalogue of proposals for change. These proposals still await implementation. In contrast, the compensation provisions of the 1927 Act have been regarded in a less favourable light and, if the Law Commission's Report of 1989 is followed, will be consigned to the dustbin of legal history. Again Parliament has not yet acted on these reform proposals. Such proposals for change will, however, be considered in detail in the course of the text and a running comparison will throughout be drawn with the revamped scheme as operated in Northern Ireland since 1996. The book also tackles, where relevant, the intricacies and mysteries of the Civil Procedure Rules 1998.

My aim in writing this book is to provide a detailed and comprehensive analysis of the law regulating the termination and renewal of business tenancies. I have attempted to provide an accurate and in-depth examination of the statutory provisions and the case law (both reported and unreported), while paying attention to the policy which underpins the present law and will continue to shape it over future years. I have also attempted to look at the practical realities which relate to the operation of the provisions. In short, my hope is that the text will appeal to any-one whose work, research or studies concern business leases.

The law is as stated at 1 January 2000.

CONTENTS—SUMMARY

CONTENTS

TABLE OF CASES

TABLE OF LEGISLATION

STATUTORY INSTRUMENTS

EUROPEAN COMMUNITY

1

THE DEVELOPMENT OF LEGISLATIVE CONTROLS

A. Introduction

In the modern and purposive age of statutory interpretation, the antecedents of **1.01** legislation, Hansard, government Green and White Papers and other official publications (such as Law Commission Reports) have become crucial. As Lord Griffiths demonstrated in *Pepper v Hart*:

> The days have long passed when the courts adopted a strict-constructionist view of interpretation which required them to adopt the literal meaning of the language. The courts now adopt a purposive approach which seeks to give effect to the true purpose of legislation and are prepared to look at much extraneous material that bears upon the background against which the legislation was enacted.[1]

While it was intended by the House of Lords that external aids should be used sparingly and only when there is ambiguity, obscurity or absurdity, it has become clear that they are used more widely than anticipated.[2] Seemingly, judges are now prepared to make far more effort than previously to ascertain the true intention of

---

[1] [1993] 1 All ER 42 at 50; see, for example, the judgment of Chadwick LJ in *Ropaigealach v Barclays Bank Plc* [1999] 4 All ER 235. This tendency has also become evident in the county court: see *Busby v Co-operative Insurance Society Ltd* (1994) 6 EG 141.

[2] See R Cross, *Statutory Interpretation* (3rd edn, 1995) 155–164. An example of the liberal use of Hansard can be found in the judgment of Lord Lowry in *A-G v Associated Newspapers Ltd* [1994] 1 All ER 556.

Parliament and to apply it to cases before them.[3] As a result, it is beyond doubt that, in order to understand the present, it has become necessary to grapple with the past.[4] Hence, this chapter aims to provide an understanding of the origins and policy of the current law and to examine, with recourse to Hansard and other official publications, how the law has developed into its present form. Possible future reforms will be considered, as appropriate, in subsequent chapters.

B. The Movement for Reform

1.02   As early as 1889, the Select Committee on Town Holdings accepted the need for legislation to protect business tenants from exploitation by their landlords.[5] The Committee acknowledged that some landlords were demanding high rents as a condition of a lease renewal and that, if these demands remained unmet, their tenants would be evicted at the end of the contractual term. In addition to the loss of the premises, the tenant would sacrifice the value of any improvements made and, of course, whatever goodwill had been established.[6] In order to eradicate this mischief, the Committee recommended that tenants should, on quitting the premises, be entitled to compensation for improvements and goodwill. Although it was not suggested that business tenants be given security of tenure, it was anticipated that an effective compensation scheme would encourage many landlords to grant a lease renewal as an alternative to digging deep into their pockets. The Select Committee therefore worked on the far-sighted assumption that State intervention had, in these circumstances, to prevail over the sanctity of a contract freely entered into by commercial parties. The emphasis, however, was upon safeguarding the financial interests of the tenant rather than ensuring the continuation of that tenant's business. Although the mischief persisted throughout, it was to take thirty-eight years before Parliament made any serious effort to curtail the exploitation of business tenants.

---

[3] See, for example, the invocation of policy by the Court of Appeal in *Bell v General Accident Fire & Life Assurance Corporation Ltd* (1998) 17 EG 144 when deciding that a tenancy by estoppel fell within the ambit of Part II of the Landlord and Tenant Act 1954.

[4] See, for example, the judgment of Leggatt LJ in *Church Commissioners for England v Baines* [1998] 1 All ER 657 (which concerned the meaning of a dwelling house for the purposes of the Rent Act 1977) and the historic analysis of Chadwick LJ in *Ropaigealach v Barclays Bank Plc* above (relating to the scope of statutory relief available to a mortgagor in a possession action).

[5] Reports from Committees, 1892, vol 7. The Select Committee had been established in 1886 to undertake a full inquiry into the operation of the leasehold system. The Committee did not propose abolition, but concentrated instead upon improvement.

[6] Goodwill being '. . . the advantage or benefit which is acquired by a business, beyond the mere value of the capital, stock, premises or lease in consequence of the general public patronage and encouragement which it receives from constant or habitual customers' (D Yates and AJ Hawkins, *Landlord and Tenant Law* (2nd edn, 1986) 739); see also *Trego v Hunt* (1896) AC 7.

The first piece of permanent legislation, designed to regulate the relationship **1.03** between the parties to a commercial lease, emerged in the form of Part I of the Landlord and Tenant Act 1927. The relevant provisions derived their inspiration from the Select Committee's recommendation and, hence, concerned themselves with safeguarding the tenant's goodwill and improvements. The policy was to prevent the landlord from gaining from the unjust exercise of common law rights relating to termination and renewal and to shield the tenant from financial loss. While the intentions of the legislature were laudable, the principle of compensation was deficient in addressing the needs of the business community. The imposition of financial sanctions as a deterrence was a mere second-best and did not strike at the prevention of abuse. Such inadequacy demonstrated that security of tenure was the only vehicle through which the tenant's interests could be effectively safeguarded. As will be shown, the movement from market forces to paternalistic intervention, and the associated transition from compensation to renewal rights, was slow and tortuous. The primary impediments were an entrenched opposition to the modification of the landlord's common law rights, coupled with a timidity and uncertainty of both Parliament and the reform agencies as to whether reform was appropriate and, if so, the form it should adopt.

Traditional Resistance

The history leading up to the Landlord and Tenant Act 1927 provides a striking **1.04** example of Parliamentary caution and uncertainty. This is in contrast to the pioneering legislation which had imposed controls over agricultural lettings since 1875 and residential tenancies from 1915.[7] The slowness of Parliamentary action is highlighted further by the fact that, by 1918, most European countries had in place a statutory code for the protection of tenants of business premises.[8] In Eire, for example, a system of compensation for goodwill and improvements had operated since the Town Tenants (Ireland) Act 1906.[9] The motivation underlying the enactments of 1875 and 1915 was to quieten civil unrest and, it is to be admitted, no major threat was perceived in relation to business tenants. Nevertheless, tenant militancy was a crucial motivating force in the enactment of protective legislation in the commercial sector. Particularly active were small shopkeepers who lived on the premises because they, holding under mixed tenancies, were hit hard by spiralling residential rents. It was their protests and activism which entailed that they

---

[7] The Agricultural Holdings Act 1875 and the Increase of Rent and Mortgage Interest (War Restrictions) Act 1915, respectively.

[8] See the *Leasehold Committee Interim Report, Tenure and Rents of Business Premises* (1949) Cmd 7706 at paras 12–24. For a brief overview of the present European position see S Bright and G Gilbert, *The Nature of Tenancies* (1st edn, 1995) 66–67.

[9] This scheme encouraged landlords to grant a lease renewal rather than pay compensation (which was based on disturbance to the tenant). In the Eire Landlord and Tenant Act 1931, compensation was replaced by a system which afforded the tenant the right to a new lease (this also was over 20 years in advance of the equivalent reforms in England and Wales).

(unlike other business tenants) would fall within the Rent Restrictions Act of 1915 and later benefit exclusively from the Leasehold Property (Temporary Provisions) Act 1951. Although it was of more general application, the Rent Restrictions Act 1920 also emerged in order to quell the fear of discontent among shopkeepers.[10]

1.05 Although the latter half of the nineteenth century was to produce many radical and wide-ranging suggestions for the reform of English land law, it remained geared to the interests of an aristocratic state.[11] As Simpson commented, 'The Legislature was indeed very tender of the rights of property.'[12] Until the election of the Liberal government of 1906, the House of Commons was comprised largely of members drawn from the landed gentry and they, not surprisingly, proved resistant to fundamental change.[13] The Liberal Party, however, offered a different approach as signalled in its election slogan 'God gave the land to the people'. Accordingly, in the wake of the 1889 Select Committee Report, there was scant Parliamentary enthusiasm towards extending rights to business tenants, and the notion of *laissez faire* and the preservation of vested interests remained prevailing influences. The law of supply and demand was thought to be an adequate mechanism by which tenants' interests could be protected, and the problem of exploitative landlords was regarded as insufficiently widespread and serious to warrant legislative controls. Although there were hard cases which excited some sympathy, the uneasiness of business tenants was perceived as arising from a fear of what could happen rather than from anything that was likely to happen.

1.06 The anti-reform camp clearly benefitted from the fact that the degree of tenant exploitation was impossible to gauge with accuracy. As neither Parliament nor the reform agencies were able to consider details of individual cases, much reliance was placed upon impressionistic intelligence gleaned from politicians and lobbyists. Such surveys were broad brush, partisan and eminently challengeable. The case for maintaining the *status quo* was, undoubtedly, easier to make out. The potential for abuse was very localised and concerned merely those tenants whose leases were drawing to a close. Accordingly, only a small proportion of the total number of businesses could be affected at any one time. If considered from the perspective of the business community as a whole, the potential for exploitation

---

[10] The legacy of shopkeeper activism is still evident in Scotland where business tenants in general do not enjoy statutory protection, but shopkeepers are protected by the Tenancy of Shops Act 1949. For an overview of the Scottish system, see R Linton [1999] EG 28 August 66.

[11] See generally AV Dicey, *The Paradox of the Land Law* (1905) 21 LQR 221. As D Englander put it, 'The 1880s, it is now clear, mark a turning-point that failed to turn' (*Landlord and Tenant in Urban Britain 1838–1918* (1983) p. xii).

[12] AWB Simpson, *An Introduction to the History of English Land Law* (1st edn, 1961) 257.

[13] See generally WS Holdsworth *The Reform of the Land Law: A Historical Retrospect* (1926) LQR 158. As Englander makes clear there had long been a tacit agreement between the political parties to do nothing of significance (n 11 above).

appeared insignificant. Furthermore, as the conventional wisdom was that the majority of landlords acted reasonably and fairly towards their tenants, extremely few tenants were thought to be at risk of exploitation at the renewal stage. Hence, there appeared little justification for imposing controls over all landlords merely to curtail the activities of a small minority and, thereby, threaten future investment and building. It is, therefore, no coincidence that reforms eventually came about in the post-war periods when, on both occasions, it was felt strongly that the law had to be modernised to suit the needs of a commercialised, industrial nation. This appetite for change was whetted by extreme market distortions, an anti-profiteering ethos and the need to maintain economic recovery. Although traditional resistance yielded before national adversity, those opposed to change continued to exert a restraining influence upon the development and form of legal controls. Until the Landlord and Tenant Act 1954, both the 'low risk' and 'good landlord' counter-arguments prevailed to the extent that reforms were both modest and limited.[14]

Politicisation and the National Interest

Despite effective resistance from the landlord lobby, the calls for legislative intervention did not disappear. As a result of growing urbanisation and the increased population in cities and towns, the pressure for reform became heightened. In 1906, the Town Tenants' League was established and political lobbying for change began in earnest. Subsequently, the cause was championed also by the Leasehold Reform Association and the National Chamber of Trade. From 1908 onwards, the proposal of a Town Tenants Bill (usually dealing with both residential and business premises) became a regular feature of the House of Commons order paper. None, however, was destined to reach the Statute Book. This lack of success was primarily due to continued objections from the Conservative benches coupled with an unprecedented party animosity and rancour which almost paralysed the House of Commons between the years 1906 and 1914. Undaunted, in 1913 the Town Tenants' League extracted from both Mr Asquith (then Prime Minister) and Mr Lloyd George (his eventual successor) the admission that protective legislation was desirable, and the assurance that the Liberal government would respond accordingly. **1.07**

Although the momentum for reform was suspended during the years of the First World War, by 1920 the issue had again been brought to the fore. Indeed, the post-war case for reform was more vital. A shortage of new building and the revival of trade and commerce ensured that competition for business premises was great. This abnormal demand and inadequacy of supply created a sellers' market **1.08**

---

[14] See, for example, the recommendations of the *Final Report of the Leasehold Committee* (1950) Cmd 7982.

in which landlords were able to abuse their superior bargaining power. Although the potential for exploitation was no recent phenomenon, it now assumed a higher profile. It was feared that unscrupulous landlords were keen to capitalise on the distorted market and to raise rents to extortionate levels. In the background, entrepreneurs and multiple shopkeepers lurked waiting for the opportunity to buy leases with established goodwill over the heads of sitting tenants. The spectre of the profiteering landlord loomed large over the tenant whose lease was about to expire.[15]

1.09 The protection of business tenants was not merely desirable on the grounds of equity; the national interest introduced a new dynamic into the case for reform. It had become clear that, in order to facilitate a post-war economic recovery, existing businesses and premises had to be preserved while new buildings were constructed to cater for business expansion. Without the prospect of recompense at the end of their terms, tenants would be reluctant to sink money into development schemes and, thereby, enhance the value of the demised premises. Undue increases in rents were likely to lead to business closures and higher levels of unemployment, or to be passed on to the consumer and, thereby, stimulate inflation. The difficulty, of course, was to devise a regulatory system which prevented landlords from taking undue advantage of the abnormal demand for business accommodation and yet did not discourage new investment in property development. Unfortunately, there was no consensus as to what form that control should adopt. The tenant lobby did not speak with one voice, whereas landlords simply sought the preservation of contractual rights. As the existing market distortions (and, hence, the scope for tenant exploitation) were likely to be short lived, there was also disagreement as to whether statutory intervention was to be of a permanent or a temporary nature. It was, as Mr Bonar Law (the Leader of the House under the Liberal and Conservative coalition government) admitted, 'a very complicated subject' for which it was 'difficult to find a remedy'.[16]

Temporary Expediencies

1.10 Prior to the Landlord and Tenant Act 1927, there existed two experimental provisions which extended limited rights to the business tenant. First, under the Increase of Rent and Mortgage Interest (War Restrictions) Act 1915, as interpreted by the courts, protection was offered to single lettings of small dwellings which had a mixed business and residential user. In a time of housing shortage, this emergency Act was designed primarily to protect living accommodation

---

[15] 'In perceptual terms the landlord was an ogre, the hardest of hard-faced men, one who preyed upon and tormented the lives of millions' (Englander, n 11 above at 5).

[16] HC Deb vol 205, col 556, 1920 (22 April); vol 206, col 635, 1920 (15 May). This difficulty persisted over the next three decades: see, for example, the divergent recommendations of the Leasehold Committee in its Interim Report (1949) above and its Final Report (1950) above.

which fell within prescribed rateable or rental values.[17] The protection of business premises was, therefore, by a side wind. As Bankes LJ said in *Epsom Grand Stand Association Ltd v Clarke*, 'The object of the legislature was to include all houses which were occupied as dwelling houses, provided they were within the class named, irrespective of whether the premises were also used for some other purpose.'[18] Such protection took the form of a non-assignable prolongation of the tenancy beyond its contractual term and a system of rent control designed to maintain rents at the 1914 level. This was a mechanism clearly unsuited to the needs of business tenants and, in 1920, the Salisbury Committee concluded that commercial premises should be taken outside the ambit of the 1915 Act.[19] The Committee acknowledged, however, that safeguards were necessary for business tenants and envisaged that control would be better achieved by offering tenants the opportunity to secure a new lease. It recommended that a separate inquiry be undertaken into the needs of commercial tenants and, later that same year, the Select Committee on Business Premises was established and reported.[20]

Second, section 13 of the Rent and Mortgage Restrictions Act 1920 exclusively **1.11** related to leases of business premises which fell within prescribed rateable values. For the first time, protection was extended to tenants of business premises without the need to establish an element of residential user. Although it had been the intention of the government to exclude business tenancies entirely from the Act, pressure from all political parties ensured the inclusion of this special and temporary provision. The immediate concern was to ensure that the hybrid class of tenants, which had fallen within the 1915 Act, would not face immediate eviction when that Act was repealed.[21] The provision operated on two levels: it prevented the landlord from increasing the rent by more than 35 per cent and inhibited the recovery of possession at the end of the contractual tenancy. This control was designed only to last for a period of one year and lapsed on 24 June 1921. It was intended merely to span the period of the deliberations of the Select Committee on Business Premises and the time it would take to enact permanent legislation. Although the Select Committee had called for immediate legislation to safeguard business tenants, its recommendations were ignored. Accordingly, and until the

---

[17] It was later amended and its duration extended by the Increase of Rent and Mortgage Interest (Restrictions) Act 1919.

[18] (1919) 35 TLR 525 at 526; see also *Colls v Parnham* [1922] 1 KB 325. It operated where, say, a shopkeeper lived over the shop or a doctor resided over consulting rooms: see *Hicks v Snook* (1928) 27 LGR 175; *Vickery v Martin* [1944] 2 All ER 167.

[19] *Departmental Committee on Increase of Rent and Mortgage Interest (War Restrictions) Acts* (1920) Cmd 658.

[20] *Reports from Committees*, 1920, vol 5.

[21] Mixed user premises, however, remained governed by the Rent Restriction Acts until the Rent Act 1957. Broadly speaking, from that time a tenancy of a dwelling house partly used for business purposes was within the residential code; business premises used in part for residential purposes were to be governed by Part II of the Landlord and Tenant Act 1954: *Whiteley v Wilson* [1953] 1 QB 77.

Landlord and Tenant Act 1927, market forces were again allowed to prevail and, excepting mixed tenancies, commercial tenants were compelled to rely solely upon their contractual rights.

Recommendation and Inaction

1.12 The short-term remedy proposed by the 1920 Select Committee was to offer the business tenants the right, on the expiry of the contractual term, to apply to a tribunal for the continuation of their tenancies (akin to the statutory tenancy already available to residential tenants). The landlord would be given the ability to oppose the application on strictly delimited grounds and, if successful, the tribunal would have the power to award compensation to the tenant. The underlying assumption was that legislative intervention should be kept to a minimum so as not to discourage new building. The Committee believed also that controls were necessary only as a temporary measure to cater for the immediate post-war shortage of premises. Two major limitations were associated with the proposed scheme. First, only buildings erected before the date of the proposed legislation would be caught by its provisions. Second, as it was widely anticipated that the post-war recovery would be achieved rapidly, the modification of the landlord's common law rights were intended to last only for a period of two and a half years from the date of the Report. Parliament, however, preferred to adopt a 'wait and see' policy and the Committee's proposals were never implemented. Subsequent to the Select Committee's Report, there were four general elections within an equal number of years and once more the impetus for reform was lost.

1.13 Although unsuccessful attempts had been made to introduce Bills which would give business tenants security of tenure with compensation in default, by 1924 the market had corrected itself. There was no longer an acute shortage of commercial premises and concerns over the national interest were less urgent. Parliament's time and attention became focused instead upon the major overhaul of the conveyancing system which was to emerge in the legislative package of 1925. Contrary to the expectations of many politicians, however, the problems experienced by business tenants did not disappear. An increased demand for retail outlets ensured that speculation in properties with established goodwill persisted. Tenants now complained of the additional abuse that, in order to obtain consent to make improvements, some lessors demanded the payment of a fine and/or increased rent. The situation was perceived to be so dire that, in 1927, Parliament was warned: 'In London and most of our large towns there are innumerable cases of tenants who have been penalised and fined, and in many instances ruined by the operation of the present system.'[22]

---

[22] *Per* Major Owen, HC Deb vol 202, col 1769, 1927 (23 February).

Political Expediencies

Although the injustices suffered by leaseholders were widely regarded as a pressing   **1.14**
problem, in 1926 the Conservative government again blocked the progress of a
Town Tenants' Bill. The Prime Minister did, however, accept the need for a public debate and, indeed, the next King's Speech promised reform. It was during this
Parliamentary session that the Home Secretary successfully piloted the Landlord
and Tenant Bill through Parliament. In doing so, and some three years into its
term of office, Mr Baldwin's government had, in the words of one MP, 'learned to
transgress the canons of historical Conservatism'.[23] This change of direction was
only partially induced by the convincing case put forward by tenants and the more
emotive stance adopted by some politicians.[24] Primarily, it was a political ploy
which, at a time when public support was slipping away from the government,
was designed to keep on board the votes of the disgruntled trading and shopkeep-
ing community. The rising price of land since the War had added greatly to the
concerns of the business sector. Dissatisfaction was acute in the West End and
Westminster areas of London where leases were falling due every day, and during
the subsequent five years or so, these areas would witness a cascade of expired
terms. In particular, government-regulated building in Regent Street had, in the
words of Viscount Sumner, 'rubbed tenants up the wrong way for three or four
years'.[25] With one year to go before the next election, the government clearly saw
profit in placating a growing sense of injustice. The simple tactic was to appease
the business community while assuring lessors (and, of course, the more reac-
tionary element of the Conservative party) that reform would do no more than
codify the current practices of reasonable landlords.

Reform was, therefore, destined to be a compromise measure. The government   **1.15**
stance was that, when worked by an ideal landlord, the leasehold system operated
perfectly well to the benefit of both parties and of the general community.[26] By
necessity, however, it had to be acknowledged that there were unscrupulous landlords who did take unfair advantage of their tenants, particularly when the time
came to make an improvement or to obtain a renewal. It followed that legislative
controls would merely serve as a code of practice designed to put all landlords in
the same category as the good landlord. Hence, the reasonable lessor would have
nothing to fear from an enactment framed 'to protect the tenant against the action

---

[23] *Per* Mr MacClaren HC Deb Vol 204, col 2321, 1927 (7 April).
[24] A typical response from the Labour benches was that of Mr Dalton, 'The present law . . . permits landlords to confiscate the fruits of the past labour and past enterprise of their tenants and also
permits them sometimes to hamper and to penalise the future enterprise and future labour of those
same tenants' (HC Deb vol 204, col 2315, 1927 (7 April)).
[25] HL Deb vol 69, col 330, 1927 (29 November).
[26] See Sir William Joynson-Hicks (Home Secretary) HC Deb vol 204, col 2301, 1927 (7 April).

of a harsh and unconscionable landlord'.[27] The public interest, moreover, demanded that the commercial position of the country be improved and that Parliament make 'a real and genuine effort to remove a real and genuine grievance'.[28] In the light that, as regards both agricultural and residential tenancies, legislation had been in place for many years, it was both illogical and untenable to deny similar safeguards to town tenants. The Home Secretary, somewhat curtly, reminded his party that they were no longer living in the eighteenth century. Although the Bill had a stormy ride through the Commons,[29] it was rushed through the House of Lords and received the Royal Assent on 22 December 1927.

C. Policy and Practice

1.16 Part I of the Landlord and Tenant Act 1927 was modelled on the general recommendations of the Select Committee on Town Holdings (1889) and the more specific and contemporary advice of the Council of the Surveyors' Institute. The scheme was to echo legislation which was thought to operate well in both Eire and France. The protection of the business tenant's interests was, therefore, to be achieved by a system which offered compensation for loss of goodwill and improvements. The theory was simple: if the landlord gained through the presence of the tenant, then compensation must be paid or a renewal granted. It was a measure which, at first blush, appeared to go some way both in redressing the inequality of bargaining power and in tackling the mischief of which business tenants had long complained. Business tenants were, at least in the short term, satisfied by the fact that some protective legislation was in place and the hope that it would facilitate reasonable security of tenure. In reality, the scheme was defective and provided little assistance to the business community.[30] It was a timid measure which did not go far enough. The failure to offer security of tenure as a direct right prompted one contemporary politician to describe its provisions as 'very small ... very niggardly and very unsatisfactory'.[31] More specifically, the primary failing

---

[27] ibid at col 2307. Not all opponents to change were convinced by the government's rhetoric. The Property Owners Protection Society, for example, feared that the Bill would prove injurious to the prosperity of the country as a whole: The Times 30 April 1927. Similarly, the Council of Auctioneers and Estate Agents Institute warned of the perils and potential evils arising from the Bill: The Times 6 May 1927.

[28] *Per* Sir William Joynson-Hicks, ibid at col 2314. As Lord Greene explained in *Stuchbery & Son v General Accident Fire & Life Assurance Corporation Ltd* [1949] 2 KB 256 at 264, 'It was obviously thought by the legislature to be unjust that the landlord should obtain that type of unearned increment at the termination of a lease ...'.

[29] There were, for example, nearly 300 amendments suggested following the second reading of the Bill.

[30] To Lord Phillimore it illustrated 'a very melancholy fact that once again bad landlords were likely to make bad laws' (HL Deb vol 69, cols 353, 354, 1927 (29 November)).

[31] Mr Dalton (Labour) HC Deb vol 204, col 3215, 1927 (7 April).

of the Act was that the key goodwill provisions were ill-thought out, largely unworkable and easily side-stepped by a well-advised landlord.[32] Consequently, and as admitted some twenty-two years later in the Interim Report of the Leasehold Committee, 'business tenants enjoy virtually no protection outside the terms of their tenancies in respect of either tenure or of rent'.[33] Although the Act may (with much validity) be viewed as a wasted opportunity, it did recognise the necessity that business tenancies be subject to permanent statutory regulation.

From there on, the principle was unchallengeable and there could be no retreat. **1.17** Indeed, the abject failure of the statutory scheme encouraged the later adoption of more radical solutions to the problems faced by the business community. Unarguably, the most significant aspect of Part I was the machinery whereby, in admittedly rare circumstances, the tenant could be awarded a new lease. For the first time, the court was given the jurisdiction to order the grant of a new tenancy of business premises. Although at that stage renewal was inextricably wedded to the provisions governing compensation for goodwill, this was to set a broader precedent for future reforms.[34] The 1927 Act also went some distance in rationalising reform options. It laid to rest the notion that controls be restricted according to the size of the premises or rateable values and (by omission) served to highlight the need of professional tenants for some protection. It also rejected the idea of a system of rent control as operated in the residential sector and ensured that the tenant's entitlement was to be proprietary in nature and not to take the form of a personal statutory tenancy.

The Mechanics of the Act

As regards business tenancies, the 1927 Act addressed the mischief of bad land- **1.18** lordism in several discrete ways. First, the general attempt was made to minimise the effect of leasehold covenants which prohibited the alienation, development or improvement of premises. This was achieved by section 19 which implies into qualified covenants (those which expressly require the consent of the landlord) the proviso that this consent cannot be unreasonably withheld. Although this provision does not strike at absolute covenants, as regards improvements of business premises only section 3 gives the court power to override a blanket prohibition.

---

[32] As Lord Paramour remarked, 'the gift given by one hand is almost withdrawn by the mass of detail by which it is accompanied' (HL Deb vol 69, col 316, 1927 (29 November)). This is a criticism not confined to business tenancies. In relation to the Rent Restriction Acts, it has been said, 'One must sympathise with the difficulties of the time, but, nevertheless, the example is there of the cure masking some of the symptoms whilst the disease gets worse' (VW Taylor, *Social Purpose of Land Law* [1966] Conv 305 at 307).

[33] Above at para 4.

[34] '[T]he focus of debate changed to the best means of providing the business tenant with the security of tenure he needed to enable him to establish, develop and preserve his business' (Law Reform Advisory Committee for Northern Ireland, *A Review of the Law relating to Business Tenancies in Northern Ireland* (1992) Discussion Paper No 3 at para 2.2.3).

With some minor amendment, these measures remain in force to the present day.[35]

1.19   Second, section 1 allows the business tenant to claim compensation for approved structural improvements (which cannot be removed as tenant's fixtures) at the end of the lease. As shown in Chapter 10, the essential preconditions of a successful claim are that the improvement adds to the letting value of the premises and that notice has been served on the landlord prior to the making of the improvement. Unfortunately, the procedure is unwieldy, difficult to operate and remains in urgent need of simplification. The Law Commission has recommended the abolition of this compensation scheme, but the proposal is not unassailable and, although approved in principle by the government, it is doubtful when (and possibly whether) it will be implemented.[36]

1.20   Third, section 4 allowed the business tenant to claim compensation for goodwill at the end of the contractual term. As goodwill is an intangible form of personal property which can be assigned and/or protected against unlawful interference, it was a logical progression to allow a tenant to be recompensed for its loss.[37]

Adherent Goodwill

1.21   As regards compensation, the burden lay with the tenant to show that, as a result of carrying on a trade or business for at least five years (by the tenant or a predecessor), the letting value of the premises had increased. Accordingly, the provision applied only to what is curiously termed 'adherent goodwill', which stayed with the site and made it a more valuable asset for a succeeding tenant.[38] As such, the calculation of goodwill did not reflect the potential loss to the tenant, but rather the potential gain to the landlord.[39] Hence, the tenant could not succeed if the premises were to be demolished or if the landlord intended to re-let for a different and, perhaps, more valuable purpose. Similarly, compensation did not extend to professional tenants because they were regarded as having only 'personal goodwill'

---

[35]   In so far as they relate to the authorisation of tenants' improvements, the provisions are considered in detail in Chapter 10.

[36]   *Landlord and Tenant Law: Compensation for Tenant's Improvements*, (1989) Law Com No 178.

[37]   See Yates and Hawkins, *Landlord and Tenant Law* (1986) 740–747. As Lord Macnaghten accepted in *IRC v Muller & Co's Margarine Ltd* [1901] AC 217 at 234, '[Goodwill] has no independent existence. It cannot subsist by itself. It must be attached to a business. Destroy the business, and the goodwill perishes with it, though elements remain which may perhaps be gathered up and be revived again.'

[38]   See *Hudd v Matthews* [1930] 2 KB 197. For an analysis of the difficulties raised by section 4 see RE Megarry [1953] 69 LQR 305.

[39]   As made clear in the Final Report of the Leasehold Committee (n 14 above) at para 126, 'In truth "adherent goodwill" is not goodwill at all in the sense in which that term is understood either in law or in ordinary business parlance.'

which would follow them to new premises.[40] The concept of adherent goodwill, therefore, proved to be a manifestly inappropriate measure of compensation. Although it was relatively straightforward to show what the premises were worth, it was rarely possible to know how much of that figure had been contributed by the tenant's business.[41]

In addition, there were various types of business (for example, manufacturers) and **1.22** bodies (such as charitable institutions and trade associations) that did not attract such goodwill and, therefore, were deprived of both compensation and renewal rights. Even if adherent goodwill was identified, tenants still faced a long and complicated procedure to prove entitlement to compensation. The lessee had to make a written claim, containing certain prescribed particulars, as appropriate, within one month following the service of a notice to quit or, in any other case, at least twelve months and no more than thirty-six months preceding the contractual termination of the tenancy. The tenant was disentitled to compensation in circumstances where the landlord, within two months of the tenant's claim, made a written offer to renew the lease on reasonable terms. If the offer was not accepted within one month, the tenant was deemed to have declined it. Those tenants who were ignorant of their rights and/or the statutory procedure faced the real risk of losing any entitlement by default. There was, moreover, no obligation on the landlord to inform the tenant of the statutory rights. In addition, and on surmounting such hurdles, as the Act did not offer compensation for disturbance the amount awarded would rarely reflect accurately the value of the premises to the tenant. The availability of compensation, moreover, was of little solace to those tenants who wanted to continue in occupation of the premises.

Renewal in Lieu

Section 5 of the 1927 Act, moreover, facilitated the grant of a new lease in cir- **1.23** cumstances where the lessee was entitled to compensation for goodwill, but the sum to be awarded (based on landlord's gain) would be insufficient to compensate the tenant for the loss of 'personal goodwill'. Although there was no compensation for this type of loss, in this situation the tenant could claim a new lease in lieu of the inadequate compensation.[42] The emphasis here was shifted from the landlord's gain and placed upon the tenant's loss. The tenant's claim could, however, be defeated by a landlord on the grounds that suitable alternative accommodation

---

[40] Section 17(3)(a). Being wholly related to the personal skill and reputation of the tenant, this type of goodwill is unsaleable and does not increase the value of the property. See the 'cat', 'rat' and dog' metaphor provided by Scrutton LJ in *Whiteman Smith Motor Co v Chaplin* [1934] 2 KB 35 at 42 and interpreted in *Mullins v Wessex Motors* [1947] 2 All ER 727.

[41] As recognised by Lord Jessel: 'this question of goodwill is a sort of elusive will-o'-the wisp which you cannot grasp' (HL Deb vol 69, Col 414, 1927 (1 December); see also *Charrington & Co v Simpson* [1935] AC 325.

[42] The court, moreover, could make an interim order authorising the tenant to continue in occupation until the claim was resolved.

was available, the premises were required for landlord's occupation (or by a son or daughter of the landlord), the premises were to be demolished or redeveloped, or the grant of a new lease would be inconsistent with good estate management. If the tenant's claim was successful there could only be one renewal and its term could not exceed fourteen years. The rent was to be fixed by the court on the basis of what a willing lessee would pay to a willing lessor, disregarding any value attributable to goodwill and tenant's improvements. The major defect, of course, was that the tenant still had to prove the existence of adherent goodwill before statutory renewal became a possibility and, as shown, many tenants (including all professional tenants) were unable to prove this fact.

D. The Momentum Continued

1.24 It was only in the aftermath of the Second World War that concern for the business tenant again became a pressing issue. For almost a decade there had been no new building, and bombing had seriously depleted the stock of pre-existing premises, particularly in the larger cities. Since 1945, there had been a major revival and expansion of commercial activity, and existing businesses now found themselves in fierce competition with new firms seeking premises from which to trade. As in 1918, this increased demand created a seller's market in which landlords were able to take advantage of their sitting tenants. It became clear that the Landlord and Tenant Act 1927 had failed to achieve its purpose, and that business tenants remained vulnerable to exploitation. Accordingly, in December 1948 the government set up the Leasehold Committee with the remit to determine whether business tenants should be given security of tenure and/or enhanced rights to compensation for improvements at the expiry of their tenancies. Provision was allowed for the publication of an interim report as regards any matters which were deemed sufficiently urgent to merit attention. In January 1949, the Committee, then under the chairmanship of Lord Uthwatt, published its *Interim Report on Tenure and Rents of Business Premises.*[43] The Interim Report acknowledged that business tenants remained dissatisfied by the ability of landlords to charge a much increased rent and/or fine on a lease renewal.

The Interim Report

1.25 Due to the inequality of bargaining power, renewals were still offered on a non-negotiable 'take it or leave it' basis. This was particularly harsh on small shopkeepers whose trade was subject to price controls and who could not pass on the increased costs to their customers. In addition, such renewals might be for periods that bore no resemblance to those originally granted. In order to maximise the

---

[43] See n 8 above. Two minority reports were appended.

investment potential of the demised premises, some lessors preferred to grant only periodic tenancies whereas others insisted on the tenant taking a long term of years. The menace of the unscrupulous speculator was also invoked, but in the modern guise of a purchaser who bought up a large office-block with the sole ambition that the current tenants would be evicted and the premises re-let as a single unit to a large corporation.[44] These observations, therefore, bore a striking similarity to those rehearsed some thirty years earlier.

The Committee's defence of landlords also toed the traditional line. Albeit pre- **1.26** dictable and by now somewhat hackneyed, it was concluded that lessors generally exercised proper restraint in setting rent levels on renewal and that there was no evidence of widespread abuse.[45] Rent increases alone (even large ones) were no proof of exploitation and often simply reflected the fall in the value of money (and associated increased costs of repair and service charges).[46] It was unrealistic to view the 1939 level of rents as a standard by which to judge the fair level of the subsequent decade. Nevertheless, the Committee acknowledged that a minority of landlords did abuse their superior bargaining power and that this was sufficient to cause uneasiness to the majority of business tenants. As with the Landlord and Tenant Act 1927, it was intended that the proposed reforms would not seriously damage the interests of reasonable landlords and would merely impose, 'as a kind of "professional code" for property owners the moral standards of good landlords'.[47] On this occasion, however, higher standards would be ensured and the tenant given greater protection than that previously afforded. No immediate action was taken by the government of the day.

Interim Recommendations

The Interim Report based its recommendations on the assumption that business **1.27** tenants did not want rent control; rather they sought security of tenure and the ability to carry on trade without interruption. Compensation was viewed as being insufficient to achieve this stability.[48] The Committee felt that there was an immediate need to secure the sitting tenant against the risk of unreasonable disturbance by the landlord.[49] This enabled it to make the crucial leap and recommend that a

---

[44] ibid at para 29.

[45] ibid at para 30.

[46] ibid at para 31.

[47] ibid at para 51. This complacency was not, however, endorsed by Sir Edward Gillett who feared that the proposed cure would prove to be worse than the disease: ibid at 36; see also the doubts of Sir Edwin Herbert at 37–40.

[48] 'Compensation is a very desirable alternative in cases where continuity of tenure is for special reasons out of the question, but it is only a second best and it should remain in the background— the exceptional procedure, rather than the normal remedy. The business tenant occupies his premises in order to trade, or to pursue his profession: he does not wish to be compensated for being prevented from doing so' (ibid at para 38).

[49] This protection was necessary at least until the availability of business accommodation increased and some equality of bargaining power restored: ibid at para 36. Whether the proposed

general entitlement to security of tenure for existing tenants was the only way to ensure fair dealing. A simple, predictable and easily enforced renewal scheme would obviate the need for any system of rent control and largely overcome the defects associated with the goodwill provisions contained in the 1927 Act. Accordingly, the Interim Report advocated a sweeping system whereby sitting tenants, excepting those in new buildings, would be given the prima-facie right to a new lease. This renewal could not exceed seven years, but the tenant would then be able to apply for further renewals. Only in special circumstances would the landlord be able to defeat the tenant's claim. The right to renewal was to extend to all types of business and professional activity and was not to be limited according to size of the premises or rateable values. There was also to be no minimum period of occupation as a condition of entitlement. The scheme was to interlock with the Landlord and Tenant Act 1927 to the extent that a failure to secure renewal would not deprive the tenant of any claim for compensation for goodwill and improvements and that a notice of a claim for a new lease would operate also as notice of an alternative claim to compensation.

An Alternative Agenda

1.28 The Final Report of the Leasehold Committee (now under the chairmanship of Jenkins LJ) was published in June 1950.[50] The new chairman distanced himself from the majority recommendations of the Interim Report (of which he had not been party).[51] Not surprisingly the Committee's final conclusions varied greatly, both in principle and in detail, from its previous recommendations. Jenkins LJ felt that the business tenant's predicament had been overstated in the Interim Report and did not justify placing drastic restrictions on the contractual rights of all landlords of commercial premises. Unlike the previous report, Jenkins LJ refused to accept that lessees had a specific and occupational interest in the premises which, outweighing that of their landlords (who were interested primarily in the financial return from the property), should be translated into tenants' rights. Instead, the extent of intervention was to be tempered by the fact that safeguards were necessary only for a minority of tenants who had to deal with a small class of unscrupulous landlords. As Jenkins LJ explained: 'If abuse is the exception rather than the rule, I do not see how it can be right in principle to subject the whole business community to a new system of control . . . merely for the purpose of preventing the relatively few cases of unfair dealing which might otherwise occur'.[52]

---

scheme was to be permanent or temporary was an issue to be left until the Committee's Final Report.

[50] See n 14 above. The Committee again was not unanimous.
[51] ibid at 122–125.
[52] ibid at 122, para 4.

This attitude represented a fundamental shift in ideology from that which per-   **1.29**
vaded the Interim Report. Although the Final Report was to favour renewal rights
over compensation, it did not advocate a prima-facie right to security of tenure.
Instead, it proposed a scheme under which the tenant had to establish special circumstances in order to justify a new lease. This reflected the basic tenet of the
Final Report that the landlord's right of property should not be overridden in any
fundamental fashion. In marked contrast to its interim recommendations, the
Committee now sought to protect the legitimate claims of the landlords and to
avoid unduly favouring tenants. As the Committee explained:

> [Tenants] should not have such a degree of security as will protect the bad tenant or
> perpetuate the inefficient business; or will prevent the due expansion of existing
> businesses or the setting up of new ones; or will in other ways promote stagnation
> and interfere with redevelopment or other desirable change.[53]

The interim proposals were felt not only to prejudice unjustifiably the interests of
landlords, but also to be capable of producing anomalies and inequalities amongst
business tenants. It was feared that startling results would follow on from the ability of a tenant to claim protection by the mere fact of occupation on a certain date
regardless of how short that period of occupation might have been. Such a 'first
come, first served' principle was arbitrary and failed to take on board the interests
of those who were in need of premises.[54] Consequently, it would distort the market in original tenancies, and entail that a purchaser would have to pay much more
for a lease which carried with it the right to renewal. In addition, it would drive up
the rents of new premises which fell outside the scheme. Finally, as the controls
were mooted only as a temporary expedient, they offered no assistance to those
who had taken a long lease which was not to due to expire in the immediate future.

Security of Tenure

In its Final Report, the Leasehold Committee accepted that reasonable security of   **1.30**
tenure was essential for the development of business and acknowledged that the
Landlord and Tenant Act 1927 failed to provide adequate safeguards. The
Committee had two general choices open to it. First, to persist with a scheme
under which compensation was the primary claim. If so, it was apparent that the
amount claimable by a dispossessed tenant would have to be increased so as to
reflect the actual loss incurred by removal.[55] This would entail that the refusal of
renewal would be so expensive that the landlord would only deny the tenant a new
lease on good grounds. The Committee, however, rejected this option on the
basis that it would be difficult to operate and, in any event, would be no more

---

[53] ibid at para 143.
[54] 'The result of such a plan must inevitably be to benefit the man in possession of the premises
at the expense of the man in search of premises for no better reason than that the former has managed to get in first' (*per* Jenkins LJ, ibid at 123, para 5).
[55] ibid at paras 145–146.

acceptable to landlords than if tenants were given direct security of tenure. The second choice was to entitle the tenant to renewal as the primary claim.[56] In line with its stance that the sins of a few landlords should not unduly punish the majority, the Committee refused to accept that there should be an automatic right to renewal.[57] Instead, it resolved that the existing machinery contained in the Landlord and Tenant Act 1927 should be modified to allow the tenant to apply for a new lease without first proving the case for compensation.[58] This was subject to what the Committee described as 'just exceptions' whereby the tenant's claim would be debarred. There was also to be no contracting out, except where the tribunal was prepared to authorise a pre-tenancy agreement to that effect.

Entry Conditions and Entitlement

1.31   To qualify under the proposed scheme, the tenant (or predecessor) must have carried on a trade, business or profession from the premises for a minimum period of three years. Entitlement to a renewal was conditional on there being an absence of suitable alternative accommodation available to the tenant. Unlike the Landlord and Tenant Act 1927, the burden of proving this negative was to rest with the tenant. Hence, the tenant would have to demonstrate the non-existence of suitable alternative premises as a condition of entry to the renewal provisions. The criterion upon which renewal was to be decided was, moreover, cumbersome and varied according to whether the tenant used the premises for profit-making purposes, non-profit-making purposes or for professional purposes.[59] Within these parameters, the tenant had to convince the tribunal that it was reasonable for it to order a new tenancy against the wishes of the landlord. The tribunal was, thereby, to take into account all considerations relevant to the merits of the tenant's claim, and was not to be restricted merely to the issue of goodwill.[60]

1.32   The inherent complexity of the scheme entailed that the tribunal's task would be neither simple nor straightforward. Indeed, as feared by a minority of the Committee:

> [I]t is too much to hope that these three definitions, involving complicated considerations and hypothetical calculations, and necessarily somewhat novel in some

---

[56]   ibid at paras 147–151.

[57]   'Security of tenure is not to be at the expense of the landlord and is not to subsidise the inefficient business' (ibid at para 151).

[58]   '[R]enewal would become the principal relief and compensation would take what we conceive to be its proper place as a substitute in cases where renewal is not obtained' (ibid at para 207).

[59]   As regards profit-making use, the test was whether failure to obtain renewal would cause substantial diminution in the value of the business as a going concern; in connection with non-profit-making activities, the test was whether it would cause a substantial increase in costs or loss of efficiency; and relating to the professions, the ground for claiming renewal was a substantial diminution in net profits.

[60]   Hence, businesses which did not generate 'adherent goodwill' would no longer be excluded from renewal rights: n 14 above at paras 149–150.

respects, will avoid professional wrangles. They may go far towards defeating the cheap, speedy and certain conclusion of a claim to renewal and therefore the very purpose of the scheme itself.[61]

If the tenant's claim was successful, any new lease ordered by the tribunal could not exceed fourteen years. The tenant was, however, entitled to apply for a further renewal at a later date. The rent was to be a fair market rent, disregarding any goodwill and tenants' improvements. The other terms of the new lease, subject to the discretion of the tribunal, were to mirror those in the original tenancy. If the claim for renewal was refused, compensation would remain as the alternative. Although the Committee had criticised the method of calculation as embodied in the 1927 Act, it was intended that it remain the general basis of compensation. The tribunal, however, was to be given the power to depart from the 'adherent goodwill' mode of assessment in one special case. This was where renewal had been refused on the ground that the landlord wanted the premises for personal occupation. If the tenant's business had made the premises more valuable to the landlord (in light of their intended use), then compensation should be awarded on the basis of that increased value.[62]

E. A New Deal for Tenants

Although it was apparent that further legislative controls were necessary to protect **1.33** business tenants, the irreconcilable differences, both in tone and content, between the Interim and Final Reports of the Leasehold Committee obscured the way forward. Hence, it was to take a further four years before a revamped code for commercial premises was introduced. Although many of the Committee's recommendations were never to be followed, within the two reports can be found the framework of what was to become the Landlord and Tenant Act 1954. The enduring legacy of these protracted and divergent deliberations was, undoubtedly, the shift of emphasis from compensation towards renewal rights. It entailed that security of tenure was to become the indelible hallmark of subsequent legislation. The outstanding difficulty, of course, was to design a scheme which, while derogating from the landlord's common law rights, would operate fairly and effectively. In the aftermath of the publication of the Final Report, however, the Leasehold Property (Temporary Provisions) Act 1951 was passed through Parliament. This was destined to have a lifespan of only three years, and Part II of the Act gave tenants (of retail shop premises only) the ability to apply to the

---

[61] The Hale/Ungoed-Thomas Minority Report, ibid at 130, para 19.
[62] ibid at para 210. The Hale/Ungoed-Thomas Minority Report felt that the broader base of compensation should apply in all cases where renewal was refused and the tenant was not in default (ibid at 131, para 25).

county court for a new tenancy, not exceeding one year, at a reasonable rent.[63] Further applications could be made later and, in theory at least, a series of extensions built up. The temporary scheme, albeit popular with shop tenants, was merely a stop-gap measure until Parliament could decide on a permanent and generally applicable system. It did, however, provide a valuable opportunity for experimentation with a system which afforded security of tenure as a prima-facie right. It was an experiment which appeared to work well.

Governmental Policy

1.34   In January 1953, a White Paper entitled *Government Policy on Leasehold Property in England and Wales* was published.[64] Within it, the Conservative government accepted the general proposition of the Leasehold Committee that improved security of tenure should be made available as a permanent measure to business and professional tenants.[65] It admitted that rent control and the concept of a statutory tenancy (both pivotal to the Rent Restriction Acts) should not feature in the regulation of business tenancies. Nevertheless, the White Paper concluded that neither scheme put forward by the Leasehold Committee was wholly satisfactory and that 'a new approach' was required.[66] Notwithstanding the fact that the details of this scheme differed markedly from that contained in the Interim Report of 1949, it was to embody a similar principle. The tenant was to be offered the automatic right to a new lease on fair market terms, defeasible only on limited grounds. The twin tenets of this new deal for commercial lessees were as follows. First, a tenant in occupation had a greater right than any alternative tenant to the premises. Second, if the landlord successfully opposed renewal, the tenant should (in defined circumstances) be entitled to claim compensation for disturbance. Although the precise mechanics of the new approach were left to be worked out at a later date, the paramount aim of government policy was to produce a scheme under which:

> The respective rights of the parties would be clear, and could if necessary be established before the Tribunal without undue trouble, dubiety or expense, because they would depend primarily on the facts of the case, not on the prior satisfaction of a formula or formulae whose application to the particular case would be a matter for legal argument with results not always consonant with the real deserts of the parties. Under such a scheme the parties would have every incentive to settle by agreement on reasonable terms without going to the Tribunal.[67]

---

[63] See *Deeble v Robinson* The Times, 11 November 1953. Although in Scotland there remains no security of tenure or compensation generally available for business tenants, shopkeepers are protected by the Tenancy of Shops Act 1949.

[64] (1953) Cmd 8713.

[65] ibid at paras 39–53.

[66] ibid at para 42.

[67] ibid at para 53.

The Landlord and Tenant Bill was introduced before Parliament in December **1.35** 1953 by Sir David Maxwell Fyfe. Part II of the Bill was to adhere to the policy previously described in the White Paper and was as the Lord Chancellor, Lord Simonds, appreciated, 'an attempt to do what was imperfectly and unsatisfactorily done by the Landlord and Tenant Act 1927'.[68] The Bill, however, was to approach the problem of tenant abuse from a different angle than that adopted by its predecessor. The landlord's common law rights of termination were to be abrogated to the extent that the tenant would be allowed to stay in possession and to apply to the court for a new lease. For the unsuccessful tenant, flat-rate compensation was to be available in lieu of a new lease.[69] The central strand of policy was that the business tenant would be given legal rights sufficient to enforce the standards expected from a reasonable landlord. As Lord Rochdale commented, 'A good landlord certainly will not complain of that. The poor landlord has no right to complain and the tenant cannot expect any more.'[70] In addition, the Bill was framed so that the poor tenant (ie one in breach of covenant) would be disentitled to renewal and compensation. By these means, the disturbance of business premises was to be reduced to a minimum and the parties encouraged to settle by agreement without recourse to the courts. Although the Bill provoked much debate in the House of Commons, primary attention was focused on Part I which dealt with residential tenancies.[71] As it applied to business tenancies, however, the general principles underlying the proposed legislation were non-controversial and widely welcomed in both Houses. On 1 October the Landlord and Tenant Act 1954 came into force and the new deal for business tenants finally materialised.

Extending Protection

The new scheme offered security of tenure to tenants of shops, offices, and facto- **1.36** ries, as well as professional tenants and bodies such as charities and trade associations. It ensured this by providing for the continuation and renewal of commercial tenancies. Until the issue of renewal is determined, the tenant is allowed to remain in possession of the premises. The original lease is, thereby, automatically and indefinitely prolonged beyond the date of its contractual termination, the continuation being on the same basic terms as the original tenancy. As Megarry explained:

> Statutory security of tenure for business premises has undergone many vicissitudes in recent years. The Landlord and Tenant Act, 1927, was relatively ineffective, and

---

[68] HL Deb vol 188, col 114, 1954 (29 June).
[69] This measure of compensation was favoured because it was simple and certain and, perhaps more to the point, because Parliament could not devise a better alternative: see Lord Simonds LC, HL Deb vol 188, col 116, 1954 (June 29).
[70] HL Deb vol 188, col 135, 1954 (June 29).
[71] The issue of leasehold enfranchisement, for example, dominated the Second Reading of the Bill. As to the residential reforms, see A Bramall, *Landlord and Tenant Act 1954* [1954] Conv 437.

was restricted in its field; the Leasehold Protection (Temporary Provisions) Act, 1951, was puissant yet even more limited in its scope; but the Landlord and Tenant Act, 1954, is both strong and wide in its application.[72]

Renewal itself is not, however, automatic. Instead, being the subject of a highly technical procedure, the new lease has to be earned by the tenant through timely form filling and process serving.[73] If the tenant does not obtain a renewal, financial compensation remains a possible alternative.

1.37 Although compensation for improvements remains under the auspices of the Landlord and Tenant Act 1927, the provisions relating to goodwill were repealed and replaced by a new right to compensation for the loss of the renewal right.[74] Part II of the 1954 Act, therefore, marks the culmination of the long drawn-out movement away from the sanctity of contract towards an effective system of control which protects business tenancies. It is designed to redress the inequality of bargaining power which traditionally pervades the relationship of landlord and tenant. By offering the right to a new lease, the 1954 Act has done much to eradicate the mischief which had plagued tenants for more than seventy years. At the end of the contractual term, the tenant should no longer face the unenviable prospect of business closure or being compelled to take a new lease at an exorbitant rent. The shift from compensation to renewal has, moreover, de-personalised the system in that it is no longer geared to safeguarding the financial interests of a particular tenant: it is not the tenant, but the tenant's business which is now the subject of protection. This has eliminated much subjectivity and discretion from the process and serves to emphasise the proprietary nature of a tenant's entitlement.

A Conflict of Interests

1.38 Although the 1954 Act represents an enormous improvement for those tenants who are now able to secure a renewal, it should not be viewed as a tenants' charter.[75] Unlike with the residential sector, the reforms were intended only to make limited inroads on the free market and are not designed to deprive the lessor of any investment value in the demised premises.[76] As Viscount Simonds accepted in *Re*

---

[72] RE Megarry [1956] 71 LQR 21.

[73] As D Macintyre [1955] CLJ 42 at 44 recognised, 'Meticulous compliance with the rules of procedure . . . is essential. Rigid time limits are imposed, designed, it seems, to strike a balance between minimising delay and allowing the parties to reach an agreement without going to court.'

[74] In Northern Ireland, a broadly equivalent system of security of tenure and compensation was introduced by the Business Tenancies (Northern Ireland) Act 1964. This has been repealed by the Business Tenancies (Northern Ireland) Order 1996.

[75] As the Law Reform Advisory Committee for Northern Ireland pointed out in its Discussion Paper (n 34 above at para 2.1.1), 'The policy of the legislation reflects three potentially conflicting interests: the landlord's property rights in the land, the tenant's property rights in the goodwill of his business, and the public's interest in the promotion of stability, growth and modernisation in the business sector'.

Wonderland Cleethorpes, 'if there is any ambiguity about the extent of that dero-gation, the principle is clear that it is to be resolved in favour of maintaining common law rights unless they are clearly taken away'.[77] Although the landlord's ability to let the premises is severely impeded by the tenant's rights, beyond that the Act preserves the core advantages of landlordism. Accordingly, there is no rental subsidy for the tenant on renewal and the landlord can oppose the claim for a new lease on the basis of legitimate self-interest. For example, a new lease cannot be granted if either the tenant is in breach of the tenancy agreement, the premises are to be redeveloped or used for the landlord's own purposes, or possession of sublet property is required so that the premises can be disposed of as a whole.

Similarly, the Act does not perpetuate the terms of the original lease, but instead **1.39** gives the court the discretion to redefine, where deemed appropriate and reason-able, the contractual relationship between the parties.[78] The new compensation provisions may also work favourably in the landlord's interest as the amount to be awarded reflects neither the tenant's loss nor the landlord's gain. Instead, it is based on an arbitrary formula of a sum equal to the rateable value of the premises, mul-tiplied by one if the tenant had been in occupation for less than fourteen years, or by two if occupation was for more than fourteen years. Undoubtedly, this rough and ready measure can work unfairly for tenants and lead to substantial injus-tice.[79] The statutory scheme, therefore, neglects the interests of those who are unable to obtain a new lease. The abandonment of direct protection for goodwill, supplanted by compensation for disturbance which takes no heed of the true loss incurred, produces the irony that a dispossessed tenant may have fared better under the discredited 1927 Act scheme. A striking injustice may arise, for exam-ple, where the landlord has successfully opposed renewal on the ground that it wishes to occupy the premises for the purposes of a business. If the business is to be the same as that of the dispossessed tenant, the landlord will inevitably profit from any established goodwill. In such circumstances, and particularly if the ten-ant has occupied for less than fourteen years, the 1954 Act may offer woefully inadequate compensation and, thereby, permit the landlord to benefit (perhaps substantially) from the type of unearned increment which Parliament had long intended to eradicate.[80]

---

[76] See *Garston v Scottish Widows' Fund & Life Assurance Society* [1998] 3 All ER 596.

[77] [1963] 2 All ER 775 at 778. Similarly, in *Weinbergs Weatherproofs Ltd v Radcliffe Paper Mill Co Ltd* [1958] 2 WLR 1 at 7, Harman J admitted, 'The principle must be that the bargain should not be altered by the statute more than is necessary to give the statute its proper effect.'

[78] See *O'May v City of London Real Property Co Ltd* [1983] 2 AC 726 where Lord Wilberforce accepted that 'there certainly is no intention . . . to freeze or . . . petrify the terms of the lease' (at 747).

[79] See Mr Turner-Samuels, HC Deb vol 536, cols 1825–1827, 1954 (27 January). As the Lord Chancellor (Lord Simonds) admitted, 'To some the amount will seem too much; to others undoubtedly it will seem too little' (HL Deb vol 188, col 116, 1954 (29 June)).

[80] This benefit is one which the Final Report of the Leasehold Committee specifically sought to deny the landlord: n 14 above.

From Principle to Detail

1.40 As part of its first programme of reform, the Law Commission considered the operation of Part II of the Landlord and Tenant Act 1954.[81] The Commission adopted the stance that the Act worked quite successfully and had proved advantageous both to the landlord and to the tenant. Although there was no attempt to redefine principle or policy, the Report accepted that certain anomalies and failings had emerged during the preceding fifteen years which 'had given rise to uncertainty or are likely to cause inconvenience or even injustice'.[82] Nevertheless, the Commission did not intend to investigate all known shortcomings and a number of issues were left over for future consideration. The neglected problem areas included the definition of the term 'business'; the complexity, timing and service of the statutory notices and counter notices; and the lack of sanctions for the failure by landlords and tenants to provide information as required by the Act. Ironically, it was to take a further twenty years before these issues were aired again.

1.41 As a result of its survey, the Law Commission recommended a number of changes and these were to form the basis of the Law of Property Act 1969. In line with the mission statement contained in the 1953 White Paper, the Commission sought to make the provisions more certain, workable and just. The reforms were designed to ensure that both parties to the lease obtained fair treatment. The Law of Property Act 1969 was, therefore, an exercise in fine-tuning and clarification.[83] The landlord's position was, however, strengthened in several substantive ways.

1.42 The introduction of an interim rent procedure, whereby the landlord could apply for a new rent to cover the period of the tenant's continuation tenancy, was designed purely to improve the landlord's income stream from the premises.[84] The landlord's future investment interests were also safeguarded in that the court was enabled to include a rent review clause within the new lease.[85] In order to allow the landlord the flexibility to create leases which fell outside regulatory controls, the

---

[81] *Report on the Landlord and Tenant Act 1954 Part II* (1969) Law Com No 17; see also the Working Paper (1967) Law Com No 7.

[82] ibid. For example, the Commission identified problems which had arisen in connection with partnerships, trusts and associated companies. See, for example, *Tunstall v Steigmann* [1962] 2 All ER 417 (landlord could not claim that intended to occupy through medium of own company); *Sevenarts Ltd v Busvine* [1969] 1 All ER 392 (landlord could claim occupation where acted as trustee for a company); and *Jacobs v Chanduri* [1968] 2 All ER 124 (one partner could not apply for new lease without other partner joining in).

[83] See D Macintyre [1970] Conv 16.

[84] Previously, the tenant stood to gain financially by dragging out proceedings for as long as possible and, thereby, maintaining the old rent: see *Espresso Coffee Machine Co Ltd v Guardian Assurance Co Ltd* [1958] 1 WLR 900. The interim rent was not, however, to be a full market rent and fell to be discounted to reflect the ephemeral nature of the continuation tenancy.

[85] It had been doubted whether the court could impose a variable rent on renewal. Although this occurred in practice (see *Re 88 High Road, Kilburn* [1959] 1 All ER 527), the Law Commission Report suggested that it was a somewhat dubious exercise of power: n 81 above at para 20.

court was given the power to sanction 'contracting out' and the scope for tempo-rary lettings to fall outside the statutory provisions was extended.[86] Both of these latter innovations were intended purely as an encouragement to landlords to grant short-lets of properties which would otherwise stand empty. Contracting out has, however, been utilised much more generally than was envisaged. In 1989, for example, 24,070 applications were made and, of them, 18,879 were granted by the court. The facility, moreover, is used regardless of the length of the lease to be granted. Accordingly, the statutory scheme has largely become optional and the protection of the Act potentially undermined. Such landlord-friendly reforms, moreover, emphasise that the statutory scheme modifies the common law rights of the lessor only to the extent necessary to safeguard the tenant's occupation of the premises. Beyond this, it is clear that the protection of the landlord's capital investment is of paramount concern.[87]

Tenant's Benefits

From the tenant's perspective, the Law of Property Act 1969 contained three ben-efits. First, by way of promoting certainty, the disregard of tenant's improvements in setting the new rent was, subject to conditions, to embrace improvements made during previous tenancies. Under the pre-existing system the disregard applied only to improvements made during the current tenancy.[88] Second, by way of simplification, the condition precedent that a formal application for a new lease must precede a claim for compensation for disturbance was abandoned. As the Law Commission accepted, this spares tenants the unnecessary trouble and expense in applying for a new lease, which they knew would not be granted, merely as a means of securing compensation.[89] An application does, however, postpone the date of eviction and gives the tenant more time to look for alterna-tive premises. Third, by way of clarification, where the landlord claimed posses-sion the basis of redevelopment, the court could grant the tenant a new lease of part of the original holding (for example, where possession of only part of the ten-ant's holding was reasonably required to carry out the works). Previously the court had no power to grant a new tenancy of part of the tenant's holding and there was no ability for the tenant to move out temporarily.[90] These provisions were, there-fore, introduced to facilitate the exercise of the tenant's rights and to ensure that the policy of the 1954 Act was more effectively translated into practice.

1.43

---

[86] The exclusion of short tenancies was extended to leases of up to six months duration. Longer tenancies, therefore, could be taken out of the Act only with the court's authorisation. The Law Commission Report devoted only two paragraphs to the issue of contracting out (ibid at paras 32, 33) and it was not subjected to full debate in Parliament.

[87] As was admitted by the Law Reform Advisory Committee for Northern Ireland in its 1994 *Business Tenancies' Report*: 'any interference with the initial contract between a landlord and a ten-ant should be kept to a minimum' (Report No 1 at para 2.1).

[88] *Re Wonderland Cleethorpes*, n 77 above.

[89] N 81 above at para 46.

[90] *Fernandez v Walding* [1968] 2 WLR 583.

Subsequent Developments

1.44 Little further development occurred until 1984, when the Department of the Environment undertook a review of the workings of the statutory scheme. This review concluded that no legislative changes were required. It was accepted that the 1954 Act operated satisfactorily and maintained an even balance between the rights of both landlord and tenant.[91] Nevertheless, there remained areas of detail which were widely held to be in need of reform. Subsequently, the cause was again championed by the Law Commission. In 1988, a Working Paper was published which focused attention upon a number of technical defects evident in the statutory scheme, but did not propose any fundamental reform.[92] In 1992, a Law Commission Report embodied an extensive catalogue of detailed reforms with the intention of producing a more streamlined and fair procedure.[93] Significantly, the Commission again stressed that no fundamental changes were necessary and accepted that the objectives of the 1954 Act had stood the test of time. In this light, it is perhaps surprising that contracting out has attracted no major criticism. Although it drives the proverbial coach and horses through the protective legislation, the Law Commission recommended that it be extended and that the supervisory role of the court be abandoned.[94]

1.45 This lack of controversy is, however, explainable on two fronts: first, the landlord's rental advantages (namely, an interim rent during a continuation tenancy and a market rent, with reviews, on renewal) when granting a tenancy within the catchment of the Act have overcome most of the traditional fears of the legislation. Second, as for the last thirty years or so market forces have been kind to the tenant, the freedom to contract on attractive terms has been a ready possibility for new tenants.[95] Hence, the deprivation of statutory protection is not necessarily important because the landlord is likely to want to renew and, because of the availability of alternative premises, will be unable to impose exorbitatnt rents and premiums. It follows that, in a stable or tenant-friendly market, the Act loses much of its potency because the parties can agree on an equal footing without recourse to the renewal scheme. If the market distorts, however, it is a certainty that attention will become focused on the appropriateness of a device which potentially negates all protection for the tenant. In the foreseeable future, therefore, the basis

---

[91] HC Deb vol 87, col 245, 1985 (20 November).

[92] Law Commission, *Part II of the Landlord and Tenant Act 1954* (1988) Working Paper No 111, paras 1.5–1.6.

[93] *Business Tenancies: A Periodic Review of the Landlord and Tenant Act 1954* (1992) Law Com No 208.

[94] ibid at paras 2.14–2.20.

[95] As the Law Reform Advisory Committee for Northern Ireland acknowledged in its 1994 Report, '[the property market] has experienced changes in the balance of supply and demand for business accommodation with corresponding shifts in the balance of bargaining power between landlord and tenant' (n 87 above at para 2.1).

of the statutory scheme is destined to stay intact. While decontrol has prevailed recently in both the residential and agricultural sectors, the business tenancy code survives, seemingly immune from shifts in policy and changes in economic climate.[96] This is primarily due to the existence of contracting out which undermines the need for total deregulation and to the fact that decontrol is designed to revitalise a flagging letting market. Such revitalisation is, simply, unnecessary in the business sector as some 60 per cent of all commercial properties remain leasehold.

Monitoring the Provisions

It is hardly surprising that periodic reviews of the workings of the 1954 Act detect **1.46** flaws and uncertainties. Any legislative code which attempts to safeguard landlords' vested interests while giving novel rights to their tenants is apt to produce tensions.[97] This is particularly so in relation to the provisions and procedures contained in Part II which, being notoriously technical and complex, generate much litigation.[98] The operation of the Act requires, therefore, to be monitored periodically so that the intended balance between the tenant's occupational rights and the landlord's financial interests is maintained. It is also crucial that the provisions are kept in step with the exigencies of contemporary commerce. There are two main vehicles through which this may be achieved. First, the supervision of the court is of major importance in ensuring the development of the statutory scheme. Albeit limited to a case-by-case basis, the court can act as a watchdog, identifying defects and drawing them to the attention of Parliament and law reform agencies.[99] The judiciary may also, where necessary, adopt a creative stance by interpreting the statutory provisions purposively so as to make the scheme work more effectively and equitably.[100] Second, the role of the Law Commission in the development of the law is, undoubtedly, crucial. The Commission enjoys the ability to take an overview of the workings of the 1954 Act and consults widely to elicit evidence and views as to grievances and the remedies that are appropriate. The danger which exists is that, by placing heavy emphasis upon the biased and

---

[96] The business tenancy code, as recognised by the Law Reform Advisory Committee for Northern Ireland in its Discussion Paper, n 34 above at para 2.2.5, '[now] stands alone as a code of major practical significance involving restrictions on the landlord's freedom of contract'.

[97] '[A] fact which is not surprising, considering the rise in land values and the rapid development of business and industrial property' (A Samuels [1961] JBL 374).

[98] As Lord Silkin had accurately predicted, 'this Bill is exceedingly difficult and will, I have no doubt for many years to come provide ample occupation for members of my [the legal] profession' (HL Deb vol 188, col 120, 1954 (29 June)). For example, the skills of the Parliamentary draughtsman came under vehement attack in *Connaught Fur Trimmings Ltd v Cramas Properties Ltd* [1965] 1 All ER 148 at 151,152.

[99] See, for example, *Mark Stone Cars Ltd v Howard De Walden Estates Ltd* (1997) 30 January CA.

[100] See, for example, Lord Diplock in *Kammins Ballrooms Co v Zenith Investments* [1970] 2 All ER 871 at 882.

impressionistic responses to its Working Papers, the Commission may end up with patchy and unscientific data. Undue reliance upon this evidence, moreover, obscures wider issues which, if identified, may be deemed unworthy of redress.

1.47 There is, clearly, the need for an objective reappraisal of the philosophy of the 1954 Act and a critical evaluation as to whether policy is being translated into practice. Unfortunately, this seems unlikely to occur and, therefore, reform will continue on an unorchestrated and piecemeal basis. Furthermore, it is apparent that reform does not come speedily, if at all. Although approved by the government,[101] the Law Commission's recommendations of 1992 still await presentation to Parliament, and amending legislation is hardly an immediate prospect. This lack of legislative action is, perhaps, not surprising as, at the beginning of 1999, around one-third of the Law Commission Reports so far published have failed to result in legislation.[102] It is, moreover, likely that the government will wait and see how the revamped Northern Irish system operates before implementing the broadly similar changes proposed for England and Wales.

---

[101] On 5 July 1996, the Department of the Environment issued a consultation paper which endorsed the majority of the Law Commission's recommendations.

[102] cf Northern Ireland where it took only two years for the recommendations of the Law Reform Advisory Committee Report to be put into effect by the Business Tenancies (Northern Ireland) Order 1996.

2

THE STATUTORY SCHEME

A. Introduction

As demonstrated in the preceding chapter, the fundamental aim of Part II of the **2.01** Landlord and Tenant Act 1954 is to confer on business tenants security of tenure without otherwise interfering with market forces. Provided that the tenant complies, within prescribed time limits, with a series of complex and technical statutory formalities, and on the understanding that the landlord cannot establish a ground of opposition as listed in section 30(1), the entitlement is to a new lease at a market rent. If the tenant is unable to obtain a renewal, flat-rate compensation for disturbance may be available under section 37. Until the contractual tenancy is terminated, however, the relationship between landlord and tenant is regulated by the general law. Although the Act does nothing to prevent the original lease being brought to an end by any method provided by the contract (for example, the exercise of a break clause), termination of the contractual term serves to activate its protective provisions. Provided that the lease is not contracted out of the Act, a section 24 continuation tenancy arises immediately and the relationship between landlord and tenant indefinitely maintained. The continuation tenancy, more-over, may only be terminated by one of the methods permitted by the Act.[1] Of these methods, the landlord's section 25 termination notice and the tenant's sec-tion 26 request for a new tenancy serve also to engage the renewal procedure. These latter notices, however, may only be served by and on a limited class of land-lord or tenant, as appropriate. It is with the adaptation of the common law and the mechanisms, concepts and characters pivotal to the statutory scheme that this chapter is concerned.

B. Contracting Out

2.02 In its original form, the 1954 Act contained a blanket prohibition on contracting out. Indeed, in Northern Ireland contracting out still remains impermissible.[2] As a result of the Law of Property Act 1969, a radical facility was introduced by which the parties can make a joint application to the court, requesting the approval for the grant of a fixed-term lease to which sections 24–28 of the Act will not apply.[3] The contracting out of a head lease entails that any later unauthorised sub-tenan-cies granted will also fall outside the statutory scheme.[4] This tactic, therefore, guarantees that the landlord can recover possession at the end of the contractual term. Not surprisingly, therefore, contracting out has become the primary method by which landlord's avoid tenants enjoying security of tenure. As the facil-ity is available only in relation to a proposed lease, however, there can be no con-tracting out of a subsisting lease.[5] Although the drafting of section 38, seemingly did not anticipate that the landlord and tenant would already have an existing relationship, in *Tottenham Hotspur Football & Athletic Co Ltd v Princegrove Publishers Ltd*, Lawson J concluded, 'The language is apt to cover—and, clearly, in my judgment, the sub-section does cover—a situation in which an existing landlord and tenant agree that there shall be a new lease of the demised premises, to come into existence between them at some future date.'[6] Accordingly, at the end of a current lease any new lease can be contracted out of the Act.

---

[1] See *Weinbergs Weatherproofs Ltd v Radcliffe Paper Mill Co Ltd* [1958] Ch 437.

[2] Article 24 of the Business Tenancies (Northern Ireland) Order 1996.

[3] Section 38(4). Subject to the special provisions relating to government departments and statu-tory undertakings which are contained in sections 57–58, other agreements purporting to exclude or to modify the tenant's renewal rights remain void: section 38(1).

[4] *St Giles Hotel Ltd v Microworld Technology Ltd* (1997) 75 P & CR 380. Authorised sub-lettings may, however, be caught by the statutory provisions. This should not cause problems for the head landlord as contracting out will normally be a condition of giving consent to the sub-lettings. Assignments of a contracted out lease always fall outside the Act.

[5] See *Shops Centres Plc v Derby City Council* (1996) October 11 HC. A tenancy granted uncon-ditionally cannot later be brought before the court for approval: *Essexcrest Ltd v Evenlex Ltd* [1988] 1 EG 56.

[6] [1974] 1 All ER 17 at 21.

It is also established that, as the court enjoys an exclusively statutory jurisdiction **2.03**
to make the order, no additional power can be bestowed on the judge by the parties.[7] Hence, a departure from the criteria laid down by Parliament will make the
order inherently invalid and always a nullity.[8] Similarly, any agreement between
the parties entered under the auspices of an irregularly exercised power is also
invalid.[9] It is also arguable that where a lease is lawfully contracted out, but the
terms of that lease are subsequently varied (for example, by the agreement of a
break clause) this change could take the tenancy outside the scope of the order,[10]
the logic being that the lease will now be different from that formerly approved.

Approval of the Court

The approval of the correct court is necessary for there to be a valid contracting **2.04**
out of the Part II provisions. This entails that before the tenancy is granted, both
parties must apply to the appropriate court for sanction of the agreement. This
joint application can be made either to the High Court[11] or to the county court.[12]
The correct High Court or county court is one within the area of the property or
where one the claimant resides or carries on business. It is as yet unclear whether,
under the Civil Procedure Rules 1998, an application made to the wrong court
will invalidate the approval once given.[13] Prior to that stage, however, it remains
possible for an application to be made to the judge for an order that the case stays
where it is (that is, in the wrong court).[14] Accordingly, the appliction should
always make this express request. Usually, the proceedings will not require the
attendance of the parties, but if one party has acted without legal advice both parties may be required to attend a hearing. The process requires that the parties set
out in their joint application the reason why they wish to contract out of the statutory provisions. Normally, but not necessarily, the application will be supported
by affidavit(s) showing the circumstances underlying the application and a

---

[7] *Barton v Fincham* [1921] 2 KB 291.

[8] *Nicholls v Kinsey* [1994] 2 WLR 622. The order does not maintain any legal force prior to
being declared void.

[9] As Hirst LJ recognised, any other conclusion would render section 38, 'a virtual dead letter'
(ibid at 628).

[10] See *Shops Centres Plc v Derby City Council*, n 5 above.

[11] By claim form issued by one solicitor acting on behalf of both parties: Rules of the Supreme
Court Order 97, r 6A (as preserved in Schedule 1 of the Civil Procedure Rules 1998). The application may be heard and determined in private.

[12] The application may be dealt with by the district judge in chambers: County Court Rules
Order 43, r 15(2) (as preserved in Schedule 2 of the Civil Procedure Rules 1998). The application
should be made on a Part 8 claim form (High Court: Form N208 County Court: Form N397) as
modified to cater for a statement of truth by both parties: see District Judge S Gold, *Civil Way*,
(1999) NLJ May 14, 718 at 721.

[13] If so, this will, for example, cause potential problems in the City of London where solicitors
routinely apply to the Mayor's and City Court. See District Judge Walker, *The Business of Litigation*
(1999) Law Society's Gazette 29 September, 96.

[14] CPR rr 30.2(2), 30.2(3).

specimen draft of the order sought by the parties. There is, however, no guidance as to when the court will refuse an application properly made. As the agreement is usually reached between business people who have received legal advice, there is little scope for the court to refuse on the merits of the application.[15] Although the facility was designed to cater for the letting of business premises on a temporary basis, it is not unknown for a lease of twenty-five years duration to be contracted out. Nevertheless, refusals do occur, for example, when there is a suspicion of coercion or oppression. For example, in its Working Paper the Law Commission relied upon statistics which showed that the county court had a refusal rate of 15 per cent, but it did admit that there were no means of knowing whether these refusals were for lack of merit or on technical grounds.[16]

2.05   By virtue of section 38(4), the agreement must be contained in (or endorsed on) the lease or (presumably, when it is an oral tenancy) noted in any other document as specified by the court. In *Tottenham Hotspur Football & Athletic Co Ltd v Princegrove Publishers Ltd*, Lawson J explained the purpose behind this requirement: '[T]hese procedural devices were introduced in order that third parties, prospective assignees, or prospective mortgagees of the tenant's interest under a lease should know . . . that this is a lease which . . . has a special restriction.'[17] Nevertheless, there the sanctioned agreement took effect even though it was neither contained in nor endorsed on the lease or other document. The court had directed that the agreement be endorsed on the lease, but no lease was ever executed. The tenant merely continued in possession and paid an increased rent under the new tenancy. Relying upon the principle in *Walsh v Lonsdale*,[18] the court took the view that the tenant should be treated as being in the same position as if there had been the execution of an instrument creating the tenancy. Hence, when the contractual term ended, the tenant could not claim security of tenure. Although possibly the just decision on the facts, Lawson J's legal reasoning is difficult to follow because it is unclear how *Walsh v Lonsdale* could be invoked once specific performance has ceased and the contractual lease ended. Fortunately, this problem has not been encountered since.

A Term of Years Certain?

2.06   Only a tenancy granted for 'a term of years certain' can be contracted out of the 1954 Act. For over twenty years it has been the conventional wisdom that, for these purposes, the expression 'a term of years certain' includes any fixed term

---

[15] See *Hagee (London) Ltd v AB Erikson & Larson* [1976] 1 QB 209 where at 215 Denning MR admitted that, 'The court has no materials on which to refuse it.'

[16] *Part II of the Landlord & Tenant Act 1954* (1988) Working Paper no 111 at para 3.5.10.

[17] N 6 above at 23. It was concluded that the court order did not constitute a document for these purposes.

[18] (1882) LR 21 Ch D 9.

(including a term for a year and for less than a year). It does not matter, moreover, whether the lease contains an option to surrender before its term ends or a break clause.[19] Although it can be regarded as a term of years, a periodic tenancy falls outside the 1954 Act because such tenancies are not certain.[20] In *Re Land & Premises at Liss, Hants*, for example Goulding J recognised that a six-months' tenancy fell within the catchment of section 38.[21] In the light that the contracting out provisions do not apply to a periodic tenancy, he explained: 'But it seems very unlikely that having decided to permit contracting out with regard to fixed terms, the legislature should think it was inappropriate where the fixed term was very short although appropriate where the fixed term was long. One would have thought that if a distinction had been made it would have been much more likely to be the other way.'[22] In *Nicholls v Kinsey*, however, a twelve-month term to be followed by a yearly tenancy was held to fall outside the scope of section 38. While it could be properly regarded as a term of years, the yearly tenancy arising at the end of the fixed term prevented it from being 'certain'. It could not, moreover, be construed as a fixed term of at least two-years' duration.[23] If the rider of the periodic tenancy had not been added, however, the tenancy would have been validly contracted out.

Other Avoidance Methods

A series of potential avoidance measures have long been thought to be adequate to **2.07** sidestep the provisions of Part II.[24] All include the grant of a lease for a duration longer than the parties really intend with, in each instance, a tenant's option to surrender at the end of the 'true' term. The danger exists that such agreements could be disregarded as shams and they are, in the light of the contracting out facility, now unnecessary. For example, avoidance might arise in the following situations. First, the grant of a term intended to be for five years could be granted for eight years with a heavily inflated rent being reserved for the final three years. This should guarantee surrender before the contractual term expires. Second, a lease could be granted for a term two years longer than intended and, at the same time, a sublease of the whole premises could be executed in favour of the landlord for

---

[19] *Scholl Manufacturing Co Ltd v Clifton (Slimline) Ltd* [1967] 1 Ch 41; *City Land Plc v Maidstone Builders Ltd* (1992) January 20 (HC).

[20] See M Haley *A Term of Years Uncertain?* (1995), AALR Vol 24 No 2, 236.

[21] [1971] 3 All ER 380. Support for this liberal approach is to be derived also from the Law Commission Report which instigated the contracting out facility: (*Landlord & Tenant Act 1954 Part II* (1969) Law Com No 17 para 33). A term for less than six months would, of course, be excluded from the Act as a short tenancy: section 43(3).

[22] ibid at 384.

[23] *EWP Ltd v Moore* [1992] QB 460. In the Business Tenancies (Northern Ireland) Order 1996, a 'term certain' is expressly defined as meaning any definite period of certain duration whether or not the tenancy is renewable: article 2(2). It is arguable that this definition, if employed in England and Wales, would embrace the *Nicholls v Kinsey* type lease.

[24] See T Aldridge, *Letting Business Premises* (6th edn, 1989) 86.

the last two-year period. This ensures that the tenant is not in occupation when the right to renew the headlease arises. Third, the lease may be granted for two years longer than intended with a covenant prohibiting absolutely all business use for the last two years.[25] Once again, the tenant will have little option but to surrender the lease.

Reform

2.08 Although the involvement of the court may be viewed as a safeguard to prevent wholesale avoidance, the judiciary most certainly does not adopt an interventionist stance. In reality, the current procedure does little more than bring the significance of exclusion formally to the attention of the tenant. In order to minimise expense and delay, and yet maintain the tenant's awareness, the Law Commission has recommended the introduction of a new system under which contracting out will be a matter solely for agreement.[26] In order that an assignee of the tenancy or reversion will have advance notification of its existence, the agreement will be contained in or endorsed on the lease. The proposed system contains the safeguard that the tenant will be furnished with prescribed information and must sign a declaration that the implications of contracting out are understood. In its 1996 Consultation Paper, the Department of Environment added the gloss that this warning should be given to the tenant some time before the lease is entered (for example, a week in advance). The Law Commission's proposals will also prevent the contracting out of oral leases and reinforce the existing rule that periodic tenancies cannot be contracted out.

2.09 This *laissez-faire* approach, however, creates the real risk that, in a letting market which favours the landlord, the door is once more opened to tenant exploitation. Indeed, this threat was recognised by the Law Reform Advisory Committee for Northern Ireland who rejected the need for any contracting out whatsoever and concluded: 'We are not convinced that there is sufficient equality of bargaining power between landlords and tenants to make that an acceptable solution. We are exercised by the fact that the prohibitions against contracting out were intended to reflect the tenant's need to establish and protect goodwill, and are not persuaded that that need has disappeared.'[27] In the light that contracting out is now an established feature of the law in England and Wales, reform might perhaps be better focused upon retaining the court's involvement, while devising guidelines upon which refusals may be based.

---

[25] Such a covenant is not void for restraint of trade: *Alec Lobb (Garages) Ltd v Total Oil Great Britain Ltd* [1983] 1 WLR 87; nor would it offend the Unfair Contract Terms Act 1977: *Star Rider v Inntrepreneur Pub Co* (1998) 16 EG 140.

[26] *Business Tenancies: A Periodic Review of the Landlord & Tenant Act 1954 Part II* (1992) Law Com No 208, paras 2.19–2.20.

[27] *A Review of the Law Relating to Business Tenancies in Northern Ireland* (1992) Discussion Paper No 3, para 3.4.8.

C. The Continuation Tenancy

It is not necessary that a new tenancy come into being as soon as the contractual **2.10** tenancy ends. This is because of the 'continuation tenancy' which arises at the end of the contractual term and operates to keep the relationship of landlord and tenant alive beyond that time. By virtue of section 65 the continuation of a headlease will also support an underlease for a longer term than would otherwise be possible. Due to this mechanism, the time between the determination of the original lease and the grant of a new tenancy may often be measured in years. The continuation is, however, not to be treated as a holding over at common law[28] nor can any periodic tenancy be implied by reason of continued occupation and the payment of rent.[29] Being of an uncertain duration, the continuation tenancy simply has no equivalent under the common law. The continuation allows the tenant to remain in possession, essentially on the same terms as before.[30]

The only departures from this rule concern the ability of the landlord to apply to **2.11** the court for an increased (albeit discounted) interim rent under section 24A and the additional restrictions placed upon the termination of a continuation tenancy. It follows, therefore, that the tenant is entitled to the same premises as under the original lease. This entails that, although the tenant may only occupy part of the demised premises at the end of the contractual lease, it is the whole of the tenancy that is continued under section 24.[31] The statutory continuation, moreover, ensures that both parties remain liable on their leasehold covenants[32] and that rights of way (and other incorporeal hereditaments) enjoyed under the original tenancy remain enforceable.[33] Any guarantor of the tenant will, however, normally be released from prospective liability.[34] A right to remove tenant's fixtures will also persist during the continuation period.[35]

---

[28] In relation to Northern Ireland, this is expressly stated in article 34 of the Business Tenancies (Northern Ireland) Order 1996.

[29] *Thorne (Sandown Lodge) v New Sherwood School* (1962) 181 EG 849; *Lewis v MTC (Cars) Ltd* [1975] 1 All ER 874.

[30] *Bowes-Lyon v Green* (1963) AC 420. As Fox LJ commented in *Cadogan v Dimovic* [1984] 2 All ER 168 at 172: 'There are not two terms, one created by the original grant, and on the expiry of that, a new one created by statute.' In Northern Ireland, article 15(2) speaks of the continuation as being 'a graft upon the tenancy previously subsisting . . .'.

[31] *Poster v Slough Estates* [1969] 1 Ch 495.

[32] *GMS Syndicate Ltd v Gary Elliott Ltd* [1982] Ch 1. As regards pre-1996 leases, original tenant liability for an assignee's breaches will not normally continue beyond the end of the original term: *City of London Corporation v Fell* [1994] 1 AC 458. Post-1996 tenancies no longer support original tenant liability by virtue of the Landlord and Tenant (Covenants) Act 1995.

[33] *Nevil Long (Boards) Ltd v Firmenich & Co* (1984) 47 P & CR 59.

[34] The continuing liability of a guarantor can, however, be expressly catered for in the guarantee: *Junction Estates v Cope* (1974) 27 P & CR 482. In Northern Ireland, this cannot occur: article 15(3).

[35] *New Zealand Government Property Corp v HM&S Ltd* [1982] 1 QB 1145.

Assignment of a Continuation Tenancy

2.12 Although described by Sellers J in *Castle Laundry (London) v Read* as 'a business statutory tenancy',[36] this epithet is misleading. Unlike a statutory tenancy under the Rent Act 1977, a continuation tenancy confers an estate in land which can be assigned or forfeited for breach of covenant. As Denning MR acknowledged in *Cheryl Investments Ltd v Saldanha*, 'This "continuation tenancy" is nothing like a statutory tenancy. It is not a personal privilege of the tenant. It is a piece of property which he can assign or dispose of to a third person, provided that it was not prohibited by the terms of the contract.'[37] As Ross makes clear, however, there are a number of practical considerations to be taken on board before any such assignment should be taken.[38] First, the assignee must be aware of the possibility the landlord might oppose a renewal on grounds concerning which the assignee has no previous knowledge and no possible defence. Second, the assignee must check carefully that the assignor has satisfied, as relevant, the requirements concerning the service of a counter notice, application to court and the service of proceedings on the landlord. Third, the assignee will often be unsure as to what the terms of any renewal will be and this will entail that, as Ross observes, 'few purchasers will be prepared to offer more than a nominal premium for the assignment of the tenancy'.[39] Finally, as the right to renew is dependant on continuing occupation, the assignee must ensure that the assignor had not ceased to occupy prior to the assignment.

D. Termination of Tenancies

2.13 The Act draws a distinction between the termination of the contractual relationship between the parties and the termination of the tenancy. As previously mentioned, the contract can be determined by any of the established common law methods (expiry of time and notice to quit, for example). The relevance of the Act, however, is that the tenancy continues notwithstanding that the contract which previously underpinned it has been brought to an end.[40] The central tenet of the statutory scheme is that a tenancy within its ambit can be terminated only by one of the methods prescribed in the Act itself.[41] As the legislative design is to prevent the landlord from exercising common law rights to refuse a renewal or to

---

[36] [1955] 1 QB 586 at 591, 592.
[37] [1979] 1 All ER 5 at 9. See RE Megarry [1955] 70 LQR 329.
[38] M Ross, *Drafting and Negotiation of Commercial Leases* (4th edn, 1994) 292.
[39] ibid.
[40] See *Castle Laundry (London) v Read,* n 36 above.
[41] Section 24(1); see *Orman Brothers v Greenbaum* [1955] 1 All ER 610. A similar approach is adopted in Northern Ireland: articles 5 and 8 of the Business Tenancies (Northern Ireland) Order 1996.

offer a new lease on a 'take it or leave it' basis, not surprisingly it is the landlord's rights that are primarily curtailed. Nevertheless, the Act throughout attempts to strike a compromise between the conflicting interests of the parties. As the Law Reform Advisory Committee for Northern Ireland acknowledged in its Discussion Paper:

> The landlord's rights of ownership are respected and preserved to the extent that if he requires the premises for his own use or for redevelopment, the tenant will not be granted a renewal. Similarly, the landlord's powers of forfeiture and ejectment are preserved, so that he may recover possession from a defaulting tenant at any time, or, alternatively, he may rely on the tenant's defaults as a ground for opposing renewal under the Act.[42]

The permitted methods of termination represent an amalgam of conventional modes of termination (albeit sometimes with minor modification) and novel, statutory rights exclusively fashioned for the renewal scheme. The majority depend upon the action or inaction of the tenant; the others can be activated only by the landlord or with the joint agreement of the parties. In contrast to the retained common law methods under which the tenant is denied any rights under the 1954 Act, the key statutory methods (that is, termination by a landlord's section 25 notice and tenant's section 26 request) operate both to preserve renewal rights and to activate the renewal procedure.

Tenant's Notice to Quit

The Act does not oblige the tenant to seek a renewal nor does it aim to tie the tenant to an unwanted continuation: it exists to benefit the tenant and not to act as a fetter. Hence, there is express provision enabling the tenant, by service of a notice to quit on the immediate landlord, to prevent a continuation tenancy arising or to terminate one that has arisen. The term 'notice to quit' is defined in section 69(1) as being a notice to terminate the lease given in accordance with its terms (for example, a notice served in the exercise of a break clause). This definition does not, however, include section 25 notices or section 26 requests.[43] In all cases, however, the effectiveness of the tenant's notice is subject to the qualification that the tenant had been in occupation in right of the tenancy for one month.[44] This is designed to prevent any device whereby the tenant is persuaded to give a notice to quit at the commencement of the tenancy thereby bringing the tenancy to an end at the expiry of the notice. In addition, no notice to quit can be served by the tenant after the service of a section 26 request for a new lease.[45] Nothing in the Act, however, **2.14**

---

[42] N 27 above at para 2.1.2.

[43] cf the view of Winn LJ in *Rene Claro (Haute Coiffure) Ltd v Halle Concerts Society* [1969] 2 All ER 842. The Business Tenancies (Northern Ireland) Order 1996 expressly draws the distinction between a 'notice to quit' and the landlord's statutory 'notice to determine': article 2(2).

[44] Sections 24(2)(a), 27(1),(2).

[45] Section 26(4). These procedures are mutually exclusive and the first to be served in time prevails: *Long Acre Securities Ltd v Electro Acoustic Industries Ltd* [1990] 1 EGLR 91.

allows termination on a date earlier than that on which the lease could or would have ended at common law.[46] The precise means to be employed depend upon whether the tenancy is periodic or fixed term. In the case of a periodic tenancy, the tenant can serve on the immediate landlord an ordinary notice to quit in accordance with the terms of the lease.[47] This will terminate the tenancy in the ordinary way whether or not it is already being continued under the Act. Although at common law the notice would normally also terminate a sub-tenancy,[48] as will become clear an underlease protected by the 1954 Act will be continued.

2.15 As regards a fixed term, and with the exception of a break clause, the tenant is unable unilaterally to terminate the lease early. Nevertheless, the tenant is entitled to serve a section 27(1) notice on the immediate landlord so as to prevent a continuation tenancy automatically arising at the end of the contractual term. This leaves unaffected any protected sub-tenancies. Although no special form of notice is required, it must be served not less than three months before the contractual date of expiry.[49] If either a continuation tenancy is in existence or the notice is served within three months of the end of the contractual tenancy, the tenant's written notice must, however, be timed to expire on a quarter day.[50] These types of notice are particularly useful where the landlord refuses to accept a surrender and shows no sign of issuing a section 25 termination notice.[51] Provided that the notice is appropriately timed to expire after the continuation tenancy arises, it can be served before or after the date that the contractual term lapses. The reliance upon quarter days does, however, give rise to an anomaly in that the actual period of the notice differs according to when it was given. The Law Commission Working Paper provided the telling comparison between a notice served on 24 September which can expire on 25 December (92 days) and a notice served on 30 September which cannot expire until 25 March (176 days).[52] Not surprisingly, in its later Report the Commission recommended that the tenant should be allowed to give three-month's notice expiring at any time so that the period of notice would always be standard.[53]

---

[46] Section 25(4). As Sellers J explained in *Castle Laundry (London) Ltd v Read*, n 36 above, at 593, 'the date on which the tenancy could be determined by a notice under the Act can be no earlier than that which the contract itself specifies'.

[47] Section 24(2). See generally RE Poole, *Common Law Notices and Business Tenancies* [1959] Conv 156.

[48] *Barrett v Morgan* [1998] 4 All ER 179. The sub-tenant might, however, make a claim against the immediate landlord for breach of the covenants of quiet enjoyment and non-derogation from grant.

[49] As regards Northern Ireland, the equivalent provision is contained in article 8(2).

[50] Section 27(2). These are 25 March (Lady Day), 24 June (Mid-summer), 29 September (Michaelmas), and 25 December (Christmas).

[51] Of course, the tenant remains liable on the covenants until the expiry date of the notice: *Long Acre Securities Ltd v Electro Acoustic Industries Ltd*, n 45 above.

[52] N 16 above at para 3.2.33.

[53] N 26 above at para 2.49. In Northern Ireland, the comparable reference to 'gale' days has been abandoned: article 8(3).

Tenant's Section 26 Request

The tenant who seeks a renewal may terminate the contractual tenancy by the ser-   **2.16**
vice of a request for a new tenancy upon the competent landlord. The tenant is
prevented from serving a request if the tenant has already served a section 27
notice or the landlord has served a section 25 notice.[54] Not every tenant, moreover, is empowered to serve such a request. To qualify for this entitlement, the tenancy had to be granted for a term of years exceeding one year (whether or not
continued under the Act) or be a term of years and thereafter from year to year.[55]
Subject to the latter exception, periodic tenants are unable to serve a request for a
new tenancy. The request must, moreover, adhere to a prescribed form and content, set out the tenant's proposals for a new lease and specify a date, not less than
six and not more than twelve months from its service, on which the lease is to terminate. The contractual term will end automatically on the stipulated date. This
gives the tenant control over when the contractual term will terminate and, therefore, enables the tenant to keep alive both the current tenancy and (subject to the
order of an interim rent) the existing rent for the maximum twelve months. The
landlord has two months within which to serve a counter notice stating opposition and the ground(s) upon which the opposition is based.[56] A landlord who does
not serve an effective counter notice loses the right to object to the new lease. If the
tenant applies to the court for a renewal within two and four months of the service of the request, the continuation tenancy will, due to section 64, subsist until
the application is disposed of. If the tenant fails to make a timely application, the
tenancy will end on the date set out in the request.[57]

Tenant's Cessation of Occupation

It was decided in *Esselte AB & British Sugar Plc v Pearl Assurance Plc* that, where the   **2.17**
tenant has ceased to occupy the premises by the end of the contractual lease, no
continuation tenancy can arise.[58] This is because the tenancy is no longer one
to which the Act applies.[59] This entails that, as regards a periodic tenancy, the

---

[54] Section 26(4).
[55] Section 26(1); see Chapter 5.
[56] Section 26(6).
[57] *Smith v Draper* (1990) 60 P & CR 252. If the tenant complies with the time-limits, but later
withdraws the renewal application, the current tenancy ends three months after the date of withdrawal: section 64(2).
[58] [1997] 1 WLR 891; see also *Morrison Holdings Ltd v Manders* [1976] 1 WLR 533. The contrary decision on this point of *Long Acre Securities Ltd v Electro Acoustic Industries Ltd* (n 45 above)
was criticised and not followed in the *Esselte* case. For the meaning of cessation of occupation see
Chapter 3.
[59] As Morritt LJ concluded in the *Esselte* case, '[the Act] cannot be construed so as to include the
past' (ibid at 897); see also S Higgins [1997] Conv 119. In Northern Ireland this outcome is
expressly catered for by article 5(2)(c). This provides that, where the immediate landlord serves a
notice to quit within 12 months of the expiry of a fixed term, a tenant who is not in occupation at
the time of service falls outside the statutory scheme.

landlord is able to serve an effective common law notice to quit on the tenant.[60] Similarly, in relation to a fixed term, the exercise of a break clause or effluxion of time will terminate a non-occupying tenant's interest. This approach, moreover, is not disturbed by the fact that the tenant has already served a section 27 notice which has yet to expire. It also entails that, if the landlord serves a section 25 notice after the tenant has quit occupation, the notice will be invalid and cannot prolong the tenancy until the stated termination date.[61] Nevertheless, if a fixed term ceases to be protected during its statutory continuance, it does not determine automatically.[62] Instead, it can be brought to an end by the immediate landlord, under section 24(3), by the service of written notice. This notice period must be between three and six months.[63] In this situation, the tenant might seek to shorten the notice period by serving a section 27(2) notice of three months, timed to expire on a quarter day.[64] If the tenancy drifts back into the scope of the Act following the service of the landlord's notice, the notice remains valid.[65]

Landlord's Forfeiture

2.18 The Act ensures that forfeiture of the lease (including the forfeiture of a superior lease) remains unaffected.[66] Forfeiture, therefore, precludes a tenant from claiming security of tenure. The tenant, however, has the right to claim relief and, if relief is sought, the Act continues to apply to the tenancy. Termination occurs only when the forfeiture is absolute and not while relief can still be granted by the court under section 146(4) of the Law of Property Act 1925.[67] This is so even if the contractual term has already expired by effluxion of time.[68] Accordingly, until the matter of relief is disposed of, the tenant remains able to apply for a new ten-

---

[60] The notice will be effective even if the tenant subsequently resumes occupation: section 24(3)(b).

[61] *Cheryl Investments Ltd v Saldanha*, n 37 above.

[62] Note the contrary argument, mooted by DL Evans and PF Smith, *The Law of Landlord and Tenant* (5th edn, 1997) 462, that the continuation tenancy should end as soon as the tenant ceases to occupy. The notice must be served on the tenant or, if the tenant is a company which has become defunct, the Crown. The danger exists that, if after service on the Crown the tenant is restored to the register of companies, the notice will be invalid: *Blenheim Leisure (Restaurants) Ltd v Registrar of Companies* (1999) The Times 13 August.

[63] Section 24(3)(a). In relation to Northern Ireland, the equivalent provision is contained in article 5(2)(a).

[64] See *Longacre Securities Ltd v Electro Acoustic Industries Ltd* (n 45 above) which on this issue, seemingly, remains good authority.

[65] Section 24(3)(b). This protects the landlord from post-notice change of tactic by the tenant: see *Teasdale v Walker* [1958] 3 All ER 307.

[66] Section 24(2).

[67] *Meadows v Clerical Medical & General Life Assurance Society* [1981] Ch 70 where Megarry VC demonstrated that section 24(2) contemplates the situation where the tenancy has truly come to an end and the process completed. See further DG Barnsley, *Termination of Leases by Forfeiture: Writ or Judgment?* [1965] Conv 267.

[68] *Cadogan v Dimovic*, n 30 above.

ancy or to pursue any ongoing application.[69] Clearly, there is some overlap between forfeiture for breach of covenant and the landlord's ability to oppose the grant of a new lease. The grounds for forfeiture are likely also to constitute grounds of opposition under section 30(1). This entails that, if the lease is drawing to a close, the landlord may decide to forego forfeiture proceedings and concentrate upon defeating the tenant's claim for renewal. It is, however, open for the landlord to pursue both courses of action.[70]

As regards sub-tenancies, at common law they fall with the head lease: the rule is **2.19** that forfeiture ends all inferior interests. The sub-tenant may apply to the court for relief and, if successful, the relief granted can comprise of the order of a new lease, but for a term no longer than the original sub-tenancy.[71] The court, otherwise, enjoys an extremely wide discretion as to the form relief may take.[72] Where the sub-tenancy is already being continued under the 1954 Act, however, a different scenario emerges within which the sub-tenant is entitled in the normal way to a new lease on terms (including duration) as agreed or determined by the court.[73] The forfeiture of the superior interest will, in this latter instance, leave the sub-tenancy totally unaffected.[74]

Landlord's Statutory Notice

The landlord is able to serve a notice to quit as reserved in the lease, but as regards **2.20** tenancies protected by the 1954 Act the notice will only sever the contractual relationship between the parties. Even if accepted by the head tenant, the notice cannot effect any protected sub-tenancy. Accordingly, in *Scholl Manufacturing Co Ltd v Clifton (Slimline) Ltd* the exercise of a break-clause in the lease ended the contractual tenancy, but the competent landlord still needed to serve the special statutory notice under section 25 in order to regain possession.[75] It is, however, possible that the notice of break and the statutory notice could be framed within one document and timed so as to satisfy both the contractual and the statutory

---

[69] *Meadows v Clerical Medical & General Life Assurance Society*, n 67 above.

[70] See *Norton v Charles Deane Productions Ltd* (1969) 214 EG 559 where the landlord's forfeiture action failed, but the tenant was still denied a new lease under the 1954 Act.

[71] *Ewart v Fryer* [1901] 1 Ch 499; section 146(4) of the Law of Property Act 1925. As Kekewich J concluded, at first instance at 504, relief is available to the sub-tenant, 'in order that injustice may not be done to an innocent man, who for no fault of his own has been deprived of that which he had contracted to acquire'.

[72] This is a new grant and not merely the restoration of the old one. The terms may, therefore, differ from the previous tenancy: *Chelsea Estates Investment Trust Co Ltd v Marche* [1955] Ch 328.

[73] Section 65(2); see *Cadogan v Dimovic*, n 30 above.

[74] The mesne landlord will not be liable for failing to give up vacant possession: *Reynolds v Bannerman* [1922] 1 KB 719.

[75] [1967] 1 Ch 41; see also *Castle Laundry (London) Ltd v Read*, n 36 above. Similarly, the service of a landlord's notice to quit on a periodic tenant would not prevent a continuation tenancy coming into existence: *Wheeler v Mercer* [1955] 3 WLR 714, CA.

requirements.[76] In deciding whether the notice will operate for the purposes of section 25, the document must be construed in a common-sense way and the court must not adopt an over-technical approach in the face of clear language.[77] Nevertheless, for a dual notice to be effective the immediate landlord must also be the tenant's competent landlord. It must be remembered that, while the severance of contractual ties is to be undertaken by the immediate landlord, the termination of the protected tenancy falls within the remit of the competent landlord. It is, however, generally to be recommended that the documentation be kept distinct so as to minimise the impact of error. This, of course, is inevitable when the immediate landlord and the competent landlord are not one and the same person.

2.21 The form and content of a valid section 25 notice are closely prescribed. If the notice does not follow this prescription, it is likely to be invalid. If so, it becomes necessary for the landlord to serve a further and effective section 25 notice. The notice, which must state a termination date not less than six and not more than twelve months in the future, operates on three levels. First, when the termination date is reached, an existing contractual tenancy ends and is replaced by a continuation tenancy. Second, it engages the renewal procedure and places the onus upon the tenant to serve a counter notice and to apply to the court within strict time-limits. Third, the notice must disclose whether the landlord opposes a new lease and, if so, upon what grounds. The section 25 notice is, therefore, the first step taken in an attempt by the landlord either to recover possession or to obtain renewal at a market rent. Following the landlord's section 25 notice, the tenant must respond within two months by service of a counter notice;[78] and apply to the court for a new lease within between two and four months following the service of the initial renewal notice.[79] If a counter notice is not served or an application not made within these time-frames, the tenant loses the right to apply for a new lease.[80] The court cannot extend these time-limits[81] and the lease will come to an end on the date stipulated in the landlord's notice.[82]

---

[76] *Weinbergs Weatherproofs Ltd v Radcliffe Paper Mills Co Ltd*, n 1 above; *Keith Bayley Rogers & Co v Cubes Ltd* (1975) 31 P & CR 412.

[77] *Giddens v Dodd* (1856) 3 Drew 485. The landlord should make clear (for example, in a covering letter) that the notice is designed to achieve this dual purpose: *Aberdeen Steak Houses Group Plc v Crown Estate Commissioners* (1997) 31 EG 101.

[78] Section 25(2). An invalid counter notice cannot be served afresh out of time and will prove fatal to the tenant's claim for a new lease.

[79] Section 29.

[80] Section 29(3).

[81] *Dodds v Walker* [1981] 2 All ER 609 where the tenant was one day late in the application for a new lease.

[82] Section 29(2). A similar consequence arises when the counter notice indicates the tenant's willingness to give up possession.

Merger and Agreement

Although merger (that is, the tenant buying out the landlord's interest) is not **2.22** specified in section 24(2) as being an approved method of termination, it is an inevitable conclusion that there can be no statutory continuation of a lease which is no longer legally in existence.[83] Merger does not, however, arise automatically: it must be intended to occur. If merger is intended by the tenant, the lease will end and be absorbed by the superior interest. Merger of a head lease does not, however, affect the interests of a sub-tenant.[84]

As regards other agreements, the emphasis of the Act is to encourage settlement **2.23** between the tenant and the competent landlord as to both the grant and the terms of a renewal. A full agreement between the parties, therefore, ousts the jurisdiction of the court.[85] Not surprisingly, where the landlord and tenant agree in writing to a new lease, the original tenancy (whether or not already being continued under the Act) will subsist until the commencement date for the new term.[86] This is so even when the new tenancy is timed to commence during the existence of the contractual term. Common practice, however, is for the commencement of the agreed lease to occur on the day after the original one has terminated. If a continuation has arisen, the tenancy comes to an end on the date specified in the agreement and, during the intervening period, is not protected by the Act. If agreement for a renewal is not achieved by the parties, the matter must be resolved by the court. In that situation, the court is empowered to reject the tenant's application only on the grounds specified in section 30(1)(a)–(g). The tenancy will, however, be continued under section 64 until three months after 'final disposal', that is, until all proceedings including appeals have come to an end. This rule gives way where final disposal occurs earlier than the termination date specified in the statutory notice or request. In such a case, the tenancy will end at the later date.

Surrender

Surrender is the yielding up of the leasehold estate to the immediate landlord and **2.24** the causing of the lease to be extinguished by the reversion. As such, surrender can never be unilateral as it requires the agreement of both parties.[87] It can, however,

---

[83] See *Watney v Boardley* [1975] 1 WLR 857.

[84] See section 65(2).

[85] If agreement is reached after an application for a new tenancy is lodged, that application (if not withdrawn) is automatically invalidated by section 28: *Hancock & Willis v GMS Syndicate Ltd* (1983) 265 EG 473.

[86] Once a binding agreement is reached, the tenant cannot have a change of mind and apply for a new lease under the Part II machinery: section 28.

[87] As regards joint tenants, the rule is that all of them must join in or acquiesce in the surrender: *Hounslow London Borough Council v Pilling* [1994] 1 All ER 432.

either be express by deed[88] or implied by operation of law (without writing) from the conduct of the parties.[89] As the doctrine of estoppel forms the foundation of surrender by operation of law[90] there must be conduct by the tenant unequivocally amounting to an acceptance that the tenancy has been terminated. As Peter Gibson LJ explained in *Gibbs Mew Plc v Gemmell*, 'That conduct can be relinquishment by the tenant of possession and its acceptance by the landlord or other conduct by the tenant inconsistent with the continuation of the tenancy, and in addition the circumstances must be such as to render it inequitable for the tenant to dispute that the tenancy has ceased'.[91]

2.25 Although this common law method of termination is retained,[92] the Act adds the requirement that, for a valid surrender to occur, the tenant must have been in occupation in right of the tenancy for at least one month before the instrument of surrender is executed.[93] This time-period is calculated from the date of the grant and not, if different, the commencement date of the lease. The policy is that a tenant, having been in occupation for one month, should not be shackled unnecessarily to an unwanted lease.[94] This proviso is also designed to prevent the avoidance of the statutory provisions by the simple method of having the lease and the document of surrender executed at the same time. In its 1992 Report, the Law Commission recommended the removal of this one-month safeguard as regards immediate surrenders, and, if implemented, this will entail their effectiveness regardless of occupation.[95] This abandonment of the one-month qualifying period should not, however, have deleterious consequences for the tenant.

Agreements to Surrender

2.26 An actual surrender must be contrasted with an agreement to surrender (whether immediately or at a future date) which, unless authorised by the court, is rendered void by virtue of section 38(1).[96] The distinction, however, applies only to express

---

[88] Section 52(1) of the Law of Property Act 1925. Accordingly, a surrender of the legal estate by letter will be ineffective: *Tarjomani v Panther Securities Ltd* (1983) 46 P & CR 32; cf the position in Northern Ireland.

[89] Section 54(2)(c) of the Law of Property Act 1925.

[90] *Tarjomani v Panther Securities Ltd*, n 88 above; *Gibbs Mew Plc v Gemmell* (1998) 1 EG 117.

[91] ibid at 119. There the original lease was surrendered by the tenant accepting a tenancy at will intended to supersede the former lease and granted on more advantageous terms. See also *Fordgate Wandsworth Ltd v Bernard Neville & Co* (1999) 7 July HC.

[92] Hence, there is no need for the landlord to follow the procedure under the Landlord and Tenant Act 1954: *Lansdown Tutors Ltd v Younger* (1998) October 10 (HC).

[93] Section 24(2)(b).

[94] See *Woodruff v Hambro* [1991] 62 P & CR 62. Based on the notion of non-derogation from grant, surrender of the head lease does not effect the interests of a sub-tenant: section 65(2); see also section 139(1) of the Law of Property Act 1925. As in *Bolton (HL)(Engineering) Ltd v Graham* [1957] 1 QB 159 where the tenant accepted a notice to quit and left the premises, the landlords still had to serve a termination on the sub-tenants who remained in occupation.

[95] N 26 above at para 2.21. This does not affect agreements to surrender.

[96] See *Tarjomani v Panther Securities Ltd*, n 88 above. A similar provision exists in Northern Ireland under article 25.

surrenders and has no resonance as regards surrender by operation of law.[97] The reason for this dual approach is as explained by the Law Commission in its Working Paper:

> To prevent the tenant surrendering the property to his landlord would be an encroachment on his freedom which is not necessary to defend the statutory right of renewal. On the other hand, to obtain from a tenant an undertaking in advance that he will surrender the lease sometime later is to invite him to forego those rights before he is in a position to judge how matters will stand at the date in question. The Act, therefore, limits the parties' freedom of contract when the tenant might be susceptible to undue persuasion by the landlord, without unnecessarily limiting their freedom to bargain.[98]

By way of illustration, a deed of surrender which the tenant executes as a condition of the grant would clearly be viewed as an agreement to surrender and, thereby, remain unenforceable unless authorised.[99] Conversely, and as in *Tarjomani v Panther Securities Ltd*, a letter purporting to effect immediate surrender could not be viewed either as an immediate surrender or as an agreement to surrender. In addition, since the Law of Property (Miscellaneous Provisions) Act 1989, an agreement to surrender (being a bilateral contract relating to an interest in land) must be in writing and signed by both parties. If not, and subject to estoppel, the agreement can have no legal consequence. Although agreements to surrender are not common, an authorised agreement might prove helpful where, for example, one tenant seeks to move out, a new tenant wishes to move in and the parties prefer a new lease instead of the assignment of the existing tenancy. **2.27**

Offer-back Clauses

A further related area concerns the so-called 'offer-back clauses' which, traditionally, are attached to covenants against assignment and provide that, on an intended assignment, the tenant must first offer to surrender the lease. This offer back may be without consideration or in consideration of a payment (often referable to the premium value of the unexpired term). The landlord has the option to accept the tenant's surrender and, if surrender occurs, this will terminate the tenant's lease. If the landlord declines the offer, the tenant can only assign the lease with the landlord's consent (which cannot be unreasonably withheld).[100] A **2.28**

---

[97] In *Gibb Mew Plc v Gemmell*, n 90 above, for example, the tenant unsuccessfully argued that the acceptance of a tenancy at will amounted merely to an agreement to surrender which was void under section 38(1). The tenant was estopped from denying that the prior tenancy had been surrendered by conduct.

[98] N 16 above at para 3.5.18. The Working Paper concluded that the Act should not continue to invalidate agreements to surrender which are intended to take effect immediately: para 3.5.20. No recommendation to this effect, however, emerged in the 1992 Report and, interestingly, this change was never contemplated in Northern Ireland.

[99] Section 38(4)(b); *Woodruff v Hambro*, n 94 above.

[100] See *Alder v Upper Grosvenor Street investments Ltd* [1957] 1 All ER 229. The reliance upon the offer-back clause does not render the landlord's objections unreasonable.

problem which arises is where the landlord accepts the tenant's obligatory offer, but the tenant does not actually wish to surrender. Even if committed to writing, the agreement to surrender remains unenforceable by virtue of section 38.[101] Nevertheless, as the right to assign has been made dependent on the landlord rejecting the offer, the tenant will be unable to assign without being in breach of covenant. An unsatisfactory stalemate is, thereby, achieved.[102] Although the Law Commission Working Paper provisionally recommended that reform was necessary,[103] its subsequent Report made no recommendation on this issue. The Commission feared that, by favouring one party at the other's expense, the balance of the Act would be disturbed. In addition, it was concluded that such contracts would now be invalidated by the Law of Property (Miscellaneous Provisions) Act 1989 and, hence, no further action was necessary.[104] Nevertheless, the 1989 Act does not facilitate lawful assignment which will remain dependent upon the landlord's refusal of the tenant's offer. The potential stalemate, therefore, continues unabated.

E. Summary of Key Time-limits

2.29 It is necessary for the parties and their legal advisers to take the necessary procedural steps within the tightly prescribed time-limits. As the statutory rights are only exercisable in accordance with the procedures set out in the Act, where the time requirements are not satisfied the landlord may lose the right to oppose a new lease, the tenant may face eviction, and the adviser subjected to a claim in negligence. These time-limits are strict and the court has no jurisdiction to extend them. The table below depicts the major time-limits which must be satisfied.

The Corresponding Date Rule

2.30 As shown in the table, the Act imposes a variety of time-limits within which, for example, notices and counter notices are to be served and court proceedings commenced. The majority of these time-limits are measured in months which, for the purposes of the Act, means calendar months.[105] Hence, as Lord Diplock calculated in *Dodds v Walker*, 'one months notice given in a 30-day month is one day shorter than one months notice given in a 31-days month and is three days shorter

---

[101] *Stevenson & Rush (Holdings) Ltd v Langdon* (1978) 38 P & CR 208.
[102] See *Allnatt London Properties Ltd v Newton* [1984] 1 All ER 423.
[103] N 16 above at para 3.5.27.
[104] N 26 above at paras 3.16–3.19. The tenant's offer back and its acceptance will now only be binding if the contract is put in writing and signed by both parties. A deed is still necessary for an express surrender.
[105] Sections 5, 22(1) and Sch 2 of the Interpretation Act 1978. The same approach operates under the Civil Procedure Rules 1998, r 2.10.

Section	Purpose	Time-limit
40	Notice for information	No more than 24 months before end of tenant's lease
25	Landlord's termination notice	Between 6 and 12 months' notice
25(5)	Tenant's counter notice	Within 2 months of service of section 25 notice
26	Tenant's request for new tenancy	Between 6 and 12 months' notice
26(6)	Landlord's counter notice	Within 2 months of service of section 26 request
27	Fixed-term tenant's notice to quit	At least 3 months before tenancy will expire. If a continuation tenancy has arisen, notice must expire on a quarter day
29	Tenant's application to court	Between 2 and 4 months from service of section 25 notice or section 26 request
36(2)	Revocation	Within 14 days of order Tenancy continues thereafter for a reasonable period
64	Final disposal	3months after cessation of proceedings, including time for any appeal.

if it is given in February'.[106] In this context it is important to appreciate the workings of the so-called 'corresponding date rule'. This means that a period of months calculated from a specified date will end on the corresponding date in the appropriate subsequent month. As Lord Diplock further explained: 'The corresponding date rule is simple. It is easy of application . . . all that the calculator has to do is mark in his diary the corresponding date in the appropriate subsequent month.'[107] In *Hogg Bullimore & Co v Co-operative Insurance Society*, for example, a section 25 notice served on 2 April was effective to terminate the tenancy on 2

---

[106] N 81 above at 610.

[107] ibid. In addition, Lord Russell provided the following example: '[I]n a four month period, when service of the relevant notice was on 28th September; time would begin to run at midnight on 28th–29th September and would end at midnight on 28th–29th January, a period embracing four calendar months' (at 611). See also *Freeman v Read* (1863) 4 B & S 174.

October.[108] The notice, therefore, specified a termination date of 'not less than' six months in the future.

2.31 Accordingly, the Act does not require 'clear' months for, as Fox LJ concluded, 'just as there are dates which are less than two months . . . there are dates which are more than two months . . . there must be a date which is simply two months, no more and no less'.[109] It also follows that, for the landlord in the *Hogg Bullimore* case to have specified a date 'not more than' twelve months in the future, the notice must, at the latest, have been timed to expire on 2 April of the following year. Where the month does not have a corresponding date (for example, where one month's notice is served on 31 March), the period will end on the last day on the appropriate month in which it expires (that is, 30 April).[110] The expressions 'not less than' and 'not more than', therefore, result in the period allowed, in which the action is to occur, being taken to include both the date of service and the corresponding date on which the notice expires.[111] There is, however, some doubt as to the application of the corresponding date rule where the action is to be taken 'within' a specified number of months. In *Lester v Garland*, for example, it was held that, in calculating the period which has elapsed since the occurrence of a stated event, the day on which the event occurred is to be discounted.[112] If correct, this would give the parties an extra day within which to comply, say, with the service of a counter notice.[113]

F. The Competent Landlord

2.32 The Act draws a distinction between the 'immediate' landlord and the 'competent' landlord. Although the same entity may embody both characteristics (for example, where the freeholder is the tenant's landlord), this is not necessarily the case where sub-tenancies have been created. The immediate landlord, simply put, is the landlord who grants the interest to the tenant (or sub-tenant). The competent landlord is, however, a more difficult concept as it is a term of art which is subject to a complex statutory definition.[114] To satisfy the standard of competency, the landlord's interest must be an interest in reversion expectant (whether imme-

---

[108] (1985) 50 P & CR 105.

[109] *Riley (EJ) Investments Ltd v Eurostile Holdings Ltd* [1985] 3 All ER 181 at 184.

[110] *Dodds v Walker*, n 81 above. Although the corresponding date rule is well understood and part of long-standing practice, its operation when there is a full month available is less convincing. For example, one month's notice served on 30 September will expire on 30 October regardless of the fact that there is an extra day available in the latter month.

[111] cf the position at common law concerning notices terminating periodic tenancies: 'The general rule as to notices at any rate between landlord and tenant is that you exclude only one of the days and not both of them' (*per* Denning MR in *Snabel v Allard* [1967] 1 QB 627).

[112] (1808) 15 Ves 248.

[113] See S Tromans, *Commercial Leases*, (2nd edn, 1996) 248; HW Wilkinson, *How long is a week, how long is a month?* (1997) NLJ, 19 December at 1849.

[114] Section 44 in conjunction with Sch 6 of the 1954 Act.

diately or otherwise) on the termination of the relevant tenancy. In addition, it must be either the fee simple or, where sub-tenancies exist, a tenancy which will not end within fourteen months.[115] In addition, if the reversion has been severed, it is the owners of the severed parts who collectively constitute the competent landlord.[116] Severance does not create a separate tenancy in respect of each severed part.[117] A mesne landlord holding by virtue of a tenancy by estoppel (that is, where it is presumed that the landlord has a title which in reality it does not have), may qualify as the competent landlord.[118] Similarly, a mesne landlord holding under a periodic tenancy may satisfy the definition, provided that no common law notice to quit has been served by either party. An intermediate tenant with a fixed term, however, will cease to be the competent landlord once that tenant exercises a break clause designed to terminate the head lease within fourteen months.

Reduced to its basics, therefore, the term 'competent landlord' means either the freeholder or a tenant whose leasehold interest will not end for at least fourteen months.[119] The latter requirement aims to ensure that the competent landlord, having more than a nominal reversion, will have a sufficient interest and incentive to take proper action in relation to the termination and renewal of sub-tenancies. It is, however, necessary that the competent landlord hold under a legal estate and not by virtue of an equitable estate.[120] In *Pearson v Alyo*, Nourse LJ admitted that: 'The subsection is concerned only with legal owners. The Act would be unworkable if it were otherwise.'[121] Nevertheless, the Court of Appeal in *Shelley v United Artists* held that an equitable lease can sometimes be of relevance in determining the identity of the competent landlord.[122] This case is, however, of limited

2.33

---

[115] Or any further time by which it may be continued under either section 64 (to cater for court proceedings) or section 36(2) (time allowed for the revocation of an order for a new tenancy): section 44(1)(b). Note that the concept of the competent landlord is explained in more simple language within article 2(2) of the Business Tenancies (Northern Ireland) Order 1996.

[116] *Nevil Long & Co (Boards) Ltd v Firmenich & Co*, n 33 above; see also *Prudential Assurance Co Ltd v Eden Restaurants (Holborn) Ltd* (1999) December 1 CA.

[117] *Jelley v Buckman* [1974] QB 488. In this type of case, notices must be served either by (whether comprising a joint notice or separate notices operating at the same time) or on all the relevant landlords: *M&P Enterprises (London) v Norfolk Square Hotels* [1994] 1 EGLR 129; *Nevil Long (Boards) Ltd v Firmenich & Co*, n 33 above.

[118] *Bell v General Accident Fire & Life Assurance Corporation Ltd* (1998) 17 EG 144. The effect of the common law doctrine of estoppel is to require the parties and the court to treat an imaginary state of affairs as real (that is, that the landlord was entitled to a freehold or leasehold interest).

[119] This interest can be under one lease or a series of leases: *Shelley v United Artists Corporation Ltd* (1990) 16 EG 69.

[120] *Biles v Caesar* [1957] 1 WLR 56.

[121] (1990) 60 P & CR 56 at 59.

[122] N 119 above. The appellate court also accepted that a failure to correct the tenant's mistaken belief as to the identity of the competent landlord, and to disclose the identity of the new competent landlord, may give rise to an estoppel. As Dillon LJ added at 82: 'It is never a defence to a person who has made a misrepresentation to say that the person to whom the misrepresentation was made could have found out the truth if he had made appropriate inquiries.' The failure to serve a section 40 notice for particulars will not, therefore, weaken the case for an estoppel.

application and applies only where there is a specifically enforceable agreement to grant a new lease to the inferior landlord.[123] Albeit at that stage equitable, the appellate court held that the agreed term (an option to take a new lease) can be added to the end of the original lease so as to maintain a landlord's status as the competent landlord.

Where Sub-tenancies Exist

2.34   The definition of a competent landlord entails that, where there is a fixed-term head lease and a sub-lease (which is within the scope of the Act), the competent landlord will be the head lessee until the last fourteen months of the head lease. If this lease has less than fourteen months to run, the competent landlord will be the freeholder and not the sub-tenant's immediate landlord.[124] Differences emerge, however, according to whether the sub-tenancy is of the whole or merely part only of the holding comprised in the head lease. If the whole is sub-let, the matter is relatively straightforward. The head lessee will no longer occupy any part of the holding and, therefore, will not be protected by the provisions of Part II.[125] Hence, the head lease will terminate by effluxion of time. As soon as the head lease enters its final fourteen months, the head lessee will cease to be the competent landlord. The next superior landlord who satisfies the statutory definition will then be the appropriate landlord for renewal purposes.[126] As Lord Reid explained in *Bowes-Lyon v Green*: 'If the interest of the tenant's immediate landlord does not fulfill the . . . conditions then you go back until you find someone whose interest does fulfil them.'[127]

2.35   When the head lessee sublets only part of the premises and continues to occupy the remainder for the purposes of a business, the head lease remains within the protection of the Act. If the head tenant seeks a renewal, however, the new lease may only relate to those parts of the holding which are still occupied by that tenant.[128] The other parts may be the subject of a potential renewal application brought by the sub-tenant. The head lease will not be ended by expiry of the contractual term and it is necessary that the statutory procedures be employed. Unless

---

[123]   Following *Walsh v Lonsdale*, n 18 above, Dillon LJ acknowledged at 76 that, 'if a person is entitled in equity to have a lease granted, his rights ought to be dealt with in the same way as if a lease had been granted to him and do not depend upon it already having been granted'.

[124]   During the final two years of the term, the mesne landlord's control and influence is diminished. As RE Poole, *Tenancies and Subtenancies of Business Premises* [1959] Conv 458 at 466 recognised, 'the Act practically deprives a tenant, whose tenancy is drawing to a close, of the power to serve a notice under the Act to determine the interest of the subtenant, or to oppose an application by the subtenant for a new sublease, even where he remains the competent landlord'.

[125]   *Graysim Holdings Ltd v P & O Property Holdings Ltd* [1995] 4 All ER 831.

[126]   Section 44(1)(b). As explained by Poole, n 124 above at 466, 'the head landlord will become the competent landlord in place of the [mesne] tenant, who will be deprived of any power to take action under the Act to determine the interest of the subtenant'.

[127]   N 30 above at 434.

[128]   Subject to the landlord's contrary insistence: section 32.

and until a statutory notice is served to bring the head lease to an end, the immediate landlord continues to be the competent landlord of the sub-tenant.[129] If such notice is served, and regardless of when it will expire, the immediate landlord is disentitled to serve any statutory notice on the sub-tenant. The head landlord is, thereby, enabled to serve a section 25 notice directly on the sub-tenant.[130] As Ross summed up: 'Thus the "competence" of a landlord who has sub-let part of the premises but remains in occupation of the remainder for business purposes will depend upon whether or not he has been served with a section 25 notice or himself served a section 26 request or a notice under section 27'.[131]

Importance of the Distinction

This distinction between landlords is vital because for some purposes the involve-   **2.36**
ment of the 'immediate' landlord is necessary, whereas, for the majority of procedures the participation of the 'competent' landlord is required. Although the immediate landlord has a more limited role to play in the renewal procedure, it is this landlord who must, by virtue of section 24(2), receive service of a notice to quit given by a periodic tenant; accept any surrender from the tenant; serve a section 24(3) notice on a non-occupying tenant; and instigate forfeiture proceedings. The immediate landlord must also receive service of any section 27 notice given by the tenant to end a fixed-term lease. Excepting the above procedures, a tenancy to which Part II extends can be terminated or renewed only with the participation of the competent landlord. It is the competent landlord who must serve a section 25 notice and a section 26 request may be served only on this landlord. The involvement of the competent landlord is also necessary concerning the section 24A interim rent procedure,[132] the agreement of a new tenancy, and the resistance of the tenant's application for a new lease.

Changes in Identity

Although there may only be one competent landlord at any given time, changes   **2.37**
of identity may occur during the period when renewal or termination is sought.[133]
The material times for adjudging who is the competent landlord are at the service of the section 25 notice or section 26 request and, later, at the date of the hearing.

---

[129] *Cornish v Brook Green Laundry Ltd* [1959] 1 QB 394.

[130] *Lewis v MTC (Cars) Ltd*, n 29 above. The superior landlord, therefore, must serve a section 25 notice on the mesne landlord before serving notice on the sub-tenant. In the *Bowes-Lyon* case, Lord Reid described this innovation as 'a radical method by-passing the immediate landlord' (n 30 above at 433).

[131] N 38 above at 286.

[132] The weakness of this requirement is that, where sub-tenancies exist, the competent landlord will have nothing to gain by activating the interim rent machinery. In such a situation the benefit will enure for the immediate landlord only.

[133] See *XL Fisheries v Leeds Corporation* [1955] 2 QB 636 where the change of landlord came after the service of the tenant's section 26 request.

As the new competent landlord steps into the shoes of the predecessor, it is necessary that this new party be joined to any existing renewal proceedings.[134] Accordingly, in *Rene Claro (Haute Coiffure) Ltd v Halle Concerts Society*, where the tenant requested a new tenancy, but omitted to make the new competent landlord a party to the action, the proceedings failed.[135]

2.38   The problem of correctly identifying the competent landlord is particularly acute where sub-underleases have been created. In this scenario the sub-underlessee may experience different parties becoming the competent landlord within rapid succession. Ross provides the following example:

> [F]reeholder A has let to headlessee B who has in turn sublet to sublessee C, retaining a nominal one day reversion, and C has himself created subunderleases. It is possible that B may become the competent landlord of the subunderlessees for that one day alone. If one of those subunderlessees were to serve a counter-notice . . . on A or C on that day it would be ineffective, and unless another effective notice was subsequently served, the subunderlessee would lose his rights under the 1954 Act.[136]

In the situation where the interest of the competent landlord is subject to a mortgage, under which either the mortgagee is in possession or a receiver has been appointed by the mortgagee or by the court, section 67 deems the mortgagee to be the competent landlord.[137] This rule applies for all purposes except as regards receiving a tenant's section 40(2) notice for particulars (this provision expressly deals with mortgagees and the service of information notices). The mortgagee is, therefore, as Upjohn LJ commented in *Meah v Mouskos*, 'putting it quite generally, virtually substituted for the landlord'.[138] The mortgagee in possession must, therefore, give and receive relevant notices under the Act, grant any new lease and, of course, be joined to the tenant's renewal proceedings. The purpose of section 67 is, as described by Russell LJ, 'to apply the position which obtains at law in general in relation to the [mortgagees's] ability to grant leases and extensions of leases, to the grant of leases or extensions of leases under the Act of 1954'.[139]

---

[134] *Piper v Muggleton* [1956] 2 QB 569 where Jenkins LJ said (at 578), 'it is necessary that at every stage of the proceedings down to final judgment the person claiming to be or joined as being "the landlord" should in fact answer that description according to the statutory definition'.

[135] N 43 above. The issue concerned the identity of the competent landlord when the sub-tenant's renewal application was heard. As the mesne landlord had dropped from the picture and the new competent landlord had not been joined to the proceedings, the sub-tenant's action was not properly constituted.

[136] N 38 above at 287, note 10.

[137] For the purposes of the Act, the definition of mortgagee includes the holder of a charge or lien: section 69(1). In the scenario where, after the tenant has commenced proceedings, the landlord's mortgagee takes possession or appoints a receiver, the court will normally allow the existing proceedings to be amended or, if necessary, order a rehearing.

[138] [1964] 2 QB 23 at 36. For Northern Ireland, the equivalent provision is contained in article 36.

[139] ibid at 40.

G. Relationship with other Landlords

The Act contains a series of rules which govern the relationship between the com- **2.39** petent landlord and any other landlords. These rules concern the ability of the competent landlord to take action which will bind either a mesne landlord or a superior landlord. Not surprisingly, the ability to bind a superior landlord is particularly restricted.

Mesne Landlords

Under paragraph 3(1) of Schedule 6, a notice served by the competent landlord **2.40** can bind all mesne landlords. This rule extends to any notice given to terminate the lease and to any agreement made with the tenant as to the grant and terms of a new tenancy. The competent landlord is empowered to execute a new lease, and this takes effect as if the mesne landlord was a party to it.[140] It is of no consequence that the competent landlord will not be the tenant's immediate landlord when the new lease commences. There is no requirement that the consent of a mesne landlord be obtained because a landlord who stands between the competent landlord and the relevant tenant has no role to play in the renewal scheme. Nevertheless, if the competent landlord acts without the consent of the mesne landlord, there may be liability on the former to pay the latter compensation for any consequential loss.[141] There is, however, the proviso that the mesne landlord's consent cannot unreasonably be withheld, but may be given subject to reasonable conditions. Such conditions might include the payment of compensation or the modification of any notice to be served on, or agreement to be reached with, the tenant. Questions of reasonableness are to be decided by the court.[142] Liability to pay compensation does not arise where consent has been sought, but the mesne landlord has unreasonably withheld that consent.

Superior Landlords

Any agreement which the competent landlord proposes to enter may have an **2.41** effect on the interest of a superior landlord. Accordingly, the consent of every superior landlord, who will become the immediate landlord of the sub-tenant during any part of the period covered by the agreement, is necessary before the agreement can be effective.[143] Accordingly, the competent landlord cannot

---

[140] Sch 6, para 3(2). The equivalent provisions for Northern Ireland are contained in Sch 1, paras 2(1), 2(2) of the Business Tenancies (Northern Ireland) Order 1996.

[141] Sch 6, para 4(1).

[142] These matters do not directly concern the sub-tenant: Sch 6, para 3. In relation to Northern Ireland, these provisions are mirrored in Sch 1, para 3 of the 1996 Order.

[143] Sch 6, para 5. In Northern Ireland, this rule is contained within Sch 1, para 4 of the 1996 Order.

unilaterally bind either a superior landlord or the freeholder where the agreement with the sub-tenant is to run beyond the end of the competent landlord's lease. A superior landlord who has a reversionary term upon which any new lease ordered by the court may encroach, therefore, should be made a party to the proceedings.[144] If not, the court will not be able to order a reversionary tenancy.

Additional Rules

2.42   Two further rules are relevant and both were introduced as a result of amendments by the Law of Property Act 1969. First, in circumstances where the competent landlord's contractual tenancy is one which can or will be brought to an end within sixteen months,[145] and following service of a section 25 notice or a section 26 request, the competent landlord must forthwith send a copy of the relevant documentation to the landlord next in the chain.[146] The underlying rationale for this is that, if a change of competent landlord is to occur within the near future, the next competent landlord should have full information concerning what acts have been taken by the predecessor. The process once initiated must then be continued up the chain until notification reaches the freeholder.[147] For some non-apparent reason the documentation must still be forwarded to other landlords higher in the chain, even when the superior landlord's lease will endure beyond any lease that could be granted to the tenant by the court.

2.43   Second, if the competent landlord serves a section 25 notice and a superior landlord then becomes the competent landlord, that notice may be withdrawn by the replacement landlord.[148] A prescribed form of withdrawal must be followed and it is without prejudice to any future notices given by the new landlord.[149] It is necessary, however, that the superior landlord becomes the competent landlord and withdraws the notice within two months of it being served. This period reflects the provision in section 29(3) which allows proceedings to be commenced two months after the service of the termination notice/request. This facility, however, does not extend to a landlord's counter notice served in pursuance to a tenant's section 26 request.

---

[144]   *Birch (AW) v PB (Sloane) & Cadogan Settled Estates Co* (1956) 106 LJ 204.

[145]   Or any further time by which the tenancy may be continued under either section 36(2) (revocation of new lease) or section 64 (final disposal of unsuccessful renewal application).

[146]   Sch 6, para 7(a).

[147]   Sch 6, para 7(b).

[148]   Sch 6, para 6.

[149]   See the Landlord and Tenant Act 1954 Part II Notices Regulations 1983 SI No 133 as amended by the Landlord and Tenant Act 1954 (Notices) (Amendment) Regulations 1989 SI No 1548. The appropriate notice here is Form 12.

H. Provisions as to Reversions

By virtue of section 69(1), the protection of the 1954 Act extends to a sub-tenant   **2.44**
as to any other tenant. It is, therefore, possible that under the Act a sub-tenancy
can be continued beyond, or a reversionary lease granted to the sub-tenant which
subsists beyond, the termination of the immediate landlord's tenancy.[150] At common law, this would be impossible because the sub-tenancy would fall with the
head lease[151] and, in any event, the rules of privity of contract and estate would
render the covenants in the sub-tenancy unenforceable by or against the head
lessor. Accordingly, section 65 regulates the rights and obligations of the parties
where a reversionary lease is created. Although the statutory provision is detailed
and complex, its effect may be described more simply. An overview was provided
by Poole who identified the general consequence of this provision as, 'usually
ensuring that the interests of the intermediate landlord will eventually drop out
unless he has vested in him a term with a good many years still to run; and section
65(2) ensures that when the interest of the intermediate landlord comes to an end
the interest of the superior landlord shall be deemed to be the reversion for all purposes'.[152] This result is engineered in a variety of ways.

First, and for as long as it subsists, the immediate superior tenancy is preserved   **2.45**
and deemed to be an interest in reversion expectant (immediately expectant if no
intermediate tenancy exists) upon the termination of the inferior tenancy. This is
so even though the inferior tenancy will continue beyond it.[153] As a result of this
fiction, and while the head tenancy and the sub-tenancy exist, both parties to the
underlease remain able to sue and to be sued on the covenants. Second, when the
immediate superior tenancy ends, the 'continuing' sub-tenancy becomes a tenancy held directly under the superior landlord next in the chain.[154] This landlord
has no option other than to accept this, perhaps unwanted, change of status and,
of course, will now be bound by the terms of a sub-lease negotiated by others.[155]
This simply could not occur at common law. Third, if a continuation tenancy
extends beyond the date on which a lease of the reversion, granted by the landlord,

---

[150] See generally JA Andrew, *Creation of Reversionary Leases* [1960] Conv 462.

[151] *Sherwood v Moody* [1952] 1 All ER 389.

[152] N 124 above at 458.

[153] Section 65(1). The equivalent provision in Northern Ireland is to be found within article 33(1).

[154] Section 65(2). This incorporates section 139(1) of the Law of Property Act 1925 which otherwise facilitates such transference of responsibility only when the intermediate tenancy is ended by merger or surrender: see *Barrett v Morgan*, n 48 above. Section 65(2), however, is wider in scope and covers also where the superior lease ends by effluxion of time, notice to quit and forfeiture: see *Electricity Supply Nominees Ltd v Thorn EMI Retail Ltd* [1991] 2 EGLR 46. The same rule applies in Northern Ireland: article 33(2) of the 1996 Order.

[155] Nevertheless, the landlord appears able to claim from the sub-tenant any rent arrears out-standing at the expiry of the head lease: see *Electric Supply Nominees Ltd v Thorn EMI Retail Ltd*, ibid.

is to commence, the latter takes effect subject to the former, including the tenant's renewal rights.[156] Fourth, if the statutory renewal is to commence after a landlord's lease of the reversion will take effect, the reversionary lease takes subject to the new tenancy and the new tenant enjoys the right to possession.[157] Such reversionary lease then being an interest expectant on the termination of the renewed tenancy.

Order of Reversionary Leases

2.46 The court is given the express power to order reversionary leases. Under Schedule 6, paragraph 2, the court is able to grant a new tenancy under the renewal scheme which, whether by agreement or otherwise, can extend beyond the date that the immediate landlord's interest comes to an end. This is achieved by creating such reversionary tenancies as may be necessary to secure the grant of the new lease and to ensure that what the Act refers to as the 'inferior tenancy' may be prolonged beyond the term of a superior tenancy.[158] An example of this arising would be where the head tenant has three years remaining under a head lease not protected by the Act and the sub-tenant has obtained a renewal for a fourteen-years' term. The court must order two leases: one for three years to be granted immediately by the current competent landlord; and one for eleven years to be granted when the first lease ends by the next landlord able to grant such a term. These two leases are, however, deemed to comprise a single fourteen-year term and no continuation rights emerge at the end of the first tenancy.

I. A Notice for Particulars

2.47 As demonstrated, the Part II procedures require that certain steps be taken by the correct person at the correct time. Central to the statutory machinery is that both parties be able to identify each other and to ascertain the nature and extent of their respective interests. It is an important preliminary step that the parties should have all the necessary information in order to exercise their statutory rights. This is of paramount importance where sub-letting has occurred. The tenant will need to know the identity of the competent landlord and the competent landlord will need to know whether the tenant is still in occupation and (where relevant) the details of any sub-tenancy. Hence, the facility exists within section 40 whereby either party may serve notice on the other so as to acquire the requisite information. It is to be appreciated, however, that a section 40 notice cannot be served by

---

[156] Section 65(3). The same rule applies in Northern Ireland: article 33(3) of the 1996 Order.

[157] Section 65(4). As regards Northern Ireland, this approach is adopted in article 33(4) of the 1996 Order. cf at common law where the tenant under a reversionary lease would be entitled to possession.

[158] In Northern Ireland, the Lands Tribunal is similarly empowered to grant reversionary tenancies: article 17(2) of the 1996 Order.

or on a tenant more than two years before the date on which (discounting the statutory renewal provisions) the lease is either due to expire or can be brought to an end by a landlord's notice to quit.[159] This restriction is intended to avoid purposeless and vexatious notices being served by either party.

Tenant's Notice

A tenant can serve a notice (in the prescribed form)[160] provided that the tenancy is **2.48** of premises used wholly or partly for the purposes of a business and is either for a term certain exceeding one year or for any term certain and thereafter from year to year.[161] There is no requirement that the tenant be in occupation nor that it is the tenant's business which is carried on at the premises. The notice may be served on the immediate landlord and any person having a superior interest, including any mortgagee in possession of such an interest.[162] Following service, it is the duty of the recipient to respond in writing within one month and to state whether the recipient is the freeholder.[163] If a mortgagee is in possession, the lender must provide its name and address. If the recipient is not the freeholder, the tenant must be notified, to the best of the recipient's knowledge and belief, of the name and address of the person who is the recipient's immediate landlord (or, where relevant, the mortgagor's immediate landlord); the term of the recipient's tenancy; and the earliest date (if any) at which that tenancy is terminable by notice to quit given by the relevant landlord. There is, however, no requirement that the recipient reveal whether any notices have been served by or on a superior landlord.

Landlord's Notice

In a like vein, the immediate or a superior landlord can serve a notice (again in the **2.49** prescribed form) on the tenant requiring the tenant to respond in writing and

---

[159] Section 40(4). A similar scheme operates in Northern Ireland: see article 29. Article 29(4), however, prohibits the service of a notice after, as appropriate, a landlord's notice to determine or a tenant's request for a new lease.

[160] See the 1983 Regulations (as amended) above. The tenant's notice is Form 10 and the landlord's notice is Form 9. In Northern Ireland, and by virtue of the Business Tenancies (Notices) Regulations (Northern Ireland) 1997, there is one universal notice for these purposes (Form 5).

[161] Section 40(2). As regards Northern Ireland, the tenancy must be for either a term certain exceeding 9 months; a tenancy granted for a term certain not exceeding 9 months, but in circumstances where, when the tenancy is granted, the tenant (including a predecessor in business) has been in occupation for over 18 months; or a term certain exceeding one year and thereafter continued from year to year: article 29(2). In both jurisdictions, the respective limitations apply also to qualify the tenant's ability to serve a request for a new tenancy.

[162] Section 40(3). For the purposes of section 40 the expression 'mortgagee in possession' includes a receiver appointed by the mortgagee or by the court who is in receipt of rents or profits: section 40(5). Form 11 is the notice to be served on the mortgagee. In Northern Ireland, the class is expanded to include any person in receipt of rent or any person who the tenant reasonably believes to be superior landlord, mortgagee in possession or agent of either: article 29(2) of the 1996 Order.

[163] Or the mortgagee of such an owner: section 40(2)(a). In Northern Ireland, the recipient must merely furnish the information as expressly requested in the notice: article 29(5).

within one month. The information to be supplied concerns whether the tenant occupies the premises or part of them wholly or partly for the purposes of a business carried on by him and the details of any sub-tenancy granted.[164] The information as to occupation assumes obvious importance as it will disclose whether, at the time of response, the tenancy is protected by the 1954 Act. The landlord should be aware, however, that the tenant may at some time resume occupation and, thereby, regain the protection of the Part II provisions. In the light of the *Esselte* case, it may be necessary to serve a further section 40 notice before attempting to engage the renewal provisions. The details to be furnished in the notice as to sub-tenancies are general in nature. The recipient must identify the premises comprised in the sub-tenancy, its term (including the provisions for termination by notice to quit), the rent, the name of the sub-tenant, whether the sub-tenant is (to the best knowledge and belief of the respondent) in occupation of the premises and, if not, the sub-tenant's address.[165] There is no provision requiring the tenant to reveal whether or not the sub-tenant is carrying on a business at the premises nor any duty to provide any further details of the sub-tenancy (for example, as to any user clause). As the information is limited to an immediate sub-tenancy, if further underleases have been created then it is advisable for the landlord to serve additional notices on all tenants.

Existing Limitations

2.50   There are a variety of criticisms that have been levelled against the current facility by the Law Commission. First, although section 40 imposes duties, it provides no redress for their non-observance.[166] The absence of any specified penalty may be seen as undermining the effectiveness of what might otherwise be an important safeguard for those who seek to exercise their statutory rights. Short of fraud, the only possible redress for a party suffering loss is for breach of statutory duty[167] or, where appropriate, for breach of an express covenant to observe statutory requirements. In its Working Paper, the Law Commission considered the issue and proposed that an express sanction be incorporated into the Act.[168] The Working Paper was unsure as to whether this sanction should be a criminal one and/or one to prevent the defaulter taking other statutory steps.[169] It did, however, propose in broad terms that there should be an express right of damages against the defaulter.

---

[164] Section 40(1).

[165] Section 40(1)(b).

[166] cf the position in Northern Ireland where the Lands Tribunal may make such order as it thinks necessary with a view to compelling the recipient to furnish information and any such order may be enforced by mandamus or compensation: article 29(6).

[167] This is, however, an untried and untested threat; see Aldridge, n 24 above at 97.

[168] N 16 above at para 3.2.37.

[169] ibid at para 3.2.38.

In its subsequent Report, the Law Commission was content to recommend that civil liability for breach of statutory duty should be imposed.[170]

Second, once the information is provided by a party, there is no obligation to keep **2.51** it up to date. In its Report, the Law Commission recommended that there should be an ongoing duty to ensure that the information remains accurate for a period of six months from the service of the request. Early curtailment of this responsibility should occur when the informant disposes of the interest in the property and communicates details of the transfer to the serving party.[171]

Third, as a section 40 notice cannot be withdrawn or cancelled, the duty to **2.52** respond persists despite any assignment of the serving party's estate. The Report believed that the duty should continue, but only until the informant is alerted both to the transfer and to the identity of the transferee. On this occurring the duty will then be owed to the assignee.[172]

Fourth, the Report argued that the information to be supplied should be **2.53** extended.[173] In order to achieve alignment with its proposed reforms concerning the treatment of companies, the Commission recommended that the tenant's response should include details as to whether the tenant's *alter ego* is in occupation. It was also recommended that the landlord should be advised as to any contracted out sub-letting and, where there is a severed reversion, details should be provided by the landlord about the other reversioners. There is no doubt that the present system is under-used. Much of the information sought by the landlord can, indeed, be gained from a physical inspection of the holding. The service of a section 40 notice, moreover, alerts the other party that a termination notice or request for a new tenancy is in prospect. As this may encourage the recipient to seize the initiative, the notice should normally be served shortly before the service of a notice or request, as appropriate. In addition, and following the lead in *Shelley v United Artists*,[174] either party can later be estopped from denying any representation made in response to a section 40 notice. Any replies should, therefore, be careful and accurate.

---

[170] N 26 above at para 2.32.
[171] ibid at paras 2.29, 2.30.
[172] ibid at para 2.31.
[173] ibid at paras 2.27, 2.28. As Ross points out, 'The questions asked in the notices are insufficiently extensive to enable the server to establish all the relevant facts from the replies' (n 38 above at 288). In Northern Ireland, such limitations have been overcome by the broader approach that the server can request any information which it is reasonable for the recipient to furnish: article 29(3).
[174] N 119 above.

3

SCOPE OF THE ACT

A. Introduction

Subject to a number of common law and statutory exceptions, section 23(1) **3.01**
extends the protection of the 1954 Act to 'any tenancy where the property comprised in the tenancy is or includes premises which are occupied by the tenant and
are so occupied for the purposes of a business carried on by him or for those and
other purposes'. Not surprisingly, as the Law Reform Advisory Committee for
Northern Ireland pointed out, 'almost every phrase of that provision has been the
subject of judicial discussion and interpretation, with the result that its meaning
is now largely clear'.[1] The requirements are, therefore, first, that a tenancy exists.
This is defined in section 69(1) to include leases, sub-tenancies and agreements
for a lease, but excludes a demise by way of mortgage. Tenancies by estoppel fall
within the 1954 Act.[2] Second, the tenancy must be of premises which are occupied by the tenant. Third, this occupation must be wholly or partly attributable

---

[1] *A Review of the Law relating to Business Tenancies in Northern Ireland*, (1992) Discussion Paper
No 3 at para 3.2. Note that an identical catchment clause is to be found in article 3(1) of the Business
Tenancies (Northern Ireland) Order 1996.
[2] *Bell v General Accident Fire & Life Assurance Corporation Plc* [1998] 17 EG144.

to the tenant's business. Finally, the tenancy must not be otherwise excluded from the ambit of statutory protection. Each of these conditions is to be examined in depth in the course of this chapter and attention also focused on the special provisions which relate to public bodies.

B. Lease or Licence?

3.02 As the Act applies only to tenancies, licence agreements necessarily fall outside its catchment.[3] A landlord who wishes to side-step the protective provisions might, therefore, attempt to do so by creating a licence instead of a tenancy. The employment of this tactic is not against public policy and it does constitute a valid avoidance measure.[4] As Buckley LJ emphasised in *Shell-Mex & BP Ltd v Manchester Garages*: 'One should not approach the problem with a tendency to attempt to find a tenancy because unless there is a tenancy the case will escape the effects of the statute.'[5] It is to be appreciated that a licence is fundamentally different from a lease in that it cannot confer a legal estate and, at best, bestows only a personal privilege on the licensee.[6] The classic exposition is that of Vaughan CJ in *Thomas v Sorrell*, 'a dispensation or licence properly passeth no interest, not alters or transfers property in any thing, but only makes an action lawful which without it had been unlawful'.[7] As evident from the mass of associated case law, however, the distinction between a lease and licence is, traditionally, difficult to draw. In order to impose a test which would make identification of a tenancy more effective, in *Street v Mountford* Lord Templeman advocated the working rule that, where 'accommodation is granted for a term at a rent with exclusive possession, the landlord providing neither attendance or services, the grant is a tenancy . . .'.[8] This rule is, however, somewhat easier to state than it is to apply and, being subject to a variety of qualifications, is apt to be misleading.

---

[3] *Shell-Mex & BP Ltd v Manchester Garages* [1971] 1 All ER 841. Licences are seemingly destined always to remain outside purview of the statutory scheme: see Law Commission, *Business Tenancies: A Periodic Review of the Landlord & Tenant Act 1954 Part II* (1992) Law Com No 208 at para 3.13.

[4] See *Buchmann v May* [1978] 2 All ER 993.

[5] N 3 above at 846. This view was shared also by Lord Templeman in *Street v Mountford* [1985] AC 809 at 819.

[6] *Ashburn Anstalt v Arnold* [1988] 2 All ER 147. Albeit personal, the rights of a licensee may, however, be enforced both at law (in contract) and in equity (if harnessed to a constructive trust or an estoppel). A lease, however, does not necessarily have to create an estate in land and can exist as a purely contractual relationship between the parties: *Bruton v London & Quadrant Housing Trust* [1999] 3 All ER 481. As Lord Hoffmann commented: 'It is putting the cart before the horse to say that whether the agreement is a lease depends upon whether it creates a proprietary interest' (at 487).

[7] (1673) Vaugh 330 at 351.

[8] N 5 above at 818.

Certainty of Term

The 'term' must be certain in that the lease must have an ascertainable and certain **3.03** duration (that is, a defined beginning and a defined end).[9] If the lease does not state a commencement date, none will be implied.[10] By way of illustration, in *Lace v Chantler* a lease granted for the duration of the War was held to be void for uncertainty.[11] In its place, however, the court was able to find a weekly, implied periodic tenancy arising from the tenant's taking of possession and the landlord's acceptance of a weekly rent. As Lord Greene explained:

> A term created by a leasehold tenancy agreement must be expressed either with certainty and specifically or by reference to something which can, at the time when the lease takes effect, be looked at as a certain ascertainment of what the term was meant to be. In the present case, when this tenancy agreement took effect the term was completely uncertain.[12]

Until recently some uncertainty existed as to whether the *Lace v Chantler* rule applied to periodic tenancies. The Court of Appeal in *Canadian Bank v Bello*, for example, held that the rule applied exclusively to fixed terms and only then when the determining event was outside the control of the parties.[13] This limitation was, however, abandoned by the House of Lords in *Prudential Assurance Co Ltd v London Residuary Body* where it was concluded that the rule applied even-handedly to both fixed terms and periodic tenancies.[14] Although the House of Lords did not seize the opportunity to overrule its previous decision, Lord Browne-Wilkinson was at a loss to understand why the rule existed. He commented, 'This bizarre outcome results from the application of an ancient and technical rule of law . . . No one has produced any satisfactory rationale for the genesis of this rule. No one has been able to point to any useful purpose that it serves at the present day.'[15] By way of comparison, in Northern Ireland it is still possible to have a valid tenancy for life or until some other uncertain event occurs.

---

[9] *Say v Smith* (1563) Plowd 269; *Oakley v Wilson* [1927] 2 KB 279.

[10] *Brown v Gould* [1972] Ch 53. A stated commencement date is not necessary for a licence: *James v Lock* [1978] 1 EGLR 40.

[11] [1944] 1 KB 368. A term expressed to be from year to year subject to the landlord's right to determine the lease before the expiry of the five years unless the war ends would, however, be valid: see *Parc Battersea Ltd v Hutchinson* [1999] 22 EG 149.

[12] ibid at 370. As the rule is concerned with maximum duration, forfeiture provisions or break clauses do not offend certainty: *Bass Holdings Ltd v Lewis* [1986] 2 EGLR 40.

[13] (1991) 64 P & CR 48 (a lease until the payment of a debt upheld); see also *Ashburn Anstalt v Arnold*, n 6 above.

[14] [1992] 2 AC 386 (a purported grant until the land was needed for road-widening purposes). Subsequently, in *Onyx (UK) Ltd v Beard* (1996) March 14 HC it was held that an agreement, relating to the use of a social club, expressed to continue indefinitely unless determined by either party giving one month's notice could not create a valid tenancy.

[15] ibid at 396. See further P Sparkes, *Certainty of Leasehold Terms* (1993) 109 LQR 93; S Bright, *Uncertainty in Leases: Is it a Vice?* (1993) Legal Studies 38.

The renewal procedure there has been expressly adapted to accommodate this possibility.[16]

Rent

3.04 The reservation of a rent (albeit normally present) is not an essential feature of a lease. Accordingly, a 'no rent, no tenancy' principle does not exist.[17] Indeed, section 205(1)(xxvii) of the Law of Property Act 1925 defines a term of years absolute 'whether or not at a rent'. Unlike the Rent Act 1977, moreover, there is no requirement that any rent be payable before a tenancy can be protected by the Part II provisions. The payment of 'rent', however, remains indicative that a lease has been created, whereas the absence of any payment whatsoever may support the proposition that a licence has been entered.[18] Hence, the tendency for purported licence agreements to describe payments as licence fees or accommodation charges.

Exclusive Possession

3.05 Exclusive possession is the legal right to exclude all others from the demised property. As Lord Templeman concluded in *Street v Mountford*: 'A tenant armed with exclusive possession can keep out strangers and keep out the landlord unless the landlord is exercising limited rights reserved to him by the tenancy agreement to enter and view and repair.'[19] Exclusive possession, however, must be distinguished from exclusive occupation which is, essentially, an issue of fact and physical use.[20] The distinction is of importance as an occupier can have the sole occupation of premises without having exclusive possession.[21] Although exclusive possession is a pre-requisite of a tenancy, it offers no guarantee that a tenancy has been created. As accepted in *Street v Mountford*, the grant of exclusive possession may, in exceptional circumstances, be consistent with a licence agreement.[22] These exceptions include where there is a lack of intention to create legal relations (for example, the arrangement is an act of friendship or charity)[23] and where possession is referable to some other legal relationship (for example, employer and employee or vendor and purchaser).[24] In these and similar circumstances it is open to the court to con-

---

[16] See Article 8 of the Northern Ireland (Business Tenancies) Order 1996.

[17] *Ashburn Anstalt v Arnold*, n 6 above, where the tenant occupied a shop rent free prior to redevelopment; see also *AG Securities v Vaughan* [1990] 1 AC 417.

[18] *Onyx (UK) Ltd v Beard*, n 14 above. This case illustrates also that, for a tenancy to be implied at common law, a rent must be payable.

[19] N 5 above at 816.

[20] *Smith v Northside Developments* (1988) 55 P & CR 164.

[21] *AG Securities v Vaughan*, n 17 above; *Westminster City Council v Clarke* [1992] 2 AC 288.

[22] See also *Essex Plan v Broadminster* [1988] 2 EGLR 73; *Ogwr BC v Dykes* [1989] 2 All ER 880; *Carroll v Manek* (1999) 12 July (HC).

[23] The absence of any payment by the occupier could put the agreement within the 'generosity' exemption: see *Onyx (UK) v Beard*, n 14 above.

[24] But not where it is only the goodwill which is to be bought and sold: *Vandersteen v Agius* (1993) 65 P & CR 266.

clude that occupation is referable to a relationship other than a tenancy.[25] Although the list is not exhaustive, the courts appear reluctant to extend the already approved categories.[26]

Exclusive Possession and its Denial

Exclusive possession has become the crucial factor in marking the distinction **3.06** between a lease and a licence.[27] Accordingly, in *Smith v Northside Developments* the Court of Appeal admitted that, when in doubt, the court should look for exclusive possession with particular emphasis upon whether the landlord can be excluded.[28] This might be difficult to discern where the agreement calls itself a licence and purports to deny the occupier exclusive possession by reserving a degree of control over the premises for the grantor.[29] For example, in *Shell-Mex & BP Ltd v Manchester Garages*, a licence was upheld in circumstances where the possession and control retained by the licensor (particularly concerning the products that could be sold) ran contrary to the grant of exclusive possession.[30] While such tactics alone are insufficient to guarantee the creation of a licence, it is an inescapable conclusion that, if exclusive possession is denied both at law and in fact, there can be no tenancy.[31] Nevertheless, the court must be concerned with the true bargain, as opposed to the apparent bargain, struck between the parties and it is this which must be examined.[32] Hence, it is the objective intentions of the parties and their real rights under the agreement which must be identified. Each case will, therefore, turn upon its own facts and be examined in the light of all the surrounding circumstances.[33]

In order to create a licence, there will normally be a written agreement which **3.07** expressly denies the existence of exclusive possession. As regards such agreements, the court must approach the document in an even-handed manner and apply the usual rules of construction.[34] The descriptive label attached by the parties to the

---

[25] See further R Smith, *Property Law* (2nd edn, 1998) 352–356.
[26] *Dellneed Ltd v Chin* (1986) 53 P & CR 172; *Camden BC v Shortlife Community Housing Ltd* (1992) 25 HLR 330.
[27] See P Sparkes, *Breaking Flat Sharing Licences* (1989) 5 JSWL 295.
[28] N 20 above.
[29] See, for example, *Lee-Verhulst (Investments) Ltd v Harwood Trust* [1973] 1 QB 204 where the landlord provided chambermaids, took incoming calls and messages, undertook general porterage work and prepared meals for the occupants when required.
[30] N 3 above. As regards petrol stations and public houses, restraint of trade provisions may offend Article 85 of the Treaty of Rome (see *Gibbs Mew Plc v Gemmell* (1998) 1 EG 117), but this does not entail that a tenancy as opposed to a licence has been created: see *Parks v Esso Petroleum Company Ltd* (1998) November 23 CA; *Star Rider Ltd v Inntrepreneur Pub Co* (1998) 16 EG 140. The position will, moreover, be unaffected by the implementation of the Competition Act 1998.
[31] See *Esso Petroleum Co Ltd v Fumegrange Ltd* (1994) 46 EG 199.
[32] *Aslan v Murphy* [1989] 3 All ER 130; *Dellneed v Chin*, n 26 above.
[33] *Stribling v Wickham* (1989) 27 EG 81; *Westminster City Council v Clarke*, n 21 above.
[34] *Hadjiloucas v Crean* [1987] 3 All ER 1008.

transaction is inconclusive: 'If the agreement satisfied all the requirements of a tenancy, then the agreement produced a tenancy and the parties cannot alter the effect of the agreement by insisting that they only created a licence.'[35] The court's function, moreover, is to detect any sham or pretence agreements and misleading labels. All depends on the interaction between the wording of the agreement and the factual matrix in which the agreement exists.[36] As *Street v Mountford* demonstrated, where the language of the licence contradicts the reality of the lease, the facts are to prevail.[37] Unrealistic provisions in the contract can, therefore, be disregarded.[38] It remains, however, for the occupier to show that the agreement is a sham or pretence and, if this burden is not discharged, the contract must be construed as it stands. As Millett J explained in *Camden LBC v Shortlife Community Housing Ltd*, 'Unless the parties' professed intentions differed from their true intention, or failed to reflect the true substance of the real transaction, this is conclusive.'[39]

3.08   Where there is no written agreement, there is of course nothing for the courts to construe. A different approach is to be adopted and the decision of the court based purely upon the surrounding circumstances, for example, the relationship between the parties, the nature and extent of the accommodation, and the intended and actual mode of occupation. The judge's task, as Sir John Arnold explained in *Smith v Northside*, is to determine 'whether there was or was not exclusive possession from the circumstances and the facts of the case in order to see whether the proper inference is that such a term was intended by means of and derived from a history of such a right being recognised'.[40] There the evidence of a particular conversation indicated that exclusive possession had not been granted.

Licences of Business Premises

3.09   As the *ratio* of *Street v Mountford* is confined to residential premises, doubt has been expressed as to whether it applies fully in the commercial sector. As Glidewell LJ admitted, 'the indicia, which may make it more apparent in the case of a residential tenant or a residential occupier that he is indeed a tenant, may be less applicable or be less likely to have that effect in the case of business tenancies'.[41]

---

[35] *Per* Lord Templeman in *Street v Mountford*, n 5 above at 819; see also *BJ Dunnel Properties v Thorpe* (1989) 33 EG 36. Nevertheless, the label might constitute prima-facie evidence of the parties' intentions: *Dresden Estates Ltd v Collinson* (1988) 55 P & CR 47.

[36] See PH Petit, *Judge Proof Licences* [1980] Conv 112.

[37] N 5 above. In previous times, a purely contractual approach dominated legal thinking: see *Somma v Hazelhurst* [1978] 2 All ER 1011.

[38] *Brooker Settled Estates v Ayres* (1987) 282 EG 325.

[39] N 26 above at 345; see also *Essex Plan v Broadminster*, n 22 above; *Baron Raglan v Harris* (1998) December 7 CA

[40] N 20 above at 167.

[41] *Dresden Estates Ltd v Collinson*, n 35 above at 52. In relation to agricultural property, a similar approach was adopted in *Baron Raglan v Harris*, n 39 above.

Although subsequent cases have stressed that Lord Templeman's approach applies equally to all forms of tenancies,[42] it is undeniable that commercial arrangements lend themselves to the creation of licences more readily than their residential counterparts.[43] So, for example, in *Venus Investments Ltd v Stocktop Ltd* it was held that the presence of exclusive possession was not to be inferred in the case of commercial property as readily as with residential premises.[44] This distinction is logical in the light that the attributes of commercial property are usually completely different from those of residential premises and the premises themselves are open to a far wider range of potential uses. Accordingly, *Street v Mountford* is capable of being distinguished when the court deems it appropriate. As Hutchison LJ accepted:

> [The exercise] is not to be undertaken in a vacuum, but rather with a proper regard to the context in which the issue arises . . . while one would ordinarily expect that someone in occupation of a small house for a fixed term at a rent had exclusive possession, one would I suggest have no such preconceptions about a person given the right to tip rubbish in the excavated parts of a large plot of land, on other parts of which, it seems, quarrying was continuing.[45]

It has to be admitted, however, that any attempt to create a licence agreement has become an unpredictable venture. In the light of the availability of contracting out, and the exemption of short leases it is, moreover, often unnecessary.[46]

There does, however, remain scope for the creation of licences of commercial **3.10** property. This was illustrated in *Mehta v Royal Bank of Scotland*[47] where, in connection with the long-term rental of a hotel room, the court upheld a licence despite the presence of Lord Templeman's three hallmarks of a tenancy. Indeed, Southwell QC limited Lord Templeman's observations in *Street v Mountford* to cases in which those hallmarks were the factors of overriding importance and where the landlord had deliberately set out to try to exclude the Rent Act protection for the tenant. He added, ' Those observations cannot be applied indiscriminately, and particularly not in a case in which there are other equally significant factors to be taken into account . . . in my judgment there is no simple all

---

[42] See *London & Associated Investment Trust Plc v Calow* [1986] 2 EGLR 80; *University of Reading v Johnson-Houghton* [1985] 2 EGLR 113.

[43] See *Minimet Enterprises v Mayor & Burgesses of Croydon* (1989) August 24 CA; *Onyx (UK) Ltd v Beard*, n 14 above, which concerned council land and buildings used by a social club.

[44] [1996] EGCS 173. There it was held that, as the agreement contained neither a forfeiture clause nor a right for the grantor to enter and inspect the premises, it did not resemble a commercial lease and, therefore, must be a licence.

[45] *Hunts Refuse Disposals Ltd v Norfolk Environmental Waste Services Ltd* [1997] 1 EGLR 16 at 18.

[46] Following the decision in *Graysim Holdings Ltd v P&O Property Holdings Ltd* [1995] 4 All ER 831, however, it might be tempting for a mesne landlord (who wishes to remain within the 1954 Act) to attempt to create a licence instead of a sub-tenancy.

[47] (1999) January 14 (HC).

embracing test for such a distinction. The search for such a test would be a search for a chimaera.'

3.11   Some remaining potential for licences of business premises can be identified in the following areas.[48] First, a licence will emerge where there is genuinely no grant of exclusive possession. This could arise where there is a sharing of floor space, as in *Smith v Northside Developments* where market traders moved into joint occupation of part of a shop unit.[49] As the others who used the premises could gain access only via the part occupied by the market traders, there could be no exclusive possession.[50] A licence would be appropriate also where there is a trade concession agreement, for example, to sell refreshments in a theatre[51] or to sell petrol on a garage forecourt.[52] Other contexts in which exclusive possession would not arise include where occupation is limited to only part of the day or week;[53] where the right is to occupy part of the premises for storage and the licensor has the right to vary which part can be used;[54] and where there is occupation of a lock-up market stall.[55]

3.12   Second, where the occupation is to allow a prospective tenant into occupation pending the grant of a lease.[56] This was a possibility recognised in *Street v Mountford*, but for a licence to be produced it has to be genuinely intended that the transaction will actually take place.[57] In *Essex Plan Ltd v Broadminster*, for example, exclusive possession was not granted when the occupants took a licence for a year with a mere option to take a lease.[58] Hoffmann J concluded that the taking of possession was ancillary to the option and did not arise from the legal relationship of landlord and tenant. In any event, if the licence fails it is likely that the

---

[48]   It was once thought that a licence would be created where the landlord genuinely had no power to create a lease. This traditional view has now been discredited by the House of Lords in *Bruton v London & Quadrant Housing Trust*, n 6 above. A lease can be created regardless of whether the grantor has the legal ability to create a legal estate.

[49]   N 20 above.

[50]   See also *Hunts Refuse Disposals Ltd v Norfolk Environmental Waste Services Ltd*, n 45 above, where the exclusive right to dump waste at a quarry, which was being worked by the owners, did not amount to exclusive possession and constituted a licence.

[51]   *Frank Warren & Co Ltd v London CC* [1904] 1 KB 713; *Clore v Theatrical Properties Ltd* [1936] 3 All ER 483.

[52]   *Shell-Mex & BP Ltd v Manchester Garages Ltd*, n 3 above; *Esso Petroleum Company Ltd v Fumegrange Ltd*, n 31, above.

[53]   *Minimet Enterprises v Mayor & Burgesses of Croydon*, n 43 above. In *Manchester City Council v NCP Ltd* [1982] 1 EGLR 94, the Court of Appeal saw sound commercial sense in such an arrangement; see also *City Securities (London) Ltd v Berkshire Car Parks Ltd* (1998) December 8 CA.

[54]   *Dresden Estates Ltd v Collinson*, n 35 above.

[55]   *Gloucester City Council v Williams* [1990] The Times, 15 May. In *Graysim Holdings Ltd v P&O Property Holdings Ltd*, n 46 above, however, the finding at first instance that the stall holders were licensees and not sub-tenants was, unfortunately, not the subject of appeal. It is submitted that the mesne landlord's case might have fared better if this had been put before the appellate courts.

[56]   *Isaac v Hotel de Paris Ltd* [1960] 1 WLR 239.

[57]   *Bhattacharya v Raising* (1987) March 25 CA.

[58]   N 22 above.

parties will have created a tenancy at will which falls outside the ambit of the 1954 Act.[59]

Third, a licence might arise where the term granted is uncertain (for example, **3.13** 'until the landlord requires the premises for other purposes'), the agreement expressly denies that any tenancy is to be implied and the rent is set to vary from, say, month to month. Although untested, this could prevent a periodic tenancy occurring by implication[60] and, at worst, give rise to a tenancy at will which, as mentioned, is itself outside the 1954 Act.[61]

C. Premises

For the 1954 Act to apply there must be a letting of property which is or includes **3.14** 'premises'. Although the Act does not define 'premises', what falls within the scope of the term is usually self-evident: offices, warehouses, shops and factories, for example. Nevertheless, the expression is construed widely as embracing land and any buildings on it.[62] There is, however, no need for any building whatsoever because bare land can constitute premises.[63] An example of this is *Bracey v Read* where gallops used for the purposes of training and exercising horses were held to be premises.[64] Other illustrations include *Harley Queen v Forsyte Kerman* where the protection of the Act extended to open land used as a car park;[65] and *Botterill v Bedfordshire CC* where the tenancy of land used for a gun club was protected.[66]

Incorporeal Hereditaments

Part II of the Act does not extend to tenancies of incorporeal hereditaments such **3.15** as a right of way,[67] a right to fish[68] or a lease of chattels. The rationale is that, although these rights and easements can be enjoyed, they do not constitute premises and cannot be occupied.[69] They do, however, qualify for protection if

---

[59] *Javad v Aqil* [1991] 1 All ER 243.
[60] See *Hi-Lift Elevator Services Ltd & Freshfields (Plant & Machinery) Ltd v British Gas Plc* (1993) March 19 CA, where it was held that there must be a common agreement that an implied periodic tenancy will arise; *Phillips v Bexleyheath Golf Club* (1993) February 4 CA, where there was no agreement as to term.
[61] See *Morris v Carey* [1989] EGCS 53.
[62] In Northern Ireland, this is expressly stated: article 2(2).
[63] *Wandsworth BC v Singh* (1991) 62 P & CR 219 (a park); *Coppen v Bruce-Smith* (1998) March 27 CA (tennis courts).
[64] [1963] Ch 88; see also *University of Reading v Johnson-Houghton*, n 42 above.
[65] (1983) 6 CLY 2077.
[66] [1985] 1 EGLR 82.
[67] *Land Reclamation Co Ltd v Basildon DC* [1979] 2 All ER 993.
[68] *Jones v Christy* (1963) 107 SJ 374.
[69] *Nevil Long & Co (Boards) Ltd v Firmenich & Co* (1984) 47 P & CR 59.

granted as ancillary rights under a lease of corporeal premises.[70] The Law Commission, in its Working Paper, provisionally concluded that this distinction was untenable and that, for the purposes of the Act, leases of incorporeal hereditaments should be classified as 'premises'.[71] The suggestion was that the word 'occupy' currently employed within section 23(1) should be replaced by the term 'use'. It is arguable, however, that this change would fail to achieve its objective. An analogous provision requiring the premises to be used for the purposes of a business can be found in Part I of the Landlord and Tenant Act 1927, but incorporeal hereditaments still remain outside its scope. Of course, if the Act embraced incorporeal hereditaments, and because such hereditaments have no rateable value, the present compensation scheme for disturbance would need to be radically reformed. Although the subsequent Law Commission Report concluded that change was unjustified, it did acknowledge that, 'There will be some circumstances in which the renewal of such a lease is just as important to protect the goodwill and future of a business as the renewal of a normal lease of business premises.'[72]

D. Occupation

3.16 The premises must be occupied by the tenant or the tenant's employee before the statutory provisions can apply. In this sense, the concept of occupation attributes eligibility.[73] Once within the ambit of the Act, the tenant is entitled to a grant of a new lease, but only of the holding as it exists at the time of the hearing. Under section 23(3), the tenant's holding comprises of all the property demised under the original lease, excepting any part which is no longer occupied by the tenant or the tenant's employees. Accordingly, the parcels of the new lease might not necessarily correspond with those under the previous tenancy. The use of 'occupation' in this context is determinative of the property (if any) which will be the subject matter of the new lease: that is, it prescribes entitlement. As Lord Nicholls explained in *Graysim Holdings Ltd v P&O Property Holdings Ltd*, 'Although a business tenancy may include property not occupied by the tenant, property not occupied by him or his employees is excluded from the holding and, accordingly, it is not property in respect of which the tenant is entitled to obtain a new tenancy or to recover compensation.'[74] As the design of the Act is to protect the continuing use of the

---

[70] See Shaw LJ in *Land Reclamation Co Ltd v Basildon DC*, n 67 above at 1007.

[71] *Part II of the Landlord and Tenant Act 1954*, (1988) Working Paper 111, paras 3.1.21- 3.1.22. The Law Reform Advisory Committee for Northern Ireland in its Discussion Paper No 3, n 1 above, made a similar recommendation.

[72] N 3 above, at para 3.2. Similarly, no recommendation for reform was advocated by the Law Reform Advisory Committee for Northern Ireland, *Business Tenancies* (1994) Report No 1.

[73] See *Teasdale v Walker* [1958] 3 All ER 307.

[74] N 55 above at 834.

premises for business purposes,[75] occupation must exist not only at the end of the contractual term, it must also persist throughout any proceedings for a new lease.[76] Accordingly, if the condition ceases to be fulfilled while proceedings are ongoing, the competent landlord can apply to have the tenant's application dismissed for a lack of *locus standi*.[77]

Occupation in Context

Although the notion of 'occupation' is crucial within the renewal process, it **3.17** remains undefined in the Act. It is, however, well established that occupation turns upon issues of fact, must be real and genuine[78] and is to be given an ordinary and commonsense meaning.[79] It was acknowledged by Lord Nicholls in *Graysim Holdings Ltd v P&O Property Holdings Ltd* that 'occupation' is not a term of art and is incapable of having a precise meaning applicable in all circumstances. As Lord Nicholls explained:

> The circumstances of two cases are never identical, and seldom close enough to make comparisons of much value. The types of property, and the possible uses of property, vary so widely that there can be no hard and fast rules. The degree of presence and exclusion required to constitute occupation, and the acts needed to evince presence and exclusion, must always depend on the nature of the premises, the use to which they are being put, and the rights enjoyed or exercised by the persons in question.[80]

Lord Nicholls recognised that there are various shades of possible interpretation according to the statutory context in which the term is employed.[81] Accordingly, in difficult cases the decision will be reached with close regard to the purpose for which the concept of 'occupation' is employed and the consequences flowing from the presence or absence of occupation. As the interpretation must be one which best suits the spirit and intent of the 1954 Act, it is unsafe to rely on decisions concerning, for example, the Rent Act 1977 or rating law. This is, however, no new wisdom.[82] Occupation turns essentially upon the degree of control and use exercised by, and the physical presence of, the tenant.[83] In *Wandsworth LBC v Singh*, for example, the local authority took a tenancy of some 500 square metres

---

[75] Rather than the actual business carried on by the tenant: *Narcissi v Wolfe* [1960] 1 Ch 10.

[76] *Domer v Gulf Oil (Great Britain) Ltd* (1975) 119 SJ 392.

[77] *Demetriou v Poolaction* (1991) 63 P & CR 536.

[78] *Pulleng v Curran* (1982) 44 P & CR 58, *Hancock & Willis v GMS Syndicate Ltd* [1983] 1 EGLR 70.

[79] *Lee-Verhulst Ltd v Harwood Trust*, n 29 above.

[80] N 46 above at 836. As Ralph Gibson LJ put it in *Wandsworth LBC v Singh*, n 63 above at 230, the issue is whether it was likely that, 'an observer knowing the facts and applying the ordinary and popular meaning of the phrase "occupation for the purposes of a business or activity", would hold that tenant to be in occupation'.

[81] ibid. See also *Bacchiocchi v Academic Agency Ltd* [1988] 2 All ER 241 where occupation was considered in relation to compensation for disturbance under section 37.

[82] See *Narcissi v Wolfe*, n 75 above; *Bagettes Ltd v GP Estates Ltd* [1956] I Ch 290.

[83] *Hancock & Willis v GMS Syndicate Ltd*, n 78 above.

of public open space which they and their sub-contractors visited periodically. As the authority's activity was more than mere passive management of the land, it was held sufficient to constitute occupation.

Effect of Sub-letting

3.18 Within the context of the 1954 Act, the term 'occupation' requires some business activity to be carried on by the tenant on the demised property. In circumstances where the tenant has not parted with possession of the premises, the position is straightforward. The court adopts a liberal approach and both 'business' and 'occupation' are readily discernible. This is because the attention of the court is focused upon the legal right to occupy and the control and use which is attendant upon that right.[84] A different approach is adopted where it is clear that the premises are occupied, but it is uncertain who the occupier is for the purposes of the Act. This situation arose in *Graysim Holdings Ltd v P&O Property Holdings Ltd* where, following the sub-letting of stalls in the tenant's market, more than one party claimed to exercise rights and control over the same premises and all had a potential claim to the status of occupier.[85] The issue is further complicated, as in the *Graysim* case, where it is the business of the tenant to permit others, in return for payment, to use the property for their own business purposes. Lord Nicholls did acknowledge that a tenant can remain in occupation of the premises even though others have been permitted to come on to the property and to use it temporarily for their business purposes. He provided the examples of a hotel company which provides rooms and facilities once a month for an antiques fair and a farmer who permits his field to be used periodically for a car-boot sale. Nevertheless, he realised that it is an entirely different matter when the tenant has allowed another to carry on a business on the premises in circumstances where the tenant is entirely excluded from the property. By way of illustration, Lord Nicholls considered the position of a tenant who carries on the business of letting office accommodation: 'He acquires a lease of the property, which he sub-lets. Under the sublease he has the usual right as landlord to enter the sublet property for various purposes, and he derives financial profit from the property in the form of rent, but plainly he would not occupy the property.'[86] In comparison the Northern Ireland (Business Tenancies) Order 1996 expressly states that a person who is the business of subletting, whether or not services are provided, is not in occupation of the sub-let premises.[87]

---

[84] *Wandsworth LBC v Singh*, n 63 above.
[85] N 46 above; see also *Groveside Properties Ltd v Westminster Medical School* (1983) 47 P & CR 507.
[86] N 46 above at 836. see *Latif v Hillside Estates (Swansea) Ltd* [1992] EGCS 75, where the tenant, following the sub-lease of a shop, was held not to be in occupation.
[87] Article 3(3).

It is to be accepted that there is no clear dividing line between the two extremes: **3.19**
the difference is one of degree, not of kind. As Bridge concludes: 'Although the
line is difficult to draw, and the area consequently grey, the policy of the Act is
being advanced. It is a statute for the protection of business tenants, who are trading from the property which they are occupying, not for commercial landlords,
intermediate or otherwise, whose principal objective is security of income rather
than tenure.'[88] Although the decision as to who occupies is a question of fact heavily dependant upon the circumstances of any given case, Lord Nicholls was able to
offer some general guidance. He felt that, if the premises are sub-let, there would
usually be little difficulty. The sub-tenant would have exclusive possession of the
premises; the tenant would cease to be in occupation of them and would, thereby,
lose all renewal rights. In the *Graysim* case, for example, the tenant retained occupation only of the common parts and service rooms in the market hall. Once the
head-lease ended the tenant could no longer be said to occupy those parts for business purposes.[89] It is the sub-tenant who will have a sufficient degree of sole use of
the property so as to enable the business to be carried on at the premises to the
exclusion of everyone else.[90]

Where, however, the permission takes the form of a licence, there is more scope **3.20**
for debate.[91] As the rights granted to a licensee are usually less extensive than those
granted to a tenant (in particular, licences rarely afford exclusive possession), the
licensor will clearly have a stronger claim to occupation. A sufficiency of control
could be evidenced by, for example, the provision of services, continued presence
through the medium of a manager, and the amount of time and resources allocated to management of the premises.[92] A clear example of this would usually
emerge when the premises are a boarding house or hotel.

Co-extensive Occupation?

A number of authorities lend support to the proposition that occupation under **3.21**
the 1954 Act can be shared.[93] The belief that occupation is not unitary and indi-
visible promotes the conclusion that the sub-tenant can occupy part of the building while, simultaneously, the tenant occupies the whole. In the *Graysim* case,

---

[88] S Bridge [1996] CLJ 197 at 198
[89] See also *Bagettes Ltd v GP Estates Ltd*, n 82 above.
[90] See *Bassari Ltd v London Borough of Camden* (1998) EGCS 27, where it was held that the letting of furnished apartments took the mesne landlord outside the protection of the 1954 Act.
[91] See *J Reid (D&K) Co Ltd v Burdell Engineering Co Ltd* (1958) 171 EG 281; *Hancock & Willis
v GMS Syndicate Ltd*, n 78 above. Obviously, if the premises are occupied by a trespasser this would
not necessarily stop the rightful occupier claiming a new lease.
[92] See *William Boyer & Sons Ltd v Adams* (1975) 32 P & CR 89.
[93] For example, *Lee-Verhulst Ltd v Harwood Trust*, n 29 above (co-existence within a single room
of the tenant's business occupation and the residential occupation of a licensee); *William Boyer &
Sons v Adams*, n 92 above (co-existence of both the tenant's and the sub-tenant's business occupan-
cies).

however, Lord Nicholls rejected this argument and felt that such an approach was untenable: 'I am unable to accept that a tenant of a business tenancy can sublet part of the property to a business subtenant on terms which would have the legal result that thereafter the sublet property would form the holding of the sub-tenant's business tenancy and yet, at the same time, remain part of the holding of the tenant's business tenancy'.[94] Lord Nicholls, therefore, concluded that the notion of dual occupation was inconsistent with the wording of section 23(3) which excludes from the tenant's holding those parts not occupied by the tenant. This provision necessarily entails that property occupied by some other party must be excluded: 'One would not expect to find that two persons, other than persons acting jointly, could each be in occupation of the same property for this purpose.'[95] If it were otherwise, somewhat curious results would ensue. First, if the sub-let part formed part of the holding of both the tenant and the sub-tenant, each would prima facie be entitled to the grant of a new lease from the same landlord in respect of the same property. Second, if the landlord successfully opposed the grant, both the tenant and the sub-tenant might be entitled to recover compensation for disturbance. Not surprisingly, Lord Nicholls adopted the view that such repercussions ran contrary to the scheme and policy of the Act: 'The Act looks through to the occupying tenants, here the traders, and affords them statutory protection, not their landlord. Intermediate landlords, not themselves in occupation, are not within the class of persons the Act was seeking to protect.'[96]

Vicarious Occupation?

3.22 Occupation through an agent, representative (including a company) or employee will suffice.[97] The occupier must, however, genuinely be acting on behalf of the tenant and this will be evidenced by the tenant's degree of control, financial interest in the business and the right to resort to the premises.[98] Where there is doubt, the agreement must be construed to determine whether the respective rights and obligations of the tenant and the *de facto* occupier show that the occupier is conducting the tenant's business or an entirely different business.[99] Since the *Graysim*

---

[94] N 46 above at 837. It should make no difference whether the sub-tenancy is commercial or residential: *Bassari Ltd v Camden LBC*, n 90 above.

[95] N 46 above. See further G Ferris [1996] JBL 592; S Higgins, *The Continuation Conundrum: Part II of the Landlord and Tenant Act* [1997] Conv 119.

[96] N 46 above at 842. Note, however, that if the tenant has sub-let only part of the premises, and seeks a renewal merely relating to the part retained, the landlord can insist that the new tenancy include all the original holding (including any parts sublet): section 32(2).

[97] *Cafeteria (Keighley) Ltd v Harrison* (1956) 168 EG 668; *Pegler v Craven* [1952] 2 QB 69; *Wandsworth LBC v Singh*, n 63 above.

[98] *Teasdale v Walker*, n 73 above, where the new occupier was allowed in, purportedly, under a management agreement, but the court held that there had, in reality, been the grant of a sub-tenancy.

[99] *Teeside Indoor Bowls Ltd v Stockton on Tees BC* [1990] 2 EGLR 87; *Parkes v Westminster Diocese Trustee* (1978) 36 P & CR 22; *Ross Auto Wash Ltd v Herbert* (1979) 250 EG 971.

case, it appears that an institutional landlord sub-letting rooms to its students will no longer be in occupation (actual or vicarious) of those premises.[100]

Companies

Problems may arise where the premises are occupied, and the business run, by a **3.23** separate legal entity from the tenant. As this clearly cannot be regarded as representative occupation, the rule is that, where the tenant runs a business through a company, it is the company that is the occupier and not the tenant who controls it.[101] Such was illustrated in *Christina v Seear* where the tenants ran a business through several companies, but were unable to claim a renewal.[102] As Wilmer LJ pointed out in *Tunstall v Steigmann*, 'There is no escape from the fact that a company is a legal entity separate from its corporators . . . This is no matter of form; it is a matter of substance and realty.'[103] There would, of course, have been no difficulty had the lease been assigned to the company because then the company would be both tenant and occupier. In order to overcome this potential trap for the tenant who decides to incorporate the business, the Law Commission Report recommended that the corporate veil be lifted and that, for these purposes, companies should be equated with those individuals (landlords and tenants alike) who control them.[104] This would entail that a tenant would still be able to claim renewal even though an *alter ego* is in occupation. It would not, however, extend protection beyond the existing tenant.[105] As the Law Reform Advisory Committee for Northern Ireland admitted in its Report, 'the rights and liabilities under the . . . Act should not be dependant upon how individuals choose to arrange their business affairs. Moreover, we feel that lifting the corporate veil . . . is doing no more than giving statutory recognition to commercial reality.'[106]

Groups of Companies

Where the tenant is a company, representative occupation through an employee, **3.24** manager or agent is clearly essential.[107] It is possible, moreover, that one company

---

[100] cf *Groveside Properties v Westminster Medical School*, n 85 above.

[101] *Nozari-Zadeh v Pearl Assurance Plc* [1987] 2 EGLR 81, where the running of a restaurant business by a series of companies was not the same as a business carried on by the tenant.

[102] (1985) 275 EG 595. The distinction between this and *Ross Auto Wash Ltd v Herbert*, n 99 above concerns the degree of control and management of the premises retained by the tenant.

[103] [1962] 2 QB 593 at 605.

[104] N 3 above at paras 2.7–2.10.

[105] ibid at para 2.10.

[106] N 72 above at para 3.2.14. This is now embodied within article 3(2) of the Business Tenancies (Northern Ireland) Order 1996. cf the lack of sympathy shown by Danckwerts LJ in *Tunstall v Steigmann*, n 103 above at 607, 'if persons choose to conduct their operations through the medium of a limited company with the advantages in respect of responsibility for debts thereby conferred, they cannot really complain if they have to face some disadvantages also'.

[107] *Lee-Verhulst (Investments) Ltd v Harwood Trust*, n 29 above; *Methodist Secondary Schools Trust Deed Trustees v O'Leary* [1993] 1 EGLR 105 (occupation through a school caretaker). Note that a lease to an unincorporated association is construed as a grant to those members who execute the

can manage another company's business.[108] The general rule is that the representative must occupy in the sense that it has control and user of the premises on behalf of the tenant.[109] By virtue of section 42(2), however, a special rule applies in relation to a group of companies. This provides that the occupation and carrying on business by one company within the group shall be treated as occupation and carrying on business by the tenant company. For these purposes section 42(1) provides that two bodies corporate are members of a group only when one is a subsidiary of the other or both are subsidiaries of a third company.[110] In its Report, the Law Commission advocated that this definition of a group of companies be extended to include pyramid companies controlled by the same individual notwithstanding that there may be lacking any connected share holding.[111] In addition, the Report recommended that the test of 'control' by an individual should be widened to equate with the test employed in relation to 'control' by a company.[112] The current test employed to determine whether a person has control of a company is to be found in section 30(2), but is limited to where that person either is a member of the company and can alone hire and fire the majority of directors; or holds beneficially more than half the share capital.[113] In contrast, the test of control of a subsidiary by its holding company is defined as either holding a majority of voting rights in the subsidiary; being a member of the subsidiary with the right to hire and fire a majority of its board; being a member of the subsidiary with the control of the majority of the voting rights in it; or controlling a company which itself controls the subsidiary.[114]

Trusts

3.25   Where a tenancy is held on an express or implied trust, section 41(1) provides that occupation by any or all of the beneficiaries is to be treated as being occupation by the tenant trustee(s).[115] This is of great practical importance because trustees are not usually given a power to trade. A change in the identity of the trustee, moreover, is not to be treated as a change in the person of the tenant.[116] The provisions

---

lease: *London Borough of Camden v Shortlife Community Housing Ltd,* n 26 above. The lease is then held on trust for the other members of the association: *Teba Fabrics v Conn* (1958) 121 EG 495.

[108] *Ross Auto Wash Ltd v Herbert,* n 99 above.

[109] *Trans-Britannia Properties Ltd v Darby Properties Ltd* [1986] 1 EGLR 151 where, following the sub-letting of lock-up garages, the tenant's representative only had nominal control over the premises. The very nature of the business amounted to parting with occupation and control.

[110] In Northern Ireland, the identical provision is contained in article 31.

[111] N 3 above at para 2.8.

[112] ibid at para 2.13.

[113] The test of control by an individual applicable in Northern Ireland is different and wider than that suggested for England and Wales: see article 2(3).

[114] See section 42(1) and Sch 18 of the Companies Act 1989.

[115] See *Secretary of State for Transport v Jenkins* (1997) October 30 CA. The equivalent provision for Northern Ireland is to be found in article 30(1).

[116] Section 41(1)(c).

as to trusts necessarily apply to property which is co-owned regardless of whether the co-owners are, in equity, joint tenants or tenants in common.[117] It is to be appreciated, however, that any statutory notices must still be served by and on the tenant and proceedings commenced by the tenant trustee.[118] The ambit of this provision was explained by Evershed MR in *Frish Ltd v Barclays Bank* as:

> [D]ealing only, with the case where, although the tenancy is vested in someone who is properly described as the tenant, nevertheless it is found that the tenant himself happens to be a trustee and the premises are actually occupied by, and the business is actually being carried on, not by the tenant trustee himself but by the beneficiary or beneficiaries, or one of them, for whom the tenant is a trustee.[119]

For the trustees to take advantage of this special provision, the occupier must be a beneficiary entitled to occupy by virtue of the equitable interest under the trust and must not be in occupation under some independent contractual relationship.[120] For example, in *Frish v Barclays Bank* the trustees could not take advantage of this provision where the beneficiary occupied *qua* sub-tenant and not under the terms of the trust. The terms of the trust , moreover, must either give the beneficiaries the right to occupy or be such that it is proper to allow the beneficiaries into occupation.[121] In the *Frish* case, the property was held under a trust for sale with the income to be held on discretionary trusts for the beneficiaries. It was held that none of the beneficiaries had a right to occupy under this discretionary trust.[122]

Similarly, the trustees cannot allow a non-beneficiary to occupy and still claim the **3.26** benefit of the statutory provision. This is illustrated by *Methodist Secondary Schools Trust Deed Trustees v O'Leary* where the management board of a school occupied the property, but were not entitled to any personal benefit under the trust.[123] The provision also does not cater for occupation under a charitable purpose trust. It does, however, remain possible for a tenant who carries on business through a distinct company to argue that a trust exists and that the occupation of the company should be caught by section 41(1).[124]

---

[117] See *Hodson v Cashmore* (1973) 226 EG 1203 (where the tenancy was a partnership asset).

[118] See *Sevenarts Ltd v Busvine* [1968] 1 WLR 1929.

[119] [1955] 2 QB 541 at 549–550. This does not include occupation by a remainderman of settled land.

[120] *Meyer v Riddick* [1990] 1 EGLR 107 (occupation was by virtue of a separate lease granted to two joint tenants by all the joint tenants and not by reason of being beneficiaries under a trust).

[121] It is to be noted that section 12 of the Trusts of Land and Appointment of Trustees Act 1996 gives beneficiaries the right to occupy where the purposes of the trust include occupation and the land is held by the trustee to be available for occupation. A more vague right to occupy had previously been available at common law: *Bull v Bull* [1955] 1 QB 234.

[122] See also *Carshalton Beeches Bowling Club Ltd v Cameron* (1979) 249 EG 1297.

[123] N 107 above; see also *Meyer v Riddick*, n 120 above.

[124] See Woodfall, *Landlord & Tenant*, Vol 2, Part 3 at 22.015; such was also tacitly accepted by the Court of Appeal in *Nozari-Zadeh v Pearl Assurance*, n 101 above.

Cessation of Occupation

3.27   If the tenant moves out of occupation or hands over control of the premises to another, prima facie section 23 is no longer satisfied and the right to a new lease is lost. There is, however, no obligation on the tenant physically to occupy throughout the contractual term and, in the situation where the tenant resumes occupation while the contractual lease is in existence, the renewal right will generally be rekindled. A lack of occupation may, however, prove crucial at two key stages: first, when the contractual term ends; and, second, when the application for a new lease is made and heard. Although an absence of *de facto* occupation at any of these times is potentially fatal to the tenant's statutory entitlement, it is not in itself decisive.[125] If the tenant has abandoned the premises, the protection of the Act will clearly cease. Temporary absence or intermittent use, however, will not usually produce such drastic consequences.[126] In *Pulleng v Curran*, for example, it was made clear that the tenancy will remain within the 1954 Act where the premises are temporarily unoccupied due to illness, bankruptcy or economic recession.[127] The distinction between occupation and non-occupation is, therefore, one of fact and degree.

3.28   A number of influential factors were, however, identified in *Bacchiocchi v Academic Agency Ltd*.[128] First, the extent of the tenant's physical presence on, use of, and control over the premises. In this context even a small amount of business use would suffice to show that the business has not ceased.[129] Second, whether the tenant vacated the premises voluntarily or involuntarily, that is, in the sense of leaving for reasons beyond the tenant's control. In the *Flairline Properties* case, for example, the fact that the tenant's restaurant had been damaged by fire was significant. Third, whether, having vacated, the tenant evinced an intention to return. This would embrace 'live' evidence of the tenant and others about the tenant's intention to return and any relevant correspondence. It does not necessitate that the landlord be informed of this intention. In the *Flairline Properties* case, it was held that the tenant is not required to establish a reasonable prospect of bringing about re-occupancy within the near or reasonable future. The court also made clear that there was no need even for the tenant to show a genuine, firm and set-

---

[125]   See *Aspinall Finance Ltd v Viscount Chelsea* (1989) 9 EG 77. Nevertheless, the High Court admitted that this absence of occupation was likely to be fatal when the tenant has moved out voluntarily.

[126]   *Hancock & Willis v GMS Syndicate Ltd*, n 78 above. Accordingly, in *Bell v Alfred Franks & Bartlett & Co Ltd* [1980] 1 All ER 356, the tenant occupied premises which were sometimes (but not always) used for storage purposes.

[127]   N 78 above; cf *Teasdale v Walker*, n 73 above where the tenant granted a sub-tenancy of seafront premises, yet intended to resume business the following season. The continuity of occupation was broken and the tenant was no longer entitled to a renewal.

[128]   N 81 above.

[129]   *Flairline Properties Ltd v Aziz Hassan* (1998) November 20 (HC).

tled intention to occupy. Fourth, whether the thread of continuity of occupation was broken.[130]

Case Law Examples

In *I&H Caplan Ltd v Caplan (No2)*, the tenant voluntarily moved out for seven **3.29** months while the renewal application was ongoing.[131] Cross J regarded this as a a borderline case, but held that the thread of continuity of occupation was not broken. He said:

> I think it is quite clear that a tenant does not lose the protection of this Act simply by ceasing physically to occupy the premises. They may well continue to be occupied for the purposes of a business although they are *de facto* empty for some period of time. One rather obvious example would be if there was a need for urgent structural repairs and the tenant had to go out of physical occupation in order to enable them to be effected . . . On the other hand . . . a mere intention to resume occupation if you get a new tenancy will not preserve the continuity of the business user if the thread has once been definitely broken.[132]

In *Morrison's Holdings Ltd v Manders Property (Wolverhampton) Ltd*, the tenants ceased trading as a result of a fire in an adjoining property, but required the landlords to reinstate so that they could continue trading as soon as possible.[133] It was held that, in order to obtain a renewal, the tenant must show that there is continuing occupation or, if events beyond the tenant's control have caused the tenant to vacate, that the tenant continues to exert and claim the right of occupancy. Although no longer in physical occupation, the tenants were, therefore, entitled to a new lease.

This is to be contrasted with the situation where the premises are rendered unin- **3.30** habitable by reason of disrepair, the landlord is under no obligation to repair, and the tenant cannot afford to effect the works. It would then be impracticable for the tenant to continue in business at those premises and, regardless of the professed intentions of the tenant, occupation will have ceased.[134] The concept of occupation was subject to further elaboration by Sir Gordon Wilmer:

> [I]n order to be in occupation one does not have to be physically present every second of every minute of every hour of every day. All of us remain in occupation, for instance, of our houses even while we are away doing our day's work. It follows, therefore, that occupation necessarily must include an element of intention as well as

---

[130] Other factors of relevance recognised in the *Flairline Properties* case included the tenant's retention of keys and continuing liability under the Occupiers Liability Act 1957.

[131] [1963] 1 WLR 1247.

[132] ibid at 1260. A similar justification would arise where the interruption of business user was due to seasonal closure (*Artemiou v Procopiou* [1966] 1 QB 878).

[133] [1976] 1 WLR 533.

[134] *Demetriou v Poolaction*, n 77 above. cf *Flairline Properties Ltd v Aziz Hassan*, n 129 above where the tenant intended to reoccupy following the landlord's reinstatement of fire-damaged premises.

a physical element . . . [I]f as a shopkeeper I close my shop for a fortnight in the summer to enable my staff to have a holiday, I apprehend that no one would contend that during that fortnight I ceased to be in occupation of my shop.[135]

3.31　Conversely, in *Hancock & Willis v GMS Syndicate Ltd*, the tenants moved to larger premises and for six months licensed their former premises to others, reserving a wine cellar and the right to use the dining room twice a month.[136] The tenants' furniture, carpets and files remained at the premises, but this could not constitute constructive occupation as the tenants reserved no right to enter and were not in the business of storage. The thread of continuity on these facts was, therefore, clearly broken. As Eveleigh LJ concluded:

> The words with which we are concerned import, in my judgment an element of control and user and they involve the notion of physical occupation. That does not mean physical occupation every minute of the day, provided the right to occupy continues. But it is necessary for the judge trying the case to assess the whole situation where the element of control and use may exist in variable degrees. At the end of the day it is a question of fact for the tribunal to decide, treating the words as ordinary words in the way in which I have referred to them.[137]

E. For the Purposes of a Business

3.32　The tenant must not merely occupy the premises; the occupation must be (in whole or part) for the purposes of a business carried on by the tenant. There is, however, no requirement that the tenant's business actually be conducted on the premises because ancillary use will suffice provided that it is in the furtherance of the tenant's business. Occupation preparatory to the operation of a business might, however, be insufficient.[138] As Megaw LJ commented in *Hillil Property & Investment Co v Naraine Pharmacy*: 'It is not a question of whether the building at which one is looking is the main seat of the business, but whether it is occupied for the purposes of the business.'[139] In *Bell v Alfred Franks & Bartlett & Co*, for example, the passive storage of cartons in a lock-up garage was held to constitute occupation for business purposes.[140] This is be contrasted with *Chapman v Freeman* where it was held an employer's tenancy of a nearby cottage, for the purpose of

---

[135] N 133 above at 542. cf *Aireps Ltd v Bradford Metropolitan Council* [1985] 2 EGLR 143 where, once the tenant had voluntarily relocated to temporary accommodation, the former premises were demolished. As the original premises no longer existed and could not be reinstated, the tenant could not be said to occupy the airline desk in dispute.

[136] N 78 above.

[137] ibid at 70.

[138] See *Latif v Hillside Estates (Swansea) Ltd*, n 86 above where the tenant carried out roof works to the premises before taking up occupation.

[139] (1979) 39 P& CR 67 at 73.

[140] N 126 above. See also *Bracey v Read*, n 64 above; *Groveside Properties Ltd v Westminster Medical School*, n 85 above.

housing hotel staff, fell outside the Act.[141] There the Court of Appeal held that the tenant was in (vicarious) occupation, but that the occupation was not for business purposes. As Denning MR explained, 'Speaking generally, the test is whether it is necessary for any of the staff to live in this cottage for the better performance of their duties. It is no doubt highly convenient that they should live there, but that is not enough.'[142] As made apparent in subsequent cases, this does not impose a 'necessity test'.[143] Instead, the requirement is that the occupation be for business reasons and not merely for the convenience of the person carrying on the business. Accordingly, a car park for customers and visitors would qualify as ancillary use.[144] A car park solely for staff away from the place of business would, however, not to be regarded as furthering the tenant's business.

Mixed User

For the purposes of section 23(1) there is no requirement that the property **3.33** demised be occupied solely for the purposes of a business. Wholly residential tenancies, however, automatically fall outside the scope of the business tenancy legislation. Nevertheless, it is permissible that the premises be used for a mixture of business and residential purposes.[145] As a rule of thumb, it might be argued that, when there is more than a nominal authorised business user, the prima-facie presumption is that the 1954 Act applies.[146] The threshold is, therefore, low in that the business user does not have to be the predominant, main or principal purposes.[147] All that is necessary is that the commercial use be of some significant degree. Hence, the tenancy will not fall within the 1954 Act if the business use is shown to be incidental.[148] The determination turns primarily upon issues of fact

---

[141] [1978] 3 All ER 878.

[142] ibid at 879. He added: 'it is a dwelling house simply for the convenience of the person carrying on the business. It is not a business tenancy.' He likened it to a barrister who rented a flat near chambers which would be used for residential rather than business purposes. As Geoffrey Lane LJ acknowledged, the conclusion would be different if the employee had been required to be on hand at all times to perform the duties (at 880).

[143] See *Methodist Secondary Schools Trust Deed Trustees v O'Leary*, n 107 above (occupation of a house by a school caretaker); *Groveside Properties Ltd v Westminster Medical School*, n 85 above (occupation of a flat by the College's students).

[144] *Hunt v Decca Navigator* [1972] EGD 331. The court made clear that a similar approach would be adopted in relation to a staff canteen and other facilities for staff.

[145] *Cheryl Investments v Saldanha, Royal Life Savings Society v Page* [1979] 1 All ER 5. In these conjoined appeals the premises concerned were used as residence and also for business purposes, that is, respectively an accountant's business and a doctor's surgery.

[146] *Kent Coast Properties v Ward* (1990) 45 EG 107; *Church Commissioners for England v Baines* (1998) 1 All ER 657. If the lease prohibits all business use, section 23(1) cannot apply to that tenancy: *Bell v Alfred Franks & Bartlett & Co Ltd*, n 126 above. If the tenant is engaged in a particular class of business which is prohibited under the lease, the protection of the Act is also denied: section 23(4).

[147] *Wright v Mortimer* [1996] 28 HLR 719.

[148] *Lewis v Weldcrest Ltd* [1978] 3 All ER 1226; *Wright v Mortimer*, ibid (a residential flat in which an art historian carried out a third of his work and used part of his sitting room as an office did not constitute business premises).

(including the nature of the business) and degree.[149] As Waite LJ admitted in *Wright v Mortimer*, 'issues involving a fine balance . . . may depend in the last analysis upon the general impression created in the mind of the judge by the evidence'.[150] Accordingly, in *Gurton v Parrot*, where the tenant resided and carried out a dog breeding and kennelling business at the premises, it was held that the commercial use (there akin to a hobby) was insufficiently substantial and that the tenancy fell outside the 1954 Act.[151] Similarly, in *Royal Life Saving Society v Page* the tenant (a doctor who had consulting rooms elsewhere) made professional use of his maisonette once or twice a year, but the tenancy was held to fall within the Rent Act 1977.

3.34   As regards residential sub-tenants, where the mesne landlord holds under a business lease, it was once thought that they could not be protected by the housing legislation.[152] It has now been established by the Court of Appeal in *Church Commissioners for England v Baines* that, at the end of the superior letting, the subtenants may be protected under the Rent Act 1977.[153] This development, as Cafferkey recognises, 'serves to remind us that statutory provisions affecting residential property should be construed in a paternalistic and pragmatic fashion'.[154]

3.35   It should be appreciated that protection under the 1954 Act ousts any protection that could otherwise be afforded to the tenant under the Rent Act 1977 or Housing Act 1988.[155] It is, however, possible that changes in use during the currency of the lease might take the tenancy from one statutory code to another.[156] Although a cessation of business will take the tenancy outside the 1954 Act, the persistence of some residential use will not automatically engage the provisions of, say, the Rent Act 1977.[157] A new tenancy agreement would, therefore, be necessary. A wholly residential tenancy, which later develops a substantial, authorised business user will, it seems, transfer more readily to the business code.[158] This is

---

[149]   *Simmonds v Egyed* [1985] CLY 1908; *Willis-Hills v Walskin Ltd* (1997) November 28 CA.

[150]   N 147 above at 725.

[151]   [1991] 1 EGLR 98.

[152]   *Pittalis v Grant* [1989] 2 EGLR 90; see C Rodgers, *Shopping Residential Sub-Tenants* [1990] Conv 204.

[153]   N 146 above, where *Pittalis v Grant* was declared *per incuriam*; see also *Wellcome Trust Ltd v Ebied* [1998] 1 All ER 657.

[154]   A Cafferkey, *Protecting the sub-tenant on termination of headlease* [1999] Conv 232.

[155]   Section 24(3) Rent Act 1977; Sch 1, para 4 Housing Act 1988; see *Webb v London Borough of Barnett* (1989) 11 EG 80. A similar approach is adopted in Northern Ireland: article 4(1)(a).

[156]   *Pulleng v Curran* n 78 above; *Wetherall v Smith* [1980] 1 WLR 1290. This is so even if the landlord is not aware of the change of use: *Cheryl Investments v Saldanha*, n 145 above.

[157]   *Webb v London Borough of Barnet*, n 155 above. This is because the premises were not originally let as a separate dwelling: *Christina v Seear*, n 102 above; cf the position with residential subtenants above.

[158]   *Cheryl Investments v Saldanha*, n 145 above. If it is a statutory tenancy, however, the 1954 Act cannot apply because the tenancy has ceased to be an estate in land and has become instead a mere personal right: see *Durman v Bell* [1988] 2 EGLR 117.

particularly so when the change of user is expressly permitted by the landlord.[159] Such possibility entails, as Tromans advises, 'that the practitioner should be alert to detect such problems, that borderline cases will require very detailed scrutiny of the background and present use of the premises, and that to avoid disputes it is important that accurate records of changes of use be kept . . .'.[160]

Business

Within section 23(2) the term 'business' is defined as including 'a trade, profes- **3.36** sion or employment and includes any activity carried on by a body of persons whether corporate or unincorporate'. This definition applies throughout the Part II provisions. Accordingly, the Act draws a distinction between those tenants who are individuals and those that are bodies (for example, trade unions and friendly societies) or corporations (for example, local authorities, statutory undertakers and private companies). It is only for bodies and corporations that the extension to 'any activity' is made.[161] Accordingly, for other tenants the business must constitute a trade, profession or employment.[162] As the 1954 Act was designed to regulate a wide range of tenancies and to embrace a wide range of commercial activity, the understanding of the term 'business' is, not surprisingly, broad-based. Lindley LJ in *Rolls v Miller* described it as including, 'almost anything which is an occupation, as distinguished from a pleasure—anything which is an occupation or a duty which requires attention is a business'.[163] The term, therefore, connotes some commercial activity with the ambition of making a gain or a profit.[164]

The actual making of a profit is not, however, essential, nor does payment itself **3.37** necessarily indicate a business.[165] In *Abernethie v AM & J Kleiman*, for example, the running of a Sunday school without reward was not a business for, as Widgery LJ admitted:

> [I]t certainly does not follow . . . that Parliament intended to push the tentacles of the Act . . . into domestic lettings and the activities which a man carries out in his private rooms as part of his hobby or recreation . . . what a man does with his spare time in his home is most unlikely to qualify for the description 'business' unless it has some

---

[159] *Henry Smith's Charity Trustees v Wagle & Tippet* (1990) 1 QB 42; *Wolfe v Hogan* [1949] 2 KB 194.

[160] S Tromans, *Commercial Leases* (2nd edn, 1996) 239.

[161] *Abernethie v AM&J Kleiman* [1970] 1 QB 10. The activities of a government department are expressly included within this provision: section 56(3). As will be shown, the reference to 'activity' embraces use which would not normally be thought to be commercial.

[162] *Lewis v Weldcrest Ltd*, n 148 above.

[163] (1884) 27 Ch D 71 at 88.

[164] *Re Incorporated Council of Law Reporting for England & Wales* [1888] 22 QBD 279; *Smith v Anderson* [1880] 15 ChD 247.

[165] *Rolls v Miller*, n 163 above; *Portman v Home Hospitals Association* (1879) 27 Ch D 81. See article 2(2) of the Business Tenancies (Northern Ireland) Order 1996 which expressly states that a business need not be carried on for gain or reward.

direct commercial involvement in it, whether it be a hobby or a recreation or the performance of a social duty . . .'[166]

Similarly, in *Secretary for State for Transport v Jenkins* the tenants ran a community farm as a non-commercial enterprise and this prompted Millett LJ to conclude: 'Not only is the enterprise not carried on with a view to profit, it is not carried on as a trading activity, but rather in the spirit of public benevolence. As such it is not a trade, profession or employment, nor is it any kind of business.'[167]

Trade, Profession and Employment

3.38　The term 'trade' is viewed as being of narrower meaning than the general expression 'business'.[168] It connotes the activity of buying and selling and will normally involve a profit-making aspect.[169] A guest house run on a non-profit basis was, however, held to be a trade in *Ireland v Taylor*[170] and, in *Brighton College v Marriott*, a college was carrying on a trade even though it was a charitable institution.[171] The concept of a 'profession' enjoys a scope less certain than a 'business' or a 'trade'. In *IRC v Maxse*, Scrutton LJ provided the working definition of a profession as being, 'an occupation requiring either purely intellectual skill or manual skill controlled, as in painting, sculpture or surgery, by the intellectual skill of the operator, as distinguished from an occupation which is substantially the production or sale or arrangement for production and sale of commodities'.[172] Accordingly, the category of professionals is wide and includes clergy, lawyers, doctors, accountants, surveyors, architects and the like. If in doubt, the court will adopt a common-sense interpretation. This is illustrated in *Abernethie v AJ&M Kleiman* where Harman LJ said of a voluntary Sunday school: 'It is not carried on professionally: it is carried on amateurishly, just the opposite to "professionally".'[173]

3.39　In the context of the 1954 Act, the term 'employment' is used as meaning a calling and is broad enough to cover most business occupations. This is in recognition that profits may be earned in many ways.[174] The term 'employment' has, therefore, included the occupation of a lecturer[175] and the carrying on of a teaching hospital.[176] In *Abernethie v AM & J Kleiman Ltd*, the tenant gratuitously ran a

---

[166] N 161 above at 20; see also *Lewis v Weldcrest Ltd*, n 148 above.
[167] N 115 above. Millett LJ felt able, however, to assume that it was an 'activity'.
[168] *Harris v Amery* (1865) LRI CP 148.
[169] *Wetherall v Bird* (1834) 2 AD & EL 161.
[170] [1949] 1 KB 300.
[171] [1926] AC 192. This case also made clear that a given activity might be classified both as a trade and as a business.
[172] [1919] 1 KB 647 at 657. See also *Stucbery & Son v General Accident Fire & Life Assurance Corporation* [1949] 2 KB 256.
[173] N 161 above at 17.
[174] See *Partridge v Mallandine* (1886) 18 LCD 276.
[175] *Lecture League Ltd v LCC* (1913) 108 LT 924.
[176] *Hills (Patents) Ltd v University College Hospital Board of Governors* [1956] 1 QB 90.

weekly Sunday school from his premises (previously a shop). This was clearly neither a trade nor a profession and, in considering whether it was an employment, Harman LJ added: 'In my view, it clearly is not. "Employment" in that sense must mean something much more regular than that. It means, I should have thought, either employing somebody else or being employed by someone else.'[177]

Activity by a Body of Persons

This expression has been given a liberal interpretation by the courts. In **3.40** *Addiscombe Garden Estates Ltd v Crabbe*, the meaning embraced the 'activity' of a member's tennis club[178] and, in *Wandsworth LBC v Singh*, the activity of the local authority was in providing a public park.[179] Other cases have extended the meaning to include the running of an NHS hospital;[180] the provision of a community centre;[181] use of a garage for storage;[182] the running of a restaurant and the use of storage areas for restaurant purposes;[183] and the supply of residential accommodation for staff.[184] One limitation, however, was imposed by the Court of Appeal in *Hillil Property & Investment Co v Naraine Pharmacy* where Megaw LJ concluded that, although different from a trade, profession or employment, 'an activity for this purpose . . . must be something which is correlative to the conceptions involved in those words'.[185] There the casual dumping of waste building materials on empty shop premises was held not to be an activity on those premises. A similar approach was adopted in *Abernethie v AM&J Kleiman* where the appellate court was sceptical as to whether the running of a Sunday school for one hour per week could amount to an activity for these purposes.[186] Hence, there has to be a business element to the activity for it to qualify for protection under the Act.

As regards 'a body of persons' a generous meaning is to be given. In *Secretary of* **3.41** *State for Transport v Jenkins*, for example, Millett LJ recognised that a very loose and informal farming collective might suffice for these purposes. This was so even though there was no evidence of any membership list, constitution or rules, or of any membership fee being charged. Nevertheless, he acknowledged that joint tenants are not *ipso facto* a body of persons: 'The expression must connote some involvement or participation in a common activity other than the mere joint ownership of the property.' Although there need not be a precise identity between the

---

[177] N 166 above at 17.
[178] [1958] 1 QB 513. Similarly, in *Bowering v Tanner* (1993) October 13 (CA) the activity of running a caving club (even though the actual caving occurred elsewhere) sufficed because various club activities were carried on at the demised premises.
[179] N 64 above.
[180] *Hills (Patents) Ltd v University College Hospital Board of Governors*, n 176 above.
[181] *Parkes v Westminster Roman Catholic Diocese Trustee*, n 99 above.
[182] *Bell v Alfred Franks & Bartlett & Co*, n 126 above.
[183] *Ye Olde Cheshire Cheese Ltd v The Daily Telegraph* [1988] 3 All ER 217.
[184] *Lee-Verhulst Investments Ltd v Harwood Trust*, n 29 above.
[185] N 139 above at 74.
[186] N 161 above.

persons who are in occupation as tenants and those who carry on the activity, it remains necessary that the activity carried on there is the tenants' business activity. This condition is overcome, however, when the tenant holds the lease on trust for the association or acts as the association's agent.

Unauthorised Business User

3.42 There is no straightforward rule which entails that a tenant who carries on a business which constitutes a breach of a user covenant is outside the protection of the 1954 Act.[187] Instead, there is a somewhat elaborate provision within section 23(4) which deals with use unauthorised by the current tenancy.[188] This provides that a business carried on in breach of certain types of covenant does not qualify for protection.[189] This rule of non-protection applies where there is a blanket prohibition against business use (for example, 'not to use the premises for business purposes' or 'to use the premises for the purposes of a dwelling only') or a covenant prohibiting the general carrying on of a trade, profession and/or employment (for example, 'not to use the premises for the purposes of any trade'). The deprivation of protection does not, therefore, arise in the following situations: first where the prohibition relates only to part of the premises (for example, a covenant which requires that only the upper floor of the demised premises be used only for residential purposes). Second, where the covenant is directed against use for the purposes of a specified business (for example, 'not to use the premises as a solicitors' office'). Third, where it restricts use to a particular business (for example, 'to use the premises only as a solicitors' office').[190] As Tromans appreciated: 'Thus the sub-section protects the landlord where the tenant is flouting a blanket ban on all business use, but not where the tenant changes from one business use which is authorised to another which is not.'[191]

Consent and Acquiescence

3.43 This limited rule of non-protection, moreover, gives way either where the tenant's immediate landlord (or the landlord's predecessor in title) consented to the breach

---

[187] A breach which does not take the tenancy outside the 1954 Act might, however, still be the basis for forfeiture and/or opposition to a new lease under section 30(1)(c). Unlike in Northern Ireland, an unauthorised sub-letting does not deprive the sub-tenant of protection because the sub-tenant was not a party to the covenant: *D'Silva v Lister House Developments Ltd* [1971] Ch 17. In Northern Ireland any tenancy granted in breach of an alienation covenant is excluded from protection: article 4(1)(I).

[188] Note that by virtue of section 3(5) of the Landlord and Tenant (Covenants) Act 1995 restrictive user covenants, in relation to tenancies created after 1 January 1996, can be enforced directly by the head landlord against the sub-tenant.

[189] In Northern Ireland, there is no provision equivalent to section 23(4). The rule there is that the tenancy is always protected, subject to forfeiture proceedings.

[190] See K Reynolds and W Clark, *Renewal of Business Tenancies* (2nd edn, 1997), 41–42.

[191] N 160 above at 239. cf Northern Ireland where the conviction of the tenant for using demised premises, or permitting them to be used, for an illegal purpose deprives the tenancy of protection under the 1996 Order: article 4(1)(h).

or where the immediate landlord (but not a predecessor in title) acquiesced in it. The difference in approach concerning the predecessor in title reflects the fact that the current landlord could not be aware of a predecessor's state of mind. For these purposes 'consent' connotes a positive act of acceptance and requires more than a mere absence of objection.[192] 'Acquiescence', however, is the passive failure to take steps concerning a known breach.[193] Hence, an acceptance of rent by a landlord who has a full knowledge of the facts could amount to an acquiescence in the breach. Conversely, the absence of actual knowledge that a business is been carried on at the premises necessitates that there can be no acquiescence.[194] In its 1988 Working Paper, the Law Commission expressed the view that: 'The way in which the position is at present expressed provides the opportunity for evading the Act.'[195] This could occur where a landlord has acquiesced in the establishment of an unauthorised business, but now wishes to escape the security of tenure provisions. The landlord can potentially achieve this by assigning the freehold to an associate who, having neither consented or acquiesced in the user, can terminate the tenancy without going through the statutory machinery.[196] To avoid this happening, the Working Paper concluded provisionally that the same test for both the current and former landlords be used, 'so that ownership of the reversion is not critical to whether the tenant enjoys renewal rights'.[197]

F. Excluded Tenancies

There are a variety of exclusions from the scope of Part II of the 1954 Act and invariably this withholding of protection is based upon sound reasoning, for example, where the tenancy is protected by another statutory code or as an encouragement to grant temporary lettings. Most are expressly listed in section 43, some arise under other statutory provisions and one is derived from the common law. These exceptions to the general availability of security of tenure now fall to be considered. **3.44**

---

[192] *Bell v Alfred Franks & Bartlett & Co*, n 126 above. In *Daimar Investments v Jones* (1962) 112 LJ 424, it was held that the landlord could not consent to a change of use at a stage when planning permission had not been obtained.

[193] *Methodist Secondary Schools Trust Deed Trustees v O'Leary*, n 107 above

[194] *Brown v Myerson* (1998) July 21 CA where the tenant conducted the business of a licensed conveyancer from home. Although the business was advertised at the front of the house, the landlord had no actual knowledge that the user covenant was breached.

[195] N 71 above at para 3.1.26.

[196] ibid at para 3.1.30.

[197] ibid at para 3.1.31–32. In the 1992 Report, however, no reform was recommended by the Law Commission (n 3 above at para 3.6.).

Agricultural Holdings and Farm Business Tenancies

3.45 Leases governed by the Agricultural Holdings Act 1986 or the Agricultural Tenancies Act 1995 are excluded from the protection of the 1954 Act.[198] This exemption extends also to lettings which, if they had not been excluded by section 2(3) of the Agricultural Holdings Act, would have been within the agricultural code, and to tenancies of agricultural land which have been taken outside that code with the approval of the relevant minister. Where the letting is for a business with an agricultural aspect, however, a potential difficulty arises concerning which statutory code is applicable. The resolution turns upon which is the substantial or dominant user.[199] If, however, the tenancy prima facie satisfies both codes, then it will be excluded from the 1954 Act.[200] On any subsequent change of user, the test of dominant purpose may again be invoked and could result in a former agricultural holding/farm business tenancy becoming a business lease governed by the 1954 Act. This possibility was considered in *Russell v Booker* where the Court of Appeal laid down helpful guidance.[201] First, it was acknowledged that the purpose as expressed in, or contemplated by, the agreement is the essential factor. Second, where the original agreement has been superseded by a new contract, the purpose may be considered in the light of that new contract. Third, a new contract may be inferred by the court from user known to the landlord. Fourth, a mere unilateral change cannot of itself bring the tenancy within the protection of a different statutory regime. Finally, where no particular user has been provided for in, or contemplated by, the agreement, actual and subsequent user will determine which code is to apply.

Mining Leases

3.46 By virtue of section 43(1)(b), tenancies created by mining leases do not attract renewal rights under the 1954 Act. As the Law Reform Advisory Committee for Northern Ireland accepted in its Discussion Paper: 'Mining leases are necessarily excluded since the tenant's business involves the depletion of the land's mineral resources, and accordingly, it is of the utmost importance for the landlord to have power to regain possession at the end of the contractual tenancy'.[202] A mining lease is one granted for a mining or related purpose and is defined in section 25 of the Landlord and Tenant Act 1927 as extending to mines and minerals and, thereby, includes all solid substances that can be obtained from beneath the surface of the

---

[198] Section 43(1)(a), (aa); see *EWP v Moore* [1992] QB 460. The Agricultural Tenancies Act 1995 replaces the 1986 Act as regards tenancies created after 1 September 1995. Instead of an agricultural holding, new lettings will give rise to a farm business tenancy. In Northern Ireland, article 4(1)(d) excludes 'a tenancy of agricultural land, including farm houses and farm buildings'.

[199] *Lord Monson v Bound* [1954] 3 All ER 228.

[200] *Short v Greeves* (1988) 8 EG 109.

[201] (1982) 5 HLR 10.

[202] N 1 above at para 3.3.1. In Northern Ireland, the exclusion is contained in article 4(1)(e).

earth for the purpose of profit.[203] The definition does not, therefore, exclude a tenancy for the drilling of oil and gas and there is no right to renew a tenancy for sand and gravel working.[204]

Service Tenancies

Part II does not apply to a tenancy granted to the tenant as the holder of an office, **3.47** appointment or employment when the tenancy will end (or becomes liable to end) on the termination of that service or employment. If, as is likely, the tenancy was granted after 1 October 1954, the additional requirement imposed by section 43(2) is that the tenancy must be in writing and must express the purpose of the grant. The court is left to ascertain whether the alleged service agreement is genuine or a sham.[205]

Short Tenancies

By virtue of section 43(3), the Act does not apply to a lease for a term of years certain not exceeding six months, unless there is provision for renewal or extension **3.48** beyond six months or the tenant (and/or a predecessor in business) has been in occupation for more than twelve months.[206] This provision allows for consecutive tenancies to be granted for a period totalling twelve months provided that there is no provision in the tenancy relating to the grant of a further term.[207] This facility is useful as it encourages such transactions as, for example, the letting of shop premises to charities and retail outlets over the seasonal periods. The 'occupation' limitation is designed to restrict the use of short leases to new tenants and to new businesses. It should be appreciated that the exemption appears to extend only to fixed term tenancies.

Although an argument can be put forward to support a periodic tenancy **3.49** being a term of years certain,[208] it is unsafe to rely on such a proposition. This

---

[203] Section 25(1) defines 'mining purposes' as including: 'the sinking and searching for, winning, working, getting, making merchantable, smelting or otherwise converting or working for the purpose of any manufacture, carrying away, and disposing of mines and minerals, in or under land, and the erection of buildings, and the execution of engineering and other works suitable for those purposes'. For the meaning of 'mines and minerals' see the lengthy and technical judgment of Slade J in *Earl of Lonsdale v AG* [1982] 1 WLR 887. cf Northern Ireland where the definition is much simpler and limited to the opening or working of a mine or quarry or dealing with the produce or refuse of a mine or quarry. article 4(2)

[204] *O'Callaghan v Elliott* [1966] 1 QB 601.

[205] *Teasdale v Walker*, n 73 above. For Northern Ireland, a similar provision (but without the need for writing) is to be found in article 4(1)(f).

[206] Note that the British Property Federation has produced a standard-form lease for short-term business tenancies.

[207] In Northern Ireland, the equivalent provision introduced by article 4(c) allows a landlord to grant a short-term tenancy for up to nine months, followed by another tenancy of up to nine months, without attracting security of tenure.

[208] *Leek & Moorlands Building Society v Clark* [1952] 2 QB 788.

exception was considered by Neuberger J in *Cricket Ltd v Shaftesbury Plc* where the tenant held over after two successive tenancies (of five months' duration each).[209] The holding over was as a tenant at will and this final period of occupation took the total period beyond the twelve-month ceiling. The court held that the period of occupation as a tenant at will (or licensee or trespasser) could not enter into the calculation. The basic notion being that such relationships fall entirely outside the definition of 'tenancy' for the purposes of the 1954 Act. Neuberger J, however, added by way of *obiter* that such periods of occupation could count if the occupier at the time was a predecessor in business of the tenant. It is, moreover, arguable that a tenant can be granted up to three consecutive terms of under six months. The restriction appears to bite when the tenancy is granted. Accordingly, as the tenant has not been in occupation for twelve months when the third term is granted, the final lease may also fall within the section 43 exception.

Tenancies at Will

3.50 Unlike in the residential sector, it has been determined that a business tenancy at will falls outside the ambit of statutory protection.[210] It would be, as Lord Morton admitted in *Wheeler v Mercer*, 'surprising if the legislation had intended to bring within the scope of the Act a relationship so personal and so fleeting as a tenancy at will'.[211] This is so regardless of whether the tenancy arises expressly or by implication of law.[212] The rationale underlying this exclusion is that the Act applies only to tenancies that can be brought to an end by notice to quit or by effluxion of time. For a tenancy at will to arise the arrangement must be expressly or impliedly made terminable at the will of either party and must not contain any terms that are inconsistent with a tenancy at will (for example, relating to re-entry and forfeiture). There should, therefore, be no mention of a minimum period of occupation or an advance payment of rent. Accordingly, a tenancy at will neither offers a secure period of occupation for the tenant nor a reliable income stream for the landlord. The safest use of such a tenancy occurs where the tenant is holding over at the end of the lease[213] or has moved into possession pending negotiation of the

---

[209] [1998] 28 EG 127.

[210] See *Cricket Ltd v Shaftesbury Plc*, ibid. Also excluded are a mortgage term and 'any interest arising in favour of a mortgagor by his attorning tenant to his mortgagee': section 69(1). Under the Business Tenancies (Northern Ireland) Order 1996 both tenancies at will and tenancies at sufferance are expressly excluded from protection: article 2(2).

[211] [1957] AC 416 at 428. Baron Parke described the tenancy at will as being, 'the lowest estate known to the law' (*Gray v Stanion* (1836) 1 M&W 695 at 700).

[212] *Manfield & Sons Ltd v Botchin* [1970] 2 QB 612. A landlord might prefer to create a tenancy at will instead of a licence agreement because the remedy of distress for rent cannot be used in relation to arrears under a licence: *Interoven Stove Co Ltd v Hibbard & Painter & Shepherd* [1936] 1 All ER 263. It should be noted that the levy of distress is not available in Northern Ireland.

[213] *Cardiothoracic Institute Ltd v Shrewdcrest Ltd* [1986] 3 All ER 633.

terms of the lease.[214] In other situations, a tenant might be reluctant to accept such an uncertain letting. Of course, the primary difficulty experienced by the court is distinguishing a genuine tenancy at will from a periodic tenancy or a licence agreement.[215] As Nicholls LJ advised in *Javad v Aqil*:

> Of course, when one party permits another to enter or remain on his land on payment of a sum of money, and that other has no statutory entitlement to be there, almost inevitably there will be some consensual relationship between them. It may be no more than a licence determinable at any time, or a tenancy at will. But when and so long as the parties are in the throes of negotiating larger terms, caution must be exercised before inferring or imputing to the parties an intention to give to the occupant more than a very limited interest, be it licence or tenancy. Otherwise the court would be in danger of inferring or imputing from conduct, such as the payment of rent and the carrying out of repairs, whose explanation lies in the parties' expectation that they will be able to reach agreement on the larger terms, an intention to grant a lesser interest, such as a periodic tenancy, which the parties never had in contemplation at all.[216]

Tenancies by Estoppel

In contrast to a tenancy at will, a tenancy by estoppel does fall within the 1954 **3.51** Act.[217] This was established recently by the Court of Appeal in *Bell v General Accident Fire & Life Assurance Corporation Ltd*.[218] There the lessor who did not have title to the premises at the time of the demise was regarded as the competent landlord and the lease was held to satisfy the definition of a tenancy set out in section 69. Hence, the law proceeds on the hypothesis that the landlord has a title which it does not in fact have and, moreover, that the precariousness of that title, as against a third party, is of no relevance. It follows that the consequences of treating an imaginary state of affairs as real must also be imagined as real. Furthermore, as Mummery LJ concluded:

> There is nothing in the language of the definitions or other provisions of the 1954 Act excluding a tenancy by estoppel from statutory protection. There is nothing in the evident policy of the Act excluding from its protection those tenants who occupy

---

[214] *Javad v Aqil*, n 59 above; *Banks v Clarke* (1996) March 4 CA. Once in occupation and trading, the tenant may, however, delay signing the lease.

[215] See *Hagee (London) Ltd v AB Erikson & Larson* [1976] 1 QB 209; *Mayor & Burgesses of Brent LBC v O'Bryan* (1993) 2 EG 113.

[216] N 59 above at 248. For the determination of an unagreed rent under a tenancy at will see *Dean & Chapter of the Cathedral & Metropolitan Church of Christ Canterbury v Whitbread Plc* [1995] I EGLR 82.

[217] Lord Hoffmann explained the concept of a tenancy by estoppel in *Bruton v London & Quadrant Housing*, n 6 above. He said (at 488): 'The estoppel arises when one or other of the parties wants to deny one of the ordinary incidents or obligations of the tenancy on the ground that the landlord has no legal estate. The basis of the estoppel is that having entered into the agreement which constitutes a lease or tenancy, he cannot repudiate that incident or obligation.'

[218] N 2 above; see J Morgan [1999] JBL 274.

business premises under a lease in circumstances in which they are prevented from disputing their landlords' title to grant the tenancy.[219]

G. The Crown and Government Departments: Special Provisions

3.52 Subject to certain qualifications, section 56(1) ensures that the Crown falls within the classification of a competent landlord for the purposes of the Part II provisions. Without this express inclusion, the Crown would not be bound by the security of tenure provisions.[220] The Act provides that where the landlord's interest is held by Her Majesty in right of the Crown or the Duchy of Lancaster, or is held by the Duchy of Cornwall, the tenant (who otherwise qualifies for protection under the statutory scheme) is entitled to the full benefit of the Act. Subject to some exceptions, section 56(1) (albeit unnecessarily) applies the same general rule when the landlord's interest is held by a government department.[221] For the purposes of the Act, when an interest belongs to Her Majesty in right of the Duchy of Lancaster, the Chancellor of the Duchy represents Her Majesty and is deemed to own the interest.[222] As regards the Duchy of Cornwall, such person as the Duke appoints shall be deemed to own the interest.[223]

Crown as Tenant

3.53 As a result of section 56(1), the Crown may also, in certain circumstances, take advantage of the protection of Part II in the capacity of a tenant. For such protection to exist, the premises must be occupied for the purposes of a business (not necessarily the business of the Crown) and fall within the general catchment of section 23. One modification of this rule exists in section 56(3) and exclusively relates to tenancies held by, or on behalf of, a government department. This departure is that premises occupied for the purposes of a government department are, whether or not it is in reality the case, deemed to be occupied for the purposes of a business. As Scott J explained in *Linden v DHSS*: 'In my judgment section

---

[219] N 2 above at 147. Hutchison LJ added: 'There is, I consider, no good reason why Parliament would have wished to afford to a landlord whose title happens to be deficient the advantage of being able to deprive his tenant of the protection of the Act . . .' (at 146).

[220] *Wirral Estates Ltd v Shaw* [1932] 2 KB 247. In Northern Ireland, the Crown is bound by virtue of article 43(1).

[221] Since the House of Lords decision in *Town Investments Ltd v Department of the Environment* [1978] AC 359, it is established that tenancies granted to government departments are, in reality, grants to the Crown. These provisions were, therefore, drafted on a mistaken assumption. As Scott J acknowledged, however, 'The legal misdescription established in 1978, 22 years after the 1954 Act was enacted, cannot change the true construction of the sub-sections' (*Linden v DHSS* [1986] 1 All ER 691 at 697).

[222] Sch 8, para1.

[223] Sch 8, para 2.

56(3) brings within Part II of the 1954 Act any tenancy held by a government department if the premises are being occupied for any purpose of any government department.'[224] Even if the premises are not occupied for the purposes of a government department, the department is protected by Part II provided that no rent is payable by any other occupier.[225] The government department is, thereby, deemed to still occupy for its own purposes. In addition, any provisions that require the premises to have been occupied for the purposes of a tenant's business for a period of time or that, on a change of tenant, the new occupier should have succeeded to the business of the predecessor are subject to a further deeming provision. The occupation condition is automatically deemed to be satisfied where the government department has occupied during that period; as regards a succession condition, one government department is deemed to be in the same business as another.[226]

Public Interest

Although the fact that the landlord's interest is held by a government department **3.54**
does not in itself prevent a tenant from claiming security of tenure, there are a series of provisions which, on the basis of public interest or national security, can modify the tenant's right to a new tenancy.[227] These special rights are in addition to the landlord's ordinary rights enjoyed under Part II. By way of some safeguard, section 59 ensures that the tenant will normally be entitled to compensation for disturbance. The public interest ground applies when the interest of the competent landlord (or any superior landlord) belongs to, or is held for the purposes of, either a government department or any local authority, health authority or special health authority, development corporation, statutory undertaker or the National Trust.[228] For these purposes, however, the Commissioners of Crown Lands do not constitute a government department.[229]

Certification

The Minister (or Board) in charge of the appropriate government department or **3.55**
other body may issue a certificate to the effect that the use or occupation of the

---

[224] N 221 above at 697. In Northern Ireland, article 43(2) expressly makes this point clear.
[225] Section 56(4); see *Linden v DHSS*, ibid, where Scott J considered this rental condition as envisaging occupation by another government department. It was stressed, however, that someone has to be in occupation in order for it to be said to be for the purposes of a government department. There is no comparative provision applicable in Northern Ireland.
[226] Section 56(3)(a),(b). As regards Northern Ireland, the equivalent provision is to be found in article 43(2)(a),(b).
[227] In Northern Ireland, the position is much more straightforward. There the fact that possession is sought by a public authority landlord is itself a ground of opposition, which will defeat the tenant's claim for a new lease, provided that possession is 'reasonably necessary for the public authority to carry out its functions': article 12(1)(I) of the 1996 Order.
[228] Section 57(1); sections 28, 38(2) of the Leasehold Reform Act 1967.
[229] Section 57(8).

demised property (or any part of it) will be changed from a specified date and that the property is required for the purposes of the relevant public body.[230] Certification excludes the tenant's right to renew. There is, moreover, no obligation that the proposed change be essential and it suffices that it is required in the circumstances.[231] A further alternative which is open to the landlord allows a different type of certificate to be issued (a certificate for break clause) where the tenant's renewal application is already under way and no order has yet been made. This certificate is to the effect that it is necessary, in the public interest, that the court must include in the new lease a break clause, determinable on six months' notice by the landlord.[232]

Preliminary Notice

3.56 It is provided by section 57(2) that none of these certificates may be issued unless the tenant has been given preliminary notice (no form is prescribed) that the Minister (or Board) is contemplating the issue of the document. The tenant then has twenty-one days in which to make written representations to the Minister (or Board) concerning the matter. Account must be taken of the representations of the tenant before any decision to issue the certificate is made. There is no appeal from the giving of a certificate, but it is subject to judicial review. Such scrutiny is essential for, as Dunn LJ explained in *R v Secretary of State for the Environment, ex parte Powis*:

> The result of these provisions is that business tenants of local authorities and other public bodies may be deprived . . . of the rights which they would otherwise have had of applying to the county court for a new tenancy. They are deprived of the opportunity of testing in court any objection by the landlord under section 30 of the Act to a grant of a new tenancy, with the advantages of a public hearing, discovery of documents and cross examination of witnesses.[233]

Legal Consequences

3.57 The consequences of certification hinge primarily upon whether the landlord has served a section 25 notice or the tenant has served a section 26 request. If the landlord has served a termination notice, the specified date of termination becomes significant. Section 57(3) provides that, if the date specified is not earlier than the date set out in the certificate (and the notice contains a copy of the certificate), the tenant can make no application for a new lease. When the date of termination is

---

[230] Section 57(1). In *XL Fisheries v Leeds Corporation* [1955] QB 636, for example, the local authority sought to use the tenant's fish shop for the purposes of a police station. As regards the National Trust, the certificate is issued by the Minister of Works under the terms of section 57(7) and is on the basis of securing the property. In relation to a health authority it is for the purposes specified in section 129 and Sch 15 the National Health Service Act 1977.

[231] *R v Secretary of State for the Environment, ex parte Powis* [1981] 1 All ER 788. Dunn LJ felt that the change should be 'reasonably necessary' (at 795).

[232] Section 57(5).

[233] N 231 above at 790.

earlier than the date specified in the certificate (and, again, provided that a copy of the certificate is included with the notice), the court can grant a renewal, but only for a term expiring no later than the certified date. The new tenancy will be outside the protection of the 1954 Act and there can be no further renewal.[234]

Where the tenant has served a request for a new lease, much depends upon whether the request was served after or before the issue of the certificate. If the section 26 request is served after the certificate, the landlord can serve a counter notice, within two months, containing a copy of the certificate. When the termination date specified in the request is later than the date specified in that certificate, section 57(4) disentitles the tenant from making an application for renewal. Where the termination date is earlier than the date contained in the certificate, a new tenancy can be granted, but for a duration no longer than the date set out in the certificate. The new tenancy falls outside the Part II machinery. If the tenant's request precedes the issue of the certificate, the request is invalid if either the preliminary certification notice has been given by the Minister (or Board) or is given within two months of the section 26 request. The provisions as to certification apply even where the authority using them acquired the reversion after the tenant served a section 26 request.[235] The consequence is that the current tenancy continues with the proviso that, once the decision as to whether to issue a certificate is taken, the tenant can make a fresh request for a new lease. **3.58**

National Security

Where the landlord's interest belongs to, or is held for the purposes of a government department, section 58(1)(a),(b) provides that the tenancy may be terminated on the grounds of national security. This special provision prevents the operation of the Part II machinery. The procedure involved requires a certificate from the Minister of the government department to the effect that, for reasons of national security, it is necessary that the use or occupation of the demised premises shall be discontinued or changed. Unlike the other type of certification discussed above, there is no requirement for any preliminary notice to be given to the tenant. The issue of a certificate does, however, have implications as regards the service of renewal documentation. **3.59**

Implications

Where the landlord, after the issue of the certificate, serves a section 25 notice (which contains a copy of the certificate) the tenant is unable to apply for a new lease or serve a counter notice. If the tenant makes a section 26 request for a new tenancy the landlord has two months within which to issue a certificate (if it has not already done so) and serve a counter notice (containing a copy of the **3.60**

---

[234] Section 57(3)(b).
[235] *XL Fisheries v Leeds Corporation*, n 230 above.

certificate) so as to preclude the tenant's renewal application. The counter notice should set a date on which the tenancy is to come to an end. If it precedes the termination date specified in the tenant's request, and is at least six months from the giving of the counter notice (and not earlier than the date the tenancy could be terminated at common law), the current tenancy will end on the date set out in the counter notice. In all other cases, the lease will terminate on the date specified in the tenant's request. As regards prospective certification, section 58 expressly validates any agreement between the parties that, on the giving of such certification, the tenancy may be terminated by notice to quit of such duration as agreed, provided that the notice concerns a copy of the certificate.[236] If no agreement is achieved, and the tenant has applied for a new lease, the court shall, at the behest of the landlord, make this provision for early termination a term of any new lease.[237]

Other Official Bodies

3.61 Further provisions apply when the Ministry of Technology or the Urban Regeneration Agency is the landlord and the demised property is located within a specified development area or an intermediate area. Under the auspices of section 60(1), the Minister of Technology may certify that a change of use or occupation is necessary or expedient for the purposes of Schedule 2 of the Industrial Development Act 1982. Section 58(1)(a),(b) applies in the same manner as it does to government departments. In addition, the Secretary of State for Wales may issue a similar certificate, concerning property leased by the Welsh Development Agency, for the purpose of providing employment appropriate to the needs of the area.[238] If the court makes an order for the grant of a new lease, and the Secretary of State certifies that it is necessary or expedient, the court must include a covenant against alienation.[239]

---

[236] Section 58(2)(a). The same rule applies as regards a statutory undertaker (section 58(2)(b)) where repairs on the property or elsewhere are urgently needed and are for the proper operation of the landlord's undertaking: section 58(3).

[237] Section 58(4)(a),(b). Where by virtue of a certificate given under sections 57 and 58 the tenant is precluded from obtaining an order for the grant of a new tenancy (or a tenancy of normal duration), the tenant is, however, entitled on quitting the premises to obtain compensation under section 37.

[238] Sections 60A(1).

[239] Section 60A(2). The same rules apply where the landlord is the Development Board for Rural Wales: section 60B(1),(2). Note that limitations apply to the availability of compensation as regards these bodies: section 59(1A), (1B).

4

THE LANDLORD'S SECTION 25 NOTICE

A. Introduction

The operation of the Part II machinery depends heavily upon the service of appro- **4.01**
priate notices on the correct parties. In the absence of agreement or legislative provision, notices must be served in a way that they can be proved to have been
received by the intended recipient. Accordingly, it is convenient within this chapter to consider the general rules of service as they apply to any document to be
served under the Landlord and Tenant Acts of 1927 and 1954. In addition, the
special rules relating to partnerships will be discussed. Nevertheless, the primary
focus is upon the landlord's section 25 notice which is, arguably, the most important notice within the renewal process.[1] This notice represents the usual method
by which the renewal machinery is engaged[2] and invokes the statutory jurisdiction of the court.[3] The section 25 notice is highly functional in that it not only terminates the existing contractual lease, but also brings into being a section 24
continuation tenancy and furnishes the tenant with both a record of the landlord's

---

[1] In Northern Ireland, article 6 of the Business Tenancies (Northern Ireland) Order 1996
embodies the equivalent notice and similar conditions.

[2] Note, however, that the landlord's notice cannot be served if the tenant has already served a section 26 request for a new tenancy: section 26(4).

[3] As such the court has no power to amend the notice: *Smith v Draper* (1990) 60 P & CR 252.
Similarly, the lease cannot vary the provisions of section 25: see *LCC v Farren* [1956] 1 WLR 1297
(for example, as to the form of the notice or the means of signature).

identity and intentions and a general catalogue of statutory rights. The service of this termination notice does not, however, necessarily mean that the landlord seeks to regain possession. It is common for the landlord to initiate proceedings so as to ensure the negotiation of, or court order for, a new lease at a market rent.

4.02 Owing to its technical nature and role, the form of the section 25 notice is heavily stylised and its contents closely prescribed.[4] The working rule is that, due to the mandatory tone both of the Act and the ancillary Notice Regulations, a notice which does not comply with the statutory and extra-statutory prescription will not activate the renewal process.[5] There is, however, nothing to prevent a landlord from subsequently serving a further notice which complies with the statutory provisions.[6] As Dillon LJ concluded in *Smith v Draper*, 'I cannot see any reason why, if the tenant does not agree to treating an apparently invalid notice as valid, the landlord should not immediately serve an unquestionably valid notice'.[7] The tenant who is faced with a notice which appears invalid is in a particularly acute dilemma because for the lessee there is no second chance. It is crucial, therefore, that the tightly governed formalities, which regulate the validity and effectiveness of the landlord's notice, are fully understood.

B. Who can Serve a Section 25 Notice?

4.03 The section 25 notice may be served only by, or on behalf of, the competent landlord. The competent landlord is either the owner of the fee simple or, where underleases have been created, the landlord next above the tenant in the chain who holds a reversion of at least fourteen months' duration.[8] As regards the service of a section 25 notice, the relevant time for ascertaining the correct identity of the competent landlord is at the date the notice is served and it is from this date that the fourteen-month time-limit is to be measured.[9] The competent landlord and a sub-tenant's immediate landlord need not, therefore, be one and the same person. This distinction assumes importance because, as demonstrated in *Yamaha-Kemble Music (UK) Ltd v ARC Properties Ltd*, a notice served by the wrong landlord is invalid.[10] There can, of course, be joint landlords who, because they are

---

[4] Section 66 requires the notice to adhere to the form as set out by statutory instrument: see currently the Landlord and Tenant Act 1954 Pt II (Notices) Regulations (SI 1983 No 133, as amended by SI 1989 No 1548). The task of secondary legislation is to devise the structure of the notice and to detail how, and to what extent, the tenant's rights are to be explained.

[5] *Weinbergs Weatherproofs v Radcliffe Paper Mill Co* [1957] 3 All ER 663.

[6] *Whelton Sinclair v Hyland* (1992) 41 EG 112.

[7] N 3 above at 255.

[8] As defined in section 44 and Sch 6; see further Chapter 2.

[9] *Diploma Laundry v Surrey Timber Co Ltd* [1955] 2 QB 604. The tenant may discover the identity of the competent landlord by serving a section 40 notice on the immediate landlord: see Chapter 2.

[10] [1990] 1 EGLR 261. There the invalid notice was served by the assignor of the reversionary estate following assignment to a subsidiary company.

entitled to the entirety of the land comprised in the relevant reversion, together will constitute the competent landlord.[11] In that scenario, and although preferably all should join in the giving of the notice, it has been held that one of them alone may serve the statutory notice.[12] To be effective, however, such a notice must state the name(s) of the other joint landlord(s).[13] The notice may, moreover, be signed by an authorised agent of the competent landlord or signed in the landlord's name by someone with due authority *per procurationem*.[14]

Although there can only be one competent landlord at any given time, the land-   **4.04** lord's identity can change during the course of proceedings. If the landlord ceases to be 'competent' subsequent to the service of a section 25 notice, the tenant should be informed. Otherwise an estoppel might arise which will defeat any assertion that the tenant's proceedings have been pursued against the wrong landlord.[15] The landlord's successor may, of course, adopt the notice and, where relevant, the grounds of opposition stated therein.[16] Conversely, the notice can be withdrawn by the new landlord, but only within two months of its service.[17] To effect withdrawal, the new competent landlord must serve on the tenant a notice in the prescribed form (Form 12).

Split Reversions

A split reversion arises where different landlords hold the reversions of separate   **4.05** parts of the demised property. This fragmentation can occur in a variety of ways. For example, first, a landlord may dispose of part(s) only of the reversion of the property demised to the tenant.[18] Second, a tenant who has two leases with different landlords may sub-let both properties under a single tenancy. Third, a tenant who holds two or more properties from the same landlord, under separate leases and for different terms, may sub-let both properties under a single lease. As occurred in *Dodson Bull Carpet Co Ltd v City of London Corporation*, the sub-tenant may end up with a different landlord for each property.[19] The problem with split reversions is that, although an ordinary notice to quit can be validly

---

[11] *M&P Enterprises (London) Ltd v Norfolk Square Hotels Ltd* [1994] 1 EGLR 129.
[12] *Leckhampton Dairies Ltd v Artus Whitfield Ltd* (1986) 130 SJ 225. This is so even if the other freehold owner would, if invited, have refused to join in.
[13] *Pearson v Alyo* (1990) 60 P & CR 50. This requirement applies even when only one of the statutory trustees of the legal estate is beneficially entitled.
[14] *Tennant v LCC* [1957] 55 LGR 421; *LCC v Farren*, above. As Stirling LJ acknowledged in *Bevan v Webb* [1901] 2 Ch 59 at 77, 'Now the general rule of law is that whatever a person who is *sui juris* can do personally, he can also do through his agent.'
[15] *Shelley v United Artists Corporation Ltd* [1990] 1 EGLR 103.
[16] *Marks v British Waterways Board* [1963] 1 WLR 1008.
[17] Sch 6, para 6.; see Chapter 2.
[18] See *Nevil Long & Co (Boards) Ltd v Firmenich & Co* (1984) 47 P & CR 59.
[19] [1975] 1 WLR 781.

served in relation to part of the holding,[20] this statutory fiction does not apply to the service of a section 25 notice.[21] As Goff J acknowledged in *Dodson Bull Carpet Co v City of London Corporation*: 'There is nothing . . . to authorise a landlord to serve a notice of determination under section 25 as to part only of the premises . . . and indeed quite the reverse, to allow him to do so would cut across and jeopardise the protection afforded by the Act'.[22] Accordingly, the landlord's statutory notice must relate to the whole of the property let to the tenant: and, hence, a notice which relates only to part of the demised premises is simply of no effect. Accordingly, in *Herongrove Ltd v Wates City of London Properties Plc*, where an office floor and ground floor storage space were demised to one tenant under one lease, the landlord's section 25 notice had to refer to both premises.[23] This can pose particular difficulties for landlords where the reversion has become split.

4.06 A classic illustration emerges from the *Dodson Bull* case where the head landlord could not serve a valid termination notice in relation to part of the property and was not the competent landlord as regards the remainder. Without the co-operation of both landlords, therefore, an impasse is reached. Accordingly, it is possible that the joint reversioners together serve a single section 25 notice or individually give separate notices operating at the same time.[24] In order for separate notices to take effect, however, they have to be construed as relating to one single tenancy and not, say, different buildings.[25] A covering letter should spell this out clearly. Nevertheless, this option is not always practicable and ceases to be available where, for example, one landlord does not wish to oppose the grant of a new tenancy or cannot establish a ground of opposition. Hence, when the leases are terminated in accordance with the contract(s), a continuation of the whole property will necessarily arise under section 24. A limited inroad on this general rule occurs, however, where the lease is of two distinct properties and it is clear that the document can be construed as two separate leases.[26] Only in that

---

[20] Section 140 of the Law of Property Act 1925. If the tenancy is not protected by the 1954 Act, therefore, the landlord of part can bring the tenancy of that part to an end: *Skelton v Harrison & Pinder* [1975] QB 361.

[21] As section 140 does not apply, the severance of the reversion does not create two separate tenancies: *Nevil Long & Co (Boards) Ltd v Firmenich & Co Ltd*, n 18 above.

[22] N 19 above at 785. cf agricultural holdings.

[23] (1998) 24 EG 108. The reference to the premises in the landlord's notice need not, however, be detailed and all that is required is that it will be clear to the reasonable tenant which premises are the subject of the notice: *Germax Securities Ltd v Spiegal* (1978) 37 P & CR 204.

[24] *Nevil Long & Co (Boards) Ltd v Firmenich & Co*, n 18 above at 67.

[25] *M&P Enterprises (London) Ltd v Norfolk Square Hotels Ltd*, n 11 above, where a single tenancy of five buildings was subject to five notices served by different reversioners. The notices were invalid as they did not make clear that it was a single tenancy that was being determined. Copies of the revised notices, later received by the tenant and following the service of a tenant's section 26 request for renewal, did, however, act as effective landlords' counter notices.

[26] This argument, however, failed in the *Dodson Bull* case, n 19 above, because there was clearly one lease. The existence of a break clause which allows early termination of part of the property, moreover, does not necessitate that two leases have been granted: *Southport Old Links Ltd v Naylor*

situation can a section 25 notice refer to one property without relating to the other.[27]

Reform

The Law Commission Working Paper considered the issue of split reversions and **4.07** concluded that landlords could be placed in an impossible, inconvenient and unjust position.[28] The problem was also identified by Oliver LJ in *Southport Old Links Ltd v Naylor* who admitted: 'It may well be (and I think it is) that the Act is defective in not making provisions for this rather unusual situation.'[29] The Working Paper advocated that the law should be reformed and concluded that a section 25 notice should be able to refer to part only of the demised property. In order to ensure that landlords should not be given an undue advantage over their tenants, however, the Working Paper drew a rather awkward distinction between a landlord who originally let a property and then split the reversion (a 'voluntary' landlord of part) and one who has only ever owned the reversion of part of the property (an 'involuntary' landlord). It was thought feasible that the tenant's protection should hinge upon which type of landlord served the notice. As regards a section 25 notice served by a voluntary landlord of part of the premises, the Working Paper recommended that the tenant should be allowed to require the notice to apply to the whole.[30] An alterative possibility of the notice being automatically applied to the whole of the premises demised did not curry favour.

In the case of a notice served by an involuntary landlord, however, the tenant's **4.08** right was to be curtailed. Two options were mooted. First, that the notice should always apply only to the part of the property specified. This approach would reflect the fact that, as the landlord was not responsible for the fragmentation of the reversion, the tenant should not be entitled to apply the notice to the whole of the premises. Second, and in the alternative, it was considered that the tenant be given a right to apply to the court for an order that the notice be made referable to the whole. The balance of justice could then be drawn by the court in the light of all the circumstances. Despite these somewhat elaborate suggestions, the Law Commission's subsequent Report recommended minimum reform. The recommendation was limited so as to allow, in so far as it affects the whole of the property, landlords collectively both to operate the statutory procedure and to have it

---

[1985] 1 EGLR 66. There the appellate court was again unable to spell two separate tenancies out of the single lease.

[27] *Moss v Mobil Oil* (1986) 6 EG 109 where two petrol stations were demised in a single document, but it was made expressly clear in the document that there were two tenancies. It is also to be appreciated that two separate tenancies can be converted into a single lease by the agreement of the parties: *Latif v Hillsdale Estates (Swansea) Ltd* [1992] EGCS 75.

[28] *Part II of the Landlord & Tenant Act 1954* (1988) Working Paper 111 at para 3.2.3.

[29] N 26 above at 69.

[30] N 28 above at para 3.2.12.

operated against them by a tenant.[31] Accordingly, the recommendation does nothing where co-operation between landlords is impractical and an impasse between them reached. As the existing law already caters for the collective service of a termination notice, and it is also thought possible that an effective section 26 request can currently be served on all landlords of the split reversion, the implementation of this recommendation might achieve little.

C. Person to be Served

4.09 The landlord's notice must be served on the tenant who is, for these purposes, the person entitled to claim a new lease.[32] As regards a bankrupt tenant, the notice should be served on the trustee in bankruptcy.[33] Where there are joint tenants, the general rule is that (subject to waiver) the notice must be served on all of them.[34] As will be shown, the exception to this rule lies in section 41A and concerns partnership tenants. Subject to certain conditions, this permits the notice to be served only on those partners who are involved in running the business. In relation to trusts, the landlord may experience difficulties when there has been a change of trustees of which the lessor has no knowledge. It might be impossible to guarantee that the tenants are correctly named in the notice. To cater for this situation, it will suffice if the landlord's notice describes the tenant as 'the trustees for the time being'.[35]

Effect of Subletting

4.10 As regards a tenant in occupation of the whole premises, few problems are raised. The landlord simply serves the notice on that tenant. More problematic, however, is where the premises have been sub-let. If the whole of the premises are sub-let and the sub-tenancy is within the scope of the Act, the section 25 notice is to be served directly on the sub-tenant . As the mesne landlord is no longer in occupation of the holding, the protection of the Act does not extend to that head lease. As happened in *Keith Bayley Rogers & Co v Cubes Ltd,* if the landlord prematurely

---

[31] *Business Tenancies: a Periodic Review of the Landlord & Tenant Act 1954 Part II* (1992) Law Com No 208 at para 2.43. Interestingly the Law Reform Advisory Committee for Northern Ireland, *Business Tenancies* (1994) Report No 1 at para 4.5.6 declined to make any recommendation on this 'rare' problem.

[32] The section 25 notice can, moreover, terminate more than one tenancy: *Tropis Shipping Co Ltd v Ibex Properties Corporation Ltd* [1967] EGD 433 (three tenancies terminated by the same section 25 notice). It is important that the notice makes clear that it is to determine each of the tenancies on the date specified therein.

[33] *Gatwick Investments Ltd v Radivojevic* [1978] CLY 1768.

[34] *Booth Investments Ltd v Reynolds* (1974) NLJ 119; see also *Rostrun v Michael Nairn & Co Ltd* [1962] EGD 284.

[35] See *Mayor & Burgesses of the London Borough of Hackney v Hackney African Organisation* (1998) October 14 CA.

ends the head tenant's lease by the exercise of a break clause the landlord will then become the sub-tenant's competent landlord.[36] Where the premises have been sub-let in part only and the landlord wishes to grant a new lease of the whole premises, the head landlord must, however, serve the section 25 notice on the head lessee. Any new tenancy will take subject to the sub-lease(s). If, however, the landlord does not wish to grant a renewal of the whole premises, the notice must be served, first, on the mesne landlord with the result that the server becomes the competent landlord of the sub-tenant(s).[37] The competent landlord will then serve an additional termination notice directly on each sub-tenant.[38] Although the notice must be served first on the mesne landlord, if the notices are served on all the parties on the same day, the presumption is that they are served in the correct order.[39]

D. Formalities

Section 25 requires that the statutory notice be in writing, relate to the whole **4.11** premises demised and adhere to the form prescribed from time to time by statutory instrument. The notice must also specify a date on which the tenancy is to terminate and that date must fall no more than twelve months and no less than six months after the service of the notice.[40] It is not necessary that the termination date falls on a rent day.[41] If a fixed term or periodic tenancy is already being continued under section 24, only these time requirements need be satisfied. Accordingly, any date can be specified provided that it falls within the statutory time span.[42] As regards other tenancies, however, the date selected cannot be one earlier than that on which the tenancy could be terminated at common law.[43] Hence, where the contractual tenancy requires a period of notice longer than six months, the maximum period of twelve months is extended so as to equal the duration of the contractual notice plus six months.[44] The general rule entails that, with regard to a periodic tenancy, the contractual term date will be that on which

---

[36] (1975) 31 P & CR 412.
[37] *Rene Claro (Haute Coiffure) Ltd v Halle Concerts Society* [1969] 1 WLR 909.
[38] Note that the date of termination specified may be earlier than the date of expiry of the head lease: *Lewis v MTC (Cars) Ltd* [1975] 1 All ER 874.
[39] *Keith Bayley Rogers & Co v Cubes Ltd* n 36 above.
[40] Section 25(2). In *Hogg Bullimore & Co v Co-operative Insurance Society* (1984) 50 P & CR 105, Whitford J applied the 'corresponding date' rule so as to bring a notice served on April 2, but purporting to terminate the tenancy on October 2, within the ambit of this provision; see further Chapter 2.
[41] *Westerbury Property & Investment Co Ltd v Carpenter* [1961] 1 All ER 481.
[42] *Lewis v MTC (Cars) Ltd,* n 38 above.
[43] Section 25(3)(a).
[44] Section 25(3)(b). Hence, if the lease requires 10 months' notice to quit, the section 25 notice may be served up to 16 months before the date for termination specified therein.

a notice to quit could have brought the tenancy to an end.[45] In *Commercial Properties v Wood*, moreover, it was demonstrated that the section 25 notice can terminate a periodic tenancy even though the stated termination date does not fall on the first or last day of a period.[46]

4.12 As regards fixed term tenancies, the date will be the one on which its original term expires.[47] A statutory notice which specifies the last day of the contractual lease is, therefore, valid[48] whereas one which specifies the day before is not.[49] Where relevant, and if there is doubt as to the last day of the original lease, several additional days should be added on to the calculation.[50] If the landlord exercises a break clause then, although the contractual term will end, a continuation tenancy will arise under section 24. The landlord is, however, expressly allowed to serve a statutory termination notice timed to follow the break.[51] If it is the tenant who exercises the break, the contractual term ends and with it any statutory protection. Accordingly, the tenant cannot then serve a request for a new lease and there is no need for the landlord to serve a termination notice.[52]

Issues of Timing

4.13 As is well illustrated by Reynolds & Clark, the timing of service of a notice and the selection of the termination date may be driven by a variety of factors.[53] First, the service of the section 25 notice will put the landlord in the driving seat and, by taking the initiative, allow the landlord to dictate the termination date. Second, as section 37 offers double-rate compensation for disturbance payable to a tenant who has been in occupation for fourteen years immediately prior to the termination date specified, the landlord may, sensibly, elect for a termination date preceding the lapse of that fourteen-year period. Third, by virtue of section 30(1)(g), renewal can be opposed on the basis of the landlord's desire to occupy, but only if the landlord did not acquire title within the five years preceding the date of termination specified. This may tempt a landlord to postpone the termination date until the five-year requirement is satisfied. Fourth, as the lessor must be in a position to specify grounds of opposition in the section 25 notice, and must be able to put the opposition into a provable form by the date of the hearing, the landlord may wish to maximise time allowed within which to finalise plans.

---

[45] See *Jones v Daniels & Davidson (Holdings) Ltd* [1981] CLY 1513.
[46] [1968] 1 QB 15; see also *Rene Claro (Haute Coiffure) Ltd v Halle Concert Society*, n 37 above. cf the common law position.
[47] *Lewis v MTC (Cars) Ltd*, n 38 above.
[48] *Re Crowhurst Park* [1974] 1 WLR 583.
[49] *Central Estates (Belgravia) v Webster* (1969) 209 EG 1319.
[50] See *Whelton Sinclair v Hyland*, n 6 above.
[51] Section 25(3); see *Willison v Shaftesbury Plc* (1998) May 15 CA. If the break clause is irregularly exercised, the section 25 notice which is timed to follow it will be invalid: *Craddock v Fieldman* (1960) 175 EG 1149.
[52] *Garston v Scottish Widow's Fund & Life Assurance Society* (1998) 3 All ER 596.
[53] K Reynolds and W Clark, *Renewal of Business Tenancies* (1997) at 130–133.

Form

Although it is advisable for a pro forma document to be used, the Notice **4.14**
Regulations permit a limited variation in form by allowing a form 'substantially to
the like effect' to be effective for these purposes.[54] This clearly indicates that some
departure from the extra-statutory prescription is permissible. While the majority
of detail emanates from the delegated legislation, the enabling Act does itself set
out certain matters which must be addressed in the notice. The latter are deemed
to be of sufficient importance to merit express mention within the statute and to
attract the ultimate sanction that, on their omission, the notice 'shall have no
effect'.[55] It is to be noted that, in contradistinction to these primary requirements,
there is no express sanction attached to a non-compliance with the secondary legislation.

Contents

The Act requires the notice to state whether or not the landlord will oppose the **4.15**
grant of a new lease and, if so, to stipulate the ground(s) of opposition upon which
the lessor will rely.[56] The landlord should think carefully before stipulating any
ground as the notice cannot later be amended.[57] Furthermore, as it may be necessary at a later stage to substantiate the ground stated, a cavalier citation of all or
most of the statutory grounds will reduce dramatically the credibility of that landlord's opposition.[58] It is not necessary, however, that the landlord set out the
ground(s) of opposition in full.[59] Instead, it is sufficient that the ground(s) be
identified by reference to the appropriate paragraph of section 30(1)[60] or by other

---

[54] This is not the case in Northern Ireland where the prescribed form of landlord's notice must always be used and, moreover, there is only one prescribed form, that is, Form 3 of the Business Tenancies (Notices) Regulations (Northern Ireland) 1997.

[55] Section 25(2),(5), (6).

[56] Section 25(6). In *Lewis v MTC Cars*, n 38 above, the landlord failed to delete the sentence which stated that the renewal would be unopposed. The landlord did, however, state a ground of opposition in the notice. The notice was upheld because it was clear to the tenant that the landlord would oppose renewal.

[57] *Nursey v P Currie (Dartford) Ltd* [1959] 1 All ER 497; *Hutchison v Lamberth* [1984] 1 EGLR 75. It should be remembered that the notice cannot be unilaterally withdrawn by the landlord except where a new competent landlord retracts a predecessor's notice within two months of its service: Sch 6. para 6.

[58] The landlord's opposition must be genuine and, if not, the notice is, arguably, void: *Earl Stradbroke v Mitchell* [1991] 1 EGLR 1; *Rous v Mitchell* [1991] 1 All ER 676. The same rule would apply if a ground was stated recklessly: *Shecrum Ltd v Savill* (1996) April 1 CA.

[59] *Bolton's (House Furnishers) Ltd v Oppenheim* [1959] 3 All ER 90. There the landlord set out ground (f) of opposition, but did not state that the work could not be reasonably undertaken with-out the recovery of possession. The notice was upheld.

[60] *Biles v Caesar* [1957] 1 All ER 151. In *Harvey Textiles Ltd v Hillel* [1979] 1 EGLR 74, the notice specified ground (g), but did not specify that the landlord intended to carry out business via a company controlled by him. The notice remained valid.

expression which indicates the particular ground(s).[61] The overriding issue is that the tenant be given adequate warning of what contention will have to be refuted at the subsequent hearing.[62]

4.16 If the landlord does not state opposition in the section 25 notice, the tenant will be entitled to a new tenancy provided that the appropriate procedural steps are taken. If opposition is stated, but no statutory ground provided, the landlord's notice is invalid.[63] On that understanding, the tenant cannot then apply to the court for a new lease. The Law Commission Report recommended that, where the landlord does not oppose renewal, the section 25 notice should set out the proposed terms of the grant.[64] Unlike the tenant's section 26 request for a new lease, the present termination notice does not cater for this information.[65] By indicating the terms the landlord will accept, obstacles to agreement will be identifiable at an early stage. Nevertheless, and as Ross points out, putting forward firm proposals 'could be a problem to a landlord serving a section 25 notice 12 months before the contractual expiry date'.[66] The notice must also require the tenant, within two months, to notify the landlord in writing whether or not possession will be willingly given up.[67] Such notification will occur through the service of a tenant's counter notice. The Act, therefore, requires the service of either a 'negative' counter notice (that is, the tenant will not give up possession) or a 'positive' counter notice (that is, the tenant will give up possession). With the possible caveat of the 'positive' notice, these requirements are imposed for the benefit of the tenant.

The Notice Regulations

4.17 Schedules 1 and 2 of the Notice Regulations 1983 (as amended) prescribe different forms of section 25 notice to cater for different types of case. For example, Form 1 is the standard type notice to be employed; Form 2 applies where the landlord's notice to terminate is based upon public interest grounds; Form 4 concerns termination on grounds of national security; Form 5 relates to termination by rea-

---

[61] *Philipson-Stow v Trevor Square Ltd* (1980) 257 EG 1262 where the notice was valid although the landlord had stated the intention to carry out substantial works of 'redecoration' rather than demolition or reconstruction; see also *Housleys Ltd v Bloomer-Holt Ltd* [1966] 2 All ER 966.

[62] *Marks v British Waterways Board*, n 16 above. In *Sevenarts Ltd v Busvine* [1969] 1 All ER 392 a notice which stated that the landlord sought to occupy when, in reality, it was the landlord's company which was to occupy, was upheld. The misstatement was immaterial.

[63] *Barclays Bank v Ascott* [1961] 1 WLR 717. There the consent of the landlord to a new tenancy was made conditional on the finding of a suitable guarantor and this invalidated the notice. The notice did not state on what ground a new tenancy would be opposed if no guarantor was found.

[64] N 31 above at para 2.34. In its 1996 Consultation Paper, the Department of the Environment argued that the notice should also contain a warning explaining to the tenant that the proposed terms are subject to negotiation.

[65] This reform has, however, been implemented in Northern Ireland: see article 6(6)(a).

[66] M Ross, *Drafting and Negotiation of Commercial Leases* (4th edn, 1994) at 278, n 9.

[67] Section 25(5). Inexplicably, the unamended Notice Regulations did not state the requirement the tenant serve a positive counter notice.

son of the Local Employment Act 1972; Form 6 assumes relevance where the tenancy is of Welsh Development Agency premises; and Form 7 is employed where the landlord is the Development Board for Rural Wales. It is imperative that the appropriate form is employed because each, although similar, is tailored to convey specific and crucial information to the tenant.[68] In all cases, the Regulations prescribe that the section 25 notice is to contain a warning to the tenant that the notice is intended to bring the tenancy to an end and the recommendation that the recipient act quickly and carefully. If in doubt, the tenant is advised to consult a solicitor or the Citizen's Advice Bureau. Appended to the prescribed form are a series of general notes of guidance which explain the basic workings of the 1954 Act and the steps that the tenant should take. These notes refer to, for example, the statutory grounds of opposition, compensation for loss of renewal rights, negotiating a renewal, challenging the validity of the notice and the explanatory booklet published by the Department of the Environment.[69]

E. Defects and Omissions

Although careful drafting of the section 25 notice is imperative, it is apparent **4.18** from case law that the requirements of the Act and the Regulations are not always complied with. Nevertheless, and despite the general rule that if there is a defect or omission the notice will be invalidated, the tenant would be ill advised to ignore a notice simply in the belief that it is ineffective. This is because the courts have usually adopted a sensible approach to the application of section 25 and have upheld seemingly defective notices on the basis of a liberal construction of either the specific words used or the notice as a whole. As will be shown, however, not all decisions are as easy to justify and some are open to doubt in that they fail to make the vital distinction between those requirements imposed by the Act and those imposed by the Regulations. This is particularly so with the requirement imposed by section 25(5) relating to the service by the tenant of a positive counter notice indicating the willingness to give up possession. Although the Act states expressly that a landlord's notice which omits such information is void, the courts have, by taking a purposive interpretation, upheld notices regardless of this omission.

---

[68] See *Keepers & Governors of the Free Grammar School of John Lyon v Mayhew* [1997] 1 EGLR 88. As discussed in Chapter 3, in most of the special cases a ministerial or other certificate must be issued and a copy of it included in the notice.

[69] Or, as appropriate, the Department of the Environment and Welsh Office booklet. In Northern Ireland, Form 3 contains no similar guidance and merely cautions the tenant that professional advice should be sought as soon as possible.

Waiver and Estoppel

4.19 It is well established that an otherwise invalid notice can be cured by waiver. Following the analysis of Lord Diplock in *Kammins Ballroom Co Ltd v Zenith Investments (Torquay) Ltd*, there are two types of waiver:

> [T]he first type of waiver . . . arises in a situation where a person is entitled to alter-native rights inconsistent with one another. If he has knowledge of the facts which give rise in law to these alternative rights and acts in a manner which is consistent only with his having chosen to rely on one of them, the law holds him to his choice even though he was unaware that this would be the legal consequence of what he did . . . The second type of waiver which debars a person from raising a particular defence to a claim against him arises when he either agrees with the claimant not to raise that particular defence or conducts himself as to be estopped from raising it.[70]

The consequences of waiver by election (that is, choosing not to rely on the irreg-ularity) are that the tenant loses the right thereafter to object to the validity of the notice[71] and the landlord is prevented also from relying on the defect.[72]

4.20 It is, however, crucial that the waiving party know of the facts which give rise to the right to challenge.[73] In *Stevens & Cutting Ltd v Anderson*, for example, the ten-ant made a premature application for a new lease, but the landlord failed to raise this in the answer to the tenant's proceedings.[74] Despite lengthy and failed nego-tiations for a new lease, this first type of waiver had not occurred because the land-lord had not been aware of the defect until after the negotiations had broken down. Similarly, in *Morrow v Nadeem* the incorrect name of the landlord was inserted in the section 25 notice and, consequently, proceedings were commenced against the wrong landlord.[75] The tenant later questioned the validity of the notice and it was held that the defect had not been waived as the tenant had not been aware of the true identity of the competent landlord until after the procedural

---

[70] [1971] AC 850 at 882–883. Note that neither waiver nor estoppel can grant the court a juris-diction which it does not otherwise possess: *Benedictus v Jalaram Ltd* [1990] 58 P & CR 330; cf the role of estoppel where there is a mere irregularity of procedure or non-compliance with statutory provisions.

[71] *Smith v Draper*, n 3 above. Unlike the second type of waiver, an election is binding even though the other party has suffered no detriment. If the party has received legal advice, moreover, the rebuttable presumption is that the party knew of the legal position, that is, the right to elect: *Peyman v Lanjani* [1985] Ch 457.

[72] *Bristol Cars Ltd v RKH (Hotels) Ltd* (1979) 38 P & CR 411 where the landlord did not realise that the tenant's request was invalid and entered into negotiations for a renewal. The landlord was also estopped from denying the validity of the request.

[73] See *Tennant v LCC*, n 14 above, where the notice was self-evidently not signed by the compe-tent landlord or the landlord's agent (it was clearly marked '*per pro*') and yet the tenant proceeded with a renewal application. In those circumstances, it was held that any defect would be waived; see also *BRB v AJA Smith Transport Ltd* [1981] 2 EGLR 69 where the tenant's conduct in claiming a new lease was inconsistent with disputing the validity of the notice. The court there advised future tenants to plead their competing claims in the alternative.

[74] (1990) 11 EG 70.

[75] [1987] 1 All ER 237.

steps had been taken.[76] In contrast, the tenant in *Keepers & Governors of the Free Grammar School of John Lyon v Mayhew* was aware that the landlord had used the wrong form of statutory notice, but proceeded as if the notice was valid and effective. The attempt to challenge validity some two months after the service of the notice failed because a reasonable landlord would have believed that the defect had been waived. Furthermore, this case demonstrates that, where the notice has served the statutory purpose of starting proceedings, and no point of validity has been taken, the notice will not later be the subject of critical examination.[77]

A proprietary estoppel may arise where there has been a representation of fact by **4.21** one party and the detrimental reliance upon that representation by the other. Evidence of each ingredient should normally be presented before the court.[78] There must be a clear and unequivocal assurance (whether by words or spelled out from conduct) which is intended to be relied upon.[79] The statement or conduct must, therefore, act as an invitation for the other party to take a particular action.[80] As regards a section 25 notice, therefore, no estoppel can arise in the absence of a representation by the tenant that the defect is not going to be taken up.[81] An expression of opinion, moreover, does not constitute an assurance for these purposes.[82] Although detrimental reliance cannot be presumed, it can be inferred from the circumstances. Usually, it will be expressly proven, for example, by showing that the tenant has carried out improvements on the demised premises or incurred other forms of financial expenditure. By way of illustration, in *Keepers & Governors of the Free Grammar School of John Lyon v Mayhew* the detriment concerned the incurring of lawyers' and surveyors' fees and the omission to serve a second and valid termination notice. The overriding issue is whether or not it is unconscionable for the representor to resile from the assurance made. If it is, the court can fulfil, either in whole or in part, the representation relied upon. Accordingly, a tenant who accepts a landlord's section 25 notice (which would otherwise be invalid by reason of a defect or omission) as being valid, and

---

[76] See also *Kammins Ballrooms Co Ltd v Zenith Investments (Torquay) Ltd*, n 70 above, where the tenant made a premature application to the court for renewal and the landlord's filing of an answer, which made no reference to the tenant's early application, did not waive the defect. This was because the filing of the answer was in a prescribed form which did not require the particular point to be raised.

[77] N 68 above at 90, 91.

[78] *JT Developments Ltd v Quinn* [1991] 2 EGLR 257; see generally M Pawlowski, *The Doctrine of Proprietary Estoppel* (1996).

[79] See *Watkins v Emslie* (1982) 261 EG 1192 where the landlord's estoppel claim failed for lack of representation by the tenant.

[80] *Sidney Bolsom Investment Trust Ltd v E Karmios & Co (London) Ltd* [1965] 1 QB 529. In *Akiens v Solomon* (1994) 65 P & CR 364, the general rule was advocated that correspondence marked 'subject to lease' will prevent an estoppel arising.

[81] *Kammins Ballrooms Co Ltd v Zenith Investments (Torquay) Ltd*, n 70 above; *Stevens & Cutting Ltd v Anderson*, n 74 above; *Spence v Shell UK Ltd* [1980] 2 EGLR 68.

[82] See *E&L Berg Homes Ltd v Grey* (1979) 253 EG 473.

persuades the landlord either to take or not to take certain steps under Part II, can be estopped from relying upon the defect.[83]

Tenant's Dilemma

4.22 An invalid section 25 notice will neither engage the renewal provisions nor terminate any continuation tenancy which has arisen. It could, however, act as a notice to quit at common law and, by terminating the contractual tenancy, give rise to a section 24 continuation. It would still remain necessary for the landlord to serve a further and valid statutory notice. The risk to the tenant, when faced with a seemingly invalid notice, is demonstrated by *Smith v Draper*. In that case, the landlords served a statutory notice which they subsequently conceded was invalid (because it did not name all the joint landlords) The tenant responded by serving a counter notice and by initiating proceedings against the named landlords. The landlords' solicitors invited the tenant to join the omitted landlord to the proceedings, but the tenant's advisors refused to do so and continued to challenge the validity of the notice. The landlords then served a second (and valid) section 25 notice and, for good measure, added a further ground of opposition.[84] A counter notice was served, but the tenant did not apply to the court within the prescribed time-limits following the second statutory notice. The landlords formally abandoned their first notice. It was held that the tenant had not waived the defect in the initial notice and that the landlord was not estopped from denying the invalidity of that notice. The tenancy was, therefore, terminated by the second notice and the tenant had lost the right to renew through the unfortunate failure to take the necessary formal steps following the service of the valid notice. As Ralph Gibson LJ concluded, 'The result is harsh and in my view regrettable . . . The statute gives no power in such circumstances to the court to give relief against the consequences of an honest error on the part of the legal advisor. There is nothing that this court can do about it.'[85] The lesson to be learned from *Smith v Draper*, therefore, is that the tenant should always respond to the landlord's actions.

Tenant's Response

4.23 The appropriate action for a tenant to take, when faced with a potentially defective section 25 notice, is always to serve on the landlord a counter notice and to apply for a new tenancy. If the landlord purports to withdraw a potentially invalid notice and serves a replacement, the tenant must serve a fresh counter notice and

---

[83] In the *Free Grammar School of John Lyon* case n 68 above, the tenant's counter notice and subsequent application for renewal assumed that the landlord's termination notice was valid. The tenant, thereby, represented that the notice was good. In appropriate circumstances, the landlord may, of course, be estopped from relying upon the invalidity of the notice: *Smith v Draper*, n 3 above.

[84] The landlord is entitled to serve a second notice without prejudice to the efficacy of the first. If the first notice is invalid, the court will give effect to its valid successor: *Keith Bayley Rogers & Co v Cubes Ltd*, n 36 above.

[85] N 3 above at 257.

make a new application to the court. This should protect the tenant's position. The tenant may, however, expressly reserve the right to challenge the initial notice.[86] This can be achieved by taking the procedural steps 'without prejudice' to any contention as to invalidity.[87] This should prevent the tenant being held to have waived the defect.[88] This tactic is not, however, always sufficient to prevent an estoppel.[89] If the first notice is to be challenged, it is also necessary that the tenant makes no representation to the landlord, acts without delay and, where appropriate, adds a plea to the application for a new lease that the notice is invalid and asks for a declaration as a preliminary issue.[90]

Different Words, Same Meanings

Following *Bolton's (House Furnishers) Ltd v Oppenheim*,[91] it is clear that the court **4.24** will condone, wherever possible, minor deviations in the form and content of a section 25 notice. It remains possible that any shortcomings might be cured by a covering letter containing the omitted information.[92] The test of validity as expressed by Hodson LJ in the *Oppenheim* case is simply whether the notice provides the tenant with sufficient information to deal with the landlord's claim. Unless Parliament states that precise and exact language be used, the obligation is merely to indicate the information with sufficient clarity so as to be understood by the tenant.[93] As Hodson LJ was concerned with the chosen form of expression employed and the ability to ascribe meanings to specific words contained in a document, he did not consider the scenario where the relevant information is entirely

---

[86] This is so even if the issue of validity has been raised previously between the parties. see *Craddock v Fieldman*, n 51 above at 1150 where Paull J admitted, 'the tenant is always in an unfortunate position when he receives . . . a notice to quit under the Landlord and Tenant Act. If he takes no step at all then if that notice is a good one he may find himself without any power of asking for a new lease. He must therefore protect his position.'

[87] *Rhyl UDC v Rhyl Amusements Ltd* [1959] 1 All ER 257; see also Henry LJ in *Keepers & Governors of the Free Grammar School of John Lyon v Mayhew*, n 68 above at 91.

[88] *Tennant v LCC*, n 14 above; *Stylo Shoes Ltd v Prices Tailors Ltd* [1960] Ch 396.

[89] See *BRB v AJA Smith Transport Ltd*, n 73 above, where the tenant was estopped from denying the validity of the termination notice despite having expressly reserved the right to challenge it. The tenant had left it too late in the proceedings to keep both options open.

[90] See *Airport Restaurants v Southend-on-Sea Corporation* [1960] 2 All ER 888 where the renewal proceedings in the county court were adjourned until the preliminary issue was determined by the High Court. Note that while the county court is expressly given the jurisdiction to make a declaration as to any matter arising under the Part II provisions (section 43A), the High Court claims this power by way of inherent jurisdiction.

[91] N 59 above.

[92] *Stidolph v American School in London Education Trust* (1969) 211 EG 925 (landlord's signature omitted from the body of the notice, but was present on accompanying letter); *Germax Securities Ltd v Spiegal*, n 23 above (wrong date of termination stated in notice, but corrected by appended letter).

[93] *McMullen v Great Southern Cemetery & Crematorium Co* (1958) 172 EG 855 (where the notice was valid even though it did not refer to the 'holding', which included a small garden, but instead made reference to the 'building'). The test here concerns the knowledge of the actual tenant: see *Ladd v Sykes* [1992] 1 EGLR 1.

omitted. Nevertheless, the inapplicability of the *Oppenheim* test to omissions is sometimes overlooked by the courts and, in consequence, the case is liable to be misused as authority for a more universal proposition.[94]

Construction of the Notice

4.25 The court is guided by the normal use of grammar and construction and is not entitled to give words a meaning which they do not bear under those rules.[95] Nevertheless, as made clear by Barry J in *Barclays Bank v Ascott*, the construction can be liberal: 'provided the notice gives the real substance of the information required, then the mere omission of certain details or the failure to embody in the notice the full provisions of the section of the Act referred to will not in fact invalidate the notice'.[96] There the landlord failed to make its opposition clear and to provide any grounds of opposition in the section 25 notice. The notice was, therefore, manifestly bad: no attempt was made to identify any ground and there was nothing in the wording of the notice which could be construed as imparting the necessary information. If the notice had, on its true construction, stated what was required to be stated then it would have been saved. Nevertheless, as the omitted information was deemed fundamental to the tenant, and because the notice did not satisfy section 25(6), the defect proved fatal.

4.26 Barry J's approach was subsequently adopted by the Court of Appeal in *Sunrose Ltd v Gould* where a notice was upheld even though it failed expressly to specify the year of termination.[97] As the date was readily ascertainable from a formula provided on the back of the notice, there was sufficient specification for the purposes of section 25(5). Significantly, there was no positive inaccuracy or error on the face of the notice. If there had been, Davies LJ suspected that the notice would have been incapable of cure.[98] The *Sunrose* case, therefore, demonstrates that something can be rendered certain by reference to all parts of the document itself and that a notice can be upheld if it does communicate the required information, albeit in a different way than prescribed. In this context, moreover, it is irrelevant whether the particular requirement is imposed by the enabling Act or by the secondary legislation. As regards the latter, however, the Regulations expressly encourage a liberality of construction and, as previously mentioned, allow a form 'substantially to the like effect' to that prescribed to suffice. In gauging this degree of similarity, Stephenson LJ in *Sun Alliance & London Assurance Co Ltd v Hayman*

---

[94] See *Gudka v Patel* (1995) 69 P & CR D20; *Bridgers & Hamptons Residential v Stanford* (1991) 63 P &CR 18.

[95] See *Yamaha-Kemble Music (UK) Ltd v ARC Properties Ltd*, n 10 above.

[96] N 63 above at 722. As Lord Greene recognised in *Hankey v Clavering* [1942] 2 All ER 313 at 326: 'the court in case of ambiguity will lean in favour of reading the document in such a way as to give it validity . . .'.

[97] [1961] 3 All ER 1142.

[98] ibid at 1145.

perceived the role of the judge as being, 'to construct the few relevant words in the regulations and in the . . . notice, and to decide whether in their ordinary significance the . . . words which were in fact used do mean substantially the same as the . . . words which should have been used. If they do not, then the notice . . . is bad . . .'[99] As such the methodology of Stephenson LJ adds little to the general approach to construction. It reiterates that different wordings from those prescribed will be allowed, provided they communicate substantially the same meanings. This does not, however, cover the situations where the details are not provided anywhere within the notice or where the information is misstated.

Omissions and Mistakes

As regards either an omission to include prescribed information or a positive mistake on the face of the notice, the emphasis upon construction is different. It is no longer a matter of divining a meaning from specific words, but rather it involves the evaluation of the notice as a whole. In this context, there is a distinction between the requirements as imposed by the enabling Act and those imposed by delegated legislation. As regards the statutory requirements, section 25 unequivocally states that if such information is not provided accurately the notice is invalid. In relation to the Regulations, the phrase 'substantially to the like effect' offers some flexibility, but this of course cannot dilute the statutory provisions. Any purported modification of the statutory provisions by secondary legislation would simply be *ultra vires*.[100] Unfortunately, this is a distinction which, on occasion, even the Court of Appeal has failed to draw.[101] The liberality, as promoted in *Barclays Bank v Ascott*, invites the court to determine whether the real substance of the information is communicated to the tenant. **4.27**

The key issues are whether the notice provides the tenant with enough information to proceed (that is, serve a counter notice and apply for a renewal) and whether it clearly declares the landlord's intentions.[102] As Aldous LJ explained in *Sabella Ltd v Montgomery*: **4.28**

[T]he decision as to whether the two are substantially to like effect will depend upon the importance of the differences rather than their number or amount . . . It follows that a difference can only be disregarded when the information given as to the particular recipient's rights and obligations under the Act is in substance as effective as that set out in the form. Matter that is irrelevant to the recipient's rights and

---

[99] [1975] 1 WLR 177 at 182; see also *Snook v Schofield* [1975] 1 EGLR 69. Both cases dealt with a notice which followed an out-of-date prescription.

[100] See, for example, *Price v West London Investment Building Society Ltd* [1964] 2 All ER 318.

[101] See *Gudka v Patel*, n 94 above; *Bridgers & Hamptons Residential v Stanford*, n 94 above.

[102] A heavy reliance upon Barry J's lead was demonstrated in *Tegerdine v Brooks* (1977) 36 P & CR 261 where a notice which omitted certain marginal notes (as prescribed by the Regulations) remained valid on the basis that the omitted information was, on the facts, either irrelevant or obvious to the tenant. As the tenant's knowledge would not have been enhanced, the notes were not part of the substance of the notice.

obligations may be omitted as in such a case the notice has given the recipient information substantially to like effect as that in the form.[103]

Not surprisingly, there have been a number of occasions where the courts have felt able to overlook minor deviations in form and content. Accordingly, in *Falcon Pipes Ltd v Stanhope Gate Property*, the failure to insert the date that the notice was signed did not prove fatal.[104] Similarly, in *Bond v Graham* a misstatement as to the rateable value of the premises was condoned[105] and in *Morris v Patel* the use of an outdated prescribed form, which did not contain the same degree of detail as the up-dated version of the notice, was upheld.[106]

Prejudice and the Hypothetical Tenant

4.29   Although the *Sun Alliance* case concluded that, if the notice is bad, it cannot be saved simply because the particular tenant is not misled, prejudice (or the lack of it) does assume some relevance. It asserts importance, for example, when assessing the actual degree of similarity between the notice served and that which technically should have been served. As Neill LJ put it in *Gudka v Patel*, 'The question is: is the tenant being misled in any way or prejudiced by the omission of the particular words . . .'[107] From this perspective 'prejudice' closely links in with the notion of 'materiality' as expressed in *Tegerdine v Brooks*. In deciding whether the substance of the information is communicated by the notice, however, the court must ignore the subjective knowledge of the tenant. As Nourse LJ emphasised in *Pearson v Alyo*, 'the validity of a section 25 notice is to be judged, and judged objectively, at the date at which it is given. The question is not whether the inaccuracy actually prejudices the particular person to whom the notice is given, but whether it is capable of prejudicing a reasonable tenant in the position of that person.'[108] Accordingly, if the information is omitted or misstated, the court must decide whether that information is relevant and must be imparted to that tenant. As Nicholls LJ concluded in *Morrow v Nadeem*, 'a form made out in such a way as not to give the real substance of the information required is not a form substantially to

---

[103] (1999) 77 P & CR 431 at 434. This approach is, moreover, consistent with the wording of section 66.

[104] (1967) 204 EG 1243. cf *Panayi & Pyrkos v Roberts* (1993) 25 HLR 421, a notice (served under the Housing Act 1988) with an incorrect date was held not to be substantially to the same effect as a notice with the correct date. The mistake was not obvious.

[105] (1975) 236 EG 536. See also *BRB v AJA Smith Transport Ltd*, n 73 above, where, although the notice misstated the rateable value limits of the court's jurisdiction, the notice was 'substantially to the like effect' as that prescribed and upheld.

[106] (1987) 281 EG 419.

[107] N 94 above.

[108] N 13 above at 60. This echoes somewhat the test expounded by Goulding J in *Carradine Properties Ltd v Aslam* [1976] 1 WLR 442 at 444: 'Is the notice quite clear to a reasonable tenant? Is it plain that he cannot be misled by it?' There the notice contained the wrong year for termination, but was still valid; see also *Germax Securities Ltd v Spiegal*, n 23 above.

the like effect as the statutory form of notice'.[109] The fact that the consequences may be negligible to the particular tenant is irrelevant.

The authorities are consistent in that a material defect is one which prejudices or **4.30**
misleads the hypothetical tenant and that, subject to waiver or estoppel, a notice which embodies such a defect is bad and cannot be validated. In the *Morrow* case, for example, the notice failed to identify the landlord accurately and, as this would have misled a reasonable tenant, the misstatement could not be overlooked.[110] In *TS Investments Ltd v Langdon*, the Court of Appeal held a notice to be invalid because it omitted both a vital warning to the tenant about acting expeditiously and the landlord's name and address as well as not fully describing the premises.[111] An omission of part of the demised premises from the scope of the notice will normally be fatal,[112] but this rule gives way if it is clear to the reasonable tenant that the landlord is intending to terminate the whole of the tenancy.[113] Similarly, in *Pearson v Alyo* a notice which provided the name of only one of two joint landlords was void and of no effect. By way of contrast, in *Bridgers v Stanford* it was the tenant's name which was misstated (that is, the notice was addressed not to the tenant, but to a company carrying on the tenant's business). As this would not mislead the hypothetical tenant it did not taint the validity of the notice. In a like vein, the misstatement of the demised premises as, for example, '12 Sussex Gardens' instead of '92 Sussex Gardens' should not invalidate the landlord's notice.[114]

Sabella v Montgomery

In *Sabella v Montgomery*, the tenant was faced with a section 25 notice riddled **4.31**
with omissions from the prescribed form. The notice did not contain an 'act quick' warning, failed to reproduce a number of the notes,[115] and omitted to describe all the grounds of opposition upon which the landlord initially sought to

---

[109] N 75 above at 243.

[110] cf a minor misdescription of the landlord's name which will not nullify the effect of the notice: *M&P Enterprises (London) Ltd v Norfolk Square Hotels Ltd*, n 11 above. There the notice identified the landlord as 'Norfolk Square No 2 Ltd' whereas the correct name was 'Norfolk Square Hotels No 2 Ltd'.

[111] (1987) February 13 CA.

[112] This is because of the rule that the notice must refer to the entire holding; *Kaiser Engineers & Contractors Inc v ER Squibb & Sons Ltd* (1971) 218 EG 1731; *Herongrove Ltd v Wates City of London Properties Plc*, n 23 above.

[113] *Safeway Food Stores Ltd v Morris* [1980] 1 EGLR 59 where the notice was valid notwithstanding that it omitted reference to a disused garage and small strip of land to the rear of the premises. It was not confined to the supermarket building alone. Walton J admitted that a different conclusion might have been drawn if the garage had retained some independent use.

[114] See *M&P Enterprises (London) Ltd v Norfolk Square Hotels Ltd*, n 11 above (there it was the tenant's section 26 notice which made this typographical error and still was upheld).

[115] Relating to compensation for loss of renewal rights, disturbance payments on compulsory purchase by a local authority, negotiating a renewal, challenging the validity of the notice, and the explanatory booklet.

rely.[116] It was held that the omission of the 'act quick' notice was fatal because of the vital nature of this warning to the tenant. As Otton LJ commented, 'He may or may not have or have had legal advice in the past from a solicitor. It is conceivable that he might well not have access to legal advice. In any event, he will be bewildered or overawed by receiving such a notice. If he does not take appropriate and timeous action he may lose his right either to a new tenancy or to compensation.'[117] As to the omission to provide details of all the grounds of opposition upon which the landlord sought originally to rely, this absence of information was also regarded as being of substance. The fact that the landlord no longer wished to rely upon the omitted ground offered no excuse. As the tenant had not been informed of this change of position, the omitted information remained material to the notice.

4.32   Although the appellate court did not consider the issue, the logical consequence of this approach is that the failure to refer to compensation for disturbance must also be of invalidating effect. As the tenant was unaware that the landlord no longer sought to rely upon ground (f), equally the tenant could not know that compensation would cease to be available. In relation to the absence of the other notes, the Court of Appeal was unhelpful. It is likely, however, that the lack of reference to compulsory purchase would be condoned as irrelevant on the facts. Similarly, the failure to allude to the explanatory booklet should be overlooked where the notice contains an 'act quick' warning and the direction to seek immediate legal advice. The validity of the notice should be adjudged on the direct and internal guidance which it contains and not turn upon the presence or otherwise of a bibliographical reference to an external source. The omissions relating to the negotiation of a new tenancy and the challenging of the validity of the notice served must, however, be fatal. These notes, respectively, speak of the tenant seeking to negotiate (and not of the landlord's willingness) and alert the tenant to the possibility that the immediate landlord may not be the competent landlord for renewal purposes. Both notes, therefore, convey potentially important information to the tenant.

Positive Counter Notices

4.33   As regards the conditions imposed expressly by section 25, there is no scope for the notice to be saved by allusion to the hypothetical tenant or by a liberal construction of the document. Rather the court must rely upon skills of statutory interpretation, distil the intention of Parliament and apply that intention to the facts. As section 25 provides that if the legislative requirements are not satisfied the notice is invalid, there appears no scope for disregarding this effect. The notice

---

[116] The landlord stated the intention to rely on grounds (b) rent arrears; and (f) demolition and reconstruction. Only ground (b) was described in the notice.

[117] N 103 above at 438.

must be bad. The courts have, however, experienced a particular unease with the requirement, contained in section 25(5), that the notice must require the tenant to serve a counter notice indicating whether the property will be willingly given up. Although it is clear that an omission to require the tenant to serve a negative counter notice will render the notice invalid,[118] the courts have reached the alternative conclusion where there is a failure to require a positive counter notice (that is, one expressing a willingness to quit). This result has been achieved by the adoption of a purposive approach to statutory interpretation which, as explained by Lord Diplock in *Kammins Ballrooms Co Ltd v Zenith Investments (Torquay) Ltd,* 'can be justified only on the assumption that the draftsman of the Act omitted to state in any words he used . . . an exception to the absolute prohibition to which Parliament must have intended it to be subject'.[119] Lord Diplock advocated an intelligent interpretation of the statutory scheme as a whole and the application of Parliament's overall purpose to the problem in hand.

While this broad-brush approach is an attractive mechanism where there is an **4.34** inelegance of language or absurdity, where the Parliamentary language is clear and emphatic the use of a purposive approach is contentious. As Chadwick LJ acknowledged in *Ropaigealach v Barclays Bank Plc,* 'An English judge is not to indulge in judicial legislation. Before he can imply words into an Act, the statutory intention must be plain and the insertion not too big, or too much at variance with the language in fact used by the legislature.'[120] In section 25(5), the Parliamentary intention and language could not have been clearer: the notice is to be invalid for the failure to serve a positive counter notice. The disregard of an unequivocal dictate, on the basis that the words do not reflect the true Parliamentary intention, is palatable only if supported by specific evidence derived from Hansard. If not, and as is the case with section 25(5), the danger lies in divining a phantom intention so as to validate a departure from the text of a statute.

Disregarding Section 25(5)

There are two notable instances where, as regards the requirement to serve a **4.35** counter notice expressing the willingness to surrender possession, the courts have pushed the purposive approach to its limits. In *Bridgers & Hamptons Residential v Stanford,* the Court of Appeal was faced with a termination notice that did not

---

[118]   *Bridgers & Hamptons Residential v Stanford,* n 94 above.
[119]   Above at 882. This case directly concerned the issue of whether the time-limits, imposed by section 29, within which the tenant must make an application to court could be waived. By way of *obiter,* some reference was made to section 25(5).
[120]   [1999] 4 All ER 235. As admitted in P Devlin *The Judge* (1981) at 14, ' [I]n the end the words must be taken to mean what they say and not what their interpreter would like them to say: the statute is the master and not the servant of the judgment.' See also Lord Greene MR in *Re a Debtor* [1948] 2 All ER 533 at 536.

require the tenant to serve a positive counter notice. On a literal interpretation of the Act, the court accepted that the notice would be invalid due to this omission. Nevertheless, the purposive route was followed and the court could see no purpose at all in requiring the tenant to serve a positive notice.[121] The service of such a counter notice was regarded as being of no benefit to the tenant and only instilled certainty into the proceedings to the advantage of the landlord.[122] Consequently, Lloyd LJ concluded that Parliament could not have intended that the procedural step of requiring a positive counter notice be taken as a condition of the validity of the landlord's section 25 notice.[123] In circumstances almost identical to those in the *Bridgers* case, the High Court in *Baglarbasi v Deedmethod Ltd* similarly extolled the virtues of a purposive approach to section 25(5).[124] Baker J was convinced of the futility of the positive counter notice and, as it conferred no apparent benefit on the tenant and little on the landlord, felt that he could depart from (that is, totally ignore) the language of the statutory provision. This does not, however, address the somewhat obvious issues of why the legislature included the requirement of a positive counter notice in the first place and why the provision was not removed by the Law of Property Act 1969. It also discounts the trouble taken in 1989 to amend the Notice Regulations specifically to accommodate the reference to a section 25(5) counter notice.

4.36 Baker J drew support from the wording of section 25(6), which requires the notice to declare (and to state the grounds of) any opposition to renewal, but does not require the landlord to specify that there is no opposition. He concluded: 'There is no "whether or not" in subsection (6), but that is a case where "whether or not" would seem to have been appropriate and certainly the prescribed form proceeds on that basis. Thus it seems to me that one should not put too much weight on the presence of "or not" after "whether" in subsection (5)'.[125] This analogy is, however, somewhat unconvincing in that, regardless of opposition or the absence of it, the tenant must respond by a negative counter notice and an application to the court in order to preserve the right to renew. Consequently, and as it does not affect the actions of the tenant, Parliament may be taken to have concluded that information as to non-opposition was better conveyed by the Notice Regulations. The invention of a significance from the difference of wording in the two subsections

---

[121] cf the negative counter notice which links in directly with the renewal provisions.

[122] It discloses the tenant's stance before the termination of the current lease. As a positive counter notice cannot be withdrawn, the only foreseeable consequence of its service is one prejudicial to the tenant: *Re 14 Grafton St* [1971] 2 All ER 1.

[123] This view was shared also by Ralph Gibson LJ. Both relied heavily upon *Lock v Pearce* [1983] 2 Ch 271 where, as regards a forfeiture notice, the omission to ask for compensation, which the landlord was in any event not seeking, did not invalidate the notice under section 14(1) of the Conveyancing Act 1881. Section 25(5) of the 1954 Act is, however, of a different nature and has nothing to do with the landlord 'asking' and is focused upon the 'telling'.

[124] (1991) 29 EG 137.

[125] ibid at 142.

is simply unhelpful. In both the *Bridgers* case and the *Deedmethod* case, the conclusion that the actual service of a positive counter notice confers no advantage on the tenant proved crucial. Superficially, this conclusion appears to be correctly drawn, but it should not be overlooked that the emphasis within section 25 is not to impose a requirement on the tenant to serve a counter notice, rather it is that the landlord inform the tenant that such a notice can be served. Hence, it is the information itself, and not what the tenant does with it, which is the concern of section 25. Accordingly, it could be argued that the tenant benefits from the notification because it makes apparent that there is no obligation to take a new lease. This fundamental information is, otherwise, only to be indirectly culled from other parts of the notice.

In addition, while both cases pay homage to Lord Diplock's purposive approach **4.37** they fail to acknowledge that the issues before the House of Lords in the *Kammins Ballrooms* case were very different from those invoked by section 25(5). The House had been concerned with the issue of whether procedural time-limits could be waived by one of the parties.[126] As demonstrated by the majority, waiver was permissible without Lord Diplock's broad-sword approach to statutory interpretation.[127] In any event, as the tenant only has one chance to respond, any major doubt as to validity of the landlord's notice should surely, as a general rule, be resolved in the tenant's favour. It cannot be viewed as unreasonable, particularly as the landlord has a second chance to serve an effective notice, to expect the landlord to ensure that the notice satisfies the requirements as set out in both the Act and the Regulations.

F. Tenant's Counter Notice

Where the tenant seeks a new tenancy, the tenant must respond to the section 25 **4.38** notice by serving a counter notice on the landlord which clearly indicates the unwillingness to give up possession on the date stipulated by the landlord.[128] This is so even if the landlord has indicated that there will be no opposition to a renewal.[129] Except as regards the special provisions relating to partnerships contained in section 41A, where there is a joint tenancy all the trustees must join in the service of the counter notice or, at the least, authorise one or more of their

---

[126] Waiver here referred to the ability of one party to choose not to rely on the non-compliance of the other party with the requirement. cf the scenario in both the *Bridgers* and *Deedmethod* cases where the non-compliance was not by the other party, but by the party seeking to set up the waiver.

[127] Lords Reid and Pearson felt that there was nothing in the Act to prevent the parties from agreeing not to insist on a time-limit and, it followed, that one of them could waive the right to insist on such limits.

[128] Section 29(2).

[129] *JT Development Ltd v Quinn*, n 78 above.

number to act on their behalf.[130] Similarly, in relation to a charitable trust, one trustee may be given the authority to serve a counter notice and make an application for renewal.[131] There is no need, however, for the counter notice to expressly state that the server is acting in this capacity; it is sufficient that it indicates that it was served on behalf of all the trustees. It is advisable, however, that the document makes the position crystal clear. As Simon Brown LJ acknowledged:

> Provided only and always that the counter notice, properly construed, is recognisable as a statement on behalf of all four trustees jointly that they are unwilling to give up possession, that would represent a sufficient compliance with the requirements of the statute. There is nothing in the 1954 Act which specifies precisely how the tenant should give the section 29 notice. On ordinary principles, therefore, the document must be construed (in context) to see whether the tenants were indeed indicating their joint unwillingness to give up possession.[132]

4.39 The counter notice must be served within two months of the service of the section 25 notice[133] and the tenant must, moreover, apply to the court within two and four months of the service of the landlord's termination notice.[134] Subject to estoppel and waiver, these time-limits are strict.[135] Apart from it being in writing, there is no prescribed form for the counter notice. Provided that the intention of the tenant is manifest, it is even possible to discern a counter notice from written negotiations for a new lease which implicitly make clear that the tenant has no intention of giving up possession.[136] Although an oral communication will not suffice, a letter asking for the extension of the termination date will, seemingly, operate as a counter notice.[137] If the tenant states in the counter notice that possession will be given up, then that is an irrevocable election.[138] The counter notice

---

[130] Where necessary, the court enjoys the discretion to order a joint tenant to join in: *Harris v Black* (1983) 46 P & CR 266. A trustee who does not co-operate could also be liable for breach of duty.

[131] *Mayor & Burgesses of Hackney LBC v Hackney African Organisation*, n 35 above.

[132] ibid. In upholding the validity of the notice, he added some words of caution: 'The context will not generally favour the tenant to the extent that it does here.'

[133] *Chiswell v Griffon Land & Estates Ltd* [1975] 1 WLR 1181 where a counter notice posted within the time-limit and never delivered was insufficient notification and the tenant lost the right to apply for a renewal.

[134] Section 29(3). Although the tenant has served a timely counter notice, a failure to make an application within this time-frame is fatal to the tenant's claim: *Polyviou v Seeley* [1979] 3 All ER 853; *Newman v Belfield* (1991) May 17 (CA).

[135] *Kammins (Ballrooms) Co Ltd v Zenith Investments (Torquay) Ltd*, n 70 above.

[136] *Lewington v Trustees of the Society for the Protection of Ancient Buildings* (1983) 45 P & CR 336. cf *Taylor v Michel* [1960] CLY 1739 where a solicitor's letter stating that the tenant would like to negotiate terms and to settle the matter quickly was equivocal and did not make clear the tenant's refusal to give up possession.

[137] *Smale v Meakers* [1957] CLY 1940. cf a letter making an offer to purchase the freehold reversion which is consistent with the tenant's wishing to retain possession only as freeholder: *Mehmet v Dawson* [1984] 1 EGLR 74. There Eveleigh LJ stressed that each case turns upon its own facts.

[138] *Re 14 Grafton St*, n 122 above; *De Havilland (Antiques) Ltd v Centrovincial Estates (Mayfair) Ltd* [1971] Ch 935.

cannot be withdrawn. In practice, however, a negative counter notice is served as a matter of routine and is no real guide to the tenant's intentions. As made clear in the Law Commission's Report:

> They lose nothing in doing so: the period in which they must apply to the court is not affected and there is no sanction or penalty if they later change their mind and vacate. Indeed, it must be borne in mind that a tenant who seeks to renew but later decides to give up possession can withdraw his renewal application, and even after an order for renewal he has 14 days in which to apply that the order be revoked.[139]

Reform

In its Working Paper, the Law Commission had suggested that the present require-   **4.40**
ments for the service of a tenant's counter notice be changed. It favoured a new procedure under which the tenant would serve a counter notice only when the desire was to terminate the lease and not to apply for a renewal.[140] Hence, the tenant would not need to serve a counter notice as a prerequisite to making an application for a new lease. This approach was adopted in the subsequent Report and the recommendation which ensued was that the inconclusive negative counter notice be abolished.[141] While the proposed amendment to section 25 will provide further details of the landlord's intentions, the lessor may still remain ignorant of the tenant's true designs. Admittedly, abolishing the tenant's negative counter notice will remove what is now a superfluous procedural hurdle, but if retained and remodelled to include suggested terms of the new lease, the tenant's mind would become more focused and the landlord more informed.[142] As the landlord is expected to work out a strategy of opposition in the counter notice served in response to the tenant's section 26 request for a new lease, it is not unrealistic for the tenant to firm up renewal terms within the same period. Although the Law Commission Report believes in general that issues between the parties should be identified at an early stage,[143] these particular reforms are not on the current agenda.

G. General Rules of Service

The provisions of section 23 of the Landlord and Tenant Act 1927 apply to the   **4.41**
service of all notices under the 1954 Act.[144] Section 23(1) requires that any notice,

---

[139] N 31 above at para 2.3.8.
[140] N 28 above at para 3.3.7.
[141] N 31 above at para 2.39. In Northern Ireland, and pursuant to article 6, there is no longer any need for the tenant to serve any counter notice.
[142] Similarly, there is no reason why the landlord's counter notice to a section 26 request could not, if the application is unopposed, also set out the proposals for renewal.
[143] N 31 above at para 2.36.
[144] Section 66(4). Note that the more extensive service provisions contained in section 196 of the Law of Property Act 1925 do not apply here.

request, demand or other instrument must be in writing and stipulates that service may occur in one of a number of ways. The purpose of this specification is to ensure that the notice is duly served and to provide actual or deemed proof of service. Although not exhaustive or mandatory, the prescribed modes of service exist, therefore, to assist the serving party and to simplify matters for the court.[145] Notwithstanding that the specified methods of service are not followed, actual receipt of the notice will always constitute good service.[146] Unspecified methods would include, for example, ordinary post, document exchange and fax.[147] In *Chiswell v Griffon Land & Estates Ltd*, Megaw LJ drew the following distinction between the authorised methods of service and those not specified in section 23:

> If any of those methods are adopted, they being the primary methods laid down, and in the event of dispute, it is proved that one of those methods has been adopted, then sufficient service is proved. Thus if it is proved, in the event of dispute, that a notice was sent by recorded delivery, it does not matter that that recorded delivery letter may not have been received by the intended recipient. It does not matter, even if it were to be clearly established that it had gone astray in the post . . . But . . . if the person who gives the notice sees fit not to use one of those primary methods, but to send the notice through the post, not registered and not by recorded delivery, that will nevertheless be good notice, if in fact the letter is received by the person to whom the notice has been given. But a person who chooses to use that method instead of one of the primary methods is taking the risk that, if the letter is indeed lost in the post, notice will not have been given.[148]

Can a Notice be Withdrawn Pre-Service?

4.42 In *Kinch v Bullard*, a notice to sever a joint tenancy, which was delivered by first class post to the joint home of the sender and the recipient, was destroyed by the sender before it was seen by the addressee. The issue before the High Court was whether valid service had occurred and whether this was affected by the sender's change of mind. Neuberger J stated the general rule as being: 'Once the sender has served the requisite notice, the deed is done and cannot be undone . . . Once the procedure has been set in train, and the relevant notice has been served, it is not

---

[145] *Tennant v London County Council*, n 14 above; *Galinski v McHugh* (1989) 21 HLR 47. In *Kinch v Bullard* [1998] 4 All ER 650, it was recognised that if a third party picks up the notice (and, say, files it away or destroys it) good policy reasons dictate that the risk is that of the addressee and not the sender. As will be considered, the position is much different, however, if it is the sender who retrieves the notice and prevents actual receipt.

[146] *Stylo Shoes Ltd v Prices Tailors Ltd*, n 88 above.

[147] As to the scope for service by fax, e-mail and document exchange see the supplemental Practice Direction 6 of the Civil Procedure Rules 1998. As regards electronic service, the prior agreement of the other party is necessary and a hard copy should be forwarded at a later date. In *Hastie & Jenkerson v McMahon* [1991] 1 All ER 255 the Court of Appeal accepted that a fax transmission could constitute good service provided that the document received was intact and legible. Service occurs when the transmission is complete.

[148] N 133 above at 1188, 1189. There a counter notice put in the normal post was not received by the landlord's solicitors and it was held that, on a balance of probabilities, it had gone astray.

open to the giver of the notice to withdraw the notice . . .'[149] By way of *obiter*, however, Neuberger J outlined two possible qualifications to this general rule. First, that the position would be different if, before the notice was given, the sender had informed the addressee that the notice was withdrawn. His view was that, while it is still in the post and until it is given, the notice can be withdrawn provided that withdrawal is communicated to the addressee before it is served. Second, that the sender could not destroy the notice before it is seen by the addressee and later argue that valid service had occurred. The statutory presumption of service could not be relied on by the sender of a notice as an engine of fraud. The very purpose of serving a notice is to convey information, with legal consequences, on the addressee: it cannot be right that the sender of a notice can take positive steps to ensure that the notice does not come to the attention of the addressee, after it has been statutorily deemed to have been served, and then fall back on the Statute to allege that service has none the less been effected.[150]

The Primary Methods of Service

Actual Delivery

The physical delivery of the notice to the recipient is clearly the most effective and **4.43** certain means of service. In the case of a local or public authority or statutory or public utility, service can be made on its secretary or other proper officer. Section 23(1) also authorises service on the landlord's duly authorised agent.[151] In *Railtrack Plc v Gojra*, for example, where the section 26 request was not addressed to the new landlord, but instead to the former landlord, the latter was on the facts held to be acting as the agent of the successor.[152] There is, however, no statutory provision for service on the tenant's agent.[153] Nevertheless, the normal rules of agency apply and, hence, the tenant's solicitor or other agent with actual or ostensible authority will be able to accept service.[154]

Service at Last Known Place of Abode

Leaving the notice at the party's last known place of abode in England and Wales **4.44** will suffice for effective service. The term 'leaving' is interpreted as meaning that

---

[149] N 145 above at 655. He explained at 656 that, if it were otherwise, 'The addressee would not be able to rely confidently upon a notice after it had been received, because he might subsequently be faced with the argument that the sender had changed his mind after sending it and before its receipt . . . [I]t is scarcely realistic to think that the legislature intended that the court could be required to enquire into the state of mind of the sender of the notice in order to decide whether the notice was valid.'

[150] ibid at 658.

[151] See *Sector Properties Ltd v Meah* (1974) 229 EG 1097.

[152] (1998) 8 EG 158.

[153] cf the Business Tenancies (Northern Ireland) Order 1996 which expressly caters for service on and by the agent of either party: article 41.

[154] *Galinski v McHugh*, n 145 above; *Italica Holdings SA v Bayadea* (1985) 273 EG 888.

the document must be deposited in such a place as is reasonable for it to be drawn to the attention of the intended recipient. As Russell LJ commented in *Lord Newborough v Jones*, '[the notice] must be left there in the proper way, that is to say, in a manner which a reasonable person, minded to bring the document to the attention of the person to whom the notice is addressed, would adopt'.[155] Hence, if the premises are shared by a number of firms, and there is only one central letter box, posting through that communal box will suffice.[156] The expression 'last known' caters for the situation where one party has moved address and this fact and/or the new address is not known to the other party. It does not mean the address last notified as being the appropriate address for service.[157] In *Kinch v Bullard*, a notice was 'left' at the husband's last place of abode as soon as it was delivered by post regardless that the husband never actually received it.[158] There Neuberger J explained the simple and clear rule:

> [S]ervice of a notice at the last known place of abode . . . of the addressee is good service, and there is no suggestion that it matters how that service is effected, that is, whether it is by the giver of the notice, his agent, courier service, ordinary post, recorded delivery, or registered post or some other method. Provided that it can be established that, irrespective of the identity of the person who delivered the notice to a particular address, it was delivered to that address, then the notice has been validly served at that address, provided that it is the addressee's last known abode or place of business.[159]

Not surprisingly, for the purposes of the business tenancy legislation, the term 'abode' includes place of business as well as home address.[160] Accordingly, service at the registered office of a company would be regarded as being its place of abode.[161] As regards a local authority, service may occur at an office designated for receiving such notices.[162] In relation to the other bodies, service may be at their principal office. As demonstrated in *Stylo Shoes Ltd v Prices Tailors Ltd*,[163] however, delivery is the overriding issue. There the document was addressed to the former registered office of a company, but was redirected by the post office to the new reg-

---

[155] [1975] Ch 90 at 94. There the notice was slid under the recipient's door, but unfortunately became hidden under the floor covering. It was held to be valid service.

[156] *Henry Smith's Charity Trustees v Kynakou* [1989] 2 EGLR 110.

[157] *Price v West London Investment Building Society*, n 100 above.

[158] N 145 above. This should be contrasted with *Rostran v Michael Nairn & Co Ltd*, n 34 above, where a section 25 notice was sent by letter to the matrimonial home of the joint tenants, but was addressed only to the husband. This was held to be insufficient for service to occur on the wife.

[159] ibid at 654. A notice sent to the addressee's home is valid service even though the sender knows that the addressee is in prison at the time: *Van Haarlam v Kasner* [1992] 2 EGLR 59. See also *Commercial Union Life Assurance Co Ltd v Monstafa* [1999] 24 EG 155. The reasoning is that it is up to the absent addressee to make arrangements for mail to be forwarded on.

[160] *Robertson v Banham & Co* [1997] 1 All ER 79; *Morecambe & Heysham Corporation v Warwick* (1958) 9 P & CR 307; *Italica Holdings SA v Bayadea*, n 154 above.

[161] *National Westminster Bank v Betchworth Investments* (1975) 234 EG 675.

[162] Section 231(1) Local Government Act 1972.

[163] N 88 above.

istered office. The service was complete even though the envelope had been addressed incorrectly.

Registered or Recorded Mail

The use of the ordinary post is not authorised by the 1954 Act.[164] Nevertheless, as **4.45** both registered and recorded post are permitted, the presumptions as to service contained in section 7 of the Interpretation Act 1978 may have some resonance.[165] Section 7 contains two rules of evidence; first, the non-rebuttable presumption that service is effected by properly addressing, pre-paying and posting a letter containing the document. Although there is no need for the sender to provide a certificate of posting, in cases of dispute the court may require proof that the correct postage fee was paid.[166] The second rule of evidence is the rebuttable presumption that the letter has been delivered in the ordinary course of the post. This presumption is particularly relevant where the notice has to be served within strict time-limits because it leaves it open for the recipient to show that a notice was served too late. Although both presumptions assume obvious importance as regards authorised service by the conventional post, their practical relevance in relation to registered and recorded delivery should not be overstated. Nevertheless, it is to be admitted that the potential interaction between section 26 and section 7 is somewhat opaque.

It is to be appreciated that for these types of special post, service is complete when the letter is taken and signed for.[167] It is the signed receipt which proves that service has occurred. In this context, the decision in *R v County of London Quarter Session Appeal Committee, ex parte Rossi* becomes readily understandable.[168] There a registered letter was returned marked 'Undelivered. No response' and this amounted to clear evidence that service was incomplete. Normally, as regards registered and recorded mail there will be documentary proof of service and this will also be determinative of exactly when service has taken place. The existence of the second presumption, however, enables the recipient to challenge the timing of service. This could occur, for example, where the delivery is signed for by someone other than the addressee or an agent.[169] The onus of rebutting the presumption,

---

[164] Consequently, section 26 of the Interpretation Act 1978 has no application where service occurs by conventional post; cf section 725(1), Companies Act 1985 which authorises service on a limited company to occur by sending the notice to the company's registered office by ordinary post.

[165] See James J in *Moody v Godstone RDC* [1966] 2 All ER 696; and Megaw LJ in *Chiswell v Griffon Land & Estates Ltd*, n 133 above.

[166] *Mayor & Burgesses of the London Borough of Lewisham v Gopee* (1999) March 12 CA.

[167] *Railtrack Plc v Gojra*, n 152 above. Hence, there needs to be an available recipient to sign for the letter: *Stephenson & Sons v Orca Properties Ltd* [1989] 2 EGLR 129.

[168] [1956] 1 QB 682; see also *Hewitt v Leicester Corporation* [1969] 1 WLR 855. cf the view of Sedley J in *Commercial Union Life Assurance Co Ltd v Monstafa*, above, where, even though the notice was returned, service had taken place.

[169] See *Price v West London Investment Building Society*, n 100, above, where the registered letter was signed for by the tenant's cleaner and, on becoming mixed up with other papers, was not

however, appears to be a heavy burden to shoulder. This was illustrated in *Lex Service Plc v Johns* where, in circumstances when a recorded delivery letter was illegibly signed for someone (identity unknown) and asserted not to have been received by the tenant, the addressee failed to rebut the statutory presumption.[170] There was simply no positive evidence that the document had not been received by the recipient. The Court of Appeal added that, even if there was evidence that the document had been received by some other person, it was still necessary to establish that it had not been brought to the addressee's attention.

Partnerships and Joint Tenancies

4.46   Prior to amendment by the Law of Property Act 1969, a difficulty existed concerning a tenancy held by a partnership in circumstances where not all of the partners were active in the business. Previously, it had been necessary that all of the joint tenants joined in the renewal and termination procedures.[171] In order to remedy this situation, modifications to that rule were introduced by section 41A. Subject to certain conditions, this provision allows the tenant(s) who carry on the business to act on behalf of any other partner(s).[172] If any of these conditions are unmet, however, it is still necessary for all joint tenants to join together as regards the service and receipt of statutory notices.[173] The conditions are to be found in section 41A(a)–(d) and, with one exception, refer to the circumstances existing at the end of the contractual term. These conditions are, first, that a tenancy is held jointly by two or more persons. This necessarily entails that where the tenancy is vested in one partner only, the other partners receive no assistance from section 41A. Second, that the property comprised in the tenancy is or includes premises occupied for the purposes of a business. If it does not, the tenancy simply falls outside the catchment of the 1954 Act. Third, that at some time during the subsistence of the current tenancy a business was carried on upon the premises in partnership with all other joint tenants (not just some of them), with or without others, and that the tenancy was held as partnership property. Consequently, if the tenancy is held jointly, but each tenant has always carried out a distinct business, section 41A cannot apply and the landlord's termination notice must be served on all joint tenants.[174] Fourth, that the business is carried on (whether alone or in

---

physically received by the tenant for six days. The date of service was, however, held to be that on which the letter was delivered.

[170]   (1990) 10 EG 67. This was so even though Mr Johns claimed to be the only person authorised to sign for letters and suggested that the letter had been signed for by someone from another business in the premises.

[171]   *Jacobs v Chaudhuri* [1968] 2 QB 470; see generally J Goudie, *Leases and Partnerships* [1971] Conv 17.

[172]   A similar provision applies in Northern Ireland: article 32.

[173]   *Harris v Black*, n 130 above.

[174]   *Booth Investments Ltd v Reynolds*, n 34 above.

partnership with other persons) by one or more of the joint tenants and no part is occupied for a business carried on by the other partners.

Where these conditions are met, the tenants carrying on the business at a given **4.47** time are called 'the business tenants' and it is they who derive benefit from the provision. The remaining partners are termed 'the other joint tenants'.[175] The benefit afforded by section 41A is that key notices and applications may be served on or by the business tenants only. It would seem, moreover, that notices must be served by and on all the business tenants for the provision to be relied upon. It is stated in section 41A(3) that, as regards section 26 requests and section 27 notices, service by the business tenants will be deemed to be service by all the joint tenants, but only when the notice states that it is given by virtue of this provision and sets out the facts showing that it is served by the business tenants. In relation to section 25 notices, section 41A(4) provides that a notice served on the business tenants will automatically be deemed to be service on all the joint tenants. The business tenants may also apply for a new lease under section 24(1), without joining the other joint tenants to the application,[176] and when this occurs it is the business tenants who, at the discretion of the court, may obtain the new lease or will be entitled to compensation in lieu.[177] The new lease may be subject to such conditions (for example, relating to the provision of guarantors and sureties) as the court thinks equitable, having regard to the omission of the other joint tenants from the grant. It is unclear whether this adds anything to the court's general discretion, under section 35, to include new terms in the renewed lease. It does, however, highlight that the interests of the other joint tenants should be safeguarded.[178] As section 41A is a facilitating provision, there is, of course, nothing to stop all the joint tenants making the application and receiving the grant.

---

[175] Section 41A(2). In Northern Ireland, the tenants are called the 'remaining tenants' and the 'departed tenants', respectively: article 32(2).

[176] Section 41A(5). This also provides that the business tenants alone will be liable for the payment of rent and other outgoings under the current tenancy once it is continued under the Act.

[177] Section 41A(6), (7).

[178] It is noteworthy that the Business Tenancies (Northern Ireland) Order 1996 does not expressly mention the ability to attach conditions.

5

TENANT'S RIGHTS

A. Introduction

The right to obtain a new lease, timed to follow on from the termination of the **5.01** contractual or continuation tenancy, can be achieved in several ways. First, there is nothing to prevent the parties from agreeing a new lease without recourse to the statutory machinery. If a written agreement is concluded, the current lease continues until the date set for the commencement of the new tenancy. In the intervening period, it is not a lease to which the provisions of Part II apply and the tenant is precluded from making any application for a new tenancy. Second, in the absence of agreement, the tenant can apply to the court for a new lease following the service of a landlord's section 25 notice and the tenant's subsequent counter notice. Finally, where there is no agreement and a landlord's termination notice has not been served, the tenant may be able to initiate the action for a new tenancy by the service of a section 26 request on the competent landlord or that landlord's authorised agent.[1] As with the landlord's notice, the tenant's request terminates the current lease and activates the jurisdiction of the court to grant a new tenancy. The entitlement to renewal is defeasible only on the grounds specified in section

---

[1] See *Railtrack Plc v Gojra* (1998) 8 EG 158. In Northern Ireland, similar provisions regulating for the tenant's request are to be found in article 7 of the Business Tenancies (Northern Ireland) Order 1996.

30(1) and, if the landlord successfully opposes the tenant's claim, compensation in lieu might be available. This chapter is concerned with the three key rights afforded to the tenant, namely, the rights to engage the renewal provisions, to commence proceedings for a new lease[2] and to obtain compensation for loss of renewal rights.

B. The Section 26 Request

5.02   Although any protected business tenant who has been served with a section 25 notice is entitled (provided a counter notice has been served in response) to apply to the court for a new tenancy, not all tenants can make a statutory request for a new tenancy. Indeed, section 26(1) provides that only those tenants holding under a lease originally granted for either a term of years certain (that is, a fixed term) exceeding one year or a term of years certain (which can be less than one year)[3] and thereafter as a yearly tenancy are entitled to make a request. Periodic tenants are excluded because their terms are not 'certain'.[4] A request served by a tenant who does not comply with these basic requirements is invalid and cannot end the tenancy.[5] It cannot be, in any sense, regarded as a notice to quit. As regards associated companies, therefore, care must be taken to ensure that the correct company serves the request. If not, and in a similar vein to the exercise of a break clause, it should be argued that the company is acting as the agent of the tenant.[6] Not surprisingly, it is a criticism levelled at section 26 that the availability of the right is unduly restricted.

5.03   On three occasions, however, the Law Commission has refused to recommend that the right be extended to periodic tenants. In 1969, the Commission said: 'We can see no merit in this proposal since a periodic tenancy of its nature continues indefinitely until it is terminated. If the landlord serves a notice under section 25 to terminate the tenancy, a weekly or monthly tenant has the same right as other tenants . . . to apply for a new tenancy.'[7] Some twenty years later, the Commission's Working Paper reconsidered the matter and arrived at the same conclusion,

---

   [2] Although the Civil Procedure Rules 1998 have introduced major changes in the civil litigation process, as regards commercial landlord and tenant law much remains the same. The new Rules re-enact a variety of the old Rules of the Supreme Court and the County Court Rules: see Schedules 1 and 2, respectively. For present purposes, it is important to note that those provisions formerly contained in RSC Order 97 and CCR Order 43 are retained with modifications. If the body of the rules conflicts with the schedules, the retained RSC and CCR orders prevail: Practice Direction 7A.

   [3] *Re Land & Premises at Liss* [1971] 3 All ER 380.

   [4] See M Haley, *In Search of Parliamentary Meaning: A Term of Years Uncertain?* (1995) AALR Vol 24, No 2, 236.

   [5] See *Watkins v Emslie* (1982) 261 EG 1192 where the request was served by a periodic tenant.

   [6] See *Dun & Bradstreet Software Services (England) Ltd v Provident Mutual Life Assurance Association* [1998] 2 EGLR 175; *Lemmerbell Ltd v Britannia LAS Direct Ltd* (1998) 48 EG 188.

   [7] *Report on the Landlord and Tenant Act 1954 Part II* (1969) Law Com No 17 at para 53.

declaring that to extend the rights to periodic tenants would lead to a proliferation of applications and be of little benefit to such tenants.[8] Finally, in 1992 the fate of this possible reform was sealed: 'In the absence of pressing reasons for reform, we consider that this aspect of the legislation is best left as it is. The change could open a door unhelpfully to many applications by short-term tenants, and this seems to be a case in which the balance between landlords and tenants struck by the present provisions is generally accepted and should be maintained.'[9] The Law Commission did not expressly consider whether a term *simpliciter* for a year or less than a year should continue to be excluded from the ambit of section 26.[10] As accepted by Goulding J in *Re Land & Premises at Liss*, the present distinction entails that a term of exactly one year is excluded whereas a five-month term followed by a yearly tenancy falls within the catchment of section 26(1).[11] It is to be doubted whether, for example, a term of exactly one year followed by a weekly tenancy would suffice. Although it will entail that the tenancy continues for at least one week beyond a year, the periodic tenancy is not certain and will not satisfy the language of section 26(1).

Section 23(2)

Section 23(2) of the Landlord and Tenant Act 1927 provides that, unless and **5.04** until the tenant is notified that the landlord has ceased to be entitled to rents and profits and provided with the name and address of the new lessor, the tenant is entitled to treat the original landlord as still being the appropriate landlord for the service of notices.[12] As Evans LJ explained in *Railtrack Plc v Gojra*: 'The purpose of section 23(2) . . . is to validate a payment made to the original landlord before the required notice is given and has taken effect.'[13] This provision does not require the tenant to wait until the original landlord has ceased to be entitled to the rent before serving a request for a new tenancy.[14] It is always to be appreciated,

---

[8] *Part II of the Landlord & Tenant Act 1954* (1988) Working Paper No 111 at para 3.2.27.

[9] *Business Tenancies: A Periodic Review of the Landlord and Tenant Act 1954* (1992) Law Com No 208, at para 3.21. An identical approach to periodic tenancies was adopted by the Law Reform Advisory Committee for Northern Ireland, *Business Tenancies* (1994) Report No 1 at para 4.5.8.

[10] In contrast, the Business Tenancies (Northern Ireland) Order 1996 has widened the class of tenant able to serve a request. There a tenant can serve a request provided that the tenant holds under a lease granted either for a term certain exceeding 9 months; for a term certain not exceeding 9 months provided that the tenant (including a predecessor in business) has occupied the premises for over 18 months; or for a term granted to exceed 1 year and thereafter to continue from year to year: article 7(1)(a)–(d)

[11] N 3 above at 383.

[12] See *Sector Properties Ltd v Meah* (1974) 229 EG 1097 where the Court of Appeal held that merely providing the name and address of the new landlord's agents will not suffice. The section requires the name and address of the actual landlord.

[13] N 1 above at 160.

[14] ibid. Any contrary conclusion would, as Evans LJ acknowledged at 160, 'give rise to great difficulties in practice, where the change of landlord occurs at about the same time as the rent becomes due'.

however, that a landlord can still be in receipt of rents and profits and yet not be the competent landlord for renewal purposes. The provision can do nothing to assist a tenant who fails to serve a renewal notice on the correct competent landlord. Such is illustrated by *Railtrack Plc v Gojra*, where the tenant sent a request for a new tenancy by ordinary post on 31 March which was received on 6 April. On 1 April, however, Railtrack Plc had become the statutory assignee of the reversion from the British Railways Board. The request was addressed to the in-house solicitors of the former landlords. The Court of Appeal acknowledged that, because it was not addressed to the correct landlord, normally the consequence would be that the request was invalidated.[15]

Form & Content

5.05   The section 26 request must be served on the competent landlord by, or on behalf of, the tenant. The request must be in writing and in the form prescribed by the Part II (Notices) Regulations 1983 or in a form substantially to like effect.[16] The Regulations entail that the section 26 notice should contain an 'act quick' warning to the recipient and contain a series of notes relating to the grounds of opposition, compensation for disturbance and the steps and time-limits to be satisfied by the landlord. Reference should be made also to the explanatory booklet published by the Department of the Environment.[17] In addition, the Act itself expressly stipulates that the request must contain certain details and these now fall to be discussed.

Commencement Date

5.06   The request must state the commencement date for the proposed new tenancy which must be at least six months, and no more than twelve months, after the service of the request.[18] On the day before the date specified, section 26(6) provides that the existing tenancy automatically terminates. This is, however, subject to any interim continuance while the decision of the court as to the grant of a new tenancy is pending[19] and any short extension, under section 36(2), following the

---

[15]   This conclusion was averted, however, because of the operation of Sch 8 of the Railways Act 1993 which deemed that, from 1 April, Railtrack was substituted as the relevant landlord for the purposes of the renewal proceedings.

[16]   SI 1983 No 133, as amended by SI 1998 No 1548. Form 8 is the model to be adopted for these purposes. In Northern Ireland, the tenant's request is prescribed in Form 4 of the Business Tenancies (Notices) Regulations (Northern Ireland) 1997. There the actual form must be adopted and there is no leeway catering for a document of similar effect.

[17]   cf Northern Ireland where Form 4 does not contain such general guidance. It merely advises the landlord to seek legal advice quickly and to serve a counter notice within two months.

[18]   Section 26(2). This mirrors the time-limits which regulate the service of the landlord's section 25 notice.

[19]   As will be shown, section 64 provides that, where an application for a renewal has been made to the court, the tenancy will continue for three months following final disposal (which includes withdrawal of the action).

tenant's election not to accept the renewal on the terms decided by the court. A further limitation is that the commencement date cannot be earlier than that on which the current tenancy can be ended by the effluxion of time (if a fixed term) or a tenant's notice to quit (if a periodic tenancy). The rule, of course, is irrelevant when a continuation tenancy has already arisen. Where the contractual term is in existence, however, this rule entails that a fixed-term tenant cannot serve a request until the last year of the lease. Accordingly, the Act does not allow the tenant to terminate the tenancy early so as to obtain a new lease on more favourable terms. In *Garston v Scottish Widows Fund & Life Assurance Society*, for example, the tenant sought to exercise an option to break at the end of the tenth year because the premises were over-rented and to obtain a renewal at a lower rent.[20] A section 26 request was served at the same time as the break notice. The Court of Appeal held that the tenant could not exercise a break clause and then serve a request for a new lease. It would otherwise offend the rule that, as regards a fixed term lease, a request can only be served within twelve months of its contractual term date. A valid notice to break would, moreover, operate as a tenant's notice to quit under section 24(2) and should, on that basis alone, disqualify the tenant from engaging the renewal provisions. As Nourse LJ explained:

> One of the main purposes of Part II of the 1954 Act is to enable business tenants, where there is no good reason for their eviction, to continue in occupation after the expiration of their contractual tenancies. It is not a purpose of the Act to enable a business tenant who has chosen to determine his contractual tenancy to continue in occupation on terms different from those of that tenancy.[21]

Proposed Terms

5.07 By virtue of section 26(3), the tenant's request must also include the proposed terms of the new tenancy requested. A failure to do so will render the request void. These proposals must concern:

(1) the property to be comprised in the new lease (being either the whole or part of the property comprised in the current tenancy). This will normally, but not necessarily, be the tenant's holding, that is, the premises then occupied by the tenant for business purposes. The current holding need not, therefore, be identical to the premises as originally demised;

(2) the rent to be payable under the new lease;

(3) the other terms of the renewal which, most importantly, include duration. This requirement may be satisfied by a statement that, other than as to the parcels and the rent, the renewal should be on the same terms as the original lease.[22]

---

[20] [1998] 3 All ER 596.
[21] ibid at 602.
[22] *Sidney Bolsom Investment Trust Ltd v Karmios & Co (London) Ltd* [1956] 1 QB 529.

Although the court's jurisdiction is limited to the order of a fourteen-year term, the request will not be invalidated by the fact that the tenant proposes a grant of longer duration. The policy of the Act is to encourage negotiation and to facilitate agreement between the parties and, it is to be appreciated, the tenant's proposals may not necessarily be reflected in the actual terms of any new lease agreed or ordered. Similarly, a mistake in this statement of terms will not invalidate the notice. As Denning LJ explained in *Sidney Bolsom Investment Trust Ltd v E Karmios & Co (London) Ltd*:

> Whatever his inmost state of mind, once a tenant has to all outward appearances made a valid request in the prescribed form setting out his proposals, then he cannot thereafter rely on his own mistake to say that it was a nullity or invalid, no matter how important the mistake was. The validity of the request must be judged by the true interpretation of it, without regard to what happened behind the scenes. It is a formal document with specific legal consequences and it must be treated as such.[23]

Waiver and Estoppel

5.08 Although a failure to comply with the time-limits and adhere to the prescribed content prima facie renders the request invalid, the landlord should be careful when dealing with what is thought to be a defective request. As discussed in the preceding chapter in the context of the landlord's section 25 notice, waiver and estoppel may have a curative effect in such circumstances. A defect in the tenant's section 26 request can, for example, be expressly or impliedly waived by the landlord's conduct. In *Bristol Cars Ltd v RKH Hotels Ltd*, for example, neither party noticed an error as to the commencement date specified in the section 26 request.[24] The landlord indicated that it would not oppose the grant of a new lease and applied for an interim rent. Subsequently, the defect in the request was discovered and the landlord then served a termination notice. Following *Kammins Ballrooms Co Ltd v Zenith Investments (Torquay) Ltd*,[25] it was held that a tenant's failure to comply with section 26 could be condoned by the landlord. Both Megaw and Templeman LJJ held that, as the landlord had led the tenant to expect that a new lease would not be opposed and the tenant had detrimentally relied on that assurance, the lessor was estopped from denying the validity of the tenant's request. Bridge LJ, however, treated the case as one of waiver by election; that is, by applying for an interim rent and having a full knowledge of the facts, the landlord had affirmed the tenant's request and waived the defect.

---

[23] ibid at 539. He added: 'If the proposals had ripened into a contract, then the mistake might in some circumstances be a ground for setting the contract aside in equity, but it would not render the contract a nullity from the beginning, nor does it render the request invalid'.

[24] (1979) 251 EG 1279.

[25] [1971] AC 850 where it was held that a failure to comply with the timing requirements of section 29(3) could be waived because they were procedural rules. Note that under the Civil Procedure Rules 1998, the general rule is that procedural time-limits can be waived by the written agreement of the parties: r 2.11.

Similarly, in *JT Developments Ltd v Quinn* statements made in the course of com- **5.09** mercial negotiations gave rise to a proprietary estoppel because they created an expectation in the mind of the tenant that a new lease would be granted on the same terms as a specified tenancy of nearby premises.[26] There the statements made constituted more than an offer to negotiate, and amounted to an assurance that, irrespective of a formal contract, a renewal would be granted.[27] Estoppel was also raised (albeit unsuccessfully) in *Sidney Bolsom Investment Trust Ltd v E Karmios & Co (London) Ltd* where Denning MR acknowledged that a representation about the legal position can give rise to an estoppel. Nevertheless, he made it clear that a number of hurdles had to be overcome by the claimant:

> But, in order to work an estoppel, the representation must be clear and unequivocal, it must be intended to be acted upon, and it must be acted on. When I say it must be 'intended to be acted on', I would add that a man must be taken to intend what a reasonable person would understand him to intend. In short, the representation must be made in such circumstances as to convey an invitation to act on it. It seems to me that the representation in this case conveyed no such invitation.[28]

C. Effect of the Request

A variety of consequences arise from the service of a valid section 26 request. As **5.10** mentioned, the request brings to an end the current lease on the day before the date specified as being the commencement date for the new tenancy. The service of a request entitles the landlord to serve a counter notice stating any opposition to renewal itself and/or the terms proposed by the tenant.[29] The request also enables the tenant to apply to the court, not less than two months and no more than four months following its service.[30] If the tenant fails to make an application to the court within this time-frame, the current tenancy ends immediately on the expiration of the request.[31] Understandably, the tenant then loses the right to a new tenancy and ceases to benefit from the protection of the 1954 Act. This is because the tenant is allowed only to serve one request for a new tenancy and that single request, provided that it is valid (an invalid request is of no effect for these purposes), cannot be abandoned so as to make way for a replacement.[32] As Edmund Davies LJ emphasised in *Stile Hall Properties Ltd v Gooch*:

---

[26] [1991] 2 EGLR 257 (Glidewell LJ dissenting).
[27] cf *Willis v Hoare* (1998) December 3 CA, where the representation was to negotiate and this was too uncertain for there to be an appropriate remedy in equity. As Auld LJ admitted: 'There are parts that sometimes even equity may not reach . . .'.
[28] N 22 above at 540, 541.
[29] Section 26(6).
[30] Section 29(3).
[31] *Smith v Draper* (1990) 60 P & CR 252.
[32] *Polyviou v Seeley* [1979] 3 All ER 853. This rule applies whether or not a different termination date is specified.

The suggestion put forward that it is open to the tenant, without the concurrence of the landlord, to withdraw his request for a new tenancy is one which would cut entirely across the statutory scheme. The Act vests radical rights in the tenant of business premises. It also recognises that the landlord also has certain rights and must be protected against exploitation and against harassment.[33]

The Pre-emptive Strike

5.11 It is standard advice to tenants that the use of the section 26 procedure is, in most cases, inadvisable. Despite the facility of an interim rent, the tenant still may gain by prolonging the existing lease, and paying either the old rent or a subsidised interim sum for as long as possible.[34] In this light, and particularly when the landlord shows no sign of serving a section 25 notice, it is rarely advantageous for the tenant to terminate the existing tenancy.[35] Such a step would normally be appropriate only where the tenant either seeks to gain a greater business stability by securing a new lease or wishes to make a pre-emptive strike. This latter tactic assumes relevance only when the tenant suspects that landlord intends to serve a section 25 notice. The pre-emptive service of a section 26 request will, therefore, maintain the status quo (and associated rental advantages) for longer that might be desired by the landlord. This is possible because the request takes between six and twelve months to terminate the existing lease and, by choosing the longer period, the tenant may gain a half year.[36] Once the request is served, the landlord is prevented from serving a section 25 notice.[37] Accordingly, the consequence of the section 26 request might be viewed as giving the tenant an unwarranted advantage over the landlord. Indeed, the Law Commission Working Paper believed this to be an unfair manipulation of the rules and suggested that they be modified.[38]

Reform?

5.12 The following possibilities for reform were mooted in the Working Paper. First, that it be made obligatory for the tenant's request to have effect as soon after its service as possible. This would be either at the expiry of six months or at the contractual term date whichever is the later. Second, that the exclusivity of the section

---

[33] [1979] 3 All ER 848 at 852.

[34] See *Sector Properties v Meah*, n 12 above.

[35] This approach may change, however, in recessionary times where rental values fall: see D Harris and V King (1992) 20 EG 98; A Langleben and C Newnham (1993) 11 EG 120.

[36] Section 26(2). In doing so, the tenant also delays the payment of an interim rent until the later date: section 24A(2).

[37] Section 26(4). Similarly, the tenant cannot serve a section 27 notice or other notice to quit after the service of a section 26 request (and vice versa). A similar rule applies in Northern Ireland, except that there the tenant can (with the landlord's consent) serve a request after serving a notice to quit: article 7(4).

[38] N 8 above at para 3.2.20; cf *Sun Life Assurance Plc v Racal Tracs Ltd* (1999) December 1 where the technology and construction court held that where the tenant did not want a new tenancy any section 26 request is invalid. This approach is, however, somewhat dubious.

25 and section 26 procedures be ended. This would allow the landlord to serve a section 25 notice on the heels of the tenant's request, specifying a termination date six months hence. Third, that the landlord should be allowed to serve a counter notice which would require the current tenancy to end on the earliest date on which the tenant's original section 26 request could have terminated it (that is, six months). The latter alternative was favoured by the Working Paper. It was viewed as being the most even-handed modification and a practical and acceptable way to eliminate the abuse associated with the pre-emptive strike. Regardless of these proposed reforms, however, the Commission's 1992 Report recognised no justification for disturbing the present provisions.[39] The Report believed that, in light of its recommendations extending the landlord's ability to claim an interim rent, the current financial advantage enjoyed as a result of the pre-emptive strike will be abolished.[40] Hence, the lack of direct reform of the statutory request itself.

Landlord's Counter Notice

If the competent landlord seeks to oppose the grant of a new lease, a counter **5.13** notice must be served on the tenant within two months of receipt of the section 26 request.[41] There is no prescribed form for this counter notice, but it must state the landlord's opposition and the section 30(1) grounds upon which the opposition is based.[42] Accordingly, there is no positive counter notice whereby the landlord can declare the willingness to grant a new lease.[43] The landlord must respond carefully because once the counter notice is served it is both binding and limiting. The landlord and successors in title remain bound by the grounds set out in the counter notice. Where a new competent landlord emerges, an extant counter notice cannot be withdrawn.[44] If, however, the predecessor had not served a counter notice, the new landlord can serve one provided that service occurs within the two-month statutory period.[45] A landlord who does not serve a valid counter notice loses the right to oppose the tenant's application for a new lease. If the landlord has no opposition to the tenant having a renewal, there is no need for the landlord to respond to the tenant's statutory request. It should be understood that

---

[39] N 9 above at para 2.48. The same stance was adopted in the Report of the Law Reform Advisory Committee for Northern Ireland (n 9 above at para 4.5.3).

[40] See Chapter 6. Note that in Northern Ireland no interim rent facility exists.

[41] Section 26(6). An identical rule applies to Northern Ireland: article 7(6).

[42] As to this statement of opposition and the expression of the statutory grounds, the same considerations apply as previously discussed in relation to the section 25 notice: see Chapter 4. It is noteworthy that the Law Reform Advisory Committee for Northern Ireland in its Report, n 9 above at para 4.5.1, recommended that the counter notice should be contained in a 'tear off' portion of the original request. This recommendation was not to be adopted. The Report also advocated giving the Lands Tribunal a discretion to deal with challenges to the form and content of notices served and this is now contained within article 40(3) of the Business Tenancies (Northern Ireland) Order 1996.

[43] cf article 7(6)(a) of the Business Tenancies (Northern Ireland) Order 1996.

[44] cf a landlord's section 25 notice: Sch 6, para 6.

[45] *XL Fisheries v Leeds Corporation* [1955] 2 QB 636.

where a counter notice is served which contains a ground of opposition which is neither honest nor truthful, the possibility is that it might be invalidated on the basis of fraudulent misrepresentation.[46] A similar result may arise in relation to a representation which is made recklessly.[47]

D. The Tenant's Application

5.14 Section 24(1) affords the right to apply to the court for a new lease. Only one application may be entertained and it must be made subsequent to either the service of a landlord's section 25 notice (and tenant's negative counter notice) or the service of a tenant's section 26 request. The other means whereby a tenancy can be terminated under the Act do not carry with them the right to apply for renewal. The right to make an application, moreover, extends only to the tenant and it is conditional upon the tenancy being within the catchment of the 1954 Act. This entails that the tenancy must not have been contracted out of the Act and that the tenant remains in occupation for business purposes. Indeed, for the application to be successful, the tenancy must remain within the Act until the proceedings are concluded. Finally the application can be entertained only within tightly prescribed, procedural time-limits. Section 29(3) requires that the tenant's application for a new tenancy be made not less than two and not more than four months after the service of the landlord's notice or the tenant's request. The time that the application is made is when the relevant claim form is issued.[48] Subject to waiver and estoppel, it might be thought that the general rule would be that a premature application is totally invalid. Nevertheless, in *Zenith Investments (Torquay) Ltd v Kammins Ballrooms Co Ltd (No.2)* the Court of Appeal held that, for the purposes of continuation under section 64, the making of an 'application' did not turn upon whether it was valid or invalid.[49] The application (albeit premature), therefore, remained one made under the Act. This does not, however, entail that, following the service of an invalid application, a new and valid application cannot be made by the tenant and entertained by the court.[50] Indeed, it would be remarkable

---

[46] *See Betty's Cafes Ltd v Phillips Furnishing Stores Ltd* [1959] AC 20. The same rule applies to a fraudulent section 25 notice: see *Charlwood Alliance Holding v CR Vending & Electronics Ltd* (1999) 29 June CA.

[47] *Rous v Mitchell* [1991] 1 All ER 609.

[48] The date of issue is that entered on the form: CPR, r 7.2. This rule gives way when, in order to satisfy a statutory time limit, it is necessary to rely on the date the claim was received by the court: para 5.1 of Practice Direction 7A.

[49] [1971] 3 All ER 1281. Even though the application was made earlier than the two-month minimum period, the tenant was able to remain in possession at the old rent until three months following final disposal. Sachs LJ did accept that this may allow a tenant to make a frivolous application after four months and artificially prolong the tenancy, but hoped that 'the court will find robust ways of preventing tenants from gaining advantages from such abuse' (at 1286).

[50] cf the view expressed by K Reynolds and W Clark, *Renewal of Business Tenancies* (1997) at 149.

if the tenant was unable to replace an invalid notice by a valid one within the pre-scribed time-limits.[51] It is simply a procedural matter which falls to be covered by the Civil Procedure Rules 1998.

Extending the Right to the Landlord

Perhaps the most dramatic reform advocated by the Law Commission, in its 1992 **5.15** package of proposed change, is the recommendation that the landlord should also be given the right to commence proceedings.[52] This equality between the parties is intended to counter delay and, thereby, to encourage settlement. The landlord's proceedings would be either to obtain possession; to confirm that a ground of opposition is conclusive; or to obtain a renewal where the terms are in dispute. Once commenced, the landlord would, for example, be able to convert proceed-ings for possession into an application for renewal.[53] Although unobjectionable in principle, the inherent danger with such reform is that it might generate more work for the courts and impose further procedural hurdles. In order to minimise such risks, the Report envisaged certain safeguards.[54] First, if the landlord's pos-session proceedings prove unsuccessful, the tenant will not be required to instigate separate proceedings. The court will thus be able to order a new tenancy and settle its terms at the conclusion of the landlord's proceedings. Second, a multi-plicity of actions will be avoided because the commencement of proceedings by one party will prevent the other from making a separate application. Third, and so as to prevent the discontinuance of proceedings precluding the tenant from obtaining a renewal, the landlord will be barred from withdrawing an action with-out the consent of the tenant.

Timing

In the calculation of the statutory time-periods, the corresponding date rule **5.16** applies and entails that an application made exactly two months after the service of the notice or request will suffice[55] and that the period will expire, on the same date of service, four months later.[56] The general rule is that if these time-limits are not complied with, the tenant loses the right to a renewal. The court, moreover,

---

[51] cf the *Kammins* case, n 49 above, where the date had passed within which to make a new appli-cation.

[52] N 9 above at para 2.55. This extension has been introduced into Northern Ireland by article 10.

[53] ibid at para 2.56. The landlord would not be fettered by stating opposition in the termination notice or counter notice.

[54] ibid at para 2.57. As regards Northern Ireland, identical safeguards are imposed by article 10(4).

[55] See *EJ Riley Investments Ltd v Eurostile Holdings Ltd* [1985] 3 All ER 181.

[56] *Dodds v Walker* [1981] 2 All ER 609; see further Chapter 2.

has no jurisdiction to extend the statutory time-limits[57] and, subject to waiver and estoppel, they are strict.[58] Although it is permissible for the parties expressly to agree to extend procedural time-limits, care must be taken to make an application before the statutory termination date set out in the renewal documentation. This is because beyond that time, the tenant is no longer protected by the 1954 Act and, hence, has no rights to enforce.[59] Although the need to apply to the court within these time-limits is brought to the attention of the tenant in the prescribed forms of renewal documentation, tenants often lose entitlement to a new lease by the non-observance of these time conditions. This lamentable fact caused the Law Commission Working Paper to question the rigidity of the present time conditions and to conclude that it is 'undesirable that tenants should lose their statutory rights on what in some cases can be regarded as a technicality'.[60]

Reform

5.17 Not surprisingly, therefore, the Commission's subsequent Report recommended a number of changes.[61] First, that an application be allowed at any time before the date specified in the landlord's section 25 notice or the tenant's section 26 request. This would extend the current period in which an application must be made by up to eight months. Second, that the parties should be allowed to extend this period further by written agreement.[62] An initial agreement could be made after the service of a landlord's notice or tenant's request and before the termination date specified in the notice or request. Further extensions could then be agreed before the end of the period specified in the immediately preceding agreement. The tenancy would continue during such extensions and terminate either at the end of the period specified in the last agreement or when an application is made to the court. Third, that the absolute ban on the early commencement of proceedings be removed. As the Law Commission's Report concluded: 'There is only

---

[57] *Hodgson v Armstrong* [1967] 2 QB 199. One minor exception has, however, been permitted. If the last day for making an application is a Sunday or Bank Holiday, the application may be made on the next day that the court is open: r 2.8(5) of the Civil Procedure Rules 1998.

[58] *Stevens & Cutting Ltd v Anderson* (1990) 11 EG 70.

[59] See *Meah v Sector Properties Ltd* [1974] 1 All ER 1074 where the tenant made an application some three years after the termination date set out in the tenant's request. The application was struck out. Estoppel and waiver cannot assist the tenant: see *Watkins v Emslie*, n 5 above, where the Court of Appeal doubted whether an estoppel could give the court a jurisdiction to order possession which it otherwise would not have.

[60] N 8 above at para 3.3.9.

[61] N 9 above at paras 2.58–2.60. Many of these changes haven already been introduced into Northern Ireland by article 10.

[62] The Law Reform Advisory Committee for Northern Ireland in its Report rejected the idea that the parties should be able to agree variable time-limits: 'Parties would still have to remember to abide by time limits (albeit self-imposed ones), so the possibility would still remain that these could constitute a time trap' (n 9 above, para 4.4.4). Instead, it recommended that the Lands Tribunal should be given power to extend or abridge time-limits in order to achieve fairness (para 4.4.7). This jurisdiction has now been given to the Lands Tribunal by article 10(5) of the Business Tenancies (Northern Ireland) Order 1996.

one requirement which needs to be met before a court action can satisfactorily be started: it must be clear whether the landlord intends to oppose a renewal, and if so on what grounds. Once this condition is satisfied, there is no procedural reason to require that an application be delayed.'[63] Accordingly, the parties would be permitted to make an application at any time after the service of the landlord's termination notice. As regards a tenant's request, however, the application would be possible only after the landlord has responded by the service of a counter notice or the time for serving such a response has lapsed.

The Parties

Since the Civil Procedure Rules 1998, in the High Court the parties to a renewal **5.18** application are known as the claimant and the defendant. In the county court, however, the tenant seeking a new lease is called the applicant and the landlord is called the respondent.[64] The claimant/applicant is the tenant of the holding at the time the originating process is issued. If the tenant assigns the lease after proceedings have been commenced, the assignee will need to be substituted as the new tenant. Where there are joint tenants, the general rule is that all the tenants must all join in the application.[65] The court has, moreover, the discretionary power to order one joint tenant (in the capacity of statutory trustee) to become a party to the proceedings so as to protect trust property.[66] Even when the tenant is a trustee for the business occupier or where the tenant and the occupier are both members of a group of companies, it is the actual tenant who must be a party to the proceedings. In addition, on obtaining probate, the executor of a deceased tenant can make or continue with, as appropriate, the application to the court.[67] If there is a misdescription of the tenant, and provided that the landlord is not misled, the application can, however, be amended.[68]

The appropriate defendant/respondent is the competent landlord as defined in **5.19** section 44[69] and as assessed at the time the process is issued. If there is a change of competent landlord after the court application is made, the proceedings cease to

---

[63] N 9 above at para 2.60.

[64] CCR Order 43, r 6(1)–(2).

[65] *Jacobs v Chaudhuri* [1968] 2 QB 470. Note the exception in section 41A which relates to business partners and which allows the 'business tenants' to be the plaintiffs.

[66] *Harris v Black* (1983) 46 P & CR 366. Although the co-trustee refused to sign a negative counter notice, an interlocutory order was refused as the trustees were also the beneficiaries; they had for some time been in dispute concerning whether to continue with the business; and no special circumstances existed.

[67] *Re Crowhurst Park* [1974] 1 All ER 991; *Willison v Shaftesbury Plc* (1998) May 15 CA.

[68] See *Signet Group Plc v Hammerson UK Properties Ltd* (1997) The Times, 15 December, where by mistake the parent company of the tenant was wrongly named as the tenant. The landlord knew that the counter notice was given on behalf of the tenant; see also *Thistle Hotels Ltd v McAlpine & Sons Ltd* (1989) 6 April CA.

[69] Or landlord's personal representative: see RSC Order 15, r 6A; CCR Order 5, r 8 (as preserved, respectively, in Schedules 1 and 2 of the Civil Procedure Rules).

be properly constituted unless the new landlord is made a party to the application.[70] Accordingly, if a mortgagee takes possession or a receiver is appointed following the commencement of proceedings, the mortgagee/receiver must be joined.[71] Similarly, where a reversionary tenancy is sought by the tenant, the landlord next superior to the competent landlord should be joined.[72] Although it is important that the identity of the person intended to be sued is made unequivocal, an error as to the landlord's name or status will not necessarily render the proceedings nugatory. Even if the tenant names the wrong party as landlord, the court may still allow the proceedings to be amended. This is permitted by the Civil Procedure Rules 1998, but only where a mistake was genuine and not one which would cause reasonable doubt as to the identity of the party in question.[73] This, seemingly, reiterates the rule, as established in *Evans Construction Co Ltd v Charrington & Co Ltd*, that no amendment can be made when the mistake relates to responsibility.[74] Although amendments exist only to correct a simple misnomer, the distinction between name and responsibility is, however, not always easy to draw.[75]

E. Practice and Procedure

5.20   The tenant's application can be made either to the High Court or the county court. Since 1991, the county court has been given an unlimited jurisdiction to determine applications under the Landlord and Tenant Act 1954.[76] Any jurisdictional limitations based upon rateable values were, therefore, swept away. Accordingly, and although the venue of the High Court remains an option for the

---

[70]   *Piper v Muggleton* [1956] 2 QB 569. The addition and substitution of new parties is governed by Part 19 of the CPR.
[71]   *Meah v Mouskos* [1964] 2 QB 23.; see RSC Order 97, r 1(2).
[72]   *Birch (A&W) v PB (Sloane) Ltd* (1956) 167 EG 283.
[73]   CPR, r 17.4(3). See *Teltscher Bros Ltd v London & India Dock Investments Ltd* [1989] 1 WLR 770, where the application was valid even though the landlord was stated to be the 'plaintiff' and not, as was correct, the defendant. The mistake was genuine and did not mislead the landlord. Similarly, the court may also condone any misspelling and incomplete versions of the landlord's name.
[74]   [1983] QB 810. The tenant should have commenced proceedings against Bass Holdings, but instead named the landlord's managing agents and associated company (Charrington & Co) in the application. The amendment was allowed.
[75]   See the *Sardinia Sulcis* case [1991] 1 Lloyds Rep 201. In *Re 55 & 57 Holmes Road, Kentish Town* [1958] 2 WLR 975, for example, it was stressed that a misnomer will occur when the tenant has in mind one party only, but sets down the name incorrectly. It is not, however, a mere misnomer when the tenant has two entities in mind, correctly names one but wrongly makes that one a party. It is, as Beldam LJ put it in *Fluoro Engineering Plastics (Lining) Ltd v British Telecommunications Plc* (1998) March 19 CA, 'the distinction between an error in the party and an error in the name of the party'.
[76]   Section 63(2) of the 1954 Act as amended by the High Court and County Court Jurisdiction Order 1991 (SI, 1991, No 724).

tenant, the primary agency dealing with lease renewals is the county court.[77] The tenant's application, moreover, can cover a number of properties demised under different leases provided that the parties are the same, act in the same capacity and, in each case, the statutory procedures have been followed.[78] The issue of whether the tenant is to be granted a new lease may be tried as a preliminary issue before the court turns its attention to working out the terms of the grant.[79] The costs of the proceedings, moreover, are at the discretion of the court.[80] Accordingly, a landlord who withdraws opposition to the renewal after proceedings are commenced always runs the risk of costs.[81] Similarly, a tenant who is awarded a new lease, but exercises the right to have the order revoked, will face the probability that costs will be awarded in favour of the landlord.[82]

Civil Procedure Rules

The Civil Procedure Rules 1998, and associated practice directions, have dramatically altered the manner in which civil litigation is carried out.[83] The Rules embody a unified code of civil procedure which applies to all the civil courts, is written in plain English and substantially, but not entirely, dispenses with the distinctions of practice and procedure between the High Court and the county court. The laudable ambition of this major overhaul is to overcome public dissatisfaction with the delay, cost, complexity and uncertainty of litigation. The overriding objective is that the court will deal with cases more justly.[84] This entails, so far as is practicable, putting the parties on an equal footing; saving expense; dealing with the case as appropriate to the amount of money involved, its importance and complexity and the financial position of each party; ensuring that the case is dealt with expeditiously and fairly; and allotting to it an appropriate share of the court's resources.[85] In order to ensure that cases are dealt with justly, the court is **5.21**

---

[77] Para 2.4 of Practice Direction 7A of the CPR states that a High Court action should be the justified on the basis of the financial value of the claim, its factual or legal complexity, and/or its public importance.

[78] *Curtis v Calgary Investments Ltd* (1984) 47 P & CR 13. Obviously, issues concerning individual premises will then be argued separately. The court can, however, order that each application be heard individually.

[79] *Dutch Oven v Egham Estate & Investment Co Ltd* [1968] 3 All ER 100.

[80] See Part 44 of the CPR; *Decca Navigator Co Ltd v GLC* [1974] 1 All ER 1178.

[81] See *Demag Industrial Equipment Ltd v Canada Dry (UK) Ltd* [1969] 2 All ER 936.

[82] See *Re No 88 High Road, Kilburn* [1959] 1 All ER 527.

[83] The latest version of the Rules and the Forms and guidance and are available on the Internet at www.open.gov.uk/lcd/civil/procrules_fin/crules.htm and www.courtservice.gov.uk respectively. Proceedings commenced prior to 26 April 1999 are subject to transitional provisions (see Part 51). If not brought before the court before 26 April 2000, the proceedings are automatically stayed. It will then be for the tenant to get the stay lifted under Part 23.6.

[84] CPR, r 1.1(1). This overriding objective must be given effect to when the Rules are being exercised or interpreted: r 1.2. It is also the duty of the parties to help the court to further this objective: r 1.3.

[85] CPR, r 1.1(2)(a)–(e). As the commencement of lititgation under the 1954 Act is a procedural requirement, the danger exists of 'front loading' of litigation costs (for example, concerning expert evidence).

obliged actively to manage cases and take this responsibility from the parties. This management activity includes, for example, encouraging co-operation between the parties, identifying issues at an early stage, deciding promptly which issues can be disposed of summarily, helping the parties to agree a settlement, fixing timetables and giving directions to facilitate the quick and efficient disposal of proceedings.[86] The parties are, moreover, only required to undertake work which the court deems necessary to bring about a just resolution of the dispute, and the directions and orders made by the courts must reflect this realistic stance. If either party fails to comply with the directions, various sanctions can be imposed relating to, for example, the admissibility of evidence and costs. As regards non-compliance by the landlord, the tenant of course may pursue the application regardless of the lessor's default. Consequently, these changes should exert a downward pressure on costs and reduce the scope of procedural manipulation for tactical advantage. A further means of saving costs is for the parties to elect for Professional Arbitration on Court Terms (PACT). This method of alternative dispute resolution is a realistic alternative when the issues are clear and straightforward. Nevertheless, at the time of writing, PACT has proved unpopular with tenants.

5.22   Although as yet not relevant to landlord and tenant disputes, the Rules have introduced certain pre-action Protocols.[87] The Protocols prescribe pre-action behaviour, for example, relating to early exchange of information, which is designed to encourage settlement prior to the issue of proceedings. Even if settlement is not reached, compliance with the Protocols will normally mean that the case will be sufficiently well prepared to progress quickly to trial. As regards those parts that the Protocols do not reach, the parties are expected to act reasonably in exchanging information and documents and to try to achieve a settlement. Non-compliance with the Protocols may be penalised by an order of costs. Once proceedings have commenced, the court's ability to case-manage arises after the filing of a defence. The parties are invited to complete allocation questionnaires[88] and these will help determine at the case-management hearing whether the case will be allocated to the small claims track, the fast track or the multi-track.[89] Renewal cases will fall within the latter two categories and the court has the discretion sub-

---

[86] CPR, r 1.4 (2)(a)–(l). The court's case management powers are wide and are set out in Part 3 of the CPR.

[87] At the time of writing, these cover clinical negligence and personal injury claims only. Future reforms will extend the number of Protocols and, eventually, it is possible that a Protocol will be designed for landlord and tenant disputes; see further District Judge GJ Evans (1999) NLJ, March 5 at 335.

[88] CPR, r 26.3. The questions concern, for example, whether a one-month stay is required to achieve settlement; lay and expert witnesses; location of the trial; representation and estimated length of hearing; and estimated costs. In short, a comprehensive overview is to be taken of the proceedings from the outset. Sanctions for a failure to return the questionnaire may be imposed.

[89] See generally Part 26 of the CPR.

sequently to re-allocate the claim to a different track.[90] The appropriate selection is geared to a variety of factors including, for example, the financial value and complexity of the claim, the wishes of the parties and the amount of oral evidence which may be required.[91] A date for trial will normally be set when directions are given. On the application of all parties, or on the court's initiative, a stay to allow for settlement can, however, be granted. In the first instance, this is for a period of one month, but it may be extended until such date as the court deems appropriate.[92] The duty is on the claimant to inform (normally within fourteen days) the court if a settlement is reached and, where the parties remain unable to reach an agreement within the period of stay, the matter will proceed to a hearing.[93]

In both the High Court and the county court, proceedings are commenced by **5.23** claim form (usually Form N1).[94] The proceedings commence once the claim form is issued by the court. The claim form must state the title of the proceedings, the allocated number of the proceedings, the court of issue, the full names of the parties and their status in the proceedings.[95] In the county court, the claim will normally be issued in the district within which the demised premises are situated and/or the tenant resides or carries out business.[96] As regards the High Court, the claim form may be issued out of Chancery chambers or, if outside London, the district registry for the area within which the premises are located.[97] If the claim is issued in the High Court it is to be marked 'Chancery Division', whereas, if commenced in the county court, it is labelled 'Chancery Business'.[98] The claim form must contain a concise statement of the nature of the claim and specify the remedy which the claimant seeks. The claim must also identify the premises, its rateable value and the business carried on there and provide particulars of the current tenancy, renewal documentation served and the proposed terms of the new lease.[99] These proposals need not be set out with precision[100] and the claim can be

---

[90] CPR, r 26.10.

[91] CPR, r 26.8(1). The procedural rules vary according to which track is allocated.

[92] CPR, r 26.4.

[93] CPR, rr 26.4, 26.5.

[94] Para 3.1 of Practice Direction 7A. Writs, summons and originating applications have, therefore, no role to play in the new system.

[95] Para 4.1 of Practice Direction 7A.

[96] If the wrong county court is chosen, the court may order that the proceedings continue, be transferred or be struck out: CPR, r 30.2(2).

[97] RSC Order 97, r 3(1). The High Court has the power to transfer proceedings from the Royal Courts of Justice to a district registry (or vice versa) or from one district registry to another: CPR, r 30(2).4. The criteria for such transfers are set out in CPR, r 30.3.

[98] Para. 2.5 of Practice Direction 7A.

[99] RSC Order 97, r 3(1), r 6(1); CCR Order 43, r 6(1). If known to the tenant, the application must provide details of any superior landlords. A failure to include the required information will render the claim invalid.

[100] See *Williams v Hillcroft Garage Ltd* (1971) 22 P & CR 402.

amended at a later stage and outside the section 29(3) time-limit.[101] The claim form should also specify any preliminary matters to be decided[102] and the claimant is also required to verify the particulars of claim by a statement of truth.[103]

5.24 The claim form must be served on the landlord by one of the permitted methods of service. Service can be undertaken either by the court or by the claimant personally.[104] The methods are set out in Part 6 of the Civil Procedure Rules and include personal service, first class post, leaving the document at the address for service of the party, document exchange and electronic communication.[105] The Rules also stipulate deemed days of service according to which method is employed.[106] Service is to occur within two calendar months of the issue of the claim form.[107] The claimant may, however, apply for an order extending the two-month period, but an application to extend must generally be made within the two-month period or, where an extension has already been granted, within the period of that extension.[108] An application for extension may be made *ex parte* and must be supported by evidence.[109] If the application is made outside these time-frames, the court may grant an extension only if the court has been unable to serve the claim form in time or the claimant has taken all reasonable steps to serve the claim form, but had been unable to do so; and, in either case, the claimant has acted promptly in making the application.[110]

---

[101] *Nurit Bar v Pathwood Investments* (1987) P & CR 178 (extent of premises); *De Costa v Chartered Society of Queen Square* [1961] 177 EG 447 (nature of tenant's business); and *G Orlik (Meat Products) Ltd v Hastings & Thanet Building Society* (1974) 29 P & CR 126 (terms of new lease).

[102] For example, relating to the validity of a statutory notice: *Boltons (House Furnishers) Ltd v Oppenheim* [1959] 3 All ER 90.

[103] CPR, r 22.1; see generally G Exall (1999) Solicitors Journal, 12 March at 234. If the claimant is a company, the verification must come from a person holding a senior position in the company. A solicitor may, if authorised, sign a statement of truth on behalf of a client: see Practice Direction 22, para 3.8.

[104] If served by the court, the court must notify the claimant when service has occurred, whereas, if service is by the claimant, the claimant must file a certificate of service within seven days of service taking place: CPR, r 6.10.

[105] CPR, r 6.2. Rule 6.8, however, provides for the court to permit service by an alternative method. The special rules of service contained in RSC Order 14 and CCR Order 7 are preserved.

[106] For example, the next day for first class post, electronic communication and when having left the document at the permitted address. If transmitted by fax before 4 pm on a business day (that is excluding weekends and Bank Holidays), the same day; if not, the next business day: CPR, r 6.7.

[107] CCR Order 43, r 6.3; RSC Order 97. Note that the general and more generous time-limits set out in CPR, r 7.5 do not apply here. When particulars of claim are served on the landlord, they must be accompanied by relevant forms for defending or admitting the claim and for acknowledging service: CPR, r 7.8.

[108] CPR, r 7.6.

[109] CPR, r 7.6(4).

[110] CPR, r 7.6(3).

Following past practices, it is unlikely that an extension of time for service will be **5.25** granted when the initial application is made more than four months after the issue of the claim form.[111] As Bingham MR concluded in *Ward-Lee v Lineham*: 'Time limits such as these are intended to be short; it is incumbent on parties to comply with them; and if extensions were granted at all readily the time limits would very quickly become a dead letter.'[112] This limitation is not applicable, however, where the parties have agreed in writing to waive the time-limits while negotiations continue.[113] Where a claim form has been issued and not served, the landlord may serve notice on the tenant requiring either that the claim form be served or that the claim be discontinued within a specified period of at least fourteen days from the service of the notice.[114] If the claimant fails to comply, the court may dismiss the claim or make any other order it thinks just.[115]

Part 31 of the Civil Procedure Rules 1998 sets out the rules concerning disclosure **5.26** and inspection of documents.[116] The court will normally order standard disclosure which requires disclosure of those documents which are to be relied upon or which adversely affect the party's case.[117] An application for specific disclosure directed at specified documents or classes of document must be supported by evidence.[118] The parties are required to make a reasonable search in all the circumstances for such documents and the duty to disclose is ongoing throughout the proceedings.[119] Each party will serve a disclosure list and a disclosure statement. The latter must describe the extent of the search for the documents and certify that the duty to disclose is understood and has been carried out. The general rule is that a party to whom a document has been disclosed has the right to inspect and copy that document.[120]

County Court

In the county court, the court will fix a return day which, unless it otherwise **5.27** directs, shall be the day fixed for the case-management hearing of the proceedings. Different county courts are, however, inconsistent in their approach to the

---

[111] See *Leal v Dunlop Bio-Processes International Ltd* [1984] 2 All ER 207.
[112] [1993] 2 All ER 1006 at 1015. There the validity of the proceedings was upheld where the delay was entirely the fault of the county court; the tenant had not known of the default and the delay had not caused prejudice to the landlord.
[113] CPR, r .2.11; see *Ali v Knight* (1983) 272 EG 1165.
[114] CPR, r 7.7(1)–(2). References to days are to 'clear days', that is, they exclude the day the period begins and, if the day is defined by reference to an event, the day on which that event occurs: r 2.8 (3). In relation to periods of no more than five days, Saturdays, Sundays and Bank Holidays do not count: r 2.8(4).
[115] CPR, r 7.7(3).
[116] See generally District Judge C Tromans (1999) NLJ, 26 February at 307.
[117] CPR, r 31.6. The procedure is contained within r 31.10.
[118] CPR, r 31.12.
[119] CPR, rr 31.7, 31.11.
[120] CPR, rr 31.2, 31.15.

progress of renewal applications. Following service of the claim form, the respondent has fourteen days within which to file an answer.[121] The answer is required to state any objections to the tenant's renewal application and/or proposals, any counter proposals, and (where relevant) the name and address of the real competent landlord.[122] There is, however, no prescribed form for the respondent's answer. The court enjoys the discretion both to extend the time limit for filing the answer and to allow the landlord to raise objections or alter the grounds of opposition at the hearing.[123] The landlord may, moreover, insert into the answer an application for an interim rent. If the landlord fails to file a valid answer, the tenant's application for a new lease then goes unopposed. The landlord does, however, retain the right to be heard concerning the terms of the new grant.[124] The case-management hearing occurs before the district judge and it is there that preliminary issues will be aired and directions given.

High Court

5.28 Upon issue of the claim form for a new tenancy, a date for the hearing before the master must be inserted and this must be at least fourteen days after the service of the claim form.[125] At least four days before the date fixed for the first hearing, the claimant must also file a witness statement or affidavit verifying the statement of facts made in the claim form.[126] This must state, as appropriate, whether the landlord opposes the grant of a new lease and, if so, on what grounds; opposition to the tenant's proposed terms and any counter proposals; and whether the landlord will have a reversion of less than fourteen months at the date specified for the termination of the tenant's lease.[127] The landlord need not set out the grounds of opposition or counter proposals in detail. Unless contrary affidavits are sworn (as is common because such matters as the landlord's intention and the terms of the proposed lease are often contested), this process operates to avoid cross examination. The detail contained in the tenant's affidavit, however, is likely to be thin. As Reynolds and Clark explain:

---

[121] CCR Order 43, r 2(1).

[122] CCR Order 43, r 7.

[123] *Olley v Hemsby Estates* (1965) 196 EG 601; *Morgan v Jones* [1960] 3 All ER 583. This is subject to the limitation that the landlord cannot oppose or rely on a ground of opposition unless it was specified in the section 25 notice or landlord's counter notice: *Nursey v P Currie (Dartford) Ltd* [1959] 1 All ER 497.

[124] *Morgan v Jones*, ibid; see also *Willison v Shaftesbury Plc*, n 67 above, which concerned serious delay on the part of the landlord's predecessor in title and the new landlord's failed application to have opposition restored.

[125] RSC, Order 97, r 3(3).

[126] RSC Order 97, r 7(1). Any party affected by the proceedings may apply in private and *ex parte* to be made a party to the proceedings and the court may give such directions as appear necessary: Order 97, r 8. This is in addition to the general ability of the court to add or substitute parties given in Part 19 of the CPR.

[127] RSC Order 97, r 7(2). A case-management hearing will take place before the master or a district judge and, as in the county court, orders and directions will be given and a date for trial set.

The tenant may not wish to disclose his case to the other side before any directions are made by the master at the first hearing. Furthermore, he may not know at this stage whether the landlord is going to attempt to take any preliminary issue in his affidavit in reply. The purpose of the tenant's affidavit is, therefore, to enable the master to understand what the tenant wants, but without necessarily going into great detail as to why he wants those terms.[128]

F. Withdrawal of Application

It might be that, after the tenant's application to court, the parties reach an agree- **5.29** ment as to the grant of a new lease and the terms of that lease. In such a case, there are two options open to the tenant. First, the tenant may proceed with the application and have the agreement embodied in an order of the court.[129] Second, the tenant may withdraw the application on the terms agreed. The general rule is that discontinuation is as of right and constitutes the most simple and inexpensive alternative.[130] The process involves the tenant filing a notice of discontinuance and serving a copy of it on every party.[131] Pre-discontinuation costs will, however, normally be payable by the tenant.[132] In the context of the Landlord and Tenant Act 1954, withdrawal entails that the existing tenancy will come to an end three months after the date of discontinuation and precludes any change of heart and any chance of compensation for misrepresentation under section 55. The withdrawal does not, however, disentitle the tenant to compensation for disturbance under section 37. Similarly, the landlord cannot automatically avoid paying compensation by withdrawing all opposition to the tenant's application. In that situation, the Court of Appeal has acknowledged that the tenant has two options: either to obtain a new tenancy or to discontinue the application and obtain compensation.[133]

G. Compensation for Loss of Renewal Rights

Where the tenant is unable to obtain an order for a new lease, the question of com- **5.30** pensation may become the paramount concern. The landlord enjoys no comparative right to claim compensation if the tenant withdraws an application or

---

[128] K Reynolds and W Clark, n 50 above at 408. The authors make the valid point that, if a tenant wants matters to progress swiftly, more than a perfunctory response will be advisable.
[129] CPR, r 40.6.
[130] CPR, r 38.2.
[131] CPR, r 38.3. The defendant has the right to apply, within 28 days, to have the notice of discontinuance set aside: r 38.4.
[132] CPR, r 38. 6.
[133] *Lloyds Bank v City of London Corporation* (1982) 262 EG 61.

applies for the revocation of any tenancy ordered.[134] Compensation is payable by the competent landlord under section 37 for what is termed 'disturbance' or, more technically, for loss of the contingent right of renewal. As Ackner LJ recognised in *Cardshops Ltd v John Lewis Properties Ltd*, 'Parliament intended that the tenant should be properly compensated for the disturbance in having to vacate the premises'.[135] If the tenant's application is refused because of a misrepresentation by the landlord, additional compensation is available under section 55.

Disturbance

5.31 Compensation for disturbance reflects the fact that a tenant's failure to obtain a new lease can prove costly. Apart from a loss of business and goodwill, the tenant will incur expense in locating and moving to alternative premises. This is particularly harsh where the loss of a new lease is not due to any default (for example rent arrears and breach of covenant) on the tenant's part. It is this mischief against which the compensation provisions in section 37 are aimed. Before amendment by the Law of Property Act 1969, compensation was payable only when the tenant had made an application to the court for a new tenancy and the court was precluded from making the order on grounds (e) uneconomic sub-letting; (f) demolition and reconstruction; and/or (g) own occupation.[136] The need to make a renewal application was the cause of much criticism. As the Law Commission concluded in 1969, 'tenants may be put to unnecessary trouble and expense in making applications for new tenancies, which they know will be refused, in order simply to enforce their rights to compensation under the Act. Moreover, these rights are often lost through a failure to make an application by tenants who are unaware that this is necessary.'[137] Accordingly, the Law Commission recommended that compensation should not be limited to where an application has been made and refused. Instead, it should be available whether or not the tenant bothered to make such an application.[138] As Ward LJ explained in *Bacchiocchi v Academic Agency Ltd*: 'The disturbance is suffered equally when . . . the tenant withdraws his application for a new tenancy and a tenant in these circumstances

---

[134] cf Northern Ireland where the landlord can make such a claim for loss arising as a result of the tenant's action or inaction: article 21.

[135] [1983] QB 161 at 179. The payment is not liable to capital gains tax: *Drummond (Inspector of Taxes) v Brown* [1985] Ch 52. In contrast to any premium paid on surrender, the rule is that statutory compensation is not chargeable: *Davis v Henderson* [1995] STC (SCD) 308.

[136] 'The right to compensation arises where the ground of opposition asserted by the landlord is one which is a ground inserted into the Act purely for the benefit of the landlord in the sense that the landlord only has to prove its own intentions as to its own activities without proving any default of any kind on the part of the tenant' (per Pryor J): *Sight & Sound Education Ltd v Books Etc Ltd* (1999) 13 November (HC).

[137] N 7 above at para 46.

[138] ibid at para 47.

is just as much entitled to his compensation.'[139] This recommendation is now incorporated within section 37(1).[140]

Availability

For those tenants who fall within the catchment of the 1954 Act, compensation is **5.32** available under section 37 in two circumstances. First, when the court is precluded from making an order for a new tenancy solely on any of the grounds (e), (f) and (g).[141] These are the mandatory grounds of opposition which do not involve fault on the part of the tenant. If, instead, the court makes a declaration under section 31(2) that either ground (e) or (f) will be satisfied at a later date, compensation remains payable as the tenant is still denied a renewal. Refusal on any other ground takes the tenant entirely outside the compensation scheme. It has been argued that, if the application is refused because of a defect (for example, it was premature), compensation will cease to be available to the tenant.[142] Similarly, compensation should be unavailable where the tenant agrees to take a tenancy of an economically separable part of the previous holding for the purposes of section 31A, the rationale being that the tenant's application has, albeit partially, been successful. On refusing a new tenancy exclusively on one or more of the three specified grounds, the court is, at the behest of the tenant, obliged to certify that fact.[143] A request for such a certificate is usually made at the end of the renewal hearing, but it can be entertained subsequently.[144] The compensation payable to the tenant will not, however, form part of the order made by the court when dismissing the tenant's renewal application. As Brightman J recognised in *Re 14 Grafton Street*, 'It is a debt created by statute, on which the tenant may sue in other proceedings if necessary.'[145]

Second, compensation is available when the landlord has served a section 25 **5.33** notice, or counter notice in response to the tenant's section 26 request, stating only one or more of the grounds of opposition contained in section

---

[139] [1998] 2 All ER 241 at 251. See also *Sight & Sound Education Ltd v Books Etc Ltd*, n 136 above.

[140] It was not, however, made retrospective in effect: *Re 14 Grafton Street* [1971] Ch 935. Following the recommendation of the Law Reform Advisory Committee for Northern Ireland Report, n 9 above at para 8.2.2, a similar provision is now to be found in article 23(1)(b) of the Business Tenancies (Northern Ireland) Order 1996.

[141] Due to the recommendation of the Law Commission in 1992 that ground (g) should be extended to cover use for a business carried on by a company under the landlord's control or vice versa, further modification will be necessary to ensure that the right to compensation is extended accordingly: *n 9* above at 2.81. This reform has occurred in Northern Ireland: article 23(1).

[142] Reynolds and Clark, n 50 above at 355. It remains open for the tenant to withdraw the application before it is struck out.

[143] Section 37(4).

[144] In private and *ex parte*: RSC Order 97, r 10(1) (High Court); CCR Order 43, r 9 (county court).

[145] N 140 above at 942.

30(1)(e)–(g).[146] The general rule, therefore, is that compensation is available regardless of whether the tenant serves a counter notice,[147] applies for a new tenancy or withdraws any application made.[148] As Slade J explained at first instance in *Lloyds Bank Ltd v City of London Corporation*, the right to compensation is not qualified by any consideration of the tenant's motive:

> Section 37(1), as amended, says nothing whatever about the motives which may prompt a tenant either to omit to apply for a new tenancy or to withdraw his application after it has been made. The motives prompting the tenant to take either of these course, after he has received a notice under section 25 or section 26(6), relying on one or more of the grounds specified in paragraphs (e), (f) or (g) of section 30, may be many and mixed. I cannot impute an intention to the legislature to withhold compensation from a tenant . . . merely because his motives for omitting to apply to the court, or for withdrawing an application when made, may be of a particular nature.[149]

Special Provisions

5.34 Where the right to renew is excluded on the grounds of public interest or national security, or a certificate on those grounds prevents renewal beyond a specific date, compensation for disturbance is payable.[150] If the Welsh Development Agency or the Development Board for Rural Wales is the landlord, and a certificate has been issued under section 60A, 60B by the Secretary of State, compensation might not be available to the tenant.[151] The rule of non-compensation applies where the landlord acquired its interest under statute[152] or the tenant took the lease after the Agency or Development Board had acquired its interest. In Northern Ireland, the position is much simpler. Under article 23(7) disentitlement to compensation occurs when the landlord is a public authority; the tenant had been (or should have been) aware of this fact when the contract of tenancy was entered; and the contract or other agreement expressly denied compensation.

Split Reversions

5.35 It is an aspect of the catalogue of reforms advocated by the Law Commission in 1992, that, where the ownership of the reversion to a tenancy has been split, the

---

[146] If other grounds are specified, the tenant must successfully defeat those additional grounds at the hearing stage in order to be entitled to compensation. As Reynolds and Clark point out (n 50 above at 354–355), the landlord might specify an additional ground merely as a tactic to test whether the tenant will make an application.

[147] See *Re 14 Grafton Street*, n 140 above.

[148] In light of the 1992 Law Commission Report, which recommended that the landlord be able to commence renewal proceedings, the compensation scheme will need to cater for the situation where the landlord is successful in an action for possession or withdraws the action: n 9 above at para 2.81.

[149] N 133 above, at 64; but see *Sun Life Assurance Plc v Racal Tracs Ltd* n 38 above.

[150] Section 59; see further Chapter 3.

[151] The certification is that the occupation or use of the premises should be changed in order to provide employment in the area.

[152] That is, as appropriate, sections 7, 8 of the Welsh Development Agency Act 1978; and *section 24* of the Development of Rural Wales Act 1976.

owners of the parts should together be treated as the competent landlord for renewal purposes.[153] In the interests of fairness, the Commission recommended also that compensation payable under section 37 should be apportioned between each part of the property under distinct ownership.[154] Each reversioner's liability would, therefore, be capped according to the rateable value of, and higher or lower rate applicable to, their respective parts.

Amount of Compensation

The tenant is entitled, by virtue of section 37(2), to a flat rate compensation **5.36** geared to the rateable value of the premises that are occupied by the tenant for business purposes as determined at the time the landlord serves the section 25 notice or counter notice. Compensation, therefore, is only payable in respect of the tenant's holding (as defined in section 23(3)) which is not necessarily the whole of the premises enveloped within the former tenancy.[155] The amount payable is the product of an appropriate multiplier (currently one) and either the rateable value of the holding or, in certain circumstances, twice the rateable value.[156] The appropriate multiplier to be used is that applicable when the tenant vacates the premises. It is not fixed as at the date of the landlord's notice or counter notice.[157] This general rule gives way, however, only where it is clear from the wording of the secondary legislation that a different approach is to be taken. This occurred, for example, in *Brewer v Vesco Ltd* where, due to the abolition of domestic rating, the Multiplier Order of 1990 expressly drew a distinction according to whether or not the notice was served before 1 April 1990.[158] The tenant, moreover, has no right to receive compensation until the premises are quit at the end of the tenancy. As Slade J concluded in *International Military Services Ltd v Capital & Counties Plc*: 'The entitlement arises on the quitting of the holding and not before. In my judgment, therefore, it is quite plain that the amount of the entitlement must be assessed in accordance with the law as it stands at the date of quitting.'[159] Although the compensation scheme is attractive by reason of its simplicity

---

[153] See Chapter 4.

[154] N 9 above at para 2.84

[155] In the event that there is dispute as to what constitutes the holding, the court is expressly empowered by section 37(5),(6) to determine the issue.

[156] These rates and the multiplier can be changed by ministerial order: section 37(8). Such changes have occurred previously so as to reflect significant inflation. The current multiplier is set by the Landlord and Tenant Act 1954 (Appropriate Multiplier) Order 1990 (SI. No 363). In Northern Ireland the scheme is more complex in that the net annual value of the holding is ascertained and subject to a multiplier which varies according to whether the tenant has occupied either for less than 5 years, over 5 years, but less than 10 years; over 10 years, but less than 15 years; or over 15 years: article 23(3).

[157] *Cardshops Ltd v John Lewis Properties Ltd*, n 135 above (Eveleigh LJ dissenting).

[158] (1994) March 9 CA.

[159] [1982] 1 WLR 575 at 582; see also *Garrett v Lloyds Bank Ltd* (1982) 7 April HC where Walton J added, 'quitting is the only thing that the tenant is required to do in order to obtain compensation. He is not required to serve any kind of notice or make any kind of application . . .'

and certainty, it is to be admitted that the present calculation is purely arbitrary, reflects neither the true loss to the tenant nor the real gain to the landlord and, hence, may produce unfairness.

5.37 As regards partly residential premises included within a business tenancy, the abolition of domestic rates has entailed a modification of the compensation scheme. The general rule is that the domestic property is excluded when the rateable value of the premises is calculated, that is, the domestic property does not figure in the calculation of compensation under section 37.[160] Nevertheless, the tenant can claim reasonable removal expenses for that part, as agreed with the landlord or ordered by the court.[161] Otherwise the rateable value is that as shown on the valuation list in force at the date of service of, as appropriate, the landlord's termination notice or counter notice.[162] If no separate value is given, a proper apportionment or aggregation needs to be made.[163] Where the rateable value still cannot be ascertained, it is taken to be the value which, apart from any exemption from assessment to rates, would on a proper assessment be the value which would have been entered in the valuation list as the annual value of the holding.[164] In *Plessey Co Plc v Eagle Pension Funds*, for example, the central issue was whether the rateable value of the holding was to be ascertained in accordance with section 37(5)(b) (as argued by the landlord) or under section 37(5)(c) (as argued by the tenant). The difference produced between these calculations was considerable. The landlord was claiming that the rateable value on apportionment was £17; the tenant claimed that the rateable value was £21,097. This discrepancy stemmed from the premises having been damaged by fire and the valuation list consequently being amended to reflect a massively reduced rateable value. Although the premises had been put into a restored state, the rateable value was not upgraded until after the tenant had quit. It was decided that the relevant rateable value was that at the time

---

[160] Section 37(5A). Although section 37(5C),(5D) deals with compensation where the whole of the holding is domestic property, since the House of Lords' decision in *Graysim Holdings Ltd v P&O Property Holdings Ltd* [1995] 4 All ER 831, it appears no longer possible to be in the business of subletting and to remain within the scope of the 1954 Act. In addition, the creation of residential licences, which in theory could keep the business tenant within the 1954 Act, is difficult to engineer since *Street v Mountford* [1985] AC 809. Section 37(5C),(5D) has, therefore, little (if any) modern relevance.

[161] Section 37(5A), (5B). It should be appreciated that an alternative, but transitional, scheme of compensation is available for those holdings which include domestic property: see *Busby v Co-operative Insurance Society* (1994) 6 EG 141 This is afforded by Sch 7 of the Local Government and Housing Act 1989. It provides that where the tenancy was created (or contracted for) prior to April 1990, and the landlord's termination notice or counter notice is served before April 2000, the tenant may elect for a special basis of compensation. This election must, however, be made within two and four months of the service of the landlord's notice or tenant's request. The alternative calculation will be based on the pre-April 1990 rateable valuation multiplied by 8 or 16, as appropriate.

[162] Section 37(5)(a).

[163] Section 37(5)(b). Apportionment is relevant where the holding is merely part of a rated hereditament. Aggregation would apply where the holding comprises of separately rated parts.

[164] Section 37(5)(c).

when the section 25 notice was served (that is, the lower sum). Although a harsh result, the language of section 37(5)(b) is clear and unambiguous and the landlord's argument irrefutable.[165]

Procedural Rules

Any dispute concerning the determination of the rateable value must be referred **5.38**
to the Commissioners of Inland Revenue for evaluation by an authorised valuation officer.[166] The valuation officer is not an arbitrator and enjoys much discretion under the present rules. Subject to appeal to the Lands Tribunal, the decision of this officer is final. The court has no jurisdiction to determine rateable values.[167] Pursuant to section 37(6), rules have been made by the Inland Revenue governing the procedure for such references.[168] Under the Rules, reference may be made either by one party only or by the parties jointly (rule 3(2)). The reference, moreover, must be in the form prescribed in the Rules or in a form substantially to the like effect (rule 3(1)). Unless all the parties join in the reference, copies of the form must be forwarded immediately to all other parties to the dispute (rule 4). The valuation officer is also obliged to inform all parties that referral has occurred and to invite them to make written representations, usually within twenty-eight days (rule 5). The valuation officer can request the parties to furnish such information as reasonably required to assist in the determination (rule 6). The valuation officer decides the issue in the capacity of an expert, on such evidence as is considered relevant. There is no duty to consider any evidence introduced by the parties, other than their written representations. The valuation officer, however, has the power to hold a meeting with all the parties before making a determination (rule 7). Although all must be invited, the meeting can proceed even if a party declines the invitation. On reaching the determination of rateable value, the officer must send notification of the decision to all the parties and to the Inland Revenue Commissioners and this must state the right to appeal to the Lands Tribunal (rule 8).[169]

Higher Rate Valuation

As mentioned earlier, in certain cases the rateable value is doubled for the purposes **5.39**
of compensation. The conditions for this higher rate to become payable are twofold. First, by virtue of section 37(3)(a) where, during the whole of the

---

[165] Although the Law Commission has not championed this reform, the Department of the Environment (in its Consultation Paper dated 5 July 1996) recommended that the compensation paid under section 37 should be adjusted if the rateable value of the holding is subsequently revised.
[166] Section 37(5),(7).
[167] Section 37(5).
[168] Landlord and Tenant (Determination of Rateable Value Procedure) Rules 1954, SI No 1255.
[169] Such notice being admissible as proof of the rateable value: CCR rule 11; RSC Order 97, r 13.

fourteen years immediately preceding the termination of the current tenancy,[170] the premises (being or comprised in the holding)[171] have been occupied for the purposes of a business carried on by the occupier or for those and other purposes. As the Law Reform Advisory Committee for Northern Ireland accepted in its Report: 'The rationale behind compensation is that the tenant is being paid for something he has built and then lost. The longer he has spent in the premises the more compensation he should receive.'[172]

5.40   A particularly illustrative case is *Edicron v William Whitely* where the tenants had occupied the first floor of a building for over fourteen years.[173] During that period, they had surrendered their original lease and obtained a new tenancy comprising the first, second and third floors. Although the second and third floors had not been occupied for the requisite period, the tenants were able, by virtue of their occupation of the first floor, to claim double compensation on the basis of the rateable value of the entire holding. In its Working Paper, the Law Commission thought that it was unsatisfactory that the occupation of some part of the premises for fourteen years should suffice to qualify the tenant for higher rate compensation in respect of the whole property. As the Commission rightly pointed out: 'The amount of compensation could change materially, to the profit of one party and the loss of the other, because of the period of occupation of an insignificant part of the property'.[174] As the law stands, however, no other construction of section 37 is possible. Although doubting whether such situations often arise, the Working Paper advocated the imposition of a requirement that compensation be payable on the respective parts of the property according to the periods of occupation of each part.[175] This was a theme echoed in the subsequent Report where it was recommended that a mix of higher and lower rate calculations should apply to parts that have been occupied for 14 years and those that have not.[176] If a separate calculation had been adopted for each part of the property in the *Edicron* case, double compensation would have been payable with regard to the first floor only. The second and third floors would have attracted compensation at only the lower rate. This would, undoubtedly, have achieved a more just balance between the interests of the parties.

---

[170] This is the date of termination specified in the landlord's section 25 notice or the tenant's section 26 request: section 37(7). This may be different from the date the current tenancy ends or the date the tenant quits the premises: *Sight & Sound Education Ltd v Books Etc Ltd*, n 136 above.

[171] Logically, the extent of the holding should fall to be adjudged as at the time of service of the landlord's section 25 notice or counter notice.

[172] N 9 above at para 8.3.6. Although section 37 caters for mixed user, it is not necessary that the residential use should have been for 14 years.

[173] [1984] 1 All ER 219.

[174] N 8 above at para 3.6.10.

[175] ibid at para 3.6.11.

[176] N 9 above at para 2.83. This distinction is not, however, drawn in the Business Tenancies (Northern Ireland) Order 1996.

The second condition is, that, if during those fourteen years there was a change of **5.41**
occupier of the holding, the new occupier must have succeeded to the business of
the predecessor. Of crucial relevance here is the continuity of the business and not
the identity of the occupier.[177] Accordingly, this opens the door for the argument
that, if the tenant took over the business of the freeholder, the freeholder's period
of occupation can, where relevant, count towards the overall fourteen-year period.
Of course, if the fourteen years' qualification is not satisfied, the tenant (no matter how short the period of occupation is) will be entitled to compensation at the
lower rate. As regards leases granted before 1 October 1954, an additional limitation exists. This is that no compensation for disturbance is payable unless the tenant or someone else has, on the date on which the holding is to be quit,
continuously occupied the holding (in whole or in part) for the tenant's business
purposes for at least five years.[178]

Traditionally, the requirement of fourteen years' business user was strictly **5.42**
applied.[179] The High Court in *Department of Environment v Royal Insurance Plc*,
for example, held that the claim for higher rate compensation was defeated in circumstances where the tenant took a fourteen-year lease, but entered into physical
occupation one day after the term began.[180] A much different approach was, however, adopted by the Court of Appeal in *Bacchiocchi v Academic Agency Ltd* where
the *Royal Insurance* case was held to be wrongly decided.[181] Simon Brown LJ
acknowledged that the determination of whether business occupation had persisted for the appropriate period should take into account short periods, either at
the beginning, mid-term or end of the contractual lease, where the premises stand
empty.[182] Provided that there is no rival claimant to the status of occupier during
such periods, fitting out or closing down periods should, therefore, be included in
the calculation. As Simon Brown LJ explained:

> That is to my mind how Part II of the 1954 Act should operate in logic and in just-
> ice. It has nothing to do with the *de minimis* principle. Rather it is a recognition that
> the tenant's business interests will not invariably require permanent physical posses-
> sion throughout the whole term of the lease and he ought not to have to resort to

---

[177] See *Cramas Properties Ltd v Connaught Fur Trimmings Ltd* [1965] 2 All ER 382. For these
purposes one government department is deemed to succeed to the business of another: section
56(3).

[178] Sch 9, para 5.

[179] As the period is calculated retrospectively from the date of termination specified in the landlord's notice or the tenant's request, the effect of an interim continuation under section 64 is discounted from this calculation.

[180] [1987] 54 P & CR 26. There Falconer J rejected a *de minimis* argument and worked on the
premise that the qualification period was not on the facts satisfied because there was not a complete
14 years.

[181] As Ward LJ admitted, n 139 above at 251, 'I find it very difficult to accept Falconer J's reasoning that . . . there was no intention to occupy the premises on the first day simply because the
builders began work on the second day'.

[182] ibid at 249.

devices like storage of goods or token visits to satisfy the statutory requirements of continuing occupation. If, of course, the premises are left vacant for a matter of months, the court would be readier to conclude that the thread of continuity has been broken.[183]

Contracting Out

5.43　The general rule is that the right to compensation can be excluded or modified by an agreement in writing.[184] Unfortunately, and as Yates and Hawkins point out: 'This comparatively simple idea is, however, legislated for in a characteristically complex way.'[185] This criticism refers to the fact that the general rule gives way where the premises (which comprise the holding or a part of it)[186] have been occupied for the purposes of the occupier's business (or for those and other purposes) for the whole of five years immediately preceding the date on which the occupier is to quit the holding.[187] In such circumstances, any agreement which purports to exclude or to reduce compensation before its accrual is void.[188] This is regardless of whether it is contained in the lease or in an extraneous document and whether it is entered into before or after the termination of the contractual tenancy. It is arguable that the right to compensation accrues when the landlord serves either a section 25 notice or counter notice which specifies opposition only on the grounds (e), (f) and/or (g).[189] If correct, then the insertion of other grounds of opposition will entail that the right has not accrued. Indeed, in those circumstances the right will not accrue until the landlord's additional grounds are withdrawn or dismissed by the court. When the identity of the occupier has changed within the five-year period, however, the agreement is invalidated only if the new occupier was a successor to the business of the previous occupier. Merely being a successor in title to the previous tenant is insufficient to continue the chain of

---

[183]　ibid at 250. As Pryor J explained in *Sight & Sound Education Ltd v Books Etc Ltd*, n 138 above, 'The process of moving out and timing your move is part of the general process of occupation, and a few days either at the beginning or the end—at the beginning when you take up occupation or at the end when you go out of occupation—cannot destroy the general continuity of occupation for business purposes.

[184]　Section 38(3). This extends also to tenancies terminated in the public interest or due to national security: section 59(2). The Law Reform Advisory Committee for Northern Ireland Report recommended that, excepting public authorities, there should be no contracting out of the compensation provisions (n 9 above at para 8.3.7). This approach is now embodied in article 24 of the Business Tenancies (Northern Ireland) Order 1996.

[185]　D Yates and AJ Hawkins, *Landlord & Tenant Law* (2nd edn, 1986) at 750.

[186]　See *Edicron v William Whitely*, n 173 above.

[187]　*Section 38(2)*. It is clear from *Bacchiocchi v Academic Agency Ltd*, n 139 above, that the date the tenant is to quit is that on which the tenant will legally be required to give up possession to the landlord. There, due to section 64, the tenant was to quit at the expiry of 3 months following final disposal of the proceedings. It is not necessarily the date specified in the renewal documentation.

[188]　An agreement made after the right to compensation has accrued is always valid: section 38(2).

[189]　cf Reynolds and Clark who suggest that the right accrues only when the tenant has quit the premises (n 50 above at 364). This argument, however, seemingly fails to distinguish between entitlement and payment.

occupation. Nothing in the Act, moreover, prevents the parties from entering an agreement which increases the amount of compensation beyond that payable under the statutory calculation. If the lease contains a provision as to compensation payable on termination, the tenant can choose whether to claim under section 37 or the lease. As Ward LJ commented in *Bacchiocchi v Academic Agency Ltd*:

> Section 38 operates to restrict the freedom of contract which would otherwise allow the parties to agree that no such compensation shall be paid. It operates in favour of the tenant and against the landlord. Its purpose is to ameliorate the tenant's position by imposing the statutory scheme of compensation on the landlord once the tenant qualifies for relief through five years' occupation for business purposes.[190]

The Meaning of Occupation

The references in section 38 to the 'whole of five years' and to 'immediately pre- **5.44** ceding' indicate, respectively, that continuous occupation is required and must continue up to the date of quitting. In *Bacchiocchi v Academic Agency Ltd*, the court was faced with a novel point concerning occupation in this context. From 1974 to 1994, the tenant ran a restaurant business in Bath. He held under a twenty-year lease and the tenancy fell within the catchment of the 1954 Act. In 1993, the landlords served a section 25 notice on the tenant. The notice stated that they would oppose the tenant's application for renewal on the basis of redevelopment and reconstruction and owner occupation. The tenant served a negative counter notice and applied to the court. The landlords then filed an answer that no longer opposed the application, but did object to the terms proposed by the tenant. The tenant later had a change of heart and decided to retire from business. He withdrew his application on 11 May 1994. By operation of section 64, the tenancy was continued until 11 August 1994 and terminated on that date. The tenant, however, mistakenly believed that the lease terminated on 29 July and moved out of possession on that date. In the normal course of events, the tenant would be entitled to double rate compensation under section 37. The landlords, however, contended that no compensation whatsoever was payable because the right had been excluded in the lease.

The crucial issue was whether, by moving out twelve days early, the tenant had sat- **5.45** isfied the conditions as set out in section 38(2). If so, the contracting out provision would be invalid. Ward LJ felt that to give effect to the statutory purpose, 'the question should be approached broadly rather than narrowly'.[191] The case was to turn upon the meaning to be given to the expression 'occupied for the purposes of a business carried on by the occupier'. The appellate court acknowledged that the meaning of occupation in section 38 should bear an allied meaning as to that given for the purposes of section 23.[192] On the basis that there occupation can

---

[190] N 139 above at 251.
[191] ibid.
[192] See Chapter 3.

persist even though the premises are closed (for example, seasonally), Simon Brown LJ concluded that it must follow that section 38 can be satisfied where the tenancy comes to an end during such period of closure:

> What is it, therefore, one asks about periods of mid-term closure for repairs and the like that in the eyes of the law they do not destroy the continuity of business occupation? That is the critical question and the answer is surely this: each of these events is recognisable as an incident in the ordinary course or conduct of business life. By the same token . . . so also it [occupation] may have to be delayed for the premises to be fitted out in the first place, or may have to end before the term of the lease expires so that the premises may be cleaned up and handed over with vacant possession on the due date.[193]

Accordingly, as the tenant had intended (albeit mistakenly) to quit on the proper date and to remain responsible under the tenancy until that time, it could not be said that occupation for business purposes had prematurely ceased. Instead, the tenant's conduct was viewed as a normal incident of winding down a business at the end of the lease.[194]

5.46 It is not uncommon for compensation to be excluded in a lease for longer than five years. The exclusion is not void *ab initio*, but will be rendered inoperative only when, at the end of the lease, the five years' occupation can be established. Until that time, the agreement will be effective if the lease is prematurely terminated before the qualifying period is satisfied or there is a late change in tenant and the nature of the business carried out on the holding. It is advisable, therefore, for landlords to include an exclusion in all cases and not merely those leases which are granted for a term less than five years. The tenant should, however, resist an exclusion clause because it will affect the value of the lease towards the last five or so years of its contractual term. Where relevant, both parties should remain aware of this five-year condition and, hence, the timing of a section 25 notice should be keyed in so as to ensure termination before the five-year period is reached. Conversely, the tenant's section 26 request should attempt to ensure that the five-year mark is passed before the lease can be terminated under the Act. The landlord must also bear in mind the extensions which are possible under the Act and build these into the calculation.[195]

---

[193] N 139 above at 249. Ward LJ added at 253: 'To insist . . . that there be precise coincidence of time between cessation of all activity and the moment when the obligation to quit arises, will produce commercial absurdity. It is an affront to common sense to require a pot and pan to be left on the premises till the clock strikes midnight on the last day. Common sense surely dictates that there be an allowance for reasonable leeway.'

[194] For a criticism of the Court of Appeal's approach: see F Bennion (1998) NL, 26 June at 953; 3 July at 986; see also J Morgan (1999) JBL 264.

[195] Extensions are available under section 31(2) (up to one year); section 36(2) (an agreed or reasonable period); and section 64 (three months after final disposal).

H. Misrepresentation

The Act contains a separate provision for compensation for misrepresentation or **5.47**
concealment. The tenant can obtain compensation under section 55 if the application for a new lease is rejected because of the competent landlord's misrepresentation to, or concealment of a material fact from, the court.[196] This remedy is in addition to any common law remedies.[197] The compensation payable under section 55 is not, however, punitive[198] and the measure of damages is that which is sufficient to compensate the tenant for any loss sustained as a result of the refusal. If the tenant is entitled to compensation for disturbance under section 37, that award will be taken into account in the assessment of compensation for misrepresentation. Loss of expected profits and removal expenses may, however, be included in the calculation.[199] Unlike compensation for disturbance, the scope of section 55 is not keyed in to a particular ground of opposition relied on by the competent landlord. It is, however, most likely to be relevant where the landlord bases opposition on demolition and reconstruction and/or own occupation. This is because, in both instances, the landlord will have to demonstrate the necessary intention and it is to that intention that any misrepresentation will normally strike. The misrepresentation (which can be negligent or fraudulent) or the concealment (which recognises that the landlord must act in good faith) must induce the court to reject the tenant's application. Hence, no compensation is available in circumstances where the landlord bona fide sets up a ground of opposition and subsequent to the hearing has a change of plans.

Unlike compensation for disturbance, the tenant must have applied for a renewal. **5.48**
This may involve the tenant having to go through the motions of a seemingly hopeless application so as to be eligible for compensation. In addition, the tenant must also establish that the misrepresentation or concealment actually induced the court to reject the tenant's application. As it currently stands, section 55 does not take into account any inducement which persuades the tenant to act in any particular way.[200] As Gatehouse J commented in *Deeley v Maison AEL Ltd*:

---

[196] The landlord for these purposes being the defendant/respondent to the proceedings.
[197] Such as deceit or negligence: *French v Lowen* [1925] EGD 150. The crime of perjury might also be committed by a landlord. Under article 28 of the Business Tenancies (Northern Ireland) Order 1996, fraud or wilful concealment comprises a statutory, triable-either-way offence. The maximum penalties on summary conviction being a fine and/or six months imprisonment and, on indictment, a fine and/or two years imprisonment.
[198] See *Engleheart v Catford* [1926] EGD 192. The Law Reform Advisory Committee for Northern Ireland Report rejected the notion of punitive damages because it was, 'exercised by the practical difficulty of assessing the basis on which "punitive" damages could be assessed' (n 9 above at para 5.3.1).
[199] *Clark v Kirby-Smith* [1964] Ch 506.
[200] See *Thorne v Smith* [1947] KB 307.

[T]he words in section 55 relating to business tenancies are specific and unequivocal . . . [W]e feel compelled to hold that, as a matter of plain language, the provisions of the section are not satisfied where a tenant agrees to vacate and the court, by its order, merely records that agreement. Even if that can constitute the 'refusal' of an order for the grant of a new tenancy, the court is induced into giving it not by the misrepresentation or concealment of material facts but by the agreement between the parties. An inducement of the tenant into making the agreement is not, and cannot be treated as, an inducement of the court into giving the refusal.[201]

In its Working Paper, the Law Commission expressed the view that requirement of a court application was clearly illogical.[202] Not surprisingly, its 1992 Report recommended that compensation should be available under section 55 when the tenant is also induced not to apply to court or to withdraw an application.[203] The purpose of the reform is primarily to achieve symmetry between the two compensation schemes and to avoid unnecessary applications to court.

I. Final Disposal

5.49   As previously mentioned, the date of termination set out in the section 25 notice or section 26 request is not necessarily the date on which (whether the tenant's application is successful or not) the current tenancy will end. Under section 64, where the tenant makes an application to the court for a new tenancy and the termination date specified in the renewal documentation expires within three months of the final disposal of the application, the tenancy automatically continues until the end of that three-month period.[204] The tenant need do nothing and it is the whole tenancy that is continued in this way. Final disposal occurs when all proceedings (including appeal) have been determined and any time for further appeals has expired.[205] Alternatively, it arises when an application has been withdrawn or from the discontinuance of proceedings. In *Austin Reed v Royal Insurance Co (No 2)*, for example, the date of final disposal, where the Court of Appeal refused leave to appeal to the House of Lords, was the date on which time to petition the Appeals Committee of the House of Lords expired.[206] The purpose of

---

[201] (1989) July 28 CA.

[202] N 8 above at para 3.6.16. It should not be forgotten that the tenant can still claim damages at common law.

[203] N 9 above at para 287. The same recommendation was made by the Law Reform Advisory Committee for Northern Ireland Report (above at para 5.3.3) and has since found its way into article 27(2).

[204] Although the three-month period is retained in Northern Ireland, the Lands Tribunal is the discretion to order a different termination date: article 11(1).

[205] Leave to appeal out of time may, however, be granted within the three-month period: *Rawashdeh v Lane* (1988) 40 EG 109. The principles upon which such leave is to be granted are as set out in *CM Van Stillevoldt BV v EL Carriers Inc* [1983] 1 All ER 699.

[206] [1956] 3 All ER 490. Similarly, in Northern Ireland, the meaning of 'final disposal' is expressly defined as being the earliest date by which the proceedings on the application (including appeal proceedings) have been determined: article 11(2).

section 64 (No 2) was described as follows by Sachs LJ in *Zenith Investments Ltd v Kammins Ballrooms Ltd*:

> The manifest object of section 64 as a whole was to ensure that during the periods, sometimes prolonged, whilst litigation between landlord and tenant was pending and neither party knew that a new lease would be granted, there should yet be certainty as between them relating to their interim obligations. It was intended that they should not be beset with the hazy, one is tempted to say crazy, problems that can arise under the law of landlord and tenant between parties who do not know whether the one who is in possession of the property is a trespasser or a tenant—problems which can be of great interest to lawyers but can infuriate laymen . . .[I]t simply intended to produce clarity as between the parties until all real disputes had been finally disposed of.[207]

Criticisms

Although intrinsically reasonable, section 64 is vulnerable to some criticism. First, **5.50** where the tenant enters a genuine appeal, the period of three months is hardly sufficient within which to locate new premises. If the tenant attempts to find alternative accommodation, it should be borne in mind that the tenant is under a continuing condition to remain in occupation of the premises throughout all of the proceedings.[208] If the tenant ceases to be in occupation, the protection of the Act is withdrawn and the chance of a renewal is lost. In 1969, the Law Commission thought it unreasonable to expect a business tenant to wait three months before seeking other premises and unrealistic to suppose that other accommodation will be found in that time.[209] The Commission recommended that the tenant should be required only to occupy up to the time of the court order, any later and intermediate period being of no relevance. This recommendation was not to find its way into the Law of Property Act 1969 and has not been championed since. Second, the possibility exists that a tenant can exploit the provision, and so extend the current tenancy for as long as possible, by entering a notice of appeal in circumstances where there is no reasonable prospect of an appeal succeeding. Such appeal perhaps destined to be abandoned at the last moment. The motive of the tenant may be merely to gain an extra period of occupation[210] or might be designed to deter the landlord's development plans.[211] Nevertheless, the tenant is allowed to manipulate the system and the courts feel obliged to condone unmeritorious appeals. As Glidewell LJ made clear in *Burgess v Stafford Hotels Ltd*: 'One cannot say that a person who is granted such rights [to appeal] and takes advantage of them is behaving disgracefully or is deserving of

---

[207] N 49 above at 1286.
[208] *Caplan (I&H) v Caplan No 2* [1963] 2 All ER 930.
[209] N 7 above at para 45.
[210] See *Photo Centre Ltd v Grantham Court Properties (Mayfair) Ltd* (1964) 191 EG 505.
[211] See *AJA Smith Transport v BRB* (1980) 257 EG 1257. There Brandon LJ felt that the tenant's use of section 64 was close to an abuse of the judicial process.

moral condemnation. The landlord's remedy . . . is either to apply for an order to strike out . . . or to apply for an order for security of costs, or to make both applications.'[212]

5.51 Most cases deal with the scenario where the tenant's quest for a new lease is still technically afoot, albeit perhaps doomed to failure. A different situation arose in *Mark Stone Car Sales Ltd v Howard De Walden Estates Ltd* where the tenant's interest solely concerned compensation without even the possibility of a renewal.[213] The landlord was able to oppose successfully the renewal on the basis of redevelopment, but the appeal concerned whether the landlord had also offered suitable alternative accommodation under section 30(1)(d). If so, the tenant would be deprived of compensation. As Brooke LJ explained:

> Where a landlord has established to the court's satisfaction one or more substantive grounds for opposing the grant of a new tenancy which are not the subject of an appeal it seems quite absurd, if it be correct, that the tenant's current tenancy should automatically continue until three months after the date on which an appeal against a concurrent adverse finding on a section 30(1)(d) issue is finally determined.

Although Brooke LJ hoped that Parliament would intervene and amend the 1954 Act, he felt that ' . . . imaginative judicial interpretation' might be employed in order to avoid the obvious injustice which would otherwise befall landlords. He focused attention on the word 'application' as employed in section 64 and suggested that its final disposal might be construed as meaning 'when a court's unappealed decision put paid to any question of the grant of a new tenancy'. This is a simple and straightforward solution which may readily be employed by those judges who favour the purposive route to statutory interpretation. For those who seek a literal meaning, however, the impossibility of renewal may be viewed as the disposal of an issue rather than the disposal of the application.

---

[212] [1990] 3 All ER 222 at 228. The appellate court made the point, however, that appeals will be struck out only in clear and obvious cases and not when an extensive inquiry into the facts is going to be necessary. It was also said that to raise an issue on appeal, which had not been raised below, would be an abuse of process when its argument would entail a rehearing.

[213] (1997) 30 January CA.

6

THE INTERIM RENT

A. Introduction

The facility of an interim rent was created in 1969, by the insertion of section 24A **6.01** into the Landlord and Tenant Act 1954, to offer the landlord much needed protection from financial disadvantage during the continuation period between the end of the contractual tenancy and the commencement of a new lease. It is a bridging device which caters for a variation of the former contractual rent until the time when, on renewal, a market rent becomes payable. The interim rent, therefore, constitutes a counterweight to the tenant's right to prolong the continuation tenancy under section 24(1).[1] As Lawton LJ explained in *Bloomfield v Ashwright Ltd*: 'There were probably two reasons for its introduction. First, experience between 1954 and 1969 had shown that some tenants who anticipated a rise in their rent following the grant of a new lease had delayed the day of judgment. The second reason was that by 1969 inflation was beginning to rear its head in the United Kingdom.'[2]

Nevertheless, it is to be admitted that the facility is markedly deficient. It is of lim- **6.02** ited availability, is based upon unrealistic comparables, operates only prospectively from the date of the landlord's application, and is dependant upon the vagaries of judicial discretion in both its grant and its calculation. In addition,

---

[1] Accordingly, no interim rent is available when the tenancy is being continued under section 28 (that is, in circumstances where renewal has been agreed and will commence at a future date).
[2] (1983) 47 P & CR 78 at 80.

owing to oblique draughtsmanship the statutory provisions challenge the judiciary with 'a notoriously difficult task'.[3] It is a sad commentary that even Megarry J found the law to be 'difficult and puzzling' and admitted 'to having groped my way to a conclusion . . . for reasons which defy any detailed analysis'.[4] Not surprisingly, section 24A has posed interpretational difficulties for courts and practitioners alike. The sole responsibility for the unsatisfactory state of the law, undoubtedly, lies at the door of Parliament. Although proposals for reform have been put forward by the Law Commission, the relationship of commercial landlord and tenant maintains a low political profile. It is likely that the recommendations for change (as discussed below) will eventually become law, but reform is not an imminent prospect.

B. The Old Law

6.03   As initially enacted, the 1954 Act provided that, during a section 24 continuation, the original contractual terms (other than those concerning termination) were to be preserved. This entailed that the contractual rent payable to the landlord was frozen until either the continuation tenancy was ended or a new lease came into being. The temptation was offered to the tenant to delay proceedings for as long as possible and, thereby, engineer a pecuniary advantage over the landlord. The financial incentive could prove considerable. In *Re No 88, High Road, Kilburn*, for example, the original rent of £250 per annum was increased to £3,000 per annum on the order of a new tenancy.[5] The landlords' predicament was compounded by the fact that the statutory scheme willingly lends itself to manipulation by the tenant. It is a relatively simple matter for a tenant to stall proceedings and to prolong a continuation well beyond any termination date specified in either the landlord's section 25 notice or the tenant's section 26 request.[6] As Harman J acknowledged in *Espresso Coffee Machine Co Ltd v Guardian Assurance Co Ltd*, a substantial time can elapse 'before every legal artifice is exhausted . . . That may not be a very admirable attitude, but it is one which the law entitled the tenants to take up, and they unblushingly do so.'[7] Although the widely held view was that this produced manifest injustice, the courts felt powerless to assist the landlord. As Wynn-Parry

---

[3]   *Per* Megarry J in *English Exporters v Eldonwall* [1973] 1 Ch 423 at 431.

[4]   ibid at 434. These difficulties were shared also by Stamp J in *Regis Property Co Ltd v Lewis & Peat Ltd* [1970] 1 Ch 695 and Goff LJ in *Fawke v Viscount Chelsea* [1979] 3 All ER 568.

[5]   [1959] 1 All ER 527.

[6]   In such documentation there must be stated a termination date for the existing tenancy and this can be no earlier than 6 months and no later than 12 months from the service of the notice/request: sections 25(2), 26(2).

[7]   [1958] 1 WLR 900 at 903. In *Re Sunlight House* (1959) The Times, 4 February, the tenant benefitted to the tune of £50,000 from manipulating section 64. As RE Megarry [1959] 75 LQR 180 commented: 'The vice of this provision against the background of steadily rising rents that have prevailed since the war lies in the direct incentive that it offers to the tenant to adopt delaying tactics.'

J admitted in *Re No 88, High Road, Kilburn*: 'I consider that the result at which I am compelled to arrive is one which is unjust to landlords, but I cannot mitigate that injustice as regards rent.'[8] He did, however, seek to mitigate the hardship with reference to the duration of the new lease ordered.

Prolonging the Continuation Tenancy

The most effective course for a tenant to pursue, in order to prolong the life of a **6.04** continuation tenancy, is to enter an appeal against the decision of the court of first instance. The appeal could relate to the terms of the new lease ordered or the denial of a renewal. By virtue of section 64, a continuation tenancy survives until the end of three months subsequent to the final disposal of the tenant's application. One aim of this provision is to give the tenant a reasonable period, within which to find alternative premises, following an unsuccessful application for a new lease on acceptable terms. As final disposal occurs when all proceedings (including any appeal) have been determined and any time for further appeal has expired, the tenant may have much to gain by taking a matter to appeal even when there is no reasonable prospect of that appeal being successful.[9] The appeal might then be abandoned at the last moment and the three-months period of grace will run from the date of that discontinuance. Although the product may purely be to allow the tenant to prolong the benefit of a low rent, the wording of section 64 is unambiguous and its consequences, seemingly, unavoidable.

An alternative avenue for the tenant to follow, so as to add to the life of the con- **6.05** tinuation tenancy, is afforded by section 36(2). This enables a tenant, who has successfully fought for a new tenancy (possibly one which had in truth never been wanted), to apply to the court within fourteen days of its grant for the revocation of that tenancy.[10] The tenant is, thereby, given a limited 'cooling off' period within which to decline the renewal. Although the tenant may face an order for costs, the court enjoys no power to refuse the application for revocation.[11] Following the order for revocation, section 36(2) ensures that the continuation tenancy subsists for such period as the parties may agree or, in default of agreement, for so long as the court deems reasonable.[12]

Both these statutory provisions enjoy a valid and vital function within the statu- **6.06** tory scheme, but it is likely that Parliament did not foresee the possibility of inflating rents and the scope for tenants to exploit the machinery simply for financial gain. As Wynn-Parry J admitted:

---

[8] N 5 above at 530.
[9] See *Mark Stone Car Sales Ltd v Howard De Walden Estates Ltd* (1997) 30 January CA; see further Chapter 5.
[10] As occurred, for example, in *Re No 88, High Road, Kilburn*, n 5 above.
[11] See *Rom Tyre & Accessories Ltd v Crawford Street Properties* (1996) 197 EG 565.
[12] As it is not a continuation under section 24(1), no interim rent can be applied for during this period of extension. Any existing rent will, however, continue in operation.

It is not for me to speculate whether the legislature intended as a matter of policy what I hold to have been brought about by these sections or whether there has been some mistake . . . but whether it be a matter of policy or a matter of mistake, I can find no way of giving any other construction to these sections than that which I have given.[13]

C. The Current Law

6.07 There is still little that can be done to prevent tenants utilising the statutory scheme as set out above in order to extend artificially the duration of their continuation tenancies. Instead, reform focused upon how to deter tenants from manipulating the system solely for financial profit. By virtue of the Law of Property Act 1969, and following the recommendation of the Law Commission,[14] the 1954 Act was amended. The insertion of section 24A gave the landlord the right to apply for an interim rent during the continuation tenancy. The interim rent is, essentially, the rent which the court decides is reasonable for the tenant to pay while the old tenancy is being continued, in substitution for the historic, contractual rent.[15] This rent is, thereby, intended to be of lesser amount than the market rent which would be awarded on the grant of a new lease. Interestingly, in Northern Ireland the problem is dealt with differently. Although, there is no interim rent facility, the Lands Tribunal has the power to penalise the tenant who procrastinates by directing, when hearing a renewal application, that the old tenancy shall terminate and the new tenancy (and any increased rent) shall be backdated to a time of the Tribunal's choosing.[16] In addition, and following the recommendation of the Law Reform Advisory Committee for Northern Ireland,[17] the landlord can be awarded 'compensation for interim loss of rent' where the tenant either refuses the grant of a new tenancy or withdraws an application.[18]

Who can Apply?

6.08 The interim rent facility is currently available only to the 'competent landlord' as defined in section 44 and Schedule 6 of the 1954 Act. This entails that other landlords (for example, an immediate landlord who does not qualify as being 'compe-

---

[13] *Re No 88, High Road, Kilburn*, n 5 above at 530.
[14] Law Commission Report, *Landlord and Tenant Act 1954 Part II* (1969) Law Com No 17 at paras 22–26.
[15] The liability of the original tenant for breach of an assignee's rental covenant does not, unless it is defined in the lease to include a statutory continuation, run into the continuation period: *City of London v Fell* (1994) 1 AC 458.
[16] Article 11(3) of the Business Tenancies (Northern Ireland) Order 1996.
[17] *Business Tenancies* (1994) Report No 1 at para 7.10.
[18] This right to claim compensation is contained in article 21 of the 1996 Order.

tent') and those acting in the capacity of a tenant have no such right.[19] This somewhat awkward distinction between landlords 'competent' and landlords 'immediate' is one drawn throughout Part II of the Act. Although the same body may be both, where sub-leases have been created this is not necessarily the case. As shown in Chapter 2, the 'immediate landlord' is the person who granted the interest to the tenant/sub-tenant, whereas the identity of the 'competent landlord' is more difficult to discern. This is because 'competency' for these purposes is determined on a temporal level. The Act defines the 'competent landlord' as being the person who is either a mesne landlord whose lease will not end for at least fourteen months or, if none, the freeholder.[20] The policy underlying this, somewhat arbitrary, distinction is that the landlord with less than fourteen months remaining will not be sufficiently equipped to make long-term decisions about the termination and renewal of sub-tenancies. In that context, the distinction may have the hall-mark of common sense, but whether it should extend to the interim rent machinery is questionable. Indeed, the Law Commission Working Paper accepted that, as regards the interim rent, the restrictions upon availability were both anomalous and problematic.[21]

Allowing the Tenant to Apply

The Working Paper saw no objections to the statutory right being extended to the tenant.[22] Admittedly, as the usual trend is towards rising rents, this will at times have little practical value, but at the least it would 'demonstrate the evenhandedness of the law'.[23] The present provisions overlook entirely the depressive effect of an economic recession on rental values and are firmly rooted in the traditional wisdom that commercial rents will continue to rise. This assumption is clearly a fallacy. More recent market conditions have clearly shown the financial prejudice that can arise from the existing limitation. Accordingly, the system is not designed to cater for a downward movement in market values. Scant reliance should be placed upon the court's declared (but as yet untried) ability to order an interim rent of a lesser sum than the former contractual rent.[24] If a decrease was a likely consequence, no landlord would be prepared to make or, if made, continue with an application. During times of recession, or where the premises are in major

6.09

---

[19] Section 24A(1).

[20] Section 44(1)(a),(b). Note that a lessor under a tenancy by estoppel is entitled to apply for an interim rent: *Bell v General Fire and Life Assurance Corporation Plc* (1998) 17 EG 144.

[21] *Part II of the Landlord and Tenant Act 1954* (1988) Working Paper No 111 at paras 3.4.9, 3.4.10.

[22] ibid at para 3.4.10. This was later to form a recommendation within the Law Commission Report, *Business Tenancies: A Periodic Review of the Landlord and Tenant Act 1954* (1992) Law Com No 208 (at para 2.63).

[23] Working Paper, ibid at para 3.4.10.

[24] *Fawke v Viscount Chelsea*, n 4 above, where Goff LJ felt that it would be possible to order a reduced rent where there had been a fall in property prices or, in special cases, a breach by the landlord of repairing covenant.

a new lease.[36] The tenant may then face the payment of substantial arrears as the interim rent to be payable is backdated to the termination date specified in the section 25 notice/section 26 request or the date of the landlord's application, whichever is the later.[37] Some change has, however, been advocated by the Law Commission which, in its 1992 Report, recommended the abolition of the right to make a separate application. Instead, the claim for an interim rent would then be heard only in the course of proceedings.[38] This proposal furthers the Commission's general policy to reduce the number of applications made to the courts. It should also be viewed in the light of the additional recommendation that landlords should be able to initiate a renewal application (currently within the exclusive remit of the tenant).[39]

6.14 As the landlord's application for an interim rent is in the nature of a counterclaim, it is unaffected by the discontinuance of the tenant's action for a renewal.[40] It is a distinct claim independent of the tenant's proceedings. This rule applies in both the county court and the High Court. As Stephenson LJ said in *Michael Kramer & Co v Airways Pension Fund Trustees Ltd*:

> It must be treated separately, and it cannot be discontinued simply by the discontinuance of the tenants' proceedings. However described, and whatever its form, the landlords' application is in substance an originating application. However labelled, it originates, or starts, or initiates a claim, in some sense countering the tenant's application though affording no defence to it, and has its own distinct and separate life . . .[41]

Accordingly, the application may be heard even after the order for a new lease is made.[42] If, however, the proceedings are adjourned it is up to the landlord to keep the application alive and to produce appropriate evidence before the court.[43] In addition, the assignment of the reversion does not prevent the new landlord (albeit acquiring title after the application for an interim rent is made) benefiting from those proceedings. The tenancy continues and the rent continues to be payable. If the assignor and assignee cannot agree as to who is to receive the bene-

---

[36] See *Homeville Estates Ltd v Sams* (1976) 243 EG 827 where the Court of Appeal stressed that it is, to some extent, prejudicial to a tenant if the interim rent is fixed before the terms of the new tenancy.

[37] Section 24A(2); see *Victor Blake (Menswear) Ltd v Westminster City Council* (1978) 249 EG 543; *R v Gravesend County Courts, ex parte Patchett* [1993] 26 EG 125.

[38] N 22 above at para 2.74.

[39] ibid at para 2.55; see Chapter 5.

[40] *Artoc Bank & Trust Ltd v Prudential Assurance Co* [1984] 1 WLR 1181. The same principle will apply if the Law Commission's recommendation that separate applications be abolished is adopted.

[41] (1976) 246 EG 911 at 915.

[42] *Regis Property Co Ltd v Lewis & Peat*, n 4 above.

[43] *Arora v Bose* (1998) 23 February CA where the landlord's application was adjourned and never formally restored. At the renewal hearing, some four years later, it was held too late for the landlord to resuscitate the application.

fit of the order, this is a matter for them to litigate amongst themselves. It does not concern the court's jurisdiction under section 24A. The award of an interim rent is, therefore, not a money order payable by a party, it is simply an order for the determination of rent payable under the tenancy.[44] As such, the rent concerns particular premises and not a particular person. As Lawton LJ acknowledged in *Bloomfield v Ashwright Ltd*:

> The ownership of the reversion to the premises may pass from one person to another for various reasons, but when there is such a transfer the tenancy goes on and the rent which is payable in respect of the tenancy continues to be payable. The court is concerned with determining that which is to be paid for the tenancy.[45]

The Case for Automatic Entitlement

In its Working Paper, the Law Commission considered briefly whether it was necessary to persevere with the need for an express application to the court.[46] Automatic entitlement to an interim rent was viewed as an alternative, but not favoured. It was, however, conceded that automatic entitlement would reduce the discretion of the court while circumventing any trap for the ill-advised landlord.[47] Two justifications for maintaining the *status quo* were offered in the Working Paper. First, automatic entitlement would encourage requests for a rent increase by landlords who would not otherwise bother. Second, it would deprive tenants of a positive warning that a rent increase may be on the way. The assumption that such warning is necessary is not beyond question. Indeed, the sentiment was not echoed by Nourse LJ in *French v Commercial Union Life Assurance Plc* who concluded that the shock of an increased rent occurs irrespective of whether the tenant had been forewarned or not.[48] Nourse LJ was, therefore, more concerned with the shock to the tenant's pocket than the shock to the tenant's senses. The Law Commission refused the opportunity to examine the argument for change in any greater depth and, in its subsequent Report, declined to investigate the matter further.

6.15

---

[44] Accordingly, if the tenant appeals against the interim rent, the landlord cannot levy distress until the appeal is resolved: *Eren v Tranmac* [1997] 2 EGLR 211. As an interim rent is liable to be reduced on appeal, there is no certainty as to what sum could be the subject of distraint.

[45] N 2 above at 83.

[46] N 21 above at para 3.4.14.

[47] It must always be appreciated that for the current provisions to fully benefit the landlord, the lessor must, as recognised by Pennycuick VC in *Stream Properties Ltd v Davis* [1972] 2 All ER 746 at 751, 'make application . . . at the earliest available date then the new rent will relate back accordingly'.

[48] [1993] 1 EGLR 113; see M Haley [1997] Conv at 228. It is also worthy of note that the 'new rent rules' (see below) advocated in the Working Paper, n 21 above at para 3.4.8, do not involve any advance warning of a higher rent to the tenant.

D. Period of Payment

6.16 Under section 24A(2), the revised rent is payable from either the termination date set out in, as appropriate, the section 25 notice or the section 26 request or, if later, the date that the interim rent proceedings were commenced (that is, when the application for an interim rent is issued by the court).[49] The rent then runs until the termination of the continuation tenancy. The commencement date, therefore, is not normally the day that the original lease ends and this entails that the tenant can enjoy a period of grace, potentially spanning a considerable period of time, free from any rental increase. It is hard to justify why the termination notices are keyed into the system of interim rents. It is, moreover, unrealistic to limit the provisions only to delay which occurs during the period after such notices have been served. The interim rent provisions, thereby, ignore the period, as equally profitable for the tenant, between the end of the contractual term and the initiation of the termination procedures. This is particularly harsh in the light that the court has no power to back-date an application to achieve a fairer result.[50] The disadvantage to the landlord was recognised by Lord Denning in *Secretary of State for Social Services v Rossetti Lodge Investment Co* who, in an attempt to side-step such consequences, said by way of *obiter*: 'I think that section 24A should be given a liberal interpretation in accordance with the manifest intention of the section. Under it the court can determine the interim rent to take effect as from the expiry of the old lease.'[51] On the point of construction of section 24A(2), Lord Denning unarguably arrived at the wrong conclusion.[52] The sub-section is expressed in clearest terms. Nevertheless, Lord Denning's perception of how the law should be is far less susceptible to challenge.

Suggestions for Reform

6.17 Although it was recommended by the Law Commission that the service of termination documentation as a trigger mechanism be preserved, the Report admitted that a tenant could manufacture the prolongation of a continuation tenancy simply by pre-empting the landlord and serving a section 26 request. It is then open for the tenant to insert the longest termination date possible (that is, twelve months hence) and effectively freeze the rent for that period. Consequently, a compromise measure was advocated. It was recommended that this financial advantage should be minimised by making the interim rent run from the earliest date that could have been specified in the section 26 request (that is, six months).[53] A similar principle will apply where (on the understanding that the Law

---

[49] *Stream Properties Ltd v Davis*, n 47 above. Any interest is payable from the date that the interim rent falls due. This rule is subject to any contrary provision in the lease.

[50] *R v Gravesend County Courts ex parte Patchett*, n 37 above.

[51] (1975) 18 February CA.

[52] See *Victor Blake (Menswear) Ltd v City of Westminster*, n 37 above, where the conflicting interpretation in *Stream Properties Ltd v Davis*, n 47 above, was followed.

[53] N 22 above at para 2.65.

Commission's proposal is enacted) it is the tenant who applies for an interim rent and the unfair prolongation is engineered in the landlord's termination notice.[54]

E. A Discretionary Award

Within the interim rent machinery there exist two distinct means through which **6.18** the judge must enter 'the realm of pure discretion where it is hardest to condense in words the dialogue of the intracranial jury room'.[55] First, it is at the discretion of the court whether an interim rent should be ordered.[56] Second, the actual calculation of any rent awarded involves the exercise of much discretion on the part of the judge.[57] Issues as to whether such powers are appropriate or necessary components of the system are, however, seldom considered.[58] It was established by Megarry J in *English Exporters v Eldonwall Ltd* that there is no obligation on the court to set an interim rent and that section 24A(1) is merely permissive in nature.[59] Such is, in any event, clear from the wording of that section. It has, however, become the accepted and general rule that the discretion will normally be exercised in favour of the landlord.[60] It could be argued that this has now, tacitly, been elevated to a presumption which, unless rebutted by the tenant, will prevail.[61] The circumstances in which any such presumption can be defeated, however, remain vague[62] and will be dependent on the merits of a given case.[63] Megarry J was prepared to venture into the realms of speculation:

> Nevertheless, there may be many cases in which proceedings for the fixing of an interim rent might be unreasonable or even oppressive. Thus the gap between the rent being paid and the rent sought by the landlord may be so small; or the proceedings may have marched on apace, so that the period for which any interim rent could operate would be trivial.[64]

---

[54] ibid at para 2.66.

[55] *Per* Goulding J cited in *O'May v City of London Real Property* [1983] 2 AC 726 at 742.

[56] Section 24A(1) provides that: 'The landlord of a tenancy to which this Part of the Act applies may . . . apply to the court to determine a rent . . . and the court may determine a rent accordingly.'

[57] Section 24A(1) refers to 'a rent which it would be reasonable for the tenant to pay' and section 24A(3) obliges the court to 'have regard to the rent payable under the terms of the [existing] tenancy'.

[58] But see *Michael Kramer & Co v Airways Pension Fund Trustees*, n 41 above.

[59] N 3 above; see also *Charles Follett Ltd v Cabtell Investments Ltd* (1988) 55 P & CR 36.

[60] *English Exporters v Eldonwall Ltd*, ibid; see also *Bailey Organisation v UK Temperance and General Provident Insurance* (1975) 233 EG 507.

[61] See *Michael Kramer & Co v Airways Pension Fund Trustees*, n 41 above.

[62] As Lawton LJ admitted in *Bloomfield v Ashwright*, n 2 above at 84: 'There may be circumstances when it would be unjust to make a tenant pay an interim rent. I find it myself difficult to imagine such circumstances, but no doubt others with a more fertile imagination than I have can do so.'

[63] *Arora v Bose*, n 43 above.

[64] The *English Exporters* case, n 3 above at 425. In *Michael Kramer & Co v Airways Pension Fund Trustees Ltd*, n 41 above, the period of five months was held not to be trivial for these purposes. There Stephenson LJ reiterated the rule that, in normal cases, an interim rent should be awarded.

6.19 Although the rhetoric of Megarry J is seductive, such justification for persevering with this brand of judicial discretion is based on a dubious foundation. The assumption that there might be 'many cases' where an interim rent is 'unreasonable' or 'oppressive' is one incapable of substantiation. Certainly, it is arguable that the illustrations provided by Megarry J do not, in any event, offend 'reasonableness' or constitute 'oppression'. Megarry J, however, added two further justifications: first, that the tenant has no statutory escape route, akin to section 36(2), from a continuation tenancy; and, second, that it might be the landlord who delays the proceedings under the Act. Both these arguments can be countered: section 27 offers the tenant an alternative escape route and, despite any delay by the landlord, the tenant is not tied to a continuation tenancy. The tenant, therefore, has the option to quit if the rent is raised. As the primary purpose of section 24A(1) is to protect the financial interests of the landlord, the alleged benefits of retaining judicial discretion here are greatly outweighed by the disadvantage of maintaining a procedural hurdle which if not taken, or taken late, can hit hard the landlord's pocket.[65] In the context where the court will rarely (if at all) refuse the landlord's application, the filter can be seen to achieve little and, for practical purposes, to be unnecessary.[66]

F. Calculation of the Interim Rent

6.20 As to the quantum of the interim rent, the courts have experienced many problems. These arise from the somewhat obscure wording of section 24A and, in particular, its uneasy interaction with section 34.[67] Before examining the manner in which the judiciary have grappled with the technicalities of construction, it is helpful to outline the ingredients of the statutory formula through which the interim rent is to be assessed. First, account must be taken of the calculus provided within section 34(1),(2) and these provisions applied as if the court is setting a rent under a hypothetical yearly tenancy.[68] Second, regard must be had to the rent payable under the existing tenancy.[69] Third, the court has to determine a rent

---

[65] See *Arora v Bose*, n 43 above. Obviously, if delay or failure to apply for an interim rent is the responsibility of the landlord's legal adviser, liability may arise in professional negligence: see *Rogers v Bulleid Leeks & Co* (1992) 4 November CA.

[66] See *Bloomfield v Ashwright*, n 2 above.

[67] See *French v Commercial Union Life Assurance Plc*, n 48 above. Section 34(1) empowers the court to determine a rent which 'having regard to the terms of the tenancy (other than those relating to rent) the holding might reasonably expected to be let in the open market by a willing lessor'; see further Chapter 9.

[68] Section 24A(3). The operation of section 34 is itself fraught with difficulties: see, for example, *Baptist v Masters of the Bench and Trustees of the Honourable Society of Grays Inn* [1993] 2 EGLR 159 and *Ward v Soho Estates Ltd* (1994) 17 November CA.

[69] Section 24A(3).

which it would be reasonable for the tenant to pay.[70] In *Charles Follett Ltd v Cabtell Properties*, Nourse LJ concluded that this latter condition imposed what could validly be described as a 'reasonable rent'.[71]

The Approach of Stamp J

The initial occasion on which the court had the opportunity to unravel this curi- **6.21**
ous and complex formula fell to Stamp J in *Regis Property Co Ltd v Lewis & Peat*.[72]
Although it was later to be said that his analysis fell into error,[73] the decision
attempted to provide guidance as to the future operation of the interim rent
machinery. In a reserved judgment, Stamp J gave short shrift to arguments that
section 24A presented the court with an indefinite and unguided discretion as to
what rent was reasonable for the tenant to pay. If it were so, he concluded, 'the rent
will in the end be fixed by the length of the judge's foot'.[74] His approach was that
the legislature, having set out a formula, could not have 'intended to enable the
court to depart from it to an unspecified and arbitrary extent'.[75] Guided by this
appealing judicial pragmatism, it was held that the calculation of an interim rent
was a single, straightforward operation. The machinery of section 34(1),(2) was
to be applied in its normal manner modified only by the concession that, due to
section 24A(3), the existing rent could be a factor in the assessment. As section 34
was otherwise to be applied *simpliciter* to the existing tenancy, as if it were a yearly
tenancy, the weight given to the existing rent was not such as to provide the tenant with a cushion against a steep rent increase. As Stamp J explained:

> [I]f the existing terms as to rent throw no light on the rent at which the holding
> might reasonably be expected to be let under a tenancy from year to year, you are no
> more bound to take the actual rent into account as a relevant element in determin-
> ing the rent than you would an irrelevant covenant . . . Finding that some of the
> terms of the existing tenancy and the existing rent do not on the facts of a particular
> case assist you in determining what the interim rent ought to be, you ignore them.[76]

According to this view, therefore, the existing rent was of evidential value only.
Once the valuation exercise under section 34 was complete, the issue was closed
and there was to be no modification by reference to 'reasonable' in section 24A(1)
or the existing rent in section 24A(3). The attraction of this approach is that it
provides greater certainty and is more in accordance with the mischief underlying
the existence of the interim rent provisions.

---

[70] Section 24A(1).
[71] N 59 above at 43.
[72] N 4 above.
[73] *Per* Goff LJ in *Fawke v Viscount Chelsea*, n 4 above at 573; see also the *English Exporters* case, n 3 above.
[74] N 4 above at 698.
[75] ibid.
[76] ibid at 699, 670.

The Correct Approach

6.22 This simplicity of approach did not appeal to the High Court in *English Exporters v Eldonwall Ltd*.[77] While taking account of Stamp J's 'closely reasoned' and 'persuasive and powerful' judgment,[78] Megarry J did not accept that such an elaborate formula could be reduced to such a convenient and straightforward prescription. In holding that the court had to calculate the market rent of a notional yearly tenancy, identify the existing rent and, aided by the concept of reasonableness, determine the interim rent at some level between those figures, he was critical of the *Regis* approach. Megarry J's analysis in the *English Exporters* case was to set the template for future decisions. The following points can be distilled from this influential judgment. First, the conclusion drawn in *Regis* that section 24A was not concerned with rent under a new tenancy, but with a rent to be paid under an existing tenancy was viewed as wrong, giving 'scant weight' to the wording of that section.[79] The interpretation favoured by Megarry J was that, once the market rent of the hypothetical annual tenancy had been assessed under section 34, regard must, in all cases, be had to the existing rent under the continuation tenancy. This regard is a separate and independent requirement. It does not, however, entail that the market rent and the existing rent are to be given equal weight; rather it is a process 'of applying one factor, namely, the market rent, and, where appropriate, suitably tempering it by reference to the existing rent'.[80] The idea that section 24A(3) and section 34 could be applied, within one operation, to the existing tenancy was rejected. The statutory provisions spoke of two different tenancies and two different calculations.

6.23 Second, the requirement that the interim rent be one which is reasonable for the tenant to pay, did not give the court a roving commission to consider every relevant fact. It merely provides 'for the rent that it would be reasonable for the tenant to pay to be worked out in a particular way, namely, by taking the market rent and then having regard to the existing rent; and that is all . . .'.[81] It should be noted that (despite the original recommendation of the Law Commission in its 1969 Report)[82] the Act does not allude to a 'fair rent' and, accordingly, the court is precluded from considering the interests of the landlord. As Lawton LJ commented in *Bloomfield v Ashwright*, 'whether or not a particular landlord is rich or poor, flush with money or nearly impoverished is irrelevant'.[83] Instead the wording

---

[77] N 3 above.

[78] ibid at 428, 426.

[79] ibid at 428.

[80] ibid at 434.

[81] ibid at 431. The court must take into account all relevant circumstances in a broad and common-sense fashion, giving such weight as it thinks fit to the various factors, in order to reach a right and fair conclusion: *Harwood v Borough of Reigate & Banstead* (1982) 43 P & CR 336.

[82] N 14 above at para 8.

[83] N 2 above at 84.

focuses solely upon the tenant who has to pay the rent. In this way, Megarry J argued that the restrictive formula contained in section 24A undermined the 'length of the judge's foot' criticism. In the light of subsequent cases, this assertion appears little more than ill-founded optimism. Megarry J's interpretation, moreover, clearly views the old rent as being a depressive factor and does not cater for the situation where the market rent is valued at less than the old contractual rent. In the circumstances that the old rent merely provides a cushion for the tenant, the landlord would not be able to rely on the higher figure in order to produce an interim rent above the market value.

Third, the elaboration of the language used by Parliament must be for some pur-   **6.24**
pose. If a market value was to be fixed (which is, essentially, what occurred in *Regis*), then the complex formula within section 24A would stand redundant. Megarry J could not accept that the legislature would go to such elaborate lengths for nothing when it could more simply have allowed the permanent rent under a new tenancy to be back-dated or the interim rent to be calculated purely on the basis of section 34. Finally, the conclusion that the award of an interim rent is at the discretion of the court emphasises that section 24A is not designed to provide a rigid valuation according to market values. As Megarry J explained:

> If this were not so, the discretion would have to be exercised on the footing that the court must either refuse to fix an interim rent at all, and so leave the existing rent to continue, or else an interim rent at full market value, with no intermediate rent possible. To me section 24A does not read as if it were intended to provide for all or nothing.[84]

Accordingly, Parliament was seen as offering a cushion for the tenant with the extent of that temperance being decided on the facts of each case. This view does, however, appear to gloss over the additional subsidy afforded by the valuation being of a hypothetical tenancy and not the existing lease. The decision in the *English Exporters* case has subsequently received the support (albeit *obiter*) of the Court of Appeal[85] and the alternative (and equally authoritative) approach of Stamp J must be viewed as incorrect.

Practical Consequences

While the conclusion drawn in *Regis* may be considered as more consistent with   **6.25**
the spirit and intention of section 24A,[86] it is clearly at odds with its wording. Nevertheless, the divergence of statutory interpretation does not, necessarily, entail a different outcome to the case according to which construction is followed. The alternative views are, indeed, capable of producing disparate results, but the

---

[84] N 3 above at 431, 432.
[85] *Fawke v Viscount Chelsea*, n 4 above. It is also in line with the scheme as originally envisaged in 1969 by the Law Commission (n 14 above at para 25).
[86] That is, to prevent the landlord being financially prejudiced during the period of the continuation tenancy.

likelihood of that occurring in practice may not be as great as might be feared. It should not be overlooked that *Regis* recognised that the existing rent was an evidential factor to be taken on board where relevant. The *English Exporters* case, while recognising that the contractual rent must always be looked at, did not set down any rule other than that, where appropriate, the existing rent can temper the market valuation under section 34. In many cases, the 'evidential factor' will govern the discretion of the court and produce either a cushion for the tenant or no discount on this basis. The two routes, thereby, lead towards a similar destination.[87] As Goff LJ explained in *Fawke v Viscount Chelsea*:

> In the result, therefore, both agreed, though for different reasons, that the court and the expert witnesses appearing before it should have regard to the existing rent if it has evidentiary value, but the difference betwen them lies in Stamp J's view that, apart from that, it is irrelevant and the matter ends with the valuation, whereas in Megarry J's view it then has in any event to be considered in order to determine whether it is reasonable to adopt the valuation without modification.[88]

The danger, of course, lies primarily with the flexibility of discretion and the potential for its erratic exercise. The *English Exporters* case clearly opened the door wide for the unguided and uncertain use of discretion in this area. The operation of section 24A is, therefore, purely dependant upon the sense and perceptions of the individual judge. As Nourse LJ concluded in *Charles Follett Ltd v Cabtell Properties*, 'that I think is the inescapable result of Parliament having given no guidance as to the consequences which are to flow from the mandatory regard to the old rent'.[89] The potential consequences of a maverick decision, moreover, are exacerbated by the reluctance of the appellate courts to interfere with the findings at first instance. As the calculation of the interim rent is primarily a question of fact, an appeal will succeed only if there is an error of law.[90]

G. The Fiction of a Yearly Tenancy

6.26   The modifications to the normal section 34 valuation procedure operate to the advantage of the tenant and produce an interim rent discounted below the true market rent for the property. A reduction may occur because the calculation is based upon the fictional premise that what is being valued is a yearly tenancy. It is due to the continuation tenancy being a creature of indeterminate duration, that Parliament elected for the yardstick, admittedly arbitrary, of an annual lease of the

---

[87] See *UDS Trading v BL Holdings* (1982) 261 EG 49.
[88] N 4 above at 573.
[89] N 59 above at 43.
[90] *Halberstam v Tandalco Corporation NV* [1985] 1 EGLR 90; *French v Commercial Union Life Assurance Plc*, n 48 above. For example, where the judge engages in contradictory reasoning or fails to take regard of comparables: *Romulus Materials Ltd v W T Lamb Properties Ltd* (1999) 18 February CA.

holding. This is thought necessary because a market rent can have little meaning unless it can be applied to a tenancy of a calculable period. There is, however, no automatic entitlement to a discount under this head and a case must be made out by the tenant.[91] Nevertheless, by employing the gauge of a yearly tenancy a deduction will occur in the normal course of events.[92] This is because the tenant under the hypothetical lease will enjoy less security of tenure, and fewer safeguards against increasing rent levels and inflation, than a tenant under a term of years certain.[93] The assessment of this rent reduction can prove considerable. In *Regis Property*, for example, the market value otherwise calculated was, on the assumption of a tenancy from year to year, discounted by 33 per cent.[94]

Factors to be Taken into Account

Both parties have the right to be heard and to introduce expert evidence.[95] The **6.27** judge is not, however, bound to accept the uncontradicted evidence of an expert.[96] If no valuations are agreed, the court will look at comparable properties when assessing the interim rent. Before reliance can be placed on such evidence, the court will need to know how those comparables were arrived at, how the figures were calculated and the reasoning behind them.[97] Where there is nothing comparable, the rents of neighbouring properties might be used as a guide.[98] In all cases, the comparable rents to be used are those current at the time the interim rent period commences, which may be years before the application is heard.[99] Consequently, if it appears that rents are to rise sharply in the foreseeable future, the landlord may be tempted to wait and make an application later than otherwise advisable in order to take advantage of inflated comparables. In *French v Commercial Union Life Assurance Plc*, Nourse LJ accepted that the effects of an

---

[91] *Halberstam v Tandalco Corporation NV*, ibid.

[92] *Homeville Estates v Sams*, n 36 above.

[93] *Janes (Gowns) Ltd v Harlow Development Co* (1979) 253 EG 799.

[94] Such a high level of discount is, however, unusual; for example, the yearly tenancy reduction was 10% in *Lawson v Hartley-Brown* (1996) 71 P & CR 242; 12.5% in *Department of Environment v Allied Freehold Property Ltd* [1992] 45 EG 156; 15% in *Ratners (Jewellers) Ltd v Lemnoll* (1980) 255 EG 987; and 20% in *Halberstam v Tandalco*, n 90 above. For further illustrations see K Reynolds and W Clark, *Renewal of Business Tenancies* (1997) at 304–305.

[95] *Homeville Estates v Sams*, n 36 above, where the tenant was not legally represented, but its director was in court, the judge was wrong to deny the director the right to be heard.

[96] *Rogers v Bulleid Leeks & Co*, n 65 above. Nevertheless, in *Conway v Arthur* [1988] 2 EGLR 113, where the landlord introduced no evidence, and the tenant argued for an interim rent of £2,500, the judge clearly erred in setting the rent at £4,234.

[97] *Harwood v Borough of Reigate & Banstead*, n 81 above. In *Romulus Materials Ltd v W T Lamb Properties Ltd*, n 90 above, for example, the court discounted down for shortcomings that the comparables demonstrated. The appellate court also criticised the judge at first instance for plucking figures from the air.

[98] *Woodbridge v Westminster Press Ltd* (1987) 284 EG 60. This was as intended in the Law Commission's 1969 Report, n 14 above, at para 23.

[99] *Fawke v Viscount Chelsea*, n 4 above; see also Pennycuick VC in *Stream Properties v Davis*, n 47 above at 750, 751.

economic recession must be built into the calculation and that this could produce a reduced interim rent.[100] There the fact that a large supermarket was moving out of a shopping centre, and the impending refurbishment of the building, operated to depress market values and this fell to be reflected in the interim rent. In addition, the condition of the premises, and any obligation of either party as to repairs, may be taken into account when it will, for example, involve expense during the continuation period.[101]

6.28 Although the reference in section 24A is to a hypothetical letting, the court cannot simply shut its eyes to known facts existing at the commencement of the interim period. Accordingly, the court should have regard to the actual condition and state of the premises at the commencement date of the interim rent. Facts which come into being afterwards cannot, however, form part of the calculation. In addition, and if appropriate, the court can order a differential rent (that is, one varying with the state of repair of the property) but, seemingly, only where the disrepair is of a very serious character.[102] As Brandon LJ admitted, 'I should not, however, wish to encourage the view that this is a power which the court should exercise at all frequently.'[103] In theory, it is possible that a nil interim rent could be set if the state of repair of the premises was such that they would be worthless to a lessee for a certain period.

Disadvantages

6.29 There are, however, two potential disadvantages for the tenant arising from the objective yardstick of section 24A(3). First, as the hypothetical lease is from year to year, if the tenant seeks a shorter term on renewal the interim market valuation will necessarily be higher than that of the new lease.[104] Second, the valuation is of a hypothetical tenancy of the whole premises. As it may be that any new lease sought by a tenant could comprise of less property than under the original lease,[105] it might be considered unfair for the tenant to pay an interim rent for the whole

---

[100] N 48 above. The recession must, however, be shown to impact on the particular premises: *Rogers v Bulleid Leeks & Co*, n 65 above.

[101] *Woodbridge v Westminster Press*, n 98 above. In *Fawke v Viscount Chelsea*, n 4 above, for example, the premises were infested with dry rot arising from many years of neglect by the landlord. In addition to the discount for disrepair, the interim rent was also to reflect the inconvenience to the tenant and limited use of the premises while the repair work was to be carried out. There Goff LJ made clear that this leaves unaffected the tenant's right to sue for breach of covenant, except of course that credit for the reduction of interim rent must be given from any damages awarded.

[102] *Fawke v Viscount Chelsea*, ibid. Goff LJ expressed doubts as to the correctness of this approach, but the majority were certain that the court had the power to order a variable interim rent.

[103] ibid at 579.

[104] As occurred in *Woodbridge v Westminster Press Ltd*, n 98 above, where the tenant was seeking a nine-month renewal.

[105] For example, because the tenant has sub-let or is willing to accept a tenancy of an economically separable part of the holding under section 31A(1)(b).

premises.[106] This argument, however, is one lacking in force. It should not be viewed as the responsibility of the landlord to subsidise the tenant for the latter's inability to secure either an adequate financial return from any sub-letting or a new lease of the whole property. Few would argue that, as it is the original lease which is being continued, it is improper for the landlord to receive an interim rent of the entire premises which comprised the subject matter of that grant.

Although for rental purposes the calculation is on the basis of a yearly tenancy, it is not uncommon for a continuation tenancy to span a number of years.[107] As there can only be one award of an interim rent,[108] the landlord's predicament is compounded by the likelihood that, in such cases, the rent set will become unrealistically low by the end of the continuation tenancy. Nevertheless, this does not justify the court setting initially an interim rent which is above the market value as assessed at the time of the hearing.[109] Nor can the court achieve this end with hindsight where the matter of the interim rent is disposed of at the same time as the application for a new lease. Such is illustrated in *Conway v Arthur* where proceedings were delayed for three years and, eventually, the interim rent was fixed at a level some 330 per cent above the contractual rent.[110] This assessment was reduced on appeal because, for part of the three years, the rent ordered exceeded the market rent of a yearly tenancy. **6.30**

H. The Effect of the Existing Rent

The need to have regard to the existing rent may, as shown, have a further depressive effect. As Nourse LJ concluded in *Charles Follett Ltd v Cabtell Investments Ltd*, this cushion exists to protect the tenant from the shock of an inflated rent taking effect in full as soon as the lease determines.[111] Accordingly, the market rent of the hypothetical tenancy will, where appropriate, be suitably tempered with reference to the contractual rent. It was made clear in the *English Exporters* case that there is no obligation on the court to make such an adjustment and that it is necessary for the tenant to establish a case for reduction. This is, however, solely at the discretion of the court and is not an issue for expert evidence.[112] Once the case has been made out, however, the weight given to it (and, hence, its translation into monetary terms) can vary dramatically. As Paul Baker QC acknowledged: 'One does **6.31**

---

[106] See the Law Commission Working Paper, n 21 above, at para 3.4.5.
[107] For example, in *French v Commercial Union Life Assurance Plc*, n 48 above, the continuation tenancy spanned more than six years.
[108] Section 24A(2).
[109] *Halberstam v Tandalco Corporation NV*, n 90 above.
[110] N 96 above.
[111] N 59 above. Goff LJ in the *Tandalco* case stressed that there will not be a cushion in every case (n 90 above at 394).
[112] *French v Commercial Union Life Assurance Plc*, n 48 above.

have regard to it, but with the weight from zero to perhaps predominant in a continuous line'.[113]

6.32 This scope for variation is readily apparent from case law. In *Halberstam v Tandalco Corporation NV* no discount was allowed because there had been a three-year delay, since the application for a new lease, before the landlord applied for an interim rent.[114] A modest reduction of 6.66 per cent was made in the *English Exporters* case in circumstances where the tenant had entered into the lease three years before the Law of Property Act 1969 and had held the expectation that the lease would continue for some time at a low rent.[115] In *Ratners (Jewellers) Ltd v Lemnoll* a 10.63 per cent discount was given[116] and in *Charles Follett Ltd v Cabtell Investments Ltd* the Court of Appeal approved an astonishing 50 per cent reduction.[117] Although the *Charles Follett* case is to be regarded as exceptional, the computation was justified on the basis of a dramatic increase in market rental value.[118] Nevertheless, to give as much weight to the old rent as to the hypothetical market value is both unduly harsh on the landlord and seems to overlook the purpose of why section 24A was enacted. Admittedly, each case turns on its own facts, but the variations indicated above do little to erase the imprint of the 'judge's foot' from the proceedings. This is particularly so in the light of judicial admissions that mathematical precision is not necessary and the adoption of a broad-brush approach.[119]

Side-stepping the Machinery

6.33 It is hardly surprising that landlords often negotiate and agree (from a position of weakened bargaining strength) a figure for an interim rent without taking part in

---

[113] *Woodbridge v Westminster Press*, n 98 above at 68. Normally, the discount will be evaluated as a percentage of the yearly interim rent: *French v Commercial Union Life Assurance Plc*, ibid.

[114] N 90 above. In *Department of the Environment v Allied Freehold Trust Ltd*, n 94 above, again no cushion was warranted. The tenant had already had the considerable benefit of a low rent in inflationary times and the shock element was unreal. There was seen to be no reason to perpetuate what inflation and the passage of time had turned into an injustice for the landlord; see also *Woodbridge*, ibid.

[115] N 3 above.

[116] N 94 above.

[117] N 59 above. As Nourse LJ concluded: 'I cannot see that there was intended to be any invariable rule that the interim market rent should be given greater weight than the old rent, or that regard to the latter should only be capable of resulting in some marginal or not very significant reduction' (at 43). He commented, on the suggestion that a 10 per cent reduction would be appropriate, that it 'would be paying not more than lip service to the old rent' (at 44). cf Finlay J in *Janes (Gowns) Ltd v Harlow Development Corporation*, n 93 above at 805.

[118] See Nourse LJ in *French v Commercial Union Life Assurance Plc*, n 48 above, where he defended his previous judgment (in the *Charles Follett* case) as being no more than holding that the lower court had not erred in principle. He feared, however, that the decision had been taken out of context and stressed that it should be confined to the facts of that case.

[119] See *Ratners (Jewellers) Ltd v Lemnoll*, n 94 above at 991; *Lawson v Hartley Brown*, n 94 above.

this uncertain and financially risky courtroom lottery.[120] As regards interim rents settled by agreement, a practice of deducting an amount in the region of 10 per cent from the agreed market value is discernible. Indeed, landlords might be better served if they sidestep the interim rent machinery totally. This may be done by the insertion in the original lease of an 'upwards only' rent review which would be geared to take effect prior to the termination of the original fixed term (for example, the day before). Due to the provision against contracting out of the 1954 Act, contained in section 38, a review clause designed to operate during the continuation itself would be void as being repugnant to the nature of a continuation tenancy.[121] A 'last day' review would be based on the assumption that the tenant will remain in occupation under the aegis of section 24 and is likely to produce a figure higher than any interim rent as fixed by the court. Interest on rent falling due may also be dealt with in the review clause. There would also be no need for the service of a section 25 notice or section 26 request to activate the rent increase and that increase would be based upon contemporary valuations and run from the date of the review. In short, this produces a much more advantageous position for the landlord. It should be appreciated that, if the continuation period spans a number of years, the landlord may later apply for an interim rent.

I. The Proposed 'New Rent Rules'

Although the Law Commission Report of 1992 acknowledged that there was discontent amongst landlords, unfortunately it could find no consensus as how best to proceed.[122] Hence, it attempted to provide a fair compromise between landlord and tenant in promoting a revised scheme under which 'the interim rent should be raised in those cases in which there is no sustainable case for a discount from the full market figure, but in other cases the rent should be assessed in accordance with the present formula'.[123] This novel proposal was drawn from the deliberations of its previous Working Paper. As regards those tenants whose renewals are not in doubt, a system of 'new rent rules' was advocated as a replacement to the current interim rent. For this class of tenancy, no special interim rent would be necessary and, instead, the tenant would be under a 'continuous' obligation to pay a market rent.[124] As the Working Paper explained: 'Effectively, therefore, that new

6.34

---

[120] See Millett J in *Coates Brothers Plc v General Accident Life Assurance Ltd* [1991] 3 All ER 929 at 931, 932.

[121] *Willison v Cheveral Estates* [1996] 1 EGLR 116. The review clause has relevance only to a fixed term while it exists and, therefore, cannot apply to the post-termination yearly tenancy which arises under section 24A. The landlord must then look solely to the interim rent facility.

[122] N 22 above at para 2.67.

[123] ibid at para 2.68.

[124] Working Paper, n 21 above at 3.4.6. The rent would be equal to the rent to be payable at the commencement of the renewed term.

rent would date back to the date given, in the landlord's notice or the tenant's request, for ending the current lease.'[125] The advantages of the proposed scheme are that it would avoid the need for reference to a hypothetical yearly tenancy and side-step the requirement that regard be had to the existing rent. Where renewal is guaranteed, therefore, there would no longer be any cushion for the tenant. This should not, however, be conflated with an automatic entitlement to an interim rent as whether or not an award should be made would remain within the discretion of the court. In addition, as the procedure would remain tied to the service of renewal documentation, the new rent would not necessarily operate from the expiry of the contractual term.

Conditions

6.35 The conditions which would need to be satisfied before the new rent rules can apply were identified as follows. First, the landlord's section 25 notice or tenant's section 26 request must relate to all the property let under the existing lease. Hence, the new rent must be calculated by reference to the premises which the tenant is entitled to enjoy under the current tenancy. Second, the tenant must be in occupation of the whole property demised. Third, the landlord's section 25 notice or counter notice (served in response to the tenant's section 26 request) must state that there will be no opposition to the tenant's application for a new tenancy. Fourth, the court must have ordered a new lease and the landlord must have granted it.[126] Finally, the tenant must not have applied for a revocation order under section 36(2). The latter two conditions were imported by the Law Commission Report on the basis that it would be unfair for a market rent to be payable under the revised scheme if the tenant withdraws while the case is pending or escapes after it is granted.[127]

---

[125] Working Paper, n 21 above at 3.4.8.
[126] It was envisaged that new procedural rules would make the order for an interim rent conditional on the new lease being granted.
[127] N 22 above at para 2.69.

7

DEFEATING THE TENANT'S CLAIM: ILLEGALITY AND THE DISCRETIONARY GROUNDS

A. Introduction

Under section 29 of the Landlord and Tenant Act 1954, the primary right of the **7.01** business tenant is to apply for and obtain the grant of a new lease following on from the determination of the current tenancy. In default of agreement, the grant or refusal of a new tenancy must be determined by the court. The terms of any such renewal may also be worked out by the court. This jurisdiction is limited by the requirement that the tenant must have adhered to any prescribed time-limits and procedures.[1] Accordingly, the right to renew can be sacrificed through slowness and inaction. In order for the court to grant a renewal, it is, moreover, necessary that the tenancy is within the catchment of the Act and remains so until the proceedings are concluded.[2] The tenancy must, therefore, still be in existence and

---

[1] Section 29(2),(3). As to the tenant's failure to make a timely application in *Sommer v Isik* (1998) 24 April CA, Hirst LJ commented: 'That was a misfortune on his part which it is not possible for this court to correct.' This outcome is subject to waiver and estoppel: see Chapter 6.
[2] *Domer v Gulf Oil (GB) Ltd* (1975) 119 SJ 392. As Cross J admitted in *Caplan (I&H) v Caplan* [1963] 2 All ER 930 at 936, 'the contrary view would lead to some astonishing results which I can hardly think would be consistent with the policy underlying the Act'.

the premises demised must be occupied for the purposes of a business carried on by the tenant.[3] As it is necessary that the tenant holds under a subsisting tenancy, where the landlord forfeits the contractual or continuation tenancy, for example, there will be nothing remaining with which the renewal machinery can engage. The tenant then simply falls outside the statutory provisions.[4] It is to be appreciated that an objection by the landlord that the Act no longer applies to the tenancy can be raised at any time after the termination of the contractual lease or the service of the renewal documentation, whichever is the earlier.

7.02 If the tenancy remains within the protection of the Act, and the tenant pursues an application for a new lease, the court can decline a renewal only in strictly delimited circumstances. Refusal may be based either on the common law ground of illegality or on one of the seven statutory grounds as set out in section 30(1)(a)–(g). These grounds are:

(a) failure to repair;
(b) persistent rent arrears;
(c) other breaches of obligation or prejudicial acts connected with the use and management of the holding;
(d) suitable alternative accommodation;
(e) uneconomic subletting;
(f) demolition and reconstruction;
(g) and owner occupation.[5]

With the exception of ground (d), the listed grounds divide broadly into two main categories: those that require fault on the part of the tenant (grounds (a)–(c)) and those that are based upon the promotion of good estate management (grounds (e)–(g)). As will be discussed, grounds (a)–(c) and (e) confer a discretion on the court, whereas the other grounds are mandatory. Accordingly, if one of the mandatory grounds is made out, the court has no option other than to reject the tenant's application.[6] It is, however, with illegality and the discretionary grounds that this chapter is concerned.

---

[3] See, for example, *Esselte AB & British Sugar Plc v Pearl Assurance Plc* [1997] 1 WLR 891 where the tenancy fell outside the ambit of the renewal provisions as soon as the tenant ceased to occupy the premises; *Manoocher Nozari-Zadeh v Pearl Assurance Plc* (1987) 283 EG 457.

[4] As shown in Chapter 2, the landlord's common law termination rights are heavily curtailed. The tenant's rights to terminate are not as restricted. The exact means to be employed by the tenant depend upon whether the lease is periodic or fixed term and whether a continuation tenancy has already arisen.

[5] As regards Northern Ireland, almost identical grounds of opposition are listed in article 12(1)(a)–(g) of the Business Tenancies (Northern Ireland) Order 1996.

[6] Section 31(1); see also *Housleys Ltd v Bloomer-Holt Ltd* [1966] 1 WLR 1244.

B. Illegality

No renewal can be granted in circumstances where the tenant intends to use the   **7.03**
property for an illegal purpose. Although as will be shown this is closely allied to
section 30(1)(c), it is undoubted law that where the illegality is directly concerned
with the use of the land, and is implicit in the proposed new tenancy, the court
cannot enforce the tenancy. As the court will neither countenance nor facilitate
the illegal user of the land, the lease is void and its terms unenforceable. In *Beard
v Williams*, however, the common law did not avail the landlord because the
actual user of the land was not illegal. The 'illegality' (arguably a trespass only)
consisted of parking a decrepit van on or near the adjacent highway.[7] Conversely,
in *Udechuku v Lambeth LBC* a lease granted by a landlord, who was aware that a
demolition order had become operative in relation to the premises, was void and
any rent irrecoverable.[8] This approach is illustrated further in *Turner & Bell v
Searles (Stanford-le-Hope) Ltd*[9] where, contrary to a planning enforcement notice,
the tenant continued to operate its coaching business from the demised premises.
Although no prosecution had been brought, this conduct constituted a criminal
offence. The tenant then applied for a new lease so as to carry on the same business, but the application was unsuccessful. As Bridge LJ explained:

> [Q]uite independently of the express provisions of the statute, this is a case where the
> court would be bound to refuse the relief claimed on the simple ground that if the
> court were to order a new tenancy in the circumstances indicated it would be order-
> ing the parties to enter into an illegal contract which the court could not enforce
> because the illegal purpose of the tenant was clearly known to both parties. That
> would be an absurdity.[10]

The attractions of relying upon the common law, in circumstances where the
premises are actually being used for an illegal purpose, are that, in contradistinction to section 30(1)(c), the landlord does not have to specify this reliance in any
of the renewal documentation and the court does not enjoy any discretion.
Instead, it is the duty of the court, whether or not the point is taken by the parties,
to raise on its own motion any issue of illegality.[11]

---

[7] (1986) 278 EG 1087. It was, therefore, relevant only in so far as it was 'connected with the tenancy or management of the holding' under section 30(1)(c) below.

[8] (1982) 262 EG 1308. The grant amounted to a criminal offence.

[9] (1977) 33 P & CR 208.

[10] ibid at 211. If the unlawful user was in the past, however, the court will not deny the tenant a
renewal on the basis of illegality. Nevertheless, it would be a consideration under ground (c) below.
cf Northern Ireland where the conviction of the tenant (after 1 January 1965) of using, or permitting the premises to be used, for an illegal purpose automatically takes the tenancy outside statutory
protection: article 4(1)(h).

[11] See Roskill LJ ibid at 212.

C. Relevance of Forfeiture

7.04 As discussed in Chapter 2, forfeiture for breach of covenant is the landlord's only common law remedy which emerges unscathed from the statutory regime. It is, therefore, possible that questions of forfeiture and relief and the grant of new tenancies may overlap within the same proceedings. It is, therefore, useful to outline the influences which might persuade a landlord to adopt one course of action in preference to the other. Always providing that the lease contains a re-entry clause, forfeiture might well be a desirable option when the contractual expiry date is a distant prospect. As forfeiture is concerned with the termination of the original contractual tenancy (whether or not being continued), it not only ends the existing contractual lease, but also deprives the tenant of any renewal rights. It should be appreciated, however, that relief from forfeiture is routinely granted to the tenant, for example, on the payment of rent arrears and the remedy of other breaches of covenant.[12] Indeed, the lease does not end until a claim for relief, or any challenge by the tenant as to validity, is determined.[13] The danger, therefore, is that a forfeiture action may merely ensure the performance of covenants without enabling the landlord to re-take possession.

7.05 Matters are somewhat different, however, when the lease is drawing to a close. If the motive of the landlord is solely to recover possession, the most effective course is usually to employ the machinery of the 1954 Act. First, as a breach of covenant is a prerequisite of a forfeiture action, that breach is likely also to fall within one of the fault-based grounds of opposition. Second, and unlike forfeiture, the court enjoys at best a discretion and is under no obligation to grant relief to the tenant. There is, as Jenkins LJ explained in *Dellenty v Pellow*, 'no ground for holding that the landlord is to be denied possession . . . because in similar circumstances a tenant under a contractual tenancy would have had a statutory right to relief from forfeiture'.[14] Third, and although breaches of covenant for the purposes of forfeiture can be waived (often inadvertently) by the landlord, waiver is relevant only to those statutory grounds which invoke the court's discretion and even then only to the extent that it can influence the exercise of that discretion. Fourth, until any forfeiture proceedings are concluded the Act continues to apply to the tenancy and renewal proceedings are kept in abeyance. This potential for delay is magnified as the forfeiture is not complete when the writ is served. Instead there is, as Megarry VC admitted in *Meadows v Clerical Medical & General Life Assurance*

---

[12] See generally DL Evans and PF Smith, *The Law of Landlord and Tenant* (5th edn, 1997) at 252–257

[13] *Billson v Residential Apartments Ltd* (1992) 1 AC 495; see also *Ivory Gate Ltd v Spetale* [1998] 2 EGLR 43.

[14] [1951] 2 All ER 716 at 717.

Society, a 'twilight period'[15] within which '[t]he tenancy has a trance-like existence *pendente lite*, none can assert with assurance whether it is alive or dead . . . at least it cannot be said to be dead beyond the hope of resurrection.'[16] This delay and uncertainty can only work to the disadvantage of the landlord who could regain possession under the 1954 Act. This is particularly so when the competent landlord is not the sub-tenant's immediate landlord and forfeiture proceedings have been initiated by the immediate landlord.

Admittedly, it is possible that, if a forfeiture action is unsuccessful, the court may **7.06** still decline to grant the tenant a new lease.[17] This is particularly so when the landlord opposes the renewal on the estate management grounds or suitable alternative accommodation. Where however, the landlord's complaint concerns repair, rent or other breaches then a forfeiture action may be unproductive. As mentioned, commonly the tenant will remedy the breach in order to obtain relief and, thereby, potentially undermine the landlord's opposition to renewal. This is particularly pertinent in the light of the House of Lords' view, as expressed in *Betty's Cafes Ltd v Phillips Furnishing Stores Ltd*, that the breach must exist at the time the landlord's termination notice or counter notice is served and that its remedy prior to the hearing is a factor that the judge must take into account.[18] Conversely, where the tenant is either unable or unwilling to perform the covenant, the landlord should still be able to regain possession without the need for a forfeiture action. Hence, the only discernible advantage to the landlord in pursuing both lines of action is to intensify the pressure upon the tenant to quit the premises, spurred on by a heightened fear of costs.

D. The Statutory Grounds: General Observations

Role of Discretion

Grounds (a)–(c) invoke the court's discretion by adding the requirement that the **7.07** tenant 'ought not to be granted a new tenancy'. Ground (e) also employs this discretion, but the emphasis there is upon the landlord's needs and not the tenant's default.[19] As admitted by Ormerod LJ in *Lyons v Central Commercial Properties Ltd*, this general discretion exists 'to enable the judge to refuse to grant a new lease

---

[15] [1981] Ch 70 at 78.

[16] ibid at 75. He explained: 'Until the application [for relief] has been decided, it will not be known whether the lease will remain forfeited or whether it will be restored as if it had never been forfeited' (ibid).

[17] See *Norton v Charles Deane Productions Ltd* (1969) 214 EG 559 which involved an extensive catalogue of breaches ranging from prostitution to disrepair.

[18] [1959] AC 20.

[19] With the exception of ground (e), the non-fault grounds are not discretionary and merely require the proof of certain facts (for example, in respect of ground (f) that the landlord intends to carry out works of demolition or reconstruction on the premises).

to a tenant who has shown himself to be unsatisfactory in the performance of his obligation under the contract of tenancy'.[20] It is, therefore, a discretion to deprive the tenant of statutory rights which must be adaptable to the facts of individual cases.[21] Accordingly, as Millett LJ pointed out in *Jaggard v Sawyer*:

> Reported cases are merely illustrations of circumstances in which particular judges have exercised their discretion . . . Since they are all cases on the exercise of a discretion, none of them is binding authority on how the discretion should be exercised. The most that any of them can demonstrate is that in similar circumstances it would not be wrong to exercise the discretion in the same way. But it does not follow that it would be wrong to exercise it differently.[22]

Timing

7.08 In *Betty's Cafes v Phillips Furnishing Stores*, the House of Lords considered when the landlord must be able to prove the statutory grounds of opposition.[23] This may differ according to which ground the landlord relies on.[24] Although the appeal concerned ground (f), wide-ranging *obiter* provided guidance relating to the other grounds. While it is to be admitted that the Law Lords did not entirely speak with one voice on the timing issue, three points may be safely distilled from the case. First, notwithstanding the fact that grounds (e)–(g) involve a future element relating to the landlord's intentions and use of the property, the time for proving intention is at the date of the hearing and not at the date the notice or counter notice is served.[25] Second, as regards grounds (a)–(c), there must be a breach by the tenant at the date of the landlord's notice or counter notice and that default must be proven at the hearing.[26] Third, in connection with ground (d), the landlord must express the willingness to provide or secure suitable alternative accommodation in the notice or counter notice and persist in this willingness throughout the proceedings. These basic propositions will be considered again as each ground is analysed during both this and the subsequent chapter.

---

[20] [1958] 1 WLR 869 at 878.

[21] As Morris LJ acknowledged, ibid at 876: 'It is to be noted that the discretion is one whereby a tenant may be deprived of that which under the Act he was in a position to receive. The discretion does not operate to give something, but to take something away.'

[22] [1995] 1 WLR 269 at 288.

[23] N 18 above.

[24] There is, as Viscount Simonds admitted, ibid at 35, 'no reason why different grounds of opposition should not relate to different periods of time'.

[25] As Viscount Simonds accepted, ibid: 'All is still in the future, and except for purposes of challenging his [the landlord's] *bona fides* . . . nothing that has happened in the past has any relevance.'

[26] This requirement does not give rise to any difficulties for as Lord Keith explained: 'I cannot understand a landlord, who wishes to terminate a tenancy, being thought to state a ground of opposition to a possible application for a new tenancy that did not exist at the time of his notice' (ibid at 46).

Compensation

The ground(s) of possession relied on by the landlord also dictate whether the ten-   **7.09**
ant is entitled to flat rate compensation for disturbance under section 37.[27] This
entitlement applies only when the landlord's opposition is based exclusively upon
one or more of grounds (e)–(f).[28] The fundamental reasoning is, first, that the tenant in default does not deserve compensation; second, the tenant deprived of possession in furtherance of the landlord's management interests should be
recompensed; and, third, the tenant offered suitable alternative accommodation
has no need of compensation. Clearly, in the hope of defeating the tenant's entitlement to compensation, the landlord might be well advised, if relevant, to rely
also upon a ground drawn from the categories (a)–(d).

Identifying the Statutory Grounds

Although in the interests of clarity and convenience this chapter will analyse only   **7.10**
the discretionary grounds ((a)–(c) and (e)), leaving the non-discretionary grounds
to be considered in the following chapter, unless stated to the contrary the following observations apply generally to all statutory grounds.

First, each of the statutory grounds are distinct and, as mentioned, proof of any   **7.11**
allows the landlord to defeat the tenant's claim. The grounds can be pleaded either
exclusively, cumulatively or in the alternative. It is necessary, however, that the
statutory ground(s), upon which the landlord intends to rely, are stated in the section 25 notice or section 26(6) counter notice served in response to the tenant's
request for a new tenancy.[29] The reverse sides of each of the pro forma versions of
these documents set out the statutory grounds in their full form.[30] On the front of
both forms, the landlord is required to indicate such ground(s) that are relevant to
the opposition and to do so with sufficient clarity so that the tenant can appreciate the basis of the landlord's objection.[31] In *Sevenarts v Busvine*, for example, the
trustee landlord stated ground (g), but wrongly claimed to want occupation for its
own business.[32] Although occupation was, in reality, sought for occupation by the

---

[27] Note that the court must state all the grounds upon which the refusal is based: County Court
Rules, Order 43 r 8; Rules of the Supreme Court, Order 97, r 9 (as preserved by the Civil Procedure
Rules 1998).

[28] Section 37(2). The tenant may apply to the court for a certification of the grounds on which
the landlord succeeded: section 37(4). In the High Court, this application is made either at the trial
or by *ex parte* summons in chambers: RSC, Order 97, r 10(1). In the county court, the application
may be made at the hearing or *ex parte* before the district judge CCR, Order 43, r 9.

[29] This requirement does not, however, apply to illegality: see above.

[30] These forms are prescribed by the Landlord and Tenant Act 1954, Part II (Notices)
Regulations 1983 SI No 133, as amended.

[31] *Biles v Caesar* [1957] 1 All ER 151 where it was made clear that there is no need to refer to subsidiary portions of the ground on which the tenant seeks to rely; see also *Philipson-Stow v Trevor
Square Ltd* (1980) 257 EG 1262.

[32] [1969] 1 All ER 392; see further Chapter 5.

beneficiary, the notice remained valid because it did not mislead the tenant and was of no practical importance. Second, when the tenant has commenced proceedings for a new lease the landlord may plead only the grounds as previously stated in the renewal documentation. In the county court, the pleaded grounds will appear in the answer to the tenant's proceedings,[33] whereas, in the High Court they are disclosed in the landlord's affidavit.[34] In both courts, the landlord may abandon grounds at this stage. Although a landlord who fails to submit an answer/affidavit loses the right to oppose the tenant's application, the landlord can still challenge the terms of the new lease. It was made clear by Upjohn LJ in *Morgan v Jones* that the fact that the landlord fails to oppose does not amount to an agreement to accept the tenant's proposals as to the terms of the new lease.[35]

Election and Evidence

7.12   It is, therefore, obvious that the landlord must decide upon tactics prior to the service of the section 25 notice or counter notice. The landlord's election of grounds must, moreover, be taken with care. Although once stated a ground can subsequently be abandoned, grounds cannot otherwise be amended or added to. As the landlord's ability to defeat the tenant's claim is limited to the ground(s) set out in the renewal documentation,[36] not surprisingly, this election will also bind any successor in title of the landlord.[37] Hence, if the landlord omits to specify any grounds of opposition, or states only one(s) that cannot be established, the opposition will fail and the tenant will be granted a new lease. This occurred in *Nursey v P Currie (Dartford) Ltd* where the landlord failed to establish the stated ground that the premises were wanted for owner occupation and was unable to rely upon the intended demolition and reconstruction of the premises because the latter ground had not been disclosed in the notice.[38]

7.13   Nevertheless, as regards the fault-based grounds ((a)–(c)) the landlord may still be able to adduce evidence of an unexpressed ground, but only in so far as it throws light upon a stated ground. This was illustrated in *Hutchinson v Lamberth* where the landlord introduced evidence concerning a nuisance (which is covered by ground (c), but which had not been stated) and this was regarded as relevant in

---

[33] CCR, Order 43, r 7.
[34] RSC, Order 97, r 7. The affidavit must be filed not less than four days before the specified hearing date: Order 97, r 7(2).
[35] [1960] 3 All ER 583 at 586: '[The judge] can only determine whether the terms of the tenancy are reasonable in all the circumstances . . . if he hears evidence on that matter. In my opinion mere proposals put forward by the applicants for a new tenancy are quite insufficient to enable the judge, on those proposals alone, to come to any conclusion on the matter at all.'
[36] *Hutchinson v Lamberth* (1983) 270 EG 545.
[37] *Marks v British Waterways Board* [1963] 3 All ER 28. Special provisions allow the withdrawal of a section 25 notice (but note, not a counter notice) by a superior landlord: Sch 6, para 7; see further Chapter 5.
[38] [1959] 1 All ER 497.

establishing whether the tenant should be denied a renewal under the pleaded grounds (a)–(b).[39] It was, therefore, open to the landlord to lead evidence of all collateral matters relating to the occupancy of the premises. Similarly, in *Eichner v Midland Bank Executor and Trustee Co Ltd* the judge was allowed to take into account matters not specified in the landlord's notice of opposition.[40] There Denning MR held that, in relation to grounds (a)–(c), the judge was entitled to consider a wide range of factors, including the tenant's conduct and the history between the parties. He said: 'It was, I think, open to him to look at all the circumstances in connection with that breach; also I may add, to look at the conduct of the tenant as a whole in regard to his obligations under the tenancy. The judge was not limited to the various grounds stated in the notice.'[41] Although ground (b) was not relied upon by the landlord, the court could look at the tenant's past rental defaults as demonstrating the unhappy relationship between the parties.

Misrepresentation

The insertion of any ground of opposition must, however, be bona fide. It was **7.14** suggested by Denning LJ, sitting in the House of Lords in *Betty's Cafes Ltd v Phillips Furnishing Stores Ltd*, that an absence of bona fides could taint and invalidate the effect of the notice:

> It would be deplorable if a landlord could be allowed to get an advantage by misrepresenting his state of mind or any other fact . . . I should have thought it clear that the notice would be bad—voidable—liable to be set aside for fraudulent misrepresentation . . . If it was avoided, the original tenancy would continue . . . If it was too late to avoid the notice, the landlord would be liable at common law in damages for fraud: just as he would under section 55 if the misrepresentation was made to the court.[42]

In the context of farm tenancies, this approach was later described by Nourse LJ as being, 'a fundamental principle of our jurisprudence'.[43] It is, therefore, a principle that deserves further comment.

First, the landlord is throughout entitled to have a change of heart and to abandon **7.15** any ground of opposition before the close of the proceedings. This demonstrates clearly that, where the landlord initially states a ground that cannot subsequently

---

[39] N 36 above.

[40] [1970] 2 All ER 597

[41] ibid at 599. cf the narrower view (that is, the court should look to past conduct only) taken by Harman J in *Lyons v Central Commercial Properties Ltd*, n 20 above at 880: 'the discretion vested in the court under section 30(1)(a), (b) and (c) is a narrow one: it is limited to the question whether having regard only to the grounds set out a new tenancy "ought not" to be granted'.

[42] N 18 above at 50, 51. Denning LJ based his approach upon that which he had previously stated in *Lazarus Estates Ltd v Beasley* [1956] 1 All ER 341 (a fraudulent claim for rent in connection with a residential letting). There he had said (at 345): 'No court in this land will allow a person to keep an advantage which he has obtained by fraud. No judgment of a court . . . can be allowed to stand if it has been obtained by fraud. Fraud unravels everything.' cf Morris LJ at 349.

[43] *Rous v Mitchell* [1991] 1 WLR 469 at 496.

be made out, the notice is not void *ab initio*. If a fraudulent intention is made out while the notice is extant then it is open to challenge and, seemingly, impeachable at the election of the tenant.[44] Second, if the abuse only becomes apparent after the hearing, the tenant will have to be content with compensation under section 55 or, in the alternative, redress at common law.[45] It is noticeable, therefore, that the court is given no power to re-open proceedings and that the provision implicitly operates on the basis that the notice or counter notice was effective despite the *mala fide* intent of the landlord. Third, it is unclear whether the invalidating tendency identified by Lord Denning could extend even-handedly to both the section 25 notice and the landlord's counter notice.[46] If so, the consequences would vary dramatically. When a section 25 notice is rendered void, the landlord can serve a fresh notice immediately and no great hardship will be incurred. If, however, it is a counter notice which is invalidated, it is unlikely that the landlord will be able to serve a replacement within the statutory time-limit. Hence, the tenant's application is likely to proceed as if it were unopposed and there would be nothing further that the landlord could do. It could be argued that the degree of the landlord's prejudice should not be dictated according to whether it is the lessor or lessee who initiates the demise of the existing tenancy. It is instead possible that, in both cases, the court would be content merely to strike out the fraudulent ground as an abuse of process. This would leave the remainder of the notice or counter notice untainted.

E. Ground (a): Disrepair

7.16 Ground (a) offers the court the discretion to refuse renewal if, due to the failure to observe repairing and maintenance obligations under the existing lease, the tenant ought not, in view of the state of repair of the holding, to be granted a renewal. This ground, therefore, has relevance only where there is some repair obligation (express or implied) imposed upon the tenant and when that obligation is breached. This will normally be evidenced by the competent landlord serving a schedule of dilapidations on the tenant.[47] Obviously, the breach of repair or maintenance must exist at the date when the landlord serves the notice or counter

---

[44] This appears to be so even if the tenant is not deceived: ibid.

[45] In *Kruggers & Co v R&J Evans* (1994) 31 January (CA), for example, the landlords successfully opposed on the basis of owner occupation, but it was later alleged by the tenant that the landlords had neither occupied nor had intended to occupy the premises. Glidewell LJ admitted: 'The Act itself contains a specific provision which enables him [the tenant] to obtain compensation from them [the landlords] for that misrepresentation . . . it is there to deal with this precise situation . . . That is his remedy in my judgment.'

[46] As is suggested by K Reynolds and W Clark, *Renewal of Business Tenancies* (1997) at 161.

[47] If the competent landlord is not the immediate landlord, it is the latter who should serve the schedule. It is up to the competent landlord to engage the co-operation of the mesne landlord.

notice. This should not cause the landlord undue difficulties because, as Viscount Simonds commented in *Betty's Cafes Ltd v Phillips Furnishing Stores Ltd*: 'It is not to be supposed that a landlord will base his opposition under ground (a) . . . if in fact the state of repair at that date gives him nothing to complain of. He will state that he will rely on ground (a) if and only if at the date of the notice it gives him solid support.'[48] If the disrepair is remedied during the intervening period before the date of the hearing, the landlord can still rely upon ground (a). The state of the premises at the time of the hearing may, however, be relevant when the judge decides, as a matter of discretion, whether to grant the landlord possession.[49] Hence, it might prove beneficial for the tenant to carry out any repair work before that time. If the breach has been remedied then, akin to forfeiture, there may be no convincing reason why the tenant should not be given relief.

Meaning of Repair

The Act offers some guidance to the meaning of 'repair' which is widely defined   **7.17** in section 69(1) as including maintenance, decoration and restoration. As the term 'premises' is here not limited to buildings, a failure to maintain landlord's fixtures, fencing or garden area, for example, should fall within ground (a). Subject to contrary wording in the lease, the repair obligations imposed will survive the contractual tenancy and bind the tenant during any section 24 continuation tenancy.[50] In addition, section 30(1)(a) concerns only disrepair to the tenant's 'holding' which may be less in extent than the premises originally demised. Accordingly, where the tenant is in occupation of the entire premises for business purposes, disrepair to any part will enable the landlord to oppose the tenant's application. Different considerations apply, however, when the tenant has ceased to occupy part of the premises as originally leased. Under section 23(1), the tenant's holding excludes any part not occupied by the tenant for the purposes of a business. Hence, if the tenant has granted a sub-tenancy, the landlord cannot rely upon the disrepair to the sub-tenant's premises when opposing the mesne tenant's application for a new lease. Similarly, if the tenant has discontinued business use of part of the premises, renewal rights in relation to that part are lost and, correspondingly, the landlord cannot rely on the disrepair of that part under ground (a).[51]

---

[48] N 18 above at 35, 36.

[49] As Viscount Simonds stressed, ibid at 36: 'At the hearing, the judge . . . will necessarily take into consideration the state of repair or disrepair, not only at the date of the notice, but also at the date of the hearing.'

[50] *Wilson v Cheverell Estates Ltd* [1996] 1 EGLR 116; *Junction Estates v Cope* (1974) 27 P & CR 482.

[51] The disrepair of premises no longer comprising the tenant's holding can, however, be a relevant consideration under section 30(1)(c) below.

Discretion

7.18 As mentioned above, ground (a) is a discretionary ground for possession. This entails that it is insufficient for the landlord merely to show a breach of repairing covenant existing at the date of the hearing. The court must also be satisfied that the breach is of such a serious nature as to justify the tenant losing the right to a new lease.[52] It follows that where there is disrepair, but the landlord intends to demolish the premises, the court is unlikely to decline renewal on the basis of section 30(1)(a). The breach would there be seen to have no deleterious effect on the landlord and the performance of the tenant's obligation would stand redundant. In such circumstances, therefore, the landlord would be wise to place primary reliance upon ground (f). In deciding whether the tenant 'ought not' to be granted a new tenancy, the court must examine the factual matrix and look to all the circumstances.[53] This will normally include factors such as the extent of the tenant's liability, the physical state of the premises, the conduct of the tenant, the relationship of the parties, the reasons for the breach, and the consequences of the tenant's failure.[54]

7.19 It is on the basis of such wide-reaching evidence that the court must then decide how to exercise its discretion.[55] In doing so, the court will adopt a broad-brush approach in order to determine, 'whether it would be unfair to the landlord, having regard to the tenant's past performance and behaviour, if the tenant were to enjoy the advantage which the Act gives to him'.[56] Accordingly, the tenant's willingness at the hearing to remedy the breach is not necessarily decisive. In the *Lyons* case, for example, there was a serious breach of repair obligation which the tenant had left unremedied for one year. Although the tenant offered an undertaking to carry out the necessary works, the court declined to award a new lease. The tenant was viewed as being unworthy of relief. As Harman J acknowledged, a new lease should not be granted to a bad tenant unless there exist exculpatory circumstances

---

[52] As Ormerod LJ put it in *Lyons v Central Commercial Properties Ltd*, n 20 above at 878, there must be 'substantial' disrepair.

[53] *Eichner v Midland Bank Executor & Trustee Co Ltd*, n 40 above. In the *Lyons* case, Morris LJ explained: 'But when Parliament has not precisely defined, I would hesitate to adopt any particular formulation as being all embracing or which might be thought to be restrictive or definitive' (ibid at 877).

[54] *Lyons* case, ibid. There the fact that the tenant had a small business and faced the loss of livelihood was regarded as a persuasive factor.

[55] *Horowitz v Ferrand* (1956) 5 CL 207. The appellate court, moreover, will only interfere with the exercise of this discretion when it can be shown that the judge erred at law, that is, the judge took into account irrelevant matters or failed to take into account relevant matters: *Paddington Churches Housing Association v Sharif* (1997) 29 HLR 817.

[56] *Per* Morris LJ in *Lyons v Central Commercial Properties Ltd*, n 20 above at 877; see also *Eichner v Midland Bank Executor & Trustee Co Ltd*, n 40 above. In *Lyons* case, it was made apparent that it is only the relationship between the landlord and the present tenant which must be adjudged. The willingness of, say, a proposed assignee to perform the covenants is irrelevant.

which can forgive the past misdoing.[57] In contrast, however, the tenant in *Nihad v Chain* was given the benefit of the doubt on the basis that he was prepared to consent to the new lease containing both a covenant to put the property into immediate repair and a forfeiture clause.[58] The provisions offered sufficient protection to the landlord against future defaults occurring. These two cases, therefore, demonstrate that existing breaches may be overlooked, but only when the court is satisfied as to the future performance of the repair obligations.

F. Ground (b): Persistent Rent Arrears

Ground (b) is that the tenant ought not to be given a new tenancy because of persistent delay in the payment of rent which has become due. The term 'rent' was defined by Lord Diplock in *United Scientific Holdings Ltd v Burnley BC* as being, 'a payment which a tenant is bound by his contract to pay to the landlord for the use of his land.'[59] The lease will normally contain a rental covenant in which the sum payable is expressed. It is, however, possible that the lease will describe other types of payment as being 'rent', for example, service charges and insurance premiums.[60] This entitles the landlord to exercise the remedy of distress to defaults in such payments and to proceed in forfeiture. Ground (b) will, therefore, extend to any non-payment of sums which are described in the lease as 'rent'. The reference to 'persistent', moreover, necessitates either that there has been a delay on more than one occasion or that at least one instalment of arrears has been outstanding for some time.[61] **7.20**

Accordingly, the issue is one of fact and degree. As Stocker LJ admitted in *Gill v Moore*: 'The word "persistent" must import some consideration of past events, although these events should be considered at the time of the hearing, and if there were then no arrears at that time then that would be a factor to be taken into account by the judge in the exercise of his discretion.'[62] The landlord should, therefore, support the opposition with a schedule of rental payments which can be served either before or at the time of the hearing.[63] The size and duration of the arrears need not be substantial[64] and the arrears need not cover the whole duration of the lease. All that is necessary is that some arrears have been sustained over a **7.21**

---

[57] ibid at 880.
[58] [1956] EGD 234.
[59] [1978] AC 904 at 935.
[60] See *Roynton Industries Ltd v Lawrence* [1994] 1 EGLR 110.
[61] See *Maison Kaye Fashions Ltd v Horton's Estate Ltd* (1967) 202 EG 23 where for over three years every monthly payment of rent was paid after the due date, mostly one to two months late.
[62] (1989) 3 August CA.
[63] *Gill v Moore*, ibid. This is not a requirement, but it does save time and avoids going through each item orally. It assists both parties and the court.
[64] *Horowitz v Ferrand*, n 55 above.

period of time.[65] The landlord is, therefore, required to demonstrate a history of bad payment. A classic example is to be found in *Gill v Moore* where the tenant had been persistently late in paying rent throughout a long period, had given the landlord dishonoured cheques and had been subject to the landlord's distraint on two occasions.[66] The court was of the opinion that, in this type of case, it would be very unfair to the landlord if a new tenancy was granted. Indeed, Fox LJ admitted: 'This is really an overwhelming case, and it would be perverse of me to grant a new tenancy in the light of this admitted record.'

Tenant's Response

7.22 In order to persuade the court to grant a renewal, the tenant has two potential counter-strategies. First, to show that there was good reason why the rent fell into arrears. In *Electricity Supply Nominees Ltd v Truman*, it was made clear that the effects of a recession do not offer the tenant a good reason for these purposes.[67] Although a lack of financial organisation or oversight will not provide any justification,[68] some mitigation might be found where, for example, the rent has been withheld because of breach of landlord's covenant and the tenant is pursuing a genuine counterclaim against the landlord.[69] It is, however, necessary for the tenant to have informed the landlord in writing why the rent was being withheld.[70] If the counterclaim succeeds, the tenant has a defence to any action for rent arrears.[71] Even if the counterclaim fails, the fact that the rent was withheld for this reason will be a factor in favour of the tenant.[72] It is, however, necessary for the tenant to be equipped to make immediate payment or, at least, to make some provision for the discharge of outstanding arrears.[73] This does not

---

[65] *Hopcutt v Carver* (1969) 209 EG 1069.

[66] N 62 above. An appalling record of late payment emerged also in *Hutchinson v Lamberth*, n 36 above (where no rent was paid for the first four years of the lease) and *Rawashdeh v Lane* [1988] 2 EGLR 109 (where payments were regularly months overdue).

[67] (1994) 14 December CA. The appellate court also announced a wariness of tenants who resist payments of rent and then seek a pretext to justify having done so.

[68] See *Gill v Moore*, n 62 above, where the tenant claimed that the late payment and bounced cheques arose from uncleared items in her bank account and the fact that she had overstretched her business interests.

[69] *London Borough of Haringey v Stewart* (1991) 23 HLR 557.

[70] *Page v Sole* (1991) 24 January CA.

[71] *British Anzani (Felixstowe) Ltd v International Marine Management (UK) Ltd* [1980] 1 QB 137. In *Televantos v McCullock* (1991) 23 HLR 412, the tenant's well-founded counterclaim was for a sum in excess of the rent withheld. This prompted Nicholls LJ to conclude that, 'when one takes that into account, I have the greatest difficulty in seeing how it could be regarded as reasonable in the circumstances of this case to say that an order for possession should be made' (at 416).

[72] It is a factor which relates to discretion, but may still be outweighed by a record of persistent late payment: *Dellenty v Pellow*, n 14 above.

[73] *London Borough of Haringey v Stewart*, n 69 above, where Waite J said (at 559): 'In ordinary circumstances it will not be reasonable to make a possession order if the tenant has made arrangements in the event of failure of his counterclaim to clear the arrears by an anticipatory payment into court (to give one example), or by setting aside funds which can be devoted for that purpose (to give another), or, at the very least, to put forward proposals for an early discharge of the arrears.'

invariably offer any guarantee because, as Waite J explained in *London Borough of Haringey v Stewart*:

> In exceptional circumstances, however, as for example where the tenant has already a very poor record for persistent late payment of rent, the ordinary benevolent course will not be followed, and the making of an order would be regarded as reasonable upon the ground that the tenant has disqualified himself from the court's sympathy by the persistency of his past defaults . . .[74]

The second counter-strategy is to offer a rent deposit and/or a surety for the new lease. This additional protection for the landlord might persuade the court to overlook previous defaults and to favour the tenant's application.[75] As Birkett LJ commented *obiter* in the Court of Appeal in *Betty's Cafes Ltd v Phillips Furnishing Stores Ltd*, 'if the tenant has some very good reasons to explain delays and very good grounds for assuring the court that the like situation would never arise again, it seems difficult to say that the court should not listen to evidence to show how completely the situation had changed at the date of the hearing, from what it was at the date of the notice . . .'.[76]

Discretion

Whether or not a renewal is declined turns upon the perceptions of the judge and the evidence put before the court. As Russell LJ explained in *Page v Sole*: 'Once he [the judge] had made the finding that there had been persistent delay, there remained in the judge a discretion as to whether, in all the circumstances, this was a case where the landlord was entitled to possession.'[77] In *Maison Kaye Fashions Ltd v Horton's Estate Ltd*, it was demonstrated that the court may, in exercising this discretion, have regard to such matters as the frequency of delay, the reasons for the delay, the measures taken by the landlord to secure payment and any safeguards that the landlord has against future arrears.[78] Accordingly, it is arguable that the landlord's forbearance of rental breaches could operate to encourage non-payment and that the court's discretion should, in that situation, favour the tenant. The inconvenience and expense to the landlord incurred in having had to chase a tenant for rent is also a material factor for the court to take on board.[79] The court

7.23

---

[74] ibid.

[75] *Hopcutt v Carver*, n 65 above.

[76] [1957] 1 All ER 1 at 7.

[77] N 70 above. As Lord Greene said (of a similar provision) in *Cumming v Danson* [1942] 2 All ER 653 at 655, the judge must act in a 'broad commonsense way as a man of the world, and come to his conclusion giving such weight as he thinks right to the various factors in the situation. Some factors may have little or no weight, others may be decisive, but it is quite wrong for him to exclude from his consideration matters which he ought to take into account.'

[78] N 61 above.

[79] Note, however, *Freeman v Barclays Bank* (1958) 171 EG 171, where the landlord had not raised the issue of the tenant's long and substantial rent arrears until the service of the section 25 notice and yet the claim for possession under ground (b) was unaffected. The landlord, therefore, is

can, moreover, take account of the tenant's cavalier attitude towards the payment of other creditors as indicating that it is unsatisfactory to foist a further term on the landlord.[80] As the court has to rely on past conduct in order to predict future behaviour, the poorer the tenant's record the more likely that the landlord's opposition will succeed.[81] As Millett LJ commented in *Secretary of State for Transport v Jenkins*, 'a landlord is not to be saddled with a poor tenant who habitually pays rent late and is, therefore, unlikely if any new tenancy is granted, to be punctual in his payments'.[82]

7.24 It should be recalled that, unlike relief against forfeiture, the payment of arrears pending proceedings does not necessarily protect the tenant.[83] This is particularly so in the context that a substantial rent increase is likely to occur on renewal and this will cast even further doubt upon the tenant's ability and willingness to pay. In *Gill v Moore*, for example, Fox LJ considered the tenant's punctuality following the service of the landlord's section 25 notice and commented: 'The resistance to the tenant's claim and the onset of proceedings may have caused her to beware. It does not alter the fact that the persistent delay previously occurred and it is highly conjectural whether, if a new tenancy were granted, she would not revert back to her old practices.'[84]

Exercise of Discretion

7.25 The wide discretion given to the court entails that one case is no sure guide to another. Although it is up to the landlord to establish the ground, there is an obligation on the tenant to explain away the past failures and to satisfy the court that there will be no recurrence. Accordingly, each case turns upon its own facts and falls to be determined by the county court or the High Court. Unless the judge errs at law, the decision of these fact-finding tribunals will not be disturbed by the higher courts. In *Hurstfell Ltd v Leicester Square Property Co*, for example, a renewal was ordered even though the tenant had been in arrears for eleven con-

---

allowed to overlook the tenant's shortcomings for some time and then have a change of heart and become unwilling to grant any further indulgence.

[80] *Bede Securities (Property Management) Ltd v Margolis* (1985) 7 March CA where the court also took account of the bankruptcy of one of the tenants and the judgment debts that were outstanding against the other tenant; see also *Patel v Norwich Union Life Insurance Society* (1995) 27 June CA.

[81] *Dellenty v Pellow*, n 14 above, where, in the context of the Rent Restriction Acts, the tenant had a long history of non-payment during which the landlord regularly took proceedings, receiving payment on the court steps.

[82] (1997) 30 October CA. As Pennycuick J explained in *Maison Kaye Fashions Ltd v Horton's Estate Ltd*, n 61 above at 24: 'It could not be right to saddle the landlords with tenants who had been continuously in arrear with rent for the last three years of their term and who had given endless trouble in the collection of their rent, and this was all the more so when one bore in mind that the rent would almost certainly be increased if an order for a new tenancy was made.'

[83] ibid; see also *Dellenty v Pellow*, n 14 above.

[84] N 62 above.

secutive rent instalments and had given the landlord dishonoured cheques.[85] There the judge was satisfied that there would be no future repetition, notwithstanding that the viability of the tenant's business was questionable.[86] In *Rawashdeh v Lane*, however, a renewal was refused to the tenant, who had been late in rent payments regularly during the course of the lease, because the delays were regarded as sufficiently serious to justify the rejection of the application.[87] This was so even though the tenant was prepared to pay a quarter's rent in advance and to agree to payment by a monthly standing order. Similarly, in *Hopcutt v Carver* the tenant had occupied for twenty years, but the evidence showed that, during the last two years, he had regularly been in arrears with rent.[88] The judge carefully prepared a table relating to past payments which showed that, while proceedings were pending, the tenant had become more punctual. The renewal was, however, refused and the appellate court felt that it was significant that the tenant had made no offer for the rent to be payable in advance and offered no security to the landlord. There was simply no certainty that the rent would be paid if the renewal was granted. These cases demonstrate that the onus is on the tenant to persuade the court that there will be no future arrears and that this will normally require the offer of effective safeguards for the landlord.

G. Ground (c): Other Breaches

Ground (c) enables the landlord to oppose the renewal application on the basis   **7.26**
that the tenant ought not to be granted a new lease in the light of other substantial breaches of the obligations under the lease or for any other reason connected with the use or management of the holding.[89] In opposing the new lease on the basis of ground (c), the landlord should take care to specify all allegations made and be able to support them with evidence. A vague, general statement of the tenant's conduct will not suffice. The wording of ground (c), moreover, makes it apparent that this ground deals with two distinct sets of circumstances.

---

[85] [1988] 2 EGLR 105. As Nicholls LJ put it (at 106), 'at the end the matter comes down to this. Here was a question of fact on which the judge . . . saw the witnesses, heard their evidence, heard the submissions and reached a conclusion for which there was supporting evidence. In those circumstances it seems to me that there is no justification for this court interfering with the judge's conclusion of fact . . .'

[86] Although Nicholls LJ (ibid) upheld the decision of the county court, he expressed the view that, on the evidence, he 'would not have been wholly surprised if the judge had reached a different conclusion on the crucial question'.

[87] N 66 above.

[88] N 65 above. At one stage the tenant went five months without making any payment; see also *Horowitz v Ferrand*, n 55 above, where the tenant was refused a new lease on the basis of a long history of late payment of rent, even though the payments were always forthcoming.

[89] By virtue of the Interpretation Act 1978, the reference to 'breaches' in section 30(1)(c) includes also the singular.

Breach of Covenant

7.27 Any substantial breach of leasehold covenant (except one caught by grounds (a) and (b)) can be relied upon by the landlord, for example, a breach of a user covenant[90] or a covenant prohibiting the tenant from causing a nuisance or annoyance.[91] It would also include a breach of repairing obligation which fell outside ground (a) because it referred to premises which were not comprised in the tenant's holding. Similarly, it would embrace rent arrears which were not persistent and non-payments of sums not designated as rent in the lease. For the landlord to be successful in this opposition, however, the breach must be more than trivial and its consequences must be serious. The determination lies at the court's discretion and, in its exercise, the court will take into account the nature of the breach, whether it can be remedied, any proposals made by the tenant for remedy, and whether the landlord has either acquiesced in or waived the breach.[92] In deciding whether the breach is substantial, the court will look at the whole of the tenant's conduct during the tenancy and is, therefore, not restricted to issues set out in the landlord's notice or counter notice. The tenant's expected, future conduct should also be of relevance.[93] There must, however, be cogent evidence introduced by the landlord proving the breach. In *Jones v Jenkins*, for example, the county court erred in finding a breach in the absence of evidence.[94] Despite the fact that another breach was established (relating to the use of a flat as a massage parlour), the court's exercise of discretion was tainted and a retrial ordered.

Any Other Reason

7.28 Ground (c) is widened considerably by the allusion to 'any other reason' relevant to the use and management of the holding.[95] The court can, seemingly, look to both past and future use[96] and there is no requirement of substantiality here. Clearly, this includes matters which are beyond the tenant's legal obligations to the landlord, but it is not certain how far this extension reaches. It covers, for example, a breach of either criminal law or planning law by the tenant. It might

---

[90] *Jones v Jenkins* (1986) 277 EG 644.

[91] *Norton v Charles Dean Productions Ltd*, n 17 above.

[92] See *Eichner v Midland Bank Executor and Trustee Co Ltd*, n 40 above. In relation to waiver see *Jones v Christy* (1963) 107 SJ 374.

[93] *Turner & Bell v Searles (Stanford-le-Hope) Ltd*, n 9 above.

[94] N 90 above, where the landlord alleged that three rooms in a basement flat had been converted into a laundry in breach of user covenant. No evidence of this was, however, introduced and the landlord could not succeed under ground (c).

[95] If the reason impacts solely upon land which has been sub-let by the tenant then, as it will no longer concern the tenant's holding, it falls outside this second limb of ground (c).

[96] See the majority view in *Turner & Bell v Searles (Stanford-le-Hope) Ltd*, n 9 above (Cairns LJ being unsure on this point). Roskill LJ (at 212) took a very liberal approach and suggested that any factor which could be said to be relevant to the use or management might legitimately be taken on board.

cater for the situation where, following a change in the neighbourhood, it is no longer desirable that the tenant's business be continued on the premises. It could be invoked, moreover, when the tenant has run the business in such a fashion that, although in compliance with the terms of the lease, it is undesirable that the business continues to operate as before.[97] The conduct of the tenant on land not comprised in the demise is also relevant to the extent that it reflects on the tenant's ability to manage the holding properly.[98] An underlying consideration is whether the landlord will be prejudiced by the tenant's conduct.[99] Albeit normally present, fault on the part of the tenant is not, however, a necessary ingredient under this second set. Nevertheless, the absence of fault would be a material consideration for the court to take on board in exercising its discretion. Similarly, the ready availability of alternative accommodation for the tenant is a factor which may influence the court to deny renewal.[100]

H. Ground (e): Uneconomic Sub-letting

Ground (e) is relevant where the current tenant is a sub-lessee of part only of the premises which previously had been let by the competent landlord under a superior tenancy of the whole.[101] It is a discretionary ground which can only be relied upon when the competent landlord can demonstrate the reasonable expectation that the aggregate of the rents, reasonably obtainable on separate lettings of the sub-tenant's holding and the remainder of the premises, would be substantially less than if the property was let as a whole. In addition, it must be shown that, on the termination of the current tenancy, the landlord requires possession of the holding for the purpose of letting or otherwise disposing of the whole premises. Consequently, ground (e) enables the competent landlord to recover possession in order to effect a more lucrative re-letting or sale. This ground is, however, seldom used in practice due to its difficulties and limited application. Indeed, Viscount Simonds in *Betty's Cafes Ltd v Phillips Furnishing Stores Ltd* described ground (e) as not being 'wholly intelligible'.[102]

7.29

---

[97] See *Cheryl Investments Ltd v Saldanha* [1979] 1 All ER 5 where Lord Denning (at 12) contended that even a lawful change of user might give the landlord the ability to oppose renewal.

[98] See *Beard v Williams*, n 7 above, where the unlawful parking of a van (in which the tenant lived) 100 yards from the demised premises entailed that the van could be moved on, which would jeopardise the tenant's dog breeding business and, thereby, potentially prejudice the landlord. These precarious living arrangements were clearly connected to the tenant's use and management of the holding.

[99] See *Eichner v Midland Bank Executor & Trustee Co*, n 40 above.

[100] *Beard v Williams*, n 7 above.

[101] See *Greaves Organisation Ltd v Stanhope Gate Property Co Ltd* (1973) 228 EG 725.

[102] N 18 above at 32.

Hurdles

7.30 For ground (e) to have relevance it is necessary that a number of features be present. First, it must be the sub-tenant who applies for a new lease and the sub-tenancy must be of part only of the premises (not the whole). Second, the intermediate landlord's interest must be due to end within fourteen months, following the notice or counter notice, as otherwise the head landlord would not be the sub-tenant's competent landlord for the purposes of the renewal procedure.[103] This is crucial as the ground cannot be used by a landlord against an immediate tenant. Third, the time for determining whether a sub-tenancy is in existence is the date of the tenant's application.[104] Previous relationships are to be ignored. Accordingly, if a merger of the interests of the competent landlord and the mesne landlord occurs before this date, the competent landlord will be unable to rely upon ground (e).[105] The opposition should not, however, be affected if, after the date of the tenant's application, the mesne landlord's tenancy ends, for example, by expiry of time or surrender. If it were otherwise, and as Reynolds and Clark argue, '[it] would be entirely fortuitous, depending on how quickly it was possible to obtain a date for hearing'.[106] Fourth, the head landlord must demonstrate at the hearing that substantially more rent (presumably calculated at a net value) would be received if the premises were let as whole, rather than subject to separate lettings. This difference in rental values may be difficult to prove and will necessarily hinge upon detailed, comparative valuation evidence of the premises as let on different tenancies and as let in their entirety on a hypothetical single lease. The court will then make a comparison between these competing valuations and decide whether the former is substantially less than the latter. The court cannot consider the effect on other property outside the under lease. This limited calculation, therefore, overlooks the possibility that the sub-letting may diminish the value of the landlord's reversion from an investment viewpoint.[107] Nevertheless, if there is no substantial diminution of rental income then ground (e) is unavailable.[108]

7.31 Finally, the landlord must demonstrate at the hearing a genuine intention and ability to dispose of the property as a whole when possession of the tenant's hold-

---

[103] See section 44.

[104] *Greaves Organisation Ltd v Stanhope Gate Property Co Ltd*, n 101 above. The guiding *obiter* of the House of Lords in *Betty's Cafes Ltd v Phillips Furnishing Stores Ltd*, n 18 above, did not expressly encompass the timing element of ground (e).

[105] The *Greaves* case, ibid.

[106] N 46 above at 183.

[107] As M Ross, *Drafting and Negotiation of Commercial Leases* (4th edn, 1994) at 294 n 6 makes clear, the landlord's complaint is that the paragraph is too narrowly drafted: 'Thus it is suggested that the rental value should not be the sole possible ground of opposition—a wider test such as 'damage to the reversion' should be used.'

[108] See the *Greaves* case, above, where a diminution could be proved, but was not shown to be substantial.

ing is recovered. This entails that the competent landlord must be able to convince the court that vacant possession of the remainder of the building can be obtained. In the context of the limited sphere of ground (e), the remainder will be occupied by the mesne landlord and, where relevant, any other sub-tenants. If, for example, the mesne landlord's tenancy is protected by the 1954 Act, then ground (e) will, except where the mesne landlord's co-operation is obtained, stand redundant. Even if the above matters can be proved, the court must be persuaded to exercise its discretion. In order to decide whether the sub-tenant 'ought not to be granted a new tenancy', the court will take into account all the circumstances of the case and, particularly, whether the superior landlord had originally consented to the sub-letting. Adopting a broad-brush approach, the court will balance the respective hardship to the competent landlord and to the sub-tenant. The landlord's case is presumably strengthened by the fact that, if the renewal is denied under ground (e), compensation for disturbance is available to the tenant under section 37.

8

DEFEATING THE TENANT'S CLAIM: THE MANDATORY GROUNDS

A. Introduction

As evident from the preceding chapter, three further grounds for possession exist **8.01** and these are neither dependant upon the tenant being in default nor do they invoke the discretion of the court. Ground (d) (suitable alternative accommodation) is, however, attractive only where the landlord is both able and prepared to offer the tenant other premises from which to conduct business. Due to the restrictions upon what is suitable, many landlords will not be in a position to satisfy the necessary requirements and, even if they can, the temptation may exist (although compensation for disturbance will then become payable) to rely instead upon one of the other non-discretionary grounds. Conversely, grounds (f)–(g) (demolition/reconstruction and owner occupation) constitute the most popular avenues through which landlords attempt to regain possession of the tenant's holding.

B. Ground (d): Suitable Alternative Accommodation

8.02 Under ground (d), the tenant's application can be successfully opposed if the land-lord has offered, and is willing to provide or to secure, suitable alternative accom-modation on reasonable terms. The court enjoys no discretion here and, if the landlord can establish certain facts, must refuse the tenant's application. There is, however, much that remains unclear about the operation of ground (d) for, as Judge Aron Owen acknowledged in *Chaplin (M) Ltd v Regent Capital Holdings Ltd*: 'The Act has now been in operation for nearly three decades, but it appears that the implications of this paragraph have never had to be fully and directly con-sidered.'[1] Little assistance, moreover, is to be drawn from the cases decided in rela-tion to residential tenancies. This is, as stressed by the House of Lords in *Singh v Malayan Theatres*,[2] because of the different considerations which apply to resi-dential property and the different wording of the respective statutory codes.

An Offer

8.03 Suitable alternative must have been offered by the landlord to the tenant and this offer must be firm, bona fide and capable of immediate acceptance. This neces-sarily entails that the landlord must be able to comply with the offer. As to the tim-ing of the offer, in *Chaplin (M) Ltd v Regent Capital Holdings Ltd* the county court held that it was unnecessary for the offer to be made prior to the service of the landlord's section 25 notice or counter notice.[3] Indeed, it would be impractical always to expect the landlord to make an offer within the period of two months following the service of the tenant's section 26 request for a new tenancy. Such was recognised *obiter* also by Viscount Simonds, in the House of Lords in *Betty's Cafes Ltd v Phillips Furnishing Stores Ltd*, who felt that it would, 'not be reasonable to reduce the time within which the landlord should have the opportunity of find-ing and offering alternative accommodation'.[4] While being preferable that the landlord makes the offer either before or at the time of the notice/counter notice, it will suffice if ground (d) is merely indicated at that stage and details provided later. This is consistent with a central tenet of ground (d) which is that matters which need to be established must be established at the date of the hearing. It is

---

[1] [1994] 1 EGLR 249.

[2] [1953] AC 632. As Lord Porter admitted at 639, 'principles applicable to the retention by ten-ants of places which are required as a home have very little bearing on the position of a tenant who requires a place in which to conduct his business'.

[3] To tie the landlord's hands prematurely would, as Romer LJ commented in the Court of Appeal in *Betty's Cafes Ltd v Phillips Furnishing Stores Ltd* [1957] 1 All ER 1 at 12, 'be a disadvantage to the landlord without securing any corresponding benefit to the tenant, it is surely a legitimate inference that the legislature did not intend to impose it'. cf Denning LJ sitting in the House of Lords in the *Betty's Cafes* case [1959] AC 20 at 50.

[4] ibid at 36. See *Trendgrove Properties Ltd v Deeks* (1999) 23 July (CA).

also sensible in the light that, as will be shown, the landlord can revise an offer both before and during the court proceedings.

Suitability

The landlord must be willing to provide or to secure the accommodation and this   **8.04**
willingness must continue throughout the hearing. It is also at the hearing that questions of suitability are to answered. There the judge will normally see plans and photographs of both the existing and the alternative premises and consider the reports of surveyors. The judge might even feel obliged to inspect the respective premises personally. As regards suitability, it is not necessary that the accommodation is identical or even similar to the present premises. As Judge Aron Owen admitted, 'alternative accommodation does not have to mirror exactly the existing accommodation'.[5] Indeed, the alternative accommodation may consist of part only of the premises currently leased to the tenant.[6] In gauging suitability, the court is expressly directed by section 30(1)(d) to consider a variety of issues: the preservation of goodwill (where relevant), the nature of the tenant's business as permitted by the lease, the location of the existing holding and the extent of the holding and facilities presently afforded. Accordingly, the alternative might (but not necessarily) be regarded as unsuitable where the tenant can show that existing goodwill will be detrimentally affected as a result of the business being moved.[7] Similarly, if the premises are less spacious than the current holding, it might be argued that they are ill-suited to the tenant's needs.

Although the landlord carries the primary burden to show that the current business   **8.05**
can be adequately carried out in the alternative premises, the tenant should be ready to produce evidence so as to demonstrate some deleterious impact upon that business. In the *Chaplin* case, for example, accommodation offered on the second floor of a building was held to be a suitable alternative to the existing ground floor premises because the change would not affect the tenant's business as a wholesale jeweller. It is a working rule that the premises cannot, however, be regarded as suitable when their occupation would cause change to the conduct of the tenant's business and require it to be carried out in a different or diminished fashion.[8]

---

[5] *Chaplin (M) Ltd v Regent Capital Holding Ltd*, n 1 above at 253.

[6] *Lawrence v Carter* (1956) L Jo 259 (county court); see *Singh v Malayan Theatres*, n 2 above, where Lord Porter was 'not disposed to lay down a general rule to the effect that a multiple business can never be so dealt with as to make the closing of one of their multiple shops possible by the provision of alternative space in another or others' (at 641).

[7] A loss of goodwill will be easier to show as regards a retailing business than, say, a wholesale or manufacturing enterprise: see *Chaplin (M) Ltd v Regent Capital Holdings Ltd*, n 1 above.

[8] See *Gold v Brighton Corporation* [1956] 3 All ER 442. cf Lord Porter in *Singh v Malayan Theatres*, n 2 above at 639, 'the respondent's business must be regarded as a whole . . . provided that they can carry on that business in some alternative accommodation, even if the business is to some extent diminished, their rights are maintained: the fact that one source of profit is eliminated is not a vital matter'.

Reasonable Terms

8.06   The alternative accommodation must be available on terms which, having regard to the terms of the 'current tenancy' and all other relevant circumstances, are deemed to be reasonable. Somewhat remarkably, in the *Chaplin* case the county court accepted the concession that, ' "terms of the current tenancy" in this context refer not to the old terms under which the tenant holds his existing tenancy, but to such terms as the parties agree or the court would determine in a grant of the tenant's application for a new tenancy of his holding'.[9] This interpretation simply cannot be correct and it totally disregards the clear and obvious meaning of Parliamentary expression. Accordingly, the terms which the tenant currently enjoys should have some bearing on what is to be judged reasonable. Nevertheless, the reference to all other circumstances does invite some comparison between the terms of the tenancy which would be granted on renewal and those of the proposed alternative. The expense to be incurred in moving premises is not, however, a factor which will affect reasonableness nor, it is submitted, suitability. It is, instead, an inevitable risk which all tenants face at the expiry of their contractual terms.[10] The accommodation must, moreover, be available on those reasonable terms throughout the hearing. Although the landlord will normally take care to specify all the terms of the offer, it is permissible for the landlord to invite the court to determine terms as a preliminary issue.[11] Hence, in the *Chaplin* case, the judge assessed what a reasonable rental figure would be for the alternative premises.

Revising the Offer

8.07   A novel argument was put before the Court of Appeal in *Mark Stone Car Sales Ltd v Howard De Walden Estates Ltd* and concerned the evidence upon which issues of suitability fall be adjudged.[12] There the tenant argued that the court was limited solely to considering the terms of the original offer and could not have regard to the terms of an improved offer made by the landlord during the trial. The Act provides no direct assistance on this matter of timing and there is no definite answer to be drawn from case law. Unfortunately, the appellate court found it unnecessary to promote a solution and this important issue remains in some doubt. It is, however, not unduly difficult to discern a meaning from the current provisions and to justify a conclusion that the Act allows the offer of alternative accommodation to be revised while the hearing is continuing.[13] First, the general policy of

---

[9] *Per* Judge Aron Owen, n 1 above at 251.

[10] If, however, the landlord's payment of such costs is a term of the offer then the adequacy of the sum prescribed might be relevant in deciding whether the offer is on reasonable terms: see the *Chaplin* case, ibid.

[11] As if working out the terms for a new lease: see Chapter 9.

[12] (1997) 30 January (CA).

[13] Albeit *obiter*, some support for this conclusion can be drawn from the decision of Birkett LJ in *Betty's Cafes Ltd v Phillips Furnishing Stores Ltd*, n 3 above (CA) at 8.

the 1954 Act is to encourage negotiation and to promote agreement between the parties. The court is intended to be a venue of last resort. Enabling the bargaining process to continue for as long as possible is overtly consistent with this goal. It would, thereby, be curious if the landlord's pre-trial offer was regarded as immutable and the landlord denied the opportunity to overcome the tenant's objections which, in all likelihood, would then remain undisclosed until the commencement of the trial. A landlord would be placed in the awkward position of having to couch an offer in such terms as would overcome any future pitfalls which might emerge at the trial stage. As Judge Aron Owen admitted: 'It would be an impossible, or almost impossible feat for a landlord to make an offer which is "spot on" from inception and will remain so throughout the lengthy period that is going to elapse.'[14] As this would frustrate rather than facilitate negotiation, this approach would seriously undermine the flexible spirit and intention of the statutory scheme.

Second, there is nothing within the wording of section 30(1)(d) which supports a **8.08** restrictive approach. Indeed, the emphasis upon reasonableness and suitability as measured at the time of the hearing seemingly reinforces the notion that the landlord can refine the offer once the trial is under way. Certainly, the Act envisages that the tenant's circumstances may change between the landlord's initial offer and the conclusion of the trial and allows challenge on this basis at the hearing. In like vein, it must surely follow that the landlord should be able to amend an offer at an equivalently late stage so as to reflect the tenant's change of circumstances. It would then be for the tenant to apply for an adjournment so as to consider the landlord's revised offer. Third, the county court in *Chaplin (M) Ltd v Regent Capital Holdings Ltd* has already established that an offer of alternative accommodation can be revised after the service of the landlord's section 25 notice or counter notice. Although the scope of that judgment was limited to pre-trial amendments, it would seem illogical to prevent further revision merely because the trial has commenced.[15] There is certainly no rule of evidence or procedure to justify such limitation. Further support for a liberal interpretation emerges from section 31(2) which provides that, where the landlord fails to establish the alternative accommodation at the hearing, but the court believes that it could be established within a specified period, a new tenancy cannot be ordered.[16] If at the end of that period the landlord again fails to satisfy the court, it is only then that a new lease can be granted. This surely drives the proverbial horse and coaches through any argument that the landlord's hands are tied from the commencement of the hearing.

---

[14] The *Chaplin* case, n 1 above at 251.

[15] This is not a novel proposition as ground (f) (demolition and/or reconstruction) allows the landlord's case to be put in a provable form once the trial is under way: *Betty's Cafes Ltd v Phillips Furnishing Stores Ltd* (HL), n 3 above.

[16] The period, however, cannot exceed one year from the termination date specified in the landlord's notice or tenant's request, as appropriate. This section applies also to grounds (e) and (f).

It would be most peculiar for the landlord to be denied the opportunity to revise the offer during the hearing and yet be allowed to prove the ground of opposition during the subsequent months.

8.09 Finally, it should be remembered that the statutory scheme is designed to protect the tenant's business and not the tenant *per se.* The central issue for the court to decide is whether the alternative premises are suitable for that business, and considerations such as the tenant's reluctance to relocate or desire to obtain compensation are irrelevant. Meanwhile the tenant is safeguarded in that the landlord's opposition will succeed only if the alternative accommodation is both suitable and reasonable. If it is, then the business will not be prejudiced and can be carried out from the new premises. In this light, continued negotiations about the suitability of the proposed accommodation are of even-handed benefit. While the landlord can strengthen the case for rejection of the tenant's application, the tenant's business will benefit by having more reasonable and suitable premises from which it can operate in future. In the context of a provision which attempts to achieve a compromise between the commercial interests of the parties, it would be distinctly odd for the tenant to be able to reject the landlord's enhanced offer and yet rely on the inadequacy of the original.

Keeping the Offer Open

8.10 The landlord's offer of, and willingness to provide/secure, suitable accommodation must be maintained throughout the hearing. There is, however, no requirement that the offer be kept open for acceptance after that time, for example, while the tenant's appeal is pending. Similarly, the tenant is not compelled to accept the landlord's offer. If the offer is withdrawn post-hearing, therefore, the tenant may be placed in an unenviable situation. There is no provision for the court to order that the landlord keep the offer on the table for a reasonable period. Subject to section 55 compensation being payable for any misrepresentation by the landlord which induced the court to reject the tenant's application, the tenant will be unable to accept the offer, must quit the premises and will be unable to claim compensation for disturbance. There can be no argument that a binding contract exists at this stage because, regardless of any oral offer and acceptance, the provisions of the Law of Property (Miscellaneous) Provisions Act 1989 remain unsatisfied. If an appeal is outstanding, the tenant's only remaining hope is that it is successful.[17] Where the appellate court determines that the accommodation is not suitable, the tenant may, depending on the circumstances, be entitled to a renewal or, if the landlord has established other grounds of opposition, compensation for loss of renewal rights.

---

[17] It should be appreciated that, by virtue of section 64, the existing tenancy continues until three months after the final disposal of the proceedings, including appeals.

C. Ground (f): Redevelopment

By virtue of ground (f) the tenant's application will be dismissed if the competent **8.11** landlord can show that, on the termination of the existing lease, it is the bona fide intention that the premises (or a substantial part of them) comprised in the holding are either to be demolished or reconstructed; or that substantial works of construction are to be carried out on the holding. Work carried out on property other than the tenant's holding, therefore, falls to be disregarded for these purposes.[18] As regards demolition and reconstruction, this ground is only available where there is some building already on the holding.[19] In relation to construction, however, bare land would suffice provided that there is the intention either to erect some building on it or to convert it for a different use such as, for example, a roadway or runway.[20] The landlord must also show that the development could not occur without first gaining possession of the tenant's holding.[21]

Where the landlord takes the initiative by serving a section 25 notice, a strategy **8.12** should be planned in advance. This may be more difficult, however, when it is the tenant who initiates the renewal proceedings by the service of a section 26 request. An unprepared landlord may then have to respond with some haste to ensure that the intention to develop is put into a provable form. Nevertheless, the landlord does not have to prove the full extent of what is claimed in the notice or counter notice.[22] For these purposes it is the genuineness of the landlord's intention which is crucial and the burden rests with the tenant to show that the landlord's professed intention is colourable. The motives underlying that intention are, moreover, irrelevant.[23] In *Betty's Cafes Ltd v Phillips Furnishing Stores Ltd*, for example, the landlord's opposition was successful even though the reconstruction was designed

---

[18] *Joel v Swaddle* [1957] 3 All ER 325. Hence, work undertaken on common parts would be disregarded. It does not, therefore, matter how substantial the works are on other parts of the premises; it is only works on the tenant's holding which count: *Barth v Pritchard* (1990) 20 EG 65.

[19] *Coppen v Bruce-Smith* (1998) 77 P & CR 239 at 245 where Robert Walker LJ accepted that, 'premises in section 30(1)(f) cannot mean bare land with no building on it'.

[20] *Housleys Ltd v Bloomer-Holt Ltd* [1966] 1 WLR 1244. Preparatory works for a caravan site will suffice for these purposes: *Cook v Mott* (1961) 178 EG 637.

[21] *Fernandez v Walding* [1968] 1 All ER 994 This rule is subject to two qualifications contained in section 31A below.

[22] *Biles v Caesar* [1957] 1 All ER 151. There the landlord claimed the intention to reconstruct the whole of the premises, whereas it was really intended to reconstruct a substantial part. The landlord was able to recover possession. As Denning MR explained: 'It is a settled rule of pleading that if a pleader alleges more than is necessary, he is entitled to rely on any lesser facts covered by the allegation which are sufficient for the purpose he has in hand ... The greater allegation includes the less' (at 153).

[23] *Turner v Wandsworth London BC* (1995) 69 P & CR 433; see J Morgan [1995] JBL 189. In Al Malik Carpets Ltd v London Buildings (Highgate) Ltd (1999) 12 August HC, Neuberger J made clear that, even if the sole intention is to regain possession, the ground can still be made out.

merely to allow the landlord to occupy the premises.[24] As Evershed MR explained in *Craddock v Hampshire CC*, where the landlord 'establishes a bona fide intention to demolish, it is not made ineffective because it is what might be called ancillary to or subsidiary to some other purpose, namely to incorporate it into someone's agricultural holding'.[25] At the outset, however, it should be appreciated that ground (f) is unavailable in circumstances where the landlord intends to gain possession, sell the site to a developer and then leave the premises.[26] It must be the competent landlord who intends to develop.

A Firm and Settled Intention?

8.13 The competent landlord must have an unequivocal and fully formed intention to demolish, reconstruct or carry out works of construction.[27] This requires the landlord to have both a genuine desire to carry out the works and a reasonable chance of putting those plans into effect.[28] A vague or general assertion of intention will not suffice.[29] The classic exposition of what constitutes an intention emerges from the *obiter* of Lord Asquith in *Cunliffe v Goodman*:

> Not merely is the term 'intention' unsatisfied if the person professing it has too many hurdles to overcome, or too little control of events; it is equally inappropriate if at the material date that person is in effect not deciding to proceed but feeling his way and reserving his decision until he shall be in a possession of financial data sufficient to enable him to determine whether the payment will be commercially worth while . . . In the case of neither scheme did she [the landlord] form a settled intention to proceed. Neither project moved out of the zone of contemplation—out of the

---

[24] N 3 (HL) above. See also *Fisher v Taylors Furnishing Stores Ltd* [1956] 2 All ER 78 where the Court of Appeal stressed that the use to which the premises are ultimately put is of no concern. Hence, the landlord may wish to dispose of the premises or may not have come to any decision as to their future use.

[25] [1958] 1 WLR 202 at 209.

[26] *Ahern (PF) & Sons Ltd v Hunt* (1988) 21 EG 69. cf where the landlord intends to lease or sell after the development is completed: *Craddock v Hampshire CC*, ibid. Note that if the landlord in the *Ahern* case had sold the reversion following the service of the section 25 notice, the relevant intention to develop would have easily been shown by the new competent landlord.

[27] *Marks v British Waterways Board* [1963] 3 All ER 28. The capacity in which the competent landlord has the required intention is irrelevant: *Shiel v St. Helens Metropolitan BC* (1997) Current Law Week 6/97. There the landlord council owned both the freehold and, following a building lease to a developer, the sub-lease in a covered market. The landlord later sought to redevelop by surrendering its sub-tenancy to the developer and accepting the surrender of the building lease. This scheme of clearing the title back to the freeholder did not amount to an outright sale of the landlord's interest. The county court held that it would be artificial to require the council to have the requisite intention in its capacity as underlessee.

[28] As Denning MR stated in *Reohorn v Barry Corporation* [1956] 2 All ER 742 at 744: 'Intention connotes an ability to carry it into effect. A man cannot properly be said to intend to do a work of reconstruction when he has not got the means to carry it out. He may hope to do so; he will not have the intention to do so.' Accordingly, a mere wish to develop is insufficient as what is required is some objective ability of development being available: see *New Ash Green Village Association Ltd v Bovis (New Ash Green) Ltd* (1998) 12 February (CA).

[29] *Adams (E&B) Ltd v Chesterfield Properties Ltd* (1961) 178 EG 561.

sphere of the tentative, the provisional and the exploratory—into the valley of decision.[30]

In order to move into this 'valley of decision', the landlord must have a definite attitude to redevelopment, formed plans and overcome any serious obstacles. There is, however, no requirement that the landlord has taken all necessary steps towards the achievement of the development and the proposal need not be examined by the court in detail.[31] It is sufficient that there is a reasonable prospect of bringing about that which is intended and, hence, there must not be so many obstructions which undermine that prospect.[32] In this context, a reasonable prospect was described by Saville LJ in *Cadogan v McCarthy & Stone Developments Ltd* as, 'a real chance, a prospect that is strong enough to be acted on by a reasonable landlord minded to go ahead with plans . . . as opposed to a prospect that should be treated as merely fanciful or as one that should sensibly be ignored by a reasonable landlord'.[33]

As will be shown, intention is primarily evidenced by the ability, both financial **8.14** and legal, of the landlord to put the plans into operation. The fact that the landlord proposes a technical breach of planning conditions does not, however, prevent the landlord from establishing the requisite intention.[34] In addition, entrusting the work to another (for example, an agent or a contractor) does not disentitle the landlord from relying upon ground (f), provided that some form of control is retained over the works.[35] In the absence of control, the landlord will be regarded as merely intending to dispose of the property with vacant possession. It is, however, argued by Ross that the current provisions inadequately cater for the contemporary trend towards redevelopment on a grand scale: 'The 1954 Act did not contemplate the major redevelopment schemes of the type that are seen today. The "development process" may be so long and complex that the landlord will be unable to satisfy the intended requirement when the first leases of properties forming part of the site expire.'[36] It is suggested that, in such cases, the landlord should argue for a short term on renewal and the insertion of a development break clause.[37]

---

[30] [1950] 2 KB 237 at 254. He added, 'an intention to my mind connotes a state of affairs which the party "intending" does more than contemplate; it connotes a state of affairs which, on the contrary, he decides, so far as in him lies to bring about, and which, in point of possibility, he has a reasonable prospect of being able to bring about by his own act of volition' (at 253).

[31] *Aberdeen Steak Houses Plc v Crown Estates Commissioners* (1997) 31 EG 101.

[32] See *Levy (AJ) & Son Ltd v Martin Brent Developments* (1987) 283 EG 646.

[33] (1996) 16 May (CA).

[34] *Palisade Investments Ltd v Collin Estates Ltd* [1992] 2 EGLR 94. There it was stressed that prospective illegality was relevant only to the extent that it concerned the ability to carry out the works. Thus ground (f) is unavailable when the works themselves can only be carried out illegally.

[35] *Gilmour Caterers Ltd v St Bartholomew's Hospital* [1956] 1 All ER 314.

[36] M Ross, *Drafting and Negotiation of Commercial Leases* (4th edn, 1994) at 295, n 2.

[37] See further Chapter 9.

Evidencing Intention

8.15 As mentioned above, the landlord must show an ability to undertake the works and demonstrate the reasonable prospect of them being carried out.[38] This is a question of fact and degree[39] and there are a number of ways in which the landlord can establish the firm and settled intention to redevelop. It is possible, for example, that the court may accept the uncorroborated sworn testimony of the landlord,[40] but to rely on this course alone is somewhat unsafe.[41] As Denning LJ stressed in *Reohorn v Barry Corporation*, the court must be careful as the landlord may assert the intention at the hearing, but may have a change of heart once in possession.[42] In such cases, short of awarding compensation for misrepresentation, there is nothing that the court can do.[43] Although it may add evidential weight to the landlord's case, an undertaking to the court does not of itself prove that the landlord has the necessary intention.[44] Indeed, in *London Hilton Jewellers Ltd v Hilton International Hotels Ltd* the landlord's undertaking tipped the scales in favour of rejecting the application for a new lease.[45] The undertaking does, however, have to be both specific and realistic as a vague or implausible undertaking is of little evidential worth.[46] Furthermore, as illustrated in *Coppen v Bruce-Smith*, the terms of any undertaking given should be carefully scrutinised by the landlord. There the undertaking included the demolition of recreational facilities which entailed that planning permission would remain unavailable. If the undertaking had not made reference to these works, the landlord would have succeeded on the basis of the demolition of the buildings situated on the property.[47]

---

[38] An objective test is, therefore, applied: *Capocci v Goble* (1987) 284 EG 230.

[39] See *Fleet Electrics Ltd v Jacy Investments Ltd* (1956) 3 All ER 99.

[40] *Mirza v Nicola* (1990) 30 EG 92. This could include, for example, the testimony of an executor under a will whether or not probate has been obtained: *Biles v Caesar*, n 22 above.

[41] See *Levy (AJ) & Son Ltd v Martin Brent Developments*, n 32 above.

[42] N 28 above. Denning LJ also suggested that, where the premises are old and worn out, the court is more easily persuaded than when the premises are comparatively new or where the desirability of the project is open to doubt.

[43] As accepted by the Law Reform Advisory Committee for Northern Ireland in its *Review of the Law relating to Business Tenancies in Northern Ireland* (1992) Discussion Paper No 3 at para 5.2.2, compensation for misrepresentation 'does not appear to have been wholly successful'. Accordingly, in its subsequent Report (*Business Tenancies* (1994) Report No 1), the Committee recommended that the Irish equivalent to section 30(1)(f) should be amended so as to require evidence that planning permission has been obtained (at para 5.3.4). This is now incorporated within article 13(1) of the Business Tenancies (Northern Ireland) Order 1996.

[44] *Chez Gerard Ltd v Greene Ltd* (1983) 268 EG 575. Such is apparent from *Betty's Cafes Ltd v Phillips Furnishing Stores Ltd* (HL), n 3 above, where an undertaking given while the hearing was ongoing, coupled with other evidence of a board resolution, was thought to demonstrate the fixity of intention.

[45] (1990) 20 EG 69.

[46] *Lennox v Bell* (1957) 169 EG 753 where it was clear to the court that the landlord could not carry out the undertaking. The undertaking may be to use 'best endeavours' and might be accompanied by a bond: *Adams (E&B) Ltd v Chesterfield Properties Ltd*, n 29 above.

[47] N 19 above.

Although there are no hard and fast rules, it is not surprising that the court will normally look for some outward sign that the landlord is serious in intent.

Planning Permission

Usually this will entail that the landlord has obtained planning permission[48] or **8.16** can demonstrate a reasonable prospect that planning permission will be granted if the landlord is awarded possession.[49] The issue is determined, therefore, according to whether a reasonable man would expect permission to be granted.[50] As demonstrated in *Coppen v Bruce-Smith*, where there is no reasonable prospect of obtaining planning permission it cannot be said that the landlord has the requisite intention. There, as the landlord had previously been refused permission because the proposed construction would entail a loss of recreational facilities, it was apparent that planning permission would again be refused on the same grounds, even though the landlord now sought to turn the tennis courts into a derelict 'brown field' site. Although planning permission will normally be needed by the landlord,[51] if there is uncertainty as to whether such permission is necessary the court normally should not try to resolve the issue. As Upjohn LJ concluded in *Gregson v Cyril Lord*:

> [A]n inquiry whether the landlords on the evidence have established a reasonable prospect either that planning permission is not required or, if it is, that they would obtain it . . . does not necessitate the determination by the court of any questions which may one day be submitted to the planning authority or to the Minister; it is the practical appraisal upon the evidence of the court as to whether the landlords, upon whom, let me stress, the onus lies, have established a reasonable prospect of success.[52]

Nevertheless, in *Coppen v Bruce-Smith* the Court of Appeal did consider whether the landlord's proposed works of demolition fell within planning constraints. This point had (unnecessarily) been decided in the lower court, and due to expediency and the concession by counsel that if planning permission was needed it would not be granted, the appellate court felt obliged to consider the planning point.[53]

---

[48] *Joss v Bennett* (1956) 167 EG 207. As regards Northern Ireland, planning permission must be granted before the landlord can rely on this ground of opposition: article 13(1) of the Northern Ireland (Business Tenancies) Order 1996.

[49] *Gregson v Cyril Lord Ltd* [1963] 1 WLR 41. As made clear by Saville LJ in *Cadogan v McCarthy & Stone Developments*, n 33 above: 'A reasonable prospect does not entail that it is more likely than not that [planning] permission will be obtained.' A similar approach must apply also to any listed building consent which the landlord requires.

[50] *Westminster City Council v British Waterways Board* [1985] 1 AC 676.

[51] See section 57 of the Town and Country Planning Act 1990.

[52] N 49 above at 48. This passage was approved by the House of Lords in *Westminster City Council v British Waterways Board*, n 50 above at 680.

[53] N 19 above. If it arises, this determination involves issues both of law and fact: *Heron Service Stations v Coupe* [1973] 1 WLR 502.

Financial Viability

8.17 The landlord should also be able to demonstrate the availability of adequate finance.[54] This demonstration can adopt a number of forms and the court is entitled to look at any relevant documentation, even if such documents remain undisclosed before the hearing.[55] For example, in *DAF Motoring Centre (Gosport) Ltd v Hutfield & Wheeler* a letter from a bank manager promising finance was held to suffice for these purposes.[56] Similarly, in *Adams v Glibbery (JR) & Sons Ltd* a faxed message from the landlord's bank proved decisive.[57] The court is not, however, concerned with the precise source of the funds and, instead, simply concentrates upon whether the funds available are sufficient to implement the proposed development.[58] Accordingly, where the landlord has cashflow problems and is dependant upon the support of a bank, it will be expected that some evidence of the bank's willingness to provide continued (and increased) finance will be brought before the court.[59] If the landlord does not have the necessary financial resources, it will generally follow that the intention to redevelop is incomplete. It is, however, open to the landlord to arrange for the work to be carried out by another. This occurred in *Gilmour Caterers Ltd v St. Bartholemew's Hospital* where the landlord established its intention by entering into an agreement for a building lease under which the lessees were to do the rebuilding.[60] This flexibility, therefore, leaves it open to the landlord to have a change of tactics prior to the hearing. This is illustrated in *Spook Erection Ltd v British Railways Board* where the landlord had initially intended to develop through the sale of the site with vacant possession.[61] This would have taken the landlord outside ground (f), but a successful change of strategy occurred when the landlord then decided to grant a long building lease to a developer who would undertake the work.

---

[54] The tenant should, therefore, require the landlord (under Part 31 of the Civil Procedure Rules 1998) to produce for inspection any disclosed documents which purport to support this intention, ability and preparations to carry out the works. This approach is equally applicable to ground (g) below.

[55] *Mirza v Nicola*, n 40 above.

[56] (1982) 263 EG 976.

[57] (1991) 22 January (CA).

[58] *Levy (AJ) & Sons Ltd v Martin Brent Developments Ltd*, n 32 above, where the mere fact that the landlord was part of a group of companies which had previously carried out many developments convinced the court that the necessary finances would be available.

[59] *Keddie (GJ) & Sons Ltd v Norwich Union Life Assurance Society* (1985) 20 November (HC).

[60] N 35 above. The duration of the building lease for these purposes may be long (125 years in *Ahern (PF) & Sons Ltd v Hunt*, n 26 above or relatively short (4 years in *Turner v Wandsworth London BC*, n 23 above). In the *Turner* case, Staughton LJ expressed the view (at 437) that a short lease 'is not a stronger case for saying that he does not want to do the work; it is a stronger case for saying that he does intend it'.

[61] (1988) 21 EG 73.

Although for these purposes it is not necessary that binding contracts have been **8.18** entered between reversioner and developer,[62] in *Edwards v Thompson* the landlord was deemed unable to carry out the works because, at the time of the hearing, he had not selected an independent developer and had not reached any agreement as to the cost of the redevelopment.[63] There was, simply, no guarantee that the whole development would go ahead if the landlord obtained possession. Similarly, in *Reohorn v Barry Corporation* Denning MR examined the landlords' plans and concluded that they were insufficiently advanced: 'Plans for development are hardly started . . . It is obvious that there will be required long and detailed negotiations about the plans, nature of the buildings, amount of rent, terms of the leases, timetable and so forth.'[64] There Parker LJ rejected the argument that the landlords should not be expected to spend money on developing plans until possession was obtained: 'If such proof can only be adduced by incurring expense, then the landlords must incur expense and risk failure to obtain possession.'[65] This does not, however, pose a great risk for the landlord. In *Peter Goddard & Sons Ltd v Hounslow London BC*, for example, the fact that the landlord had spent £70,000 by way of preparatory expenditure indicated strongly that the works would go ahead.[66]

Corporate Intentions

As regards a company, it is necessary to evidence a corporate intention to rede- **8.19** velop. The mere evidence of a company representative, whether secretary or director, should not of itself suffice.[67] This is because the mere appointment of such officers does not give them adequate powers to form a company intention. Usually, therefore, a corporate intention will be evident from a formal board resolution,[68] but even then it should be coupled with an additional resolution authorising a specified director or manager to give evidence of the company's intention, if required. Alternatively, a director could be given express or implied authority to

---

[62] *Ahern (PF) & Sons Ltd v Hunt*, n 26 above; *Smith (AJA) Transport Ltd v British Railway Board* (1980) 257 EG 1257 (where a builder had been approached and was willing to carry out the works); *Capocci v Goble*, n 38 above (where it was probable that an agreement would be reached).
[63] (1990) 60 P & CR 222. Although the landlord was unable to show a firm and settled intention, as the prospects looked good for the future the tenant was given merely a one-year renewal.
[64] N 28 above at 744.
[65] ibid at 749.
[66] [1992] 1 EGLR 281. This was despite the tenant's objections that the plans and specifications were not advanced, that there might be financial problems and that sub-tenants existed who might be removed only with difficulty.
[67] *Birch (A & W) Ltd v Sloane (PB) Ltd* (1956) 167 EG 283.
[68] In *Espresso Coffee Machine Co Ltd v Guardian Assurance Co Ltd* [1959] 1 All ER 458 the intention to develop was not undermined by the fact that the company was unsure whether to occupy the holding. In the case of a local authority, a similar stance should be adopted with a formal resolution made by the authority or an authorised sub-committee. In *Poppett's (Caterers) Ltd v Maidenhead BC* [1970] 3 All ER 289, however, the local authority's approval of committee minutes was sufficient to show the necessary intention.

take the necessary decisions and, in this case, the director's intention would constitute the corporate intention.[69] It may, moreover, be possible to overcome the absence of a formal resolution where the intention of a number of directors is such that it is to be regarded as the company intention. As Denning LJ famously remarked:

> A company may in many ways be likened to a human body. They have a brain and a nerve centre which controls what they do. They also have hands which hold the tools and act in accordance with directions from the centre. Some of the people in the company are mere servants . . . who are nothing more than hands to do the work . . . Others are directors and managers who represent the directing mind and will of the company and control what they do. The state of mind of these managers is the state of mind of the company and is treated by the law as such.[70]

Much turns upon the officers' positions within the company, the nature of the matter under consideration and other relevant circumstances.[71] If, however, the directors do not possess adequate powers either to pass a resolution or to formulate the company's intention, a resolution in a general meeting will be necessary.[72]

Timing of Intention

8.20   Although the landlord's intention must be established at the hearing,[73] it can be put into a provable form after the hearing has begun.[74] In order to promote convenience and to keep costs at a minimum, however, it is normally desirable that the determination of intention be dealt with as a preliminary matter before any other issue in the proceedings. The attraction of a two-stage trial is that, if the landlord succeeds on ground (f) there is no need for the parties to collate valuation evidence as to the new rent. As Megarry J explained, 'in cases such as this the advantage of directing that there should first be one bite at the cherry is that thereafter either it will be plain that no other bite is possible or else the second bite will

---

[69] *Branhills Ltd v Town Tailors Ltd* (1956) 168 EG 642; *Manchester Garages Ltd v Petrofina (UK) Ltd* (1974) 233 EG 23. In *Fleet Electrics Ltd v Jacey Ltd*, n 39 above, the landlord company passed a resolution, but the evidence of the director was inconsistent and revealed that no thought had gone into the cost of the works and the financial implications for the company. The landlord, therefore, failed to show a firm and settled intention.

[70] *Bolton (HL) Engineering Co Ltd v Graham (TJ) & Sons Ltd* [1956] 3 All ER 624 at 630. There three directors formed the intention of the landlord company. As RE Megarry [1957] 73 LQR 15 at 16 conceded: 'Such a view may represent a departure from the requirement of formalism to be found expressed in certain nineteenth-century decisions, but it is . . . a realistic approach.' In this way the 1954 Act made a valuable contribution to the development of company law.

[71] See Megarry, ibid.

[72] *Birch (A & W) Ltd v PB (Sloane) Ltd*, n 67 above.

[73] *DAF Motoring Centre (Gosport) Ltd v Hutfield & Wheeler Ltd*, n 56 above; *Marks v British Waterways*, n 27 above.

[74] *Betty's Cafes Ltd v Phillips Furnishing Stores Ltd* (HL), n 3 above; *Branhills Ltd v Town Tailors Ltd*, n 69 above (during an adjournment). cf *Gallant (A&B) Ltd v British Home Stores Ltd* [1957] EGD 128 where the county court refused to allow into evidence a company resolution passed once the landlord had given evidence.

be made on due consideration after the need for it has been established'.[75] The intention, moreover, need not be supported by evidence at the date of service of the landlord's notice or counter notice and there is no need for the landlord, at that time, to disclose precise intentions. It is sufficient for the landlord merely to indicate that ground (f) will be relied upon.[76] This means that the landlord is able to advance the development plans in the intervening period between the service of the renewal documentation and the hearing.[77] It is also permissible for the landlord to express alternative schemes of proposed development and to maintain both up to and throughout the hearing. All that is necessary is the intention to carry out one of them.

In addition, last minute changes to the proposals do not automatically damage the credibility of the landlord's claim.[78] Neither does it matter if the identity of the competent landlord changes between the service of the landlord's renewal documentation and the date of the hearing. If this occurs, it is the new competent landlord's intention which is relevant and this will be unaffected by the seriousness or otherwise of the intention of the former landlord. As Denning MR said in *Marks v British Waterways Board*: 'If the subsequent landlord can prove that at the date of the hearing he has the requisite intention, the new lease must be refused.'[79]   **8.21**

Timing of Works

While it is at the time of the hearing that the competent landlord must establish the existence of a firm and settled intention, that intention is necessarily one that cannot be put into effect until the termination of the existing lease. Accordingly, the landlord must also demonstrate the intention to start work on, or within a reasonable time after, the date vacant possession will be obtained.[80] An intention to commence work within three months of termination, for example, was held to be sufficient in *Livestock Underwriting Agency v Corbett & Newton*.[81] The tenant's cause, moreover, will not be advanced by deferring the termination date (for example, lodging an appeal against the refusal of a new lease) and then arguing that the landlord is less able to effect the development.[82] It should also be recalled   **8.22**

---

[75] *Dutch Oven Ltd v Egham Estate & Investment Co Ltd* [1968] 3 All ER 100 at 103; see also *Barth v Pritchard*, n 18 above. One hearing might be appropriate when the terms of the new lease sought by the tenant are not much in dispute.

[76] *Biles v Caesar*, n 22 above.

[77] *Manchester Garages Ltd v Petrofina (UK) Ltd*, n 69 above.

[78] See *Birch (A & W) Ltd v PB (Sloane) Ltd*, n 67 above.

[79] N 27 above at 31.

[80] *Fisher v Taylors Furnishing Stores Ltd*, n 24 above; *London Hilton Jewellers v Hilton International Hotels Ltd*, n 45 above. Because of the operation of section 64, it will be unclear at the hearing date exactly when vacant possession will be obtained.

[81] (1955) 165 EG 469.

[82] *Smith (AJA) Transport v British Railways Board*, n 62 above. In addition, the tenant is not entitled to argue that the landlord should use a contractor as a way of speeding up the development process: *Jones v Thomas* (1963) 186 EG 1053.

that, once possession is gained, the landlord is free to have a change of mind and the tenant (except if there has been misrepresentation) is left with no remedy. This explains why it is necessary for the landlord to have a fixed and settled intention to redevelop.

Section 31(2)

8.23 If there is no intention to start the works within a reasonable time, but the landlord can show that they will be commenced within a year of the termination date stated in the section 25 notice or section 26 request, the court must dismiss the tenant's application and declare when the landlord will be able to satisfy the court.[83] This provision leaves unaltered the date when the intention must be established and focuses instead upon when it is to be implemented. Following the declaration, the tenant has fourteen days to make an *ex parte* application in chambers (High Court) or to the district judge (county court) requiring the court to substitute the date specified in the declaration for the original termination date.[84] This fourteen-day period cannot be extended. If the tenant fails to respond promptly to the declaration, the tenancy will end on the date specified in the renewal documentation.[85] On the tenant taking the positive step envisaged by section 31(2), the existing tenancy continues beyond the original termination date until the later date specified in the declaration.[86] It is to be stressed that the tenant has the choice of whether or not to accept this extension.

The Works

8.24 Ground (f) details what it is that the landlord must intend. The landlord is required to intend to demolish or reconstruct the premises comprising the holding (or a substantial part of the premises); or to carry out substantial construction work on the holding. Whether or not the proposed works fit within one of these categories is an issue of fact and degree. In *Bewlay (Tobacconists) Ltd v British Bata Shoe Co Ltd*, Evershed MR demonstrated that the court must, 'look at the totality of what is proposed to be done and, as a matter of fact and commonsense, to ask . . . whether these proposals . . . satisfy the language of ground (f)'.[87]

---

[83] Section 31(2) (which applies also to grounds (d) and (e)). As regards Northern Ireland, a similar provision is contained in article 14(2) of the Business Tenancies (Northern Ireland) Order 1996.

[84] County Court Rules, Order 43, r 9; Rules of the Supreme Court, Order 97, r 10(1).

[85] Or later if the proceedings have not by then been finally disposed of: section 64.

[86] See *Accountancy Personnel Ltd Worshipful Company of Salters* (1972) 116 SJ 240 where it was proven that the landlord's redevelopment plans were dependant on planning permission which would be granted in the near future.

[87] [1958] 3 All ER 652 at 655. There the removal of a wall and its replacement by screens amounted to works of reconstruction. It was also made clear that the landlord's opposition is not limited to works appropriate to turn to modern use an old or out-of-date building.

Demolition

Where the landlord intends to demolish all the buildings on the holding, this is **8.25** clearly within the scope of ground (f). Similarly, if the intention is not to destroy all the buildings, but to demolish a substantial part of the premises, the landlord will also be able to rely upon this ground of opposition. Some difficulty, however, has existed in determining what is 'substantial' for these purposes. General guidance emerged from Denning LJ in *Atkinson v Bettison* where he interpreted 'substantial' as meaning 'big', 'solid' and 'considerable'.[88] This approach, however, led to what was later described by Diplock LJ in *Housleys v Bloomer-Holt Ltd* as 'a short lived fallacy' that the intention of the landlord is to be regarded as colourable where the premises to be developed are not themselves substantial.[89] This is clearly not good law.[90] In *Housleys* case, for example, the demolition of a brick wall and a wooden garage (covering one-third of a timber yard) and replacement with concrete hard-standing for lorries, was held to be sufficient for the purposes of ground (f). As Sellers LJ said:

> The fact is that what was to be demolished was all that there was to demolish on the site, the garage and the wall, and all that seems to be demolishing the whole of the premises so far as any structure was to be demolished. It seems to me that that fulfils the requirements sufficiently. I am not concerned at the moment to consider what would be the position if the structure to be demolished had been some very small dog-kennel or very small hut on a very large area.[91]

In *Coppen v Bruce-Smith*, therefore, the demolition of a clubhouse and garage alone would have satisfied ground (f).[92] If it had been left at that, planning permission would not have been necessary[93] and the landlord's ground of opposition most certainly made out. Unfortunately for the landlord, however, the additional intention to demolish the tennis courts both required and prevented the grant of planning permission and defeated the claim to possession.

---

[88] [1955] 3 All ER 340. There the Court of Appeal confirmed that the removal of an existing shop front and its replacement with an arcade entrance, together with the removal of a wall, was not substantial. The landlord's intentions were deemed to be colourable because he really sought to occupy, but as he fell foul of the five-year rule (see below) he claimed instead possession under ground (f).

[89] N 20 above at 1252; see also *Craddock v Hampshire CC*, n 25 above. RE Megarry [1956] 72 LQR 23 described the *Atkinson* case as, 'remarkable, both as an exercise in statutory interpretation and in its practical consequences'.

[90] *Fisher v Taylors Furnishing Stores*, n 24 above; *Bettys Cafes Ltd v Phillips Furnishing Stores Ltd* (HL), n 3 above.

[91] ibid at 1250. Although the latter examples might still amount to demolition, it is probable that the landlord would not succeed under ground (f) because the need for possession to carry out the works could not be made out.

[92] N 19 above. Note that if the tenant had pre-empted the landlord and carried out the demolition works, the landlord would no longer have been able to rely on ground (f).

[93] See The Town and Country Planning (Demolition—Descriptions of Development) Direction 1995.

Reconstruction

8.26 It has been held that the term 'reconstruct' is akin to a building exercise following a measure of demolition and entails more than mere works of improvement and repair or mere changes of identity.[94] To be categorised as reconstruction the works must involve a substantial interference with the structure of a building, but not necessarily to the outer walls and roof.[95] Accordingly in *Cook v Mott* the term 'reconstruction' was viewed as involving the demolition of an existing fixed structure in whole or part as opposed to 'construction' which connotes works of an original or additional nature.[96] The terms 'demolition' and 'reconstruction' here fall to be construed conjunctively. The court will, therefore, assess the degree of the proposed demolition and building work against the background of the premises as they currently exist.[97] Work which is not constructional, but is subsidiary to work that is, can be taken into account in this overall evaluation of substantiality.[98] Hence, in *Romulus Trading Co Ltd v Henry Smiths Charity Trustees* the plastering of a new load-bearing wall was regarded as being part of the reconstruction of the wall itself.[99]

8.27 In *Joel v Swaddle* the proposed change from a small shop with two storage areas into part of a large amusement arcade was held to be reconstruction.[100] Similarly, in *City Offices (Regent St) Ltd v Europa Acceptance Group Plc* the physical removal of most of an office suite and its replacement by a different floor level, new suspended ceilings, new partition walls and the removal of a brick wall had such 'far-reaching physical effect on the state of the demised property' that it constituted reconstruction.[101] In *Cadle (Percy E) & Co Ltd v Jacmarch Properties Ltd*, however, the turning of three floors, in separate occupation, into a self-contained unit was not regarded as falling within ground (f).[102] The actual construction work to be done was very little indeed. In a like vein, the installation of a new shop front was held not to be reconstruction in *Atkinson v Bettison*.[103] Similarly, the landscaping of a field, removal of material and infilling was not classified as work of recon-

---

[94] *Cadle (Percy E) & Co Ltd v Jacmarch Properties Ltd* [1957] 1 All ER 148. As Denning LJ said (at 149): 'The word "reconstruct" here is best expressed . . . by the synonym "rebuild".'

[95] *Romulus Trading Co Ltd v Henry Smiths Charity Trustees* (1990) 32 EG 41.

[96] N 20 above.

[97] *Joel v Swaddle*, n 18 above, where Romer LJ stated (at 329) that it was necessary 'to regard the whole position as one total or entire picture'.

[98] *Barth v Pritchard*, n 18 above.

[99] N 95 above.

[100] N 18 above. Evershed MR added (at 329) that 'one does not fail to rebuild in a structural sense because one does not substitute for a wall another and different wall but leaves a space, as where girders resting on pillars are substituted for the wall and perform the structural function which the wall previously performed'.

[101] (1990) 5 EG 71 at 75 (*per* Nicholls LJ).

[102] N 94 above.

[103] N 88 above.

struction in *Botterill v Bedfordshire CC*.[104] There Sir John Arnold concluded that the Council were merely intending to alter the shape of the land and to give a slightly new composition to the field. It was not open to the Council to contend that it was constructing a domed field with some trees.

Construction

Ground (f) deals also with new construction, whether on the whole holding or on **8.28** part of it (for example, an extension to an existing building). Construction, there-fore, connotes either new building or adding to what is already there. The con-struction work, however, needs to be substantial which again raises issues of fact and degree. It was recognised in *Housleys Ltd v Bloomer-Holt Ltd* that the laying of a sufficient area of concrete and the resurfacing with hard-standing could be regarded as construction for these purposes.[105] The work must, however, directly affect the structure of the building in some way and not merely constitute refur-bishment or improvement. In *Barth v Pritchard*, for example, electrical re-wiring, provision of new toilet facilities and installation of a new central heating system were, in relation to the holding, deemed neither to be works of construction nor to be substantial.[106] Conversely, in *Fernandez v Walding* the extension of a factory by the building of a second storey on top of one section and erection of a wall between that section and the tenant's holding were designated as being works of construction.[107] In *Cook v Mott*, the making of a road and the laying of pipes, cables and drains so that the land could be used as a caravan site was sufficient.[108] In *Betty's Cafes Ltd v Phillips Furnishing Stores Ltd*, the removal and replacement of existing staircases and lift, the taking down of party walls, the strengthening of floors and the installation of lavatories were also held to constitute substantial works of construction.[109]

Reform?

Although in its Working Paper the Law Commission did not discuss any reforms **8.29** of the landlord's ability to oppose the tenant's application for renewal,[110] its

---

[104] (1985) 273 EG 1217.
[105] N 20 above.
[106] N 18 above. The works proposed there could more properly be classified as refurbishment or improvements. Stocker LJ also rejected an argument that, as none of the items could be separately classified as construction, the works as a whole should be so categorised. This shows that other works are relevant only when the landlord has carried out some construction work on the holding. The problem, as recognised by Ross, n 36 above at 297, n 1, is that 'work taken as a whole is clearly sub-stantial. And yet it might well be that in relation to the particular holding in question, the works would be trivial . . . In order to deal with this the landlord may undertake more comprehensive work than was needed . . .'
[107] N 21 above.
[108] N 20 above.
[109] N 3 above (HL).
[110] *Part II of the Landlord and Tenant Act 1954* (1988) Working Paper No 111.

subsequent Report did briefly consider whether the ground (f) was sufficiently wide.[111] It has been suggested that ground (f) should be extended to better protect the landlord's interests.[112] If, for example, ground (f) was revised so as to include the landlord's intention to 'refurbish' the premises then a landlord would be able to recover possession in the *Barth v Pritchard* scenario considered above. Indeed, the Report admitted that substantial works could be carried out without there being any demolition or reconstruction and that refurbishment can change a building's use, lengthen its economic life and increase its value. Nevertheless, no change was proposed as it would mark a major shift in the policy of the Act and would create problems in distinguishing between 'redecoration, which could hardly be a ground for depriving a tenant of his security of tenure, and the more extensive refurbishment'.[113]

8.30 Although mere redecoration should never justify the denial of a new lease, substantial refurbishment is a much different issue, as regards which it can validly be argued that the present confines of ground (f) are unduly restrictive. The invocation of policy so as to exclude major refurbishment is somewhat unconvincing. In that ground (f) is concerned with the landlord's management interests and the need to regain possession in order to further those interests, the present demarcation is, seemingly, unjustifiable on policy grounds. The exact nature of the landlord's works (and, importantly, their classification) should ideally be secondary to the need to obtain possession so as to put them into effect. In this sense the Law Commission may be criticised for confusing policy with detail. It is, moreover, illogical that the landlord can regain possession by demolishing the few buildings that lie on the tenant's holding (which may, in reality, be inconsequential to the tenant's business) and yet not be able to oppose a renewal on the basis of an extensive improvement of existing buildings (which might prove pivotal to the tenant's business). As to the implication that the court would experience difficulty in separating decoration from substantial refurbishment, this is also untenable. Already standing at the heart of the current provision is the assumption that the court can distinguish between qualifying works and non-qualifying works and, as regards the former, categorise them as being works of demolition, reconstruction and construction.

---

[111] *Business Tenancies: A Periodic Review of the Landlord and Tenant Act 1954 Part II* (1992) Law Com 208 at para 3.26.

[112] For example, Ross, n 36 above at 297, suggests two reforms. First, to allow possession where there is a substantial redevelopment scheme of the whole premises, even though the work on the tenant's holding is not substantial. Second, to give the court express powers to insert terms in the new lease to facilitate refurbishment and to provide for a rent review which will operate when the works are complete.

[113] N 111 above at para 3.2.6. In total contrast, the Law Reform Advisory Committee for Northern Ireland Report, n 43 above at para 5.2.4 came to the conclusion that the scope of ground (f) was too wide. It recommended that demolition should always be linked to substantial development. This is now embodied within article 12(f)(I) of the Business Tenancies (Northern Ireland) Order 1996.

The Need for Possession

The landlord has to show that the works of demolition, reconstruction or con- **8.31**
struction cannot be reasonably carried out without obtaining possession of the
tenant's holding. Possession in this context means both physical and legal possession and, hence, the landlord is required to establish that the work could not be
undertaken without bringing the tenancy to an end. Accordingly, in *Bewlay
(Tobacconists) Ltd v Bata Shoe Co Ltd* Sellers LJ felt that the installation of a new
shop front did not require possession of the holding as the business could continue as usual.[114] In *Reohorn v Barry Corporation*, the landlord's claim failed
because it was not necessary to regain possession in order to build a proposed
road.[115] Similarly, in *Heath v Drown* it was concluded that, where there is an
express right to enter and to carry out works reserved in the lease, the landlord cannot successfully oppose the tenant's application for a new lease under ground
(f).[116] This is because legal possession is not then dependent upon the termination
of the tenancy. Instead, the legal right to undertake the works was granted by the
lease itself and this reasoning applies even though the tenant will have to close
business for a temporary period.[117] This general rule will give way, however, where
the work when completed would deprive the tenant of facilities necessary to carry
on trade and amount to a derogation from the landlord's grant.[118] To carry out
such works lawfully, the landlord will still need to acquire legal possession as well
as physical possession.

Section 31A: Calling the Landlord's Bluff

Even though the landlord can show the necessary intention, and where there is no **8.32**
existing term in the lease which gives a right to enter, the tenant can still obtain a
renewal where possession of the entire holding is not required in order to carry out
the redevelopment. This brings into relevance the somewhat complicated section
31A which, by way of an escape for the tenant, provides that the landlord is unable
to demonstrate the need for possession in two circumstances.[119] These are when

---

[114] N 87 above at 656.

[115] N 28 above.

[116] (1973) AC 498. If the landlord is under an obligation to repair, a right to enter is in any event
implied: *Saner v Bilton* (1878) 7 Ch D 815. It was suggested in *Barth v Prichard* n 18 above that a
right to enter to remedy a breach of a tenant's repair covenant is not relevant for these purposes.

[117] *Romulus Trading Co Ltd v Henry Smiths Charity Trustees*, n 95 above, where it was predicted
that the tenant would not be able to occupy the premises for up to nine months. See also *Price v Esso
Petroleum Co Ltd* (1980) 255 EG 243; *Little Park Service Station Ltd v Regent Oil Co Ltd* [1967] 2
All ER 257.

[118] *Leathwoods Ltd v Total Oil (GB) Ltd* (1986) 51 P & CR 20 where the landlord, having a right
to carry out alterations, improvements and additions, proposed a scheme of works which would
have prevented the tenant continuing the business of selling and repairing cars.

[119] As no equivalent previously existed in Northern Ireland, the Report of the Law Reform
Advisory Committee for Northern Ireland recommended the introduction of a similar provision,

the landlord requires possession of part only of the holding or requires possession of the whole for a short time only. As this provision is relevant only when the landlord can establish the necessary intention to carry out works within the scope of ground (f), it does not concern a landlord who is unable to show such intention. Section 31A is designed to benefit the tenant and does not offer assistance to the landlord who wants to repossess. The relationship between ground (f) and section 31A was considered in *Romulus Trading Company Ltd v Trustees of Henry Smith's Charity (No. 2)*.[120] There the Court of Appeal made clear that the court is bound to apply ground (f) in the light of section 31A. This entails that the tenant can put forward conditional arguments. Accordingly, it is proper for the tenant, in the alternative, to dispute the genuineness of the landlord's intention; to contend that the work does not fall within ground (f); to propose that the work can be carried out by the means of access and facilities contemplated by section 31A(1)(a); and to suggest that the work can be done if there was a grant of part only of the premises under section 31A(1)(b). This avoids the need for any election on the tenant's part.

New Terms

8.33 The first is where the tenant agrees to the inclusion within the new lease of terms which facilitate the landlord's access and ability to carry out the work, and the landlord can reasonably execute the work without either retaking possession or disrupting to a substantial extent and for a substantial time, the tenant's use of the holding.[121] This provision is relevant only where the existing lease does not contain a term allowing the landlord to carry out the work. The tenant will not, moreover, be able to utilise this provision if the landlord's works will be made unreasonably more protracted or expensive. In addition, the provision is unavailable also when the landlord intends to demolish the entire premises.[122]

8.34 The assessment of interference, moreover, is one of fact and degree.[123] The meaning of 'possession' refers to legal possession[124] and the terms 'extent' and 'time' are to be read conjunctively and, therefore, treated together.[125] The key issue is whether the work can go ahead with only minor and temporary inconvenience to the tenant's use of the holding or whether it will involve a total disruption of that use. The onus rests upon the tenant to show that the proposed term will allow the

---

'to do justice to both parties: the tenant obtains his new tenancy and the landlord's plans to modernise the premises are facilitated . . . Moreover, if the landlord is not genuine in his intention to redevelop . . . [it] would allow the tenant to call his bluff (n 43 above at para 5.2.7). This recommendation is now enacted within article 13(2).

120 (1991) 11 EG 112.
121 Section 31A(1)(a).
122 *Mularczyk v Azralnove Investments Ltd* (1985) 276 EG 1064.
123 *Blackburn v Hussain* (1988) 22 EG 78.
124 *Spalding v Shotley Point Marine (1986) Ltd* (1989) 24 January (CA).
125 *Cerex Jewels Ltd v Peachey Properties Corporation* (1986) 52 P & CR 127.

landlord to undertake the work and the court's determination will be based upon a detailed description of the works intended.[126] The aim is to reduce the ability of the landlord to recover possession, except where major demolition or reconstruction is proposed. For these purposes it is the effect on the tenant's present use which is relevant and not the effect on the tenant's business.[127] In *Cerex Jewels Ltd v Peachey Property Corporation*, for example, the closure of the tenant's business for two weeks was regarded as a minor interference,[128] whereas in *Blackburn v Hussain* a closure for twelve weeks was sufficiently disruptive to prevent the operation of section 31A.[129] These cases illustrate the basic proposition that the longer the interruption the less likely it is that the court will protect the tenant. The tenant, moreover, is unable to waive the interference with the use of the holding for, as made clear in *Redfern v Reeves*, section 31A(1)(a) does not confer on the tenant the ability to disregard any disruption.[130] The landlord, moreover, is under no duty to minimise the interference.

New Letting of Part

The second is where the tenant is willing to accept a tenancy of an economically separable part of the holding.[131] This offers the tenant a partial shield, in that the new lease will be granted, but only of part of the existing holding.[132] The meaning of 'an economically separable part' is provided by section 31A(2). This stipulates that a part is economically separable when, after the completion of the intended work, the aggregate of the rents which would be reasonably obtainable on separate lettings of that part and the remainder of the premises is not less than the rent which is reasonably obtainable on a letting of those premises as a whole. Accordingly, whether the separation of the part is economic depends purely upon valuation evidence of the landlord's alternative rental incomes. It has nothing to do with the tenant's business. For the tenant to rely upon this provision, it is necessary that a further condition be satisfied. This additional requirement is expressed in the alternative: first, that the tenant is willing to grant access and facilities (under section 31A(1)(a)) in respect of the economically separable part and the proposed works can be carried out without substantially affecting the tenant's business. Second, that the landlord can reasonably carry out the proposed works

8.35

---

[126] *Spalding v Shotley Point Marine (1986) Ltd*, n 124 above. In fairness to the landlord, the court may require the tenant to particularise the case put under section 31A(1)(a).

[127] *Redfern v Reeves* (1978) 37 P & CR 364 where the fact that the tenant's goodwill would not be affected by the tenant moving out of possession, for an estimated period of between two and four months, was irrelevant.

[128] N 125 above.

[129] N 123 above. Similarly, in *Price v Esso Petroleum Ltd*, n 117 above, a 16-week exclusion was held to constitute a substantial disruption.

[130] N 127 above.

[131] Section 31A(1)(b).

[132] Section 32(1A). For hypothetical situations in which section 31A could operate see K Reynolds and W Clark, *Renewal of Business Tenancies* (1997) at 214, 216.

(without being granted access and facilities over the separable part) on the excluded part which, of course, will no longer form part of the tenant's holding. The burden of proof lies on the tenant and it is necessary that the tenant's willingness be established at the date of the hearing.

8.36 It should be borne in mind, however, that the tenant cannot insist that there be an alteration to the landlord's plans so as to minimise the impact of the redevelopment. It is the bona fide intentions of the landlord which prevail and, hence, the court cannot consider whether the landlord's proposals are reasonable or modify those plans.[133] This was illustrated in *Decca Navigator Co Ltd v GLC* where the tenant argued that the landlord did not need all of the holding for the purposes of building a fire station and that a fifteen-feet strip should be retained for the tenant's car-parking purposes.[134] The contention was that the landlord could construct a perfectly adequate fire station in a different way. Cairns LJ rejected the tenant's proposal:

> I can see no warrant for reading this [section 31A] to mean that the court must be satisfied that it is reasonable for the landlord to execute the intended work. Still less can I see any warrant for requiring the court to balance the advantages to the landlord of executing the intended work against any disadvantage to the tenant or any disadvantage to the public of the work being executed.[135]

D. Ground (g): Owner Occupation

8.37 Under ground (g) the tenant's application for a new tenancy can be opposed if the competent landlord intends to occupy the entirety of the tenant's holding for use (either in whole or part) as a residence or for a business carried on therein by the landlord or a company controlled by the landlord.[136] To succeed under this ground there are a variety of factors which must be established.

Intention

8.38 The requirement as to the landlord's settled and genuine intention to occupy is subject to a similar standard of proof (and similar judicial gloss) as considered above in connection with ground (f).[137] It contains, therefore, both subjective and objective elements. Consequently, the landlord must be able to demonstrate both a bona fide intention to occupy for business/residential purposes and the reason-

---

[133] *Levy (AJ) & Son Ltd v Martin Brent Developments*, n 32 above.

[134] [1974] 1 All ER 1178.

[135] ibid at 1181. If it were otherwise the court would be compelled to become embroiled in planning considerations.

[136] Section 30(1)(g). As will be shown, this is qualified by the so-called five-year rule imposed by section 30(2).

[137] *Chez Gerard Ltd v Greene Ltd*, n 44 above; *Gregson v Cyril Lord Ltd*, n 49 above.

able prospect of bringing about this occupation. A noticeable difference between grounds (f) and (g), however, is that it is not normally appropriate to test the reasonable practicability of the landlord's intention under ground (g) by reference to the presence or absence of detailed financial and structural plans, consents and planning permission. In *Dolgellau Golf Club v Hett*, for example, the landlord succeeded even though he produced little to demonstrate the detail and practicality of his intentions.[138] As Balcombe LJ explained in *Palisade Investments Ltd v Collin Estates Ltd*, 'the Act was intended to be construed sensibly, so as to hold a fair balance between landlord and tenant. It is not . . . to be construed so as to create a series of artificial hoops through which the landlord must jump before he must satisfy the necessary intention.'[139]

It is also important to appreciate that ground (g) is concerned only with the reality of the landlord's intention of setting up a business and not the probability of achieving its start or its ultimate success. In *Cox v Binfield* the evidence was that the landlord would have difficulties in financing the necessary equipment and that the economic advantages of the venture were doubtful.[140] Nevertheless, the opposition succeeded even though the future plans for the holding were ill thought out and might fail. As O'Connor LJ observed: 'Objectively, the judge must be able to say that this intention is one which is being capable of being carried out in the reasonable future in the circumstances which will prevail when possession is achieved by the landlord.'[141] Similarly in *Dolgellau Golf Club v Hett*, where the landlord's plans were incomplete and the proposed business likely to fail in the longer term, the landlord's opposition prevailed because the proposal was at the least capable of succeeding.[142] As Auld LJ concluded:

8.39

> It is not an incident of the statutory formula, nor of the present judicial gloss on it, that a landlord, in seeking to satisfy the court of the reality of his intention, should be subjected to minute examination of his finances with a view to determining the financial viability and durability of the business he intends to establish. The Court is not there to police a landlord's entitlement to recover possession of his own property by examining the financial wisdom of his genuinely held plans for it.[143]

---

[138] (1998) 76 P & CR 526 ; see J Morgan [1999] JBL 269.

[139] N 34 above at 97. Nevertheless, where there is a proposed change of use, the likelihood of being granted planning permission will become a relevant factor: *Westminster CC v British Waterways Board*, n 50 above. cf *Dolgellau Golf Club v Hett*, ibid, above where there was established planning use of the land as a golf club and club house.

[140] [1989] 1 EGLR 97.

[141] ibid at 101.

[142] N 138 above. This case also shows that the landlord's business proposals can be modified during the intervening period between the service of the renewal documentation and the hearing. There the landlord's counter notice stated that the landlord sought to operate an 18-hole golf course. Because of financial constraints, at the hearing the landlord successfully claimed possession to run a 9-hole course.

[143] ibid at 90.

Proving Intention

8.40 In *Europark (Midlands) Ltd v Town Centre Securities* the landlord's intention to occupy was demonstrated by the minutes of a board meeting, an affidavit of a director, and obtaining quotations for equipment to be used by the landlord on regaining possession.[144] In *Page v Sole* a minute of a partnership meeting and the evidence of one partner was sufficient for the court to make the factual finding of intention.[145] Similarly, in *Skeet v Powell-Sneddon* the evidence of the landlord that she wanted to go into the hotel business with her husband and to give employment to her daughter sufficed, even though no partnership agreement had been entered and no application had been made for a liquor licence.[146] Although some doubt has been expressed concerning the appropriateness of an undertaking to occupy,[147] it is common for such an undertaking to support the landlord's claim.[148] Regardless of its binding status, at the least an undertaking evidences intention and, therefore, can only help the landlord's case. If alternative accommodation is available for the landlord's occupation, and the landlord seeks to preserve both options until the conclusion of the hearing, this may have an adverse effect on the landlord's claim. It may be seen as undermining the firmness of the landlord's intention to occupy the tenant's holding.[149]

8.41 As shown, the landlord will usually experience no difficulties in showing the financial resources to start a business. The finances of the competent landlord might, however, be questioned in circumstances where the premises need expensive refurbishment before they can be occupied.[150] In this instance, a detailed examination of the financial viability of the landlord's proposals might be appropriate and become a key factor in determining whether the intention is genuine and realistic. The landlord may also have difficulties where occupation is sought for business purposes which are prohibited under a head lease.[151] In such a situa-

---

[144] (1985) 274 EG 289.

[145] (1991) 24 January (CA).

[146] (1988) 40 EG 116. See also *Pelosi v Bourne* (1957) 169 EG 656 where the landlord sought to expand his successful business into the tenant's existing premises. The facts that the landlord's present accommodation was cramped and that the business was financially strong persuaded the court that the intention to occupy was settled. It was not necessary that the landlord be able to detail the proposed layout of the extended premises.

[147] See *Chez Gerard Ltd v Greene Ltd*, n 44 above. This argument is based upon the inability at law to enforce an undertaking to occupy.

[148] But an undertaking alone is not conclusive: *Lennox v Bell* (1957) 169 EG 753; *Lightcliffe District Cricket & Lawn Tennis Club* (1978) 245 EG 393.

[149] *Espresso Coffee Machine Co Ltd v Guardian Assurance Co Ltd*, n 68 above. The landlord cannot always, as Lord Evershed explained, 'have his bun and his penny' (at 460).

[150] *Adams v Glibbery (JR) & Sons Ltd*, n 29 above.

[151] *Wates Estate Agency Services Ltd v Bartleys Ltd* (1989) 47 EG 51 where the landlord was disentitled to rely on ground (g).

tion, the competent landlord should secure the relaxation of the user covenant before the hearing date.

Occupation

It is necessary that the evidence shows that the competent landlord will actually **8.42** occupy the holding. The landlord, however, need not seek to occupy the holding personally as it is well established that there are a number of other ways in which occupation can arise. The landlord can occupy, for example, through an agent,[152] a manager,[153] a partnership,[154] a beneficiary under a trust,[155] and a company which is a member of a group of companies which includes the landlord company.[156] Following its introduction by the Law of Property Act 1969, section 30(3) provides that occupation can also be through a company controlled by the landlord.[157] Short of agency, the current provisions do not, however, apply where a company landlord seeks possession so as to allow its controlling shareholder to occupy. To overcome this duality of treatment, the 1992 Law Commission Report recommended that the corporate veil be lifted and that companies be treated as identical to the individuals who control them. Hence, ground (g) should apply where the landlord company wants possession for the purposes of a business carried on by an individual who controls it or who controls another company in the group.[158] A controlling interest in a company arises when the landlord holds over half of the equity share capital of that company (disregarding nominee and fiduciary holdings) or is a shareholder and can alone appoint and dismiss the holders of a majority of the directorships.[159] By virtue of section 42(1), however, a different test applies to the control of one company by another.[160] Sensibly, the

---

[152] *Skeet v Powell-Sneddon*, n 146 above.

[153] *France v Shaftward Investments* (1981) 25 June (CA); *Hills (Patents) Ltd v University College Hospital Board of Governors* [1955] 3 All ER 365.

[154] *Re Crowhurst Park* [1974] 1 All ER 991; *Clift v Taylor* (1948) 2 KB 394 (which related to a similar provision contained in section 5 of the Landlord and Tenant Act 1927).

[155] Section 41(2); see also *Morar v Chauhan* [1985] 3 All ER 493; *Sevenarts Ltd v Busvine* [1969] 1 All ER 392. As regards occupation by a beneficiary, the occupation must be by virtue of the interest under a trust and not otherwise, for example by virtue of a lease or assignment: *Meyer v Riddick* (1990) 60 P & CR 42; see Chapter 3. Note also the provisions of the Trusts of Land and Appointment of Trustees Act 1996 with regard to occupational rights of a beneficiary.

[156] Section 42(3). The Act provides that two companies are regarded as being in a group only when one is subsidiary to the other or both are subsidiary to a third corporate body: section 42(1).

[157] See *Harvey Textiles Ltd v Hillel* (1979) 249 EG 1063. It is uncertain whether, for these purposes, a company can occupy for residential purposes except through an agent or employee.

[158] N 111 above at para 2.10. In Northern Ireland this has been achieved by article 12(1)(h).

[159] Section 30(3). This test was drawn from section 154 of the Companies Act 1948.

[160] This follows section 144 of the Companies Act 1989 which defines control for these purposes as either holding a majority of the voting rights in a subsidiary; being a member of the subsidiary with the right to approve or remove a majority of its board or controlling a majority of the voting rights of it; or controlling a company which itself controls the subsidiary.

Law Commission Report has recommended that the latter test should apply also to the control of a company by an individual.[161]

8.43 Occupation need not be immediate and the court may accept the landlord's undertaking to occupy at a later date.[162] Nevertheless, in *Method Developments Ltd v Jones* it was made clear that occupation must be intended to be within a reasonable time following the date of termination.[163] This gives rise to an issue of fact and, in approaching the matter, the court must adopt a sensible and businesslike attitude.[164] There is also no mention within ground (g) as to how long the landlord must intend to occupy the holding.[165] The rule which has emerged, however, is that it will not be sufficient for the landlord to show the intention to occupy for a temporary period before selling the property.[166] Hence, the landlord cannot rely upon ground (g) when the occupation is merely to redecorate.[167] In other circumstances, an intended occupation of a number of months may suffice, but as mentioned only when there is intended to be no outright sale of the premises to a cash purchaser.[168] In *Willis v Association of Universities of the British Commonwealth*, Salmon LJ stated, by way of analogy, that a landlord who has not long to live, and who seeks possession under ground (g), could not be said by the tenant to intend to pass the property to the heirs.[169] He also considered the situation where, following a restructuring exercise, the landlord company was to be dissolved. If dissolution occurred before the hearing, the new landlord would stand in the shoes of the old. In relation to a dissolution planned to occur after the hearing, he felt that the landlord could still rely on ground (g): 'the law does not make the rights of the parties depend on the fortuitous circumstance whether the transfer is executed sooner than later'.[170]

Occupation of What?

8.44 It should be appreciated that the landlord must intend to occupy the whole of the tenant's holding and not merely part of it, no matter how substantial that part may be.[171] This does not, however, require that each and every part of the holding be

---

[161] N 111 above at para 2.13: 'a single definition must make the Act easier to understand and to operate'.

[162] *Chez Gerard Ltd v Greene*, n 44 above.

[163] [1971] 1 All ER 1027.

[164] *London Hilton Jewellers v Hilton International Hotels Ltd*, n 45 above, where it was said that, for these purposes, a month or so would not be unreasonable.

[165] cf article 12(1)(g) of the Business Tenancies (Northern Ireland) Order 1996 which requires occupation for 'a reasonable period'.

[166] *Willis v Association of Universities of the British Commonwealth* [1964] 2 All ER 39.

[167] *Jones v Jenkins* (1985) 277 EG 644.

[168] In the *Willis* case, n 166 above, Denning MR expressed the view that a short period of occupation before, for example, a father passing the business over to his son would be sufficient (at 43).

[169] ibid at 46.

[170] ibid.

[171] *Shecrum Ltd v Savill* (1996) 1 April (CA). This may be regarded as an unduly onerous and unreasonable requirement; cf section 31A(1)(b) which relates to part development.

physically used for the landlord's business or residential purposes.[172] In the context of ground (g), the term 'holding' has been subject to judicial scrutiny. In *Nursey v P Currie (Dartford) Ltd*, the Court of Appeal concluded that the landlord could not successfully oppose the tenant's renewal under ground (g) where it was the intention to demolish the buildings on the current holding and to build replacements,[173] the reasoning being that the landlord could then no longer occupy the holding as it was. As Wynn-Parry J commented, 'it is not permissible to take into account the wider scheme which the landlords had in mind, and merely to treat the land comprised in the holding as land which, in one way or another, will be used for the purpose of the wider undertaking'.[174] This decision, however, appears to confuse the meaning of the terms 'holding' and 'premises' and has been confined only to situations where there is to be the demolition and replacement of existing buildings.[175] Hence, it has been held that, where the holding consists of a vacant site (such as a car park), the landlord can rely upon ground (g) even though the intention is to build upon the site once in occupation.[176]

The above distinction is, however, arguably untenable as there is nothing within the 1954 Act which warrants the imposition of such an artificial, double standard. The policy of ground (g) is simply to allow the recovery of possession so that the landlord can occupy for business or residential purposes. It should not matter what type of business the landlord intends to pursue, whether there are any buildings on the holding and, if there are, whether the landlord intends to physically occupy every building in pursuit of that business. Unlike ground (f), moreover, there is no attempt to distinguish expressly between 'holding' and 'premises' and it is highly unlikely that Parliament intended that the landlord could recover the holding only on the understanding that it remains in an unaltered state. Accordingly, whether or not the holding has buildings on it should not effect the landlord's ambitions to occupy.[177] Not surprisingly, therefore, the *Nursey* approach was doubted by Salmon LJ in *Method Developments Ltd v Jones*.[178] Due

8.45

---

[172] *Method Developments Ltd v Jones*, n 163 above, 'just as one can plainly occupy a dwelling house as one's residence even though one leaves a couple of rooms empty' (*per* Fenton Atkinson LJ at 1030); see also *Shecrum Ltd v Savill*, ibid.

[173] [1959] 1 All ER 497. The landlord intended to occupy and use it as a petrol station.

[174] ibid at 500. A Willmer LJ added, 'in applying section 30(1)(g) one must look at the particular holding comprised in the particular tenancy which is before the court in the particular case' (at 501).

[175] *Cam Gears Ltd v Cunningham* [1981] 2 All ER 560 where the holding consisted of a vacant site with hard-standing for the parking of cars. The landlord sought to take possession and to erect a building which would cover about a third of the site. The claim under ground (g) was successful. Note that the landlord would also, if it had been expressed in the counter notice, have been able to rely upon ground (f) in these circumstances.

[176] *Leathwoods Ltd v Total Oil (GB) Ltd* (1986) 51 P & CR 20; *Thornton (JW) Ltd v Blacks Leisure Group Plc* [1986] 2 EGLR 61. Both were able to distinguish the *Nursey* case, n 173 above.

[177] See *McKenna v Porter Motors* (1956) AC 688.

[178] N 163 above at 1030. He felt that the uncertainty was due to poor drafting and commented that section 30(1)(g) was, 'not very felicitously worded. Its meaning could perhaps have been made clearer than it is. The same criticism is possible about much of this Act' (at 1029).

to this uncertainty, however, if the landlord intends to redevelop before taking up occupation it is advisable to rely on both grounds (f) and (g). Provided that the necessary intentions are established, it is practicable for both to be relied upon together.[179] A further point of interest arises in the context of the amalgamation of the premises. In *JW Thornton Ltd v Blacks Leisure Group*, it was held that a landlord who wished to demolish two partition walls (between the landlord's present premises and those of the tenant) and to occupy the enlarged holding remained within ground (g).[180] The Court of Appeal distinguished the *Nursey* case on the ground that here the demolition and reconstruction work was not substantial.

Business or Residential Purposes?

8.46   The occupation needs to be wholly or partially for the landlord's business or residence and a mixed user is permissible.[181] As shown, the landlord must occupy the whole of the holding, but it is not necessary that the entirety is used for business or residential purposes.[182] The term 'business' is widely interpreted for these purposes. It has, for example, been held to include the running of a community centre, managed in conjunction with a local church.[183] It extends to storage purposes ancillary to the business and advantageous for the development of the business in the future.[184] In *Jones v Jenkins* it was accepted that, where the landlord is in the business of letting accommodation and intends to let the property to others while providing services and management, this may constitute occupation for business purposes.[185] Following *Graysim Holdings Ltd v P & O Property Holdings Ltd*, however, this approach can no longer be sustained because, as Lord Nicholls emphasised, the sub-lessor would neither occupy the property nor be said to be carrying on a business from the premises.[186] A further potential problem arises for the landlord where, on the grant of the original tenancy, the existing goodwill of the business was assigned to the tenant and the landlord now seeks to resume that same business. It was held in *Daleo v Iretti* that, as this use could be restrained by

---

[179] *Fisher v Taylor's Furnishing Stores Ltd*, n 24 above. There Parker LJ did, however, make the observation that, if the landlord relies upon both grounds (f) and (g) and cannot show the fixity of intention to occupy, the landlord's intention to redevelop should be viewed with some suspicion.

[180] (1987) 53 P & CR 223.

[181] As regards residential use, it should be of no consequence that the landlord has other residences provided that the intention to occupy the tenant's holding is made out.

[182] *Method Developments Ltd v Jones*, n 163 above.

[183] *Parkes v Westminster Roman Catholic Diocese Trustee* (1978) 36 P & CR 22.

[184] *Page v Sole*, n 145 above. In *Hunt v Decca Navigator* (1972) 222 EG 605 it sufficed that the holding was to be used for car parking purposes for visitors and staff to the landlord's adjacent premises.

[185] N 167 above.

[186] [1995] 4 All ER 831 at 836, 839. This decision also exploded the myth of co-existential occupation which had previously been supported by Denning MR in *Hills (Patents) Ltd v University College Hospital Board of Governors*, n 153 above at 367; see further Chapter 3.

the tenant, the landlord could not rely on ground (g).[187] In other circumstances, the continuation by the landlord of the tenant's business is acceptable.[188]

The Five-Year Rule

It is a curious, but general rule of the 1954 Act that a change in the personality of the landlord during the course of the opposition to a new tenancy does not alter the landlord's position.[189] As Robert Walker LJ commented: 'For the purposes of Part II . . . therefore, one successive landlord is very closely identified with any successor of his.'[190] An exception to this rule concerns the right of the landlord to oppose the tenant's application under section 30(1)(g). This is subject to an important qualification contained in section 30(2) which is commonly called 'the five-year rule'.[191] This precludes the competent landlord from relying upon ground (g) where the landlord's interest was purchased or, if leasehold, created[192] within the five years preceding the termination of the tenancy and the holding has throughout that time been subject to a business tenancy within the protection of the 1954 Act. The aim of this restriction is simply to prevent a speculator buying over the head of a sitting tenant and then, as soon as possible, claiming possession on the ground of owner occupation.[193] This explains why the rule has no relevance where the current landlord is the grantor of the tenancy.[194] It does, however, mean that a landlord who acquired the reversion in the last five years will be unable to use ground (g) unless there was no business tenancy in existence at any given time within that period (for example, there had been a cessation of occupation or business user).[195]

Although the operation of section 30(2) may prevent the landlord successfully opposing the tenant's application for a new tenancy, it might still be to the landlord's advantage to rely upon ground (g). If the landlord can satisfy the other aspects of this ground, the court might be persuaded to order a new lease of shorter duration than it would otherwise have granted.[196] Conversely, in the scenario where the landlord is waiting until the five-year period expires before

8.47

8.48

---

[187] (1972) 224 EG 61.
[188] *Wates Estate Agency Services Ltd v Bartleys Ltd*, n 151 above.
[189] See *Wimbush (AD) & Sons Ltd v Franmills Property Ltd* [1961] Ch 419.
[190] *Willison v Shaftesbury Plc* (1998) 15 May (CA).
[191] The equivalent rule for Northern Ireland is contained in article 13(4).
[192] Or is an interest which has merged in that interest and, but for the merger, would be the interest of the landlord. The crucial date for determining whether, apart from merger, it would have been the interest of the landlord is the time when the landlord serves a section 25 notice or counter notice: *Diploma Laundry Ltd v Surrey Timber Ltd* [1955] 2 All ER 922.
[193] *Artemiou v Procopiou* [1965] 3 All ER 539.
[194] *Northcote Laundry Ltd v Frederick Donnelly Ltd* [1968] 2 All ER 50.
[195] It is noteworthy that the five-year rule does not apply to ground (f) and that reliance on the latter may be an attractive possibility for a new landlord.
[196] *Upsons Ltd v E Robbins Ltd* [1956] 1 QB 131; see Chapter 9.

serving a section 25 notice, the tenant might be able to defeat this tactic by the pre-emptory service of section 26 request.[197]

Key Points

8.49 A series of further observations needs to be made about the intricacies of the five-year rule. First, the landlord's interest may be either in the freehold or leasehold estate. The rule applies, for example, if the landlord has been granted a reversionary lease.[198] For the purpose of determining when the landlord acquired a leasehold interest, a succession of tenancies is to be treated as a single tenancy.[199] Seemingly, it does not matter that the capacity in which the landlord held the interest has changed during the five-year period as what counts is the interest which originally arose.[200]

8.50 Second, the term 'purchased' is to be given its ordinary meaning (that is, buying for money) and does not included a surrender by operation of law or acquisition in consideration of a covenant.[201] The date of purchase is deemed to be the time that contracts are exchanged.[202] If there is doubt as to whether a purchase has occurred, the court will look at the whole transaction, including any preceding contract.[203]

8.51 Third, the term 'created' refers to the creation of the competent landlord's interest. This can give rise to difficulties where the landlord's interest is subject to a trust and it is a beneficiary who seeks to be treated as the landlord and to rely upon section 30(1)(g). In this situation, the landlord's interest will be treated as being created when the trust was declared and not the date when the beneficiary landlord actually acquires the interest.[204] Where the landlord's interest is leasehold, and a contract preceded the acquisition of that interest, the date of creation is the date of the contract. Otherwise, the general rule is that the relevant date is when the lease is executed.[205]

---

[197] See Chapter 5.
[198] *Wimbush (AD) & Sons Ltd v Franmills Properties Ltd,* n 189 above.
[199] *Artemiou v Procopiou,* n 193 above, where the landlord acquired a lease which was later renewed. The renewal did not bring the landlord within section 30(2). In *VCS Car Park Management Ltd v Regional Railways North East Ltd* (1999) November 16 (CA), it was made clear that successive periods as freeholder and then leaseholder fall to be counted together.
[200] *Morar v Chauhan,* n 155 above, where the Court of Appeal held that it was of no consequence that the identity of the landlord trustee and the beneficiaries had changed in the preceding five years.
[201] *Frederick Lawrence Ltd v Freeman Hardy & Willis Ltd* [1959] 3 All ER 77. In *Willis v Association of Universities of the British Commonwealth,* n 166 above at 46, Salmon LJ provided the example of the tenant dying and the reversion being inherited by next of kin. The new landlord would not be caught by the five-year rule.
[202] *Bolton (HL) Engineering Ltd v Graham (TJ) & Sons Ltd,* n 70 above.
[203] *Frederick Lawrence v Freeman Hardy & Willis,* n 201 above.
[204] *Northcote Laundry Ltd v Frederick Donnelly Ltd,* n 194 above. This does not apply, however, where it is a trustee landlord who seeks possession: *Morar v Chauhan,* n 155 above.
[205] *Northcote Laundry Ltd,* ibid. If, however, the lease was executed before it became effective, the date of commencement is, arguably, the relevant date: *Denny Thorn & Co Ltd v George Harker & Co Ltd* (1957) 108 LJ 348.

Fourth, the termination date of the current lease is the date specified in the land- **8.52**
lord's section 25 notice or the tenant's section 26 request.[206] As it is from this point
that the five years are counted back, the situation emerges that the landlord could
serve a section 25 notice, then sell the reversion, leaving it open for the new landlord to rely on paragraph (g).[207] Any possible extension under section 64 is ignored
for these purposes. When issuing a notice or request, the date selected for termination should take into account the five-year rule. Hence, the landlord might
insert a date more distant in time and the tenant might be wise to choose an earlier date.

Finally, the five-year rule does not operate where the landlord is a company and **8.53**
the interest has been acquired by another company landlord within the same
group of companies.[208] The Law Commission Report has, however, recommended that the five-year rule should apply to both a company or an individual
who acquires control of a reversioner company.[209]

Further Reforms?

In its 1992 Report, the Law Commission addressed two concerns which had been **8.54**
raised by landlords.[210] First, that ground (g) should be available if it was intended
that part only of the premises were to be occupied by the landlord. Although this
would mirror the provision contained in section 31A which, as shown, allows for
the recovery of part of the premises for demolition and/or reconstruction, this
suggestion was not favoured. It was viewed as marking a significant change of policy which would need wide consultation before any proposal could be made.
Second, that ground (g) could work unfairly where the landlord intends to take
over the tenant's goodwill. The Law Commission believed that Parliament has
already catered for this situation by making available compensation for disturbance in such circumstances and that no further action was necessary. The fact
that flat rate compensation is wholly inadequate for such tenants was, therefore,
of no influence.

---

[206] *Frederick Lawrence Ltd v Freeman Hardy & Willis Ltd,* n 201 above.
[207] See *Diploma Laundry Ltd v Surrey Timber Ltd,* n 192 above. This gives rise to a curious result
and Ross (n 36 above at 299) doubts whether the courts will in future adopt this approach.
[208] Section 43(2); see *Harvey Textiles Ltd v Hillel,* n 157 above.
[209] N 111 above at para 2.11. This proposal has not been universally welcomed: 'This provision
may be unduly restrictive for the good of business. Where there is a takeover of a business, the purchaser may intend to expand the business in to the premises let, but would not be able to oppose
renewal . . .' (S Bright and G Gilbert, *The Nature of Tenancies* (1995) at 62). Nevertheless, it has now
become law in Northern Ireland: article 13(5) of the Business Tenancies (Northern Ireland) Order
1996.
[210] ibid at paras 3.28, 3.29.

9

THE NEW LEASE

A. Introduction

The most significant aspect of Part II of the Landlord and Tenant Act 1954 is, **9.01**
arguably, that which deals with the new lease and the form it will adopt. It is on
renewal that the delicate balance between interventionism and the free market is
attempted. Nevertheless, the primary purpose of the Act is to encourage agreement between the landlord and the tenant as to the grant and the terms of the new
lease. This agreement may be comprehensive or might be limited to terms, without acknowledgment of the tenant's right to a new lease.[1] The statutory rights
afforded to the tenant are, thereby, designed to ensure that the parties negotiate
upon a more equal footing. Although the Act strengthens the position of the lessee
at the negotiation table, thereafter the tenant is left to strike the best bargain available. In the achievement of such an agreement, the parties' freedom to contract on
whatever terms they see fit is, essentially, reinstated. As Judge Brandt admitted in
Ganton House Investments v Crossman Investments: 'We are dealing with business
people who are perfectly entitled to drive as hard a bargain as they can.'[2] While

---

[1] Any agreement for a new lease without an agreement of terms would, of course, be void for
uncertainty and contrary to the prescription contained in the Law of Property (Miscellaneous
Provisions) Act 1989.
[2] [1995] 1 EGLR 239 at 240.

243

negotiations between the parties are ongoing, it remains imperative that the tenant complies with any time-limits and procedural requirements imposed by the 1954 Act. If the tenant fails to do so, and a binding agreement is not reached, all rights to a new lease will be lost.[3]

9.02 The tenant is not, however, obliged to negotiate. If agreement is unachieved, and where the landlord does not successfully oppose the tenant's application for a renewal, the court must, by virtue of section 29(1), order a new lease. Again in default of agreement, section 28 provides that the court must also determine the terms of that grant. It is as a last resort, therefore, that the judiciary are entrusted with translating the tenant's rights into practical realities. As the new lease is pivotal to the statutory scheme, it might be imagined that the parameters of the judge's function would be prescribed, detailed and certain. Somewhat surprisingly, this is not the case. Admittedly, sections 32–35 of the Act classify the constituent features of the new tenancy under four headings: property, duration, rent, and other terms, but these provisions merely offer sketchy directions and guidance. Beyond this, Parliament has abrogated responsibility and, within this crucial part of the statutory process, abandoned judges to their own discretion.[4] It becomes crucial, therefore, for an adviser to have some working understanding of the terms which the court will or may be likely to impose. This knowledge is an essential prerequisite to effective negotiation.

B. Agreement as to Grant

9.03 By virtue of section 28 the jurisdiction of the court will be ousted in circumstances where the competent landlord[5] (as ascertained at the date of the agreement)[6] and the tenant agree to the grant of a new lease at a future date. Such an agreement would otherwise be void under section 38.[7] The effect of section 28 is that it automatically maintains the current lease (whether or not it is a contractual or continuation tenancy) until the date agreed for the commencement of the new tenancy. This agreed commencement date can be earlier than the original tenancy could otherwise have been determined at common law. Following agreement, the former tenancy is taken outside the ambit of Part II of the Landlord and Tenant Act 1954. This entails that the parties lose the *locus standi* to commence proceedings

[3] *Solomen v Akiens* [1993] 1 EGLR 101.
[4] As the Law Reform Advisory Committee for Northern Ireland recognised, 'If a fair balance between the parties is to be mainitained, it is vital that these guidelines, and Tribunal practice, reflect current trends in commercial lettings' (*A Review of the Law relating to Business Tenancies in Northern Ireland* (1992) Discussion Paper No 3 at para 6.1).
[5] As defined in section 44 and Schedule 6 of the Act; see Chapter 2.
[6] *Bowes-Lyon v Green* (1963) AC 420.
[7] See *Joseph v Joseph* (1967) Ch 78.

and that any extant application is invalidated. In relation to the former tenancy, the statutory protection cannot be revived. Unless there is contracting out of the statutory scheme, however, the Part II provisions will apply to the new lease.

Formalities

In order to satisfy section 28, the agreement must constitute a valid and enforce-   **9.04**
able contract.[8] Accordingly, if the duration of the proposed lease exceeds three years, it would seem that the formalities of section 2 of the Law of Property (Miscellaneous Provisions) Act 1989 must be complied with. If so, such contracts must be in writing, signed by both the tenant and the competent landlord and contain all the express terms agreed. Although the 1989 Act has no application to leases for three years or less,[9] even then it is necessary that the section 28 agreement be in writing and its terms expressed.[10] Nevertheless, *obiter* of Laws J in *Lambert v Keymood Ltd* suggests that the section 28 agreement falls entirely outside the ambit of the 1989 Act. While admitting that both the 1989 Act and section 69(2) of the Landlord and Tenant Act 1954 were designed to ensure a degree of certainty and the avoidance of dispute, he contended that the courts will not here insist upon legal formalities. He commented:

> I do not think it necessarily requires the execution of a document exhaustively con-
> taining all the terms agreed, such that no parol evidence could be introduced to
> explain the full intentions of the parties. The writing must, in my judgment, demon-
> strate that the parties have come to terms upon a new contract for the tenancy of the
> property . . . if it is only signed by the party against whom it is raised in later pro-
> ceedings . . . that will be sufficient.[11]

If correct, the approach of Laws J could be said to drive the proverbial horse and coaches through the prescription contained in the 1989 Act. It is, however, strongly arguable that this departure from the general formalities is unjustified: the section 28 agreement is clearly a mutual contract concerning 'the sale or other disposition of land' and as such should fall squarely within the catchment of sec-tion 2(1) of the 1989 Act.[12]

---

[8] *Stratton (RJ) Ltd v Wallis Tomlin and Co Ltd* [1996] 1 EGLR 104 where under section 40 of the Law of Property Act 1925 (now repealed) a contract by correspondence between the parties was upheld.

[9] Section 2(5)(a) of the 1989 Act; see *Lambert v Keymood Ltd* (1997) 43 EG 131.

[10] Section 69(2) of the 1954 Act (writing); section 28 (terms). cf the views of Laws J in the *Keymood* case ibid

[11] ibid at 136. The language of Laws J here being more in tune with the old section 40 than the new legislative regime.

[12] See *Spiro v Glencrown Properties* [1991] Ch 537; see also M Haley, *Land Contracts: Injudicial Facts and Judicial Fictions* (1993) AALR Vol. 22 at 176.

Parcels

9.05 It is, moreover, necessary that the parcels of this future lease include, at the least, the tenant's holding as at the date of the agreement. The parcels may, however, include other land. This entails that an agreement relating to property which is less than the current holding cannot comply with section 28. Instead, it would be viewed as an agreement to surrender at a future date and rendered void by section 38(1).[13] The court's jurisdiction would, thereby, remain unaffected. Similarly, section 28 is inapplicable when the agreement concerns the grant of an immediate tenancy. This agreement would operate as a surrender by operation of law by virtue of which the original tenancy would terminate.[14] From its ashes the new lease would emerge which, on this occasion, may concern property less in extent than the former holding. Unless contracting out occurs, the new lease will fall within the catchment of the 1954 Act.

Enforcement

9.06 Although subsequent to a valid section 28 agreement the tenant loses statutory protection, neither party can unilaterally withdraw from the transaction.[15] The normal contractual remedies are available and, hence, the agreement may be specifically enforced and the landlord compelled to execute the lease. If the agreement does not reflect the common intention of the parties, the court has the discretion to rectify the contract. Rectification was appropriate in *Coles v William Hill Organisation Ltd* where the landlord submitted a draft lease mistakenly including a break clause in favour of the tenant.[16] As the tenant's solicitor was aware of the mistake, the High Court concluded that it would be unconscionable to deny the landlord the remedy of rectification. The contract was rewritten to reflect the true agreement reached between the parties. As with any land contract, however, it is imperative that the agreement will also bind any third party purchasers. To ensure this the tenant should, if the title is unregistered, enter a Civ land charge under the auspices of the Land Charges Act 1972.[17] In relation to registered land, the agreement may be passively protected as an overriding interest (by virtue of the tenant's actual occupation)[18] or, alternatively, may be actively protected by the entry of a notice or caution on the Land Register. The danger which exists in both systems is that an unprotected contract will fail to bind a purchaser of the landlord's reversion. This would produce the unfortunate situation that the

---

[13] *Tarjomani v Panther Securities Ltd* (1983) 46 P & CR 32.
[14] Surrender is one of the ways which a tenancy protected by Part II can be terminated: section 24(2); see Chapter 2.
[15] See *Boots the Chemist Ltd v Pinkland Ltd* (1992) 28 EG 118.
[16] (1998) March 6 (HC).
[17] See *Stratton (RJ) Ltd v Wallis Tomlin & Co Ltd*, n 8 above.
[18] See section 70(1)(g) of the Land Registration Act 1925.

agreement would exclude the jurisdiction of the court while, at the same time, it would be unenforceable against the new reversioner.[19]

C. Agreement as to Terms

Under section 29 the parties may agree the terms, whether in whole or in part, of **9.07** a prospective tenancy.[20] For the purposes of this provision, however, the landlord does not necessarily have to accept the tenant's right to a new lease.[21] If any opposition is unsuccessful, the agreed terms will then be embodied in the order for a new tenancy with the court filling in the remaining gaps. To be effective for these purposes, the Act requires the agreement to be in writing[22] and to be intended by the parties to be binding.[23] The agreement must, therefore, be unconditional and final. Although the issue is free from binding authority, it is thought that here the formalities of the Law of Property (Miscellaneous Provisions) Act 1989 do not apply.[24] It is arguable that the agreement is for the purposes of an application to court and not for the grant of a lease. In addition, the terms abstracted in this way from a grant would not, seemingly, constitute a land contract. If this general approach is correct, it will be possible for a formal offer to be made, for example, in correspondence or in the pleadings of the application which, on acceptance, becomes binding.[25] If, however, a section 29 agreement is subject to the provisions of the 1989 Act, it would no longer be possible for any valid contract to emerge from pleadings.[26]

D. The Property

As referred to above, the court will prescribe the terms of the new lease in circum- **9.08** stances where the parties fail to agree. Of key importance is the property which

---

[19] See *Stratton (RJ) Ltd v Wallis Tomlin & Co Ltd*, n 8 above.

[20] See *Bowes-Lyon v Green*, n 6 above.

[21] cf the Business Tenancies (Northern Ireland) Order 1996 which does not contain a similar provision. Seemingly, the requirement there is that there is an agreement to grant before there can be an agreement as to terms: article 9.

[22] Section 69(2).

[23] See *Derby & Co Ltd v ITC Pension Trust Ltd* [1997] 2 All ER 890 where 'without prejudice' correspondence and a 'subject to contract' agreement were insufficient for these purposes. This was so even though the lease had been put into draft form by solicitors.

[24] See Oliver J, ibid. This view is adopted also by K Reynolds and W Clark, *Renewal of Business Tenancies* (1997) at 244.

[25] *Lovely & Orchard Services Ltd v Daejan Investments (Grove Hall) Ltd* (1997) 246 EG 651; see S Shaw, *Applications for Business Tenancies* (1990) 24 EG 30.

[26] Note also that contracts by correspondence also do not appear to have survived the 1989 Act: *Commission for New Towns v Cooper* [1995] 2 All ER 929; cf *Hooper v Sherman* (1994) 30 November (CA).

will constitute the parcels of the new tenancy. The court is empowered by *section 32* to grant a new lease of the holding as it determines and designates.[27] The meaning of 'holding' is provided by section 23(3) and this embraces those parts demised that are occupied by the tenant (or the tenant's employee) for the purposes of a business, but excludes those parts not so occupied.[28] This is in contradistinction to section 24 under which, at the expiry of the contractual term, it is the whole of the tenancy which is continued. Section 32(1), moreover, requires the 'holding' to be ascertained as at the date of the court order for renewal. In *Caplan (I&H) v Caplan*, therefore, the House of Lords stressed that the time for determining the tenant's holding is when the new tenancy is ordered rather than the commencement of the hearing or the date of any ancillary or preliminary order.[29] As Lord Reid explained:

> The policy of the Act appears to be that not only the extent of the holding but also the rent, duration and other terms of the new tenancy should be determined as nearly as may be at the time when the tenancy is granted, and this seems right because circumstances may alter and the tenancy ought not to be granted in light of obsolete conditions. It is quite true that section 32 cannot be applied with literal accuracy because there may have to be some interval between the hearing of the evidence and the making of the order, but circumstances are unlikely to change in so short a time.[30]

Subtractions and Additions

9.09 The new lease may embrace all the property contained in the original, but (subject to the exception in section 32(3), considered below) cannot comprise any part which is sub-let or on which no business is carried out.[31] Accordingly, for the renewal provisions to operate the tenant has to be in 'occupation' of something.[32] Hence, a tenant who wishes to sub-let part or whole of the premises should be advised of the effect that this can have on renewal.[33] If sub-letting has occurred, it is the sub-tenant who benefits from the renewal rights.[34] A tenant might, therefore, wish to terminate any sub-lease and move back into occupation before the

---

[27] An identical provision is to be found in article 16(1) of the Business Tenancies (Northern Ireland) Order 1996.

[28] As regards occupation by another, it is necessary that this occupation be related to the business by virtue of which the tenant claims the protection of the 1954 Act (ie the business carried out on the premises): *Nurit Bar v Pathwood Investments Ltd* (1987) 54 P & CR 178; see further Chapter 3. Note that landlords' fixtures fall to be included within the definition of 'holding': *Poster v Slough Estates Ltd* [1969] 1 Ch 495.

[29] [1962] 1 WLR 55. Accordingly, it is irrelevant that the tenant misstates the extent of the holding in the claim form: *Nurit Bar v Pathwood Investments*, ibid.

[30] ibid at 59. He accepted that, if a considerable time elapses and there has been a material change of circumstances, the court should be prepared to hear new evidence.

[31] ibid.

[32] *First Leisure Trading Ltd v Dorita Properties Ltd* (1991) 23 EG 116.

[33] See *Graysim Holdings Ltd v P&O Property Holdings Ltd* [1995] 4 All ER 831.

[34] *William Shelton Ltd v Howson & Pinder Ltd* [1975] QB 361.

court order is made. For these purposes, it is the fact of occupation which is important and not its lawfulness.[35] Such retaking of possession may occur even after the tenant's application for a new lease is made.[36] It should also be understood that the court cannot enlarge the tenant's holding so that the premises are greater than those granted under the original lease.[37] There is, moreover, no jurisdiction (except as catered for by section 32(1A)) to order a new tenancy of part only of the holding.[38] As explained by Winn LJ, 'it is abundantly plain that "holding" cannot mean the same as "part of the holding", nor can part of the "holding" mean the same as "holding".'[39]

Exceptions

The general rule contained in section 32(1), which allows only the holding to be   **9.10**
the subject matter of the renewal, gives way in two situations. First, where the tenant is willing to accept a new tenancy of an economically separable part of the holding so that the landlord can carry out work on the remainder,[40] section 32(1A) limits the new lease to the part that the tenant accepts. For this to operate, however, the court must be satisfied as to the tenant's willingness; assess the impact of the redevelopment; and appraise the bona fide intentions of the landlord. As section 31A provides a fall back position for the tenant, there is no need to elect in advance whether to claim a tenancy of whole or of part only of the holding. Indeed, there is no obligation to choose until the final determination of the landlord's ground of opposition.[41] If then the tenant does not agree to a lease of part as opposed to the whole of the holding, the application can be withdrawn.[42] Second, where other premises are included in the original lease, in addition to the current holding, the landlord can require that the parcels of the new tenancy include the whole of the property as originally demised.[43] The object of this provision is to protect the landlord against any fragmentation of dealings by reason of

---

[35] *Narcissi v Wolfe* [1960] Ch 10.
[36] ibid. cf the view of Parker LJ in *J Reid (D&K) Co Ltd v Burdell Engineering Co Ltd* (1958) 171 EG 281 at 282: 'I cannot see how in designating property by reference to the circumstances existing at the date of the order one can shut one's eyes to what has gone before.'
[37] *Orlik G (Meat Products) v Hastings & Thanet Building Society* (1974) 29 P & CR 126 where the landlord had subsequently allowed the tenant to use an additional amenity.
[38] *Romulus Trading Co Ltd v Trustees of Henry Smith's Charity* [1991] 1 EGLR 95; *Nurit Bar v Pathwood Investments Ltd*, n 28 above.
[39] *Fernandez v Walding* [1968] 1 All ER 994 at 997.
[40] Hence the tenant will be able to resist partially the landlord's opposition to the new lease on the ground of demolition and reconstruction contained in section 30(1)(f). This escape route is offered by section 31A(1)(b). The meaning of 'an economically separable part' is given in section 31A(2); see further Chapter 7.
[41] *Romulus Trading Co Ltd v Trustees of Henry Smith's Charity*, n 38 above.
[42] *Fribourg & Treyer Ltd v Northdale Investments Ltd* (1982) 44 P & CR 284.
[43] Section 32(3). If this occurs all subsequent references to the holding are to be understood as referring to the whole of the property: section 32(2). In Northern Ireland this result is achieved by article 16(2).

sub-interests in the property.[44] Although employed to maintain a *status quo* between the landlord and the tenant, it does not give the landlord the opportunity to select which sub-let parts are to be excluded or included in the new lease.[45] The court has no discretion here and must accede to the landlord's wishes. This marks a rare occasion within the renewal provisions where the landlord's convenience overrides the interests of the tenant and the designs of the judge. It serves also as a reminder that the Act aims to preserve the position of the landlord as well as to protect that of the tenant.

Ancillary Rights

9.11 Subject to contrary agreement between the parties, section 32(3) provides that any ancillary rights which are enjoyed by the tenant under the current tenancy will normally be included in the new tenancy. This provision represents a curious mix of the mandatory and the permissive in that it states that the rights enjoyed *shall* be included in the new tenancy except as otherwise agreed or determined by the court.[46] Such rights, moreover, may be as granted in the original lease or have been acquired subsequently.[47] Although the Act is silent on the matter, it is to be assumed that this rule applies only to property rights and does not extend to personal rights.[48] The provision would, thereby, include such incorporeal matters as fishing rights, access, drainage and light, for example.[49] Otherwise, the court is, seemingly, given an unqualified discretion and in its exercise is likely to exclude or modify rights granted at the beginning of the current lease which are no longer necessary or appropriate. This discretion, of course, adds further uncertainty to the renewal process. Obviously, if there is dispute, ambiguity or mistake as to the parcels of the original lease, the court can admit extrinsic evidence to settle the matter.[50] It is, however, preferable for the original lease to be clear as to what ancillary rights have been granted.

9.12 The court cannot, however, use section 32 as a means of enlarging the holding beyond that contained in the original grant. It is not the intention that the tenants acquire a more valuable asset by the addition of new rights. In *Orlik G (Meat Products) v Hastings & Thanet Building Society*, for example, the Court of Appeal held that a licence to park two vehicles on the landlord's land, which was not a term of the original lease, could not pass as part of the tenant's hold-

---

44 *See Alkey v Collman* (1995) 105 LJ 396.
45 See *Southport Old Links Ltd v Naylor* (1985) 273 EG 767.
46 In Northern Ireland this provision is mirrored in article 16(3).
47 *Land Reclamation Co Ltd v Basildon DC* [1979] 2 All ER 993.
48 *Re No 1 Albermarle Street* [1959] 1 All ER 250.
49 See *Nevil Long & Co (Boards) Ltd v Firmenich & Co* (1984) 47 P & CR 59; *Whitley v Stumbles* [1930] AC 544.
50 *Mills (IS) (Yardley) Ltd v Curdworth Investments Ltd* (1975) 119 SJ 302.

ing.[51] There was no irrevocable licence or estoppel between the parties nor was there any ground for rectification of the original lease. The case demonstrates, therefore, that distinct contractual arrangements and mere *de facto* use are to be regarded as insufficient. It was suggested by Upjohn J in *Re No 1 Albermarle Street* that section 32(3) should be confined only to the type of right which, being connected to the holding, can be said to touch and concern the land demised.[52] Any rights granted after the lease should, therefore, be contained in a deed which is expressed to be supplemental to the lease. Although it was left undecided whether a personal licence to exhibit advertisements on the landlord's property could be viewed as part of the tenant's holding and, thereby, pass under section 32, it was held that the licence could pass under section 35 (below).[53] It is, moreover, to be appreciated that section 32 passes rights only if they are alive at the date the original tenancy ends and cannot resurrect past rights.[54]

Landlord's Rights

As regards any rights originally reserved for the landlord, section 32 is inexplicably silent. It is apparent that nothing in that provision allows the court to reduce, add to or modify such provisions contained in the old lease.[55] The limitation of this approach could, for example, promote difficulties for a landlord who may seek to refurbish a building in which the tenant has a lease of a part. When the new lease is granted the landlord cannot be given any new rights, under section 32, over the tenant's holding. As it is unlikely that the rights would be given by virtue of section 35 (below), the refurbishment scheme might thus be thwarted. Accordingly, there is some force in the argument that the court should be given the power to extend the landlord's rights beyond that currently available. For example, as Ross points out:

9.13

> One could imagine situations in which the rigidity of these sections could give insufficient scope to reflect changes in the physical circumstances surrounding the tenancy . . . and that this could cause problems for a landlord who wanted, for example, to run conducting media through the demised premises, or to have access to the demised premises to carry out work to the common parts.[56]

---

[51] N 37 above. In appropriate circumstances, such a right could, however, be elevated to the status of a legal easement by virtue of section 62 of the Law of Property Act 1925: *Borman v Griffith* [1930] 1 Ch 493.

[52] N 48 above.

[53] As will be shown, new rights can be created under section 35 without the need for the right to 'touch and concern' the demised premises. This case serves as a useful reminder of the interrelationship between section 32 and section 35.

[54] *Cairnplace Ltd v CBL (Property Investment) Co Ltd* [1984] 1 All ER 316; *Kirkwood v Johnson* (1979) 38 P & CR 392 where an option to purchase had lapsed and, as it was no longer appurtenant to the land, could not pass under section 32.

[55] *Fernandez v Walding*, n 39 above.

[56] M Ross, *Drafting and Negotiation of Commercial Leases* (4th edn, 1994) at 303, 304, n 3.

E. Duration

9.14 Unless the parties agree in writing as to the duration of the new lease, the court can order a term up to a maximum of fourteen years, as considered reasonable in all the circumstances.[57] An agreed duration can, however, be incorporated into the court order, even though it exceeds the statutory maximum.[58] The statutory ceiling is designed to offer adequate security of tenure, without unduly prejudicing the landlord's position, and yet is to be sufficiently flexible to cater for the tenant who does not wish to be bound too far into the future. At the end of the renewal, of course, the provisions of Part II can still apply and the tenant may be entitled to another term. In addition, as the Law Reform Advisory Committee for Northern Ireland pointed out in its Report, 'the existence of a statutory maximum helps negotiations between parties on the question of duration'.[59] As Brandt J appreciated in *Ganton House Investments v Crossman Investments*:

> [The Act] is to be used by tenants as a shield. It is not an Act which is intended to be used by them as some kind of sword. They can resort to it in order to make sure that they can continue conducting their businesses, but they cannot use it as a weapon or something that even approaches blackmail.[60]

Nevertheless, section 33 gives the court a wide discretion, limited only by the concept of reasonableness, and offers no guidance as to its exercise.[61] No directions are given as to what duration is appropriate and, in determining what is reasonable, the Act provides no hint as to what factors are relevant and the weight to be given to them. Although it is to be accepted that no one case is a sure guide to another, a variety of influential factors have, however, been highlighted on a case by case basis and have formed part of the balancing exercise which the judge is required to perform.[62] These have, for example, included 'market forces';[63] the age and state of

---

[57] Section 33. If appropriate, the court could order a periodic tenancy.

[58] *Janes (Gowns) Ltd v Harlow Development Corporation* (1979) 253 EG 799 (20 years). If the tenant has agreed a term length, but has a change of mind at the hearing, the court will order the agreed term unless the landlord consents to the change: *Boots the Chemist Ltd v Pinkland Ltd*, n 15 above.

[59] *Business Tenancies* (1994) No 1 at para 6.2.3.

[60] N 2 above at 240.

[61] See *Morgan v Jones* (1960) 1 WLR 1220.

[62] As the Law Reform Advisory Committe for Northern Ireland acknowledged in its Discussion Paper, the court's exercise of this wide discretion 'is clearly affected not only by current practice and prevailing market conditions but by any other circumstances it considers relevant' (n 4 above at para 6.2.3).

[63] In *Ganton House Investments v Crossman Investments*, n 2 above, Judge Brandt held that the court had to take into account the state of the market as a material circumstance. He added that it was, in general terms, desirable in the letting market to achieve stability and that this aim was served by the granting of long renewals. Such factors do not, however, always carry weight: see *CBS (UK) Ltd v London Scottish Properties Ltd*, [1985] 2 EGLR 125 where the tenant's desire to relocate its business was the main factor in this decision to grant a one-year term instead of the 14-year lease sought by the landlord.

the repair of the premises;[64] the age and nature of the tenant's business;[65] and the interests of good estate management.[66] The major influences, however, require somewhat closer attention.

The Duration of the Original Lease

This provides a useful starting point[67] as the court will be reluctant to grant a lease **9.15** for a term longer than the current lease.[68] Although it is common for the new lease to be of the same duration as its predecessor, the judge is not obliged to order a new lease of identical duration.[69] It is also likely that, if the original lease contained a break clause, the new lease will contain a similar provision.[70] This tendency marks an arbitrary concession to the landlord's interests and has little to do with market forces, reasonableness or the circumstances of the case (which are likely to have changed since the original grant).

The Duration of the Continuation Tenancy

The longevity of the continuation may exert some influence over the length of **9.16** lease ordered on renewal.[71] Unfortunately, its precise influence is unpredictable. Accordingly, if the tenant has been holding over for a long time, it could be argued that the new lease should be longer than the original.[72] Conversely, however, it might offer a justification for a shorter lease.[73] To add further confusion, in *Becker v Hill Street Properties* Dillon LJ felt that the length of the continuation was of no effect at all.[74] The appellate court in *Upsons Ltd v E Robins*, however, felt that the fact that the tenant had already benefited from a one-year extension to his lease was a relevant and reductive factor for the judge to take into account.[75]

---

[64] *London & Provincial Millinery Stores v Barclays Bank* [1962] 2 All ER 163.
[65] The preservation of the tenant's goodwill might influence the order of a long lease. cf the disregards in relation to rent contained in section 34(1)(b) below. In *Upsons Ltd v E Robins Ltd* [1956] 1 QB 131, the Court of Appeal concluded that the fact that the tenant had been in business since 1927 was a pertinent consideration.
[66] *Turone v Howard De Walden Estates* (1983) 267 EG 440.
[67] *CBS (UK) Ltd v London Scottish Properties Ltd* n 63 above; *London & Provincial Millinery Stores v Barclays Bank*, n 64 above.
[68] See, for example, the Court of Appeal stage in *Betty's Cafes Ltd v Phillips Furnishing Stores Ltd* [1957] 1 All ER 1 where, on this basis, the court reduced a 14-year term as ordered by the lower court to a five-year lease.
[69] See *Orenstein v Donn* (1983) 5 May (CA).
[70] See *Leslie & Godwin Investments Ltd v Prudential Assurance Co Ltd* [1987] 2 EGLR 95.
[71] *Frederick Lawrence v Freeman Hardy & Willis* (1960) 176 EG 11; *Aldwych Club Ltd v Copthall Property Co Ltd* (1963) 185 EG 219.
[72] *London & Provincial Millinery Stores v Barclays Bank*, n 64 above.
[73] *CBS (UK) Ltd v London Scottish Properties Ltd*, n 63 above.
[74] (1990) 38 EG 107.
[75] N 65 above.

The Comparative Hardship to, and Needs of, Either Party

9.17　The inequality of bargaining power between the parties is a relevant factor for the court to consider. As Morris LJ explained in *Upsons Ltd v E Robins Ltd*: 'A consideration of "all the circumstances" of a case, if it is careful and complete . . . may inevitably involve considering how the "circumstances" tell on the fortunes of those concerned.'[76] Accordingly, if the tenant seeking renewal is a one-shop company, the potential hardship to, and the need of, that tenant might persuade the court to grant a lease longer than that desired by the landlord.[77] Conversely, if the landlord owns only one shop, whereas the tenant is a company with numerous retail outlets, from the perspective of comparative hardship it is likely that the tenant will be granted only a short-term lease. For example, in *Upsons* case the tenant operated some 250 retail outlets, but the landlord (apart from the demised premises) owned only one shop. The landlord, moreover, was facing potential eviction from his current premises. This cumulative hardship tipped the scales in favour of a one-year renewal instead of the seven-year term sought by the tenant. Hardship can also become relevant in other ways. If, for example, the tenant seeks a short-term lease which would damage the value of the landlord's reversion, the court might be inclined to order a lease of longer duration than the tenant wishes.[78] As Judge Brandt accepted in *Ganton House Investments v Crossman Investments*, the tenant is not entitled 'to have his cake and eat it'.[79]

9.18　This is, however, not a hard and fast rule for in *CBS (UK) Ltd v London Scottish Properties Ltd*, Micklem J acknowledged that the value of the reversion would be substantially reduced if a short lease was ordered, but (although the landlord sought a fourteen-year term) went on to grant the tenant a one-year lease. The court suggested that the case might have been decided differently had the landlord intended to sell the reversion.[80] The term allowed sufficient time to put into effect the tenant's intention to relocate its business. Micklem J argued that section 33 invoked concepts of reasonableness, fairness and justice, but as the policy of the Act was primarily to protect the tenant it could not justify more protection than the tenant needed. His decision discounted a market forces argument put forward by the landlord. This approach differs from that adopted in *Rumbelows v Tameside Metropolitan BC* where the tenant's policy of taking only short-term renewals was

---

[76]　ibid at 141,142.

[77]　*CBS (UK) Ltd v London Scottish Properties Ltd*, n 63 above; see also the *obiter* of Hodson LJ in *Upsons* case, ibid at 141.

[78]　*Charles Follett Ltd v Cabtell Investments Co Ltd* (1988) 55 P & CR 36 (a 10-year term).

[79]　N 2 above at 240. The tenant wanted a one-year term, but the court ordered a 14-year lease with a potential break after six months if the tenant decided to relocate.

[80]　The case is, therefore, easily distinguishable on this basis. Judge Brandt in *Ganton House Investments v Crossman Investments*, ibid, agreed with the decision of Micklem J, but stressed that the facts of that case were extraordinary.

a factor disregarded by the court.[81] Micklem J was, however, influenced by the fact that the landlord would be better placed to re-let the premises during the one-year term than the tenant would be to assign a fourteen-year lease.[82]

The Landlord's Bona Fide Future Plans for the Property

The lessor's intentions are to be taken on board.[83] In the situation where the land-   **9.19**
lord intends to demolish and reconstruct or to occupy the premises, but cannot establish this intention at the date of the hearing of the tenant's application, the court must grant a new lease. Nevertheless, the duration of that new tenancy might be significantly affected by those intentions.[84] Accordingly, in *Millet (Peter) & Sons Ltd v Salisbury Handbags Ltd* the tenant sought a twelve-year lease, but as the landlord genuinely intended to occupy the property at a future date the court granted a three-year term subject to a break clause exercisable on six-months' notice.[85] Similarly, in *Upsons Ltd v E Robins Ltd* the landlord's opposition to the tenant's application under section 30(1)(g) (owner-occupation) failed because he had acquired the property two months before the end of the statutory five-year disqualification period. This influenced the court to grant a short term. The court's approach was put into the following context by Denning LJ in *Wig Creations v Colour Film Services*:

> Section 33 is in very wide terms. It empowers the court to do what is reasonable in all the circumstances. Suppose a landlord bought five years ago, plus one day. He could resist a new tenancy altogether on the ground that he wanted the place for his own business. Suppose he buys it five years ago less one day. Should he be kept out of the place for several years simply by the two day difference? I think not. The policy of the Act is to give a landlord (who has purchased more than five years ago) an absolute right to get possession for his own business; leaving it to the court to do what is reasonable if he has purchased less than five years. In doing what is reasonable, the five-year period is a factor which is permissible for the judge to take into account. The weight is for him.[86]

Two alternative strategies, therefore, emerge from case law: first, the court might   **9.20**
order a short letting so as to allow the tenant to find alternative premises. Hence, in *London & Provincial Millinery Stores v Barclays Bank*, where the landlord wanted to redevelop dilapidated premises, the nine-year lease ordered at first

---

[81] (1994) 13 EG 102.
[82] cf *Re Sunlight House* (1959) 173 EG 311 where the tenant was given a longer lease than was wanted because of the landlord's difficulty to re-let in the short term.
[83] *Becker v Hill Street Properties Ltd*, n 74 above.
[84] The landlord does not have to show a firm and settled intention to develop or to occupy, but the intention must be genuine: *Adams (E & B) Ltd v Chesterfield Properties* (1961) 178 EG 561. There the landlord's evidence was unconvincing and the court ordered a 10-year lease instead of the two-year (maximum) contended for by the lessor.
[85] [1987] 2 EGLR 104.
[86] (1969) 20 P & CR 870 at 874. There a three-year lease was granted instead of the 12-year term sought by the tenant.

instance was reduced to a one-year term on appeal.[87] Similarly, in *Reohorn v Barry Corporation* a short fixed-term lease, determinable by either party on six-months' notice, was deemed appropriate.[88] Second, a longer lease may be granted, but subject to a break clause allowing for early termination.[89] It is possible, moreover, that a mutual break clause will be included. A break clause appears appropriate where the development is not immediately in prospect, but is reasonably likely.[90] Here the emphasis is upon the landlord's genuine intentions and not what the judge thinks is desirable.[91] The judge is not to speculate as to any alternative strategies that the landlord could adopt.[92] In *NCP Ltd v Paternoster Consortium Ltd*, for example, the court felt able to insert a break clause to allow comprehensive redevelopment which was a real possibility within the next ten years, even though the plans were unfinalised.[93]

9.21 The general attitude of the court is that landlords should not be inhibited from development by being saddled with a long lease without provision for an early determination. It is, as Fox LJ admitted *in Edwards & Sons Ltd v Central London Commercial Estates Ltd*, 'wrong in principle . . . to order the grant of new leases for such substantial periods as 12 and 10 years respectively without development "break" clauses'.[94] Clearly, the court has to counterweight the landlord's aspirations with a degree of security of tenure for the tenant. Its task is to strike a reasonable balance between the conflicting interests in the light of all the circumstances of the case.[95] Accordingly, in order to preserve the tenant's position, it is standard practice for the break clause to be made operative only on the expiry of an initial fixed period.[96] Although the market value of the lease with a break

---

[87] N 64 above.

[88] [1956] 2 All ER 742; see also *Joss v Bennett* (1956) CLY 4858 where a short tenancy was justified in circumstances where the premises were ripe for development.

[89] Inserted under the auspices of section 35 below: see *McCombie v Grand Junction Co Ltd* [1962] 1 WLR 581. The rent to be paid under the renewal would be reduced accordingly: *Amika Motors Ltd v Colebrook Holdings Ltd* (1981) 259 EG 243.

[90] *Adams v Green* (1978) 247 EG 49 where the county court ordered a seven-year term without a break clause, but this was increased on appeal to a 14-year lease including an option to break for rebuilding exercisable on two-years' notice.

[91] *Becker v Hill Street Properties*, n 74 above, where a four-and-one-half year lease without a break clause was ordered.

[92] *Michael Chipperfield v Shell UK Ltd* (1980) 42 P &CR 136.

[93] (1990) 15 EG 53.

[94] (1984) 271 EG 697 at 698. The landlord must, however, exercise the break in a bona fide manner. On the termination of the tenancy, the tenant would be entitled to compensation for disturbance under section 37: see Chapter 6.

[95] See *Becker v Hill Street Properties*, n 74 above, where the tenant intended to retire on a stated date and the court declined to insert an option to break on the basis that it would cause undue hardship on the tenant if he had to relocate prior to retirement.

[96] *Amika Motors Ltd v Colebrook Holdings Ltd*, n 89 above (a five-year term with the break exercisable at the end of the third year); *Edwards & Sons Ltd v Central London Commercial Estates Ltd*, n 94 above (a seven-year lease with the break exercisable after the fifth year).

clause is reduced, it is not the intention of the 1954 Act to maintain the value of the lease, rather it is to protect the the enjoyment of the tenant's business.[97]

The Relationship between (and the Conduct and History of) the Parties

The past and present behaviour of the parties may be of relevance. If, for example, **9.22** the court believes that one party has acted unreasonably during the original lease, the term of the renewal may be influenced by that behaviour. A poor tenant could, thereby, be punished by being given a new lease of a lesser duration than would otherwise have been granted. As Ackner LJ explained:

> The relationship between landlord and tenant is important. It is a business relationship, and if the conflict between the parties is such that it is not a relationship which should continue longer than is really necessary, there is, in my judgment, no reason why a judge in that situation should not grant a somewhat shorter term rather than the longer term in the hope that the parties, if they cannot maintain a harmonious relationship, can sever that relationship, the tenant going somewhere else, thereby enabling both parties to achieve the advantage of a peaceful and quiet existence which *ex hypothesi* their continued relationship would not make possible.[98]

It might be the case, therefore, that a good relationship between the parties could be put forward as an argument to justify a longer lease than might otherwise be ordered.

Commencement Date

Section 33 provides that the new tenancy commences when the current one ter- **9.23** minates under the provisions of the Act. Due to the possibility of appeal from the court order, and with it an interim continuance under section 64, the commencement date will, however, be uncertain. As Dunn LJ admitted in *Turone v Howard De Walden Estates*: 'The difficulty is that it is impossible to say with precision at the time when the judge of first instance makes the order granting a new tenancy when that new tenancy will commence; and if one does not know when it will commence and nothing is said, it is equally impossible to ascertain when it will expire.'[99] This gives rise to potential difficulties where it is necessary to synchronise the termination date with other leases forming part of the same premises. Accordingly, it is standard practice for the order to state that the lease will begin from the date of final disposal of the application (whenever that may be) and to specify the end-date of the new tenancy.[100] As the Court of Appeal stressed in *Michael Chipperfield v Shell (UK) Ltd*,[101] this is particularly important in relation to short-term leases. In this way, the court may not know exactly when the lease

---

[97] *Gold v Brighton Corporation* [1956] 1 WLR 1291.
[98] *Orenstein v Donn*, n 69 above.
[99] N 66 above at 442.
[100] See ibid; *Re 88 High Road, Kilburn* [1959] 1 WLR 279.
[101] N 92 above.

will begin, but it will be sure of when it will end. The parties can, however, agree a different commencement date and that will then be incorporated into the order.[102] Such an agreed date might, for example, be the day immediately following the expiry of the original contractual term.[103]

Suggestions for Reform

9.24   As previously shown, under section 33 the length of renewal, unless agreed, cannot exceed fourteen years. Owing to changing market practices, this ceiling is now outmoded because it fails to match modern rent review clauses (usually at five-yearly intervals) and does not raise accurate comparables (fourteen-year leases are uncommon). Rents negotiated for new lettings are usually based on five, fifteen, twenty-five and thirty-five-year terms. Accordingly, the Law Commission has recommended that the ceiling be raised to fifteen years.[104] Obviously, any limitation is arbitrary, but the Commission felt that this period was 'about right'.[105] The difficulty which persists, however, is whether any limitation is warranted and this is particularly questionable when the original lease was for longer than the statutory ceiling. As the landlord's interests can be protected by the insertion of a rent review clause, there appears little justification for retaining any arbitrary restriction. Instead, the matter could be left open to the court's judgment with guidelines provided by Parliament. This approach was not, however, favoured by the Law Commission.

F. The Rent

9.25   As with the other terms of the new lease, the rent is to be that which is agreed between the parties or, in default, as determined by the court.[106] The court is faced with a most difficult undertaking and to assist it a general, statutory formula is prescribed.[107] Under section 34 the new rent to be ordered is that at which, having

---

[102]   *Bradshaw v Pawley* [1979] 3 All ER 273.

[103]   It should be remembered that until the commencement of the new lease, the tenant will be paying the old contractual rent or any interim rent awarded under section 24A. In Northern Ireland things are very different. First, there is no interim rent. Second, the new rent can be backdated by the Lands Tribunal: article 18(4),(5).

[104]   *Business Tenancies: A Periodic Review of the Landlord and Tenant Act 1954* (1992) Law Com No 208 at para 2.79. The preceding Working Paper, *Part II of the Landlord and Tenant Act 1954* (1988) No 111 had been unsure whether to abandon the ceiling altogether or to increase it to 15, 25 or 35 years. In relation to Northern Ireland, article 17 already imposes a 15-year ceiling.

[105]   By way of comparison, in the Republic of Ireland renewal is for 35 years unless the tenant elects for a shorter period: section 23 of the Landlord and Tenant (Amendment) Act 1980.

[106]   Section 34(1).

[107]   In *R v Huddersfield County Court Judge ex p Beaumont Ashton Ltd* (1967) 19 P & CR 62 the landlord local authority attempted to rely on the provisions of local legislation as taking the letting of a lock-up shop outside the scope of the 1954 Act. The appellate court held that there was no conflict and that, even if there had been, the general act would have repealed the provisions of the

regard to the terms of the new lease, the holding might reasonably be expected to be let in the open market by a willing lessor.[108] As will be discussed, a number of disregards are also specified. The courts, however, have been compelled to put flesh on the bare bones of section 34. Consequently, it has been decided that the rent so calculated is to be the open market rent of the premises at which a business of the type carried on by the tenant can be carried on there, and the evaluation is based upon the hypothesis that the premises are empty and without regard to the tenant's previous trading.[109] In line with the philosophy of the Act, it is dependent on market forces and not upon what is considered to be a reasonable rent. As Denning LJ commented in *McLaughlin v Walsall Arcade Ltd*, 'on a new lease the tenant has to pay the fair market value of the premises . . . the only advantage which the tenant gets . . . is security of tenure provided that he is ready to pay the fair market price'.[110]

The timing element within section 34 necessitates that the issue of rent is the final **9.26** matter to be concluded after all other terms are settled.[111] Accordingly, if on appeal a variation of any other term occurs, this must be reflected in a reconsideration of the rent.[112] The appropriate date for calculation is the time of the order, but the court should, where appropriate, take into account any foreseeable changes that might occur between that date and the time that the new lease will take effect.[113] The calculation of rent must, therefore, have a prospective element. This may, however, open the door to dangerously speculative evidence.

Open Market

There is no statutory definition of the term 'open market', but in *Baptist v Masters* **9.27** *of the Bench and Trustees of the Honourable Society of Gray's Inn* Judge Aron Owen provided guidance as to its meaning.[114] In response to an argument that a tenancy of chambers in Gray's Inn was not in the open market (that is, it was a closed letting), the judge commented that 'open market' is not a technical term and is an ordinary and commonly used expression. In the context of section 34, he added that an open market should include various features.[115] First, there must be a sufficient number of lessors and lessees to constitute a market and to create the

---

earlier local Act. If, however, the fixing of the rent is affected by any other statutory restriction, the court must take that factor into account.

[108] Once the market rent has been determined, therefore, the court cannot order either a lower or higher rent: *McLaughlin v Walsall Arcade* (1956) 167 EG 356. A similar provision applies in Northern Ireland: see article 18.

[109] *Barton (WJ) Ltd v Long Acre Securities* [1982] 1 WLR 398.

[110] N 108 above.

[111] *O'May v City of London Real Property* [1982] 1 All ER 660; *Aldwych Club Ltd v Copthall Property Co Ltd*, n 71 above; *Cardshops Ltd v Davies* [1971] 2 All ER 721.

[112] *Cardshops Ltd v Davies*, ibid.

[113] *Lovely & Orchard Services v Daejan Investments Ltd*, n 25 above.

[114] [1993] 2 EGLR 136.

[115] ibid at 138, 139.

opportunity of comparing rents (that is, circumstances in which the forces of supply and demand can operate). This does not, however, exclude a monopoly situation because, although there may be only one landlord, the market is generated by the number of potential tenants.[116] Second, there must be a willing lessor and lessee in this market. The screening of tenants or a restricted user does not vitiate the concept of an open market. Third, there has to be a reasonable period in which the parties can negotiate at arm's length, taking into account the state of the market at such time.[117] Fourth, the property must be freely exposed to the market and account is not to be taken of any higher rent that might be paid by a potential lessee with a special interest.[118] As Judge Aron Owen concluded: 'In such an open market the landlord will seek to obtain the best rent for the premises on the terms offered and the tenant will seek to agree the lowest rent which he can persuade the landlord to accept.'[119]

9.28   It is possible that, if the premises are of a type not normally associated with market rack rents (for example licensed premises and units in shopping centres), the court could order a turnover rent to be determined by a prescribed formula.[120] As regards turnover rents, the tenant should always ensure that rental formula closely reflects the actual profit. Although a turnover rent may not necessarily be a 'true' market rent as it reflects the profits of an individual business, it will be deemed to be the market rent. The device of linking rents to something such as the Retail Price Index is not always to the advantage of the landlord as the base figure of the index may be altered, producing a decrease in rent. In addition rents can rise more rapidly than the index selected. Nevertheless, it can manufacture hardship for the tenant because it does not take into account practical factors which can directly affect that business.

Willing Lessor

9.29   The reference within section 34(1) to a 'willing lessor' is accepted as alluding to a hypothetical landlord and not to the actual landlord.[121] It should be appreciated that the section, unlike many rent review clauses, does not expressly assume a 'willing lessee'. This is, however, an omission without any significance as the fact that the renewal procedure is instigated by the tenant must involve the tacit assumption that the tenant is 'willing'. In addition, the allusion to an 'open mar-

---

[116] See *Law Land Co Ltd v Consumers Association Ltd* (1980) 255 EG 617; *Air Canada v Heathrow Airport Ltd* (1993) 30 March CC.

[117] Accordingly, if there is a downturn in the market, this must be taken into account: *Ganton House Investments v Crossman Investments*, n 2 above.

[118] As Judge Aron Owen explained, 'a market may still be an open market and does not cease to be such market even though most of the persons occupying premises in the market belong to a particular profession or engage in a particular trade' (n 114 above at 139).

[119] ibid at 139.

[120] See *Naylor v Uttoxeter UDC* (1974) 23 EG 619.

[121] *Evans FR (Leeds) Ltd v English Electric Co* (1977) 245 EG 657.

ket rent' within section 34 must, seemingly, be in contemplation of a 'willing tenant' as otherwise it might be said that no market would exist. The objective standard imposed by section 34 also prevents the court fixing a rent, on the basis of what the tenant can afford, which is below the market level.[122] The emphasis is upon what rent the landlord could command for the premises and not what the tenant is able and willing to pay.[123] This was illustrated in *Northern Electricity Plc v Addison* where the Court of Appeal felt that the application of the statutory formula so as to calculate the rental value of an electricity substation was straightforward.[124] The judge had merely to determine the rent for the new tenancy subject to a restrictive and specialist user clause. This case demonstrated also that any 'ransom' element, whereby in order to relocate the tenant would have to incur great cost (for example, the payment of a premium for a lease not subject to such a restrictive user provision) was to be ignored and could not justify a higher rent. As the Court of Appeal concluded, to base a rent on a ransom value presupposes a lessor 'unwilling' to let premises for the restricted use contemplated by the lease.[125]

Repair

The state of repair of the premises is also a relevant factor.[126] If the premises are in disrepair, due to a breach of covenant by one of the parties, the issue is whether the premises should be valued as they stand or, alternatively, on the assumption that the covenants have been performed. Although the Act makes no reference to this issue, and the courts have not always spoken with one voice, the answer seemingly lies according to which party is in breach. If the tenant is in default, the assumption is that the covenants have been performed.[127] Where the landlord is in breach, the court will conclude that the proper market rent is less than it would have been had the repair covenants been observed.[128] The court has also empowered itself, in exceptional circumstances, to order a differential rent until the landlord's obligations are fulfilled.[129] The general policy running through these disrepair cases is that the tenant is not allowed to set up breaches of the tenant's repair covenant in order to depress the market rent and that the landlord cannot profit from its failure to observe repairing obligations.

9.30

---

[122] *Giannoukakis Ltd v Saltfleet Ltd* [1988] 1 EGLR 73.

[123] *Barton (WJ) Ltd v Long Acre Securities Ltd*, n 109 above.

[124] (1997) 39 EG 175.

[125] Presumably, the same line of reasoning would prevent a ransom value creeping in to private rent reviews where the hypothetical negotiation is expressed to be between willing lessor and willing lessee: see *National Grid Co Plc v M25 Group Ltd* (1998) 32 EG 90.

[126] See generally *Crown Estate Commissioners v Town & Investment Ltd* (1992) 8 EG 111.

[127] *Family Management v Gray* (1974) 253 EG, 369; *Re 5 Panton St Haymarket* (1959) 175 EG 49.

[128] *Fawke v Viscount Chelsea* [1980] 2 QB 441; *Crown Estate Commissioners v Town & Investment Ltd*, n 126 above.

[129] *Fawke*, ibid It should be appreciated that no differential rent can be read into a private rent review clause: *Clarke v Findon Developments Ltd* (1983) 270 EG 426.

Covenants

9.31 Since the enactment of the Landlord and Tenant (Covenants) Act 1995, a new sub-section, in the form of section 34(4), has been added to the Part II scheme. This expressly requires the court to take into consideration any effect on rent of the new covenants legislation. As the Act abolishes original tenant liability following assignment of the lease, it is likely that this will be used by landlords as a justification for a higher rent on renewal. Presumably, if a qualified covenant against assignment is imposed on renewal (thereby, paving the way to the negotiation of an authorised guarantee agreement) the market rent might be depressed accordingly. It is, as yet, unclear what the response of the courts will be to this new dynamic in the valuation process.[130]

The Valuation Process

9.32 There is, lamentably, an absence of authoritative guidance as to how the rent is to be calculated for the purposes of section 34. The Act is of no help and it has been left to the court to devise methods by which the open market rent can be deduced. The calculation involves questions of fact and usually turns upon expert valuation evidence, often adduced on a square foot basis and supported by comparables.[131] An important feature of valuation evidence is, therefore, the rent reserved on recent lettings of comparable properties in the area, taking into account the terms of the new lease.[132] The expert evidence of the landlord will normally support the best rent for the premises on the terms offered, whereas, the tenant's expert will argue for the lowest rent which can be achieved.[133] The court must take such evidence into account and, as Mummery J warned, 'be on its guard against trespassing on the territory of the expert valuer. This is a court of law, not a court of valuation.'[134] Nevertheless, as valuation reflects vested interest and is, undoubt-

---

[130] See generally P Luxton [1996] JBL 388.

[131] In *Rogers v Rosedimond Investments (Blakes Market) Ltd* (1978) 247 EG 467, the Court of Appeal advised that reliance should not be placed on the views of local traders as to prevailing rental values.

[132] For example, if the user restriction in the new lease is more onerous than that in the comparable lease, the rent payable will be suitably depressed. *UDS Tailoring v BL Holdings* [1982] 1 EGLR 61. The court can also look at offers in relation to comparables even though the transactions did not go through: *Rombus Materials Ltd v WT Lamb Properties Ltd* (1999) 18 February (CA).

[133] As M Freedman and N Cheffings put it, 'the reality has often been that the expert's report gives the benefit of the doubt to the instructing client. It would be fair to say that some expert witnesses have also been known to go beyond the benefit of the doubt' (*The Property Expert Witness Redefined* (1999) NLJ 30 July at 1156). In theory, however, the expert's duty is to assist the court and to provide an objective, unbiased opinion: *The Ikarian Reefer* [1993] 2 EGLR 183.

[134] *British Airways Plc v Heathrow Airport* [1992] 1 EGLR 141 at 144. As regards expert evidence under the Civil Procedure Rules 1998, see District Judge J Frenkel (1999) NLJ 12 February at 197; 19 February at 254; Freedman and Cheffings, above. The provisions concerning experts and assessors are to be found in Part 35 of the Rules. It is to be appreciated that no expert can be called without the court's permission (r 35.4) and that permission will not be given unless the expert is reasonably required (r 35.1).

edly, an inexact art, disputes and conflicts of evidence invariably arise. As Mummery J further explained:

> Exercises in property valuation sometimes generate difficult demarcation disputes between the real world, occupied by the relevant property, and an abstract world peopled with spectral willing vendors and purchasers, or lessors and lessees, haggling hypothetically in accordance with stipulated assumptions.[135]

The judicial response is, however, pragmatic and, as admitted by Megarry J in *Violet Yorke Ltd v Property Holding and Investment Trust Ltd*, aims to deal with the matter with a broad sword and not by the application of exact mathematics.[136] Accordingly, it is uncommon for the evidence of an expert to be accepted in its entirety[137] and, consequently, the court must adopt the mantle of the valuer even though it is, perhaps, ill-equipped to do so.[138] Traditionally, the judge has been left to make a value judgment and choice between rival and equally authoritative views.[139]

Comparables

As was explained by Forbes J in *GREA Real Property Investment Ltd v Williams:*   **9.33**

> It is a fundamental aspect of valuation that it proceeds by analogy. The valuer isolates those characteristics of the object to be valued which in his view affects the value and then seeks another object of known or ascertainable value possessing some or all of those characteristics with which he may compare the holding he is valuing. Where no directly comparable object exists the valuer must make allowances of one kind or another, interpolating or extrapolating from his given data. The less closely analogous the object chosen for comparison the greater the allowances which have to be made and the greater the opportunity for error.[140]

---

[135] ibid at 142; see also *First Leisure Trading Ltd v Dorita Properties Ltd*, n 32 above. Mummery J (at 144) also warned of 'the danger of confusing reality and hypothesis'.

[136] [1968] EGD 74.

[137] See *Miah v Bromley Park Estates* (1992) 10 EG 91. The judge is entitled to rely on the evidence of one party only: *Northern Electricity Plc v Addison*, n 124 above. This is not, however, an obligation: 'The parties have invoked the decision of a judicial tribunal and not an oracular pronouncement by an expert' (*per* Lord President Cooper in *Davie v Edinburgh Magistrates* (1953) SC 34 at 40). Expert evidence will now normally be given in a written report (Civil Procedure Rules 1998, r 35.5) and the expert subject to pre-trial written questions (r 35.6). Importantly, the expert's report must also state the substance of all material instructions given (whether oral or written): r 35.10.

[138] In *Simonite v Sheffield City Council* (1992) 29 January (unreported), for example, Harman J felt able to disregard and modify the evidence of valuers who were 'honest, experienced and skilled . . . Since both are human neither is infallible.' He then went on, with an air of infallibility, to calculate a rent which was so detailed as to include pence as well as pounds. Nevertheless, the Court of Appeal has warned against judges plucking figures out of the air and deciding, without evidence, what is reasonable: *Rombus Materials Ltd v WT Lamb Properties Ltd*, n 132 above.

[139] See *Eren v Tranmac* (1995) 70 P & CR 39. Following the Civil Procedure Rules 1998, the use of a joint, impartial expert should become more common (r 35.8). If the court appoints a single expert, both sides will presumably employ their own experts so that the official report can be challenged in court. As Freedman and Cheffings comment, 'despite Lord Woolf's best intentions, we are more likely to see three experts rather than one' (n 133 above at 1156).

[140] [1979] 1 EGLR 121 at 123.

Although the parties will normally come to trial having exchanged lists of comparable properties, it is for the court to decide in which area the comparables should be located. In *Baptist v Masters of the Bench and Trustees of the Honourable Society of Gray's Inn*, for example, the court looked only at comparables within Gray's Inn itself.[141] In *Ganton House Investments v Crossman Investments*, however, the court looked beyond the existing location of a betting shop and drew comparables from the surrounding area.[142] In general, the precise location of the premises does not matter if the value of the business is unaffected by it. If comparables exist within the selected area, the matter is relatively straightforward and, unless one of the parties can show that special circumstances apply, the up-to-date rental figures for such properties will guide the court.[143] Unfortunately, comparables are sometimes difficult to adduce and too frequently properties are introduced in evidence which are not comparable at all to the property in question.[144] It follows that if there is nothing comparable, or no modifications which can be made to make an adduced comparable truly comparable, the court must look elsewhere for assistance.

Other Guides

9.34 A variety of alternative options are available and each can produce a different calculation. In *NCP v Colebrook Estates*, for example, the court looked to the general rent increases in the area for inspiration.[145] In *Re 52, Osnaburgh Street*, the landlord proving that he had a firm offer from a prospective tenant was accepted as good evidence of the open market rent.[146] This case marked an unusual departure from reliance upon expert valuation because the landlord's evidence was preferred to the (standard) square-foot basis of assessment. It was held in *Harewood Hotels Ltd v Harris* that, in exceptional situations, evidence of the profitability of the tenant's business becomes relevant.[147] Traditionally, however, the general rule has

---

[141] N 114 above. The cachet of having offices within this area, thereby, driving the rent upwards.

[142] N 2 above.

[143] *Oriane v Dorita Properties Ltd* (1987) 282 EG 1001. In the *Baptist* case, n 114 above, the court rejected the suggestion that the rent of different comparables should be averaged in order to produce a rental figure for the new tenancy. Instead, the judge has to find the latest letting which provides the best comparable, perhaps with some modification to reflect, for example, differences in view, parking facilities, access, ventilation and layout between the two premises.

[144] See *Newey & Eyre v J Curtis & Son Ltd* (1984) 271 EG 891 where a 'down-market' comparable had been applied to 'up-market' premises. In *Barrett & Co v Harrison* [1956] EGD 178, it was admitted that 'the ideal comparable hardly ever exists'.

[145] (1982) 266 EG 810. Traditionally, such evidence would be excluded if it entailed recourse to hearsay (*English Exporters (London) Ltd v Eldonwall Ltd* [1973] 1 All ER 726), but the hearsay rule has now been relaxed by the Civil Evidence Act 1995.

[146] [1956] CLY 1947. This is a potentially dangerous precedent as it may encourage the landlord to canvass offers without obligation on the part of those who make them. Such offers may be far from representative of the true value.

[147] [1958] 1 All ER 104 (a hotel business). The court indicated that a similar approach could be applied to other businesses with special features such as theatres, petrol stations and racecourses, for example; see also *Barton (WJ) Ltd v Long Acre Securities Ltd*, n 109 above. It serves as an indicator of the earning capacity of the business to a potential lessee. Trading records of a similar business in a different locality are not admissible.

been that the tenant's trading accounts are inadmissible in evidence and that rental comparables will normally suffice.[148] More recently, the Chancery Division, albeit *obiter*, has declared previous decisions on this issue *per incuriam* and concluded that trading accounts may never be used in the valuation process.[149] Such contradictions hardly instil confidence in the valuation process.

Further factors that may, in the absence of comparables, affect the determination **9.35** of rent include the user of the property and its rateable value. In *Aldwych Club Ltd v Copthall Property Co Ltd*,[150] the fact that the club premises could be employed for a more profitable purpose (that is, as offices) justified a higher rent valuation. Provided that the alternative use is not prohibited under the terms of the original lease or the proposed new tenancy, the more valuable use can be taken account of.[151] Although the court may have regard also to the rateable value of the holding, such a value is a rather poor guide to rental levels. The rateable value is thought to be of relevance where the new lease is to be a yearly tenancy and otherwise to be of no consequence.[152] This is because the terms of a tenancy will rarely be comparable to the underlying basis of the property's rating assessment.[153] The rent currently payable under the existing lease is not, however, a factor to be taken account of, in the setting of the new rent, unless it constitutes direct evidence of the market rent. This, of course, it will not often do.

Mandatory Disregards

As mentioned earlier, section 34 contains a series of disregards which are not to **9.36** enter into the calculation of the new rent. Although not all are free from interpretational difficulties, these disregards are, first, the effect on rent attributable to occupation by the tenant (or a predecessor in title) of the holding.[154] The premises will, therefore, be valued on the assumption of vacant possession. This prevents both the tenant from benefiting from any sitting tenant discount and the landlord claiming any accretion to the rent attributable to such occupation.[155] Although it

---

[148] *Barton's* case, ibid, which concerned an ordinary shop as regards which there were ample rental comparables available.

[149] *Cornwall Coast Country Club v Bardgrange* (1987) 282 EG 166. Support for this conclusion was derived from the House of Lords in *Lynall v IRC* (1972) AC 680 (not cited in the *Barton* case). The basis of the exclusion of trading accounts is that as 'haggling' parties in the real world cannot see trading accounts then neither should the hypothetical landlord under section 34.

[150] N 71 above.

[151] The court will not, however, relax a user covenant merely to justify a higher valuation: *Goreleston Golf Club v Links Estates* (1959) CLY 1830.

[152] *Davies v Brighton Corporation* (1956) CLY 4963.

[153] See *Jeffreys v Hutton Investment* (1956) 168 EG 203.

[154] Section 34(1)(a). The term 'predecessor in title' is undefined in the Act, but is to be given the meaning ascribed to it in section 25 of the Landlord and Tenant Act 1927: 'any person through whom the tenant has derived title whether by assignment, by will, by intestacy or by operation of law'.

[155] *Harewood Hotels Ltd v Harris*, n 147 above.

is not the policy of the Act to compel landlord's to renew at less than a market value, the Act does not allow the landlord to argue that a sitting tenant should be prepared to outbid the rest of the market.[156] As discussed above, the disrepair of the premises, due to the tenant's breach of covenant, will also be disregarded.

9.37 Second, any goodwill attaching to the premises by reason of the business carried on by the tenant (or by a predecessor in title in both title and business) is to be discounted.[157] The policy is that, if the goodwill belongs to the tenant, additional rent should not be charged because of it. The court must, therefore, calculate whether there is any difference in the value of the holding with and without goodwill.[158] If such a difference exists, it must be disregarded. The burden of proof lies with the tenant and it must be shown on a balance of probabilities that the goodwill has enhanced the letting value of the holding. Whether or not a person is a predecessor in business is an issue of fact and is determined by such matters as whether, for example, the new tenant continues to trade under the same name; had the goodwill assigned; and purchased the predecessor's stock-in-trade.

9.38 Third, in the case of a holding comprising licensed premises, any addition to its value attributable to that licence, where the benefit of the licence belongs to the tenant, must be discounted.[159] As, since 11 July 1992, the Landlord and Tenant (Licensed Premises) Act 1990 has placed all on-licensed premises within the protection of the 1954 Act, this disregard now assumes more importance than it previously enjoyed. Although clearly not within the direct contemplation of the Parliamentary draftsman, the disregard also extends to licensed betting shops.[160]

9.39 Finally, the court must disregard any increase in value attributable to relevant improvements carried out by a tenant or a predecessor in title, other than in pursuance of an obligation to the immediate landlord.[161] The term 'improvement' is not defined in the Act and most certainly does not cover every alteration made by the tenant. Case law, however, demonstrates that it is necessary to evaluate the work from the tenant's perspective.[162] In addition, so called 'tenant's fixtures',

---

[156] *O'May v City of London Real Property Co*, n 111 above.

[157] Section 34(1)(b) (which harks back to section 5(2) of the Landlord and Tenant Act 1927).

[158] 'Goodwill' was defined by Lord MacNaughten in *Commissioners of Inland Revenue v Muller & Co* (1901) AC 217 as 'the benefit and advantage of the good name, reputation and connection of a business. It is the attractive force which brings in custom. It is the one thing which distinguishes an old established business from a new business at its first start' (at 223, 224). cf 'site goodwill' arising from the convenient situation of the premises: *Whiteman Smith Motor Co v Chaplin* (1934) 2 KB 35.

[159] Section 34(1)(d).

[160] *Ganton House Investments v Crossman Investments*, n 2 above.

[161] Section 34(1)(c). See *Rombus Materials Ltd v WT Lamb Properties Ltd*, n 132 above. Accordingly, the improvement will still be disregarded when, for example, the tenant carries it out under an obligation owed to a third party (for example, a sub-tenant or licensee).

[162] *Ball Brothers Ltd v Sinclair* (1931) 2 Ch 325; *National Electric Theatres Ltd v Hudgell* (1939) Ch 553.

which by their nature are removable, do not fall within the understanding of an improvement nor do they form part of the demise.[163] An improvement would, therefore, embrace such matters as the installation of central heating, external storage spaces, suspended ceilings and double glazing.[164]

The apparent purpose of this disregard is to protect a tenant against having to pay **9.40** a higher rent by reason of such personal expenditure. As Macintyre explains: 'If tenants are successive tenants, no hardship will be caused . . . to the landlord, since he will have neither contributed to nor paid compensation in respect of the improvements: and hardship to the tenant, who will either have made the improvements himself or paid something to his predecessor in respect of them, will be avoided.'[165] In order to defeat this disregard, it is traditionally understood that a positive, legal obligation (whether general or specific) on the tenant is required,[166] but it has, somewhat dubiously, been suggested that a moral obligation will suffice.[167] The disregard is dependent upon the work being carried out by a tenant and does not apply to improvements carried out pre-term or during a licence occupancy.[168] As made clear in *Hambros Bank v Superdrug Stores Ltd*,[169] the person making the improvement must be the tenant at the time the work is carried out. A valuation difficulty which arises with this disregard is that it is uncertain whether the valuer is to assume that the works have never been carried out; or is to value the premises as improved, but with complex adjustments reflecting the cost of the work and amortisation.[170] The matter is, however, one of fact for the court to decide and, in doing so, the judge will, undoubtedly, be influenced by the state of the comparables which are introduced into evidence.

Overcoming limitations imposed by the majority of the House of Lords in *East* **9.41** *Coast Amusements Co v BRB*,[171] amendments introduced by the Law of Property Act 1969 widened the class of tenant's improvements which fall to be disregarded. Importantly, the amending legislation ensured that it was no longer necessary for the improvement to be carried out during the current tenancy. If it was not, the improvement still falls to be disregarded if it satisfies certain further conditions set

---

[163] *NZ Government Property Corporation v HM&S Ltd* [1982] QB 1145.

[164] *Department of the Environment v Allied Freehold Property Trust Ltd* (1992) 45 EG 156; see further Chapter 10.

[165] D Macintyre , *Law of Property Act 1969—Part I* [1970] Conv 17 at 19.

[166] See *Godbold v Martin the Newsagents Ltd* (1983) 268 EG 1202.

[167] *Appleton v Abrahamson* (1956) 167 EG 633.

[168] *Euston Centre Properties Ltd v H&J Wilson* (1982) 262 EG 1079. The works can be carried out personally or by a third party. As demonstrated in *Dudley House Ltd v Cadogan Estates Ltd* (1999) (HC), any arrangement whereby a third party carries out the improvements for the tenant will normally suffice. Thre, Neuberger J added by way of *obiter* that the tenant must, however, show some involvement in identifying, supervising and/or financing the works.

[169] [1989] 1 EGLR 99.

[170] See S Fogel and P Freedman, *The 1954 Act—Some Thoughts on Reform—II* (1985) 275 EG 228.

[171] [1967] AC 85.

out in the revised section 34(2) of the 1954 Act.[172] These somewhat elaborate conditions are:

(1) that the tenant can prove that the improvement was completed not more than twenty-one years before the application for a new tenancy was made. This ceiling recognises that, in relation to previous tenancies, with the passage of time it becomes impractical to assess what effect the improvement has had on the letting value under the current lease. Accordingly, in these circumstances the improvement is, beyond twenty-one years, presumed to have no enhancing effect and the building and costs are deemed to have been written off. This ceiling also serves as an encouragement for tenants to retain documentary evidence to show what improvements were carried out, when and by whom; and

(2) that the holding, or any part of it, has at all times since the improvement was completed been comprised in tenancies which fell within the catchment provisions of the Act. There is no requirement that the same business have been carried out since the improvement. This condition entails that a tenancy existing prior to the 1954 will be caught if it would, otherwise, have fallen within the scope of the 1954 Act. Similarly, the condition will not be defeated by showing that, at some stage a tenancy had been contracted out of the Act. It is unclear what consequences would arise if it could be proved that, for some time in the twenty-one-year period, a tenancy had ceased to fall within the catchment of the Act (for example, the tenant had for some reason ceased to occupy for business purposes); and

(3) that at the termination of each of those tenancies, the tenant did not quit.[173] This reaffirms the general ethos that the tenant can disregard only improvements made by himself or by an assignor.

Relationship with Rent Review Clauses

9.42 Although the disregards contained in section 34(1)((a)–(c)) were once routinely incorporated into market rent review clauses, modern thinking is that it is best to avoid reference to the statutory disregards in such clauses.[174] Primarily, this is because modern review clauses demand a more sophisticated content than is offered in the statutory calculus. In addition, the statutory disregards might instil some uncertainty. It is, for example, unclear whether, under section 34, the valuation will assume that the premises are fit for immediate occupation. Accordingly, it is possible for the tenant to argue that the premises, stripped of tenant's fixtures and plant, would be worth less on the open market. Similarly, the disregard of a

---

[172] cf the more simple approach adopted in Northern Ireland which is that the disregard automatically occurs when the improvement is carried out during a previous tenancy: article 18(2)(c).
[173] If the tenant did quit, compensation for improvements might be claimed under Part I of the Landlord and Tenant Act 1927; see Chapter 10.
[174] See Tromans, *Commercial Leases* (2nd edn, 1996) at 103.

tenant's occupation, goodwill and improvements might not extend to increases in rental value emanating from a sub-tenant. Nevertheless, following *Oscroft v Benabo*, it could be argued that the court can disregard a sub-tenant's goodwill and improvements.[175] Although this would produce a fair result for the mesne landlord, it would be preferable if this disregard was expressly catered for within section 34.

Inclusion of a Rent Review

Since the amendments introduced by the Law of Property Act 1969, and as a con-   **9.43**
cession to inflationary times, the court is expressly enabled to include a rent review clause in the order for a new tenancy.[176] The purpose of a review clause was explained by Browne-Wilkinson VC in *British Gas Corporation v Universities Superannuation Fund Ltd* as being 'to enable the landlord to obtain from time to time the market rental which the premises would command if let on the same terms in the open market at the review date. The purpose is to reflect changes in the value of money and real increase in the value of the property during the long term'.[177] Accordingly, the prospect of a rent review clause will help to reduce the landlord's opposition to a new tenancy of a reasonably long duration. There is much force in the suggestion that all renewals should automatically contain review clauses. As the tenant is expected to pay a market rent, there can be little justification for maintaining the discretion as to whether to include in the lease such a standard, market mechanism.

Discretion

The court is not obliged to include a rent review clause, but such insertion has, for   **9.44**
longer leases, become standard practice. In the interests of fairness, the tendency is to order review clauses which permit the rent to move upwards or downwards.[178] The judge is, however, entitled to take a broad view and, as in *Northern Electricity Plc v Addison*, the court may decline the inclusion of a review where it is deemed uneconomic.[179] The frequency of any review will be geared to any relevant terms

---

[175] [1967] 2 All ER 548. This case decided that the effect of a protected residential sub-letting was to be disregarded.

[176] Section 34(3). It is thought that the court had this power anyway: *Re 88, High Road, Kilburn* n 100 above; *Stylo Shoes Ltd v Manchester Royal Exchange Ltd* (1967) 204 EG 803; see also the Law Reform Advisory Committee for Northern Ireland Report, n 59 above at 6.4.2. The sub-section does, however, remove doubt.

[177] [1986] 1 WLR 398 at 401; see also *Boots the Chemist Ltd v Pinkland Ltd*, n 15 above.

[178] *Janes (Gowns) Ltd v Harlow Development Corporation*, n 58 above; *Blythewood Plant Hire Ltd v Spiers Ltd* (1992) 48 EG 117; *Amarjee v Barrowfen Properties Ltd* (1993) 30 EG 98. This is so even though the open market tendency is towards upwards-only reviews: *Forbouys Plc v Newport Borough Council* (1994) 25 EG 156.

[179] The facts of the *Addison* case n 124 above, are to be acknowledged as unusual. The renewal concerned the tenancy of an electricity sub-station for a period of 14 years at a rent of £40 pa. The cost of surveyors and negotiations involved in any review would clearly outweigh any benefit that the landlord could achieve.

of the current tenancy or, if none, prevailing market trends (currently, five-year reviews).[180] Similarly, the review clause will generally require the involvement of an arbitrator/expert if the parties fail to agree on a new rent. It is unclear what influence a review clause in the current tenancy will have on the court. Although section 34(3) does not oblige the judge to have regard to the original tenancy, the current terms will provide strong and cogent evidence and it should follow that a similar review clause will be maintained in the new lease. In such a case, however, the court should take the opportunity to update the review clause in the light of recent developments in the drafting of such provisions.[181] It appears, moreover, that section 34(3) requires the rent review clause to be considered after the market rent has been calculated.[182] If correct, this could entail a benefit for the landlord in that the market rent might be higher if the review clause has not been included in the calculation. It is, however, apparent that a potentially downward review clause will not generate a discounted rent for the tenant.

G. Other Terms

9.45 In the absence of agreement, the onus is placed on the court to determine the remaining terms of the new tenancy.[183] The court is obliged to 'have regard to' the terms of the current tenancy and to all relevant circumstances.[184] This must, therefore, involve taking account of current market trends and changes to the premises that have occurred (for example, the need for immediate or future repairs) since the original lease was granted. This general requirement is elastic in the sense that it compels something between a reproduction of the existing terms and an unfettered right to substitute others.[185] A new section 35(2) has been introduced by the Landlord and Tenant (Covenants) Act 1995 and this expressly makes the abolition of original tenant liability a relevant consideration for the court to take on board.[186] Beyond these directions, the 1954 Act offers no explanation and no indication of what was intended to be covered by the section.[187] As Upjohn J commented in *Re No 1 Albermarle St*:

---

[180] *Smith (WH) Ltd v Bath CC* (1986) 277 EG 822.
[181] *O'May v City of London Real Property*, n 111 above.
[182] *National Westminster Bank v Arthur Young McClelland Moores & Co* (1984) 273 EG 402.
[183] Section 35.
[184] The comparable provision for Northern Ireland is to be found in article 19.
[185] *O'May v City of London Real Property Co*, n 111 above. It is particularly elastic where the previous lease was oral: see *Amarjee v Barrowfen Properties Ltd*, n 178 above.
[186] This opens the door to the court imposing a qualified alienation covenant to protect the landlord from breaches by a future assignee. Note that the 1995 Act has no application to Northern Ireland.
[187] cf article 19(2) of the Business Tenancies (Northern Ireland) Order 1996 which directs the Lands Tribunal to consider the inclusion of terms to ensure that the obligations of both parties are satisfactorily performed (for example, a surety clause).

It seems to me that section [35] goes much further than section 32. I do not believe that when section 35 was framed, Parliament was contemplating that there was to be an elaborate dissection of terms contained in the lease as between those terms which touch and concern the demised premises and those terms that do not. I think that Parliament intended to give a very wide discretion to the court . . . [T]he great width of the section is shown by the fact that the court . . . must have regard . . . to all relevant circumstances.[188]

Despite its wide discretion, the court will start with the presumption that the current terms (except as to duration and rent) will pervade the new lease.[189] This does not mean that a term will be automatically reproduced in the new lease, but rather that the party arguing for change will have to convince the court that the alteration is fair and reasonable.[190] The overriding function of the court is to draw a reasonable balance between the interests of the landlord (including any superior landlord) and the interests of the tenant. As Lord Wilberforce concluded in the *O'May* case, '[a] party seeking to introduce new, or substituted, or modified terms [has] to justify the change, with reasons appearing sufficient to the court . . . [I]f such reasons are shown, then the court . . . may consider giving effect to them: there is certainly no intention shown to freeze . . . or to 'petrify' the terms of the lease.'[191] There, in relation to a short lease, the court refused to allow the landlord to impose a fluctuating service charge in return for a fixed rent reduction.

Limitations

It is unlikely that the court will impose new terms which serve merely to improve **9.46** the position of one party, particularly when the change would be detrimental to the other.[192] This is so even if the current market practices would indicate otherwise. Accordingly, in *Charles Clements (London) Ltd v Rank City Wall Ltd* the court rejected an attempt by the landlord to relax a user covenant with the purpose of increasing the rental value of the premises. As Goulding J commented: 'If the parties are to be at liberty to insist on changes in the terms of the existing tenancy simply because they consider them beneficial to themselves, a field would be opened which I think the court would find it bewildering to traverse.'[193]

---

[188] N 48 above at 254, 255.

[189] See *Gold v Brighton Corporation*, n 97 above. In *Aldwych Club Ltd v Copthall Property Co Ltd*, n 111 above, for example, the fact that rent was payable in arrears under the original lease resulted, despite the landlords' objections, in a similar term being inserted into the new lease. cf where the previous lease was oral: *Amarjee v Barrowfen Properties Ltd*, n 178 above.

[190] *Leslie Godwin Investments Ltd v Prudential Assurance* (1987) 283 EG 1565; *Becker v Hill Street Properties*, n 74 above; *Boots the Chemist Ltd v Pinkland Ltd*, n 15 above.

[191] N 111 above at 670. Indeed, it was concluded in the Law Reform Advisory Committee for Northern Ireland Report that the current provisions are sufficiently flexible to reflect current market trends without the need for further statutory guidance: n 59 above at para 6.4.7.

[192] *Cardshops Ltd v Davies*, n 112 above. Here the landlord failed, in the attempt to change a qualified covenant against assignment into an absolute covenant, because the proposal was harsh and would imperil the tenant's goodwill.

[193] (1978) 246 EG 739 at 743.

Conversely, in *Aldwych Club Ltd v Copthall Property Co* the tenant failed to tighten a user covenant so as to reduce the rental value. There Pennycuick J accepted that it would be contrary to both the policy of the Act and 'reasonable justice' to allow the tenant to depress the rent in this way. He added, however, that had it been the landlord who sought the restriction then, provided it was fair, the court would here have favoured the change.[194] The emphasis upon fairness was reiterated in *Gold v Brighton Corporation* where the Court of Appeal refused to tighten a user covenant at the request of the landlord so as to prevent the premises being used as a second-hand clothes shop.[195] To do so would have prevented the tenant carrying out her existing business and, as Parker LJ concluded, 'in the ordinary case . . . it is difficult to think of any considerations which would justify changing restriction on user in such a way as to alter or limit the nature of the business which the tenant has lawfully carried out on those premises and which it is clearly the object of the Act to preserve'.[196]

9.47 The authorities also demonstrate that the court should not exercise its discretion so as to create a new saleable asset for the tenant;[197] to enlarge the tenant's holding;[198] or to confer rights of the tenant over the landlord's land not hitherto enjoyed.[199] Outside these parameters, the change of terms is not limited to issues concerning security of tenure and the court may, as a rule of thumb, include any provision that can become contractually binding on the new lease being executed.[200] The introduction or modification of user and alienation covenants, however, feature most frequently in the case law. Although the court does not have the ability to bind third parties, it can impose a term which will depend upon third parties for efficacy and co-operation (for example, a term that the tenant provide a guarantor or insure the premises).[201] The court does not, however, enjoy the jurisdiction to deprive the tenant of statutory protection. This is well illustrated in *Cairnplace v CBL (Property Investment) Co Ltd*[202] where the court felt that it could not include a term as to the payment of the landlord's costs and, thereby,

---

[194] N 111 above.

[195] N 97 above. The burden of persuading the court lay with the landlord and there was no evidence to show that to allow this type of business to continue would, for example, depress property values in the area.

[196] ibid at 1296.

[197] *Kirkwood v Johnson*, n 54 above, where the tenant was unable to have a fresh option to purchase inserted into the new lease.

[198] *Orlik (G) (Meat Products) v Hastings & Thanet Building Society*, n 37 above.

[199] *Kirkwood v Johnson*, n 54 above. In relation to the option to purchase, Ormrod LJ suggested that if the option in the original lease had not lapsed (ie a time limit had been imposed and had now passed) it could have been transmitted under section 32. It did not, in any event, fall within the jurisdiction conferred by section 35.

[200] *O'May v City of London Real Property*, n 111 above; see also *Re Albermarle St*, n 48 above.

[201] *Cairnplace Ltd v CBL (Property Investment) Co Ltd* above where two guarantors were required in the context of a new company which took the assignment of a lease at the fag-end of its term. Note that section 41A(6) expressly deals with the provision of a surety in relation to partnerships.

[202] ibid.

deprive the tenant of the protection afforded by section 1 of the Costs of Leases Act 1958. Such a term can only be included by express written agreement between the parties.

Justifying Change

It is clear that the party seeking the change of terms (however minor) must pro- **9.48** duce evidence in support. It is usually the landlord who seeks the revision and the tenant who resists it. As mentioned earlier, the need to permit subsequent redevelopment of the property is a sufficient justification for the insertion of a break clause. A change might also be justified so as to bring the lease into line with current practice or to revamp old and unsuitable terms;[203] to overcome the previously demonstrated unreasonableness of one of the parties;[204] or to ensure that there is no default in rent payments.[205] Taking an overview, the extra-statutory framework emerges that before allowing a variation, a four-stage test must be satisfied.[206] First, a valid reason must be shown for the variation;[207] second, the other party must be adequately compensated by the effect that the new term will have on rent; third, the tenant's business must not be impaired; and finally, it must be fair and reasonable to make the change. This approach does, as Lord Wilberforce acknowledged in the *O'May* case, place the tenant on statutory renewal in a stronger position than a new tenant negotiating in the open market. There, for example, the landlords lost an estimated £2 million accretion to the freehold value because the leases were not revised according to their proposals. Whether this advantage to the tenant, and the corresponding detriment to the landlord, was envisaged by Parliament is a matter open to debate. Certainly nothing in section 35 expressly validates the approach adopted by the judiciary or suggests that the tenant be so distanced from the effect of market forces. As Ross questions, 'If the market norm had shifted during the term of the existing lease, from fixed service

[203] *O'May v City of London Real Property*, n 111 above; *Hyams v Titan Properties Ltd* (1972) 224 EG 2017. This should be more than merely revising the language of the lease and should reflect changes in the law, building techniques and management practices, for example. It was made clear in the *O'May* case, however, that new terms will not be introduced to reflect market practices if to do so would prove unfair to the tenant.

[204] See *Re 5, Panton Street, Haymarket*, n 127 above where the landlord had, in the past, been troublesome over the tenant making minor alterations to the premises, the court revised a term in order to prohibit only 'structural alterations' without the lessor's consent.

[205] *Cairnplace Ltd v CBL (Property Investment) Co Ltd*, n 54 above. As mentioned, and due to the Landlord and Tenant (Covenants) Act 1995, it is likely that any alienation covenant imported into the new lease will be qualified. This will enable the landlord to insist that the tenant enter into an authorised guarantee agreement, when the lease is next assigned, to ensure the performance of the covenants by the assignee.

[206] See *O'May v City of London Real Property Co*, n 111 above.

[207] In *Amarjee v Barrowfen Properties Ltd*, n 178 above, a service charge and a clause allowing the landlord to insure were included because other leases of premises in the parade contained such terms. A term relating to alterations was excluded because other neighbouring tenants had been denied this right.

charges to indefinite and unlimited ones, the tenant would experience this if he sought new premises. Surely it would be anomalistic for the principle not to apply if he decided instead to renew his existing lease?'[208]

H. Following the Order

Revocation

9.49 Once the tenancy is granted by the court, the tenant is given an opportunity to reconsider. Section 36(2) allows the tenant, within fourteen days of the order, to apply to the court for revocation of the grant.[209] In such a case, the court must accede to the tenant's application. The purpose of this procedure is to ensure that the tenant is not bound to accept a new lease on terms dictated by the court.[210] If more than one tenancy has been granted by the court, the tenant has the choice to apply for revocation of any of those tenancies.[211] On revocation, section 36(2) provides that the current tenancy continues for any such period as the parties agree or, in default, at least until final disposal for the purposes of section 64 or, exceeding that time, for as long as the court deems necessary so as to allow the landlord a reasonable opportunity to re-let or otherwise dispose of the property. If the tenant is appealing against part of the order, it is advisable that the application for revocation is made (within the statutory time-frame), but adjourned until the outcome of the appeal is known.

Costs

9.50 As to costs of the proceedings, section 38(1) renders void any advance agreement that the tenant pay the costs of the landlord.[212] As is usual, costs remain at the discretion of the court and are likely to follow the event (for example, if the landlord unsuccessfully opposes the grant of a new lease, costs are likely to be awarded against that landlord).[213] This working presumption can be rebutted, however, in the light of the parties' conduct, for example, where the successful party had unreasonably refused an offer, raised unjustifiable points or engaged in miscon-

---

[208] N 56 above at 311.

[209] A similar right applies in Northern Ireland: article 20(2).

[210] cf a tenancy which has been agreed with the landlord under section 28 from which the tenant has no right to withdraw.

[211] *Broadmead v Corben-Brown* (1966) 201 EG 111.

[212] See *Stevenson & Rush (Holdings) Ltd v Langdon* (1978) 37 P & CR 208.

[213] Rule 44.3 of the Civil Procedure Rules 1998. The court must also decide when the costs order must be complied with: r 44.8. The orders that can be made include, for example, an order that a party must pay either a proportion of the other's costs, a stated amount, pre-action costs or costs relating to particular steps in the proceedings: r 44.3(6). Costs can be assessed on either a standard basis or an indemnity basis: r 44.4.

duct or time-wasting activities.[214] Any 'without prejudice' offers should, therefore, be subject to the *caveat* that they can be brought before a judge when dealing with the issue of costs. Revocation does not, of itself, affect any order for costs made, but the court can, if it thinks fit, cancel or vary any such order. If no order for costs had previously been made, the court can make an award taking into account the tenant's actions.[215] In *Rom Tyre & Accessories Ltd v Crawford Street Properties Ltd*, for example, a tenant who exercised the right to revoke was ordered to pay the landlord's costs, including those connected with the revocation.[216]

Executing the New Lease

If there is no revocation, the competent landlord must execute, and the tenant **9.51** accept, the new lease on the terms agreed or determined by the court.[217] If required by the landlord, the tenant is obliged by section 36(1) to execute a counterpart or duplicate of the lease. The Act does not stipulate at what date the lease or counterpart must be executed, but this is an understandable omission as the current tenancy will be prolonged under section 64 until after the final disposal of any appeals. Consequently, there is no obligation to comply with the order until the commencement date for the new lease. The Act is also silent as to what redress is available for non-compliance with section 36(1). Nevertheless, it is clear that a refusal would amount to a contempt of court and that the court would be able to enforce the order by executing the lease (or counterpart) itself.[218] In this way, the order for a new lease would be regarded as akin to the court ordering specific performance of a contract to grant a lease. Until the necessary formalities are completed, the parties are regarded, at least in equity, as being landlord and tenant.[219]

---

[214] Rule 44.3(4)–(5), Rule 44.14.

[215] Section 36(3). Seemingly, the court would not otherwise enjoy this jurisdiction: r 44.13(1).

[216] (1966) 197 EG 565; see also *Re 88, High Road, Kilburn*, n 100 above; *Meakers Ltd v DAW Consolidated Properties Ltd* [1959] 1 All ER 527.

[217] Section 36(1). An almost identical provision is contained in article 20(1) of the Business Tenancies (Northern Ireland) Order 1996.

[218] *Pulleng v Curran* (1980) 44 P & CR 58. In Northern Ireland, the Lands Tribunal is given the express power to nominate some proper person to execute or accept or join in executing or accepting the lease: article 20(6).

[219] *Greaves Organisation Ltd v Stanhope Gate Property Co Ltd* (1973) 228 EG 725; see also *Walsh v Lonsdale* (1882) 21 ChD 839.

10

TENANT'S IMPROVEMENTS:
AUTHORISATION AND COMPENSATION

A. Introduction

At common law, any improvements made by a tenant (unless classified as 'tenant's   **10.01**
fixtures' and, thereby, removable) form part of the freehold and, at the end of the
lease, must remain for the reversioner.[1] Subject to the law of waste, and to any contrary stipulation in the lease, the tenant remains free to carry out improvements,
but is not entitled to compensation. This is so even if the landlord knew of the
works and consented to them. Admittedly, there has never been anything to prevent the parties to a lease negotiating terms to deal with the subject of improvements. Indeed, most commercial leases contain a covenant (either qualified by
the need for the landlord's consent or absolute in its prohibition) not to make

---

[1] *New Zealand Government Property Co v HM & S Ltd* [1982] 1 QB 1145.

alterations to the property demised.[2] It is, however, rare (if at all) for there to be any specific provision as to the payment of compensation to the tenant for improvements made. Under the common law, therefore, the tenant was compelled to weigh the aesthetic and practical value of the improvement against its irrecoverable cost. Not only did this offer a potential, windfall benefit for the landlord when an improvement added to the value of the reversion, but it acted also as a disincentive to those tenants who might otherwise have wished to effect improvements to their premises. Hence, the common law was both unduly harsh on tenants and contrary to the public interest that properties should be modernised and improved.

10.02 This policy of *laissez faire* continued until the enactment of the Landlord and Tenant Act 1927. A number of its provisions deal with the promotion of improvements, primarily to commercial property. The Act encourages modernisation in three ways: first, as regards qualified covenants prohibiting improvements, section 19(2) provides that the consent of the landlord cannot be unreasonably be withheld. This extends potentially to all types of lease except for agricultural holdings, farm business tenancies and mining leases.[3] Second, as regards absolute prohibitions against improvements contained in commercial leases, section 3 allows the tenant to apply to the court for certification that the proposed works constitute 'a proper improvement', thereby overriding the landlord's objections.[4] Third, section 1 offers a limited entitlement to claim compensation for improvements carried out by a business tenant or a predecessor in title. The purpose of this latter provision is clear: 'Parliament intended that a landlord whose property had been improved by a tenant so that its letting value at the end of the lease had been increased, should pay compensation for the benefit he had received.'[5] Unfortunately, the statutory machinery set up to achieve this design was to prove both deficient and defective. Although certain modifications were engineered by Part III of the Landlord and Tenant Act 1954, the compensation scheme has, however, remained fundamentally unchanged.

---

[2] In its historic form, such a covenant would prevent the maiming or injury of any walls or timbers. Its modern day manifestation is usually in the form of a prohibition of structural alterations or additions to the demised premises.

[3] Section 19(4) (as amended). The Law Commission Report, *Landlord and Tenant: Compensation for Tenants' Improvements* (1989) Law Com No 178 at para 4.11, however, recommended that the scope of section 19(2) be widened to include these types of tenancy. Excluded also are tenancies subject to special provisions in the Housing Acts 1980 and 1985 and those protected by the Rent Act 1977.

[4] Section 19 and section 3 overlap to some extent, but the primary differences are that section 19(2) has no impact on absolute covenants and is not restricted to the making of improvements which add to the letting value.

[5] *Per* Ormrod LJ in *Pelosi v Newcastle Arms Brewery (Nottingham) Ltd* (1982) 43 P & CR 18 at 22; see also *Owen Owen Estate Ltd v Livett* [1956] Ch 1 where it was accepted that, if uncertainty or ambiguity arises, the statutory provisions fall to be interpreted in a manner favourable to the tenant.

B. Consent and its Refusal

As mentioned, section 19(2) of Part II of the Act implies, into qualified covenants **10.03** restricting improvements, the proviso that the landlord's consent cannot unreasonably be withheld.[6] It is not, however, necessary that the covenant expressly employs the word 'improvement' as the proviso applies to any covenant where, on its fair construction, the making of alterations or improvements without consent is prohibited.[7] The proviso may offer a particular advantage when, for example, the tenant needs to act with urgency or where the proposed improvement will not add to the subsequent letting value of the premises. For example, in *Rivulet Properties Ltd v GLC* section 19(2) could have helped the tenant under a building lease in circumstances where the landlord refused to allow the erection of additional and different buildings.[8] Nevertheless, it is a misconception to regard the provision as if it confers some remedial jurisdiction to release the tenant from, or to modify the terms of, a covenant. As Greene MR observed in *Woolworth (FW) & Co Ltd v Lambert*:

> It is a statutory addition to the terms of a particular type of covenant . . . It is quite wrong to look upon this as something which enables the court to say that a particular set of terms or some particular results can be provided against because there is always the question in the background as to whether or not the consent has been unreasonably withheld in an extreme case.[9]

A Reasonable Refusal?

Although the section does nothing to override absolute covenants, as regards qual- **10.04** ified covenants it operates regardless of any express term to the contrary.[10] Nevertheless, it remains unclear when the landlord's refusal of consent will be condoned as being reasonable.[11] Scant guidance is to be found in the decided authorities. A liberal approach was, however, indicated by Slesser LJ in *Lambert v Woolworth (FW) & Co Ltd (No 2)*: '[M]any considerations, aesthetic, historic or even personal may be relied upon as yielding reasonable grounds for refusing

---

[6] A comparable provision has now been introduced in Northern Ireland by article 26 of the Business Tenancies (Northern Ireland) Order 1996.

[7] *Balls Brothers Ltd v Sinclair* [1931] 2 Ch 325.

[8] (1967) 204 EG 575.

[9] [1936] 2 All ER 1523 at 1542.

[10] As Clauson J commented at first instance in *Woolworth (FW) & Co Ltd v Lambert* [1936] 1 All ER 333 at 337: 'It is curious that it should be so, because, of course, if it is so in future leases a lessor who desires to be outside this subsection has nothing in the world to do except to insist on the omission of the words "without licence or consent" which will not in the least prevent his giving a licence or consent to a breach of covenant expressed in general terms.'

[11] cf Northern Ireland where directions are given in article 26(6). This provides that the refusal is unreasonable only when the improvement does not detract from the letting value; is reasonable and suitable to the character of the property; and will not diminish the value of the landlord's other property.

consent . . . The wider the connotation given to the idea of improvement, the more necessary it may be that the landlord should have his protection.'[12] Although he felt unable to catalogue such instances, Slesser LJ continued:

> In the present decline of taste and manners, a shop-keeper, looking at the matter from a purely commercial point of view, may be right in saying that the removal of some beautiful casement and the substitution of a garish window or facade of false marble may prove . . . from his point of view . . . an improvement. It is most important that the landlord should be able to be heard to say that it may be reasonable that he should withhold his consent to the perpetration of contemplated atrocities.[13]

Accordingly, in *Morris (Marylebone) Ltd v Blake & Richards Estates Ltd*, the landlord's objection to a new, neon-lit, shop-front was upheld as being reasonable in that it detracted from the character and amenities of the neighbourhood.[14] Refusal of consent may be reasonable when the tenant's proposals conflict with good estate management.[15] The refusal of consent was held to be reasonable in *Tideway Investment & Property Holdings Ltd v Wellwood* in circumstances where the tenant's proposed works involved a trespass on the landlord's neighbouring land.[16] Indeed, the accepted rule is that if the works involve a trespass the refusal of consent will always be reasonable.[17] In *Dowse v Davis*, moreover, the mesne landlord refused consent on the basis that the approval of a superior landlord had not been obtained and the refusal was held to be reasonable.[18] It is, however, likely that the landlord would not be able to object merely in order to maintain a collateral advantage not catered for by the lease.[19] This is because the ground of objection must be connected with the use and occupation of the holding.[20] In addition, a minor disruption caused to the landlord while the works are to be carried out will not justify the refusal of consent.[21] There is also no right for the landlord to insist upon carrying out the improvement personally in return for a rent increase.

---

[12] [1938] 2 All ER 664 at 675.

[13] ibid at 675. MacKinnon LJ agreed: 'No court, as I hope and believe, will ever hold that . . . a landlord must consent to the hideous degradation of the front of his building by the fitting of a sheet of place glass, and be satisfied by a money payment for the loss of graceful eighteenth century windows' (at 678).

[14] (1956) 168 EG 96.

[15] *Re Town Investments Underlease* [1954] Ch 301.

[16] [1952] 1 All ER 1142. There the tenant sought to install a heating system which entailed that flue pipes would run over the landlord's property.

[17] See *Haines v Florensa* (1990) 9 EG 70.

[18] (1961) 179 EG 335. In Northern Ireland, this situation is specifically catered for in article 26(2) which provides that the consent of the superior landlord cannot be unreasonably withheld.

[19] See *Barclays Bank Plc v Daejan Investments (Grove Hall) Ltd* (1995) 18 EG 117.

[20] *Re Gibbs & Houlder Brothers & Co Ltd* [1925] Ch 575.

[21] In *Haines v Florensa*, n 17 above, the proposed work (and associated disruption) was to take six weeks. The appellate court held that this was not a justification for withholding consent.

Improvement?

For the tenant's works to fall within section 19(2) they must constitute an **10.05** improvement. In this context, works can be classified as an 'improvement' even though they produce a diminution of the letting value of the premises.[22] This is because what amounts to an improvement for these purposes is solely to be adjudged from the tenant's perspective.[23] As the Court of Appeal demonstrated in *Woolworth (FW) & Co Ltd v Lambert,* any alteration which makes the tenant's enjoyment and occupation of the holding (as opposed to other premises) more convenient and comfortable will fall within the scope of section 19(2).[24] It is, however, argued by Tromans that, 'work which has the effect of destroying the identity of the subject matter demised cannot be regarded as an improvement to that subject matter'.[25] Nevertheless, in *Lilley & Skinner Ltd v Crump* the tenant's proposal to connect two adjacent premises was held to be an improvement as regards which the landlord could not withhold consent unreasonably.[26] Similarly, in *Pleasurama Properties Ltd v Leisure Investments (West End) Ltd* the improvement comprised of converting existing shop premises into a dolphinarium and an auditorium.[27] It was, however, acknowledged by Brown-Wilkinson VC in *Billson v Residential Apartments Ltd* that, if the works are to facilitate a use which is prohibited by the lease, they cannot be said to constitute an improvement.[28]

Conditions

Not surprisingly, section 19(2) contains the safeguard that allows the landlord to **10.06** attach reasonable conditions to the giving of consent. The provision expressly preserves for the landlord the right to require the payment of reasonable compensation for any diminution of, or damage to, the value of the premises or

---

[22] *Balls Brothers Ltd v Sinclair,* n 7 above; *Lambert v Woolworth (FW) & Co Ltd (No 2),* n 12 above. cf the Part I provisions below which provide that no authority can be made, and no compensation paid, as regards such detrimental works.

[23] See *Haines v Florensa,* n 17 above, where the works concerned the conversion of a loft to increase living space. As pointed out in DL Evans and PF Smith, *The Law of Landlord and Tenant* (5th edn, 1996) at 127, 128: 'This beneficial view to tenants may explain why the rules in this branch of the law have remained relatively stable: the present law may induce landlords to prefer to impose absolute prohibitions where possible.'

[24] N 9 above. There the tenant's improvement consisted of the demolition of an outside wall and the building of an extension.

[25] S Tromans, *Commercial Leases* (2nd edn, 1996) at 171. This view is not new and derives from *obiter* in *Lambert v Woolworth (FW) & Co Ltd (No 2),* n 12 above at 672, where Slesser LJ hinted that, if the demised premises are described in the lease with great particularity, the removal of, say, one floor might amount to a destruction of the subject-matter. Hence, it would fall outside the scope of section 19(2). This is, indeed, the position in Northern Ireland due to article 26(8) of the Business Tenancies (Northern Ireland) Order 1996.

[26] (1929) 73 SJ 366; see also *Davies v Yadegar* [1990] 1 EGLR 71.

[27] [1986] 1 EGLR 145.

[28] (1991) 60 P & CR 392.

other premises of the landlord; the reimbursement of legal and other expenses connected with the consent; and, if reasonable and where the improvement does not increase the letting value of the premises, the reinstatement of the premises at the end of the lease.[29] Conditions as to payment and reinstatement will otherwise be unreasonable. The fact that it would be reasonable to impose conditions does not justify an unconditional refusal of consent.[30] As to compensation, a figure may be specified by the landlord or left to the court to determine. In *Woolworth (FW) & Co Ltd v Lambert,* for example, the landlord demanded the payment of £7,000 as a requirement of giving consent.[31] The Court of Appeal held the sum to be reasonable and to reflect the damage to be sustained to the reversion. When making the offer, the landlord might be advised to specify a sum which is thought to be reasonable and state that, if the tenant does not agree, the dispute can be resolved by the court. The danger exists that, where the landlord stipulates a sum and states that no lesser amount will suffice, the demand might be regarded as excessive and unreasonable. In such cases, the tenant would be allowed to carry out the works.[32]

10.07 Where the improvement does not enhance the residual letting value of the premises, and particularly when the landlord intends to recover possession of the premises at the end of the lease, a requirement to reinstate will normally be attached to the consent. If the tenant later fails to reinstate, the landlord will be able to claim damages for loss incurred.[33] The tenant may also be asked to provide a deposit by way of an indirect guarantee that the premises will be restored.[34] Other reasonable conditions commonly attached concern the approval of plans by the landlord, the tenant's obligation to adhere to such plans, the obtaining of planning and other building consents, the avoidance of nuisance and annoyance to other occupiers, the expeditious and good workmanlike carrying out of the works, the making good of any damage, and the indemnity of the landlord against all damage and liability arising from the works.[35]

Tenant's Response

10.08 If the landlord either withholds consent or imposes what the tenant believes to be an unreasonable condition, the tenant may apply to the court for a declaration

---

[29] cf Northern Ireland where article 26(4) speaks merely of reasonable conditions.
[30] *Lambert v Woolworth (FW) & Co Ltd (No 2),* n 12 above.
[31] N 9 above. This was so even though the tenant offered a covenant to reinstate at the end of the lease and undertook to enter a guarantee approved by an insurance company.
[32] *Young v Ashley Gardens Properties Ltd* [1903] 2 Ch 112.
[33] See *Duke of Westminster v Swinton* [1948] 1 KB 524. If no actual loss is incurred by the landlord, damages, of course, will be nominal: *James v Hutton* [1950] KB 9.
[34] *Tideway Investment & Property Holdings Ltd v Wellwood,* n 16 above.
[35] See Tromans, n 25 above at 172.

which will allow the tenant to proceed with the works.[36] In such circumstances, the general rule is that the burden rests upon the tenant to show that either the withholding of consent or the imposition of a condition was unreasonable.[37] If the condition imposed is determined to be unreasonable, the landlord will be regarded as having unreasonably withheld consent. The court must, moreover, make a declaration to this effect.[38] Although while challenging the reasonableness of the landlord's refusal the tenant is entitled go ahead and execute the improvement,[39] this action is ill advised as the landlord might, in response, successfully instigate forfeiture proceedings or claim reinstatement and damages.[40]

C. The Catchment of Part I of the Landlord and Tenant Act 1927

As mentioned above, it is within the provisions of Part I that the statutory rights **10.09** to make improvements and to claim compensation for improvements made are to be found. Both these provisions focus upon works carried out on the tenant's 'holding' which, as defined by section 17, comprises of premises held under a lease which are used wholly or partly for the carrying on thereat of any trade or business. While both the 1927 Act and the Landlord and Tenant Act 1954 extend protection to business leases, the respective Acts do not have identical catchment provisions and do not contain identical sets of exclusions. Consequently, it is possible that a tenant may qualify under one scheme while being excluded under the other. For example, short tenancies and tenancies lawfully contracted out of the 1954 Act enjoy no security of tenure, but remain within the compensation scheme concerning improvements.[41] Similarly, a tenant carrying out a business in contravention of a blanket prohibition against business use in the lease will usually be deprived of security, but may still be entitled to claim compensation for improvements. This lack of uniformity is largely unjustifiable and most certainly offers a potential source of confusion and complexity.[42]

---

[36] Section 53(1) of the Landlord and Tenant Act 1954 bestows on the county court, as regards a declaration as to improvements, the same jurisdiction as the High Court. Note, however, that no other relief must be sought from the county court.

[37] If the landlord does not provide any reason for the refusal, the onus is placed on the landlord to justify the denial of consent: *Lambert v Woolworth (FW) & Co Ltd (No 2)*, n 12 above.

[38] Section 53(2) of the Landlord and Tenant Act 1954

[39] *Commissioner for Railways v Avrom Investments Proprietary Ltd* [1959] 1 WLR 389.

[40] See *Mosley v Cooper* [1990] 1 EGLR 124; *Crown Estate Commissioners v Signet Group Plc* [1996] 2 EGLR 200. The damages awarded may include the cost of reinstatement: *Eyre v Rea* [1947] KB 567.

[41] The Law Commission Working Paper, *Landlord and Tenant: Compensation for Tenants' Improvements* (1987) Law Com No 102 at para 4.2 believed that the definition of tenant in both Acts should be aligned. This provisional recommendation was adopted in the subsequent Report: n 3 above at para 4.9.

[42] In recognition of this, the Law Commission advocated in its Working Paper that the concepts of 'business' as employed within the two Acts should be harmonised, but was more diffident

283

Holding

10.10 For the purposes of both authorisation and compensation, the improvement must be carried out 'on' the holding, which includes the airspace above.[43] As shown, under section 17 the term 'holding' is defined so as to include the entirety of the premises demised to the tenant and this, sensibly, entails that improvements to land other than that demised fall to be discounted. Unlike section 23(1) of the Landlord and Tenant Act 1954, therefore, the definition is not limited to those parts of the premises occupied by the tenant for the purposes of a business. Indeed, there is no requirement that the tenant occupy the premises at all. Instead, the Act requires merely that the demised premises be used wholly or partly for business purposes. The terms 'use' and 'occupy' are clearly not interchangeable for these purposes.[44] The 1927 Act, therefore, places emphasis upon the *de facto* use of the holding and does not require the business, trade or profession to be that of the tenant. This emphasis upon use, as opposed to occupation, also avoids a number of difficulties posed by the 1954 Act (for example, as regards companies, partnerships and trusts).

Premises

10.11 The meaning of the term 'premises' is, in practice, rarely disputed. At common law, premises include both the land and (if any) the buildings upon it.[45] In the context of the 1927 Act, it has been suggested that the terms 'holding' and 'premises' should be given distinct meanings: the former signifying the land, the latter referring exclusively to the buildings.[46] This suggestion was, however, rejected by Morton J in *National Electric Theatres Ltd v Hudgell* who held that, under section 17, both terms were to be ascribed a composite meaning.[47] A similar stance was adopted by Viscount Hailsham in *Whitley v Stumbles* where he defined the word 'premises' for the purposes of section 17 as being, 'not merely the actual buildings in which a trade is carried on, but also the land surrounding them, the easements granted as appurtenant to them, and any other incorporeal hereditaments which may form part of the premises in the strict legal sense of the

---

concerning the unification of the classes of specified exclusions (ibid at paras 6.8, 6.5). More specifically, the Working Paper embodied the view that compensation should not be available where the business user is in breach of the lease (at para 6.8).

[43] Section 1(1); see *Davies v Yadegar*, n 26 above; *Haines v Florensa*, n 17 above.

[44] *Land Reclamation Co Ltd v Basildon DC* [1979] 2 All ER 993; see also *Lee-Verhulst (Investments) Ltd v Harwood Trust* [1973] 1 QB 204.

[45] *Bracey v Read* [1963] Ch 88.

[46] This distinction is based upon the curious juxtaposition of the words within section 16 which deals with the landlord's right to reimbursement of increased taxes, rates or insurance premiums. There a demarcation between land and buildings is obviously necessary.

[47] [1939] Ch 553.

term'.[48] The term 'premises' is, therefore, one of technical meaning and embraces everything which is contained within the parcels clause of the lease. It refers to the subject-matter of the grant, but does not entail that an incorporeal hereditament (such as a right of way) standing alone can be classified as 'premises'. It is apparent from the wording of section 17 (and in particular the requirement that a trade or business be carried out 'thereat') that a physical context and connotation is intended. Accordingly, rights in the nature of an easement are relevant only in so far as they from part of a comprehensive demise.[49]

Lease

The requirement that there be both a lease and a tenant is designed to exclude licences from the ambit of Part I.[50] A wide definition of 'lease' is contained within section 25(1) and extends to tenancies, under-leases, assignments and agreements to create such interests.[51] There is no minimum term of lease stated and the definition embraces both fixed-term and periodic tenancies. The provisions of Part I apply, moreover, to a lease whether or not it was granted after the commencement date of the 1927 Act (24 March 1928).[52] By analogy with Part II of the Landlord and Tenant Act 1954, it would seem that a sub-letting, granted in breach of the terms of the head lease, would fall within the extensive definition of a tenancy.[53] A tenancy at will should, however, fall outside the catchment of the 1927 Act.[54]

10.12

Business User

The 1927 Act makes no attempt to define the terms 'trade', 'business' or 'profession' and, accordingly, the common law understanding of these terms is relevant. It is, however, important to note that the statutory gloss, as provided by section 23(2) of the Landlord and Tenant Act 1954, does not apply here. Under the 1954 Act, the definition of a business extends to a trade, profession, employment and any activity carried on by a body of persons, whether corporate or incorporate. The catchment of the 1927 Act is, however, narrower in scope and does not include, for example, activities carried on by a members' club or lettings for recreational purposes. In cases of dispute, it is for the court to determine, as an issue of fact, whether a particular activity falls within one category or another. The task will often prove straightforward for, as Greene MR explained in *Stuchery v Life*

10.13

---

[48] [1930] AC 544 at 547.

[49] See *Land Reclamation Co Ltd v Basildon DC*, n 44 above.

[50] *Euston Centre Properties Ltd v H & J Wilson Ltd* (1982) 262 EG 1079; *Wigan BC v Green & Son* [1985] 2 EGLR 242. The sometimes difficult distinction between a lease and a licence is analysed in Chapter 3.

[51] 'Tenant' is defined in the same section as being a person entitled in possession under any contract of tenancy however acquired.

[52] Section 17(1). Note that the parties cannot contract out of the Part I provisions: section 9.

[53] *D'Silva v Lister House Developments Ltd* [1971] Ch 17.

[54] *Hagee (London) Ltd v AB Erikson & Larson* [1976] 1 QB 209.

Assurance Co, 'there may be difficult cases, in general any person with a reasonable knowledge of affairs would not have much difficulty in saying what the legislation intended in regard to some particular activity'.[55] Although there is no requirement for a trade or business to be regularly carried on at the premises, by virtue of section 17(3) a profession must be practised on a regular basis in order to fall within the Part I provisions. This entails that seasonal, occasional and part-time business user will suffice, whereas irregular professional use most certainly will not. It can be argued, moreover, that mere ancillary or incidental use (for example, lettings to garage business vehicles, to accommodate employees or to store goods) will not attract the protection of the Act because such activities will not constitute a business carried on 'thereat' for the purposes of section 17.

Mixed User

10.14   The allusion within section 17(1) to partial or whole business user contemplates that a mixed use (that is, trade and residential) may be made of the holding. This is, indeed, accepted in section 17(4) which provides that, in cases of mixed use, the provisions of Part I apply if, and in so far as, the improvement relates to a trade, business or profession. Consequently, an improvement to be carried out on the residential part of the holding can neither be authorised nor be eligible for compensation under the 1927 legislation. Unlike the 1954 Act, however, Part I does not necessarily prevent a holding falling within the compensation scheme because it is (as a consequence of the mixed use) protected by other legislation such as the Rent Act 1977. As Greene MR observed in *Stucbery & Son v General Accident Fire & Life Assurance Corporation Ltd*:

> Once you have shown that a trade or business has been carried on the premises, you are not to have your claim for compensation . . . defeated by having it pointed out to you that, in addition to the trade or business, you are doing something else there. A very common class of case is where you have a shop and dwelling rooms over it. It is not to be said that a tenant is not entitled to compensation when the lease of his shop comes to an end merely because the demised premises include the dwelling rooms.[56]

Specified Exclusions

Mining Leases

10.15   A mining lease is defined in section 25(1) as a lease for any mining purposes or purposes connected therewith. The purpose of the lease will normally be apparent from its user clause, but at the end of the day, it is a question of fact.[57] To this end,

---

[55] [1949] 1 All ER 1026 at 1030.
[56] ibid at 1031.
[57] The court must ascertain whether it is a mining lease within the vernacular of 'the mining world, the commercial world and landowners at the time of the grant' (*per* James LJ in *Hext v Gill* LR 7, Ch App 699 at 719). In the absence of evidence to the contrary, however, the vernacular meaning at the date of the trial will prevail.

the court may, if necessary, admit extrinsic evidence to show whether or not a mining lease has been granted. As the exclusion refers to the purpose of the tenancy, it is not necessary to show that the land is actually used for mining purposes.[58] The expression 'mines and minerals' is not a definite term and potentially embraces all substances below the ground that are capable of being worked for profit.[59] For these purposes, however, it would appear that the expression is limited to solid substances which are capable of being excavated from the land.[60] Tenants under mining leases may, however, receive some security by virtue of the Mines (Working Facilities and Support) Act 1966, but there is no right whatsoever to compensation for improvements. This omission is justifiable in the context that mining necessarily involves the wasting of assets and resources. A similar exclusion is to be found in the 1954 Act.[61]

Agricultural Holdings and Farm Business Tenancies

Tenants of those agricultural holdings still governed by the Agricultural Holdings **10.16** Act 1986 have security of tenure and compensation for improvements offered under that legislative regime. Tenancies created after 1 September 1995, however, are classified as farm business tenancies and are subject to the Agricultural Tenancies Act 1995. Although the latter legislation offers farm tenants no security of tenure, it has innovated a new and, seemingly, more effective compensation scheme for farming tenants' improvements.[62] In relation to mixed user (for example, a partly agricultural and partly non-agricultural business), it may still prove difficult to determine whether the tenancy is protected by the business tenancy code or by the appropriate agricultural legislation. Nevertheless, under whichever scheme is appropriate the tenant has the potential entitlement, at the end of the lease, to claim compensation for improvements.[63] Again these tenancies also fall outside the catchment of the 1954 Act.

Service Tenancies

A holding let to a tenant as the holder of any office, appointment or employment **10.17** is excluded provided that the agreement is in writing and expresses the purpose for which the tenancy is created.[64] It is necessary that the landlord and the employer

---

[58] *O'Callaghan v Elliot* [1966] 1 QB 601.

[59] ibid.

[60] *Earl of Lonsdale v AG* [1982] 1 WLR 887. Following the lead given by Slade J, it is considered by K Reynolds and W Clark, *Renewal of Business Tenancies* (1997) at 370 that, 'On a literal reading the definition . . . would apparently include the lease of a factory where sand is graded and put into sacks (because that is the "making merchantable" of a mineral) and also the lease of an iron smelting plant'.

[61] See further Chapter 3.

[62] See generally Evans and Smith, n 23 above at 545–562.

[63] As regards farm business tenancies, however, the landlord can ensure that the tenancy remains governed by the provisions of the 1995 Act. Provided that the landlord and tenant give each other notice that they intend the tenancy to be, and to remain, governed by that Act, any future change of use will not affect the declared status of the tenancy.

[64] Section 17(2).

are the same person. Although open to some doubt, the agreement referred to in section 17(2) appears to be the contract which creates the tenancy and not the contract of employment. In addition, it is necessary that the letting is expressly made dependant upon the tenant continuing to hold the appropriate position. Service tenancies are also excluded from the protection of the 1954 Act.

Sublettings

10.18 A tenancy under which the premises are used for the business of residential sub-letting is excluded.[65] This is irrespective of whether the head tenant provides meals or services to the occupiers. Following *Graysim Holdings Ltd v P&O Properties Ltd*, such tenancies now also fall outside the catchment of Part II of the Landlord and Tenant Act 1954.[66]

Improvement

10.19 It is apparent that not every change to the tenant's holding can be classified as an 'improvement' for the purposes of Part I. It is unfortunate, therefore, that there is no definition of the term within the 1927 Act and no schedule of works (as, for example, contained in the Agricultural Holdings Act 1986) expressed to be within the ambit of the statutory scheme. In order to discern a meaning, it is necessary to look to the common law. As far as possible, the courts will give effect to the ordinary meaning of the word 'improvement'[67] and, hence, the term has been held to refer to an addition or alteration to an existing building which makes the demised property in some way better than before.[68] As Denning LJ concluded in *Morcam v Campbell-Johnson*: 'If the work which is done is the provision of something new for the benefit of the occupier, that is, properly speaking an improvement.'[69] Hence, the improvement must be assessed from the perspective of the tenant[70] and regard must be had to the demised premises and the context in which the issue arises.[71] Although a matter of construction in each case, the central issue is whether the tenant has achieved a more beneficial use of the holding.

10.20 The meaning of improvement is, therefore, to be given a liberal interpretation. Indeed, section 1(1) expressly states that 'the erection of any building' is within its ambit for these purposes. This opens the door to the classification of redevelopment as an improvement. Accordingly, in *National Electric Theatres Ltd v Hudgell* the demolition of a derelict cinema and its replacement by a row of shops and res-

---

[65] Section 17(3)(b).
[66] [1995] 4 All ER 831.
[67] *Leathwoods Ltd v Total Oil (GB) Ltd* (1986) 51 P & CR 20.
[68] *Wates v Rowland* [1952] 2 QB 12; *Re Scottish & Newcastle Breweries Ltd* (1985) 276 EG 77.
[69] [1956] 1 QB 106 at 115.
[70] *Balls Brothers Ltd v Sinclair*, n 7 above.
[71] *Haines v Florensa* above.

idences was held to constitute an improvement.[72] This was so even though a different business was to be carried on by the tenant and no part of the original structure was to remain. Similarly, in *Price v Esso Petroleum Co Ltd* the demolition of a service station and its replacement by another was held to be an improvement both in the ordinary meaning of the word and the framework of the lease in question.[73] Examples of other improvements for the purposes of Part I of the 1927 Act include the installation of a toilet;[74] the replacement of granite cladding with stainless steel cladding;[75] the removal of internal walls and the installation of a lift;[76] and the building of a wall, connecting electricity and fitting locks.[77] The common denominator is that the works all relate to the physical property. Accordingly, incorporeal improvements (for example, securing better access over neighbouring land and obtaining covenants restricting business competition) fall outside the scope of the Part I provisions.[78] The Law Commission, however, expressed the view in its Working Paper that such 'improvements' should be included when they enhance the value of the holding.[79]

D. The Statutory Right to Make Improvements

Section 3(4) of Part I of the 1927 Act enables certain tenants to obtain the authority of the court to carry out improvements which are prohibited by the lease. The only restrictions not overidden are those created for naval, military, air force and civil aviation purposes or for securing public rights over the foreshore or sea bed.[80] No equivalent right, however, is afforded to the landlord. In the High Court, the application for a certificate is made by claim form which must state the nature of the claim, the tenant's holding, the business carried on there and the particulars of the proposed improvement.[81] No witness statement or affidavit is to be filed in the first instance in support or in answer to any such claim form.[82] In the county court, the application is also by way of claim form which must state similar

10.21

---

[72] N 47 above.

[73] (1980) 255 EG 243.

[74] *Bresgall & Sons v London Borough of Hackney* (1976) 32 P & CR 442.

[75] *Land Securities v Receiver for the Metropolitan Police District* [1983] 2 All ER 254.

[76] *Billson v Residential Apartments Ltd*, n 28 above.

[77] *C & P Haulage v Middleton* [1983] 3 All ER 94.

[78] *Haines v Florensa*, n 17 above; see also *Land Reclamation Co Ltd v Basildon DC*, n 44 above.

[79] N 41 above at paras 6.10, 6.12. This did not form part of the recommendations contained in the Commission's 1989 Report, n 3 above.

[80] Section 3(4). No right to override absolute covenants exists in Northern Ireland: see the Law Reform Advisory Committee for Northern Ireland, Discussion Paper 3, *A Review of the Law Relating to Business Tenancies in Northern Ireland* (1992) at para 9.3.3. In its later Report, *Business Tenancies* (1994) Report No 1, however, it recommended that the Lands Tribunal should have the power to authorise tenant's improvements notwithstanding any term in the lease (at para 9.2.4).

[81] Rules of the Supreme Court, Order 97, r 2; Order 97, r 5.

[82] RSC, Order 97, r 5 1(3).

information as required in the High Court.[83] Here the respondent must in response file an answer to the claim. In both courts the defendant/respondent is the tenant's immediate landlord[84] and the certificate when issued must be embodied in the order.[85] The mechanism can be applied so as to allow the tenant to side-step the objections of a non-consenting landlord and, importantly, it offers a rare opportunity whereby the terms of an absolute covenant can be overridden.[86] The tenant enjoys the additional benefit that, once an improvement is permitted by the Act, the foundation for a later claim for compensation is laid. It is, however, a pre-condition of a successful compensation claim that the section 3 procedures have been followed. Even where the lease does not prohibit improvements, it is still necessary for the tenant to serve a preliminary notice in order to be eligible for compensation. The court's jurisdiction to certify that the proposed works constitute 'a proper improvement', however, does not depend upon whether the tenant intends subsequently to claim compensation, nor is it relevant that the landlord's objection is that compensation might become payable.[87]

Tenant's Notice

10.22   The Act enables a tenant, who seeks to make an improvement, to serve a preliminary notice on the immediate landlord declaring this intention.[88] The notice may be served by the tenant at any time during the lease subject to the proviso that the landlord must be given three months within which to object.[89] As the Law Commission's Working Paper recognised, prior notice is necessary as: 'Improvements can affect a property's value for insurance, rating and other purposes. The landlord's own financial plans may be significantly affected by the knowledge or the lack of knowledge.'[90] It is imperative that this preliminary notice is served because without it there exists no right to carry the improvement out, or subsequently to obtain compensation for it, under the 1927 Act. The Act, however, offers no prescribed form for the notice to adopt and states only that it must be in

---

[83]   County Court Rules, Order 43, r 2(1).

[84]   RSC, Order 97, r 5(2); CCR, Order 43, r 4(3).

[85]   RSC, Order 97, r 5(4); CCR, Order 43, r 4(4).

[86]   It is arguable that an absolute prohibition can also be disregarded when the improvement is required in order to comply with a statutory requirement, for example, under the Factories Act 1961.

[87]   See Reynolds and Clark, n 60 above at 372: 'In other words, the landlord is entitled to object to the granting of a certificate only upon the merits of the proposed works.'

[88]   If the immediate landlord is also a tenant, it is the mesne landlord's duty to serve copies forthwith on any superior landlord: RSC, Order 97, r 4(2); CCR, Order 43, r 3(2). A failure to do so will debar the mesne landlord from claiming, from the superior landlord, the compensation paid to the tenant: section 8(1).

[89]   See below. Although the tenant must still serve a preliminary notice, if the improvement is to be made under a statutory obligation the landlord cannot object: section 48(1) of the Landlord and Tenant Act 1954.

[90]   N 41 above at para 5.9.

writing.[91] In *Deerfield Travel Services Ltd v Wardens & Society of the Ministry or Art of the Leathersellers of the City of London*, the Court of Appeal accepted that, as no prescribed form exists for this type of notice, whether a document is to be treated as sufficient for these purposes is to be judged objectively.[92] The yardstick advocated was what a reasonable, sensible businessman would make of the documentation served. There the tenant wrote to the landlord, enclosing outline plans, asking for consent to carry out the improvement. Although the letter did not expressly refer to the 1927 Act, it made plain that a contribution was expected from the landlord. As no obligation to contribute to costs arises except under the 1927 Act, it was necessarily implicit that the tenant was serving a section 3 notice. Both Lawton and Templeman LJJ declined to decide whether a notice which does not refer, expressly or impliedly, to the Act would be valid, whereas, in *Oldschool v Caplin*, Gray QC had no such reservation. He concluded that a notice, which did not inform the landlord that it was the first step in a compensation claim, was ineffective: 'In order for it to be an adequate notice, the attention of the landlord must be directed to the existence of a liability under the Landlord and Tenant Act 1927. If it does so, in whatever terms and although the Act of 1927 is not mentioned, it constitutes a sufficient notice for the purposes of section 3.'[93] This approach is clearly sensible in the light that the notice triggers off an array of statutory rights for both parties.

Specifications and Plans

Section 3(1) provides that this notice of intention must be served on the landlord **10.23**
or landlord's agent 'together with a specification and plan showing the proposed improvement and the part of the existing premises affected thereby'.[94] The initial plan may be in outline form, but it must provide sufficient information so as to enable the landlord to make a considered response to the tenant's proposal. The landlord need not be informed as to the quality of the proposed works because it is assumed that the works will be done in the ordinary way and with proper materials and workmanship.[95] There is, however, no requirement that the notice, specification and plan be served at the same time. It is, indeed, common for the tenant to serve a notice of intention and to supply the plans when they have been drawn up. If not contemporaneous, the documents must refer, either expressly or

---

[91] Section 23(1).
[92] (1983) 46 P & CR 132.
[93] (1994) 8 August (HC).
[94] In the *Deerfield* case, n 92 above, it was accepted that there might be difficult distinctions to be drawn between proposed works of improvement and works of repair; see Denning LJ's examples of the distinction in *Morcam v Campbell-Johnson*, n 69 above at 114, 115. This lack of certainty will not, however, invalidate the notice. The court can decide the issue later when the lease has ended and the tenant has made a claim for compensation.
[95] In *Oldschool v Caplin*, n 93 above, the High Court held that, where the plan/specifications omit certain works proposed, the notice is not invalidated, but the tenant cannot claim compensation for the undisclosed aspects of the improvement works.

implicitly, to the tenant's notice of intention and, understandably, the process is initiated only when the last part is served.[96] A failure to request additional details, provided that the landlord is aware of the purpose of the notice, will imply that the stated details are sufficient. Where further details are requested by a landlord, who is aware of the purpose of the notice, the effective date of the notice is not the original date of service, but the date when the additional information is provided.[97]

Landlord's Response

10.24 Within three months of the date of service of the tenant's preliminary notice, the landlord may serve a notice of objection in response.[98] Where an objection is raised, which cannot be resolved by agreement between the parties, the onus is upon the tenant to obtain the authorisation of the court. Although no form is prescribed, the landlord's notice must make clear that there is objection to the carrying out the proposed improvement by the tenant. It is not enough for the landlord merely to dispute the status of the works (for example, to argue that they are in reality works of repair) and to contend that they are outside the scope of section 3.[99] If no effective notice is served by the landlord, the improvement can then be carried out according to the tenant's stated proposals.

Landlord's Counter-Offer

10.25 As an alternative (but preferably in addition) to serving a notice of objection, the landlord may offer to carry out the improvement in return for a reasonable increase of rent. As the Law Commission pointed out in its Working Paper, this option is available so as to allow the landlord 'to choose to invest ascertainable amounts immediately rather than face contingent claims [for compensation] whose amount and timing must be uncertain. It means that the improvement that the tenant wants can be made, although the financial consequences will be different from those expected.'[100] It is not open to the landlord to suggest that different works be carried out and the offer must encompass all the works proposed by the tenant. There is, of course, no guarantee that the workmanship will be of the same quality or that the costs of the works will be the same. The tenant, therefore, has

---

[96] Although no obligation rests upon the tenant to serve the preliminary notice on a superior landlord, the tenant is obliged to comply with a request from any landlord to supply copies of plans and specifications of the proposed improvement: section 3(3).

[97] In the *Deerfield* case, n 92 above, the notice was completed only when the tenant forwarded to the landlord the architect's final drawings some two months after the letter of intention. It was, as Templeman LJ put it, '[the] last nail in the coffin so far as the notice was concerned' (at 141).

[98] As regards a superior landlord, a notice of objection will be served directly on the tenant intending to carry out the works. Section 8(1), however, only entitles the superior landlord to object if the mesne landlord has previously served on the superior landlord copies of the tenant's proposals.

[99] *Deerfield Travel Services Ltd v Wardens & Society of the Ministry or Art of the Leathersellers of the City of London*, n 92 above.

[100] N 41 above at para 5.10.

the option to decline the landlord's offer (which will necessitate the withdrawal of the improvement proposal) or to accept it. There appears to be no right of the landlord to insist upon carrying out the work against the tenant's wishes. On the tenant's acceptance of the offer, under section 10 the landlord is given the right to enter on the holding, at all reasonable times, in order to execute the works. Unlike a notice of objection, however, there is no requirement that the landlord's offer be made within a three-month period following the tenant's preliminary notice.

Rentalisation

As to the proposed rental increase following the performance of the landlord's **10.26** offer, the landlord can suggest a figure and/or leave it to the determination of the court. It is implicit that the new rent will be payable only from the completion of the landlord's works. Unlike the setting of an interim rent, however, no machinery is provided by which the reasonable increase in rent can be calculated. There is, in addition, no decided authority concerning how this calculation is to be undertaken. Nevertheless, it is strongly arguable that the rental increase should reflect the increased letting value of the premises after completion of the works by the landlord. This emphasis upon value (and not cost) is, moreover, consistent with the approach, pivotal to the Part I provisions, that the improvement is to increase the letting value of the holding at the end of the lease.[101] It is to be appreciated that this rentalisation of the costs of the works may have VAT implications for the tenant. As the tenant will not be paying directly for the improvements, VAT is irrecoverable on those costs. As Tromans argues, the tenant should ask the landlord to make the election to waive exemption to VAT in such circumstances so as to enable the landlord to recover VAT and, thereby, reduce the capital payments recovered through the increased rent.[102]

Certification by the Court

Where the landlord has not formally objected to the works, the tenant can carry **10.27** out the improvement as proposed. In this case, it is not necessary that the works be calculated to add to the letting value, nor is it of relevance that the improvement is unreasonable, unsuitable and injurious to the value of other property of the landlord. The court simply has no jurisdiction to intervene and cannot, therefore, modify the tenant's plans or attach conditions. The moral which emerges is that the landlord should serve a notice of objection in all cases where there exists some dissatisfaction with the tenant's proposals. If the landlord makes a timely and formal objection to the tenant's proposals, and provided that the works have not been completed,[103] the tenant must apply to the court so that the improvement can be

---

[101] See further Reynolds and Clark, n 60 above at 377–378.
[102] N 25 above at 336.
[103] The court has no jurisdiction when the works have already been carried out by the tenant (or the landlord): *Hogarth Health Club Ltd Westbourne Investments Ltd* (1990) 2 EG 69. The mere fact

authorised.[104] At the outset, the court will seek to ascertain whether the preliminary notice was served on the landlord(s) and that all landlords have been offered an opportunity to be heard.

Conditions of Certification

10.28 Before the court can certify the intended works as being a 'proper improvement', section 3(1) requires the tenant to establish three further issues. First, that the improvement is of such a nature as to be calculated to add to the letting value of the holding at the end of the tenancy.[105] This requirement envisages that an improvement can have detrimental as well as beneficial aspects and that, regardless of its utility to the tenant, authorisation should not be given unless there is some measurable gain for the landlord.[106] If the lease has many years left to run, the tenant might find it difficult to convince the court that the improvement will add to the letting value in the long term. As the improvement is likely to become obsolete with the passage of time, it may, thereby, generate no benefit to the reversion which will survive the term of the lease. Expert evidence, on behalf of both parties, will normally be appropriate here. Second, the tenant must establish that the improvement is reasonable and suitable to the character of the holding. Either party is able to introduce expert evidence on this issue. By way of preventing the involvement of third parties, section 3(2) allows only the landlord and any superior landlord (whether or not served with a copy of the tenant's preliminary notice) to argue that 'the improvement is calculated to injure the amenity and inconvenience of the neighbourhood'. This prevents neighbouring property owners and local action groups from having a direct voice in the proceedings. Third, it must be shown that the works will not diminish the value of any other property belonging to the landlord or a superior landlord. There is no requirement that this diminution be substantial and it would follow that (excepting *de minimis*) proof of any diminution will undermine the tenant's application. Again expert evidence may assist the parties.

Discretion of the Court

10.29 Once vested with jurisdiction the court can adopt an interventionist role. If satisfied that, on a balance of probabilities, the three conditions are made out by the

---

that the works have been commenced, however, does not deprive the court of the ability to issue a certificate.

[104] As shown, the manner of this application is prescribed by RSC, Order 97, r 5; CCR, Order 43, r 4.

[105] Where the improvement increases the rateable value of the holding and/or insurance premiums, and the landlord is liable to meet such payments, the landlord can claim extra rent corresponding to the increase in liability: section 16. If the tenant refuses to pay the additional amount, the landlord can exercise the remedies of distress and forfeiture.

[106] Section 1(1); see also *National Electric Theatres Co Ltd v Hudgell*, n 47 above.

tenant, the court enjoys the discretion whether or not to issue a certificate. Section 3(1), therefore, imposes no obligation on the court to grant the application. Unlike the gauging of reasonableness and suitability, there is no prescription as to what evidence may or may not influence the exercise of the court's discretion. Hence, the court could draw its own conclusion that the improvement is undesirable, out of keeping with the neighbourhood or otherwise against the local interest.[107] The court may also make modifications as it sees fit to the tenant's specifications or plans or attach reasonable conditions to the certification. As mentioned above, the discretion to approve the improvement is abrogated when the landlord has offered to carry out the works in return for a reasonable increase in rent. In that instance, a certificate can be granted only when the tenant can show that the landlord has failed to carry out the undertaking. Although no statutory time limit is set within which the landlord must perform the offer, the agreement (or, if a notice of objection was served, the undertaking to the court) should stipulate a completion date. If not, presumably it will be implied that the works are to be completed within a reasonable period.

Carrying out the Works

In the situation where either no landlord's notice of objection has been served **10.30** (within the permitted time limit of three months) or the court has certified that the improvement is proper, section 3(4) allows the tenant to carry out the works despite any contrary provision in the lease. The provision, therefore, legitimises what might otherwise constitute a breach of covenant. If the improvement was not objected to by the landlord, the tenant may execute the works as detailed in the plan and specifications. As previously mentioned, this ability is unaffected by the fact that the improvement is unreasonable or unsuitable. There is, moreover, no time-frame prescribed within which the works are to be carried out by the tenant. Accordingly, the right to make an improvement which is not objected to by the landlord will, seemingly, extend across the remainder of the lease. If the tenant had accepted an offer by the landlord to execute the improvement, without the landlord having lodged a formal objection, the tenant remains free to carry out the works if the landlord fails to do so. Where the improvement is to be made subsequent to the court's authorisation, however, the works as certified (which may be different from those originally proposed) should be executed within such time as the court stipulates or as agreed between the parties.

A distinction is drawn within section 3(5) which suggests that the authorisation **10.31** does not lapse if the work is not commenced or completed within the specified time frame. Although in this scenario the provision expressly disallows the tenant's claim for compensation, it does not taint the authorisation itself. There is

---

[107] See Megarry J in *English Exporters (London) Ltd v Eldonwall Ltd* [1973] Ch 415.

also no right given to the court to revoke a certificate once granted (for example, where the tenant does not comply with a condition). The deprivation of compensation appears to be the only sanction available. If the court had been prevented from issuing a certificate on the basis of a landlord's offer to carry out the works, and where the landlord fails to carry out that undertaking, the tenant remains free to reapply to the court for a certification. This does not, however, require a new preliminary notice to be served by the tenant.

Certification of Execution

10.32 Once the works have been carried out by the tenant, the landlord may be asked to provide a certificate of execution to confirm that the work has been duly completed. Although there is no obligation upon the tenant to obtain such certification, the documentation could be of future evidential benefit because it proves that the improvement was carried out and establishes the date of its completion. This is of particular worth when a compensation claim is likely to be made many years in the future. A certificate will also be useful in establishing the extent of the disregard for improvements on renewal. The tenant is, however, obliged to pay the landlord's reasonable costs involved with the issue of this certificate.[108] If the landlord declines to issue a certificate of execution, or fails to do so within one month of the tenant's request, the tenant can apply to the court which, if satisfied that the improvement has been duly completed, must issue a certificate to that effect.[109]

Relationship with Compensation Scheme

10.33 The rights to make an improvement and to obtain compensation are inextricably interlinked to the extent that the tenant is not entitled to claim compensation for an improvement unless the formal procedures in section 3 have been followed: 'Unless he does that, he can never be eligible to make a compensation claim, even if the terms of his lease allow him to make whatever improvements he likes.'[110] The purpose of this interrelationship is, as the Law Commission acknowledged:

> [T]o ensure that the evidence identifying, and proving the eligibility of an improvement for compensation, will be available from the time the work was done. When the claim is finally made, the tenant (or the landlord) can produce plans and specifications, documents or a court order to show whether the improvement qualifies for consideration, and (if it was requested) a certificate that the improvement was duly executed by the tenant.[111]

---

[108] Section 3(1). Such costs may include, for example, the fees of a surveyor, architect and/or lawyer. Questions of reasonableness fall to be determined by the court.

[109] Section 3(6). This must be embodied in an order of the court: CCR, Order 43, r 4(4); RSC, Order 97, r 5(4).

[110] Law Commission Working Paper, n 41 above at para 1.10.

[111] ibid at para 5.2. The Working Paper, however, admitted that the preliminary procedure seemed unnecessary for claiming compensation: 'No formalities should be required before the tenancy comes to an end, other than a bare notification which it is fair for the landlord to have . . .' (at para 5.20).

The present process, thereby, necessitates that the tenant serves a preliminary notice on the landlord and, if the landlord objects to the works, obtains a certificate declaring the proposed works to be a proper improvement. Any conditions or modifications imposed by the court must, moreover, be complied with in order to ensure that the prospect of compensation exists. Hence, if the tenant does not adhere to any time-scale as set out by the court (or agreed with the landlord), no right to compensation arises.[112] If the landlord failed to object in the prescribed manner, the tenant is entitled to carry out the works and to obtain a certification of execution. This enables the tenant to make the improvement as originally proposed, but compensation is payable only if the improvement actually increases the letting value at the termination of the tenancy.

The Scope for Delay

Although in its Report the Law Commission advocated the abolition of the compensation scheme, it did recommend the retention of the authorisation procedure without alteration.[113] The usefulness of section 3 was neither doubted not questioned. Although not frequently relied upon, the Commission acknowledged that the provision serves a useful purpose in its own right and acts as a negotiating lever with landlords. Nevertheless, the major defect with the current scheme is that, due to the formalities and time-limits inherent in the system, the authorisation procedure is patently not expeditious. Delay can be worked by a landlord to the disadvantage of a tenant. As Staughton LJ observed: 'There may in these days be some injustice in this area of the law. A landlord may object to the tenant's proposed improvement for little or no reason, and thus hold it up until the county courts can provide a hearing with no penalty other than costs.'[114] He also accepted that landlords might use delay in order to obtain a better bargain than that which would be achieved before the court. Although the Law Commission Working Paper put forward some suggestions as to how the operation of the present formalities could be improved, these reforms were not advocated in the subsequent Report.

10.34

E. Compensation for Tenant's Improvements

Subject to a variety of limitations and conditions, section 1(1) facilitates the payment of compensation for an improvement which has been previously authorised

10.35

---

[112] Section 5(5).

[113] N 3 above at para 4.6. At para 4.1 it was admitted that: 'The modernisation of business property is probably more effectively encouraged by statutory intervention which deters landlords from unreasonably preventing their tenants from making improvements than by the statutory compensation scheme.'

[114] *Hogarth Health Club Ltd v Westbourne Investments Ltd*, n 103 above at 73.

under the provisions of Part I. Although compliance with the section 3 procedure is a prerequisite to any claim for compensation and might establish that the improvement may qualify for compensation, compliance does not itself guarantee payment. As Ormrod LJ demonstrated in *Pelosi v Newcastle Arms Brewery (Nottingham) Ltd*, 'section 1 of the 1927 Act clearly distinguishes between the right to compensation and the right to payment'.[115] In addition to the authorisation hurdles, it is necessary that the tenant makes a separate claim for compensation within strict time-limits. Further qualifying conditions also need to be satisfied before compensation becomes payable and payment can occur only when the lease has ended and the tenant has quit the premises.[116]

Ability to Claim

10.36 As demonstrated above, for the tenant to claim compensation the lease must fall within the catchment of the 1927 Act. This general condition must be satisfied both when the improvement was carried out and, it appears, when the lease ends.[117] The Act imposes further limits upon the tenant's right to compensation. First, the compensation provisions apply only to improvements effected after 24 March 1928.[118] Second, there is no compensation payable for an improvement carried out in pursuance of a statutory obligation unless that improvement was carried out after 1 October 1954.[119] Third, the improvement must not consist of a trade or other tenant's fixture which can be taken away at the end of the lease.[120] It is irrelevant whether such fixtures are actually removed or left for the landlord. This is simply a matter of choice for the tenant. Fixtures introduced by the tenant which are not removable (that is, landlord's fixtures) may, however, constitute an improvement and attract compensation.[121] Fourth, the improvement must also be calculated to add to the letting value of the holding following the termination of the tenancy.

Letting Value

10.37 If the improvement either detracts from or fails to increase the letting value, compensation for the tenant is, understandably, neither merited nor available. The

---

[115] N 5 above at 21.

[116] *Smith v Metropolitan Properties Co Ltd* [1932] 1 KB 314. The tenant's claim is, however, to be made before the end of the tenancy. The right to compensation and the amount can, moreover, be determined while the tenant is in possession.

[117] Section 1 employs the expression 'a tenant of a holding to which this Part of the Act applies'. Any intervening period of non-protection is of no consequence: see *Smith v Metropolitan Properties Co Ltd*, n 116 above.

[118] Section 2(1)(a).

[119] Section 48(1) of the Landlord and Tenant Act 1954.

[120] As Reynolds and Clark, n 60 above at 388 conclude: 'Presumably the question of whether the tenant is or is not entitled to remove his fixtures is to be considered at the date of termination of the tenancy, since otherwise a tenant who has wrongfully held over and failed to remove his fixtures within a reasonable period of time would, ironically, obtain the right to be compensated for them.'

[121] *New Zealand Government Property Corporation v HM & S Ltd*, n 1 above.

tenant's entitlement to compensation, therefore, remains throughout defeasible if the landlord can show that there is no enhancement of rental value. In making this assessment, section 1(2) requires that regard must be had to the purposes for which the landlord intends to use the premises following the termination of the tenancy. If the premises are to be demolished, structurally altered or used for a different purpose, the court must take on board these factors in so far as they effect the residual value of the improvement. The court is also directed to have regard to the time likely to elapse between the termination of the tenancy and the works of development or change of use coming to fruition. It should be appreciated, moreover, that the 1927 Act does not offer the landlord compensation for any loss of value to the reversion resulting from the tenant's works.[122] In its Working Paper, however, the Law Commission suggested that the Act should offer landlords compensation, payable by the tenant, if the value of the reversion is diminished by an improvement.[123] For the purposes of compensation, it is not a requirement that the improvement be reasonable and suitable to the character of the holding, nor is it relevant that it has produced a diminution of the value of any other property of the landlord. While these requirements are crucial as regards certification as a 'proper improvement', if no formal objection was raised by the landlord to the tenant's proposals then compensation might be payable for the works, regardless that they could not, if challenged, have been approved by the court.

Contractual Obligation

The improvement must not have been undertaken in consequence of an obliga- **10.38**
tion in a contract (including a building lease) supported by valuable considera-
tion.[124] There is, for example, no reason why this contractual obligation cannot be contained in the same instrument which grants the landlord's consent to carry out the works. The problem there lies in identifying valuable consideration which will normally require the landlord to offer some form of payment or rent reduction to the tenant. An obligation merely to carry out the works in a certain way, if the tenant decides to undertake the improvement, is insufficient to preclude compensation.[125] The obligation must be to make the improvement. It is also irrelevant whether the contract was entered into before or after the commencement of the 1927 Act. Nevertheless, there is no requirement that the contract be between landlord and tenant. In *Owen Owen Estate Ltd v Livett*, for example, the tenant was precluded from claiming compensation for new lavatories because of an obligation to carry out improvements contained in a contract

---

[122] In such circumstances, the landlord will have to seek redress in the tort of waste or to enforce any covenant/condition taken from the tenant to reinstate at the end of the tenancy: see *Mancetter Development Ltd v Garmanson Ltd* [1986] 1 All ER 449.
[123] N 41 above at para 6.24.
[124] Section 2(1)(b).
[125] *Godbold v Martin the Newsagents Ltd* (1983) 268 EG 1202.

with a sub-tenant.[126] If it were otherwise, the tenant could benefit under the Act in addition to having received consideration for carrying out the works. A potential disadvantage for the mesne landlord was, however, identified by Upjohn J:

> [A]lthough he [the tenant] may be in a position to obtain from the under-tenant valuable consideration as recompense for the improvement, that will be only for the term of the sub-tenancy. It may be that the effect is to deprive the tenant of compensation for his improvement in so far as it will inure for the benefit of the reversioner . . . But I find it impossible to give other than a liberal interpretation to the words of the section . . .[127]

Predecessor in Title

10.39　For the purposes of compensation, it is necessary that the improvement was made, and the appropriate procedures satisfied, by the claimant or a predecessor in title. The definition of 'a predecessor in title' is provided in section 25(1) as being 'any person through whom the tenant . . . has derived title, whether by assignment, by will, by intestacy, or by operation of law'. In short, this means any person who had the title to the premises to which the tenant succeeded.[128] Prospective asignees of a lease should, therefore, raise requisitions as to whether the statutory procedure has been complied with. Although it is important that the expression is not too narrowly defined, it is insufficiently wide to encompass each and every person who at some time had some interest in the premises. Accordingly, improvements made by tenants under previous tenancies are currently not within the scheme.[129] In its Working Paper, however, the Law Commission believed that there should be a roll-over entitlement from one tenancy to the next.[130]

10.40　In *Pelosi v Newcastle Arms Brewery (Nottingham) Ltd*, Ormrod LJ commented on the curious nature of the statutory definition of a predecessor in title and the peculiar conjunction between 'any' and 'person' and 'has' and 'derived'.[131] Nevertheless, on somewhat complicated facts, the court experienced little difficulty in ensuring a common-sense (as opposed to a technical) application of the definition.[132] There the sub-tenant had carried out extensive works to the demised

---

[126] [1956] Ch 1.

[127] ibid at 6, 7.

[128] *Corsini v Montague Burton Ltd* [1953] 2 QB 126; *Pasmore v Whitbread & Co Ltd* [1953] 2 QB 226.

[129] See *Trustees of Henry Smith's Charity v Hemmings* (1983) 265 EG 383 where (in the context of the Rent Act 1977) it was stressed that the improvement must be carried out by a predecessor during the subsistence of the relevant tenancy. As Slade LJ admitted: 'A contrary conclusion would, I think, lead to ludicrous results which the legislature cannot conceivably have intended' (at 384).

[130] N 41 above at para 6.26.

[131] N 5 above at 23.

[132] The attitude of Ormrod LJ was that, if the usual meaning of 'predecessor in title' was to be employed, Parliament would not have included a definition of the term within the 1927 Act. He added, at 23: 'The Act is not concerned with proof of title, as such, but with entitlement to and

premises. The sub-tenancy was later assigned and the assignee subsequently bought out the mesne landlord's residual interest. The assignee then sought £60,000 compensation for the improvement carried out by, it was argued, a predecessor in title. The appellate court held that, although the assignee ended up with a different title from that of the predecessor, the assignee's title was historically derived from the sub-tenant and that this sufficed for these purposes.[133] The approach advocated by the landlords entailed that they would have been able to take the benefit of an improvement, carried out with their knowledge and approval, without the payment of compensation. As Fox LJ concluded, 'That would be a very surprising and unfair result'[134] and, as Bush J added, 'artificial in the extreme'.[135]

Notice of Claim

In order to claim compensation, the tenant must serve a notice of claim on the landlord towards the end of the lease. At the stage when the claim must be initiated, the tenant may be unsure whether a statutory renewal will be granted under the Landlord and Tenant Act 1954. Nevertheless, the tenant would be wise to serve the notice of claim within the time-limits considered below as, if renewal is eventually refused, no compensation for improvements will otherwise be payable. The notice, moreover, must be in writing and be signed by the tenant or tenant's agent. It must also contain certain prescribed details. The details to be provided are the names and addresses of the claimant and the immediate landlord; the holding to which the claim refers and the trade or business carried on thereat; the nature of the claim; the costs and particulars of the improvement (including its completion date); and the amount of compensation claimed.[136] If the notice omits such information, it will be rendered invalid.[137]

10.41

Time Limits

As mentioned, the notice of claim must be served within certain time-limits and these are imposed by section 47 of the Landlord and Tenant Act 1954. The time-limits vary, however, according to how the lease was terminated and, it is to be

10.42

---

liability to pay compensation. The scheme of the Act is to pass this liability back eventually to the person who benefits financially.'

[133] As Fox LJ made clear (ibid) the Act is referring to the predecessor in title to the tenant's entitlement in possession to the holding under the tenancy. See *Williams v Portman* [1951] 2 KB 948 where the tenant did not derive title from the sub-tenant. As regards an improvement carried out by a sub-tenant, the mesne landlord cannot claim compensation unless the mesne landlord has paid, or is liable to pay, compensation to the sub-tenant.

[134] ibid at 24.

[135] ibid at 26.

[136] RSC, Order 97, r 4; CCR, Order 43, r 3.

[137] *British & Colonial Furniture Co Ltd v William McIlroy Ltd* [1952] 1 KB 107.

appreciated, they cannot be extended by the court.[138] Following the House of Lord's decision in *Kammins Ballrooms Ltd v Zenith Investments (Torquay) Ltd*,[139] however, these time-limits can be waived by the landlord. The somewhat cumbersome rules relating to timing are as follows:[140]

(a) where the tenancy expires by effluxion of time, the notice must be served within a period not earlier than six nor later than three months before the contractual expiry date;[141]

(b) where, as is most common, the lease is ended by the service (by either party) of a notice to quit, whether at common law or under the Landlord and Tenant Act 1954, the claim must be made within the period of three months beginning on the date the notice was served.[142] This may be different from the date from which the notice takes effect;[143]

(c) where the tenancy is terminated by forfeiture or re-entry, the notice of claim must be served within the three months commencing with the effective date of the possession order (or the date on which it ceases to be the subject of an appeal, if later) or, if there is no order, the date of actual re-entry;[144]

(d) where the tenancy is terminated by the tenant's section 26 request for a new tenancy under the 1954 Act, the claim must be made within three months starting from the date on which the landlord gave a counter notice or, if none, the latest date on which such counter notice could have been given.[145]

Quantum

10.43 Section 1(3) provides that, in the absence of agreement, all issues of quantum are to be determined by the court. As mentioned above, the tenant must state the amount claimed in the notice of claim, but it is clear from the wording of section 1(3) that this may be subject to later negotiation with the landlord. A statutory formula is, however, employed to calculate compensation so as to ensure that the amount payable mirrors the residual value of the improvement to the landlord. As the value falls to be calculated at the end of the lease, inflation can make compensation an onerous obligation for the landlord. Interest, however, becomes payable

---

[138] *Donegal Tweed Co Ltd v Stephenson* (1928) 98 LJKB 657 (a case decided under the repealed section 5 of the 1927 Act).

[139] [1971] AC 850.

[140] Note that the Law Commission's Working Paper recommended the simplification of these time-conditions and concluded that a claim should be made during the three months following the end of the tenancy (howsoever determined) and that no earlier or later applications should be entertained: n 41 above at para 6.55.

[141] Section 47(2).

[142] Section 47(1). In *Allied Iron Founders Ltd v John Smedley Ltd* [1952] 1 All ER 1344 it was held that, although an unexpired notice to quit had been served on the sub-tenant, the sub-tenancy terminated at the earlier point when the head lease ended.

[143] *Hare v Gocher* [1962] 2 QB 641.

[144] Section 47(3),(5).

[145] Section 47(1).

only from the time of the tenant's proceedings. The current formula is set out in section 1(1) and provides that the compensation awarded cannot exceed the lesser of two amounts.[146] First, the net addition to the value of the holding as a whole which is directly attributable the improvement. This balances the benefit of the improvement less against any detriment to the landlord.[147] Second, the reasonable cost of carrying out an identical improvement at the end of the tenancy, making allowance for any necessary repairs. The cost of these hypothetical works will be the subject of expert evidence. The proviso as to repair is designed so as to prevent the tenant obtaining a new-for-old, windfall gain and caters for a deduction equivalent to the cost (if any) of putting the improvement into a reasonable state of repair. This deduction does not apply, however, where the tenant is under a covenant to repair or to meet the cost of repair. In that situation, the landlord will have to rely upon a financial action for breach of covenant.

Landlord's Intended Use

As previously mentioned, the court is directed by section 1(2) to look at the purposes for which the landlord intends to use the premises. Consequently, the tenant's claim may be refused or reduced where the landlord intends to demolish or alter the premises, or to establish a different business user, at the end of the tenancy. The notion being that this may negate or diminish the value of the improvement to the landlord. In order to gauge whether the benefit is affected by the landlord's plans, it is necessary to look at the time-scale for the proposed change. As the measure of compensation is geared to the value of the improvement to the landlord, if the landlord's plans will take effect in, say, two years from the termination date of the lease then the tenant's compensation will be calculated to reflect the limited gain to the landlord. The tenant enjoys the safeguard, however, that if the landlord fails to translate the stated intention into reality, within such time as fixed by the court, a fresh application would be entertained.

10.44

Other Deductions

Within the calculation of compensation, the court is directed to discount any benefits which the tenant (or predecessors in title) may have received from the landlord (or predecessors in title) in consideration of the improvement.[148] The term 'consideration', as employed here, should not be given its technical, contractual meaning and, seemingly, requires only that there be some nexus between the benefit and the improvement. The benefit must, however, be expressly or

10.45

---

[146] The Law Commission Working Paper, n 41 above at para 3.9, criticised the present formula as being 'capricious'.

[147] *National Electric Theatre v Hudgell*, n 47 above.

[148] Section 2(3). Normally, such benefit will form part of a contractual obligation on the tenant to carry out the improvement and, hence, will preclude the operation of the compensation scheme: section 2(1)(b).

impliedly referable to the improvement and cannot arise from any source other than the landlord or the landlord's predecessor in title. An example of when this discount may arise is where the landlord has gratuitously contributed to the tenant's expenditure or, in some cases, where the landlord has informally forgone or reduced rent as a result. Although unclear, it is likely that the value of the benefit will be assessed as at the time it is provided and not translated into current values. A further factor which may produce a depressive effect on the calculation of compensation is the ability of the landlord to deduct any sum outstanding from the tenant under the lease.[149] Rent arrears, or an agreed claim for lack of repair or dilapidations, for example, can be set off against the compensation payable.

Superior Landlords

10.46 Where a chain of tenancies exist in relation to the holding, the sub-tenant will make the claim for compensation against the immediate landlord as defined in section 25(1). Seemingly, the identity of the landlord is adjudged as at the time of the termination of the tenancy.[150] The mesne landlord may, however, be entitled to pass on the burden to the landlord immediately superior in title. For this right to arise, the mesne landlord must have served all copies of the documentation, relating to the sub-tenant's authorisation and compensation claims, upon the superior landlord within the prescribed time-frames discussed above.[151] This requirement is in recognition that otherwise the superior landlord would not have been able to join in the sub-tenant's proceedings and would not have been heard by the court. Accordingly, if the superior landlord is denied the opportunity to object and to present evidence, the mesne landlord is not entitled to claim compensation. On the understanding that the above procedures have been followed, the mesne landlord must make a claim for compensation in the same way as the sub-tenant.[152] In this instance, it will suffice that the claim is made at least two months before the end of the mesne landlord's term. It is, however, still necessary for the mesne landlord to show that the improvement has increased the letting value of the holding. This reaffirms the central notion that compensation is to be paid by the landlord to whom the benefit has accrued.[153] If there is no residual

---

[149] Section 11(1). The tenant can in turn deduct any amounts owed to the landlord from the compensation payable by the landlord: section 11(2).

[150] *Nuthall (GC&E) Ltd v Entertainments & General Investment Corporation Ltd* [1947] 2 All ER 384. There is special provision for the situation where there has been a change of ownership of the reversion. Section 23(2) provides that, unless and until a tenant has received notice of the change and details of the new landlord, the original landlord will be deemed to be qualified so as to accept delivery and service of documents.

[151] Section 8(1).

[152] CCR Order 43, r 3(1); RSC, Order 97, r 4(1). In addition, Sch 1 of the Act allows the mesne landlord who has paid compensation (or carried out an improvement) to charge the holding as security for repayment from the superior landlord.

[153] See *Pelosi v Newcastle Arms Brewery (Nottingham) Ltd*, n 5 above.

benefit at the end of the mesne landlord's lease, no compensation can be claimed from the superior landlord.

Landlord's Tactics

Irrespective of the safeguards and restrictions contained in the 1927 Act, a land- **10.47** lord can be placed in a vulnerable position as against a tenant committed to the carrying out of improvements. In *National Electric Theatres v Hudgell*, Morton J recounted the following illustration of how grave hardship can befall the landlord:

> For instance, an investor might invest a small sum in a comparatively modest prop-
> erty, which was subject to a lease, and the lessee might pull down this small property
> and erect, for example, an expensive block of shops with flats over it and thereby
> impose on the landlord against his will an obligation to pay a very substantial sum by
> way of compensation at the end of the lease.[154]

There are, however, two ways in which a landlord can achieve self-protection and side-step the compensation provisions. The first, is to take a covenant from the tenant requiring reinstatement, at the end of the lease, on the landlord's demand. If reinstatement occurs, then there is no addition to the letting value of the holding and no compensation becomes payable. The second method concentrates on section 2(1)(b) which excludes from compensation an improvement carried out under a contractual obligation. This provides that, where the lease obliges the tenant to carry out the improvement (a term almost invariably found in building leases) compensation for that improvement is unavailable. A similar end can be achieved where the landlord issues a licence for alterations to be made by the tenant (that is, under a qualified covenant or on the relaxation of an absolute covenant). Provided that the landlord's consent obliges (as opposed to permits) the tenant to carry out the works, is unconditional and immediate and, crucially, is supported by valuable consideration, the compensation provisions will not apply. Consideration can be inserted into the licence itself or may be found in the relaxation of an absolute covenant. It should not be overlooked that landlords are compelled to take such indirect routes because, since 10 December 1953, it has not been possible directly to contract out of the compensation provisions.[155] Nevertheless, avoidance is widespread and, as shown, is simple to achieve. In its Working Paper, the Law Commission thought that control of such measures should be tightened and suggested specifically that reinstatement covenants should be limited in their effect.[156]

---

[154] N 47 above at 556.
[155] Section 49 of the Landlord and Tenant Act 1954.
[156] N 41 above at paras 6.48, 6.49.

F. Reform or Abolition?

10.48 There is much dissatisfaction with the present statutory provisions and there can be no doubt that the compensation scheme is in need of simplification and is unduly difficult to operate. The primary weaknesses of the existing provisions concern the inherently wasteful, complicated and cumbersome nature of the claims procedure; the unrealistic manner in which compensation is calculated; and the ease by which landlord's can circumvent the scheme. This was a sentiment echoed in the Law Commission Working Paper:

> [T]he aim of any reform should be to make it as effective as possible. This means that unnecessary preliminary formalities should be cut out; the details of the scheme should be clarified; it should as far as possible be integrated with other and more familiar legislation relating to business tenancies; and it should be related to perceived current needs.[157]

Although the Working Paper was impressive in that it put forward a series of straightforward proposals through which the existing weaknesses of the scheme could be overcome, the later Report of the Law Commission recommended the total abolition of the compensation provisions. The Report's thesis was simple: 'The statute book would be simplified by deleting a complex procedure of little practical use.'[158] This abolitionist stance is solely based upon the ground that, as the compensation provisions are seldom invoked, they must be devoid of practical worth.[159] The weight of a Law Commission recommendation is undeniable, but its judgments are, however, not beyond question.[160] This must be particularly so when there is a real threat that the rights of tenants are to be eroded. On a further examination of the reasoning underlying the move towards abolition, the case put forward in the Report appears distinctly shaky. The reasons given, which are considered below, may serve as an illustration of why there is a low take-up of the statutory right, but it is contentious to conclude that they (jointly or severally) justify the extinction of the scheme. Although the Conservative government later agreed that the compensation scheme should be abolished,[161] such action is unlikely within the foreseeable future. The change of government and the low political profile of the subject area should ensure that the present system will continue, at the least, for some years to come.

---

[157] ibid at para 4.7.

[158] N 3 above at para 3.21. As regards Northern Ireland, the Law Reform Advisory Committee for Northern Ireland Report recommended that the compensation scheme in operation there should also be abolished (n 80 above). As the Advisory Committee acknowledged: 'This matter is thus best left to market conditions and commercial decision' (at para 9.1.7). Such abolition has now occurred following the Business Tenancies (Northern Ireland) Order 1996.

[159] ibid at para 3.19.

[160] In its evidence to the Law Commission, for example, the Law Society concluded that more harm would be done by abolishing the scheme than by retaining it with modifications.

[161] See Department of the Environment, Press Release No 434, 19 July 1994.

Impact of the Landlord and Tenant Act 1954

In the light of the general availability of security of tenure for business tenants **10.49** under the 1954 Act, the Report argued the probability that: 'It is now no longer the case that a tenant who has made an improvement will necessarily lose the benefit of it at the end of the lease term; indeed, it is more likely that he will be entitled to retain possession under a new lease'.[162] There is no doubting that Part II of the 1954 Act gives comprehensive protection to those tenants within its scope. It is evident also that most potential claimants for compensation will, if both options are available, elect for a new tenancy (at a rent which will usually disregard the improvement) rather than reimbursement. Accordingly, the need for a compensation scheme is much less strong now than it was prior to 1954. Nevertheless, this is a far cry from the claim that the later Act renders its forerunner obsolete. First, there exist business tenants who do not seek a new tenancy because, for example, they intend to relocate or to cease trading. Second, the cautious business tenant may wish to have the fail-safe of compensation for improvements (as well as compensation for disturbance) in case the landlord successfully resists the application for a new lease. Third, certain tenants may fall outside the ambit of the 1954 Act and yet still be able to claim compensation under the Landlord and Tenant Act 1927. As shown, this possibility arises because the two Acts have different catchment provisions and different exclusions. Although this was known to the Law Commission, it concluded that disadvantage rarely occurs.

Complexity of the Claim Procedure

The elaborate procedure involved in the making of a compensation claim is advo- **10.50** cated as a contributory reason for the unpopularity of the statutory scheme.[163] The unwieldy and protracted nature of the claims procedure, and its last gasp defeasibility, can be viewed as a disincentive to potential claimants. In the context that for some tenants, such a claim may represent the only statutory right available, this would suggest logically that the scheme be made more accessible and convenient. It is an intriguing notion that the failure of the scheme to be user-friendly supports the extinction of the right it enshrines. As the Working Paper explained: 'The apparent paucity of compensation claims may be attributable in no small measure to the cumbersome preliminary formalities, neglect of which prevents many tenants even contemplating a claim, let alone succeeding in one.'[164]

Unsuitability to Retail Properties

The unsuitability of the compensation scheme to particular types of commercial **10.51** property was a further ground upon which the Report relied.[165] Despite the

---

[162] N 3 above at para 3.7.
[163] ibid at para 3.8.
[164] N 41 above at para 4.5.
[165] N 3 above at para 3.5.

misleading use of the plural, the Report managed only to conjure up retail properties as an example. The inappropriateness of the compensation provisions was alleged, once again, to be due to the slow and cumbersome nature of the claims machinery. It is curious that, irrespective of the Law Commission's view, the British Retailer's Association argued in favour of retaining the compensation scheme. It must be assumed that the Association see some practical worth in the present provisions. Once again the inescapable conclusion is that there is need for the simplification of the claims procedure.

Exclusion by Contract

10.52 The fact that the compensation provisions can be effectively side-stepped by the landlord was seized upon in the Report as being a major reason for the paucity of compensation claims.[166] Although it is not now possible directly to contract out of the Landlord and Tenant Act 1927, as shown there exist ways in which a landlord can arrange matters so that there is nothing to which the Act can apply. The Law Commission considered avoidance to be widespread and drew the conclusion that this evidenced the willingness of landlords and tenants to do without the scheme. This line of reasoning is hard to support. The tendency of landlords to use avoidance measures indicates that there is still potential value for tenants in the statutory right and suggests that the existing loopholes should be tightened. Indeed, the Working Paper recommended that the ability of the landlord to contract out of the scheme indirectly should be restricted by the legislature.[167]

Short Life-Span of Improvements

10.53 The Report accepted that tenants will usually invest in improvements that will pay for themselves within the term of the tenancy.[168] This is supported by the tendency of refurbishment and other improvements, due to changes in fashion and manufacturing techniques, to have a much shorter lived benefit and value. Accordingly, a tenant will calculate the value of the improvement in the context of the remainder of the lease and write off the expenditure over that period. It would be strange, indeed, for a business tenant not to take on board this type of commercial reasoning. To do so with accuracy will often render the compensation provisions redundant. As the compensation provisions relate only to improvements which benefit the landlord at the end of the lease then, as is likely to be the case with a short-term improvement, there is no benefit accruing to the landlord and there can be no compensation. This exercise in sensible accounting cannot, however, always be relied upon. There is no guarantee that a new lease will be obtained under the Landlord and Tenant Act 1954, but such an expectation could figure largely (and erroneously) in the tenant's overall calculation. Improvements

---

[166] ibid at para 3.12.
[167] N 41 above at para 6.48.
[168] N 3 above at para 3.13.

forced upon a tenant in compliance with a statutory obligation might also distort this balance-sheet approach. In addition, it overlooks the possibility that the tenant might contemplate a major improvement (for example redevelopment) which will maintain some practical benefit for the landlord at the end of the lease. To rely upon the short life-span of certain improvements, as the justification for the abolition of a scheme which caters primarily for long-term benefits is, therefore, myopic.

Ignorance

The Commission believed that the statutory right to compensation has lapsed into a modern obsolescence because tenants are ignorant of it.[169] Certainly, from the alleged prevalence of the lessor's avoidance tactics, the same cannot be said of commercial landlords. There can be no doubt that many business tenants are small traders who are unwilling to incur the cost of legal advice. In all probability, the same tenants would be unwilling to incur expenditure on major, long-term improvements. If such works are contemplated, it would be most unwise for legal advice not to be sought. It is likely, therefore, that those who remain ignorant of the scheme are often those who would not carry out works of improvement sufficiently substantial or long-term to be caught by the compensation provisions. It is unmeritorious to argue that the ignorance of the many should support abolition at the expense of the few. As the Working Paper recognised, many landlords and tenants may be ignorant of the provisions or consider them unimportant, but a substantial number regard the statute as relevant.[170]

10.54

No Residual Value

A ground for retention of the statutory right was advocated by the Law Society. The Society suggested that, although seldom invoked, the scheme operated in the background as a bargaining factor. This argument, seemingly based on an encouragement of the parties to agree compensation privately, was rejected in the Report. The Law Commission saw little evidence of express bargains for improvements and concluded that it was not a normal term of the lease.[171] To a limited extent the Law Commission was correct. It has to be admitted that a lease will not be likely to embody a compensation clause. It was, after all, this realisation which resulted in the enactment of the statutory right in 1927. Nevertheless, the Report failed to appreciate the other forms of private agreement that may be struck against the back-cloth of the compensation scheme. Such agreements may suggest that it is only in rare cases that the tenant need enforce the statutory right.

10.55

---

[169] ibid at para 3.14.
[170] N 41 above at para 1.12.
[171] N 3 above at para 3.20.

10.56 First, except where there is objection raised to a proposed improvement or dispute concerning the quantum of compensation, there is no need to go to court. Provided that the tenant complies with the procedural requirements, much scope is left for negotiation between the parties. Claims may be settled by valuers in the knowledge of the tenant's right. Second, the existence of the statutory scheme may spur the landlord into executing the improvement personally in return for a reasonable increase in rent. This would also take the matter outside the compensation provisions, provided always that the landlord carries out the undertaking. This can be beneficial to both parties. Third, the exclusion of improvements under a contractual obligation, supported by valuable consideration, may produce a contribution from the landlord (for example, a stay of a rent increase). Provided that the consideration is not nominal, this could prove mutually satisfactory to both parties. If the compensation scheme is abolished, these ancillary benefits for the tenant will cease also. The issue was put into perspective by the Working Paper, when it considered whether the machinery offered a standard against which landlords and tenants could negotiate for compensation: 'Looked at in this way, rather than by saying that the scheme is only rarely used, one should perhaps rather say that the figures show that it is still necessary for tenants regularly, although not in large numbers, to resort to their statutory rights.'[172]

---

[172] N 41 above at para 3.11. It remains a mystery, however, as to what 'figures' the Working Paper was referring.

APPENDICES

APPENDIX A

Landlord and Tenant Act 1927

Tenant's right to compensation for improvements

1.—(1) Subject to the provisions of this Part of this Act, a tenant of a holding to which this Part of this Act applies shall, if a claim for the purpose is made in the prescribed manner and within the time limited by section forty-seven of the Landlord and Tenant Act 1954 be entitled, at the termination of the tenancy, on quitting his holding, to be paid by his landlord compensation in respect of any improvement (including the erection of any building) on his holding made by him or his predecessors in title, not being a trade or other fixture which the tenant is by law entitled to remove, which at the termination of the tenancy adds to the letting value of the holding:

Provided that the sum to be paid as compensation for any improvement shall not exceed—

(a) the net addition to the value of the holding as a whole which may be determined to be the direct result of the improvement; or

(b) the reasonable cost of carrying out the improvement of the termination of the tenancy, subject to a deduction of an amount equal to the cost (if any) of putting the works constituting the improvement into a reasonable state of repair, except so far as such cost is covered by the liability of the tenant under any covenant or agreement as to the repair of the premises.

(2) In determining the amount of such net addition as aforesaid, regard shall be had to the purposes for which it is intended that the premises shall be used after the termination of the tenancy, and if it is shown that it is intended to demolish or to make structural alterations in the premises or any part thereof or to use the premises for a different purpose, regard shall be had to the effect of such demolition, alteration or change of user on the additional value attributable to the improvement, and to the length of time likely to elapse between the termination of the tenancy and the demolition, alteration or change of user.

(3) In the absence of agreement between the parties, all questions as to the right to compensation under this section, or as to the amount thereof, shall be determined by the tribunal hereinafter mentioned, and if the tribunal determines that, on account of the

intention to demolish or alter or to change the user of the premises, no compensation or a reduced amount of compensation shall be paid, the tribunal may authorise a further application for compensation to be made by the tenant if effect is not given to the intention within such time as may be fixed by the tribunal.

Limitation on tenant's right to compensation in certain cases

[NB See amendments in Part III of Landlord and Tenant Act 1954 s. 48]

2.—(1) A tenant shall not be entitled to compensation under this Part of this Act—

(a) in respect of any improvement made before the commencement of this Act; or

(b) in respect of any improvement made in pursuance of a statutory obligation, or of any improvement which the tenant or his predecessors in title were under an obligation to make in pursuance of a contract entered into, whether before or after the passing of this Act, for valuable consideration, including a building lease; or

(c) in respect of any improvement made less than three years before the termination of the tenancy; or

(d) if within two months after the making of the claim under section one, subsection (1), of this Act the landlord serves on the tenant notice that he is willing and able to grant to the tenant, or obtain the grant to him of, a renewal of the tenancy at such rent and for such term as, failing agreement, the tribunal may consider reasonable; and, where such a notice is so served and the tenant does not within one month from the service of the notice send to the landlord an acceptance in writing of the offer, the tenant shall be deemed to have declined the offer.

(2) Where an offer of the renewal of a tenancy by the landlord under this section is accepted by the tenant, the rent fixed by the tribunal shall be the rent which in the opinion of the tribunal a willing lessee other than the tenant would agree to give and a willing lessor would agree to accept for the premises, having regard to the terms of the lease, but irrespective of the value attributable to the improvement in respect of which compensation would have been payable.

(3) The tribunal in determining the compensation for an improvement shall in reduction of the tenant's claim take into consideration any benefits which the tenant or his predecessors in title may have received from the landlord or his predecessors in title in consideration expressly or impliedly of the improvement.

Landlord's right to object

3.—(1) Where a tenant of a holding to which this Part of this Act applies proposes to make an improvement on his holding, he shall serve on his landlord notice of his intention to make such improvement, together with a specification and plan showing the proposed improvement and the part of the existing premises affected thereby, and if the landlord, within three months after the service of the notice, serves on the tenant notice of objection, the tenant may, in the prescribed manner, apply to the tribunal, and the tribunal may, after ascertaining that notice of such intention has been served upon any superior landlords interested and after giving such persons an opportunity of being heard, if satisfied that the improvement—

(a) is of such a nature as to be calculated to add to the letting value of the holding at the termination of the tenancy; and

(b) is reasonable and suitable to the character thereof; and

(c) will not diminish the value of any other property belonging to the same landlord, or to any superior landlord from whom the immediate landlord of the tenant directly or indirectly holds;

and after making such modifications (if any) in the specification or plan as the tribunal thinks fit, or imposing such other conditions as the tribunal may think reasonable, certify in the prescribed manner that the improvement is a proper improvement:

Provided that, if the landlord proves that he has offered to execute the improvement himself in consideration of a reasonable increase of rent, or of such increase of rent as the tribunal may determine, the tribunal shall not give a certificate under this section unless it is subsequently shown to the satisfaction of the tribunal that the landlord has failed to carry out his undertaking.

(2) In considering whether the improvement is reasonable and suitable to the character of the holding, the tribunal shall have regard to any evidence brought before it by the landlord or any superior landlord (but not any other person) that the improvement is calculated to injure the amenity or convenience of the neighbourhood.

(3) The tenant shall, at the request of any superior landlord or at the request of the tribunal, supply such copies of the plans and specifications of the proposed improvement as may be required.

(4) Where no such notice of objection as aforesaid to a proposed improvement has been served within the time allowed by this section, or where the tribunal has certified an improvement to be a proper improvement, it shall be lawful for the tenant as against the immediate and any superior landlord to execute the improvement according to the plan and specification served on the landlord, or according to such plan and specification as modified by the tribunal or by agreement between the tenant and the landlord or landlords affected, anything in any lease of the premises to the contrary notwithstanding:

Provided that nothing in this subsection shall authorise a tenant to execute an improvement in contravention of any restriction created or imposed—

(a) for naval, military or air force purposes;

(b) for civil aviation purposes under the powers of the Air Navigation Act 1920;

(c) for securing any rights of the public over the foreshore or bed of the sea.

(5) A tenant shall not be entitled to claim compensation under this Part of this Act in respect of any improvement unless he has, or his predecessors in title have, served notice of the proposal to make the improvement under this section, and (in case the landlord has served notice of objection thereto) the improvement has been certified by the tribunal to be a proper improvement and the tenant has complied with the conditions, if any, imposed by the tribunal, nor unless the improvement is completed within such time after the service on the landlord of the notice of the proposed improvement as may be agreed

between the tenant and the landlord or may be fixed by the tribunal, and where proceedings have been taken before the tribunal, the tribunal may defer making any order as to costs until the expiration of the time so fixed for the completion of the improvement.

(6) Where a tenant has executed an improvement of which he has served notice in accordance with this section and with respect to which either no notice of objection has been served by the landlord or a certificate that it is a proper improvement has been obtained from the tribunal, the tenant may require the landlord to furnish to him a certificate that the improvement has been duly executed; and if the landlord refuses or fails within one month after the service of the requisition to do so, the tenant may apply to the tribunal who, if satisfied that the improvement has been duly executed, shall give a certificate to that effect.

Where the landlord furnishes such a certificate, the tenant shall be liable to pay any reasonable expenses incurred for the purpose by the landlord, and if any question arises as to the reasonableness of such expenses, it shall be determined by the tribunal.

Rights of mesne landlords

8.—(1) Where, in the case of any holding, there are several persons standing in the relation to each other of lessor and lessee, the following provisions shall apply:—

Any mesne landlord who has paid or is liable to pay compensation under this Part of this Act shall, at the end of his term, be entitled to compensation from his immediate landlord in like manner and on the same conditions as if he had himself made the improvement . . . in question, except that it shall be sufficient if the claim for compensation is made at least two months before the expiration of his term:

A mesne landlord shall not be entitled to make a claim under this section unless he has, within the time and in the manner prescribed, served on his immediate superior landlord copies of all documents relating to proposed improvements and claims which have been sent to him in pursuance of this Part of this Act:

Where such copies are so served, the said superior landlord shall have, in addition to the mesne landlord, the powers conferred by or in pursuance of this Part of this Act in like manner as if he were the immediate landlord of the occupying tenant, and shall, in the manner and to the extent prescribed, be at liberty to appear before the tribunal and shall be bound by the proceedings:

. . .

(2) In this section, references to a landlord shall include references to his predecessors in title.

Restriction on contracting out

[NB See amendments in Part III of Landlord and Tenant Act 1954 s. 49]

This Part of this Act shall apply notwithstanding any contract to the contrary, being a contract made at any time after the eighth day of February, nineteen hundred and twenty-seven:

. . .

Right of entry

The landlord of a holding to which this Part of this Act applies, or any person authorised by him may at all reasonable times enter on the holding or any part of it, for the purpose of executing any improvement he has undertaken to execute and of making any inspection of the premises which may reasonably be required for the purposes of this Part of this Act.

Right to make deductions

11.—(1) Out of any money payable to a tenant by way of compensation under this Part of this Act, the landlord shall be entitled to deduct any sum due to him from the tenant under or in respect of the tenancy.

(2) Out of any money due to the landlord from the tenant under or in respect of the tenancy, the tenant shall be entitled to deduct any sum payable to him by the landlord by way of compensation under this Part of this Act.

Application of 13 and 14 Geo 5 c 9, s 20

Section twenty of the Agricultural Holdings Act 1923 (which relates to charges in respect of money paid for compensation), as set out and modified in the First Schedule to this Act, shall apply to the case of money paid for compensation under this Part of this Act, including any proper costs, charges, or expenses incurred by a landlord in opposing any proposal by a tenant to execute an improvement, or in contesting a claim for compensation, and to money expended by a landlord in executing an improvement the notice of a proposal to execute which has been served on him by a tenant under this Part of this Act.

Power to apply and raise capital money

13.—(1) Capital money arising under the Settled Land Act 1925 (either as originally enacted or as applied in relation to trusts for sale by section twenty-eight of the Law of Property Act 1925), or under the University and College Estates Act 1925, may be applied—

(a) in payment as for an improvement authorised by the Act of any money expended and costs incurred by a landlord under or in pursuance of this Part of this Act in or about the execution of any improvement;

(b) in payment of any sum due to a tenant under this Part of this Act in respect of compensation for an improvement . . . and any costs, charges, and expenses incidental thereto;

(c) in payment of the costs, charges, and expenses of opposing any proposal by a tenant to execute an improvement.

(2) The satisfaction of a claim for such compensation as aforesaid shall be included amongst the purposes for which a tenant for life, statutory owner, trustee for sale, or personal representative may raise money under section seventy-one of the Settled Land Act 1925.

(3) Where the landlord liable to pay compensation for an improvement . . . is a tenant for life or in a fiduciary position, he may require the sum payable as compensation and any costs, charges, and expenses incidental thereto, to be paid out of any capital money held on the same trusts as the settled land.

In this subsection "capital money" includes any personal estate held on the same trusts as the land, and "settled land" includes land held on trust for sale or vested in a personal representative.

Power to sell or grant leases notwithstanding restrictions

Where the powers of a landlord to sell or grant leases are subject to any statutory or other restrictions, he shall, notwithstanding any such restrictions or any rule of law to the contrary, be entitled to offer to sell or grant any such reversion or lease as would under this Part of this Act relieve him from liability to pay compensation thereunder, and to convey and grant the same, and to execute any lease which he may be ordered to grant under this Part of this Act.

Provisions as to reversionary leases

15.—(1) Where the amount which a landlord is liable to pay as compensation for an improvement under this Part of this Act has been determined by agreement or by an award of the tribunal, and the landlord had before the passing of this Act granted or agreed to grant a reversionary lease commencing on or after the termination of the then existing tenancy, the rent payable under the reversionary lease shall, if the tribunal so directs, be increased by such amount as, failing agreement, may be determined by the tribunal having regard to the addition to the letting value of the holding attributable to the improvement:

Provided that no such increase shall be permissible unless the landlord has served or caused to be served on the reversionary lessee copies of all documents relating to the improvement when proposed which were sent to the landlord in pursuance of this Part of this Act.

(2) The reversionary lessee shall have the same right of objection to the proposed improvement and of appearing and being heard at any proceedings before the tribunal relative to the proposed improvement as if he were a superior landlord, and if the amount of compensation for the improvement is determined by the tribunal, any question as to the increase of rent under the reversionary lease shall, where practicable, be settled in the course of the same proceedings.

. . .

Landlord's right to reimbursement of increased taxes, rates or insurance premiums

Where the landlord is liable to pay any . . . rates (including water rate) in respect of any premises comprised in a holding, or has undertaken to pay the premiums on any fire insurance policy on any such premises, and in consequence of any improvement executed by the tenant on the premises under this Act the assessment of the premises or the rate of premium on the policy is increased, the tenant shall be liable to pay to the landlord sums equal to the amount by which—

(a) the . . . rates payable by the landlord are increased by reason of the increase of such assessment;

(b) the fire premium payable by the landlord is increased by reason of the increase in the rate of premium;

and the sums so payable by the tenant shall be deemed to be in the nature of rent and shall be recoverable as such from the tenant . . .

Holdings to which Part I applies

17.—(1) The holdings to which this Part of this Act applies are any premises held under a lease, other than a mining lease, made whether before or after the commencement of this Act, and used wholly or partly for carrying on thereat any trade or business, and not being—

(a) agricultural holdings within the meaning of the Agricultural Holdings Act 1986 held under leases in relation to which that Act applies, or

(b) holdings held under farm business tenancies within the meaning of the Agricultural Tenancies Act 1995.

(2) This Part of this Act shall not apply to any holding let to a tenant as the holder of any office, appointment or employment, from the landlord, and continuing so long as the tenant holds such office, appointment or employment, but in the case of a tenancy created after the commencement of this Act, only if the contract is in writing and expresses the purpose for which the tenancy is created.

(3) For the purposes of this section, premises shall not be deemed to be premises used for carrying on thereat a trade or business—

(a) by reason of their being used for the purpose of carrying on thereat any profession;

(b) by reason that the tenant thereof carries on the business of subletting the premises as residential flats, whether or not the provision of meals or any other service for the occupants of the flats is undertaken by the tenant:

Provided that, so far as this Part of this Act relates to improvements, premises regularly used for carrying on a profession shall be deemed to be premises used for carrying on a trade or business.

(4) In the case of premises used partly for purposes of a trade or business and partly for other purposes, this Part of this Act shall apply to improvements only if and so far as they are improvements in relation to the trade or business.

. . .

PART II
PROVISIONS AS TO COVENANTS NOT TO ASSIGN, ETC, WITHOUT LICENCE OR CONSENT

Provisions as to covenants not to assign, etc, without licence or consent

. . .

19.—(2) In all leases whether made before or after the commencement of this Act containing a covenant condition or agreement against the making of improvements without licence or consent, such covenant condition or agreement shall be deemed, notwithstanding any express provision to the contrary, to be subject to a proviso that such licence or consent is not to be unreasonably withheld; but this proviso does not preclude the right to require as a condition of such licence or consent the payment of a reasonable sum in respect of any damage to or diminution in the value of the premises or any neighbouring premises belonging to the landlord, and of any legal or other expenses properly incurred in connection with such licence or consent nor, in the case of an improvement which does not add to the letting value of the holding, does it preclude the right to require as a condition of such licence or consent, where such a requirement would be reasonable, an undertaking on the part of the tenant to reinstate the premises in the condition in which they were before the improvement was executed.

(3) In all leases whether made before or after the commencement of this Act containing a covenant condition or agreement against the alteration of the user of the demised premises, without licence or consent, such covenant condition or agreement shall, if the alteration does not involve any structural alteration of the premises, be deemed, notwithstanding any express provision to the contrary, to be subject to a proviso that no fine or sum of money in the nature of a fine, whether by way of increase of rent or otherwise, shall be payable for or in respect of such licence or consent; but this proviso does not preclude the right of the landlord to require payment of a reasonable sum in respect of any damage to or diminution in the value of the premises or any neighbouring premises belonging to him and of any legal or other expenses incurred in connection with such licence or consent.

Where a dispute as to the reasonableness of any such sum has been determined by a court of competent jurisdiction, the landlord shall be bound to grant the licence or consent on payment of the sum so determined to be reasonable.

(4) This section shall not apply to leases of agricultural holdings within the meaning of the Agricultural Holdings Act 1986 which are leases in relation to which that Act applies, or to farm business tenancies within the meaning of the Agricultural Tenancies Act 1995, and paragraph (b) of subsection (1), subsection (2) and subsection (3) of this section shall not apply to mining leases.

. . .

PART III
GENERAL

The tribunal

The tribunal for the purposes of Part I of this Act shall be the court exercising jurisdiction in accordance with the provisions of section sixty-three of the Landlord and Tenant Act 1954.

. . .

Service of notices

23.—(1) Any notice, request, demand or other instrument under this Act shall be in writing and may be served on the person on whom it is to be served either personally, or by leaving it for him at his last known place of abode in England or Wales, or by sending it through the post in a registered letter addressed to him there, or, in the case of a local or public authority or a statutory or a public utility company, to the secretary or other proper officer at the principal office of such authority or company, and in the case of a notice to a landlord, the person on whom it is to be served shall include any agent of the landlord duly authorised in that behalf.

(2) Unless or until a tenant of a holding shall have received notice that the person theretofore entitled to the rents and profits of the holding (hereinafter referred to as "the original landlord") has ceased to be so entitled, and also notice of the name and address of the person who has become entitled to such rents and profits, any claim, notice, request, demand, or other instrument, which the tenant shall serve upon or deliver to the original landlord shall be deemed to have been served upon or delivered to the landlord of such holding.

Application to Crown, Duchy, ecclesiastical and charity lands

24.—(1) This Act shall apply to land belonging to His Majesty in right of the Crown or the Duchy of Lancaster and to land belonging to the Duchy of Cornwall, and to land belonging to any Government department, and for that purpose the provisions of the Agricultural Holdings Act 1923, relating to Crown and Duchy Lands, as set out and adapted in Part I of the Second Schedule to this Act, shall have effect.

(2) The provisions of the Agricultural Holdings Act 1923, with respect to the application of that Act to ecclesiastical and charity lands, as set out and adapted in Part II of the Second Schedule to this Act, shall apply for the purposes of this Act.

. . .

(4) Where any land is vested in the official custodian for charities in trust for any charity, the trustees of the charity and not the custodian shall be deemed to be the landlord for the purposes of this Act.

Interpretation

25.—(1) For the purposes of this Act, unless the context otherwise requires—

The expression "tenant" means any person entitled in possession to the holding under any contract of tenancy, whether the interest of such tenant was acquired by original contract, assignment, operation of law or otherwise;

The expression " landlord" means any person who under a lease is, as between himself and the tenant or other lessee, for the time being entitled to the rents and profits of the demised premises payable under the lease; The expression "predecessor in title" in relation to a tenant or landlord means any person through whom the tenant or landlord has derived title, whether by assignment, by will, by intestacy, or by operation of law;

The expression "lease" means a lease, under-lease or other tenancy, assignment operating as a lease or under-lease, or an agreement for such lease, under-lease tenancy, or assignment;

The expression "mining lease" means a lease for any mining purpose or purposes connected therewith, and "mining purposes" include the sinking and searching for, winning, working, getting, making merchantable, smelting or otherwise converting or working for the purposes of any manufacture, carrying away, and disposing of mines and minerals, in or under land, and the erection of buildings, and the execution of engineering and other works suitable for those purposes;

The expression "term of years absolute" has the same meaning as in the Law of Property Act 1925;

The expression "statutory company" means any company constituted by or under an Act of Parliament to construct, work or carry on any . . . , tramway, hydraulic power, dock, canal or railway undertaking; and the expression "public utility company" means any company within the meaning of the Companies (Consolidation) Act 1908, or a society registered under the Industrial and Provident Societies Acts, 1893 to 1913, carrying on any such undertaking;

The expression "prescribed" means prescribed by County Court Rules, except that in relation to proceedings before the High Court, it means prescribed by rules of the Supreme Court.

(2) The designation of landlord and tenant shall continue to apply to the parties until the conclusion of any proceedings taken under or in pursuance of this Act in respect of compensation.

Short title, commencement and extent

26.—(1) This Act may be cited as the Landlord and Tenant Act 1927.

(2) . . .

(3) This Act shall extend to England and Wales only.

SCHEDULES

SCHEDULE 1

PROVISIONS AS TO CHARGES (s 12)

1.—A landlord, on paying to the tenant the amount due to him under Part I of this Act, in respect of compensation for an improvement . . . under that Part, or on expending after notice given in accordance with that Part such amount as may be necessary to execute an improvement, shall be entitled to obtain from the Minister of Agriculture, Fisheries and Food (hereinafter referred to as the Minister) an order in favour of himself and the persons deriving title under him charging the holding, or any part thereof, with repayment of the amount paid or expended, including any proper costs, charges or expenses incurred by a landlord in opposing any proposal by a tenant to execute an improvement or in contesting a claim for compensation, and of all costs properly incurred by him in obtaining the charge, with such interest, and by such instalments, and with such directions for giving effect to the charge, as the Minister thinks fit.

2.—Where the landlord obtaining the charge is not an absolute owner of the holding for his own benefit, no instalment or interest shall be made payable after the time when the improvement . . . in respect whereof compensation is paid will, in the opinion of the Minister, have become exhausted.

3.—Where the estate or interest of a landlord is determinable or liable to forfeiture by reason of his creating or suffering any charge thereon, that estate or interest shall not be determined or forfeited by reason of his obtaining such a charge, anything in any deed, will or other instrument to the contrary thereof notwithstanding.

4.—The sum charged shall be a charge on the holding, or the part thereof charged, for the landlord's interest therein and for interests in the reversion immediately expectant on the termination of the lease; but so that, in any case where the landlord's interest is an interest in a leasehold, the charge shall not extend beyond that leasehold interest.

5.—Any company now or hereafter incorporated by Parliament, and having power to advance money for the improvement of land, may take an assignment of any charge made under this Schedule, upon such terms and conditions as may be agreed upon between the company and the person entitled to the charge, and may assign any charge so acquired by them.

6.—Where a charge may be made under this Schedule for compensation due under an award, the tribunal making the award shall, at the request and cost of the person entitled to obtain the charge, certify the amount to be charged and the term for which the charge may properly be made, having regard to the time at which each improvement . . . in respect of which compensation is awarded is to be deemed to be exhausted.

7.—A charge under this Schedule may be registered under section ten of the Land Charges Act 1925, as a land charge of Class A.

SCHEDULE 2

PART I

Application to Crown and Duchy Land

1.—(a) With respect to any land belonging to His Majesty in right of the Crown, or to a Government department, for the purposes of this Act, the Commissioners of Crown Lands, or other the proper officer or body having charge of the land for the time being, or, in case there is no such officer or body, then such person as His Majesty may appoint in writing under the Royal Sign Manual, shall represent His Majesty, and shall be deemed to be the landlord.
. . .

2.—(a) With respect to land belonging to His Majesty in right of the Duchy of Lancaster, for the purposes of this Act, the Chancellor of the Duchy shall represent His Majesty, and shall be deemed to be the landlord.

(b) The amount of any compensation under Part I of this Act payable by the Chancellor of the Duchy shall be raised and paid as an expense incurred in improvement of land belonging to His Majesty in right of the Duchy within section twenty-five of the Act of the fifty-seventh year of King George the Third, chapter ninety-seven.

3.—(a) With respect to land belonging to the Duchy of Cornwall, for the purposes of this Act, such person as the Duke of Cornwall, or the possessor for the time being of the Duchy of Cornwall appoints, shall represent the Duke of Cornwall or other the possessor aforesaid, and be deemed to be the landlord, and may do any act or thing under this Act which a landlord is authorised or required to do thereunder.

(b) Any compensation under Part I of this Act payable by the Duke of Cornwall, or other the possessor aforesaid, shall be paid, and advances therefor made, in the manner and subject to the provisions of section eight of the Duchy of Cornwall Management Act 1863, with respect to improvements of land mentioned in that section.

Schedule 2

Part II

Application to Ecclesiastical and Charity Land

1.—(a) Where lands are assigned or secured as the endowment of a see, the powers by this Act conferred on a landlord in respect of charging land shall not be exercised by the bishop in respect of those lands, except with the previous approval in writing of the Estates Committee of the Ecclesiastical Commissioners.

. . .

(c) The Ecclesiastical Commissioners may, if they think fit, on behalf of an ecclesiastical corporation, out of any money in their hands, pay to the tenant the amount of compensation due to him under Part I of this Act, and thereupon they may, instead of the corporation obtain from the minister a charge on the holding in respect thereof in favour of themselves . . .

2.—The powers by this Act conferred on a landlord in respect of charging land shall not be exercised by trustees for ecclesiastical or charitable purposes, except with the approval in writing of the Charity Commissioners or the Board of Education, as the case may require.

APPENDIX B

Landlord and Tenant Act 1954

PART II
SECURITY OF TENURE FOR BUSINESS, PROFESSIONAL AND
OTHER TENANTS

Tenancies to which Part II applies

23.—(1) Subject to the provisions of this Act, this Part of this Act applies to any tenancy where the property comprised in the tenancy is or includes premises which are occupied by the tenant and are so occupied for the purposes of a business carried on by him or for those and other purposes.

(2) In this Part of this Act the expression "business" includes a trade, profession or employment and includes any activity carried on by a body of persons, whether corporate or unincorporate. (3) In the following provisions of this Part of this Act the expression "the holding", in relation to a tenancy to which this Part of this Act applies, means the property comprised in the tenancy, there being excluded any part thereof which is occupied neither by the tenant nor by a person employed by the tenant and so employed for the purposes of a business by reason of which the tenancy is one to which this Part of this Act applies.

(4) Where the tenant is carrying on a business, in all or any part of the property comprised in a tenancy, in breach of a prohibition (however expressed) of use for business purposes which subsists under the terms of the tenancy and extends to the whole of that property, this Part of this Act shall not apply to the tenancy unless the immediate landlord or his predecessor in title has consented to the breach or the immediate landlord has acquiesced therein.

In this subsection the reference to a prohibition of use for business purposes does not include a prohibition of use for the purposes of a specified business, or of use for purposes of any but a specified business, but save as aforesaid includes a prohibition of use for the purposes of some one or more only of the classes of business specified in the definition of that expression in subsection (2) of this section.

Continuation of tenancies to which Part II applies and grant of new tenancies

24.—(1) A tenancy to which this Part of this Act applies shall not come to an end unless terminated in accordance with the provisions of this Part of this Act; and, subject to the provisions of section twenty-nine of this Act, the tenant under such a tenancy may apply to the court for a new tenancy—

325

(a) if the landlord has given notice under section 25 of this Act to terminate the tenancy, or

(b) if the tenant has made a request for a new tenancy in accordance with section twenty-six of this Act.

(2) The last foregoing subsection shall not prevent the coming to an end of a tenancy by notice to quit given by the tenant, by surrender or forfeiture, or by the forfeiture of a superior tenancy unless—

(a) in the case of a notice to quit, the notice was given before the tenant had been in occupation in right of the tenancy for one month; or

(b) in the case of an instrument of surrender, the instrument was executed before, or was executed in pursuance of an agreement made before, the tenant had been in occupation in right of the tenancy for one month.

(3) Notwithstanding anything in subsection (1) of this section,—

(a) where a tenancy to which this Part of this Act applies ceases to be such a tenancy, it shall not come to an end by reason only of the cesser, but if it was granted for a term of years certain and has been continued by subsection (1) of this section then (without prejudice to the termination thereof in accordance with any terms of the tenancy) it may be terminated by not less than three nor more than six months' notice in writing given by the landlord to the tenant;

(b) where, at a time when a tenancy is not one to which this Part of this Act applies, the landlord gives notice to quit, the operation of the notice shall not be affected by reason that the tenancy becomes one to which this Part of this Act applies after the giving of the notice.

Rent while tenancy continues by virtue of s 24

24A.—(1) The landlord of a tenancy to which this Part of this Act applies may,—

(a) if he has given notice under section 25 of this Act to terminate the tenancy; or

(b) if the tenant has made a request for a new tenancy in accordance with section 26 of this Act;

apply to the court to determine a rent which it would be reasonable for the tenant to pay while the tenancy continues by virtue of section 24 of this Act, and the court may determine a rent accordingly.

(2) A rent determined in proceedings under this section shall be deemed to be the rent payable under the tenancy from the date on which the proceedings were commenced or the date specified in the landlord's notice or the tenant's request, whichever is the later.

(3) In determining a rent under this section the court shall have regard to the rent payable under the terms of the tenancy, but otherwise subsections (1) and (2) of section 34 of this Act shall apply to the determination as they would apply to the determiation of a rent under that section if a new tenancy from year to year of the whole of the property comprised in the tenancy were granted to the tenant by order of the court.

Termination of tenancy by the landlord

25.—(1) The landlord may terminate a tenancy to which this Part of this Act applies by a notice given to the tenant in the prescribed form specifying the date at which the tenancy is to come to an end (hereinafter referred to as "the date of termination"):

Provided that this subsection has effect subject to the provisions of Part IV of this Act as to the interim continuation of tenancies pending the disposal of applications to the court.

(2) Subject to the provisions of the next following subsection, a notice under this section shall not have effect unless it is given not more than twelve nor less than six months before the date of termination specified therein.

(3) In the case of a tenancy which apart from this Act could have been brought to an end by notice to quit given by the landlord —

(a) the date of termination specified in a notice under this section shall not be earlier than the earliest date on which apart from this Part of this Act the tenancy could have been brought to an end by notice to quit given by the landlord on the date of the giving of the notice under this section; and

(b) where apart from this Part of this Act more than six months' notice to quit would have been required to bring the tenancy to an end, the last foregoing subsection shall have effect with the substitution for twelve months of a period six months longer than the length of notice to quit which would have been required as aforesaid.

(4) In the case of any other tenancy, a notice under this section shall not specify a date of termination earlier than the date on which apart from this Part of this Act the tenancy would have come to an end by effluxion of time.

(5) A notice under this section shall not have effect unless it requires the tenant, within two months after the giving of the notice, to notify the landlord in writing whether or not, at the date of termination, the tenant will be willing to give up possession of the property comprised in the tenancy.

(6) A notice under this section shall not have effect unless it states whether the landlord would oppose an application to the court under this Part of this Act for the grant of a new tenancy and, if so, also states on which of the grounds mentioned in section thirty of this Act he would do so.

Tenant's request for a new tenancy

26.—(1) A tenant's request for a new tenancy may be made where the tenancy under which he holds for the time being (hereinafter referred to as "the current tenancy") is a tenancy granted for a term of years certain exceeding one year, whether or not continued by section twenty-four of this Act, or granted for a term of years certain and thereafter from year to year.

(2) A tenant's request for a new tenancy shall be for a tenancy beginning with such date, not more than twelve nor less than six months after the making of the request, as may be specified therein: Provided that the said date shall not be earlier than the date on which apart from this Act the current tenancy would come to an end by effluxion of time or could be brought to an end by notice to quit given by the tenant.

(3) A tenant's request for a new tenancy shall not have effect unless it is made by notice in the prescribed form given to the landlord and sets out the tenant's proposals as to the property to be comprised in the new tenancy (being either the whole or part of the property comprised in the current tenancy), as to the rent to be payable under the new tenancy and as to the other terms of the new tenancy.

(4) A tenant's request for a new tenancy shall not be made if the landlord has already given notice under the last foregoing section to terminate the current tenancy, or if the tenant has already given notice to quit or notice under the next following section; and no such notice shall be given by the landlord or the tenant after the making by the tenant of a request for a new tenancy.

(5) Where the tenant makes a request for a new tenancy in accordance with the foregoing provisions of this section, the current tenancy shall, subject to the provisions of subsection (2) of section thirty-six of this Act and the provisions of Part IV of this Act as to the interim continuation of tenancies, terminate immediately before the date specified in the request for the beginning of the new tenancy.

(6) Within two months of the making of a tenant's request for a new tenancy the landlord may give notice to the tenant that he will oppose an application to the court for the grant of a new tenancy, and any such notice shall state on which of the grounds mentioned in section thirty of this Act the landlord will oppose the application.

Termination by tenant of tenancy for fixed term

27.—(1) Where the tenant under a tenancy to which this Part of this Act applies, being a tenancy granted for a term of years certain, gives to the immediate landlord, not later than three months before the date on which apart from this Act the tenancy would come to an end by effluxion of time, a notice in writing that the tenant does not desire the tenancy to be continued, section twenty-four of this Act shall not have effect in relation to the tenancy unless the notice is given before the tenant has been in occupation in right of the tenancy for one month.

(2) A tenancy granted for a term of years certain which is continuing by virtue of section twenty-four of this Act may be brought to an end on any quarter day by not less than three months' notice in writing given by the tenant to the immediate landlord, whether the notice is given . . . after the date on which apart from this Act the tenancy would have come to an end or before that date, but not before the tenant has been in occupation in right of the tenancy for one month.

Renewal of tenancies by agreement

Where the landlord and tenant agree for the grant to the tenant of a future tenancy of the holding, or of the holding with other land, on terms and from a date specified in the agreement, the current tenancy shall continue until that date but no longer, and shall not be a tenancy to which this Part of this Act applies.

Order by court for grant of a new tenancy

29.—(1) Subject to the provisions of this Act, on an application under subsection (1) of section twenty-four of this Act for a new tenancy the court shall make an order for the grant of a tenancy comprising such property, at such rent and on such other terms, as are hereinafter provided.

(2) Where such an application is made in consequence of a notice given by the landlord under section twenty-five of this Act, it shall not be entertained unless the tenant has duly notified the landlord that he will not be willing at the date of termination to give up possession of the property comprised in the tenancy.

(3) No application under subsection (1) of section twenty-four of this Act shall be entertained unless it is made not less than two nor more than four months after the giving of the landlord's notice under section twenty-five of this Act or, as the case may be, after the making of the tenant's request for a new tenancy.

Opposition by landlord to application for a new tenancy

30.—(1) The grounds on which a landlord may oppose an application under subsection (1) of section twenty-four of this Act are such of the following grounds as may be stated in the landlord's notice under section twenty-five of this Act or, as the case may be, under subsection (6) of section twenty-six thereof, that is to say:

(a) where under the current tenancy the tenant has any obligations as respects the repair and maintenance of the holding, that the tenant ought not to be granted a new tenancy in view of the state of repair of the holding, being a state resulting from the tenant's failure to comply with the said obligations;

(b) that the tenant ought not to be granted a new tenancy in view of his persistent delay in paying rent which has become due;

(c) that the tenant ought not to be granted a new tenancy in view of other substantial breaches by him of his obligations under the current tenancy, or for any other reason connected with the tenant's use or management of the holding;

(d) that the landlord has offered and is willing to provide or secure the provision of alternative accommodation for the tenant, that the terms on which the alternative accommodation is available are reasonable having regard to the terms of the current tenancy and to all other relevant circumstances, and that the accommodation and the time at which it will be available are suitable for the tenant's requirements (including the requirement to preserve goodwill) having regard to the nature and class of his business and to the situation and extent of, and facilities afforded by, the holding;

(e) where the current tenancy was created by the sub-letting of part only of the property comprised in a superior tenancy and the landlord is the owner of an interest in reversion expectant on the termination of that superior tenancy, that the aggregate of the rents reasonably obtainable on separate lettings of the holding and the remainder of that property would be substantially less than the rent reasonably obtainable on a letting of that property as a whole, that on the termination of the current tenancy the landlord requires possession of the holding for the purpose of letting or otherwise disposing of the said property as a whole, and that in view thereof the tenant ought not to be granted a new tenancy;

(f) that on the termination of the current tenancy the landlord intends to demolish or reconstruct the premises comprised in the holding or a substantial part of those premises or to carry out substantial work of construction on the holding or part thereof and that he could not reasonably do so without obtaining possession of the holding;

(g) subject as hereinafter provided, that on the termination of the current tenancy the landlord intends to occupy the holding for the purposes, or partly for the purposes, of a business to be carried on by him therein, or as his residence.

(2) The landlord shall not be entitled to oppose an application on the ground specified in paragraph (g) of the last foregoing subsection if the interest of the landlord, or an interest which has merged in that interest and but for the merger would be the interest of the landlord, was purchased or created after the beginning of the period of five years which ends with the termination of the current tenancy, and at all times since the purchase or creation thereof the holding has been comprised in a tenancy or successive tenancies of the description specified in subsection (1) of section twenty-three of this Act.

(3) Where the landlord has a controlling interest in a company any business to be carried on by the company shall be treated for the purposes of subsection (1)(g) of this section as a business to be carried on by him.

For the purposes of this subsection, a person has a controlling interest in a company if and only if either—

(a) he is a member of it and able, without the consent of any other person, to appoint or remove the holders of at least a majority of the directorships; or

(b) he holds more than one-half of its equity share capital, there being disregarded any shares held by him in a fiduciary capacity or as nominee for another person;

and in this subsection "company" and "share" have the meanings assigned to them by section 455(1) of the Companies Act 1948 and "equity share capital" the meaning assigned to it by section 154(5) of that Act.

Dismissal of application for new tenancy where landlord successfully opposes

31.—(1) If the landlord opposes an application under subsection (1) of section twenty-four of this Act on grounds on which he is entitled to oppose it in accordance with the last foregoing section and establishes any of those grounds to the satisfaction of the court, the court shall not make an order for the grant of a new tenancy.

(2) Where in a case not falling within the last foregoing subsection the landlord opposes an application under the said subsection (1) on one or more of the grounds specified in paragraphs (d), (e) and (f) of subsection (1) of the last foregoing section but establishes none of those grounds to the satisfaction of the court, then if the court would have been satisfied of any of those grounds if the date of termination specified in the landlord's notice or, as the case may be, the date specified in the tenant's request for a new tenancy as the date from which the new tenancy is to begin, had been such later date as the court may determine, being a date not more than one year later than the date so specified,—

(a) the court shall make a declaration to that effect, stating of which of the said grounds the court would have been satisfied as aforesaid and specifying the date determined by the court as aforesaid, but shall not make an order for the grant of a new tenancy;

(b) if, within fourteen days after the making of the declaration, the tenant so requires the court shall make an order substituting the said date for the date specified in the said landlord's notice or tenant's request, and thereupon that notice or request shall have effect accordingly.

Grant of new tenancy in some cases where section 30(1)(f) applies

31A.—(1) Where the landlord opposes an application under section 24(1) of this Act on the ground specified in paragraph (f) of section 30(1) of this Act the court shall not hold that the landlord could not reasonably carry out the demolition, reconstruction or work of construction intended without obtaining possession of the holding if—

(a) the tenant agrees to the inclusion in the terms of the new tenancy of terms giving the landlord access and other facilities for carrying out the work intended and, given that access and those facilities, the landlord could reasonably carry out the work without obtaining possession of the holding and without interfering to a substantial extent or for a substantial time with the use of the holding for the purposes of the business carried on by the tenant; or

(b) the tenant is willing to accept a tenancy of an economically separable part of the holding and either paragraph (a) of this section is satisfied with respect to that part or possession of the remainder of the holding would be reasonably sufficient to enable the landlord to carry out the intended work.

(2) For the purposes of subsection (1)(b) of this section a part of a holding shall be deemed to be an economically separable part if, and only if, the aggregate of the rents which, after the completion of the intended work, would be reasonably obtainable on separate lettings of that part and the remainder of the premises affected by or resulting from the work would not be substantially less than the rent which would then be reasonably obtainable on a letting of those premises as a whole.

Property to be comprised in new tenancy

32.—(1) Subject to the following provisions of this section, an order under section twenty-nine of this Act for the grant of a new tenancy shall be an order for the grant of a new tenancy of the holding; and in the absence of agreement between the landlord and the tenant as to the property which constitutes the holding the court shall in the order designate that property by reference to the circumstances existing at the date of the order.

(1A) Where the court, by virtue of paragraph (b) of section 31A(1) of this Act, makes an order under section 29 of this Act for the grant of a new tenancy in a case where the tenant is willing to accept a tenancy of part of the holding, the order shall be an order for the grant of a new tenancy of that part only.

(2) The foregoing provisions of this section shall not apply in a case where the property comprised in the current tenancy includes other property besides the holding and the landlord requires any new tenancy ordered to be granted under section twenty-nine of this Act to be a tenancy of the whole of the property comprised in the current tenancy; but in any such case—

(a) any order under the said section twenty-nine for the grant of a new tenancy shall be an order for the grant of a new tenancy of the whole of the property comprised in the current tenancy, and

(b) references in the following provisions of this Part of this Act to the holding shall be construed as references to the whole of that property.

(3) Where the current tenancy includes rights enjoyed by the tenant in connection with the holding, those rights shall be included in a tenancy ordered to be granted under section twenty-nine of this Act except as otherwise agreed between the landlord and the tenant or, in default of such agreement, determined by the court.

Duration of new tenancy

Where on an application under this Part of this Act the court makes an order for the grant of a new tenancy, the new tenancy shall be such tenancy as may be agreed between the landlord and the tenant, or, in default of such an agreement, shall be such a tenancy as may be determined by the court to be reasonable in all the circumstances, being, if it is a tenancy for a term of years certain, a tenancy for a term not exceeding fourteen years, and shall begin on the coming to an end of the current tenancy.

Rent under new tenancy

34.—(1) The rent payable under a tenancy granted by order of the court under this Part of this Act shall be such as may be agreed between the landlord and the tenant or as, in default of such agreement, may be determined by the court to be that at which, having regard to the terms of the tenancy (other than those relating to rent), the holding might reasonably be expected to be let in the open market by a willing lessor, there being disregarded—

(a) any effect on rent of the fact that the tenant has or his predecessors in title have been in occupation of the holding,

(b) any goodwill attached to the holding by reason of the carrying on thereat of the business of the tenant (whether by him or by a predecessor of his in that business),

(c) any effect on rent of an improvement to which this paragraph applies,

(d) in the case of a holding comprising licensed premises, any addition to its value attributable to the licence, if it appears to the court that having regard to the terms of the current tenancy and any other relevant circumstances the benefit of the licence belongs to the tenant.

(2) Paragraph (c) of the foregoing subsection applies to any improvement carried out by a person who at the time it was carried out was the tenant, but only if it was carried out otherwise than in pursuance of an obligation to his immediate landlord, and either it was carried out during the current tenancy or the following conditions are satisfied, that is to say,—

(a) that it was completed not more than twenty-one years before the application for the new tenancy was made; and

(b) that the holding or any part of it affected by the improvement has at all times since the completion of the improvement been comprised in tenancies of the description specified in section 23(1) of this Act; and

(c) that at the termination of each of those tenancies the tenant did not quit.

(3) Where the rent is determined by the court the court may, if it thinks fit, further determine that the terms of the tenancy shall include such provision for varying the rent as may be specified in the determination.

(4) It is hereby declared that the matters which are to be taken into account by the court in determining the rent include any effect on rent of the operation of the provisions of the Landlord and Tenant (Covenants) Act 1995

Other terms of new tenancy

35.—(1) The terms of a tenancy granted by order of the court under this Part of this Act (other than terms as to the duration thereof and as to the rent payable thereunder) shall be such as may be agreed between the landlord and the tenant or as, in default of such agreement, may be determined by the court; and in determining those terms the court shall have regard to the terms of the current tenancy and to all relevant circumstances.

(2) In subsection (1) of this section the reference to all relevant circumstances includes (without prejudice to the generality of that reference) a reference to the operation of the provisions of the Landlord and Tenant (Covenants) Act 1995.

Carrying out of order for new tenancy

36.—(1) Where under this Part of this Act the court makes an order for the grant of a new tenancy, then, unless the order is revoked under the next following subsection or the landlord and the tenant agree not to act upon the order, the landlord shall be bound to execute or make in favour of the tenant, and the tenant shall be bound to accept, a lease or agreement for a tenancy of the holding embodying the terms agreed between the landlord and the tenant or determined by the court in accordance with the foregoing provisions of this Part of this Act; and where the landlord executes or makes such a lease or agreement the tenant shall be bound, if so required by the landlord, to execute a counterpart or duplicate thereof.

(2) If the tenant, within fourteen days after the making of an order under this Part of this Act for the grant of a new tenancy, applies to the court for the revocation of the order the court shall revoke the order; and where the order is so revoked, then, if it is so agreed between the landlord and the tenant or determined by the court, the current tenancy shall continue, beyond the date at which it would have come to an end apart from this subsection, for such period as may be so agreed or determined to be necessary to afford to the landlord a reasonable opportunity for reletting or otherwise disposing of the premises which would have been comprised in the new tenancy; and while the current tenancy continues by virtue of this subsection it shall not be a tenancy to which this Part of this Act applies.

(3) Where an order is revoked under the last foregoing subsection any provision thereof as to payment of costs shall not cease to have effect by reason only of the revocation; but the court may, if it thinks fit, revoke or vary any such provision or, where no costs have been awarded in the proceedings for the revoked order, award such costs.

(4) A lease executed or agreement made under this section, in a case where the interest of the lessor is subject to a mortgage, shall be deemed to be one authorised by section

ninety-nine of the Law of Property Act 1925 (which confers certain powers of leasing on mortgagors in possession), and subsection (13) of that section (which allows those powers to be restricted or excluded by agreement) shall not have effect in relation to such a lease or agreement.

Compensation where order for new tenancy precluded on certain grounds

37.—(1) Where on the making of an application under section twenty-four of this Act the court is precluded (whether by subsection (1) or subsection (2) of section thirty-one of this Act) from making an order for the grant of a new tenancy by reason of any of the grounds specified in paragraphs (e), (f) and (g) of subsection (1) of section thirty of this Act and not of any grounds specified in any other paragraph of that subsection or where no other ground is specified in the landlord's notice under section 25 of this Act or, as the case may be, under section 26(6) thereof, than those specified in the said paragraphs (e), (f) and (g) and either no application under the said section 24 is made or such an application is withdrawn, then, subject to the provisions of this Act, the tenant shall be entitled on quitting the holding to recover from the landlord by way of compensation an amount determined in accordance with the following provisions of this section.

(2) Subject to subsections (5A) to (5E) of this section the said amount shall be as follows, that is to say,—

(a) where the conditions specified in the next following subsection are satisfied it shall be the product of the appropriate multiplier and twice the rateable value of the holding,

(b) in any other case it shall be the product of the appropriate multiplier and the rateable value of the holding.

(3) The said conditions are—

(a) that, during the whole of the fourteen years immediately preceding the termination of the current tenancy, premises being or comprised in the holding have been occupied for the purposes of a business carried on by the occupier or for those and other purposes;

(b) that, if during those fourteen years there was a change in the occupier of the premises, the person who was the occupier immediately after the change was the successor to the business carried on by the person who was the occupier immediately before the change.

(4) Where the court is precluded from making an order for the grant of a new tenancy under this Part of this Act in the circumstances mentioned in subsection (1) of this section, the court shall on the application of the tenant certify that fact.

(5) For the purposes of subsection (2) of this section the rateable value of the holding shall be determined as follows:—

(a) where in the valuation list in force at the date on which the landlord's notice under section twenty-five or, as the case may be, subsection (6) of section twenty-six of this Act is given a value is then shown as the annual value (as hereinafter defined) of the holding, the rateable value of the holding shall be taken to be that value;

(b) where no such value is so shown with respect to the holding but such a value or such values is or are so shown with respect to premises comprised in or comprising the holding or part of it, the rateable value of the holding shall be taken to be such value as is found by a proper apportionment or aggregation of the value or values so shown;

(c) where the rateable value of the holding cannot be ascertained in accordance with the foregoing paragraphs of this subsection, it shall be taken to be the value which, apart from any exemption from assessment to rates, would on a proper assessment be the value to be entered in the said valuation list as the annual value of the holding;

and any dispute arising, whether in proceedings before the court or otherwise, as to the determination for those purposes of the rateable value of the holding shall be referred to the Commissioners of Inland Revenue for decision by a valuation officer.

An appeal shall lie to the Lands Tribunal from any decision of a valuation officer under this subsection, but subject thereto any such decision shall be final.

(5A) If part of the holding is domestic property, as defined in section 66 of the Local Government Finance Act 1988,—

(a) the domestic property shall be disregarded in determining the rateable value of the holding under subsection (5) of this section; and

(b) if, on the date specified in subsection (5)(a) of this section, the tenant occupied the whole or any part of the domestic property, the amount of compensation to which he is entitled under subsection (1) of this section shall be increased by the addition of a sum equal to his reasonable expenses in removing from the domestic property.

(5B) Any question as to the amount of the sum referred to in paragraph (b) of subsection (5A) of this section shall be determined by agreement between the landlord and the tenant or, in default of agreement, by the court.

(5C) If the whole of the holding is domestic property, as defined in section 66 of the Local Government Finance Act 1988, for the purposes of subsection (2) of this section the rateable value of the holding shall be taken to be an amount equal to the rent at which it is estimated the holding might reasonably be expected to let from year to year if the tenant undertook to pay all usual tenant's rates and taxes and to bear the cost of the repairs and insurance and the other expenses (if any) necessary to maintain the holding in a state to command that rent.

(5D) The following provisions shall have effect as regards a determination of an amount mentioned in subsection (5C) of this section—

(a) the date by reference to which such a determination is to be made is the date on which the landlord's notice under section 25 or, as the case may be, subsection (6) of section 26 of this Act is given;

(b) any dispute arising, whether in proceedings before the court or otherwise, as to such a determination shall be referred to the Commissioners of Inland Revenue for decision by a valuation officer;

(c) an appeal shall lie to the Lands Tribunal from such a decision but subject to that, such a decision shall be final.

(5E) Any deduction made under paragraph 2A of Schedule 6 to the Local Government Finance Act 1988 (deduction from valuation of hereditaments used for breeding horses etc) shall be disregarded, to the extent that it relates to the holding, in determining the rateable value of the holding under subsection (5) of this section.

(6) The Commissioners of Inland Revenue may by statutory instrument make rules prescribing the procedure in connection with references under this section.

(7) In this section—

the reference to the termination of the current tenancy is a reference to the date of termination specified in the landlord's notice under section twenty-five of this Act or, as the case may be, the date specified in the tenant's request for a new tenancy as the date from which the new tenancy is to begin;

the expression "annual value" means rateable value except that where the rateable value differs from the net annual value the said expression means net annual value;

the expression "valuation officer" means any officer of the Commissioners of Inland Revenue for the time being authorised by a certificate of the Commissioners to act in relation to a valuation list.

(8) In subsection (2) of this section "the appropriate multiplier" means such multiplier as the Secretary of State may by order made by statutory instrument prescribe and different multipliers may be so prescribed in relation to different cases.

(9) A statutory instrument containing an order under subsection (8) of this section shall be subject to annulment in pursuance of a resolution of either House of Parliament.

Restriction on agreements excluding provisions of Part II

38.—(1) Any agreement relating to a tenancy to which this Part of this Act applies (whether contained in the instrument creating the tenancy or not) shall be void (except as provided by subsection (4) of this section) in so far as it purports to preclude the tenant from making an application or request under this Part of this Act or provides for the termination or the surrender of the tenancy in the event of his making such an application or request or for the imposition of any penalty or disability on the tenant in that event.

(2) Where—

(a) during the whole of the five years immediately preceding the date on which the tenant under a tenancy to which this Part of this Act applies is to quit the holding, premises being or comprised in the holding have been occupied for the purposes of a business carried on by the occupier or for those and other purposes, and

(b) if during those five years there was a change in the occupier of the premises, the person who was the occupier immediately after the change was the successor to the business carried on by the person who was the occupier immediately before the change,

any agreement (whether contained in the instrument creating the tenancy or not and whether made before or after the termination of that tenancy) which purports to exclude or reduce compensation under the last foregoing section shall to that extent be void, so however that this subsection shall not affect any agreement as to the amount of any such compensation which is made after the right to compensation has accrued.

(3) In a case not falling within the last foregoing subsection the right to compensation conferred by the last foregoing section may be excluded or modified by agreement.

(4) The court may—

(a) on the joint application of the persons who will be the landlord and the tenant in re-lation to a tenancy to be granted for a term of years certain which will be a tenancy to which this Part of this Act applies, authorise an agreement excluding in relation to that tenancy the provisions of sections 24 to 28 of this Act; and

(b) on the joint application of the persons who are the landlord and the tenant in relation to a tenancy to which this Part of this Act applies, authorise an agreement for the sur-render of the tenancy on such date or in such circumstances as may be specified in the agreement and on such terms (if any) as may be so specified;

if the agreement is contained in or endorsed on the instrument creating the tenancy or such other instrument as the court may specify; and an agreement contained in or en-dorsed on an instrument in pursuance of an authorisation given under the subsection shall be valid notwithstanding anything in the preceding provisions of this section.

Saving for compulsory acquisitions

. . .

39.—(2) If the amount of the compensation which would have been payable under sec-tion thirty-seven of this Act if the tenancy had come to an end in circumstances giving rise to compensation under that section and the date at which the acquiring authority obtained possession had been the termination of the current tenancy exceeds the amount of the compensation payable under section 121 of the Lands Clauses Consolidation Act 1845 or section 20 of the Compulsory Purchase Act 1965 in the case of a tenancy to which this Part of this Act applies, that compensation shall be increased by the amount of the excess.

(3) Nothing in section twenty-four of this Act shall affect the operation of the said section one hundred and twenty-one.

Duty of tenants and landlords of business premises to give information to each other

40.—(1) Where any person having an interest in any business premises, being an interest in reversion expectant (whether immediately or not) on a tenancy of those premises, serves on the tenant a notice in the prescribed form requiring him to do so, it shall be the duty of the tenant to notify that person in writing within one month of the service of the notice—

(a) whether he occupies the premises or any part thereof wholly or partly for the purposes of a business carried on by him, and

(b) whether his tenancy has effect subject to any sub-tenancy on which his tenancy is im-mediately expectant and, if so, what premises are comprised in the sub-tenancy, for what term it has effect (or, if it is terminable by notice, by what notice it can be ter-minated), what is the rent payable thereunder, who is the sub-tenant, and (to the best of his knowledge and belief) whether the sub-tenant is in occupation of the premises or of part of the premises comprised in the sub-tenancy and, if not, what is the sub-tenant's address.

(2) Where the tenant of any business premises, being a tenant under such a tenancy as is mentioned in subsection (1) of section twenty-six of this Act, serves on any of the persons mentioned in the next following subsection a notice in the prescribed form requiring him to do so, it shall be the duty of that person to notify the tenant in writing within one month after the service of the notice—

(a) whether he is the owner of the fee simple in respect of those premises or any part thereof or the mortgagee in possession of such an owner and, if not,

(b) (to the best of his knowledge and belief) the name and address of the person who is his or, as the case may be, his mortgagor's immediate landlord in respect of those premises or of the part in respect of which he or his mortgagor is not the owner in fee simple, for what term his or his mortgagor's tenancy thereof has effect and what is the earliest date (if any) at which that tenancy is terminable by notice to quit given by the landlord.

(3) The persons referred to in the last foregoing subsection are, in relation to the tenant of any business premises,—

(a) any person having an interest in the premises, being an interest in reversion expectant (whether immediately or not) on the tenant's, and

(b) any person being a mortgagee in possession in respect of such an interest in reversion as is mentioned in paragraph (a) of this subsection;

and the information which any such person as is mentioned in paragraph (a) of this subsection is required to give under the last foregoing subsection shall include information whether there is a mortgagee in possession of his interest in the premises and, if so, what is the name and address of the mortgagee.

(4) The foregoing provisions of this section shall not apply to a notice served by or on the tenant more than two years before the date on which apart from this Act his tenancy would come to an end by effluxion of time or could be brought to an end by notice to quit given by the landlord.

(5) In this section—

the expression "business premises" means premises used wholly or partly for the purposes of a business;

the expression "mortgagee in possession" includes a receiver appointed by the mortgagee or by the court who is in receipt of the rents and profits, and the expression "his mortgagor" shall be construed accordingly;

the expression "sub-tenant" includes a person retaining possession of any premises by virtue of the Rent Act 1977 after the coming to an end of a sub-tenancy, and the expression "sub-tenancy" includes a right so to retain possession.

Trusts

41.—(1) Where a tenancy is held on trust, occupation by all or any of the beneficiaries under the trust, and the carrying on of a business by all or any of the beneficiaries, shall be treated for the purposes of section twenty-three of this Act as equivalent to occupation or the carrying on of a business by the tenant; and in relation to a tenancy to which this Part of this Act applies by virtue of the foregoing provisions of this subsection—

(a) references (however expressed) in this Part of this Act and in the Ninth Schedule to this Act to the business of, or to carrying on of business, use, occupation or enjoyment by, the tenant shall be construed as including references to the business of, or to carrying on of business, use, occupation or enjoyment by, the beneficiaries or beneficiary;

(b) the reference in paragraph (d) of subsection (1) of section thirty-four of this Act to the tenant shall be construed as including the beneficiaries or beneficiary; and

(c) a change in the persons of the trustees shall not be treated as a change in the person of the tenant.

(2) Where the landlord's interest is held on trust the references in paragraph (g) of subsection (1) of section thirty of this Act to the landlord shall be construed as including references to the beneficiaries under the trust or any of them; but, except in the case of a trust arising under a will or on the intestacy of any person, the reference in subsection (2) of that section to the creation of the interest therein mentioned shall be construed as including the creation of the trust.

Partnerships

41A.—(1) The following provisions of this section shall apply where—

(a) a tenancy is held jointly by two or more persons (in this section referred to as the joint tenants); and

(b) the property comprised in the tenancy is or includes premises occupied for the purposes of a business; and

(c) the business (or some other business) was at some time during the existence of the tenancy carried on in partnership by all the persons who were then the joint tenants or by those and other persons and the joint tenants' interest in the premises was then partnership property; and

(d) the business is carried on (whether alone or in partnership with other persons) by one or some only of the joint tenants and no part of the property comprised in the tenancy is occupied, in right of the tenancy, for the purposes of a business carried on (whether alone or in partnership with other persons) by the other or others.

(2) In the following provisions of this section those of the joint tenants who for the time being carry on the business are referred to as the business tenants and the others as the other joint tenants.

(3) Any notice given by the business tenants which, had it been given by all the joint tenants, would have been—

(a) a tenant's request for a new tenancy made in accordance with section 26 of this Act; or

(b) a notice under subsection (1) or subsection (2) of section 27 of this Act;

shall be treated as such if it states that it is given by virtue of this section and sets out the facts by virtue of which the persons giving it are the business tenants; and references in those sections and in section 24A of this Act to the tenant shall be construed accordingly.

(4) A notice given by the landlord to the business tenants which, had it been given to all the joint tenants, would have been a notice under section 25 of this Act shall be treated as such a notice, and references in that section to the tenant shall be construed accordingly.

(5) An application under section 24(1) of this Act for a new tenancy may, instead of being made by all the joint tenants, be made by the business tenants alone; and where it is so made—

(a) this Part of this Act shall have effect, in relation to it, as if the references therein to the tenant included references to the business tenants alone; and

(b) the business tenants shall be liable, to the exclusion of the other joint tenants, for the payment of rent and the discharge of any other obligation under the current tenancy for any rental period beginning after the date specified in the landlord's notice under section 25 of this Act or, as the case may be, beginning on or after the date specified in their request for a new tenancy.

(6) Where the court makes an order under section 29(1) of this Act for the grant of a new tenancy on an application made by the business tenants it may order the grant to be made to them or to them jointly with the persons carrying on the business in partnership with them, and may order the grant to be made subject to the satisfaction, within a time specified by the order, of such conditions as to guarantors, sureties or otherwise as appear to the court equitable, having regard to the omission of the other joint tenants from the persons who will be the tenant under the new tenancy.

(7) The business tenants shall be entitled to recover any amount payable by way of compensation under section 37 or section 59 of this Act.

Groups of companies

42.—(1) For the purposes of this section two bodies corporate shall be taken to be members of a group if and only if one is a subsidiary of the other or both are subsidiaries of a third body corporate.

In this subsection "subsidiary" has the meaning given by section 736 of the Companies Act 1985.

(2) Where a tenancy is held by a member of a group, occupation by another member of the group, and the carrying on of a business by another member of the group, shall be treated for the purposes of section twenty-three of this Act as equivalent to occupation or the carrying on of a business by the member of the group holding the tenancy; and in relation to a tenancy to which this Part of this Act applies by virtue of the foregoing provisions of this subsection—

(a) references (however expressed) in this Part of this Act and in the Ninth Schedule to this Act to the business of or to use occupation or enjoyment by the tenant shall be construed as including references to the business of or to use occupation or enjoyment by the said other member;

(b) the reference in paragraph (d) of subsection (1) of section thirty-four of this Act to the tenant shall be construed as including the said other member; and

(c) an assignment of the tenancy from one member of the group to another shall not be treated as a change in the person of the tenant.

(3) Where the landlord's interest is held by a member of a group—

(a) the reference in paragraph (g) of subsection (1) of section 30 of this Act to intended occupation by the landlord for the purposes of a business to be carried on by him shall be construed as including intended occupation by any member of the group for the purposes of a business to be carried on by that member; and

(b) the reference in subsection (2) of that section to the purchase or creation of any interest shall be construed as a reference to a purchase from or creation by a person other than a member of the group.

Tenancies excluded from Part II

43.—(1) This Part of this Act does not apply—

(a) to a tenancy of an agricultural holding which is a tenancy in relation to which the Agricultural Holdings Act 1986 applies or a tenancy which would be a tenancy of an agricultural holding in relation to which that Act applied if subsection (3) of section 2 of that Act did not have effect or, in a case where approval was given under subsection (1) of that section, if that approval had not been given;

(aa) to a farm business tenancy;

(b) to a tenancy created by a mining lease;

. . .

(2) This Part of this Act does not apply to a tenancy granted by reason that the tenant was the holder of an office, appointment or employment from the grantor thereof and continuing only so long as the tenant holds the office, appointment or employment, or terminable by the grantor on the tenant's ceasing to hold it, or coming to an end at a time fixed by reference to the time at which the tenant ceases to hold it:

Provided that this subsection shall not have effect in relation to a tenancy granted after the commencement of this Act unless the tenancy was granted by an instrument in writing which expressed the purpose for which the tenancy was granted.

(3) This Part of this Act does not apply to a tenancy granted for a term certain not exceeding six months unless—

(a) the tenancy contains provision for renewing the term or for extending it beyond six months from its beginning; or

(b) the tenant has been in occupation for a period which, together with any period during which any predecessor in the carrying on of the business carried on by the tenant was in occupation, exceedstwelve months.

Jurisdiction of county court to make declaration

Where the rateable value of the holding is such that the jurisdiction conferred on the court by any other provision of this Part of this Act is, by virtue of section 63 of this Act, exercisable by the county court, the county court shall have jurisdiction (but without prejudice to the jurisdiction of the High Court) to make any declaration as to any matter arising under this Part of this Act, whether or not any other relief is sought in the proceedings.

Meaning of "the landlord" in Part II, and provisions as to mesne landlords, etc

44.—(1) Subject to the next following subsection, in this Part of this Act the expression "the landlord", in relation to a tenancy (in this section referred to as "the relevant tenancy"), means the person (whether or not he is the immediate landlord) who is the owner of that interest in the property comprised in the relevant tenancy which for the time being fulfils the following conditions, that is to say—

(a) that it is an interest in reversion expectant (whether immediately or not) on the termination of the relevant tenancy, and

(b) that it is either the fee simple or a tenancy which will not come to an end within fourteen months by effluxion of time and, if it is such a tenancy, that no notice has been given by virtue of which it will come to an end within fourteen months or any further time by which it may be continued under section 36(2) or section 64 of this Act

and is not itself in reversion expectant (whether immediately or not) on an interest which fulfils those conditions.

(2) References in this Part of this Act to a notice to quit given by the landlord are references to a notice to quit given by the immediate landlord.

(3) The provisions of the Sixth Schedule to this Act shall have effect for the application of this Part of this Act to cases where the immediate landlord of the tenant is not the owner of the fee simple in respect of the holding.

Interpretation of Part II

In this Part of this Act:—

"business" has the meaning assigned to it by subsection (2) of section twenty-three of this Act;

"current tenancy" has the meaning assigned to it by subsection (1) of section twenty-six of this Act;

"date of termination" has the meaning assigned to it by subsection (1) of section twenty-five of this Act;

subject to the provisions of section thirty-two of this Act, "the holding" has the meaning assigned to it by subsection (3) of section twenty-three of this Act;

"mining lease" has the same meaning as in the Landlord and Tenant Act 1927.

PART III
COMPENSATION FOR IMPROVEMENTS

Time for making claims for compensation for improvements

47.—(1) Where a tenancy is terminated by notice to quit, whether given by the landlord or by the tenant, or by a notice given by any person under Part I or Part II of this Act, the time for making a claim for compensation at the termination of the tenancy shall be a time falling within the period of three months beginning on the date on which the notice is given:

Provided that where the tenancy is terminated by a tenant's request for a new tenancy under section twenty-six of this Act, the said time shall be a time falling within the period of three months beginning on the date on which the landlord gives notice, or (if he has not given such a notice) the latest date on which he could have given notice, under subsection (6) of the said section twenty-six or, as the case may be, paragraph (a) of subsection (4) of section fifty-seven or paragraph (b) of subsection (1) of section fifty-eight of this Act.

(2) Where a tenancy comes to an end by effluxion of time the time for making such a claim shall be a time not earlier than six nor later than three months before the coming to an end of the tenancy.

(3) Where a tenancy is terminated by forfeiture or re-entry, the time for making such a claim shall be a time falling within the period of three months beginning with the effective date of the order of the court for the recovery of possession of the land comprised in the tenancy or, if the tenancy is terminated by re-entry without such an order, the period of three months beginning with the date of the re-entry.

(4) In the last foregoing subsection the reference to the effective date of an order is a reference to the date on which the order is to take effect according to the terms thereof or the date on which it ceases to be subject to appeal, whichever is the later.

. . .

Amendments as to limitations on tenant's right to compensation

48.—(1) So much of paragraph (b) of subsection (1) of section two of the Act of 1927 as provides that a tenant shall not be entitled to compensation in respect of any improvement made in pursuance of a statutory obligation shall not apply to any improvement begun after the commencement of this Act, but section three of the Act of 1927 (which enables a landlord to object to a proposed improvement) shall not have effect in relation to an improvement made in pursuance of a statutory obligation except so much thereof as—

(a) requires the tenant to serve on the landlord notice of his intention to make the improvement together with such a plan and specification as are mentioned in that section and to supply copies of the plan and specification at the request of any superior landlord; and

(b) enables the tenant to obtain at his expense a certificate from the landlord or the tribunal that the improvement has been duly executed.

(2) Paragraph (c) of the said subsection (1) (which provides that a tenant shall not be entitled to compensation in respect of any improvement made less than three years before the termination of the tenancy) shall not apply to any improvement begun after the commencement of this Act.

(3) No notice shall be served after the commencement of this Act under paragraph (d) of the said subsection (1) (which excludes rights to compensation where the landlord serves on the tenant notice offering a renewal of the tenancy on reasonable terms).

Interpretation of Part III

In this Part of this Act the expression "Act of 1927" means the Landlord and Tenant Act 1927, the expression "compensation" means compensation under Part I of that Act in respect of an improvement, and other expressions used in this Part of this Act and in the Act of 1927 have the same meanings in this Part of this Act as in that Act.

Part IV
Miscellaneous and Supplementary

Extension of Leasehold Property (Repairs) Act 1938

51.—(1) The Leasehold Property (Repairs) Act 1938 (which restricts the enforcement of repairing covenants in long leases of small houses) shall extend to every tenancy (whether of a house or of other property, and without regard to rateable value) where the following conditions are fulfilled, that is to say,—

(a) that the tenancy was granted for a term of years certain of not less than seven years;

(b) that three years or more of the term remain unexpired at the date of the service of the notice of dilapidations or, as the case may be, at the date of commencement of the action for damages; and

(c) that the tenancy is neither a tenancy of an agricultural holding in relation to which the Agricultural Holdings Act 1986 applies nor a farm business tenancy.

(2) . . .

(3) The said Act of 1938 shall apply where there is an interest belonging to Her Majesty in right of the Crown or to a Government department, or held on behalf of Her Majesty for the purposes of a Government department, in like manner as if that interest were an interest not so belonging or held.

(4) Subsection (2) of section twenty-three of the Landlord and Tenant Act 1927 (which authorises a tenant to serve documents on the person to whom he has been paying rent) shall apply in relation to any counter-notice to be served under the said Act of 1938.

(5) This section shall apply to tenancies granted, and to breaches occurring, before or after the commencement of this Act, except that it shall not apply where the notice of dilapidations was served, or the action for damages begun, before the commencement of this Act.

(6) In this section the expression "notice of dilapidations" means a notice under subsection (1) of section one hundred and forty-six of the Law of Property Act 1925.

Jurisdiction of county court where lessor refuses licence or consent

53.—(1) Where a landlord withholds his licence or consent—

(a) to an assignment of the tenancy or a sub-letting, charging or parting with the possession of the demised property or any part thereof, or

(b) to the making of an improvement on the demised property or any part thereof, or

(c) to a change in the use of the demised property or any part thereof, or to the making of a specified use of that property, and the High Court has jurisdiction to make a declaration that the licence or

consent was unreasonably withheld, then without prejudice to the jurisdiction of the High Court the county court shall have the like jurisdiction whatever the net annual value for rating of the demised property is to be taken to be for the purposes of the County Courts Act 1984 and notwithstanding that the tenant does not seek any relief other than the declaration.

(2) Where on the making of an application to the county court for such a declaration the court is satisfied that the licence or consent was unreasonably withheld, the court shall make a declaration accordingly.

(3) The foregoing provisions of this section shall have effect whether the tenancy in question was created before or after the commencement of this Act and whether the refusal of the licence or consent occurred before or after the commencement of this Act.

(4) Nothing in this section shall be construed as conferring jurisdiction on the county court to grant any relief other than such a declaration as aforesaid.

Determination of tenancies of derelict land

Where a landlord, having power to serve a notice to quit, on an application to the county court satisfies the court—

(a) that he has taken all reasonable steps to communicate with the person last known to him to be the tenant, and has failed to do so,

(b) that during the period of six months ending with the date of the application neither the tenant nor any person claiming under him has been in occupation of the property comprised in the tenancy or any part thereof, and

(c) that during the said period either no rent was payable by the tenant or the rent payable has not been paid,

the court may if it thinks fit by order determine the tenancy as from the date of the order.

Compensation for possession obtained by misrepresentation

55.—(1) Where under Part I of this Act an order is made for possession of the property comprised in a tenancy, or under Part II of this Act the court refuses an order for the grant of a new tenancy, and it is subsequently made to appear to the court that the order was obtained, or the court induced to refuse the grant, by misrepresentation or the concealment of material facts, the court may order the landlord to pay to the tenant such sum as appears sufficient as compensation for damage or loss sustained by the tenant as the result of the order or refusal.

(2) In this section the expression "the landlord" means the person applying for possession or opposing an application for the grant of a new tenancy, and the expression "the tenant" means the person against whom the order for possession was made or to whom the grant of a new tenancy was refused.

Application to Crown

56.—(1) Subject to the provisions of this and the four next following sections, Part II of this Act shall apply where there is an interest belonging to Her Majesty in right of the Crown or the Duchy of Lancaster or belonging to the Duchy of Cornwall, or belonging to a Government department or held on behalf of Her Majesty for the purposes of a Government department, in like manner as if that interest were an interest not so belonging or held.

(2) The provisions of the Eighth Schedule to this Act shall have effect as respects the application of Part II of this Act to cases where the interest of the landlord belongs to Her Majesty in right of the Crown or the Duchy of Lancaster or to the Duchy of Cornwall.

(3) Where a tenancy is held by or on behalf of a Government department and the property comprised therein is or includes premises occupied for any purposes of a Government department, the tenancy shall be one to which Part II of this Act applies; and for the purposes of any provision of the said Part II or the Ninth Schedule to this Act which is applicable only if either or both of the following conditions are satisfied, that is to say—

(a) that any premises have during any period been occupied for the purposes of the tenant's business;

(b) that on any change of occupier of any premises the new occupier succeeded to the business of the former occupier,

the said conditions shall be deemed to be satisfied respectively, in relation to such a tenancy, if during that period or, as the case may be, immediately before and immediately after the change, the premises were occupied for the purposes of a Government department.

(4) The last foregoing subsection shall apply in relation to any premises provided by a Government department without any rent being payable to the department therefor as if the premises were occupied for the purposes of a Government department.

(5) The provisions of Parts III and IV of this Act amending any other enactment which binds the Crown or applies to land belonging to Her Majesty in right of the Crown or the Duchy of Lancaster, or land belonging to the Duchy of Cornwall, or to land belonging to any Government department, shall bind the Crown or apply to such land.

(6) Sections fifty-three and fifty-four of this Act shall apply where the interest of the landlord, or any other interest in the land in question, belongs to Her Majesty in right of the Crown or the Duchy of Lancaster or to the Duchy of Cornwall, or belongs to a Government department or is held on behalf of Her Majesty for the purposes of a

Government department, in like manner as if that interest were an interest not so belonging or held.

(7) Part I of this Act shall apply where—

(a) there is an interest belonging to Her Majesty in right of the Crown and that interest is under the management of the Crown Estate Commissioners; or

(b) there is an interest belonging to Her Majesty in right of the Duchy of Lancaster or belonging to the Duchy of Cornwall;

as if it were an interest not so belonging.

Modification on grounds of public interest of rights under Part II

57.—(1) Where the interest of the landlord or any superior landlord in the property comprised in any tenancy belongs to or is held for the purposes of a Government department or is held by a local authority, statutory undertakers or a development corporation, the Minister or Board in charge of any Government department may certify that it is requisite for the purposes of the first-mentioned department, or, as the case may be, of the authority, undertakers or corporation, that the use or occupation of the property or a part thereof shall be changed by a specified date.

(2) A certificate under the last foregoing subsection shall not be given unless the owner of the interest belonging or held as mentioned in the last foregoing subsection has given to the tenant a notice stating—

(a) that the question of the giving of such a certificate is under consideration by the Minister or Board specified in the notice, and

(b) that if within twenty-one days of the giving of the notice the tenant makes to that Minister or Board representations in writing with respect to that question, they will be considered before the question is determined,

and if the tenant makes any such representations within the said twenty-one days the Minister or Board shall consider them before determining whether to give the certificate.

(3) Where a certificate has been given under subsection (1) of this section in relation to any tenancy, then,—

(a) if a notice given under subsection (1) of section twenty-five of this Act specifies as the date of termination a date not earlier than the date specified in the certificate and contains a copy of the certificate subsections (5) and (6) of that section shall not apply to the notice and no application for a new tenancy shall be made by the tenant under section twenty-four of this Act;

(b) if such a notice specifies an earlier date as the date of termination and contains a copy of the certificate, then if the court makes an order under Part II of this Act for the grant of a new tenancy the new tenancy shall be for a term expiring not later than the date specified in the certificate and shall not be a tenancy to which Part II of this Act applies.

(4) Where a tenant makes a request for a new tenancy under section twenty-six of this Act, and the interest of the landlord or any superior landlord in the property comprised in the current tenancy belongs or is held as mentioned in subsection (1) of this section, the following provisions shall have effect:—

(a) if a certificate has been given under the said subsection (1) in relation to the current tenancy, and within two months after the making of the request the landlord gives notice to the tenant that the certificate has been given and the notice contains a copy of the certificate, then,—

    (i) if the date specified in the certificate is not later than that specified in the tenant's request for a new tenancy, the tenant shall not make an application under section twenty-four of this Act for the grant of a new tenancy;

    (ii) if, in any other case, the court makes an order under Part II of this Act for the grant of a new tenancy the new tenancy shall be for a term expiring not later than the date specified in the certificate and shall not be a tenancy to which Part II of this Act applies;

(b) if no such certificate has been given but notice under subsection (2) of this section has been given before the making of the request or within two months thereafter, the request shall not have effect, without prejudice however to the making of a new request when the Minister or Board has determined whether to give a certificate.

(5) Where application is made to the court under Part II of this Act for the grant of a new tenancy and the landlord's interest in the property comprised in the tenancy belongs or is held as mentioned in subsection (1) of this section, the Minister or Board in charge of any Government department may certify that it is necessary in the public interest that if the landlord makes an application in that behalf the court shall determine as a term of the new tenancy that it shall be terminable by six months' notice to quit given by the landlord.

Subsection (2) of this section shall apply in relation to a certificate under this subsection, and if notice under the said subsection (2) has been given to the tenant—

(a) the court shall not determine the application for the grant of a new tenancy until the Minister or Board has determined whether to give a certificate,

(b) if a certificate is given, the court shall on the application of the landlord determine as a term of the new tenancy that it shall be terminable as aforesaid, and section twenty-five of this Act shall apply accordingly.

(6) The foregoing provisions of this section shall apply to an interest held by a Health Authority or Special Health Authority, as they apply to an interest held by a local authority but with the substitution, for the reference to the purposes of the authority, of a reference to the purposes of the National Health Service Act 1977.

(7) Where the interest of the landlord or any superior landlord in the property comprised in any tenancy belongs to the National Trust the Minister of Works may certify that it is requisite for the purpose of securing that the property will as from a specified date be used or occupied in a manner better suited to the nature thereof that the use or occupation of the property should be changed; and subsections (2) to (4) of this section shall apply in re-

lation to certificates under this subsection, and to cases where the interest of the landlord or any superior landlord belongs to the National Trust, as those subsections apply in relation to certificates under subsection (1) of this section and to cases where the interest of the landlord or any superior landlord belongs or is held as mentioned in that subsection.

(8) In this and the next following section the expression "Government department" does not include the Commissioners of Crown Lands and the expression " landlord" has the same meaning as in Part II of this Act; and in the last foregoing subsection the expression "National Trust" means the National Trust for Places of Historic Interest or Natural Beauty.

Termination on special grounds of tenancies to which Part II applies

58.—(1) Where the landlord's interest in the property comprised in any tenancy belongs to or is held for the purposes of a Government department, and the Minister or Board in charge of any Government department certifies that for reasons of national security it is necessary that the use or occupation of the property should be discontinued or changed, then—

(a) if the landlord gives a notice under subsection (1) of section twenty-five of this Act containing a copy of the certificate, subsections (5) and (6) of that section shall not apply to the notice and no application for a new tenancy shall be made by the tenant under section twenty-four of this Act;

(b) if (whether before or after the giving of the certificate) the tenant makes a request for a new tenancy under section twenty-six of this Act, and within two months after the making of the request the landlord gives notice to the tenant that the certificate has been given and the notice contains a copy of the certificate,—

 (i) the tenant shall not make an application under section twenty-four of this Act for the grant of a new tenancy, and

 (ii) if the notice specifies as the date on which the tenancy is to terminate a date earlier than that specified in the tenant's request as the date on which the new tenancy is to begin but neither earlier than six months from the giving of the notice nor earlier than the earliest date at which apart from this Act the tenancy would come to an end or could be brought to an end, the tenancy shall terminate on the date specified in the notice instead of that specified in the request.

(2) Where the landlord's interest in the property comprised in any tenancy belongs to or is held for the purposes of a Government department, nothing in this Act shall invalidate an agreement to the effect—

(a) that on the giving of such a certificate as is mentioned in the last foregoing subsection the tenancy may be terminated by notice to quit given by the landlord of such length as may be specified in the agreement, if the notice contains a copy of the certificate; and

(b) that after the giving of such a notice containing such a copy the tenancy shall not be one to which Part II of this Act applies.

(3) Where the landlord's interest in the property comprised in any tenancy is held by statutory undertakers, nothing in this Act shall invalidate an agreement to the effect—

(a) that where the Minister or Board in charge of a Government department certifies that possession of the property comprised in the tenancy or a part thereof is urgently required for carrying out repairs (whether on that property or elsewhere) which are needed for the proper operation of the landlord's undertaking, the tenancy may be terminated by notice to quit given by the landlord of such length as may be specified in the agreement, if the notice contains a copy of the certificate; and

(b) that after the giving of such a notice containing such a copy, the tenancy shall not be one to which Part II of this Act applies.

(4) Where the court makes an order under Part II of this Act for the grant of a new tenancy and the Minister or Board in charge of any Government department certifies that the public interest requires the tenancy to be subject to such a term as is mentioned in paragraph (a) or (b) of this subsection, as the case may be, then—

(a) if the landlord's interest in the property comprised in the tenancy belongs to or is held for the purposes of a Government department, the court shall on the application of the landlord determine as a term of the new tenancy that such an agreement as is mentioned in subsection (2) of this section and specifying such length of notice as is mentioned in the certificate shall be embodied in the new tenancy;

(b) if the landlord's interest in that property is held by statutory undertakers, the court shall on the application of the landlord determine as a term of the new tenancy that such an agreement as is mentioned in subsection (3) of this section and specifying such length of notice as is mentioned in the certificate shall be embodied in the new tenancy.

Compensation for exercise of powers under ss 57 and 58

59.—(1) Where by virtue of any certificate given for the purposes of either of the two last foregoing sections or, subject to subsections (1A) or (1B) below, sections 60A or 60B below or, subject to subsection (1A) below, section 60A below the tenant is precluded from obtaining an order for the grant of a new tenancy, or of a new tenancy for a term expiring later than a specified date, the tenant shall be entitled on quitting the premises to recover from the owner of the interest by virtue of which the certificate was given an amount by way of compensation, and subsections (2), (3) and (5) to (7) of section thirty-seven of this Act shall with the necessary modifications apply for the purposes of ascertaining the amount.

(1A) No compensation shall be recoverable under subsection (1) above where the certificate was given under section 60A below and either—

(a) the premises vested in the Welsh Development Agency under section 7 (property of Welsh Industrial Estates Corporation) or 8 (land held under Local Employment Act 1972) of the Welsh Development Agency Act 1975, or

(b) the tenant was not tenant of the premises when the said Agency acquired the interest by virtue of which the certificate was given.

(1B) No compensation shall be recoverable under subsection (1) above where the certificate was given under section 60B below and either—

(a) the premises are premises which—

    (i) were vested in the Welsh Development Agency by section 8 of the Welsh Development Agency Act 1975 or were acquired by the Agency when no tenancy subsisted in the premises, and

    (ii) vested in the Development Board for Rural Wales under section 24 of the Development of Rural Wales Act 1976, or

(b) the tenant was not the tenant of the premises when the Board acquired the interest by virtue of which the certificate was given.

(2) Subsections (2) and (3) of section thirty-eight of this Act shall apply to compensation under this section as they apply to compensation under section thirty-seven of this Act.

Special provisions as to premises provided under Distribution of Industry Acts 1945 and 1950, etc

60.—(1) Where the property comprised in a tenancy consists of premises of which the Minister of Technology or the English Industrial Estates Corporation the Urban Regeneration Agency is the landlord, being premises situated in a locality which is either—

(a) a development area . . . or

(b) an intermediate area . . .

and the Minister of Technology certifies that it is necessary or expedient for achieving the purpose mentioned in section 2(1) of the said Act of 1972 that the use or occupation of the property should be changed, paragraphs (a) and (b) of subsection (1) of section fifty-eight of this Act shall apply as they apply where such a certificate is given as is mentioned in that subsection.

(2) Where the court makes an order under Part II of this Act for the grant of a new tenancy of any such premises as aforesaid, and the Secretary of State certifies that it is necessary or expedient as aforesaid that the tenancy should be subject to a term, specified in the certificate, prohibiting or restricting the tenant from assigning the tenancy or sub-letting, charging or parting with possession of the premises or any part thereof or changing the use of premises or any part thereof, the court shall determine that the terms of the tenancy shall include the terms specified in the certificate.

(3) In this section "development area" and "intermediate area" mean an area for the time being specified as a development area or, as the case may be, as an intermediate area by an order made, or having effect as if made, under section 1 of the Industrial Development Act 1982.

Welsh Development Agency premises

60A.—(1) Where the property comprised in a tenancy consists of premises of which the Welsh Development Agency is the landlord, and the Secretary of State certifies that it is necessary or expedient, for the purpose of providing employment appropriate to the needs of the area in which the premises are situated, that the use or occupation of the property should be changed, paragraphs (a) and (b) of section 58(1) above shall apply as they apply where such a certificate is given as is mentioned in that subsection.

(2) Where the court makes an order under Part II of this Act for the grant of a new tenancy of any such premises as aforesaid, and the Secretary of State certifies that it is necessary or expedient as aforesaid that the tenancy should be subject to a term, specified in the certificate, prohibiting or restricting the tenant from assigning the tenancy or sub-letting, charging or parting with possession of the premises or any part of the premises or changing the use of the premises or any part of the premises, the court shall determine that the terms of the tenancy shall include the terms specified in the certificate.

Development Board for Rural Wales premises

60B.—(1) Where the property comprised in the tenancy consists of premises of which the Development Board for Rural Wales is the landlord, and the Secretary of State certifies that it is necessary or expedient, for the purpose of providing employment appropriate to the needs of the area in which the premises are situated, that the use or occupation of the property should be changed, paragraphs (a) and (b) of section 58(1) above shall apply as they apply where such a certificate is given as is mentioned in that subsection.

(2) Where the court makes an order under Part II of this Act for the grant of a new tenancy of any such premises as aforesaid, and the Secretary of State certifies that it is necessary or expedient as aforesaid that the tenancy should be subject to a term, specified in the certificate, prohibiting or restricting the tenant from assigning the tenancy or sub-letting, charging or parting with possession of the premises or any part of the premises or changing the use of the premises or any part of the premises, the court shall determine that the terms of the tenancy shall include the terms specified in the certificate.

Jurisdiction of court for purposes of Parts I and II and of Part I of Landlord and Tenant Act 1927

63.—(1) Any jurisdiction conferred on the court by any provision of Part I of this Act shall be exercised by the county court.

(2) Any jurisdiction conferred on the court by any provision of Part II of this Act or conferred on the tribunal by Part I of the Landlord and Tenant Act 1927, shall, subject to the provisions of this section, be exercised by the High Court or a County Court.

. . .

(4) The following provisions shall have effect as respects transfer of proceedings from or to the High Court or the county court, that is to say—

(a) where an application is made to the one but by virtue of an Order under section 1 of the Courts and Legal Services Act 1990 cannot be entertained except by the other, the application shall not be treated as improperly made but any proceedings thereon shall be transferred to the other court;

(b) any proceedings under the provisions of Part II of this Act or of Part I of the Landlord and Tenant Act 1927, which are pending before one of those courts may by order of that court made on the application of any person interested be transferred to the other court, if it appears to the court making the order that it is desirable that the proceedings and any proceedings before the other court should both be entertained by the other court.

(5) In any proceedings where in accordance with the foregoing provisions of this section the county court exercises jurisdiction the powers of the judge of summoning one or more assessors under subsection (1) of section eighty-eight of the County Courts Act 1934, may be exercised notwithstanding that no application is made in that behalf by any party to the proceedings.

(6) Where in any such proceedings an assessor is summoned by a judge under the said subsection (1),—

(a) he may, if so directed by the judge, inspect the land to which the proceedings relate without the judge and report to the judge in writing thereon;

(b) the judge may on consideration of the report and any observations of the parties thereon give such judgment or make such order in the proceedings as may be just;

(c) the remuneration of the assessor shall be at such rate as may be determined by the Lord Chancellor with the approval of the Treasury and shall be defrayed out of moneys provided by Parliament.

(7) In this section the expression "the holding"—

(a) in relation to proceedings under Part II of this Act, has the meaning assigned to it by subsection (3) of section twenty-three of this Act,

(b) in relation to proceedings under Part I of the Landlord and Tenant Act 1927, has the same meaning as in the said Part I.

. . .

(9) Nothing in this section shall prejudice the operation of section 41 of the County Courts Act 1984 (which relates to the removal into the High Court of proceedings commenced in a county court).

. . .

Interim continuation of tenancies pending determination by court

64.—(1) In any case where—

(a) a notice to terminate a tenancy has been given under Part I or Part II of this Act or a request for a new tenancy has been made under Part II thereof, and

(b) an application to the court has been made under the said Part I or the said Part II, as the case may be, and

(c) apart from this section the effect of the notice or request would be to terminate the tenancy before the expiration of the period of three months beginning with the date on which the application is finally disposed of,

the effect of the notice or request shall be to terminate the tenancy at the expiration of the said period of three months and not at any other time.

(2) The reference in paragraph (c) of subsection (1) of this section to the date on which an application is finally disposed of shall be construed as a reference to the earliest date by which the proceedings on the application (including any proceedings on or in

consequence of an appeal) have been determined and any time for appealing or further appealing has expired, except that if the application is withdrawn or any appeal is abandoned the reference shall be construed as a reference to the date of the withdrawal or abandonment.

Provisions as to reversions

65.—(1) Where by virtue of any provision of this Act a tenancy (in this subsection referred to as "the inferior tenancy") is continued for a period such as to extend to or beyond the end of the term of a superior tenancy, the superior tenancy shall, for the purposes of this Act and of any other enactment and of any rule of law, be deemed so long as it subsists to be an interest in reversion expectant upon the termination of the inferior tenancy and, if there is no intermediate tenancy, to be the interest in reversion immediately expectant upon the termination thereof.

(2) In the case of a tenancy continuing by virtue of any provision of this Act after the coming to an end of the interest in reversion immediately expectant upon the termination thereof, subsection (1) of section one hundred and thirty-nine of the Law of Property Act 1925 (which relates to the effect of the extinguishment of a reversion) shall apply as if references in the said subsection (1) to the surrender or merger of the reversion included references to the coming to an end of the reversion for any reason other than surrender or merger.

(3) Where by virtue of any provision of this Act a tenancy (in this subsection referred to as "the continuing tenancy") is continued beyond the beginning of a reversionary tenancy which was granted (whether before or after the commencement of this Act) so as to begin on or after the date on which apart from this Act the continuing tenancy would have come to an end, the reversionary tenancy shall have effect as if it had been granted subject to the continuing tenancy.

(4) Where by virtue of any provision of this Act a tenancy (in this subsection referred to as "the new tenancy") is granted for a period beginning on the same date as a reversionary tenancy or for a period such as to extend beyond the beginning of the term of a reversionary tenancy, whether the reversionary tenancy in question was granted before or after the commencement of this Act, the reversionary tenancy shall have effect as if it had been granted subject to the new tenancy.

Provisions as to notices

66.—(1) Any form of notice required by this Act to be prescribed shall be prescribed by regulations made by the Lord Chancellor by statutory instrument.

(2) Where the form of a notice to be served on persons of any description is to be prescribed for any of the purposes of this Act, the form to be prescribed shall include such an explanation of the relevant provisions of this Act as appears to the Lord Chancellor requisite for informing persons of that description of their rights and obligations under those provisions.

(3) Different forms of notice may be prescribed for the purposes of the operation of any provision of this Act in relation to different cases.

(4) Section twenty-three of the Landlord and Tenant Act 1927 (which relates to the service of notices) shall apply for the purposes of this Act.

(5) Any statutory instrument under this section shall be subject to annulment in pursuance of a resolution of either House of Parliament.

Provisions as to mortgagees in possession

67.—Anything authorised or required by the provisions of this Act, other than subsection (2) or (3) of section forty, to be done at any time by, to or with the landlord, or a landlord of a specified description, shall, if at that time the interest of the landlord in question is subject to a mortgage and the mortgagee is in possession or a receiver appointed by the mortgagee or by the court is in receipt of the rents and profits, be deemed to be authorised or required to be done by, to or with the mortgagee instead of that landlord.

Interpretation

69.—(1) In this Act the following expressions have the meanings hereby assigned to them respectively, that is to say:—

"agricultural holding" has the same meaning as in the Agricultural Holdings Act 1986;

"development corporation" has the same meaning as in the New Towns Act 1946;

"farm business tenancy" has the same meaning as in the Agricultural Tenancies Act 1995; "local authority" means any local authority within the meaning of the Town and Country Planning Act 1990, any National Park authority, the Broads Authority or . . . a joint authority established by Part IV of the Local Government Act 1985;

"mortgage" includes a charge or lien and "mortgagor" and "mortgagee" shall be construed accordingly;

"notice to quit" means a notice to terminate a tenancy (whether a periodical tenancy or a tenancy for a term of years certain) given in accordance with the provisions (whether express or implied) of that tenancy;

"repairs" includes any work of maintenance, decoration or restoration, and references to repairing, to keeping or yielding up in repair and to state of repair shall be construed accordingly;

"statutory undertakers" has the same meaning as in the Town and Country Planning Act 1947 . . .

"tenancy" means a tenancy created either immediately or derivatively out of the freehold, whether by a lease or underlease, by an agreement for a lease or underlease or by a tenancy agreement or in pursuance of any enactment (including this Act), but does not include a mortgage term or any interest arising in favour of a mortgagor by his attorning tenant to his mortgagee, and references to the granting of a tenancy and to demised property shall be construed accordingly;

"terms", in relation to a tenancy, includes conditions.

(2) References in this Act to an agreement between the landlord and the tenant (except in section seventeen and subsections (1) and (2) of section thirty-eight thereof) shall be construed as references to an agreement in writing between them.

(3) References in this Act to an action for any relief shall be construed as including references to a claim for that relief by way of counterclaim in any proceedings.

Short title and citation, commencement and extent

70.—(1) This Act may be cited as the Landlord and Tenant Act 1954, and the Landlord and Tenant Act 1927, and this Act may be cited together as the Landlord and Tenant Acts 1927 and 1954.

(2) This Act shall come into operation on the first day of October, nineteen hundred and fifty-four.

(3) This Act shall not extend to Scotland or to Northern Ireland.

SCHEDULE 6
PROVISIONS FOR PURPOSES OF PART II WHERE IMMEDIATE LANDLORD
IS NOT THE FREEHOLDER (s 44)

Definitions

1. In this Schedule the following expressions have the meanings hereby assigned to them in relation to a tenancy (in this Schedule referred to as "the relevant tenancy"), that is to say:—

"the competent landlord" means the person who in relation to the tenancy is for the time being the landlord (as defined by section forty-four of this Act) for the purposes of Part II of this Act;

"mesne landlord" means a tenant whose interest is intermediate between the relevant tenancy and the interest of the competent landlord; and "superior landlord" means a person (whether the owner of the fee simple or a tenant) whose interest is superior to the interest of the competent landlord.

Power of court to order reversionary tenancies

2. Where the period for which in accordance with the provisions of Part II of this Act it is agreed or determined by the court that a new tenancy should be granted thereunder will extend beyond the date on which the interest of the immediate landlord will come to an end, the power of the court under Part II of this Act to order such a grant shall include power to order the grant of a new tenancy until the expiration of that interest and also to order the grant of such . . . Act shall, subject to the necessary modifications, apply in relation to the grant of a tenancy together with one or more reversionary tenancies as they apply in relation to the grant of one new tenancy.

Acts of competent landlord binding on other landlords

3.—(1) Any notice given by the competent landlord under Part II of this Act to terminate the relevant tenancy, and any agreement made between that landlord and the tenant as to the granting, duration, or terms of a future tenancy, being an agreement made for the purposes of the said Part II, shall bind the interest of any mesne landlord notwithstanding that he has not consented to the giving of the notice or was not a party to the agreement.

(2) The competent landlord shall have power for the purposes of Part II of this Act to give effect to any agreement with the tenant for the grant of a new tenancy beginning with the coming to an end of the relevant tenancy notwithstanding that the competent landlord will not be the immediate landlord at the commencement of the new tenancy, and any instrument made in the exercise of the power conferred by this sub-paragraph shall have effect as if the mesne landlord had been a party thereto.

(3) Nothing in the foregoing provisions of this paragraph shall prejudice the provisions of the next following paragraph.

Provisions as to consent of mesne landlord to acts of competent landlord

4.—(1) If the competent landlord, not being the immediate landlord, gives any such notice or makes any such agreement as is mentioned in sub-paragraph (1) of the last foregoing paragraph without the consent of every mesne landlord, any mesne landlord whose consent has not been given thereto shall be entitled to compensation from the competent landlord for any loss arising in consequence of the giving of the notice or the making of the agreement.

(2) If the competent landlord applies to any mesne landlord for his consent to such a notice or agreement, that consent shall not be unreasonably withheld, but may be given subject to any conditions which may be reasonable (including conditions as to the modification of the proposed notice or agreement or as to the payment of compensation by the competent landlord).

(3) Any question arising under this paragraph whether consent has been unreasonably withheld or whether any conditions imposed on the giving of consent are unreasonable shall be determined by the court.

Consent of superior landlord required for agreements affecting his interest

5. An agreement between the competent landlord and the tenant made for the purposes of Part II of this Act in a case where—

(a)   the competent landlord is himself a tenant, and

(b)   the agreement would apart from this paragraph operate as respects any period after the coming to an end of the interest of the competent landlord,

shall not have effect unless every superior landlord who will be the immediate landlord of the tenant during any part of that period is a party to the agreement.

Withdrawal by competent landlord of notice given by mesne landlord

6. Where the competent landlord has given a notice under section 25 of this Act to terminate the relevant tenancy and, within two months after the giving of the notice, a superior landlord —

(a)   becomes the competent landlord; and

(b) gives to the tenant notice in the prescribed form that he withdraws the notice previously given,

the notice under section 25 of this Act shall cease to have effect, but without prejudice to the giving of a further notice under that section by the competent landlord.

Duty to inform superior landlords

7. If the competent landlord's interest in the property comprised in the relevant tenancy is a tenancy which will come or can be brought to an end within sixteen months (or any further time by which it may be continued under section 36 or section 64 of this Act) and he gives to the tenant under the relevant tenancy a notice under section 25 of this Act to terminate the tenancy or is given by him a notice under section 26(3) of this Act:—

(a) the competent landlord shall forthwith send a copy of the notice to his immediate landlord; and

(b) any superior landlord whose interest in the property is a tenancy shall forthwith send to his immediate landlord any copy which has been sent to him in pursuance of the preceding sub-paragraph or this sub-paragraph.

SCHEDULE 8

APPLICATION OF PART II TO LAND BELONGING TO CROWN AND
DUCHIES OF LANCASTER AND CORNWALL (s 56) 1.

Where an interest in any property comprised in a tenancy belongs to Her Majesty in right of the Duchy of Lancaster, then for the purposes of Part II of this Act the Chancellor of the Duchy shall represent Her Majesty and shall be deemed to be the owner of the interest.

2. Where an interest in any property comprised in a tenancy belongs to the Duchy of Cornwall, then for the purposes of Part II of this Act such person as the Duke of Cornwall, or other the possessor for the time being of the Duchy of Cornwall, appoints shall represent the Duke of Cornwall or other the possessor aforesaid, and shall be deemed to be the owner of the interest and may do any act or thing under the said Part II which the owner of that interest is authorised or required to do thereunder.

. . .

4. The amount of any compensation payable under section thirty-seven of this Act by the Chancellor of the Duchy of Lancaster shall be raised and paid as an expense incurred in improvement of land belonging to Her Majesty in right of the Duchy within section twenty-five of the Act of the fifty-seventh year of King George the Third, Chapter ninety-seven.

5. Any compensation payable under section thirty-seven of this Act by the person representing the Duke of Cornwall or other the possessor for the time being of the Duchy of Cornwall shall be paid, and advances therefor made, in the manner and subject to the provisions of section eight of the Duchy of Cornwall Management Act 1863 with respect to improvements of land mentioned in that section.

SCHEDULE 9
TRANSITIONAL PROVISIONS (ss 41, 42, 56, 68)

...

3. Where immediately before the commencement of this Act a person was protected by section seven of the Leasehold Property (Temporary Provisions) Act 1951, against the making of an order or giving of a judgment for possession or ejectment, the Rent Acts shall apply in relation to the dwelling-house to which that person's protection extended immediately before the commencement of this Act as if section fifteen of this Act had always had effect.

APPENDIX C

THE FORMS

Form Number 1

Landlord's Notice to Terminate Business Tenancy*

(Landlord and Tenant Act 1954, section 25)

To: (*name of tenant*)
of   (*address of tenant*)

IMPORTANT—THIS NOTICE IS INTENDED TO BRING YOUR TENANCY TO AN END. IF YOU WANT TO CONTINUE TO OCCUPY YOUR PROPERTY YOU MUST ACT QUICKLY. READ THE NOTICE AND ALL THE NOTES CAREFULLY. IF YOU ARE IN ANY DOUBT ABOUT THE ACTION YOU SHOULD TAKE, GET ADVICE IMMEDIATELY e.g. FROM A SOLICITOR OR SURVEYOR OR A CITIZENS ADVICE BUREAU.

---

1. This notice is given under section 25 of the Landlord and Tenant Act 1954.

2. It relates to ....
(*description of property*)
of which you are the tenant.

3. I/we give you notice terminating your tenancy on ....

4. Within two months after the giving of this notice, you must notify me/us in writing whether or not you are willing to give up possession of the property comprised in the tenancy on the date stated in paragraph 3.

5.** If you apply to the court under Part II of the Landlord and Tenant Act 1954 for the grant of a new tenancy, I/we will not oppose your application.

See notes 1 and 8.

See notes 2 and 3.

---

* This form must *not* be used if—
  (a) no previous notice terminating the tenancy has been given under section 25 of the Act, and
  (b) the tenancy is the tenancy of a house (as defined for the purpose of Part I of the Leasehold Reform Act 1967), and
  (c) the tenancy is a long tenancy at a low rent (within the meaning of that Act of 1967), and
  (d) the tenant is not a company or other artificial person.
     If the above apply, use form number 13 instead of this form.

**The landlord must cross out one version of paragraph 5. If the second version is used the paragraph latter(s) must be filled in.

OR

5.** If you apply to the court under Part II of the Landlord and Tenant Act 1954 for the grant of a new tenancy, I/we will oppose it on the grounds mentioned in paragraph(s) .... of section 30(1) of the Act.

6. All correspondence about this notice should be sent to †[the landlord][the landlord's agent] at the address given below.

<table>
<tr><td rowspan="9">See notes 4 and 5.
†Cross out words in square brackets if they do not apply.</td><td>Date ....</td></tr>
<tr><td>Signature of †[landlord][landlord's agent]</td></tr>
<tr><td>...</td></tr>
<tr><td>Name of landlord ....</td></tr>
<tr><td>Address of landlord ....</td></tr>
<tr><td>...</td></tr>
<tr><td>...</td></tr>
<tr><td>†[Address of agent ....</td></tr>
<tr><td>..]</td></tr>
</table>

NOTES

Termination of tenancy

1. This notice is intended to bring your tenancy to an end. You can apply to the court for a new tenancy under the Landlord and Tenant Act 1954 by following the procedure outlined in notes 2 and 3 below. If you do your tenancy will continue after the date shown in paragraph 3 of this notice while your claim is being considered. The landlord can ask the court to fix the rent which you will have to pay while the tenancy continues. The terms of any *new* tenancy not agreed between you and the landlord will be settled by the court.

Claiming a new tenancy

2. If you want to apply to the court for a new tenancy you must:—
(1) notify the landlord in writing not later than 2 months after the giving of this notice that you are not willing to give up possession of the property;

AND

(2) apply to the court, not earlier than 2 months nor later than 4 months after the giving of this notice, for a new tenancy. You should apply to the County Court unless the rateable value of the business part of your premises is above the current County Court limit. In that case you should apply to the High Court.

3. The time limits in note 2 run from the giving of the notice. The date of the giving of the notice may not be the date written on the notice or the date on which you actually saw it. It may, for instance, be the date on which the notice was delivered through the post to your last address known to the person giving the notice. If there has been any delay in

your seeing this notice you may need to act very quickly. If you are in any doubt get advice immediately.

> **WARNING TO TENANT**
> IF YOU DO NOT KEEP TO THE TIME LIMITS IN NOTE 2, YOU WILL *LOSE* YOUR RIGHT TO APPLY TO THE COURT FOR A NEW TENANCY.

Landlord's opposition to claim for a new tenancy

4. If you apply to the court for a new tenancy, the landlord can only oppose your application on one or more of the grounds set out in section 30(1) of the 1954 Act. These grounds are set out below. The paragraph letters are those given in the Act. The landlord can only use a ground if its paragraph letter is shown in paragraph 5 of the notice.

Grounds

(a) where under the current tenancy the tenant has any obligations as respects the repair and maintenance of the holding, that the tenant ought not to be granted a new tenancy in view of the state of repair of the holding, being a state resulting from the tenant's failure to comply with the said obligations;

(b) that the tenant ought not to be granted a new tenancy in view of his persistent delay in paying rent which has become due;

(c) that the tenant ought not to be granted a new tenancy in view of other substantial breaches by him of his obligations under the current tenancy, or for any other reason connected with the tenant's use or management of the holding;

(d) that the landlord has offered and is willing to provide or secure the provision of alternative accommodation for the tenant, that the terms on which the alternative accommodation is available are reasonable having regard to the terms of the current tenancy and to all other relevant circumstances, and that the accommodation and the time at which it will be available are suitable for the tenant's requirements (including the requirement to preserve goodwill) having regard to the nature and class of his business and to the situation and extent of, and facilities afforded by, the holding;

(e) where the current tenancy was created by the sub-letting of part only of the property comprised in a superior tenancy and the landlord is the owner of an interest in reversion expectant on the termination of that superior tenancy, that the aggregate of the rents reasonably obtainable on separate lettings of the holding and the remainder of that property would be substantially less than the rent reasonably obtainable on a letting of that property as a whole, that on the termination of the current tenancy the landlord requires possession of the holding for the purposes of letting or otherwise disposing of the said property as a whole, and that in view thereof the tenant ought not to be granted a new tenancy;

(f) that on the termination of the current tenancy the landlord intends to demolish or reconstruct the premises comprised in the holding or a substantial part of those premises or to carry out substantial work of construction on the holding or part thereof and that he could not reasonably do so without obtaining possession of the holding;

If the landlord uses this ground, the court can sometimes still grant a new tenancy if certain conditions set out in section 31A of the Act can be met.)

(g) that on the termination of the current tenancy the landlord intends to occupy the holding for the purposes, or partly for the purposes, of a business to be carried on by him therein, or as his residence.

(The landlord must normally have been the landlord for at least five years to use this ground.)

Compensation

5. If you cannot get a new tenancy solely because grounds (e), (f) or (g) apply, you are entitled to compensation under the 1954 Act. If your landlord has opposed your application on any of the other grounds as well as (e), (f) or (g) you can only get compensation if the Court's refusal to grant a new tenancy is based solely on grounds (e), (f) or (g). In other words you cannot get compensation under the 1954 Act if the Court has refused your tenancy on *other* grounds even if (e), (f) or (g) also apply.

6. If your landlord is an authority possessing compulsory purchase powers (such as a local authority) you may be entitled to a disturbance payment under Part III of the Land Compensation Act 1973.

Negotiating a new tenancy

7. Most leases are renewed by negotiation. If you do try to agree a new tenancy with your landlord, remember—

(1) that your present tenancy will not be extended after the date in paragraph 3 of this notice unless you *both*

(a) give written notice that you will not vacate (note 2(1) above); *and*

(b) apply to the court for a new tenancy (note 2(2) above);

(2) that you will lose your right to apply to the court if you do not keep to the time limits in note 2.

Validity of this notice

8. The landlord who has given this notice may not be the landlord to whom you pay your rent. "Business" is given a wide meaning in the 1954 Act and is used in the same sense in this notice. The 1954 Act also has rules about the date which the landlord can put in paragraph 3. This depends on the terms of your tenancy. If you have any doubts about whether this notice is valid, get immediate advice.

Explanatory booklet

9. The Department of the Environment and Welsh Office booklet "Business Leases and Security of Tenure" explains the main provisions of Part II of the 1954 Act. It is available from the Department of the Environment Publications Store, Building No. 3, Victoria Road, South Ruislip, Middlesex.

Form Number 2

Landlord's Notice to Terminate Business Tenancy on Grounds of Public Interest

(Landlord and Tenant Act 1954, sections 25 and 27)

To: (*name of tenant*)

of   (*address of tenant*)

> IMPORTANT—THIS NOTICE IS INTENDED TO BRING YOUR TENANCY TO AN END. READ THE NOTICE AND ALL THE NOTES CAREFULLY. IF YOU ARE IN ANY DOUBT ABOUT THE ACTION YOU SHOULD TAKE, GET ADVICE IMMEDIATELY e.g. FROM A SOLICITOR OR SURVEYOR OR A CITIZENS ADVICE BUREAU.

1. This notice is given under section 25 and 57 of the Landlord and Tenant Act 1954.
2. It relates to ....
                                  (*description of property*)
of which you are the tenant.
3. We give you notice terminating your tenancy on ....
4. A certificate has been given by ....
that is requisite for †[our purposes] [the purposes of ....]
that the use or occupation of all or part of the property shall be change by ....
A copy of the certificate is contained in the Schedule to this notice.
5. All correspondence about this notice should be sent to †[the landlord][the landlord's agent] at the address given below.

Date ....

Signature of †[landlord] [the landlord's agent] ....

....

Name of landlord ....

Address of landlord ....

....

....

†Cross out words in square brackets if they do not apply.

---

* This form must *not* be used if—
  (a) no previous notice terminating the tenancy has been given under section 25 of the Act, and
  (b) the tenancy is the tenancy of a house (as defined for the purpose of Part I of the Leasehold Reform Act 1967), and
  (c) the tenancy is a long tenancy at a low rent (within the meaning of that Act of 1967), and
  (d) the tenant is not a company or other artificial person.
      If the above apply, use form number 14 instead of this form.

†[Address of agent ....

....

....]

SCHEDULE

[Insert a copy of the certificate]

NOTES

Termination of tenancy

1. This notice is intended to bring your tenancy to an end. Usually tenants under tenancies to which Part II of the Landlord and Tenant Act 1954 applies can apply to the court for a new tenancy. You cannot do so because a certificate has been given under section 57 of the Act and the date in paragraph 3 of the notice is not earlier than the date specified in the certificate (set out in the Schedule to this notice) as the date by which the use or occupation of all or part of the property shall be changed.

Compensation

2. Because the court cannot order the grant of a new tenancy in your case, you are entitled to compensation under the 1954 Act when you leave the property. Also if your landlord is an authority possessing compulsory purchase powers (such as a local authority) you may be entitled to a disturbance payment under Part III of the Land Compensation Act 1973.

Validity of notice

3. The landlord who has given this notice may not be the landlord to whom you pay your rent. "Business" is given a wide meaning in the 1954 Act and is used in the same sense in this notice. The 1954 Act also has rules about the date which the landlord can put in paragraph 3. This depends on the terms of your tenancy. If you have any doubts about whether this notice is valid, get immediate advice.

Explanatory booklet

4. [The Department of the Environment and Welsh Office booklet "Business Leases and Security of Tenure" explains the main provisions of Part II of the 1954 Act. It is available from the Department of the Environment Publications Store, Building No. 3, Victoria Road, South Ruislip, Middlesex.]

Form Number 3

LANDLORD'S NOTICE TO TERMINATE BUSINESS TENANCY WHERE CHANGE REQUIRED AT FUTURE DATE ON GROUNDS OF PUBLIC INTEREST*

(LANDLORD AND TENANT ACT 1954, SECTIONS 25 AND 57)

To: *(name of tenant)*

of *(address of tenant)*

> IMPORTANT—THIS NOTICE IS INTENDED TO BRING YOUR TENANCY TO AN END. IF YOU WANT TO CONTINUE TO OCCUPY YOUR PROPERTY YOU MUST ACT QUICKLY. READ THE NOTICE AND ALL THE NOTES CAREFULLY. IF YOU ARE IN ANY DOUBT ABOUT THE ACTION YOU SHOULD TAKE, GET ADVICE IMMEDI-ATELY e.g. FROM A SOLICITOR OR SURVEYOR OR A CITIZENS ADVICE BUREAU.

1. This notice is given under sections 25 and 57 of the Landlord and Tenant Act 1954.

2. It relates to ....

(description of property)

of which you are the tenant.

3. I/we give you notice terminating your tenancy on ....   See notes 1 and 8.

4. Within two months after the giving of this notice, you must notify us in writing whether or not you are willing to give up possession of the property comprised in the tenancy on the date stated in paragraph 3.   See notes 2 and 3.

5.** If you apply to the court under Part II of the Landlord and Tenant Act 1954 for the grant of a new tenancy, we will not oppose your application.

OR

5.** If you apply to the court under Part II of the Landlord and Tenant Act 1954 for the grant of a new tenancy, we will oppose it on the grounds mentioned in paragraph(s) .... of section 30(1) of that Act.

---

* This form must *not* be used if—
  (a) no previous notice terminating the tenancy has been given under section 25 of the Act, and
  (b) the tenancy is the tenancy of a house (as defined for the purpose of Part I of the Leasehold Reform Act 1967), and
  (c) the tenancy is a long tenancy at a low rent (within the meaning of that Act of 1967), and
  (d) the tenant is not a company or other artificial person.
    If the above apply, use form number 13 instead of this form.

**The landlord must cross out one version of paragraph 5. If the second version is used the paragraph letter(s) must be filled in.
See notes 4 and 5.

See notes 1
and 6.

†Cross out
words in
square
brackets if
they do not
apply.

6. A certificate has been given by ....

that it is requisite for †[our purposes][the purposes of ....]

that the use or occupation of all or part of the property shall be changed by ....

A copy of the certificate is contained in the Schedule to this notice.

7. All correspondence about this notice should be sent to †[the landlord][the land-lord's agent] at the address given below.

Date ....

Signature of †[landlord][landlord's agent] ....

Name of landlord ....

Address of landlord ....

....

†[Address of agent ....

....

....]

SCHEDULE

[Insert a copy of the certificate]

NOTES

Termination of tenancy

1. This notice is intended to bring your tenancy to an end. You can apply to the court for a new tenancy under the Landlord and Tenant Act 1954 by following the procedure outlined in notes 2 and 3 below. If you do your tenancy will continue after the date shown in paragraph 3 of the notice while your claim is being considered. The landlord can ask the court to fix the rent which you will have to pay while the tenancy continues. The terms of any *new* tenancy not agreed between you and the landlord will be settled by the court. However, a certificate has been given under section 57 of the 1954 Act and a copy is con-tained in the Schedule to this notice. This means that if the court orders the grant of a new tenancy the new tenancy must end not later than the date specified in the certificate. Any new tenancy ordered to be granted will not be a tenancy to which Part II of the 1954 Act applies.

Claiming a new tenancy

2. If you want to apply to the court for a new tenancy you must:—

(1) notify the landlord in writing not later than 2 months after the giving of this notice that you are not willing to give up possession of the property;

AND

(2) apply to the court, not earlier than 2 months nor later than 4 months after the giving of this notice, for a new tenancy. You should apply to the County Court unless the rateable value of the business part of your premises is above the current County Court limit. In that case you should apply to the High Court.

3. The time limits in note 2 run from the giving of the notice. The date of the giving of the notice may not be the date written on the notice or the date on which you actually saw it. It may, for instance, be the date on which the notice was delivered through the post to your last address known to the person giving the notice. If there has been any delay in

---

WARNING TO TENANT

IF YOU DO NOT KEEP TO THE TIME LIMITS IN NOTE 2, YOU WILL *LOSE* YOUR RIGHT TO APPLY TO THE COURT FOR A NEW TENANCY.

---

your seeing this notice you may need to act very quickly. If you are in any doubt get advice immediately.

Landlord's opposition to claim for a new tenancy

4. If you apply to the court for a new tenancy, the landlord can only oppose your application on one or more of the grounds set out in section 30(1) of the 1954 Act. These grounds are set out below. The paragraph letters are those given in the Act. The landlord can only use a ground if its paragraph letter is shown in paragraph 5 of the notice.

Grounds

(a) where under the current tenancy the tenant has any obligations as respects the repair and maintenance of the holding, that the tenant ought not to be granted a new tenancy in view of the state of repair of the holding, being a state resulting from the tenant's failure to comply with the said obligations;

(b) that the tenant ought not to be granted a new tenancy in view of his persistent delay in paying rent which has become due;

(c) that the tenant ought not to be granted a new tenancy in view of other substantial breaches by him of his obligations under the current tenancy, or for any other reason connected with the tenant's use or management of the holding;

(d) that the landlord has offered and is willing to provide or secure the provision of alternative accommodation for the tenant, that the terms on which the alternative accommodation is available are reasonable having regard to the terms of the current tenancy and to all other relevant circumstances, and that the accommodation and the time at which it will be available are suitable for the tenant's requirements (including the requirement to preserve goodwill) having regard to the nature and class of his business and to the situation and extent of, and facilities afforded by, the holding;

(e) where the current tenancy was created by the sub-letting of part only of the property comprised in a superior tenancy and the landlord is the owner of an interest in reversion expectant on the termination of that superior tenancy, that the aggregate of the rents reasonably obtainable on separate lettings of the holding and the remainder of that property would be substantially less than the rent reasonably obtainable on a letting of that property as a whole, that on the termination of the current tenancy the landlord requires possession of the holding for the purposes of letting or otherwise disposing of the said property as a whole, and that in view thereof the tenant ought not to be granted a new tenancy;

(f) that on the termination of the current tenancy the landlord intends to demolish or re-construct the premises comprised in the holding or a substantial part of those premises or to carry out substantial work of construction on the holding or part thereof and that he could not reasonably do so without obtaining possession of the holding;
If the landlord uses this ground, the court can sometimes still grant a new tenancy if certain conditions set out in section 31A of the Act can be met.)

(g) that on the termination of the current tenancy the landlord intends to occupy the holding for the purposes, or partly for the purposes, of a business to be carried on by him therein, or as his residence.
(The landlord must normally have been the landlord for at least five years to use this ground.)

Compensation

5. If you cannot get a new tenancy solely because grounds (e), (f) or (g) apply, you are entitled to compensation under the 1954 Act. If your landlord has opposed your application on any of the other grounds as well as (e), (f) or (g) you can only get compensation if the Court's refusal to grant a new tenancy is based solely on grounds (e), (f) or (g). In other words you cannot get compensation under the 1954 Act if the Court has refused your tenancy on *other* grounds even if (e), (f) or (g) also apply. If the court *does* order the grant of a new tenancy you will be entitled to compensation under the 1954 Act because the new tenancy cannot expire later than the date specified in the certificate in the Schedule.

6. If your landlord is an authority possessing compulsory purchase powers (such as a local authority) you may be entitled to a disturbance payment under Part III of the Land Compensation Act 1973.

Negotiating a new tenancy

7. Most leases are renewed by negotiation. If you do try to agree a new tenancy with your landlord, remember—
(1) that your present tenancy will not be extended after the date in paragraph 3 of this notice unless you *both*
(a) give written notice that you will not vacate (note 2(1) above); *and*
(b) apply to the court for a new tenancy (note 2(2) above);
(2) that you will lose your right to apply to the court if you do not keep to the time limits in note 2.

Validity of this notice

8. The landlord who has given this notice may not be the landlord to whom you pay your rent. "Business" is given a wide meaning in the 1954 Act and is used in the same sense in this notice. The 1954 Act also has rules about the date which the landlord can put in paragraph 3. This depends on the terms of your tenancy. If you have any doubts about whether this notice is valid, get immediate advice.

Explanatory booklet

9. The Department of the Environment and Welsh Office booklet "Business Leases and Security of Tenure" explains the main provisions of Part II of the 1954 Act. It is available from the Department of the Environment Publications Store, Building No. 3, Victoria Road, South Ruislip, Middlesex.

Form Number 4

Landlord's Notice to Terminate Business Tenancy on Grounds of National Security

(Landlord and Tenant Act 1954, sections 25 and 27)

To: (*name of tenant*)

of   (*address of tenant*)

> IMPORTANT—THIS NOTICE IS INTENDED TO BRING YOUR TENANCY TO AN END. READ THE NOTICE AND ALL THE NOTES CAREFULLY. IF YOU ARE IN ANY DOUBT ABOUT THE ACTION YOU SHOULD TAKE, GET ADVICE IMMEDIATELY e.g. FROM A SOLICITOR OR SURVEYOR OR A CITIZENS ADVICE BUREAU.

1. This notice is given under sections 25 and 58 of the Landlord and Tenant Act 1954.

2. It relates to ....

   (*description of property*)

of which you are the tenant.

3. We give you notice terminating your tenancy on ....

4. A certificate has been given by ....

that it is necessary for reasons of national security that the use or occupation of the property should be discontinued or changed. A copy of the certificate is contained in the Schedule to this notice.

5. All correspondence about this notice should be sent to †[the landlord][the landlord's agent] at the address given below.

Date ....

Signature of †[landlord] [landlord's agent] ....

†Cross out
words in
square
brackets if
they do not
apply.

Name of landlord ....

Address of landlord ....

....

†[Address of agent ....

....]

SCHEDULE

[Insert a copy of the certificate]

NOTES

Termination of tenancy

1. This notice is intended to bring your tenancy to an end. Usually tenants under tenancies to which Part II of the Landlord and Tenant Act 1954 applies can apply to the court for a new tenancy. You cannot do so because a certificate has been given under section 58 of the Act that it is necessary for reasons of national security that the use or occupation of the property shall be changed.

Compensation

2. Because the court cannot order the grant of a new tenancy in your case, you are entitled to compensation under the 1954 Act when you leave the property. Also you may be entitled to a disturbance payment under Part III of the Land Compensation Act 1973.

Validity of notice

3. The landlord who has given this notice may not be the landlord to whom you pay your rent. "Business" is given a wide meaning in the 1954 Act and is used in the same sense in this notice. The 1954 Act also has rules about the date which the landlord can put in paragraph 3. This depends on the terms of your tenancy. If you have any doubts about whether this notice is valid, get immediate advice.

Explanatory booklet

4. [The Department of the Environment and Welsh Office booklet "Business Leases and Security of Tenure" explains the main provisions of Part II of the 1954 Act. It is available from the Department of the Environment Publications Store, Building No. 3, Victoria Road, South Ruislip, Middlesex.]

Form Number 5

Landlord's Notice to Terminate Business Tenancy by Reason of the Local Employment Act 1972*

(Landlord and Tenant Act 1954, sections 25, 58 and 60)

To: *(name of tenant)*

of   *(address of tenant)*

> IMPORTANT—THIS NOTICE IS INTENDED TO BRING YOUR TENANCY TO AN END. READ THE NOTICE AND ALL THE NOTES CAREFULLY. IF YOU ARE IN ANY DOUBT ABOUT THE ACTION YOU SHOULD TAKE, GET ADVICE IMMEDIATELY e.g. FROM A SOLICITOR OR SURVEYOR OR A CITIZENS ADVICE BUREAU.

1. This notice is given under sections 25, 58 and 60 of the Landlord and Tenant Act 1954.

2. You are the tenant of ....
                                   (description of property)
which is situated in a locality which is either—
   (a) a development area, or
   (b) an intermediate area.

3. We give you notice terminating your tenancy on ....

4. A certificate has been given by the Secretary of State that it is necessary or expedient for the purposes mentioned in section 2(1) of the Local Employment Act 1972 that the use or occupation of the property should be changed. A copy of the certificate is contained in the Schedule to this notice.

5. All correspondence about this notice should be sent to †[the landlord] [the landlord's agent] at the address given below.

†Cross out words in square brackets if they do not apply.

Date ....

Signature of †[landlord][landlord's agent] ....

....

Name of landlord ....

Address of landlord ....

....

....

---

* This form must *not* be used if—
   (a) no previous notice terminating the tenancy has been given under section 25 of the Act, and
   (b) the tenancy is the tenancy of a house (as defined for the purpose of Part I of the Leasehold Reform Act 1967), and
   (c) the tenancy is a long tenancy at a low rent (within the meaning of that Act of 1967), and
   (d) the tenant is not a company or other artificial person.
     If the above apply, use form number 16 instead of this form.

†[Address of agent ....

....

....]

SCHEDULE

[Insert a copy of the certificate]

NOTES

Termination of tenancy

1. This notice is intended to bring your tenancy to an end. Usually tenants under tenancies to which Part II of the Landlord and Tenant Act 1954 applies can apply to the court for a new tenancy. You cannot do so because the Secretary of State has certified that it is necessary or expedient for achieving the purposes mentioned in section 2(1) of the Local Employment Act 1972 that the use or occupation of the property shall be changed.

Validity of notice

2. The landlord who has given this notice may not be the landlord to whom you pay your rent. "Business" is given a wide meaning in the 1954 Act and is used in the same sense in this notice. The 1954 Act also has rules about the date which the landlord can put in paragraph 3. This depends on the terms of your tenancy. If you have any doubts about whether this notice is valid, get immediate advice.

Explanatory booklet

3. [The Department of the Environment and Welsh Office booklet "Business Leases and Security of Tenure" explains the main provisions of Part II of the 1954 Act. It is available from the Department of the Environment Publications Store, Building No. 3, Victoria Road, South Ruislip, Middlesex.]

Form Number 6

LANDLORD'S NOTICE TO TERMINATE BUSINESS TENANCY OF WELSH DEVELOPMENT AGENCY PREMISES*

(LANDLORD AND TENANT ACT 1954, SECTIONS 25, 58 AND 60A)

To: *(name of tenant)*

of   *(address of tenant)*

> IMPORTANT—THIS NOTICE IS INTENDED TO BRING YOUR TENANCY TO AN END. READ THE NOTICE AND ALL THE NOTES CAREFULLY. IF YOU ARE IN ANY DOUBT ABOUT THE ACTION YOU SHOULD TAKE, GET ADVICE IMMEDIATELY e.g. FROM SOLICITOR OR SURVEYOR OR A CITIZENS ADVICE BUREAU.

1. This notice is given under sections 25, 58 and 60A of the Landlord and Tenant Act 1954.

2. It relates to ....
(description of property)
of which you are the tenant.

3. We give you notice terminating your tenancy on ....

4. A certificate has been given by the Secretary of State that it is necessary or expedient, for the purposes of providing employment appropriate to the needs of the area in which the premises are situated, that the use or occupation of the premises should be changed. A copy of the certificate is contained in the Schedule to this notice.

5. All correspondence about this notice should be sent to †[the landlord] [the landlord's agent] at the address given below.

Date ....

Signature of †[landlord] [landlord's agent] ....

†Cross out words in square brackets if they do not apply.

Name of landlord ....

Address of landlord ....

....

....

†[Address of agent ....

---

* This form must *not* be used if—
  (a) no previous notice terminating the tenancy has been given under section 25 of the Act, and
  (b) the tenancy is the tenancy of a house (as defined for the purpose of Part I of the Leasehold Reform Act 1967), and
  (c) the tenancy is a long tenancy at a low rent (within the meaning of that Act of 1967), and
  (d) the tenant is not a company or other artificial person.
     If the above apply, use form number 16 instead of this form.

....

....]

SCHEDULE

[Insert a copy of the certificate]

NOTES

Termination of tenancy

1. This notice is intended to bring your tenancy to an end. Usually tenants under tenancies to which Part II of the Landlord and Tenant Act 1954 applies can apply to the court for a new tenancy. You cannot do so because the Secretary of State has given a certificate under section 60A of the Act that it is necessary or expedient, for the purpose of providing employment appropriate to the needs of the area in which the premises are situated, that the use or occupation of the property should be changed.

Compensation

2. Because the court cannot order the grant of a new tenancy in your case, you are entitled to compensation under the 1954 Act when you leave the property. You will *not* be entitled to compensation if either;
   (a) the premises were vested in the Welsh Development Agency under section 7 or 8 of the Welsh Development Agency Act 1975; or
   (b) you were not the tenant of the premises when the Agency acquired the interest by virtue of which the certificate contained in the Schedule was given.

3. You may be entitled to a disturbance payment under Part III of the Land Compensation Act 1973.

Validity of notice

4. The landlord who has given this notice may not be the landlord to whom you pay your rent. "Business" is given a wide meaning in the 1954 Act and is used in the same sense in this notice. The 1954 Act also has rules about the date which the landlord can put in paragraph 3. This depends on the terms of your tenancy. If you have any doubts about whether this notice is valid, get immediate advice.

Explanatory booklet

5. The Department of the Environmental booklet "Business Tenancies" explains the main provisions of Part II of the 1954 Act in more detail than these notes. It is available from Her Majesty's Stationery Office or through booksellers.

Form Number 7

LANDLORD'S NOTICE TO TERMINATE BUSINESS TENANCY OF PREMISES OF THE DEVELOPMENT BOARD FOR RURAL WALES*

(LANDLORD AND TENANT ACT 1954, SECTIONS 25, 58 AND 60B)

To: (*name of tenant*)
of   (*address of tenant*)

> IMPORTANT—THIS NOTICE IS INTENDED TO BRING YOUR TENANCY TO AN END. READ THE NOTICE AND ALL THE NOTES CAREFULLY. IF YOU ARE IN ANY DOUBT ABOUT THE ACTION YOU SHOULD TAKE, GET ADVICE IMMEDIATELY e.g. FROM A SOLICITOR OR SURVEYOR OR A CITIZENS ADVICE BUREAU.

1. This notice is given under sections 25, 58 and 60B of the Landlord and Tenant Act 1954.

2. It relates to ....
(*description of property*)
of which you are the tenant.

3. We give you notice terminating your tenancy on ....

4. A certificate has been given by the Secretary of State that it is necessary or expedient, for the purposes of providing employment appropriate to the needs of the area in which the premises are situated, that the use or occupation of the premises should be changed. A copy of the certificate is contained in the Schedule to this notice.

5. All correspondence about this notice should be sent to †[the landlord] [the landlord's agent] at the address given below.

Date ....

Signature of †[landlord] [landlord's agent] ....

†Cross out
words in   Name of landlord ....
square   Address of landlord ....
brackets if
they do not   ....
apply.   ....

---

* This form must *not* be used if—
  (a) no previous notice terminating the tenancy has been given under section 25 of the Act, and
  (b) the tenancy is the tenancy of a house (as defined for the purpose of Part I of the Leasehold Reform Act 1967), and
  (c) the tenancy is a long tenancy at a low rent (within the meaning of that Act of 1967), and
  (d) the tenant is not a company or other artificial person.
     If the above apply, use form number 18 instead of this form.

†[Address of agent ....

....

....]

....

SCHEDULE

[Insert a copy of the certificate]

NOTES

Termination of tenancy

1. This notice is intended to bring your tenancy to an end. Usually tenants under tenancies to which Part II of the Landlord and Tenant Act 1954 applies can apply to the court for a new tenancy. You cannot do so because the Secretary of State has given a certificate under section 60B of the Act that it is necessary or expedient, for the purpose of providing employment appropriate to the needs of the area in which the premises are situated, that the use or occupation of the property should be changed.

Compensation

2. Because the court cannot order the grant of a new tenancy in your case, you are entitled to compensation under the 1954 Act when you leave the property. You will *not* be entitled to compensation if either;
    (a) the premises are premises which
        (i) were vested in the Welsh Development Agency by section 8 of the Welsh Development Agency Act 1975 or were acquired by the Agency when no tenancy subsisted in the premises; and
        (ii) subsequently vested in the Development Board under section 24 of the Development of Rural Wales Act 1976; or
    (b) you were not a tenant of the premises when the Board acquired the interest by virtue of which the certificate contained in the Schedule was given.
3. You may be entitled to a disturbance payment under Part III of the Land Compensation Act 1973.

Validity of notice

4. The landlord who has given this notice may not be the landlord to whom you pay your rent. "Business" is given a wide meaning in the 1954 Act and is used in the same sense in this notice. The 1954 Act also has rules about the date which the landlord can put in paragraph 3. This depends on the terms of your tenancy. If you have any doubts about whether this notice is valid, get immediate advice.

Explanatory booklet

5. [The Department of the Environment and Welsh Office booklet "Business Leases and Security of Tenure" explains the main provisions of Part II of the 1954 Act. It is available from the Department of the Environment Publications Store, Building No. 3, Victoria Road, South Ruislip, Middlesex.]

Form Number 8

TENANT'S REQUEST FOR NEW TENANCY OF BUSINESS PREMISES

(LANDLORD AND TENANT ACT 1954, SECTION 26)

To: (*name of tenant*)

of   (*address of tenant*)

IMPORTANT—THIS IS A REQUEST FOR A NEW TENANCY OF YOUR PROPERTY OR PART OF IT. IF YOU WANT TO OPPOSE THIS REQUEST YOU MUST ACT QUICKLY. READ THE REQUEST AND ALL THE NOTES CAREFULLY. IF YOU ARE IN ANY DOUBT ABOUT THE ACTION YOU SHOULD TAKE, GET ADVICE IMMEDIATELY e.g. FROM A SOLICITOR OR SURVEYOR OR A CITIZENS ADVICE BUREAU.

---

1. This request is made under section 26 of the Landlord and Tenant Act 1954.
2. You are the landlord of ....

   (*description of property*)
3. I/We request you to grant a new tenancy beginning on ....
4. I/We propose that:
   (a) the property comprised in the new tenancy should be ....

   ....

   (b) the rent payable under the new tenancy should be ....

   ....

   (c) the other terms of the new tenancy should be ....

5. All correspondence about this notice should be sent to †[the tenant] [the tenant's agent] at the address given below.

Date ....   †Cross out

Signature of †[tenant] [tenant's agent]   words in

....   square

Name of tenant ....   brackets if

Address of tenant ....   they do not

....   apply.

†[Address of agent ....

....

....]

NOTES

Request for a new tenancy

1. This request by your tenant for a new tenancy brings his current tenancy to an end on the day before the date mentioned in paragraph 3 above. He can apply to the court under the Landlord and Tenant Act 1954 for a new tenancy. If he does, his current tenancy will continue after the date mentioned in paragraph 3 of this request while his application is being considered by the court. You can ask the court to fix the rent which your tenant will have to pay whilst his tenancy continues. The terms of any *new* tenancy not agreed between you and your tenant will be settled by the court.

Opposing a request for a new tenancy

2. If you do not want to grant a new tenancy, you *must* within two months of the making of this request, give your tenant notice saying that you will oppose any application he makes to the court for a new tenancy. You do not need a special form to do this, but you must state on which of the grounds set out in the 1954 Act you will oppose the application—see note 4.

3. The time limit in note 2 runs from the making of this request. The date of the making of the request may not be the date written on the request or the date on which you actually saw it. It may, for instance, be the date on which the request was delivered through the post to your last address known to the person giving the request. If there has been any delay in your seeing this request you may need to act very quickly. If you are in any doubt get advice immediately.

WARNING TO LANDLORD

IF YOU DO NOT KEEP TO THE TIME LIMIT IN NOTE 2, YOU WILL *LOSE* YOUR RIGHT TO OPPOSE YOUR TENANT'S APPLICATION TO THE COURT FOR A NEW TENANCY IF HE MAKES ONE.

Grounds for opposing an application

4. If your tenant applies to the court for a new tenancy, you can only oppose the application on one or more of the grounds set out in section 30(1) of the 1954 Act. These grounds are set out below. The paragraph letters are those given in the Act.

Grounds

(a) where under the current tenancy the tenant has any obligations as respects the repair and maintenance of the holding, that the tenant ought not to be granted a new tenancy in view of the state of repair of the holding, being a state resulting from the tenant's failure to comply with the said obligations;

(b) that the tenant ought not to be granted a new tenancy in view of his persistent delay in paying rent which has become due;

(c) that the tenant ought not to be granted a new tenancy in view of other substantial breaches by him of his obligations under the current tenancy, or for any other reason connected with the tenant's use or management of the holding;

(d) that you have offered and are willing to provide or secure the provision of alternative accommodation for the tenant, that the terms on which the alternative accommodation is available are reasonable having regard to the terms of the current tenancy and to all other relevant circumstances, and that the accommodation and the time at which it will be available are suitable for the tenant's requirements (including the requirement to preserved goodwill) having regard to the nature and class of his business and to the situation and extent of, and facilities afforded by, the holding;

(e) where the current tenancy was created by the sub-letting of part only of the property comprised in a superior tenancy and you are the owner of an interest in reversion expectant on the termination of that superior tenancy, that the aggregate of the rents reasonably obtainable on separate lettings of the holding and the remainder of the property would be substantially less than the rent reasonably obtainable on a letting of that property as a whole, that on the termination of the current tenancy you require possession of the holding for the purpose of letting or otherwise disposing of the said property as a whole, and that in view thereof the tenant ought not to be granted a new tenancy;

(f) that on the termination of the current tenancy you intend to demolish or reconstruct the premises comprised in the holding or a substantial part of those premises or to carry out substantial work of construction on the holding or part thereof and that you could no reasonably do so without obtaining possession of the holding; (If you use this ground, the court can sometimes still grant a new tenancy if certain conditions set out in section 31A of the Act can be met.)

(g) that on termination of the current tenancy you intend to occupy the holding for the purposes, or partly for the purposes, of a business to be carried on by you therein, or as your residence. (You must normally have been the landlord for at least five years to use this ground.)

You can only use one or more of the above grounds if you have stated them in the notice referred to in note 2 above.

Compensation

5. If your tenant cannot get a new tenancy solely because grounds (e), (f) or (g) apply, he is entitled to compensation from you under the 1954 Act. If you have opposed his application on any of the other grounds as well as (e), (f) or (g) he can only get compensation if the court's refusal to grant a new tenancy is based solely on grounds (e), (f) or (g). In other words he cannot get compensation under the 1954 Act if the court has refused his tenancy on *other* grounds even if (e), (f) or (g) also apply.

6. If you are an authority possessing compulsory purchase powers (such as a local authority) you will be aware that your tenant may be entitled to a disturbance payment under Part III of the Land Compensation Act 1973.

Negotiating a new tenancy

7. Most leases are renewed by negotiation. If you do try to agree a new tenancy with your tenant—

(1) YOU should remember that you will not be able to oppose an application to the court for a new tenancy unless you give the notice mentioned in note 2 above within the time limit in that note;

(2) YOUR TENANT should remember that he will lose his right to apply to the court for a new tenancy unless he makes the application not less than two nor more than four months after the making of this request.

Validity of this notice

8. The landlord to whom this request is made may not be the landlord to whom the tenant pays the rent. "Business" is given a wide meaning in the 1954 Act and is used in the same sense in this request. The 1954 Act also has rules about the date which the tenant can put in paragraph 3. This depends on the terms of the tenancy. If you have any doubts about whether this request is valid, get immediate advice.

Explanatory booklet

9. [The Department of the Environment and Welsh Office booklet "Business Leases and Security of Tenure" explains the main provisions of Part II of the 1954 Act. It is available from the Department of the Environment Publications Store, Building No. 3, Victoria Road, South Ruislip, Middlesex.]

Form Number 9

NOTICE BY LANDLORD REQUIRING INFORMATION ABOUT OCCUPATION AND SUB-TENANCIES OF BUSINESS PREMISES

(LANDLORD AND TENANT ACT 1954, SECTION 40(1))

To: (*name of tenant*)
of   (*address of tenant*)

> IMPORTANT—THIS NOTICE REQUIRES YOU TO GIVE YOUR LANDLORD CERTAIN INFORMATION. YOU MUST ACT QUICKLY. READ THE NOTICE AND ALL THE NOTES CAREFULLY. IF YOU ARE IN ANY DOUBT ABOUT THE ACTION YOU SHOULD TAKE, GET ADVICE IMMEDIATELY e.g. FROM A SOLICITOR OR SURVEYOR OR A CITIZENS ADVICE BUREAU.

1. This notice is given under section 40(1) of the Landlord and Tenant Act 1954.
2. It relates to ....
   (*description of property*)
   of which you are the tenant.
3. I/We require you to notify me/us in writing, within one month of the service of this notice on you—
   (a) whether you occupy the premises or any part of them wholly or partly for business purposes; and
   (b) whether you have a sub-tenant.
4. If you have a sub-tenant, I/We also require you to state—
   (a) what premises are comprised in the sub-tenancy;
   (b) if the sub-tenancy is for a fixed term, what the term is, or, if the sub-tenancy is terminable by notice, by what notice it can be terminated;
   (c) what rent the sub-tenant pays;
   (d) the sub-tenant's full name;
   (e) whether, to the best of your knowledge and belief, the sub-tenant occupies either the whole or part of the premises sub-let to him and, if not, what is his address.
5. All correspondence about this notice should be sent to †[the landlord] [the landlord's agent] at the address given below.

Date ....

Signature of †[landlord] [the landlord's agent] ....

Name of landlord ....

Address of landlord ....

....

†Cross out words in square brackets if they do not apply.

†[Address of agent ....

....

....]

NOTES

Purpose of this notice

1. Your landlord (or if he is a tenant himself, possibly his landlord) has served this notice on you to obtain the information he needs in order to find out his position under Part II of the Landlord and Tenant Act 1954 in relation to your tenancy. He will then know, for example, whether, when your tenancy expires, you will be entitled to apply to the court for a new tenancy of the whole of the premises comprised in your present tenancy; you may not be entitled to a new tenancy of any part of the premises which you have sub-let. (In certain circumstances, a sub-tenant may become a direct tenant of the landlord.)

Replying to this notice

2. Section 40 of the 1954 Act says that you *must* answer the questions asked in the notice and you *must* let the landlord have your answers in writing within one month of the service of the notice. You do not need a special form for this. If you do not answer these questions or give the landlord incorrect information he might suffer a loss for which, in certain circumstances, you could be held liable.

3. If you have let to more than one sub-tenant you should give the information required in respect of each sub-letting

Validity of this notice

4. The landlord who has given this notice may not be the landlord to whom you pay your rent. "Business" is given a wide meaning in the 1954 Act and is used in the same sense in this notice. The landlord cannot ask for this information earlier than two years before your tenancy is due to expire or could be brought to an end by notice given by him. If you have any doubts about whether this notice is valid get immediate advice.

Explanatory booklet

5. [The Department of the Environment and Welsh Office booklet "Business Leases and Security of Tenure" explains the main provisions of Part II of the 1954 Act. It is available from the Department of the Environment Publications Store, Building No. 3, Victoria Road, South Ruislip, Middlesex.]

Form Number 10

NOTICE BY TENANT OF BUSINESS PREMISES REQUIRING INFORMATION FROM LANDLORD ABOUT LANDLORD'S INTEREST

(LANDLORD AND TENANT ACT 1954, SECTION 40(2))

To: (*name of tenant*)

of   (*address of tenant*)

> IMPORTANT—THIS NOTICE REQUIRES YOU TO GIVE YOUR TENANT CERTAIN INFORMATION. YOU MUST ACT QUICKLY. READ THE NOTICE AND ALL THE NOTES CAREFULLY. IF YOU ARE IN ANY DOUBT ABOUT THE ACTION YOU SHOULD TAKE, GET ADVICE IMMEDIATELY e.g. FROM A SOLICITOR OR SURVEYOR OR A CITIZENS ADVICE BUREAU.

1. This notice is given under section 40(2) of the Landlord and Tenant Act 1954.
2. It relates to ....
(description of property)
of which you are the landlord.

3. I/We give you notice requiring you to notify me/us in writing, within one month of the service of this notice on you—

(a) whether you are the freeholder of the whole or part of the premises.

If you are *not* the freeholder:

(b) I/we also require you to state, to the best of your knowledge and belief—

    (i)   the name and address of the person who is your immediate landlord in respect of the premises or the part of which you are not the freeholder;

   (ii)   the length of your tenancy; and

 (iii)   the earliest date (if any) at which your tenancy can be terminated by notice to quit given by your immediate landlord.

4. I/We also require you to notify me/us—

(a) whether there is a mortgagee in possession of your interest in the property and, if so, his name and address; and

(b) if there is a receiver appointed by the mortgagee or by the court, his name and address also.

5. All correspondence about this notice should be sent to †[the tenant] [the tenant's agent] at the address given below.

Date ....

Signature of †[tenant][tenant's agent] ....

....

Name of tenant ....

†Cross out words in square brackets if they do not apply.

Address of tenant ....

....

†[Address of agent ....·

....

....]

NOTES

Purpose of this notice

1. Your tenant has served this notice on you to obtain the information he needs in order to find out who is his landlord for the purposes of Part II of the Landlord and Tenant Act 1954. The Act in certain circumstances enables a tenant of business premises to obtain a new tenancy from that landlord.

Replying to this notice

2. Section 40 of the 1954 Act says that you *must* answer the questions asked in the notice and you *must* let your tenant have your answers in writing within one month of the service of the notice. You do not need a special form for this. If you do not answer these questions or give your tenant incorrect information he might suffer a loss for which, in certain circumstances, you could be held liable.

Validity of this notice

3. "Business" is given a wide meaning in the 1954 Act and is used in the same sense in this notice. Your tenant cannot ask for this information earlier than two years before his current tenancy is due to expire or could be brought to an end by notice to quit given by you. If you have any doubts about whether this notice is valid, get immediate advice.

Explanatory booklet

4. [The Department of the Environment and Welsh Office booklet "Business Leases and Security of Tenure" explains the main provisions of Part II of the 1954 Act. It is available from the Department of the Environment Publications Store, Building No. 3, Victoria Road, South Ruislip, Middlesex.]

Form Number 11

Notice by Tenant of Business Premises Requiring Information from Mortgagee about Landlord's Interest

(Landlord and Tenant Act 1954, section 40(2))

To: *(name of tenant)*

of   *(address of tenant)*

> IMPORTANT—THIS NOTICE REQUIRES YOU TO GIVE THE TENANT OF PREMISES OF WHICH YOU ARE THE MORTGAGEE IN POSSESSION, CERTAIN INFORMATION. YOU MUST ACT QUICKLY. READ THE NOTICE AND ALL THE NOTES CAREFULLY. IF YOU ARE IN ANY DOUBT ABOUT THE ACTION YOU SHOULD TAKE, GET ADVICE IMMEDIATELY e.g. FROM A SOLICITOR OR SURVEYOR OR A CITIZENS ADVICE BUREAU.

1. This notice is given under section 40(2) of the Landlord and Tenant Act 1954.

2. It relates to ....

(description of property)

which I/we believe to be in mortgage to you.

3. I/We give you notice requiring you to notify me/us in writing, within one month of the service of this notice on you—

(a) whether your mortgagor is the freeholder or the holder of part of the premises. If he is *not* the freeholder:

(b) I/we also require you to state, to the best of your knowledge and belief—

    (i)   the name and address of the person who is your mortgagor's immediate landlord in respect of the premises or the part of which he is not the freeholder;

    (ii)   the length of your mortgagor's tenancy; and

    (iii) the earliest date (if any) at which this tenancy can be terminated by notice to quit given by his immediate landlord.

4. All correspondence about this notice should be sent to †[the tenant] [the tenant's agent] at the address given below.

Date ....

Signature of †[tenant] [tenant's agent] ....

....

Name of tenant ....

Address of tenant ....

....

....

†[Address of agent ....

....

....]

†Cross out words in square brackets if they do not apply.

Notes

Purpose of this notice

1. You are either the mortgagee in possession of business premises or a receiver appointed by the mortgagee or by the court. A tenant of the whole or part of the premises has served this notice on you to obtain the information he needs in order to find out who is his landlord for the purposes of Part I of the Landlord and Tenant Act 1954. The Act in certain circumstances enables a tenant of business premises to obtain a new tenancy from that landlord.

Replying to this notice

2. Section 40 of the 1954 Act says that you *must* answer the questions asked in the notice and you *must* let your tenant have your answers in writing within one month of the service of the notice. You do not need a special form for this. If you do not answer these questions or give your tenant incorrect information he might suffer a loss for which, in certain circumstances, you could be held liable.

Validity of this notice

3. "Business" is given a wide meaning in the 1954 Act and is used in the same sense in this notice. Your tenant cannot ask for this information earlier than two years before his current tenancy is due to expire or could be brought to an end by notice to quit given by you. If you have any doubts about whether this notice is valid, get immediate advice.

Explanatory booklet

4. [The Department of the Environment and Welsh Office booklet "Business Leases and Security of Tenure" explains the main provisions of Part II of the 1954 Act. It is available from the Department of the Environment Publications Store, Building No. 3, Victoria Road, South Ruislip, Middlesex.]

Form Number 12

WITHDRAWAL OF LANDLORD'S NOTICE TO TERMINATE BUSINESS TENANCY

(LANDLORD AND TENANT ACT 1954, SECTION 44 AND PARAGRAPH 6 OF SCHEDULE 6)

To: *(name of tenant)*
of *(address of tenant)*

> IMPORTANT—THIS NOTICE IS INTENDED TO WITHDRAW A PREVIOUS NOTICE TO TERMINATE YOUR TENANCY. READ THE NOTICE AND ALL THE NOTES CARE-FULLY. IF YOU ARE IN ANY DOUBT ABOUT THE ACTION YOU SHOULD TAKE, GET ADVICE IMMEDIATELY e.g. FROM A SOLICITOR OR SURVEYOR OR A CITIZENS ADVICE BUREAU.

1. This notice is given under section 44 of, and paragraph 6 of Schedule 6 to, the Landlord and Tenant Act 1954.

2. It relates to ....
        (description of property)
of which you are the tenant.

3. I/We have become your landlord for the purposes of the Act.

4. I/we withdraw the notice given to you by ....
.... *(name of former landlord)*
of ....
....
....

(address of former landlord) terminating your tenancy on ....

5. All correspondence about this notice should be sent to †[the landlord] [the land-lord's agent] at the address given below.

Date ....

Signature of †[landlord] [the landlord's agent] ....

Name of landlord ....

Address of landlord ....
....

†[Address of agent ....
....
....]

†Cross out words in square brackets if they do not apply.

391

NOTES

Purpose of this notice

1. You were earlier given a notice bringing your tenancy to an end, but there has now been a change of landlord for the purposes of the 1954 Act. This new notice has been given to you by your new landlord and withdraws the earlier notice, which now has no effect. However, the new landlord can, if he wishes, give you a fresh notice with the intention of bringing your tenancy to an end.

Validity of this notice

2. The landlord who has given this notice may not be the landlord to whom you pay your rent. "Business" is given a wide meaning in the 1954 Act and is used in the same sense in this notice. This notice can only be given within two months after the giving of the earlier notice. If you have any doubts about whether this notice is valid, get immediate advice. If it is *not* valid you may have to act quickly to preserve your position under the earlier notice.

Explanatory booklet

3. [The Department of the Environment and Welsh Office booklet "Business Leases and Security of Tenure" explains the main provisions of Part II of the 1954 Act. It is available from the Department of the Environment Publications Store, Building No. 3, Victoria Road, South Ruislip, Middlesex.]

Form Number 13

Landlord's Notice to Terminate Business Tenancy where Leasehold Reform Act 1967 May Apply*

(Landlord and Tenant Act 1954, section 25 and Leasehold Reform Act 1967, Schedule 3, paragraph 10)

To: (*name of tenant*)
of   (*address of tenant*)

> IMPORTANT—THIS NOTICE IS INTENDED TO BRING YOUR TENANCY TO AN END. IF YOU WANT TO CONTINUE TO OCCUPY YOUR PROPERTY YOU MUST ACT QUICKLY. READ THE NOTICE AND ALL THE NOTES CAREFULLY. IF YOU ARE IN ANY DOUBT ABOUT THE ACTION YOU SHOULD TAKE, GET ADVICE IMMEDI-ATELY e.g. FROM A SOLICITOR OR SURVEYOR OR A CITIZENS ADVICE BUREAU.

1. This notice is given under section 25 of the Landlord and Tenant Act 1954.
2. It relates to ....
(*description of property*)
of which you are the tenant.
3. I/we give you notice terminating your tenancy on ....
4. Within two months after the giving of this notice, you must notify me/us in writing whether or not you are willing to give up possession of the property comprised in the tenancy on the date stated in paragraph 3.   See notes 1 and 13.
5.** If you apply to the court under Part II of the Landlord and Tenant Act 1954 for the grant of a new tenancy, I/we will not oppose your application.   See notes 5 and 9.

OR

5.** If you apply to the court under Part II of the Landlord and Tenant Act 1954 for the grant of a new tenancy, I/we will oppose it on the grounds mentioned in paragraph(s) .... of section 30(1) of the Act.

---

* This form must *not* be used if—
  (a) no previous notice terminating the tenancy has been given under section 25 of the Act, and
  (b) the tenancy is the tenancy of a house (as defined for the purpose of Part I of the Leasehold Reform Act 1967), and
  (c) the tenancy is a long tenancy at a low rent (within the meaning of that Act of 1967), and
  (d) the tenant is not a company or other artificial person.
**The landlord must cross out one version of paragraph 5. If the second version is used the paragraph letter(s) must be filled in.
See notes 5 and 9.
See notes 6 and 7.

6. (a) If you have a right under the Leasehold Reform Act 1967 to acquire the freehold or an extended lease of the property comprised in the tenancy, notice of your desire to have the freehold or an extended lease cannot be given more than two months after the service of this notice on you.

(b) If you have that right and give such a notice within those two months, *this* notice will not operate.

(c) If you give such a notice within those two months—

†(i) I/we shall be entitled to apply to the court under section †[17][18] of the Leasehold Reform Act 1967 and I/we †[propose][do not propose] to do so.]

†(ii) I/we shall not be entitled to apply to the court under section †[18][18] of the Leasehold Reform Act 1967.]

†[7. The following persons are known or believed by me/us to have an interest superior to your tenancy or to be the agents concerned with the property on behalf of someone who has such an interest ....

....

....]

8. All correspondence about this notice should be sent to †[the landlord][the landlord's agent] at the address given below.

Date ....

Signature of †[landlord][the landlord's agent] ....

Name of landlord ....

Address of landlord ....

....

†[Address of agent ....

....]

NOTES

Termination of tenancy

1. This notice is intended to bring your tenancy to an end. Because your tenancy is one to which Part II of the Landlord and Tenant Act 1954 applies, you can apply to the court under that Act for a new tenancy—see notes 2 to 5 below. However, the Leasehold Reform Act 1967 may also apply to your case. If it does you may be able to buy the freehold of the property or get an extended lease under *that* Act—see notes 6 to 8 below. In some circumstances your landlord may still be able to get possession of the property. If he does, you may be able to get compensation. The amount of any compensation (see notes 9 to 11) will depend on the steps you have taken and under which Act (it is likely to be greater under the 1967 Act). If you have any doubt about what you should do, get advice immediately.

Claiming a new tenancy under the 1954 Act

2. If you apply to the court for a new tenancy you under the 1954 Act,. your present tenancy will be continued by that Act after the date shown in paragraph 3 of this notice whilst your claim is being considered. The landlord can ask the court to fix the rent which you will have to pay whilst the tenancy is continued. The terms of any *new* tenancy not agreed between you and the landlord will be determined by the court.

3. If you want to apply to the court for a new tenancy you must:—

(1) notify the landlord in writing not later than two months after the giving of this notice that you are not willing to give up possession of the property;

AND

(2) apply to the court, not earlier than two months nor later than four months after the giving of this notice, for a new tenancy. You should apply to the County Court unless the rateable value of the business part of your premises is above the current County Court limit. In that case you should apply to the High Court.

4. The time limits in note 3 run from the giving of the notice. The date of the giving of the notice may not be the date written on the notice or the date on which you actually saw it. It may, for instance, be the date on which the notice was delivered through the post to your last address known to the person giving the notice. If there has been any delay in your seeing this notice you may need to act very quickly. If you are in any doubt get advice immediately.

Landlord's opposition to claim for a new tenancy

5. If you apply to the court for a new tenancy, the landlord can only oppose your application on one or more of the grounds set out in section 30(1) of the 1954 Act. These grounds are set out below. The paragraph letters are those given in the Act. The landlord can only use a ground if its paragraph letter is shown in paragraph 5 of the notice.

Grounds

(a) where under the current tenancy the tenant has any obligations as respects the repair and maintenance of the holding, that the tenant ought not to be granted a new tenancy in view of the state of repair of the holding, being a state resulting from the tenant's failure to comply with the said obligations;

(b) that the tenant ought not to be granted a new tenancy in view of his persistent delay in paying rent which has become due;

(c) that the tenant ought not to be granted a new tenancy in view of other substantial breaches by him of his obligations under the current tenancy, or for any other reason connected with the tenant's use or management of the holding;

(d) that the landlord has offered and is willing to provide or secure the provision of alternative accommodation for the tenant, that the terms on which the alternative accommodation is available are reasonable having regard to the terms of the current tenancy and to all other relevant circumstances, and that the accommodation and the time at which it will be available are suitable for the tenant's requirements (including the requirement to preserve goodwill) having regard to the nature and class of his business and to the situation and extent of, and facilities afforded by, the holding;

(e) where the current tenancy was created by the sub-letting of part only of the property comprised in a superior tenancy and the landlord is the owner of an interest in reversion expectant on the termination of that superior tenancy, that the aggregate of the rents reasonably obtainable on separate lettings of the holding and the remainder of that property would be substantially less than the rent reasonably obtainable on a letting of that property as a whole, that on the termination of the current tenancy the landlord requires possession of the holding for the purposes of letting or otherwise disposing of the said property as a whole, and that in view thereof the tenant ought not to be granted a new tenancy;

(f) that on the termination of the current tenancy the landlord intends to demolish or reconstruct the premises comprised in the holding or a substantial part of those premises or to carry out substantial work of construction on the holding or part thereof and that he could not reasonably do so without obtaining possession of the holding;

(If the landlord uses this ground, the court can sometimes still grant a new tenancy if certain conditions set out in section 31A of the Act can be met.)

(g) that on the termination of the current tenancy the landlord intends to occupy the holding for the purposes, or partly for the purposes, of a business to be carried on by him therein, or as his residence.

(The landlord must normally have been the landlord for at least five years to use this ground.)

Rights under the Leasehold Reform Act 1967

6. If the property comprised in your tenancy is a house, as defined in the 1967 Act, you may have the right to buy the freehold of the property or to extend your lease for fifty years. You can do so if *all* the following conditions are met:

(i) your lease was originally granted for a term of more than 21 years, or it was preceded by such a lease which was granted or assigned to you; *and*

(ii) your lease is of the whole house; *and*

(iii) your lease is at a low rent. That is, your present annual rent is less than two-thirds of the rateable value of your house as assessed either on March 23, 1965, or on the first day of the term in the case of a lease granted to commence after March 23, 1965; *and*

(iv) you are occupying the house as your only or main residence and you have been doing so either for the whole of the last three years, or for a total of three years during the last ten years under this lease; *and*

(v) the rateable value of your house was at one time within certain limits.

Claiming your rights under the 1967 Act

7. If you do have the right to buy the freehold or to extend the lease and wish to exercise it you must serve the appropriate notice (on a special form prescribed under the 1967 Act) on the landlord. You must do so within two months after the date this notice was

served on you. The date of service of the notice may not be the date written on the notice or the date on which you actually saw it. It may, for instance, be the date on which the notice was delivered through the post to your last address known to the person serving the notice. If there has been any delay in your seeing this notice you may need to act very quickly. If you are in any doubt get advice immediately.

> WARNING TO TENANT
>
> IF YOU DO NOT KEEP TO THE TIME LIMITS IN NOTES 3 AND 7 YOU WILL *LOSE* YOUR RIGHT TO APPLY TO THE COURT FOR A NEW TENANCY UNDER THE 1954 ACT OR TO CLAIM THE FREEHOLD OR AN EXTENDED LEASE UNDER THE 1967 ACT.

Landlord's opposition to claims under the 1967 Act

8. If your landlord acquired his interest in the house not later than February 18, 1966 he can object to your claim to buy the freehold or to extend the lease on the grounds that he needs the house for occupation by himself or a member of his family. This objection will be under section 18 of the 1967 Act. If you claim a fifty year extension of your lease, your landlord can object under section 17 of the 1967 Act on the grounds that he wishes to redevelop the property. Paragraph 6(c) of the notice will tell you whether the landlord believes he has the right to apply to the court under sections 17 and 18 and whether or not he proposed to do so.

Compensation

9. If you cannot get a new tenancy solely because grounds (e), (f) or (g) apply, you are entitled to compensation under the 1954 Act. If your landlord has opposed your application on any of the other grounds as well as (e), (f) or (g) you can only get compensation if the Court's refusal to grant a new tenancy is based solely on grounds (e), (f) or (g). In other words you cannot get compensation under the 1954 Act if the Court has refused your tenancy on *other* grounds even if (e), (f) or (g) also apply.

10. If your landlord is an authority possessing compulsory purchase powers (such as a local authority) you may be entitled to a disturbance payment under Part III of the Land Compensation Act 1973.

11. If you have right under the 1967 Act to buy the freehold or get an extended lease of your premises but the landlord, as mentioned in note 8, is able to obtain possession of the premises, compensation under the 1967 Act is payable. This is normally higher than the compensation mentioned in note 9 above. Your solicitor or surveyor will be able to advise you on this.

Negotiations with your landlord

12. Many tenants buy their houses or renew their leases by negotiation. If you do try to by the property by agreement or to negotiate a new lease with your landlord, remember—

(1) that your present tenancy will not be extended under the 1954 Act after the date in paragraph 3 of this notice unless you *both*

    (a) give written notice that you will not vacate (note 3(1) above); *and*

    (b) apply to the court for a new tenancy (note 3(2) above);

(2) that you will lose your right to apply to the court if you do not keep to the time limits in note 3; and

(3) that you will lose your right to serve a notice claiming to buy the freehold or to have an extended lease under the 1967 Act if you do not keep to the time limit in note 7.

Validity of this notice

13. The landlord who has given this notice may not be the landlord to whom you pay your rent. "Business" is given a wide meaning in the 1954 Act and is used in the same sense in this notice. The 1954 Act also has rules about the date which the landlord can put in paragraph 3. This depends on the terms of your tenancy. If you have any doubts about whether this notice is valid, get immediate advice.

Explanatory booklets

14. The Department of the Environment and Welsh Office booklet "Business Leases and Security of Tenure" explains the main provisions of Part II of the 1954 Act. The Department of the Environment and Welsh Office booklet "Leasehold Reform" (booklet no. 9 in the series of housing booklets) gives details of the rights of leaseholders to claim to buy the freehold or to have an extension to the lease of their house. "Business Leases and Security of tenure" is available from the Department of the Environment Publications Store, Building No. 3, Victoria Road, South Ruislip, Middlesex and "Leasehold Reform" is available from council offices and housing aid centres.

Form Number 14

Landlord's Notice to Terminate Business Tenancy on Grounds of Public Interest where Leasehold Reform Act 1967 May Apply*

(Landlord and Tenant Act 1954, sections 25 and 57 and Leasehold Reform Act 1967, Schedule 3, paragraph 10)

To: (*name of tenant*)
of   (*address of tenant*)

> IMPORTANT—THIS NOTICE IS INTENDED TO BRING YOUR TENANCY TO AN
> END. READ THE NOTICE AND ALL THE NOTES CAREFULLY. IF YOU ARE IN ANY
> DOUBT ABOUT THE ACTION YOU SHOULD TAKE, GET ADVICE IMMEDIATELY e.g.
> FROM A SOLICITOR OR SURVEYOR OR A CITIZENS ADVICE BUREAU.

1. This notice is given under sections 25 and 57 of the Landlord and Tenant Act 1954.
2. It relates to ....
(*description of property*)
of which you are the tenant.
3. We give you notice terminating your tenancy on ....
4. A certificate has been given under section 57 of the 1954 Act by ....   See notes 1
that it is requisite for †[our purposes] [the purposes of ....]   and 5.
that the use of occupation of all or part of the property shall be changed by ....
A copy of the certificate is contained in the Schedule to this notice.
5. (a) If you have a right under the Leasehold Reform Act 1967 to acquire the freehold
   or an extended lease of the property comprised in the tenancy, notice of your desire   See note 2.
   to have the freehold or an extended lease cannot be given more than two months
   after the service of this notice on you.
   (b) If you have that right and give such a notice within those two months, *this* notice will not operate.   See note 4.
   (c) If within those two months you give written notice claiming to be entitled to acquire the freehold or an extended lease we will be entitled to apply to the court under
   section 17 of the Leasehold Reform Act 1967 and we propose to do so.
†6. The following persons are known or believed by us to have an interest superior to
your tenancy or to be the agents concerned with the property on behalf of someone who   †Cross out
                                                                                                words in
                                                                                                square
_____   brackets if
* This form must *not* be used if—   they do not
   (a) no previous notice terminating the tenancy has been given under section 25 of the Act, and   apply.
   (b) the tenancy is the tenancy of a house (as defined for the purpose of Part I of the Leasehold
        Reform Act 1967), and
   (c) the tenancy is a long tenancy at a low rent (within the meaning of that Act of 1967), and
   (d) the tenant is not a company or other artificial person.

has such an interest ....

....

....]

7. All correspondence about this notice should be sent to †[the landlord] [the land-lord's agent] at the address given below.

Date ....

Signature of †[landlord] [the landlord's agent] ....

....

Name of landlord ....

Address of landlord ....

....

†[Address of agent ....

....]

SCHEDULE

[Insert a copy of the certificate]

NOTES

Termination of tenancy

1. This notice is intended to bring your tenancy to an end. Usually tenants under ten-ancies to which Part II of the Landlord and Tenant Act 1954 applies can apply to the court for a new tenancy. You cannot do so because a certificate has been given under section 57 of the Act and the date in paragraph 3 of this notice is not earlier than the date in the cer-tificate (set out in the Schedule to this notice) as the date by which the use or occupation of all or part of the property shall be changed. Because of this you will be entitled to com-pensation—see note 3.

Rights under the Leasehold Reform Act 1967

2. If the property comprised in your tenancy is a house, as defined in the 1967 Act, and if *all* the following conditions are met—

   (i) your lease was originally granted for a term of more than 21 years, or it was pre-ceded by such a lease which was granted or assigned to you; *and*

   (ii) your lease is of the whole house; *and*

   (iii) your lease is at a low rent. That is, your present annual rent is less than two-thirds of the rateable value of your house as assessed either on March 23, 1965, or on the first day of the term in the case of a lease granted to commence after March 23, 1965; *and*

   (iv) you are occupying the house as your only or main residence and you have been doing so either for the whole of the last three years, or for a total of three years during the last ten years under this lease; *and*

(v) the rateable value of your house was at one time within certain limits

you would usually have the right to buy the freehold of the property or to extend your lease for fifty years under the 1967 Act. You cannot do so when a certificate has been given under section 57 of the 1954 Act, because section 28 of the 1967 Act says that any notice you give to exercise such a right shall be of no effect. However, you may be entitled to compensation—see note 4.

Compensation

3. Because the court cannot order the grant of a new tenancy under the 1954 Act you are entitled to compensation under that Act when you leave the property. Also if your landlord is an authority possessing compulsory purchase powers (such as a local authority) you may be entitled to a disturbance payment under Part III of the Land Compensation Act 1973.

4. Because in your case you cannot buy the freehold of the property or extend your lease for 50 years under the 1967 Act, you may also be entitled to compensation under that Act. You cannot, however, get compensation under both the 1954 Act and under the 1967 Act. The compensation payable under the 1967 Act is likely to be greater than that payable under the 1965 Act. In order to be able to claim compensation under 1967 Act you must, *within two months* serve a written notice on your landlord claiming to be entitled to acquire the freehold or an extended lease (*i.e.* to say, in effect, that you would have been able to acquire the freehold or an extended lease were is not for the certificate under section 57 of the 1954 Act). The notice must be on a special form prescribed under the 1967 Act. The two month time limit runs from the service of the notice. The date of service of the notice may not be the date written on the notice or the date on which you actually saw it. It may, for instance, be the date on which the notice was delivered through the post to your last address known to the person serving the notice. If there has been any delay in your seeing this notice you may need to act very quickly. If you are in any doubt about what you should do, get advice immediately.

> **WARNING TO TENANT**
>
> IF YOU DO NOT KEEP TO THE TIME LIMIT IN NOTE 4, YOU WILL *LOSE* YOUR RIGHT TO COMPENSATION UNDER THE 1967 ACT.

Validity of this notice

5. The landlord who has given this notice may not be the landlord to whom you pay your rent. "Business" is given a wide meaning in the 1954 Act and is used in the same sense in this notice. The 1954 Act also has rules about the date which the landlord can put in paragraph 3. This depends on the terms of your tenancy. If you have any doubts about whether this notice is valid, get advice immediately.

Explanatory booklets

6. [The Department of the Environment and Welsh Office booklet "Business Leases and Security of Tenure" explains the main provisions of Part II of the 1954 Act. The Department of the Environment and Welsh Office booklet "Leasehold Reform" (booklet no. 9 in the series of housing booklets) give details of the rights of leaseholders to claim to buy the freehold or to have an extension to the lease of their house. "Business Leases and Security of Tenure" is available from the Department of the Environment Publications Store, Building No. 3, Victoria Road, South Ruislip, Middlesex and "Leasehold Reform" is available from council offices and housing aid centres.]

Form Number 15

Landlord's Notice to Terminate Business Tenancy where Change Required at Future Date on Grounds of Public Interest and where Leasehold Reform Act 1967 May Apply*

(Landlord and Tenant Act 1954, sections 25 and 27 and Leasehold Reform Act 1967, Schedule 3, paragraph 10)

To: *(name of tenant)*

of *(address of tenant)*

> IMPORTANT—THIS NOTICE IS INTENDED TO BRING YOUR TENANCY TO AN END. IF YOU WANT TO CONTINUE TO OCCUPY YOUR PROPERTY YOU MUST ACT QUICKLY. READ THE NOTICE AND ALL THE NOTES CAREFULLY. IF YOU ARE IN ANY DOUBT ABOUT THE ACTION YOU SHOULD TAKE, GET ADVICE IMMEDIATELY e.g. FROM A SOLICITOR OR SURVEYOR OR A CITIZENS ADVICE BUREAU.

1. This notice is given under sections 25 and 57 of the Landlord and Tenant Act 1954.

2. It relates to ....

(description of property)

of which you are the tenant.

3. We give you notice terminating your tenancy on ....

4. Within two months after the giving of this notice, you must notify us in writing whether or not you are willing to give up possession of the property comprised in the tenancy on the date stated in paragraph 3.   See notes 1 and 9.

5.** If you apply to the court under Part II of the Landlord and Tenant Act 1954 for the grant of a new tenancy, we will not oppose your application.   See notes 5 and 9.

OR

5.** If you apply to the court under Part II of the Landlord and Tenant Act 1954 for

---

* This form must *not* be used if—

    (a) no previous notice terminating the tenancy has been given under section 25 of the Act, and

    (b) the tenancy is the tenancy of a house (as defined for the purpose of Part I of the Leasehold Reform Act 1967), and

    (c) the tenancy is a long tenancy at a low rent (within the meaning of that Act of 1967), and

    (d) the tenant is not a company or other artificial person.

**The landlord must cross out one version of paragraph 5. If the second version is used the paragraph letter(s) must be filled in.

See notes 4 and 5.

†Cross out words in square brackets if they do not apply.

6. A certificate has been given under section 57 of the 1954 Act by ....
that it is requisite for †[our purposes][the purposes of ....]
that the use or occupation of all or part of the property shall be changed by ....
A copy of the certificate is contained in the Schedule to this notice.

    7. (a) If you have a right under the Leasehold Reform Act 1967 to acquire the freehold or an extended lease of the property comprised in the tenancy, notice of your desire to have the freehold or an extended lease cannot be given more than two months after the service of this notice on you

See notes 1 and 8.

    (b) If you have the right and give such a notice within those two months, *this* notice will not operate.

    (c) If within those two months you give written notice claiming to be entitled to acquire the freehold or an extended lease we will be entitled to apply to the court under section 17 of the Leasehold Reform Act 1967 and we propose to do so.

    †[8. The following persons are known or believed by us to have an interest superior to your tenancy or to be the agents concerned with the property on behalf of someone who has such an interest ....

....

....

....]

9. All correspondence about this notice should be sent to †[the landlord][the landlord's agent] at the address given below.

Date ....

Signature of †[landlord][the landlord's agent]

....

Name of landlord ....

Address of landlord ....

....

†[Address of agent ....

....]

SCHEDULE

[Insert a copy of the certificate]

NOTES

Termination of tenancy

    1. This notice is intended to bring your tenancy to an end. Because your tenancy is one to which Part II of the Landlord and Tenant Act 1954 applies, you can apply to the court under that Act for a new tenancy. However a certificate has been given under section 57

of the 1954 Act and a copy is contained in the Schedule to this notice. This means that if the court orders the grant of a new tenancy, the new tenancy must end not later than the date specified in the certificate. Any new tenancy ordered to be granted will *not* be a tenancy to which Part II of the 1954 Act applies. However the Leasehold Reform Act 1967 may also apply in your case. If it does, you would usually have the right to buy the freehold of the property or to extend the lease for 50 years under the 1967 Act. You cannot do so when a certificate has been given under section 57 of the 1954 Act, because section 28 of the 1967 Act says that any notice you give to exercise such a right shall be of no effect. However you may be entitled to compensation. If you want to apply to the court under the 1954 Act, see notes 2 to 5 below. If you want to know about compensation, see notes 6 to 8 below. The amount of any compensation will depend on the steps you have taken and under which Act (it is likely to be greater under the 1967 Act). If you have any doubt about what you should do, get advice immediately.

Claiming a new tenancy under the 1954 Act

2. If you apply to the court for a new tenancy you under the 1954 Act,. your present tenancy will be continued by that Act after the date shown in paragraph 3 of this notice whilst your claim is being considered. The landlord can ask the court to fix the rent which you will have to pay whilst the tenancy is continued. The terms of any *new* tenancy not agreed between you and the landlord will be determined by the court.

3. If you want to apply to the court for a new tenancy you must:—

(1) notify the landlord in writing not later than two months after the giving of this notice that you are not willing to give up possession of the property;

AND

(2) apply to the court, not earlier than two months nor later than four months after the giving of this notice, for a new tenancy. You should apply to the County Court unless the rateable value of the business part of your premises is above the current County Court limit. In that case you should apply to the High Court.

4. The time limits in note 3 run from the giving of the notice. The date of the giving of the notice may not be the date written on the notice or the date on which you actually saw it. It may, for instance, be the date on which the notice was delivered through the post to your last address known to the person giving the notice. If there has been any delay in your seeing this notice you may need to act very quickly. If you are in any doubt get advice immediately.

Landlord's opposition to claim for a new tenancy

5. If you apply to the court for a new tenancy, the landlord can only oppose your application on one or more of the grounds set out in section 30(1) of the 1954 Act. These grounds are set out below. The paragraph letters are those given in the Act. The landlord can only use a ground if its paragraph letter is shown in paragraph 5 of the notice.

Grounds

(a) where under the current tenancy the tenant has any obligations as respects the repair and maintenance of the holding, that the tenant ought not to be granted a new tenancy in view of the state of repair of the holding, being a state resulting from the tenant's failure to comply with the said obligations;

(b) that the tenant ought not to be granted a new tenancy in view of his persistent delay in paying rent which has become due;

(c) that the tenant ought not to be granted a new tenancy in view of other substantial breaches by him of his obligations under the current tenancy, or for any other reason connected with the tenant's use or management of the holding;

(d) that the landlord has offered and is willing to provide or secure the provision of alternative accommodation for the tenant, that the terms on which the alternative accommodation is available are reasonable having regard to the terms of the current tenancy and to all other relevant circumstances, and that the accommodation and the time at which it will be available are suitable for the tenant's requirements (including the requirement to preserve goodwill) having regard to the nature and class of his business and to the situation and extent of, and facilities afforded by, the holding;

(e) where the current tenancy was created by the sub-letting of part only of the property comprised in a superior tenancy and the landlord is the owner of an interest in reversion expectant on the termination of that superior tenancy, that the aggregate of the rents reasonably obtainable on separate lettings of the holding and the remainder of that property would be substantially less than the rent reasonably obtainable on a letting of that property as a whole, that on the termination of the current tenancy the landlord requires possession of the holding for the purposes of letting or otherwise disposing of the said property as a whole, and that in view thereof the tenant ought not to be granted a new tenancy;

(f) that on the termination of the current tenancy the landlord intends to demolish or reconstruct the premises comprised in the holding or a substantial part of those premises or to carry out substantial work of construction on the holding or part thereof and that he could not reasonably do so without obtaining possession of the holding;

(If the landlord uses this ground, the court can sometimes still grant a new tenancy if certain conditions set out in section 31A of the Act can be met.)

(g) that on the termination of the current tenancy the landlord intends to occupy the holding for the purposes, or partly for the purposes, of a business to be carried on by him therein, or as his residence.

(The landlord must normally have been the landlord for at least five years to use this ground.)

Compensation under the 1954 Act

6. If you cannot get a new tenancy solely because grounds (e), (f) or (g) in note 5 apply, you are entitled to compensation under the 1954 Act. If your landlord has opposed your application on any of the other grounds as well as (e), (f) or (g) you can only get compensation if the Court's refusal to grant a new tenancy is based solely on grounds (e), (f) or (g). In other words you cannot get compensation under the 1954 Act if the Court has refused your tenancy on *other* grounds even if (e), (f) or (g) also apply. If the Court *does* order the grant of a new tenancy, you will be entitled to compensation under the 1954 Act because the new tenancy cannot expire later than the date specified in the certificate in the Schedule.

7. If your landlord is an authority possessing compulsory purchase powers (such as a local authority) you may be entitled to a disturbance payment under Part III of the Compensation Act 1973.

Compensation under the 1967 Act

8. If the property comprised in your tenancy is a house, as defined in the 1967 Act *all* the following conditions are met—
   (i) your lease was originally granted for a term of more than 21 years, or it is preceded by such a lease which was granted or assigned to you; *and*
   (ii) your lease is of the whole house; *and*
   (iii) your lease is at a low rent. That is, your present annual rent is less than two-thirds of the rateable value of your house as assessed either on March 23, 1965, or on the first day of the term in the case of a lease granted to commence after March 23, 1965; *and*
   (iv) you are occupying the house as your only or main residence and you have been doing so either for the whole of the last three years, or for a total of three year during the last ten years under this lease; *and*
   (v) the rateable value of your house was at one time within certain limits

you may be entitled to compensation under the 1967 Act. You cannot, however, claim compensation under both the 1954 Act and the 1967 Act. The compensation payment under the 1967 Act is likely to be greater than that payable under the 1954 Act. In order to claim compensation under the 1967 Act you must, *within two months*, serve a written notice on your landlord claiming to be entitled to acquire the freehold or an extended lease (*i.e.* to say, in effect, that you would have been able to acquire the freehold or an extended lease were it not for the certificate under section 57 of the 1954 Act). The notice must be on a special form prescribed under the 1967 Act. The two months time limit runs from the service of the notice. The date of service of the notice may not be the date written on the notice or the date on which you actually saw it. It may, for instance, be the date on which the notice was delivered through the post to your last address known to the person serving the notice. If there has been any delay in your seeing this notice you may need to act very quickly. If you are in any doubt about what you should do, get advice immediately.

> WARNING TO TENANT
> IF YOU DO NOT KEEP TO THE TIME LIMITS IN NOTES 3 AND 8 YOU WILL *LOSE*
> YOUR RIGHT TO APPLY TO THE COURT FOR A NEW TENANCY,UNDER THE 1954
> ACT OR YOUR RIGHT TO COMPENSATION UNDER THE 1967 ACT.

Validity of this notice

9. The landlord who has given this notice may not be the landlord to whom you pay your rent. "Business" is given a wide meaning in the 1954 Act and is used in the same sense in this notice. The 1954 Act also has rules about the date which the landlord can put in paragraph 3. This depends on the terms of your tenancy. If you have any doubts about whether this notice is valid, get immediate advice.

Explanatory booklets

10. The Department of the Environment and Welsh Office booklet "Business Leases and Security of Tenure" explains the main provisions of Part II of the 1954 Act. The Department of the Environment and Welsh Office booklet "Leasehold Reform" (booklet no. 9 in the series of housing booklets) gives details of the rights of leaseholders to claim to buy the freehold or to have an extension to the lease of their house. "Business Leases and Security of Tenure" is available from the Department of the Environment Publications Store, Building No. 3, Victoria Road, South Ruislip, Middlesex and "Leasehold Reform" is available from council offices and housing aid centres.

Landlord's Notice to Terminate Business Tenancy by Reason of the Local Employment Act 1972 where Leasehold Reform Act 1967 May Apply*

(Landlord and Tenant Act 1954, sections 25, 58 and 60 and Leasehold Reform Act 1967, Schedules 3, Paragraph 10)

To: *(name of tenant)*

of   *(address of tenant)*

> IMPORTANT—THIS NOTICE IS INTENDED TO BRING YOUR TENANCY TO AN END. READ THE NOTICE AND ALL THE NOTES CAREFULLY. IF YOU ARE IN ANY DOUBT ABOUT THE ACTION YOU SHOULD TAKE, GET ADVICE IMMEDIATELY e.g. FROM A SOLICITOR OR SURVEYOR OR A CITIZENS ADVICE BUREAU.

1. This notice is given under sections 25, 58 and 60 of the Landlord and Tenant Act 1954.

2. You are the tenant of ....
(description of property)
which is situated in a locality which is either—
  (a) a development area, or
  (b) an intermediate area.

3. We give you notice terminating your tenancy on ....

4. A certificate has been given by the Secretary of State that is necessary or expedient for the purposes mentioned in section 2(1) of the Local Employment Act 1972 that the use or occupation of the property should be changed. A copy of the certificate is contained in the Schedule to this notice.

5. (a) If you have a right under the Leasehold Reform Act 1967 to acquire the freehold or an extended lease of the property comprised in the tenancy, notice of your desire to have the freehold or an extended lease cannot be given more than two months after the service of this notice on you.

   (b) If you have the right and give such a notice within those two months, *this* notice will not operate.

---

* This form must *not* be used if—
  (a) no previous notice terminating the tenancy has been given under section 25 of the Act, and
  (b) the tenancy is the tenancy of a house (as defined for the purpose of Part I of the Leasehold Reform Act 1967), and
  (c) the tenancy is a long tenancy at a low rent (within the meaning of that Act of 1967), and
  (d) the tenant is not a company or other artificial person.
     If the above apply, use form number 13 instead of this form.

(c)If you give such a notice within those two months—

†[(i) We shall be entitled to apply to the court under section 17 of the Leasehold Reform Act 1967 and we †[propose] [do not propose to do so].

†(ii) We shall not be entitled to apply to the court under section 17 of the Leasehold Reform Act 1967].

†[6. The following persons are known or believed by us to have an interest superior to your tenancy or to be the agents concerned with the property on behalf of someone who has such an interest ....

....

....]

7. All correspondence about this notice should be sent to †[the landlord] [the landlord's agent] at the address given below.

Date ....

Signature of †[landlord] [the landlord's agent]

Name of landlord ....

Address of landlord ....

....

†[Address of agent ....

....]

....

SCHEDULE

[Insert a copy of the certificate]

NOTES

Termination of tenancy

1. This notice is intended to bring your tenancy to an end. Usually tenants under tenancies to which Part II of the Landlord and Tenant Act 1954 applies can apply to the court for a new tenancy. You cannot do so because the Secretary of State has certified that it is necessary or expedient for achieving the purposes mentioned in section 2(1) of the Local Employment Act 1972 that the use or occupation of the property should be changed. However, the Leasehold Reform Act 1967 may also apply in your case. If it does you may be able to buy the freehold of the property or get an extended lease under *that* Act—see notes a2 and 3 below. If you claim an extended lease your landlord may still be able to get possession of the property—see note 4. If he does, and you have served notice under the 1967 Act, you may be able to get compensation—see note 5 below. If you have any doubt about what you should do, get advice immediately.

Rights under the Leasehold Reform Act 1967

2. If the property comprised in your tenancy is a house, as defined in the 1967 Act, you may have the right to buy the freehold of the property or to extend your lease for fifty years. You can do so if *all* the following conditions are met—

(i) your lease was originally granted for a term of more than 21 years, or it was preceded by such a lease which was granted or assigned to you; *and*

(ii) your lease is of the whole house; *and*

(iii) your lease is at a low rent. That is, your present annual rent is less than two-thirds of the rateable value of your house as assessed either on March 23, 1965, or on the first day of the term in the case of a lease granted to commence after March 23, 1965; *and*

(iv) you are occupying the house as your only or main residence and you have been doing so either for the whole of the last three years, or for a total of three years during the last ten years under this lease; *and*

(v) the rateable value of your house was at one time within certain limits

Claiming your rights under the 1967 Act

3. If you do have the right to buy the freehold or to extend the lease and wish to exercise it you must serve the appropriate notice (on a special form prescribed under the Act) on the landlord. You must do so within two months after the date this notice was served on you. The date of service of the notice may not be the date written on the notice or the date on which you actually saw it. It may, for instance, be the date on which the notice was delivered through the post to your last address known to the person serving the notice. If there has been any delay in your seeing this notice you may need to act very quickly. If you are in any doubt get advice immediately.

WARNING TO TENANT

IF YOU DO NOT KEEP TO THE TIME LIMITS IN NOTE 3, YOU WILL *LOSE* YOUR RIGHT TO CLAIM THE FREEHOLD OR AN EXTENDED LEASE UNDER THE 1967 ACT.

Landlord's opposition to claims under the 1967 Act

4. If you claim a fifty year extension of your lease, your landlord can object under section 17 of the 1967 Act on the grounds that he wishes to redevelop the property. Paragraph 5(c) of the notice will tell you whether the landlord believes he has the right to apply to the court under section 17 and whether or not he proposed to do so.

Compensation

5. If you have a right under the 1967 Act to buy the freehold or get an extended lease of your premises but the landlord, as mentioned in note 4 is able to obtain possession of the premises, compensation is payable under the 1967 Act. Your solicitor will be able to advise you on this.

Negotiations with your landlord

6. Many tenants buy their houses or renew their leases by negotiation. If you do try to buy the property by agreement or to negotiate a new lease with your landlord, remember that you will lose your right to serve a notice claiming to buy the freehold or to have an extended lease under the 1967 Act if you do not keep to the time limit in note 3.

Validity

7. The landlord who has given this notice may not be the landlord to whom you pay your rent. "Business" is given a wide meaning in the 1954 Act and is used in the same sense in this notice. The 1954 Act also has rules about the date which the landlord can put in paragraph 3. This depends on the terms of your tenancy. If you have any doubts about whether this notice is valid, get advice immediately.

Explanatory booklets

8. [The Department of the Environment and Welsh Office booklet "Business Leases and Security of Tenure" explains the main provisions of Part II of the 1954 Act. The Department of the Environment and Welsh Office booklet "Leasehold Reform" (booklet no. 9 in the series of housing booklets) give details of the rights of leaseholders to claim to buy the freehold or to have an extension to the lease of their house. "Business Leases and Security of Tenure" is available from the Department of the Environment Publications Store, Building No. 3, Victoria Road, South Ruislip, Middlesex and "Leasehold Reform" is available from council offices and housing aid centres.]

Form Number 17

Landlord's Notice to Terminate Business Tenancy of Welsh Development Agency Premises where Leasehold Reform Act 1967 May Apply*

(Landlord and Tenant Act 1954, sections 25, 58 and 60A and Leasehold Reform Act 1967, Schedule 3, Paragraph 10)

To: (*name of tenant*)
of   (*address of tenant*)

> IMPORTANT—THIS NOTICE IS INTENDED TO BRING YOUR TENANCY TO AN END. READ THE NOTICE AND ALL THE NOTES CAREFULLY. IF YOU ARE IN ANY DOUBT ABOUT THE ACTION YOU SHOULD TAKE, GET ADVICE IMMEDIATELY e.g. FROM A SOLICITOR OR SURVEYOR OR A CITIZENS ADVICE BUREAU.

1. This notice is given under sections 25, 58 and 60A of the Landlord and Tenant Act 1954.

2. It relates to ....
(*description of property*)
of which you are the tenant.

3. We give you notice terminating your tenancy on ....

4. A certificate has been given by the Secretary of State that is necessary or expedient for the purposes of providing employment appropriate to the needs of the area in which   See note 1. the premises are situated, that the user or occupation of the premises should be changed. A copy of the certificate is contained in the Schedule to this notice.

5. (a) If you have a right under the Leasehold Reform Act 1967 to acquire the freehold or an extended lease of the property comprised in the tenancy, notice of your desire   See notes 2 to have the freehold or an extended lease cannot be given more than two months   to 4. after the service of this notice on you.

(b) If you have that right and give such a notice within those two months, *this* notice will not operate.

(c) If you give such a notice within those two months—

---

* This form must *not* be used if—
(a) no previous notice terminating the tenancy has been given under section 25 of the Act, and
(b) the tenancy is the tenancy of a house (as defined for the purpose of Part I of the Leasehold Reform Act 1967), and
(c) the tenancy is a long tenancy at a low rent (within the meaning of that Act of 1967), and
(d) the tenant is not a company or other artificial person.
If the above apply, use form number 13 instead of this form.

See notes 4
to 7.
†Cross out
words in
square
brackets if
they do not
apply.

†(i) We shall be entitled to apply to the court under section 17 of the Leasehold Reform Act 1967 and we †[propose] [do not propose] to do so.

†(ii) We shall not be entitled to apply to the court under section 17 of the Leasehold Reform Act 1967].

†[6. The following persons are known or believed by us to have an interest superior to your tenancy or to be the agents concerned with the property on behalf of someone who has such an interest ....

....

....]

7. All correspondence about this notice should be sent to †[the landlord][the landlord's agent] at the address given below.

Date ....

Signature of †[landlord] [the landlord's agent] ....

Name of landlord ....

Address of landlord ....

....

†[Address of agent ....

....]

SCHEDULE

[Insert a copy of the certificate]

NOTES

Termination of tenancy

1. This notice is intended to bring your tenancy to an end. Usually tenants under tenancies to which Part II of the Landlord and Tenant Act 1954 applies can apply to the court for a new tenancy. You cannot do so because the Secretary of State has given a certificate under section 60A of the Act that it is necessary or expedient, for the purposes of providing employment appropriate to the needs of the area in which the premises are situated, that the use or occupation of the property should be changed. However, the Leasehold Reform Act 1967 may also apply in your case. If it does, you may be able to buy the freehold of the property or get an extended lease under *that* Act—see notes 2 and 3 below. If you claim an extended lease your landlord may still be able to get possession of the property—see note 4. If he does, you may be able to get compensation. The amount of any compensation (see notes 5 to 7) will depend on the steps you have taken and under which Act (it is likely to be greater under the 1967 Act). If you have any doubt about what you should do, get advice immediately.

Rights under the Leasehold Reform Act 1967

2. If the property comprised in your tenancy is a house, as defined in the 1967 Act, you may have the right to buy the freehold of the property or to extend your lease for fifty years. You can do so if *all* the following conditions are met:—

(i) your lease was originally granted for a term of more than 21 years, or it was preceded by such a lease which was granted or assigned to you; *and*

(ii) your lease is of the whole house; *and*

(iii) your lease is at a low rent. That is, your present annual rent is less than two-thirds of the rateable value of your house as assessed either on March 23, 1965, or on the first day of the term in the case of a lease granted to commence after March 23, 1965; *and*

(iv) you are occupying the house as your only or main residence and you have been doing so either for the whole of the last three years, or for a total of three years during the last ten years under this lease; *and*

(v) the rateable value of your house was at one time within certain limits

Claiming your rights under the 1967 Act

3. If you do have the right to buy the freehold or to extend the lease and wish to exercise it you must serve the appropriate notice (on a special form prescribed under the Act) on the landlord. You must do so within two months after the date this notice was served on you. The date of service of the notice may not be the date written on the notice or the date on which you actually saw it. It may, for instance, be the date on which the notice was delivered through the post to your last address known to the person serving the notice. If there has been any delay in your seeing this notice you may need to act very quickly. If you are in any doubt get advice immediately.

WARNING TO TENANT

IF YOU DO NOT KEEP TO THE TIME LIMITS IN NOTE 3, YOU WILL *LOSE* YOUR RIGHT TO CLAIM THE FREEHOLD OR AN EXTENDED LEASE UNDER THE 1967 ACT.

Landlord's opposition to claims under the 1967 Act

4. If you claim a fifty year extension of your lease, your landlord can object under section 17 of the 1967 Act on the grounds that he wishes to redevelop the property. Paragraph 5(c) of the notice will tell you whether the landlord believes he has the right to apply to the court under section 17 and whether or not he proposed to do so.

Compensation

5. Because the court cannot order the grant of a new tenancy in your case, you may be entitled to compensation under the 1954 Act when you leave the property. You will *not* be entitled to such compensation if either:

(a) the premises were vested in the Welsh Development Agency under section 7 or 8 of the Welsh Development Agency Act 1975; or

(b) you were not the tenant of the premises when the Agency acquired the interest by virtue of which the certificate contained in the Schedule was given.

6. You may be entitled to a disturbance payment under Part III of the Land Compensation Act 1973.

7. If you have a right under the 1967 Act to buy the freehold or get an extended lease of your premises but the landlord, as mentioned in note 4 is able to obtain possession of the premises, compensation under the 1967 Act is payable. This is normally higher than the compensation mentioned in note 5 above. Your solicitor or surveyor will be able to advise you on this.

Negotiations with your landlord

8. Many tenants buy their houses or renew their leases by negotiation. If you do try to buy the property by agreement or to negotiate a new lease with your landlord, remember that you will lose your right to serve a notice claiming to buy the freehold or to have an extended lease under the 1967 Act if you do not keep to the time limit in note 3.

Validity of this notice

9. The landlord who has given this notice may not be the landlord to whom you pay your rent. "Business" is given a wide meaning in the 1954 Act and is used in the same sense in this notice. The 1954 Act also has rules about the date which the landlord can put in paragraph 3. This depends on the terms of your tenancy. If you have any doubts about whether this notice is valid, get advice immediately.

Explanatory booklets

10. [The Department of the Environment and Welsh Office booklet "Business Leases and Security of Tenure" explains the main provisions of Part II of the 1954 Act. The Department of the Environment and Welsh Office booklet "Leasehold Reform" (booklet no. 9 in the series of housing booklets) give details of the rights of leaseholders to claim to buy the freehold or to have an extension to the lease of their house. "Business Leases and Security of Tenure" is available from the Department of the Environment Publications Store, Building No. 3, Victoria Road, South Ruislip, Middlesex and "Leasehold Reform" is available from council offices and housing aid centres.]

Form Number 18

LANDLORD'S NOTICE TO TERMINATE BUSINESS TENANCY OF PREMISES OF THE DEVELOPMENT BOARD FOR RURAL WALES WHERE LEASEHOLD REFORM ACT 1967 MAY APPLY*

(LANDLORD AND TENANT ACT 1954, SECTIONS 25, 58 AND 60B AND LEASEHOLD REFORM ACT 1967, SCHEDULE 3, PARAGRAPH 10)

To: (*name of tenant*)
of   (*address of tenant*)

> IMPORTANT—THIS NOTICE IS INTENDED TO BRING YOUR TENANCY TO AN END. READ THE NOTICE AND ALL THE NOTES CAREFULLY. IF YOU ARE IN ANY DOUBT ABOUT THE ACTION YOU SHOULD TAKE, GET ADVICE IMMEDIATELY e.g. FROM A SOLICITOR OR SURVEYOR OR A CITIZENS ADVICE BUREAU.

1. This notice is given under sections 25, 58 and 60 of the Landlord and Tenant Act 1954.

2. It relates to ....
(*description of property*)
of which you are the tenant.

3. We give you notice terminating your tenancy on ....

4. A certificate has been given by the Secretary of State that is necessary or expedient for the purposes of providing employment appropriate to the needs of the area in which the premises are situated that the use or occupation of the premises should be changed. A copy of the certificate is contained in the Schedule to this notice.

See note 1.

5. (a) If you have a right under the Leasehold Reform Act 1967 to acquire the freehold or an extended lease of the property comprised in the tenancy, notice of your desire to have the freehold or an extended lease cannot be given more than two months after the service of this notice on you.

See notes 2 and 3.

(b) If you have the right and give such a notice within those two months, *this* notice will not operate.

---

* This form must *not* be used if—
  (a) no previous notice terminating the tenancy has been given under section 25 of the Act, and
  (b) the tenancy is the tenancy of a house (as defined for the purpose of Part I of the Leasehold Reform Act 1967), and
  (c) the tenancy is a long tenancy at a low rent (within the meaning of that Act of 1967), and
  (d) the tenant is not a company or other artificial person.
     If the above apply, use form number 13 instead of this form.

See notes 4
to 7.
†Cross out
words in
square
brackets if
they do not
apply.

(c) If you give such a notice within those two months—

†[(i) We shall be entitled to apply to the court under section 17 of the Leasehold Reform Act 1967 and we †[propose] [do not propose to do so].

†[(ii) We shall not be entitled to apply to the court under section 17 of the Leasehold Reform Act 1967].

†[6. The following persons are known or believed by use to have an interest superior to your tenancy or to be the agents concerned with the property on behalf of someone who has such an interest ....

....

....]

7. All correspondence about this notice should be sent to †[the landlord] [the landlord's agent] at the address given below.

Date ....

Signature of †[landlord] [the landlord's agent] ....

Name of landlord ....

Address of landlord ....

....

†[Address of agent ....

....]

SCHEDULE

[Insert a copy of the certificate]

NOTES

Termination of tenancy

1. This notice is intended to bring your tenancy to an end. Usually tenants under tenancies to which Part II of the Landlord and Tenant Act 1954 applies can apply to the court for a new tenancy. You cannot do so because the Secretary of State has given a certificate under section 60B of the Act that it is necessary to the needs of the area in which the premises are situated; that the use or occupation of the property should be changed. However, the Leasehold Reform Act 1967 may also apply in our case. If it does, you may be able to buy the freehold of the property or get an extended lease under *that* Act—see notes 2 and 3 below. If you claim an extended lease your landlord may still be able to get possession of the property—see note 4. If he does, you may be able to get compensation. The amount of any compensation (see notes 5 to 7) will depend on the steps you have taken and under which Act (it is likely to be greater under the 1967 Act). If you have any doubt about what you should do, get advice immediately.

Rights under the Leasehold Reform Act 1967

2. If the property comprised in your tenancy is a house, as defined in the 1967 Act, you may have the right to buy the freehold of the property or to extend your lease for fifty years. You can do so if *all* the following conditions are met:—

(i) your lease was originally granted for a term of more than 21 years, or it was preceded by such a lease which was granted or assigned to you; *and*

(ii) your lease is of the whole house; *and*

(iii) your lease is at a low rent. That is, your present annual rent is less than two-thirds of the rateable value of your house as assessed either on March 23, 1965, or on the first day of the term in the case of a lease granted to commence after March 23, 1965; *and*

(iv) you are occupying the house as your only or main residence and you have been doing so either for the whole of the last three years, or for a total of three years during the last ten years under this lease; *and*

(v) the rateable value of your house was at one time within certain limits.

Claiming your rights under the 1967 Act

3. If you do have the right to buy the freehold or to extend the lease and wish to exercise it you must serve the appropriate notice (on a special form prescribed under the Act) on the landlord. You must do so within two months after the date this notice was served on you. The date of service of the notice may not be the date written in the notice or the date on which you actually saw it. It may, for instance, be the date on which the notice was delivered through the post to your last address known to the person serving the notice. If there has been any delay in your seeing this notice you may need to act very quickly. If you are in any doubt get advice immediately.

> WARNING TO TENANT
>
> IF YOU DO NOT KEEP TO THE TIME LIMITS IN NOTE 3, YOU WILL *LOSE* YOUR RIGHT TO CLAIM THE FREEHOLD OR AN EXTENDED LEASE UNDER THE 1967 ACT.

Landlord's opposition to claims under the 1967 Act

4. If you claim a fifty year extension of your lease, your landlord can object under section 17 of the 1967 Act on the grounds that he wishes to redevelop the property. Paragraph 5(c) of the notice will tell you whether the landlord believes he has the right to apply to the court under section 17 and whether or not he proposed to do so.

Compensation

5. Because the court cannot order the grant of a new tenancy in your case, you may be entitled to compensation under the 1954 Act when you leave the property. You will *not* be entitled to such compensation if either—

(a) the premises are premises which—

(i) were vested in the Welsh Development Agency by section 8 of the Welsh

Development Agency Act 1975 or were acquired by the Agency when no tenancy subsisted in the premises; and

(ii) subsequently vested in the Development Board for Rural Wales under section 2 of the Development of Rural Wales Act 1976; or

(b) you were not a tenant of the premises when the Board acquired the interest by virtue of which the certificate contained in the Schedule was given.

6. You may be entitled to a disturbance payment under Part III of the Land Compensation Act 1973.

7. If you have a right under the 1967 Act to buy the freehold or get an extended lease on your premises but the landlord, as mentioned in note 4, is able to obtain possession of the premises, compensation under the 1967 Act is payable. This is normally higher than the compensation mentioned in note 5 above. Your solicitor or surveyor will be able to advise you on this.

Negotiations with your landlord

8. Many tenants buy their houses or renew their leases by negotiation. If you do try to buy the property by agreement or to negotiate a new lease with your landlord, remember that you will lose your right to serve a notice claiming to buy the freehold or to have an extended lease under the 1967 Act if you do not keep to the time limit in note 3.

9. The landlord who has given this notice may not be the landlord to whom you pay your rent. "Business" is given a wide meaning in the 1954 Act and is used in the same sense in this notice. The 1954 Act also has rules about the date which the landlord can put in paragraph 3. This depends on the terms of your tenancy. If you have any doubts about whether this notice is valid, get advice immediately.

10. [The Department of the Environment and Welsh Office booklet "Business Leases and Security of Tenure" explains the main provisions of Part II of the 1954 Act. The Department of the Environment and Welsh Office booklet "Leasehold Reform" (booklet no. 9 in the series of housing booklets) give details of the rights of leaseholders to claim to buy the freehold or to have an extension to the lease of their house. "Business Leases and Security of Tenure" is available from the Department of the Environment Publications Store, Building No. 3, Victoria Road, South Ruislip, Middlesex and "Leasehold Reform" is available from council offices and housing aid centres.]

Landlord and Tenant Act 1954
Section 26(6)

Landlord's Notice Opposing Grant of New Tenancy of Business Premises

To(^{1})

of(^{2})

I/we received on(^{3})   19   your request for a new tenancy

of(^{4})

TAKE NOTICE that I/we shall oppose an application to the court for the grant of a new tenancy on the grounds mentioned in paragraph(s) (^{5})   of section 30(1) of the Landlord and Tenant Act 1954, as set out overleaf in Note 3 to this notice.

DATED   19

Signed:

[As solicitor/agent for] Landlord

Name of Landlord:

Address of Landlord:

[Name and address of solicitor/agent:

(1) Name of Tenant.
(2) Address of Tenant.
(3) Date Tenant's request made, see note 1.
(4) Address of property.
(5) Insert paragraph letter(s), see note 2.

NOTES

1. A landlord who wishes to oppose an application to the court by the tenant for a new tenancy must serve this notice within two months of the tenant making his request.

2. The grounds upon which the landlord may oppose an application to the court are limited to those set out in Note 3. The landlord can only rely on grounds specified in this notice, by the insertion of the appropriate paragraph letter(s). References to more than one ground may be inserted.

3. The grounds on which the landlord may oppose the tenant's application, as specified in the Landlord and Tenant Act 1954, s 30(1), are:

Grounds

(a) where under the current tenancy the tenant has any obligations as respects the repair and maintenance of the holding, that the tenant ought not to be granted a new tenancy in view of the state of repair of the holding, being a state resulting from the tenant's failure to comply with the said obligations;

(b) that the tenant ought not to be granted a new tenancy in view of his persistent delay in paying rent which has become due;

(c) that the tenant ought not to be granted a new tenancy in view of other substantial breaches by him of his obligations under the current tenancy, or for any other reason connected with the tenant's use or management of the holding;

(d) that the landlord has offered and is willing to provide or secure the provision of alternative accommodation for the tenant, that the terms on which the alternative accommodation is available are reasonable having regard to the terms of the current tenancy and to all other relevant circumstances, and that the accommodation and the time at which it will be available are suitable for the tenant's requirements (including the requirement to preserve goodwill) having regard to the nature and class of his business and to the situation and extent of, and facilities afforded by, the holding;

(e) where the current tenancy was created by the sub-letting of part only of the property comprised in a superior tenancy and the landlord is the owner of an interest in reversion expectant on the termination of that superior tenancy, that the aggregate of the rents reasonably obtainable on separate lettings of the holding and the remainder of that property would be substantially less than the rent reasonably obtainable on a letting of that property as a whole, that on the termination of the current tenancy the landlord requires possession of the holding for the purposes of letting or otherwise disposing of the said property as a whole, and that in view thereof the tenant ought not to be granted a new tenancy;

(f) that on the termination of the current tenancy the landlord intends to demolish or reconstruct the premises comprised in the holding or a substantial part of those premises or to carry out substantial work of construction on the holding or part thereof and that he could not reasonably do so without obtaining possession of the holding;

(g) that on the termination of the current tenancy the landlord intends to occupy the holding for the purposes, or partly for the purposes, of a business to be carried on by him therein, or as is residence.

4. In section 30(1), quoted in Note 3, 'the holding' means the property comprised in the tenancy, other than any part which is occupied neither by the tenant nor by someone whom he employs for the purposes of a business which brings the tenancy within the scope of the Landlord and Tenant Act 1954: s 23(3).

INDEX